CO-ASZ-247

Brief Contents

The Academic Writer

A BRIEF GUIDE

The Academic Writer

A BRIEF GUIDE

SECOND EDITION

LISA EDE

Oregon State University

BEDFORD/ST. MARTIN'S

Boston · New York

For Bedford/St. Martin's

Senior Developmental Editor: Alexis P. Walker
Senior Production Editor: Harold Chester
Production Supervisor: Andrew Ensor
Marketing Manager: Molly Parke
Art Director: Lucy Krikorian
Text Design: Anne Carter
Copy Editor: Denise P. Quirk
Photo Research: Julie Tesser
Cover Design: Donna Lee Dennison
Composition: Achorn International, Inc.
Printing and Binding: RR Donnelley and Sons

President: Joan E. Feinberg
Editorial Director: Denise B. Wydra
Editor in Chief: Karen S. Henry
Director of Development: Erica T. Appel
Director of Marketing: Karen R. Soeltz
Director of Production: Susan W. Brown
Associate Director, Editorial Production: Elise S. Kaiser
Managing Editor: Shuli Traub

Library of Congress Control Number: 2010932690

Copyright © 2011, 2008 by Bedford/St. Martin's

All rights reserved. No part of this book may be reproduced, stored in a retrieval system, or transmitted in any form or by any means, electronic, mechanical, photocopying, recording, or otherwise, except as may be expressly permitted by the applicable copyright statutes or in writing by the Publisher.

Manufactured in the United States of America.

5 4 3 2 1 0
f e d c b a

For information, write: Bedford/St. Martin's, 75 Arlington Street, Boston, MA 02116   (617-399-4000)

ISBN: 978-0-312-60319-9

Acknowledgments

Acknowledgments and copyrights appear at the back of the book on pages 403–4, which constitute an extension of the copyright page.

It is a violation of the law to reproduce these selections by any means whatsoever without the written permission of the copyright holder.

To my students
and
(of course)
to Gregory —
and in memory of Bachelor

Preface for Instructors

What does it mean to be an "academic writer" in today's world? What is the role of traditional print texts in a world that increasingly favors visual and multimedia presentations? How can students strengthen their conventional academic writing skills while also developing their ability to employ multimedia and other forms of communication? How can students think critically and effectively evaluate the abundance of sources they can access online? In a world of YouTube, Facebook, MySpace, and other social media, what role does and should traditional print communication play? Does writing really *matter* anymore?

Most of us are asking these same questions, as the ways in which all of us read, write, and otherwise construct texts continue to evolve rapidly and in sometimes bewildering directions. In this new edition of *The Academic Writer*, I offer my (always provisional) answers to these questions and focus on the kinds of writing and research that students in college do *now*, using contemporary digital and online as well as traditional print technologies. At the same time, I have kept true to the goals that guided me in creating the first edition of the text:

- *The Academic Writer* **is a practical guide to the** *essentials* **of academic writing and research.** It does not try to be everything to everyone, and it does not try to convey everything students will need to know to succeed in college and in life: Rather, in as clear and straightforward a fashion as I could manage, it shares key concepts and practical strategies for writing and research that have helped students I have worked with over the years to become effective writers.

- **The text is flexible and open to multiple pedagogical approaches.** Depending on teachers' goals for the course and their preferred methods for teaching, the book can be used either on its own or with a collection of readings or a handbook. It reflects current research on the teaching of writing without insisting on a single theory or method, making it well suited for writing programs that use a common text but allow multiple curricular and/or thematic approaches.

■ **The text respects students and speaks to them in a language they understand.** In recognition of both the financial and time pressures students face, I have tried to make *The Academic Writer* as brief, and hence inexpensive, as possible. Every sentence has been framed with students in mind: I've included (and explained) key vocabulary students will need for composition and other courses, but I've avoided unnecessary jargon. Wherever possible, I've used examples from the media-rich lives students lead today, and the real-world contexts that matter to them.

Thinking Rhetorically: A Foundational Concept for the Book

The longer and harder I thought about the new challenges and opportunities that contemporary writers face, the more I found myself wondering about the continued relevance of the **rhetorical tradition**. Could this ancient tradition have anything left to say to twenty-first-century students?

I concluded that it still has a *lot* to say. Some of the most important concepts in western rhetoric were formulated in Greece during the fifth century B.C.E., a time when the Greeks were in the midst of a transition from an oral to an alphabetic/manuscript culture. This was also a time when principles of democracy were being developed. In Athens—an early limited democracy—citizens met in the Assembly to make civic and political decisions; they also served as jurors at trials. Those arguing for or against an issue or person made public speeches in the Assembly. Because each case varied, rhetoricians needed to develop flexible, situation-oriented strategies designed to achieve specific purposes.

Modern rhetorical practices derive from these ancient necessities. A rhetorical approach to communication encourages writers to think in terms of *purpose* and *effect*. Rather than providing "rules" about how texts should be organized and developed, rhetoric encourages writers to draw on their commonsense understanding of communication—an understanding they have developed as speakers, listeners, writers, and readers—to make local, situated decisions about how they can best communicate in specific situations.

In keeping with these principles, the rhetorical approach in *The Academic Writer* encourages writers to think—and act—like problem solvers. In its discussion of rhetoric and of the rhetorical situation, *The Academic Writer* shows students how best to respond to a particular writing challenge—whether they are writing an essay exam, designing a PowerPoint presentation for work, writing an email to *USA Today,* or posting to their personal blog. "Thinking Rhetorically" icons that appear throughout the book highlight the rhetorical advice, tips, and strategies that will help them do so, efficiently and effectively.

Organization

PART I, "WRITING MATTERS: WRITING AND RHETORIC IN THE TWENTY-FIRST CENTURY," provides the foundation for the book. In addition to introducing the principles of rhetoric—with particular emphasis on the **rhetorical situation**—Part I places particular emphasis on another central concept: that of **writing as design**.

Increasingly, scholars of rhetoric and writing argue that the most productive way to envision the act of composing texts is as a species of design: Among other things, both activities are open-ended, creative, persuasive, and problem-solving in nature. In fact, given the extent to which visual and multimedia elements are now routinely incorporated into composition classrooms and other writing spaces, the distinctions between what was traditionally conceived of as "design" and what was traditionally conceived of as "writing" are disappearing. *The Academic Writer* draws upon this research, and it does so in a clear, user-friendly manner. This discussion creates bridges between students' self-sponsored writing on such social networks as Facebook and MySpace (where they literally design self-representations) and the writing they undertake as college students.

PART II, "WRITING IN COLLEGE," focuses, as its title suggests, on the demands that contemporary students face. **Analysis**, **argument**, and **research** are central to academic writing, and this section provides chapters on each of these topics, as well as a chapter on **writing in the disciplines**.

PART III, "PRACTICAL STRATEGIES FOR READING AND WRITING," provides concise, reference-friendly advice for students on **reading**, **invention**, **planning**, **drafting**, **document design**, and **revision**.

Key Features

- Every feature of the text, in every chapter, reinforces the book's primary aim: to help students learn to think *rhetorically*. The text as a whole encourages transfer by emphasizing decision-making over rules—in other words, as the old trope goes, it teaches students to fish, rather than presenting them with a fish. **Guidelines** and **Questions boxes** summarize key concepts, and "**Thinking Rhetorically**" icons flag passages where they are fully explained. "**For Exploration**," "**For Collaboration**," and "**For Thought, Discussion, and Writing**" activities encourage students to apply and extend what they have learned.

- **A wide range of model student essays** include a multipart case study (now presented in its entirety in Chapter 5) and eleven other samples of student writing, which serve both to instruct students and to inspire them.

- **Thoughtful discussions of visuals and of writing as design** in Chapters 1, 4, 5, 6, 8, and 11 suggest strategies for reading, writing, and designing multimodal texts.

- **Chapter 7, "Writing in the Disciplines,"** helps students analyze writing tasks in the humanities, sciences, social sciences, and business.

New to This Edition

RECONCEIVED RESEARCH COVERAGE HELPS STUDENTS MASTER THE INS AND OUTS OF JOINING THE SCHOLARLY CONVERSATION IN THE TWENTY-FIRST CENTURY.

- **A brand-new Chapter 6, "Doing Research: Joining the Scholarly Conversation,"** written in close collaboration with Oregon State University librarian Anne-Marie Deitering, reframes research as a recursive process of exploration, information-gathering, evaluation, and composition. To foster deep, transferrable learning, the chapter emphasizes the rationale behind the rules. In addition, it covers the "new basics" of online research—explaining, for example, the use of online bookmarking tools and citation managers—as well as current topics most textbooks don't even address, such as copyright and "copyleft" (the principle granting the public limited rights to distribute and modify an author's intellectual property) and how students can understand and assert their rights as content creators.

- **The fully revised Writers' References** section at the end of the book provides an updated guide to MLA and APA documentation. In addition to providing abundant examples for citing print and electronic materials, this appendix offers illustrations that annotate sample sources, showing students where to find the information they need for correct documentation.

A FULLY REVISED ARGUMENT CHAPTER features advice on mastering the essential moves in academic writing: determining whether a claim can be argued, developing a working thesis, providing good reasons and support, acknowledging counterarguments, framing arguments as part of the scholarly conversation, and using visuals.

NEWLY DESIGNED GUIDELINES AND QUESTIONS BOXES present key processes in flowchart format, reinforcing the importance of decision-making and active engagement in the processes of writing, thinking, and reading, and helping students find what they need more easily than ever before.

NEW SAMPLE STUDENT ESSAYS from across the disciplines address topics students care about:

- In a new essay on bilingual education in Chapter 3, student Alia Sands uses Richard Rodriguez's *Hunger of Memory* as a frame for discussion of her experience in the Iowa public school system.

- In Chapter 7, student Tawnya Redding's essay on how music preferences correlate to suicide risk in adolescents models conventions in the social sciences.

- In Chapter 12, Stevon Roberts's essay on privacy in the age of the Internet models strategies for effective "deep" or global revision.

The Instructor's Edition of *The Academic Writer*

We have designed *The Academic Writer* to be as accessible as possible to all of the kinds of people teaching composition, including new graduate students, busy adjuncts, experienced instructors, and writing program administrators. Toward that end, we provide detailed *Instructor's Notes* (ISBN 978-0-312-63090-4), written by Lisa Ede and revised and expanded by Sara Jameson of Oregon State University. This material, bound together with the student text in a special Instructor's Edition, includes correlations to the Council of Writing Program Administrators' Outcomes Statement, multiple course plans, practical tips for meeting common classroom challenges and for teaching key concepts, detailed advice for working with each chapter in the text, and nine sample student papers. The *Instructor's Notes* are also available for download by authorized instructors at **bedfordstmartins.com/ academicwriter**.

Digital Support for *The Academic Writer*

The Academic Writer doesn't stop with a book. Online, you'll find both free and affordable premium resources to help students get even more out of the book and your course. You'll also find convenient instructor resources, such as downloadable sample syllabi, classroom activities, and even a nationwide community of teachers. To learn more about or order any of the products below, contact your Bedford/St. Martin's sales representative, e-mail sales support (sales_support@bfwpub.com), or visit the Web site at **bedfordstmartins.com/academicwriter**.

Student Resources

FREE AND OPEN RESOURCES for students, available via **bedfordstmartins .com/academicwriter**, include the following:

- **Research and Documentation Online** by **Diana Hacker** offers clear advice across the disciplines on how to integrate outside material into a paper, how to cite sources correctly, and how to format the paper in MLA, APA, *Chicago*, or CSE style. The site also includes links to specialized online resources for more than thirty disciplines.

- **Bedford Bibliographer** helps students with the process of collecting source information and making a bibliography in MLA, APA, and *Chicago* styles.

- **Exercise Central**, the largest database of editing exercises on the Web, is now a comprehensive resource for skill development as well as skill assessment. In addition to over nine thousand exercises offering immediate feedback and reporting, *Exercise Central* can help identify students' strengths and weaknesses, recommend personalized study plans, and provide tutorials for common problems.

PREMIUM RESOURCES include the following:

- **Re:Writing Plus**, now with **VideoCentral**, which gathers all of Bedford/ St. Martin's premium digital content for composition into one online collection. It includes hundreds of model documents, the first-ever peer review game, and *VideoCentral*, with over fifty brief videos for the writing classroom. *Re:Writing Plus* can be purchased separately or packaged with the print book at a significant discount. An activation code is required. To order *Re:Writing Plus* packaged with the print book, use ISBN 978-0-312-56356-1.

- **CompClass**, an easy-to-use online course space designed for composition students and instructors, complete with powerful assignment and assessment tools. *CompClass* can be purchased separately at **yourcomp class.com** or packaged with the print book at a significant discount. An activation code is required. To order *CompClass* with *The Academic Writer*, use ISBN 978-0-312-56417-9.

Instructor Resources

You have a lot to do in your course. Bedford/St. Martin's wants to make it easy for you to find the support you need — and to get it quickly.

- The *Instructor's Notes for the Academic Writer* are available in PDF format that can be downloaded by authorized instructors from **bedfordstmartins.com/academicwriter**. This material includes correlations to the Council of Writing Program Administrators' Outcomes Statement, multiple course plans, practical tips for meeting common classroom challenges and for teaching key concepts, detailed advice for working with each chapter in the text, and nine sample student papers.

- *TeachingCentral* (**bedfordstmartins.com/teachingcentral**) offers the entire list of Bedford/St. Martin's print and online professional resources in one place. You'll find landmark reference works, sourcebooks on pedagogical issues, award-winning collections, and practical advice for the classroom—all free for instructors.

- *Bits* (**bedfordstmartins.com/bits**) collects creative ideas for teaching a range of composition topics in an easily searchable blog. A community of teachers—leading scholars, authors, and editors—discuss revision, research, grammar and style, technology, peer review, and much more. Take, use, adapt, and pass the ideas around. Then, come back to the site to comment or share your own suggestion.

- **Content cartridges** for the most common course management systems—Blackboard, WebCT, Angel, and Desire2Learn—allow you to easily download Bedford/St. Martin's digital materials for your course.

Even More Options for Students

Add more value and flexibility to your textbook with one of the following resources, free when packaged with *The Academic Writer*. To learn more about package options or any of the products below, contact your Bedford/St. Martin's sales representative or visit the Web site at **bedfordstmartins.com/academicwriter**.

ISERIES ON CD-ROM includes multimedia tutorials in a flexible CD-ROM format—because there are things you can't do in a book.

- *ix:visual exercises* help students visualize and put into practice key rhetorical and visual concepts.

- *i·claim visualizing argument* offers a new way to see argument—with six tutorials, an illustrated glossary, and over seventy multimedia arguments.

- *i·cite visualizing sources* brings research to life through an animated introduction, four tutorials, and hands-on source practice.

PORTFOLIO KEEPING, SECOND EDITION, BY NEDRA REYNOLDS AND RICH RICE is the first guide that provides all the information students need to use the portfolio method successfully in a writing course. *Portfolio Teaching*, a guide for instructors, is also available. It provides the practical information instructors and writing program administrators need to use the portfolio method successfully in a writing course and is the ideal companion to *Portfolio Keeping*.

ORAL PRESENTATIONS FOR THE COMPOSITION COURSE: A BRIEF GUIDE BY MATTHEW DUNCAN AND GUSTAV W. FRIEDRICH offers students the advice they need to plan, prepare, and present their work effectively. With sections on analyzing audiences, choosing effective language, using visual aids, collaborating on group presentations, and dealing with the fear of public speaking, this booklet offers help for students' most common challenges in developing oral presentations.

Acknowledgments

Before I wrote *The Academic Writer*, acknowledgments sometimes struck me as formulaic or conventional. Now I recognize that they are neither; rather, acknowledgments are simply inadequate to the task at hand. Coming at the end of a preface—and hence twice marginalized—acknowledgments can never adequately convey the complex web of interrelationships and collaborations that make a book like this possible. I hope that the people whose support and assistance I acknowledge here not only note my debt of gratitude but also recognize the sustaining role that they have played, and continue to play, in my life and in my work.

I would like to begin by thanking my colleagues at the Center for Writing and Learning at Oregon State University. I could accomplish little in my teaching, research, and administration without the support and friendship of Dennis Bennett, Robin Pappas, and Jeanna Towns. They, along with our writing assistants, have taught me what it means to collaborate in a sustaining, productive fashion. Others in the OSU English department, my second academic home, supported me while I wrote and revised this text. I am indebted to my colleagues Chris Anderson, Vicki Tolar Burton, Anita Helle, Sara Jameson, and Susan Meyers for their friendship and their commitment to writing.

I have dedicated this book to my students, and I hope that it in some way reflects what *they* have taught me over the years. I also owe a great debt of gratitude to two other friends and teachers, Anne-Marie Deitering and Sara Jameson, who collaborated with me on, respectively, a reenvisioned chapter on research and a reenvisioned *Instructor's Notes*. Deep thanks to both.

I also wish to acknowledge the students whose writing appears in this text. I am particularly grateful to Stevon Roberts, who contributed several impressive essays to the first edition of this text and radically revised one of them (which now appears as "Identity, Rebooted") for this second edition, and Daniel Stiepleman, whose writing appears in Chapter 5 and provides students with an extended example of successful academic writing in action.

Colleagues and students play an important role in nurturing any project, but so do those who form the intangible but indispensable community of scholars that is one's most intimate disciplinary home. Here, it is harder to determine who to acknowledge; my debt to the composition theorists who have led the way or "grown up" with me is so great that I hesitate to list the names of specific individuals here for fear of omitting someone deserving of credit. I must, however, acknowledge my friend and frequent coauthor Andrea Lunsford, who writes with me even when I write alone. Andrea generously allowed me to reprint material from *The St. Martin's Handbook*, Sixth Edition, in the appendix of this text, and for that I thank her as well.

I would also like to thank the many dedicated teachers of composition I have worked and talked with over the years. By their example, comments, suggestions, and questions, they have taught me a great deal about the teaching of writing. A number of writing instructors took time from their teaching to look carefully at the first edition of *The Academic Writer* as well as drafts of this new book. Their observations and suggestions have enriched and improved this edition. These reviewers include the following instructors: Jeanne Guerin, Sierra College; Celena Kusch, University of South Carolina Upstate; Alex Blazer, Georgia College and State University; Sara Coffman, University of Tennessee at Chattanooga; Sara Jameson, Oregon State University; Matthew Moberly, California State University; Karen Overbye, Mount Royal College; Jordana Hall, Texas A&M University–Commerce; Peter Caster, University of South Carolina Upstate; Emily Cope, St. John Fisher College; Lisa Maruca, Wayne State University; Brandi Westmoreland, Texas A&M University–Commerce; Cathy Rusco, Muskegon Community College; Lori Feyh, Missouri State University; Patricia Webb, Arizona State University; Jennifer Richardson, SUNY Potsdam; Jane Hoogestraat, Missouri State University; Karen Jackson, North Carolina Central University; Elizabeth Kubek, Benedictine University; Lee-Nickoson Massey, Bowling Green State University; Debra Lohe, Washington University in St. Louis; Brock Dethier, Utah State University; and Pam Fox Kuhlken, San Diego State University.

I wish to thank the dedicated staff of Bedford/St. Martin's. Any textbook is an intensely collaborative effort, and I count myself particularly fortunate in having had Alexis Walker as the senior editor on this project. I have valued Alexis's expertise and insight on this project, and I am sure *The*

Academic Writer is a better book as a result. Kristin Bowen, the editor with whom I worked on the previous edition, and who began work with me on this one, has also been a tremendous source of valuable advice and support. I feel fortunate indeed to have been able to work with such an experienced and knowledgeable team. In addition, I want to thank senior project editor Harold Chester, whose patient attention to detail proved especially valuable, editorial assistant Nick McCarthy, who kept all of us organized and on track, and marketing manager Molly Parke, whose constant reminders about the needs of instructors and students were always appreciated.

Finally, I want to (but cannot adequately) acknowledge the support of my husband, Gregory Pfarr, whose passionate commitment to his own creative endeavors, and our life together, sustains me.

Lisa Ede

Contents

PART II

Writing in College

PART III

Practical Strategies for Reading and Writing

The Academic Writer

A BRIEF GUIDE

Rethinking Writing: A Rhetorical Process for Composing Texts

What does it mean to be a writer in the twenty-first century? In a media-saturated world where visual images surround us, how much does writing still matter? How has the increasing emphasis on the visual—and the availability of digital and online media—influenced the communicative practices of ordinary people like you and me? One need only visit Flickr, the popular online photo-sharing space, to notice the power that images hold for many people. While drafting this chapter, for instance, I typed *black labs* into Flickr's search engine and discovered that 56,487 photos of this popular breed were posted on this site. Clearly, black lab owners are using Flickr to communicate how much they love their dogs. Words still play a role in this communication, for the photos cataloged in Flickr include such titles as "Happy Black Lab," "Black Labs, Rainy Day," and "Black Lab in Truck." On Flickr, however, visual images are clearly more important than the words that accompany them (see p. 2).

As a medium, photographs are not new. People have been sharing photographs ever since the process was developed. Long before people posted photos of recent vacations on Flickr or iPhoto, many travelers mailed postcards of famous sites they visited to friends and family. Of course, the Web has changed all that, and people are increasingly posting words and images online. In the month since I drafted the previous paragraph, for instance, the number of photos of black labs posted on Flickr rose from 56,487 to 57,622.

When it was first invented, the Internet wasn't a very friendly place for the ordinary communicator. But with the development of the Web and user-friendly software programs, the situation has changed dramatically. Now just about anyone with a computer and Internet access can establish a visually

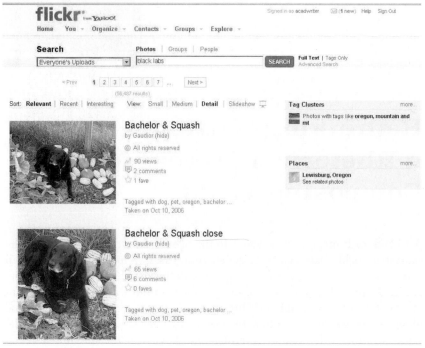

Flickr Search Results

SOURCE: Reproduced 2009 by Yahoo! Inc. YAHOO! and the image with permission of Yahoo! Inc. YAHOO! logo is a trademark of Yahoo! Inc.

rich presence on the Web. On social-networking sites such as Facebook and Twitter, on video-sharing sites like YouTube, and on many blogs, images, video clips, and audio clips can be at least as important as the written text.

Written language has hardly lost its power, however. If you have ever visited Amazon.com, you know that customer reviews are featured prominently on this site. You may not realize, however, just how many people contribute customer reviews to Amazon. On the same day that I first searched for photos of black labs on Flickr, I searched Amazon for the tenth anniversary edition of *Harry Potter and the Sorcerer's Stone,* the first novel in J. K. Rowling's Harry Potter series, and I found 5,518 reviews of the novel posted on the site for this one edition alone. In the month since my first visit, 26 additional reviews appeared.

As this example demonstrates, the written word still very much matters. In fact, in a developed country like the United States, those with access to computers and online technologies are writing more than ever before. Even

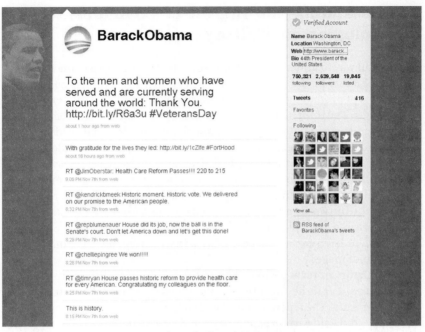

Homepage of Barack Obama's Twitter Account

outside of school, many students read and write virtually all the time, via instant messaging, texting, Twitter, blogs, Facebook, and so on. Technology, of course, has engendered many changes in the kinds of text produced. For example, the design, or look, of these texts has become increasingly important, and more and more written texts integrate video, still images, music, and the spoken word.

If you're a traditional-age student, you've grown up with the Web. You take sites like YouTube, Flickr, and Facebook for granted. You're probably more comfortable manipulating images and texts at your computer than many of your instructors are. But how will this knowledge of online communication apply to the writing you will do in college?

You may think that the writing you do for fun is irrelevant to the writing you do for your classes. While it's true that you wouldn't compose an essay for a history class the way you text message a friend, *all* of your experiences as a writer, reader, speaker, and listener can help you learn how to meet the demands of academic writing. Gaining a better understanding of the rhetorical tradition and of rhetorical sensitivity will play an important role in this process. This chapter (and this book) will help you gain that understanding.

Understanding the Impact of Communication Technologies on Writing

One helpful way to understand the impact of technology on writing is to consider the history of the printed text. For centuries in western Europe, the only means of producing texts was to copy them by hand, as scribes did in the Middle Ages. The limited number of manuscripts created meant that few private individuals owned manuscripts, and fewer people could read them. In 1440, Johannes Gutenberg invented the printing press, which could produce multiple copies of texts and therefore dramatically increase the availability of the written word. The rise of printing tended, however, to de-emphasize the role of visual elements in mass-produced texts, because the technologies for printing words and images were largely incompatible. In the 1800s, it again became possible to print high-quality illustrated texts. Since that time, readers have come to expect increasingly sophisticated combinations of words and images.

The history of texts produced by individual writers differs from that of printed texts. Until the invention of the typewriter in 1868, writers handwrote their texts. The typewriter enabled writers to produce texts much more efficiently, and with carbon paper they could even make copies. But typewriters were designed to produce only words. Writers could manipulate spacing and margins, and they could underline words and phrases, but that was about it.

The development of the personal computer, and of sophisticated software for writing, design, and imaging, changed all that. Today anyone with a computer and access to the Internet can compose texts that have most if not all of the features of professionally produced documents, including the ability to integrate visual and auditory elements. An art history student who's convinced that graffiti represents an important genre of contemporary art could write a traditional essay making this argument, but she could also create a video, develop a PowerPoint presentation, or record a podcast to make her point. If this student has an ongoing interest in graffiti art, she might even host a blog on this subject.

||||||||||||||||||||||||||||||||||||||||||||||||||||||||||||||||||||||||||||||||||||||||||

FOR EXPLORATION

Take some time to think about—and list—all the kinds of writing that you do. Obviously, you'll want to include such traditional print and handwritten texts as essays, class notes, letters, and shopping and "to do" lists. You'll also want to inventory the many forms of online writing that you do, such as instant messaging, tweeting, posting on Facebook or commenting on blogs, and writing reviews on Amazon.com or other sites. Are design elements and visual images more important to some kinds of writing that you do than to others?

Now turn your attention to the media you use to write. In writing essays for your classes, do you first brainstorm and write rough drafts in pencil or pen and then revise at your computer, or do you write entirely on your computer or laptop—or do you switch back and forth, depending on the project and situation? When you write at the computer, how many programs do you typically have open, and how often do you move back and forth from, say, the Web, email, or instant messaging as you compose? Does your cell phone play a role in your writing? Do you ever incorporate photos (yours or others) into other texts, whether emails or essays?

Take a few more minutes to reflect about what you have written. What insights have you gained from this reflection?

|||||||||||||||||||||||||||||||||||||||||||||||||||||||||||||||||||||||||||||||||||||||||||

The ability to compose in diverse media and to integrate visual and textual elements represents an exciting opportunity for writers—but opportunity can also bring difficulties and dilemmas. Consider the art history student writing an essay on graffiti as art. If she followed the conventions of traditional academic writing, she would double-space her essay and choose a readable font that doesn't call attention to itself (like 12-point Times New Roman). If she's using headings, she might make them bold; she might also include some photographs. But in general her essay would look and read much like one written twenty, or even fifty, years ago.

Suppose, however, that her instructor required the class to prepare an oral presentation using PowerPoint, in addition to writing a traditional academic essay. For her presentation, the student writing on graffiti would still need to communicate her ideas in a clear and understandable way, but she might manipulate fonts and spacing to give her presentation an urban and edgy feel. While she would hardly want to use an unusual font like the graffiti-style BROOKLYN KID throughout, she might employ it at strategic points for emphasis and to evoke the graffiti she's writing about (see p. 6). She might show visual examples of graffiti and choose and arrange her images in prominent or unusual ways, to create the kind of "in your face" feel that characterizes much graffiti.

How can this student decide on the best way to convey her ideas and meet her professor's expectations? Obviously, she can discuss the assignment with her teacher. But such consultations aren't always possible. Moreover, this student will eventually have a job where she will be required to compose and take responsibility for other important texts—from reports to Web sites, brochures, and memos. In many instances, she will have to make decisions

Settings for GRAFFITI

→ Subways eliminated in late 1980s as most popular venue

→ Moved above ground to walls and buildings

→ Freight trains took art across continent

Fig. 3. New York subway graffiti. Edward Hausner. *The New York Times Agency Photos.* The New York Times, 18 Jan. 1973. Web. 15 Feb. 2010.

Tools for GRAFFITI

→ Paint cans using custom spray nozzles

→ Keith Haring's work with chalk

→ Markers and stickers

→ Cutouts and posters applied with glue

Fig. 5. Artist "Swoon" pastes a cutout on a wall in Brooklyn. Michael Kamber. *The New York Times Agency Photos.* The New York Times, 9 July 2004. Web. 15 Feb. 2010.

PowerPoint Slides from a Student Oral Presentation

about these texts' visual and other design elements, and the medium in which the writing will appear.

Like others who value writing and recognize its importance, this student needs to develop the ability to respond effectively to a variety of writing situations. She needs to know, in other words, how to make effective *choices* as a writer—and she needs to do so in the context of the demands and opportunities that twenty-first-century writers face.

Writing and Rhetoric

thinking rhetorically

One of the most powerful resources this student, and other writers, can draw upon is one of the oldest fields of study in Western culture: rhetoric. Rhetoric was formulated by such Greek and Roman rhetoricians as Isocrates (436–338 B.C.E.), Aristotle (384–322 B.C.E.), Cicero (106–43 B.C.E.), and Quintilian (35–96 C.E.). Originally developed to meet the needs of speakers, rhetoric came to be applied to written texts as well.

When you think rhetorically, you consider the ways in which words and images are used to engage—and sometimes to persuade—others. Writers who think rhetorically apply their understanding of human communication in general, and of written texts in particular, to the decisions that will enable effective communication within a specific situation.

A rhetorical approach to writing encourages you to consider four key elements of your situation:

- Your role as a *writer* who has (or must discover) something to communicate

- One or more *readers* with whom you would like to communicate

- The *text* you create to convey your ideas. We are used to thinking of texts as comprised of words, but increasingly texts may include images and other graphics, such as charts, graphs, and borders.

- A *medium* (print text, PowerPoint presentation, poster, brochure, report, video clip, blog, etc.) that makes this communication possible

The relationship among these elements is dynamic. Writers compose texts to express their meaning, but readers are equally active. Readers don't simply decipher the words on the page; they draw on their own experiences and expectations as they read. As a student, for instance, you read your economics textbook differently than you read the comics or a popular novel. You also know that the more experience you have reading certain kinds of writing—textbooks in your major, or the sports or financial pages of the newspaper, for example—the more you will get out of them.

Rhetoric is a practical art that helps writers make effective choices within specific rhetorical situations. You'll learn more about the rhetorical situation in Chapter 3. For now, you simply need to know that when you analyze your rhetorical situation, you consider each of the four elements of rhetoric: writer, reader, text, and medium.

Let's return to the student who wants to write an essay on graffiti as art. To analyze her situation, she would first consider her own position as a writer. As a student in a class, how much freedom does she have? In academic writing, this question leads immediately to the second element of the rhetorical situation: the reader. In academic writing, the reader is primarily the teacher, so the student would want to consider the nature of her assignment—how open it is, what statement (if any) the teacher has provided about format, expectations, and so on. But she would also want to draw upon her general understanding of writing in the humanities. Instructors in the humanities often favor a conservative approach to academic writing, so while this student might use headings and images in her research paper, her safest bet would be to focus primarily on the clear and logical development of her ideas.

This student has considerably more flexibility in approaching her PowerPoint presentation. The conventions for PowerPoint presentations are less constraining and more open than those of traditional academic writing. Moreover, instructors and students alike expect that those composing PowerPoint presentations will take full advantage of the medium. Even here, though, the student will want visual and design elements to enhance and enrich the expression of her ideas. She would never want her goal of creating an urban, edgy look for her presentation to interfere with its content.

In this example, the student's teacher has specified the media she should use: a print essay and an oral presentation using PowerPoint slides. For this reason, constructing a blog or creating a video would be an inappropriate response to the assignment. In a different situation, employing one or both of these media might be not only appropriate but effective. If this student were writing an honors thesis on graffiti as art, for instance, she might well create a blog to express and explore her ideas during the year that she works on this major project. At her thesis defense, she might share relevant blog posts and comments with her committee via a PowerPoint presentation. She might also show film clips of interviews with graffiti artists.

As this example indicates, a rhetorical approach to writing encourages you to think in practical, concrete ways about your situation as a writer. It's no accident that rhetoric takes this approach to communication. The discipline of rhetoric was originally developed to meet the needs of the citizens of Athens, who, in their limited democracy, met to make civic and political decisions and also served as jurors. Those arguing for or against an issue made public speeches in the Assembly. Because each case varied, rhetoricians needed to develop flexible, situation-oriented strategies designed to achieve specific purposes, rather than a fixed set of rules for making speeches. A rhetorical approach to writing, then, encourages writers to think and act like problem solvers.

Composing—and Designing—Texts

thinking
rhetorically

When you think and act like a problem solver, you use skills that have much in common with those in the contemporary profession of design. There are many kinds of design—from industrial design to fashion design—but writing is especially closely allied with graphic design, thanks in large part to the development of the Web and of such software programs as Adobe Photoshop and PowerPoint. In fact, given ongoing developments in communication technologies, conventional distinctions between these two creative activities seem less and less relevant. While it is true that in the humanities the most traditional forms of academic writing emphasize words over images and other elements of design, increasingly student writers—like all writers—are integrating the visual and verbal in texts.

In his influential book *How Designers Think*, Bryan Lawson lists the essential characteristics of design. These characteristics apply, Lawson argues, to all kinds of design, from product design to graphic design.

- Design problems are open-ended and cannot be fully specified.
- The design process is endless.
- There is no infallibly correct process of design.
- The process involves finding as well as solving problems.
- Design inevitably involves subjective value judgments.
- Design is a persuasive activity that is concerned with what might, could, and should be.
- Designers work in the context of a need for action.

Lawson's description of design holds true in many respects for writing. Like design, writing is a creative act that occurs within a complex system of opportunities and constraints, and the writing process, too, is potentially endless in the sense that there is no objective or absolute way to determine when a project is complete. Rare is the writer or designer who thinks, "What I've just created is perfect; I couldn't improve it if I tried." Instead, writers and designers often call a halt to their process for pragmatic reasons. They may have a deadline, or they may feel they've spent as much time as they should, or they may know they've reached the limits of a fixed budget for a design project. Indeed, the open-ended nature of writing and design is typical of activities that require creativity.

Precisely because writing and design are creative processes, there is no infallibly correct process that writers and designers can follow. The more experienced writers and designers are, the better able they are to determine what strategies are appropriate for any particular task. But each time they work on a new project, they must consider their project, situation, purpose, medium, and audience.

As they do so, designers and writers do not just solve problems; they find, or create, them. This may sound intimidating at first. "I don't want to find problems," you might think. "I'm a busy student—I need to solve problems quickly and efficiently." Here's the rub: Often you can't do the latter until you do the former.

Let's say, for example, that you and your roommate are frustrated because your room is always a mess. You talk it over, and you realize that the problem is that you just don't have enough storage space, so rather than putting clothes and other items away in already-overstuffed closets and chests, you leave them out everywhere.

To address this problem, you have to go beyond the general recognition that you need more storage space to pinpoint the problem more specifically. After reading an online version of a local newspaper feature on organizing and redecorating dorm spaces (see p. 11), you realize that your real problem is that you've neglected to systematically consider all your options for storage. Once you've identified the crux of your problem, you can address it—in this case, by taking advantage of unused space under your beds and in the bottom half of your closet. So you take measurements and head to the local discount store to look for inexpensive storage units that will fit the space. You've solved your storage problem by finding, or creating, it.

In writing and in design, as in everyday life, the better you are at finding your problem, the better you will be at addressing it. In fact, the ability to create complex and sophisticated problems is one feature that distinguishes experienced from inexperienced writers and designers. Imagine, for instance, that two students in the same political science class have been asked to write an essay on the current debate over their state's mandated prison sentences for drug offenders. One student thinks, "The easiest way to approach this assignment is to figure out what my teacher believes and say that." The other student thinks, "This is a complex issue, and I've always had complicated responses to it. I'm going to use this assignment to see if I can develop a clearer sense of my beliefs." Each student in effect finds, or creates, the problem that he will solve in his writing.

Design Advice for Organizing Dorm Space

As this example suggests, writing involves subjective value judgments. The first student wants to get his assignment done as easily and quickly as possible; his motivation is external—do the assignment and get a good grade. The second student also wants to get a good grade, but he approaches the assignment as an opportunity for genuine learning and thus creates a more complex, sophisticated—and ultimately rewarding—problem. When these students' teacher reads their essays, there will be an element of subjectivity in his or her response as well. As every student knows, two teachers reading the same essay might give that essay different grades. Similarly, two clients will evaluate the sketch for a design differently. This subjectivity can be frustrating, but it's a fact of life for both writers and designers.

The potential for diverse responses is a reminder that both writing and design are persuasive activities. They both occur in the context of a need for action. As a result, writers and designers are always making decisions about what might, could, and should be. Writers do this when they develop an argument or complete an analysis. Designers do this when they determine which of the many potential designs they've created they will ultimately present to their clients.

Because both writing and design are concerned with what might, could, and should be, these activities involve ethical obligations. In the case of designers, these obligations include the responsibility to do the best work possible for their clients. Writers also have responsibilities, though they may be less obvious. For example, students writing in response to an academic assignment need to complete their assignment by the date it is due. How well they complete the assignment depends in part on their ability and understanding, but commitment to the project is central, as it is in design. Once they graduate and embark on careers, the context of a need for action for these student writers will become even stronger. Because workplace writing is pragmatic and goal-oriented, strong writing skills can make the difference between an adequate and a highly successful career—just as they can make the difference between adequate and superior grades in college.

Both writing and design offer individuals the opportunity to make a difference in the world. Someone who redesigns and in so doing improves the comfort and mobility of wheelchairs, for instance, will improve the quality of life of all who rely upon this vehicle. It's easy to think of writers who have made a difference in the world—both positively (e.g., the signers of the Declaration of Independence) and negatively (e.g., Hitler, as the author of *Mein Kampf*). Yet there are other, less visible but still important examples of the power that writing can have to effect economic, social, political, and cultural change. Writing is one of the most important ways that students can become members of a disciplinary or professional community. For example, in order to be recognized as a professional civil engineer, engineering students need to learn not only how to plan, design, construct, and maintain structures: They must also learn to write like civil engineers. Writing not only plays a key role in most careers, but it also represents an important way that citizens express their views and advocate for causes (see the poster on p. 13). Think, for example, of the role that blogs now play in politics and in public affairs. In these and other ways, writing provides an opportunity for ordinary people to shape the future of local, regional, and national communities.

||||||||||||||||||||||||||||||||||||||||||||||||||||||||||||||||||||||||||||||||||||||||||

FOR EXPLORATION

Write for five or ten minutes in response to this question: What has this discussion of the connections between writing and design helped you to better understand about written communication?

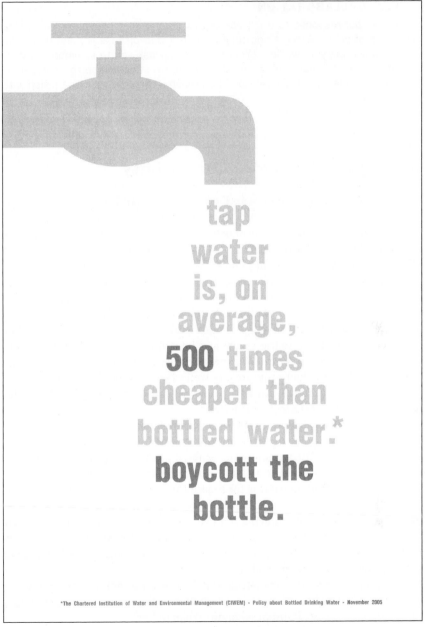

Poster Advocating for a Cause

FOR COLLABORATION

Bring your response to the preceding Exploration to class and meet with a group of peers. Appoint someone to record your discussion, and then take turns sharing your writing. (Your teacher may ask you to summarize, rather than to read, what you've written.) Be sure that your reporter includes as many people's ideas as possible. Be prepared to share your discussion with the class.

|||||||||||||||||||||||||||||||||||||||||||||||||||||||||||||||||||||||||||||||||||

Developing Rhetorical Sensitivity

thinking rhetorically

Experienced graphic designers and writers understand that they must draw on all their resources when they compose. From their prior reading and viewing, they learn about what makes texts work. (Remember, in our contemporary world texts increasingly include not only the written word but also images and graphics.) They analyze their own situations, think about the purpose and goals of particular projects—the meaning they wish to communicate, their reasons for composing—and consider their audience. They explore their own ideas, challenging themselves to express their ideas as clearly and carefully as possible. They play with words, phrases, images, and other graphic elements to make their work stylistically effective. And they take advantage of such computer and online resources as word processing, image editing, and spreadsheet programs, as well as specialized programs for their particular areas of interest. In all of these activities, experienced writers and designers practice *rhetorical sensitivity*.

Designers and writers practice rhetorical sensitivity when they explore the four elements of rhetoric—writer, reader, text, medium—in the context of specific situations. The student writing about graffiti art drew upon her rhetorical sensitivity in determining how best to respond to her assignment. She realized that as a student writing for a class she was constrained in significant ways and that her reader's (i.e., her teacher's) expectations were crucial to her decision making. In considering the two texts she was composing, an essay and an oral presentation using PowerPoint slides, this student understood that the textual conventions governing the former are more conservative than those governing the latter, and that differences in media—print text versus PowerPoint—reinforce this distinction. As a result of her analysis, this student realized that she had more freedom to experiment with visual elements of design in her PowerPoint presentation than in her essay.

thinking rhetorically

In order to respond to her assignment, this student consciously explored her rhetorical situation. Writers and designers are particularly likely to do this when they undertake new or demanding tasks. At other times, this kind of analysis is unconscious and takes the form of rhetorical common sense.

In your daily life, you already practice considerable rhetorical sensitivity. As you make decisions about how to interact with others, you naturally (if unconsciously) draw on your commonsense understanding of effective communication. Imagine, for instance, that you're preparing to interview for a job. Though you might not think of it this way, everything that you do before and during the interview is an effort to design a successful experience. Every decision that you make — what to wear, how to act, what to say during the interview — reflects your rhetorical sensitivity. Much of your attention will focus on how to present yourself best, but you also recognize the importance of being well prepared and of interacting effectively with your interviewers. If you are smart, you will consider the specific situation for which you are applying. Someone applying for a position as a bank teller might dress and act differently than someone applying for a job as a salesperson in a store that specializes in clothes for teenagers and young adults. Successful applicants know that all they do — the way they dress, present themselves, respond to questions, and interact with interviewers — is an effort to communicate their strengths and persuade the interviewers to employ them.

NOTE FOR MULTILINGUAL WRITERS

It is more challenging to "read" a rhetorical situation when you are new to the context. You may find it helpful to consult your teacher or classmates, asking specific questions in order to better understand the rhetorical situation for a particular assignment.

You also employ rhetorical sensitivity when you "read" contemporary culture. As a consumer, for instance, you're bombarded with advertisements urging you to purchase various products or services. How you respond to these ads will depend primarily on how you read them. Wise consumers know that ads are designed to persuade, and they learn ways to read them with a critical eye (even as they appreciate, say, a television commercial's humor or a magazine ad's design). You read other aspects of contemporary culture as well. Much of the time, you may do so for entertainment: While watching sports or other programs on television, for instance, your primary goal may be to relax and enjoy yourself. If you find the plot of a detective show implausible or the action of the Monday night football game too slow, you can easily click to a more interesting program.

At times, however, you may take a more critical, distanced perspective on such forms of popular culture as television, music, and magazines. After arguing with a friend about whether 50 Cent advocates homophobia and

thinking rhetorically

violence, you may watch his videos with a careful eye, comparing him with other hip-hop artists. When you compare different musicians' lyrics, type of dress, and movements, you're considering the ways in which these groups appeal to and communicate with their audience. Though you probably wouldn't have used this term to describe your viewing, you're analyzing the *rhetoric* of their performances.

thinking
rhetorically

Writers and designers who think rhetorically understand that writing and reading do not occur in a vacuum. The language you grow up speaking, the social and cultural worlds you inhabit, and the technologies available to you, among other factors, all influence how you communicate. For example, wherever they come from, most students find that the writing they do in college differs considerably from the language they use in their everyday lives. The language that feels comfortable and natural to you when you speak with your family and friends may differ considerably from that required in academic reading and writing assignments.

Like life, writing involves negotiation. When you prepare for a job interview, you must decide how much to modify your everyday way of dressing to meet the demands of the situation. Similarly, when you write—whether in college, at work, or for civic or other activities—you must consider the expectations of others. At times it can be difficult to determine, let alone meet, these expectations. In your first weeks at a new job, for instance, you probably felt like the new kid on the block. Gradually, however, you became sensitive to your supervisor's and coworkers' expectations. Likewise, as a college student you may at times feel like a new writer on the block. Both *The Academic Writer* and your composition course will help you build on the rhetorical sensitivity that you already have, so you can use all the resources available to you to meet the demands of writing in the twenty-first century.

||||||||||||||||||||||||||||||||||||||||||||||||||||||||||||||||||||||||||||||||||||||||

FOR EXPLORATION

Take a look at the two documents on the following pages. The first is an ad for Levi's jeans, which appeared in major newspapers and magazines as part of their "Go Forth/New Americans" campaign. The second is a screen shot of Levi's marketing Web site, which presents user-submitted words, pictures, and stories as a corporate-sponsored self-portrait of the "New Americans" and their country.

After reading the ad and Web page carefully, respond in writing to these questions:

1. Bryan Lawson argues that design always involves persuasion, or the effort to specify what "might, could, and should be." What are these documents trying to persuade readers/viewers to believe?

2. How do the designers of the ad and Web page use words, images, and graphics to persuade? Do some of these elements seem more important than others? Why?

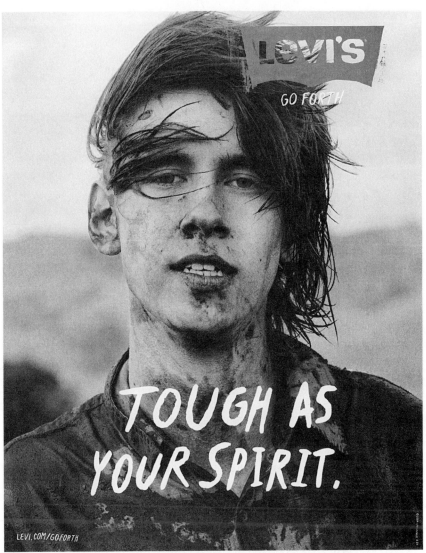

Advertisement for Levi's

3. In what ways do the ad and Web page reinforce Lawson's observation that design involves "subjective value judgments"? Do they, for instance, rely upon culturally sanctioned stereotypes? If they do, how do these stereotypes reinforce their message?

4. In what ways do these promotional pieces demonstrate rhetorical sensitivity on the part of those who created them?

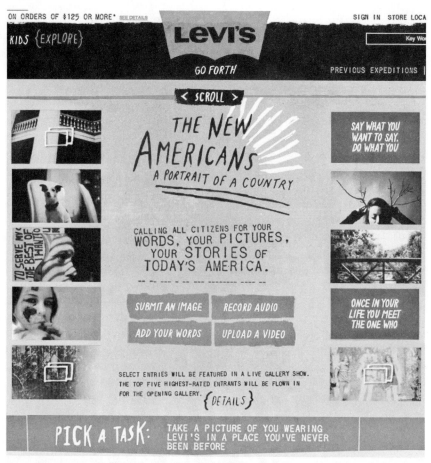

Levi's Marketing Web Site for Its "Go Forth" Campaign

NOTE FOR MULTILINGUAL WRITERS

If you learned to write in a language other than English, you may sometimes feel frustrated when teachers ask you to adapt to the conventions of academic writing in the United States. You may feel that you are being asked to stop speaking and writing in a way that feels natural to you. In fact, you are not alone in facing this challenge; many students who have grown up in the United States speaking English may also have limited experience with academic writing conventions.

Although conflicts sometimes occur between first or home languages and those you use in school, your goal as a writer should not be to abandon your first or home language. Instead, as you become more fluent in the conventions of standard written English, you should try to develop a rhetorical sensitivity that allows you to write effectively in both languages and communities.

| |

FOR THOUGHT, DISCUSSION, AND WRITING

1. Take a few moments to reflect on your understanding of the terms *rhetoric* and *rhetorical sensitivity*. You may find it helpful to recall an incident in your daily life when you were called on to demonstrate rhetorical sensitivity. Write a paragraph describing this incident. Then write a paragraph or so stating your current understanding of these terms. Finally, write one or two questions that you still have about *rhetoric* and *rhetorical sensitivity*.

2. Write an essay in which you describe and reflect upon the many kinds of writing that you do and the role that visual and design elements play in your writing. After writing the essay, create a text that uses words, images, and (if you like) graphics to convey the ideas you discuss in your essay. You can use any mix of photographs, drawings, text, or other material that will help others understand your experience.

3. Interview two or three students in your current or prospective major to learn more about writing in this field. Ask these students the following questions:

    ■ What kinds of writing are students required to do in classes in this field?

    ■ How would they characterize the role of images and other graphic elements in this writing? What role, if any, do multimedia play in their writing?

    ■ How is their writing evaluated by their professors?

    ■ What advice about writing would they give to other students taking classes in this discipline?

Your instructor may ask you to report the results of these interviews to the class. Your instructor may also ask you to write an essay summarizing and reflecting on the results of your interview.

Academic Writing: Committing to the Process

Many people think that those who write well possess a magical or mysterious power. According to this view, people are either born with the ability to write well or not, and those who write well find writing easy: They just sit down, and the words and ideas begin to flow. Interestingly, people often feel the same way about those who work with images and graphics. They believe that designers and artists have a gift that enables them to create vivid and compelling designs, paintings, or other aesthetic objects.

In fact, most successful writers, designers, and artists study their craft for many years. What some would call "talent" or "a gift" might more aptly be characterized as interest, motivation, and commitment. Successful writers and designers know that their skills take time to mature. They also know that to develop their skills they must look for opportunities to practice them. As they practice, they reflect on the strengths and limitations not only of the products they produce but also of the processes they use to create them. This reflection, in turn, allows them to develop strategies to cope with the complexities of writing and design, and thus to experience the satisfaction of a job well done.

As a student, you probably know from experience that your writing is most successful when you give yourself ample time to develop your thoughts, draft, and revise. If you're like most students, though, you don't always act upon this knowledge. This chapter will help you gain insight into your own preferences as a writer, enabling you to commit to a writing process that works for you—and that results in successful academic writing.

||||||||||||||||||||||||||||||||||||||||||||||||||||||||||||||||||||||||||||||||||||||||

FOR EXPLORATION

Take some time to reflect on your own assumptions about writing and your experiences as a writer. Set aside at least half an hour, and respond in writing to the following questions. As you do so, be sure to reflect on both your academic and your personal writing and reading experiences.

1. What are your earliest memories of learning to write? Of learning to read?

2. How were reading and writing viewed by your family and friends when you were growing up?

3. What role did reading play in your development as a writer? What kinds of texts were you drawn to—traditional print texts; visual texts, such as comics and graphic novels; a mix; or some other kind(s)?

4. Can you recall particular experiences in school or on the job that influenced your current attitude toward writing?

5. If you were to describe your history as a writer, what stages or periods in your development would you identify? Write a sentence or two briefly characterizing each stage or period.

6. What images come to mind when you hear the term *writer*?

7. What images come to mind when you think of yourself as a writer? Try drawing up a list of metaphors, such as "As a writer, I'm a turtle—slow and steady" or "As a writer, I'm a racehorse—fast out of the gate but never sure if I've got the stamina to finish." Write two or three sentences that use images or metaphors to characterize your sense of yourself as a writer.

8. What kinds of writing have you come to enjoy? To dislike? What kinds of writing do you do outside of school? Do you regularly tweet or chat via text messages? Do you keep a personal journal or blog? Do you write poetry? In answering this question, include any print or multimedia texts that you regularly create simply because you enjoy doing so.

9. What role have multimedia texts (such as Web sites, hypertext documents, or video games) played in your reading and writing experiences? What role do images and graphics play in your writing—both in and out of school?

10. What do you enjoy most about the process of writing? What do you enjoy least?

11. What goals would you like to set for yourself as a writer?

FOR EXPLORATION

Using the notes, responses, and reflections generated by the previous Exploration, write a letter to your classmates and teacher in which you describe who you are as a writer today—and how you got to be that way. Alternatively, create a text that uses words, images, and (if you like) graphics to describe who you are as a writer today. You could hand-draw your text or create it on the computer; you could also make a collage.

For her response to this assignment, student Mirlandra Ebert created a collage, which is shown on p. 22. (To read Mirlandra's analysis of her rhetorical situation, turn to p. 43.)

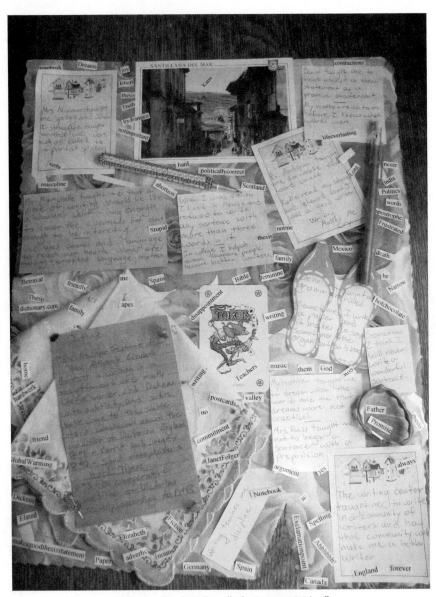

Mirlandra Ebert's Collage, "Who I Am as a Writer"

FOR COLLABORATION

Bring enough copies of the letter or visual text you created in response to the previous Exploration to share with members of your group. After you have all read one another's texts, work together to answer the following questions. Choose one person to record the group's answers so that you can share the results of your discussion with the rest of the class.

1. To what extent are your attitudes toward writing and experiences as writers similar? List three to five statements with which all group members can agree.

2. What factors account for the differences in your attitudes toward writing and experiences as writers? List two or three factors that you agree account for these differences.

3. What common goals can you set for yourselves as writers? List at least three goals you can agree on.

|||||||||||||||||||||||||||||||||||||||||||||||||||||||||||||||||||||||||||||||||||||||

Managing the Writing Process

Successful writers know that they must develop and commit to a writing process that enables them to succeed as students. But how do writers actually manage the writing process? Notice how differently the following students say that they proceed.

> My writing starts with contemplation. I let the topic I have chosen sink into my mind for a while. During this time my mind is a swirl of images, words, and ideas. Sometimes I draw clusters or diagrams that show how my ideas relate; sometimes I make lists. Whatever works works. But this period of letting my ideas develop is essential to my writing. Gradually my ideas take shape — and at a certain point I just know whether I have the right topic or approach or not. If I think I don't, I force myself to start over. If I do, then I make a plan for my essay. I can't really write without at least a skeleton plan that I can refer to: it stresses me out not to know where I'm headed. Before I get very far into my draft I try to stop and ask myself whether I should write something that is straight text — a regular academic essay — or whether this is a project that needs visuals or graphics. By the time I'm done with my plan, I usually have a pretty clear idea of where I'm going. Next I write a draft, possibly several drafts, before I do a final revision. — **Sara Steinman**

> Maybe it's just my personality, but when I get an assignment I have to leap right into it. It's hard to describe what I write at the beginning. It's part brainstorming, part planning, part drafting, part letting off steam. I

just have to write to see what I think! I make notes to myself. What's the best evidence for this argument? Would a graph strengthen my point? What do I really think about this topic? I do most of this early writing by hand because I need to be able to use arrows to connect ideas, circle important points, draw pictures. At this point, no one but me could understand what I've written. I take a break if I can, and then I sit down and reread everything I've written (it can be a lot). That's when I move to the computer. Even at this point I still basically write without doing a lot of conscious planning — I'm going on intuition. The time comes when I've got to change gears and become my own harshest critic. That's when I do a kind of planning in reverse. I might outline my draft, for instance, and see if the outline makes sense. It takes a lot of time and work for me to get to the point where my ideas have really jelled, and even then I've often got several drafts ahead of me. — **Eduardo Alvarez**

As a writer, I am first a thinker and then a doer. I've always had to think my ideas out in detail before I begin drafting. Even though for me this is essentially a mental process, it still involves words and images. I can't really describe it — I just keep thinking things through. It's always felt like a waste of time to me to sit down to write without having a clear idea of what I want to say. Since I have two children, I also don't have a lot of time to focus solely on my writing, so I try out different ideas while folding laundry, driving the kids to daycare, after they're in bed. I'm a new media major, so part of my mental planning always involves thinking about media. If the assignment specifies the medium, then I always think how to make the best possible use of it. If it doesn't, then I run through all my options. Eventually I have a pretty clear sense of what I want to say and what medium will best convey it. Sometimes I make a plan before I get to work, especially if it's a long or complicated project. But sometimes I just begin writing. With some projects, my first draft is strong enough that I just have to edit it. Of course, that's not always the case. — **Wei Liao**

thinking rhetorically On the surface, these students' writing processes seem to have little in common. Actually, however, all involve the same three activities: planning, drafting, and revising. These activities don't necessarily occur in any set order. Wei Liao plans in her head and postpones making a written plan until after she has generated a rough draft, whereas Sara Steinman plans extensively before she writes her first word. To be successful, however, all these writers must sooner or later think rhetorically and make choices about their own situation as writers, their readers, their text, and medium. Then they must try out these choices in their heads, on paper, or at the computer;

evaluate the effects of these choices; and make appropriate changes in their drafts. Rather than being a magical or mysterious activity, then, writing is a process of planning, drafting, and revising.

Identifying Composing Styles

When designers and writers take their own composing processes seriously, they attempt to build on their strengths and recognize their limitations. They understand that they must vary their approach to writing depending on the task or situation. A student who prefers to spend a lot of time developing written or mental plans for an essay simply doesn't have that luxury when writing an in-class essay exam. For this reason, it's more accurate to refer to *writing processes* rather than *the writing process*. As a writer and designer, you must be pragmatic: You decide how to approach a project based on such factors as the nature and importance of the task, the schedule, the nature and demands of the medium, the experience you have with a particular kind of writing, and so on. Most experienced writers and designers do, however, have a preferred way of managing the composing process.

HEAVY PLANNERS.   Like Wei Liao, heavy planners generally plan their writing so carefully in their heads that their first drafts are often more like other writers' second or third drafts. As a consequence, they revise less intensively and less frequently than other students. Many of these students have disciplined themselves so that they can think about their writing in all sorts of places—on the subway, at work, in the garden pulling weeds, or in the car driving to and from school.

Some heavy planners write in this way because they prefer to; others develop this strategy out of necessity. Wei Liao, for instance, says that she simply has to do a great deal of her writing in her head because she's a mother as well as a student, and at home she often has to steal spare moments to work on her writing. As a result, she's learned to use every opportunity to think about her writing while she drives, cooks, or relaxes with her family.

HEAVY REVISERS.   Like Eduardo Alvarez, heavy revisers use the act of writing itself to find out what they want to say. When faced with a writing task, they prefer to sit down at a desk or computer and just begin writing.

Heavy revisers often state that writing their ideas out in a sustained spurt of activity reassures them that they have something to say and helps them avoid frustration. These students may not seem to plan because they begin drafting so early. Actually, however, their planning occurs as they draft and especially as they revise. Heavy revisers spend a great deal of time revising their initial drafts. To do so effectively, they must be able to read their work critically and, often, discard substantial portions of first drafts. For one

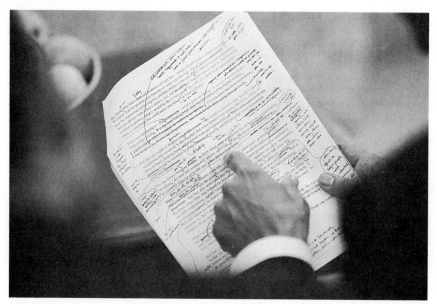

President Barack Obama and Speechwriter John Farreau Edit a Speech on Health Care, Sept. 9, 2009

example of heavy revision in action, see above, where we've reproduced a White House photo of President Obama holding the heavily revised text to one of his speeches.

As you've probably realized, in both of these styles of composing, one of the components of the writing process is apparently abbreviated. Heavy planners don't seem to revise as extensively as other writers. Actually, however, they plan (and, in effect, revise) so thoroughly early in the process that they often don't need to revise as intensively later. Similarly, heavy revisers may not seem to plan; in fact, though, once they write their rough drafts, they plan and revise simultaneously and, often, extensively.

SEQUENTIAL COMPOSERS. A third general style of composing is exemplified by Sara Steinman. These writers might best be called sequential composers because they devote roughly equivalent amounts of time to planning, drafting, and revising. Rather than trying out their ideas and planning their writing mentally, as heavy planners do, sequential composers typically rely on written notes and plans to give shape and force to their ideas. And unlike heavy revisers, sequential composers need to have greater control over form and subject matter as they draft.

Sequential composers' habit of allotting time for planning, drafting, and revising helps them deal with the inevitable anxieties of writing. Like heavy revisers, sequential composers need the reassurance of seeing their ideas written down: Generating a volume of notes and plans gives them the confidence to begin drafting. Sequential composers may not revise as extensively as heavy revisers, for they generally draft more slowly, reviewing their writing as they proceed. But revision is nevertheless an important part of their composing process. Like most writers, sequential composers need a break from drafting to be able to critique their own words and ideas.

Each of these composing styles has advantages and disadvantages. Heavy planners can be efficient writers, spending less time drafting and revising than other writers, but they must have great mental discipline. An unexpected interruption when they're working out their ideas—a child in tears, a phone call, or a friend dropping by—can cause even the most disciplined thinker to have a momentary lapse. Because so much of their work is done in their heads, heavy planners are less likely to benefit from the fruitful explorations and revisions that occur when writers review notes and plans or reread their own texts. And because heavy planners put off drafting until relatively late in the composing process, they can encounter substantial difficulties if the sentences and paragraphs that had seemed so clearly developed in their minds don't look as coherent and polished on paper.

Heavy revisers experience different advantages and disadvantages. Because they write quickly and voluminously, heavy revisers aren't in danger of losing valuable ideas. Similarly, their frequent rereading of drafts helps them remain open to new options that can improve their writing. However, heavy revisers must learn how to deal with emotional highs and lows that occur as they discover what they want to say through the process of writing itself. They must be able to critique their own writing ruthlessly, discarding large portions of text or perhaps even starting over. And because they revise so extensively, heavy revisers must leave adequate time for revision or the quality of their work can suffer.

What about sequential composers? Because they spend time planning, drafting, and revising—and do so primarily in writing—they have more external control over the writing process than heavy planners and revisers have. Sequential composers are also unlikely to fool themselves into thinking that a quickly generated collection of ideas is an adequate rough draft or that a plan brainstormed while taking the subway is adequate preparation for writing. Sequential composers can, however, develop inefficiently rigid habits—habits that reflect their need to have external control over their writing process. They may, for instance, waste valuable time developing detailed written plans when they're actually ready to begin drafting.

Good writers are aware of their preferred composing style—and of its potential advantages and disadvantages. They take responsibility for decisions about how to manage their composing process, recognizing the difference, for instance, between the necessary incubation of ideas and pro-crastination. Good writers are also flexible; depending on the task or situa-tion, they can modify their preferred approach. A person who generally is a heavy reviser when writing academic essays, for instance, might write routine business memos in a single sitting because that's the most efficient way to get the job done, and the readers of business memos tend to value directness, concision, and timeliness over finely tuned deliberation or refined prose. Similarly, heavy planners who prefer to do much of the work of writing men-tally must employ different strategies when writing collaboratively with oth-ers or when engaged in research-based writing.

PROCRASTINATORS.　There is one other common way of managing the writing process, though it might best be described as management by avoid-ance—procrastination. All writers occasionally procrastinate, but if you ha-bitually put off writing a first draft until you have time only for a final draft (and this at 3 A.M. on the day your essay is due), your chances of success are minimal. Though you may have invented good reasons for putting off writing ("I write better under pressure"; "I can't write until I have all my easier as-signments done first"), procrastination makes it difficult for you to manage the writing process in an efficient and effective manner.

Is procrastination always harmful? Might it not sometimes reflect a pe-riod of necessary incubation, of unconscious but still productive planning? Here's what Holly Hardin—a thoughtful student writer—discovered when she reflected about her experiences as a writer.

> For me, sometimes procrastination isn't really procrastination (or so I tell myself). Sometimes what I label procrastination is really planning. The trouble is that I don't always know when it's one or the other.
>
> How do I procrastinate? Let me count the ways. I procrastinate by doing good works (helping overtime at my job, cleaning house, aiding and abetting a variety of causes). I procrastinate by absorbing myself in a purely selfish activity (reading paperbacks, watching TV, going to movies). I procrastinate by visiting with friends, talking on the telephone, prolonging chance encounters. I procrastinate by eating and drinking (ice cream, coffee, cookies — all detrimental). Finally, I procrastinate by convincing myself that this time of day is not when I write well. I'd be much better off, I sometimes conclude, taking a nap. So I do.
>
> Part of my difficulty is that I can see a certain validity in most of my reasons for procrastinating. There are some times of day when my thoughts flow better. I have forced myself to write papers in the past

when I just didn't feel ready. Not only were the papers difficult to write, they were poorly written, inarticulate papers. Even after several rewrites, they were merely marginal. I would much rather write when I am at my mental best.

     I need to balance writing with other activities. The trouble is — just how to achieve the perfect balance!

Holly's realistic appraisal of the role that procrastination plays in her writing process should help her distinguish between useful incubation and unhelpful procrastination. Unlike students who tell themselves that they should never procrastinate — and then do so anyway, feeling guilty every moment — Holly knows that she has to consider a variety of factors before she decides to invite a friend over, bake a batch of chocolate chip cookies, or take a much-needed nap.

NOTE FOR MULTILINGUAL WRITERS

If your first or home language is not English, you may be familiar with different approaches to the composing process of planning, drafting, and revising. Educational systems throughout the world have different approaches to writing and to the teaching of writing. In thinking about your writing process as a student in college, reflect on how your previous experiences as a writer enhance or interfere with your efforts to compose in standard written English. (Different approaches to revision may be especially relevant.) You may want to discuss the results of your reflection with your teacher or your tutor in the writing center.

Analyzing Your Composing Process

The poet William Stafford once commented that "a writer is not so much someone who has something to say as he is someone who has found a process that will bring about new things he would not have thought if he had not started to say them." Stafford's remarks emphasize the importance of developing a workable writing process — a repertoire of strategies that you can draw on in a variety of situations.

thinking
rhetorically

Quiz: Analyzing Your Composing Process

You can use the following questions to analyze your composing process. Your teacher may ask you to respond to some or all of these questions in writing.

1. What is your general attitude toward writing?

    a. love it   b. hate it   c. somewhere in between

How do you think this attitude affects your writing?

2. Which of the composing styles described in this chapter best describes the way you compose?

    a. heavy planner   b. heavy reviser   c. sequential composer   d. procrastinator

If none seems to fit you, how do you compose?

3. How do you know when you are ready to begin writing?

    a. I have a "start-up" method or ritual.
    b. I just feel ready.
    c. It's the night before the assignment is due.

If you have a "start-up" method, what is it? If you don't have a ritual, do you think establishing one would help?

4. How long do you typically work on your writing at any one time?

    a. less than an hour   b. from one to two hours   c. more than two hours

Do you think you spend about the right amount of time at a given stretch, or do you think you should generally do more (or less)? Why?

5. Are you more likely to write an essay

    a. in a single sitting?   b. over a number of days (or weeks)?

Have you had success doing it this way? How do you think adjusting your approach would affect the essays you end up writing?

6. Do you have any writing habits and rituals?

    a. yes   b. no

If you answered "yes," what are they? Which are productive, and which interfere with your writing process? If you answered "no," can you think of any habits you would like to develop?

7. **How often do you import visuals and graphics into texts you are composing?**

    a. sometimes   b. never   c. always

    If you do use visuals and graphics, do you enjoy doing so? find it a challenge? take it for granted? How have your instructors received your efforts?

8. **What planning and revising strategies do you use?**

    a.   specific strategies (e.g., outlining, listing)
    b.   general strategies (e.g., "I think out a plan, and I reread what I've written.")
    c.   no strategies I'm aware of

    How do you know when you have spent enough time planning and revising?

9. **If your first or home language is not English, how does knowing two or more languages influence your writing process?**

    a. a great deal   b. somewhat   c. not at all

    If you do have a second language, reflect on how it affects your writing in English (or why you think it doesn't). Also consider: What language do you typically think in? In what language do you freewrite, brainstorm, or make notes?

10. **What role do exchanges with others (conversations, responses from peers or tutors) play in your writing?**

    a. an important role   b. an occasional role   c. no role

    Would you like to make more use of exchanges like these? Why or why not?

11. **How do you procrastinate? (Be honest! All writers procrastinate occasionally.)**

    a. I procrastinate very little.
    b. I start later than I should, but I get the job done.
    c. I don't start until it's too late to do a good job.

    Do you need to change your habits in this respect? If you do need to change them, how will you do so?

12. **Thinking in general about the writing you do, what do you find most rewarding and satisfying about writing? Most difficult and frustrating? Why?**

||||||||||||||||||||||||||||||||||||||||||||||||||||||||||||||||||||||||||||||||||||||||

FOR COLLABORATION

Meet with classmates to discuss your responses to the quiz on pp. 30–31. Begin by having each person state two important things he or she learned as a result of completing the quiz. (Appoint a recorder to write down each person's statements.) Once all members of your group have spoken, ask the recorder to read their statements aloud. Were any statements repeated by more than one member of the group? Working as a group, formulate two conclusions about the writing process that you would like to share with the class. (Avoid vague and general assertions, such as "Writing is difficult.") Be prepared to discuss your conclusions with your classmates.

||||||||||||||||||||||||||||||||||||||||||||||||||||||||||||||||||||||||||||||||||||||||

Writing is a *process,* and stopping to think about your own composing process can prove illuminating. One of my students, for example, formulated an analogy that helped us all think fruitfully about how the writing process works. "Writing," he said, "is actually a lot like sports." Writing—like sports? Let's see what this comparison reveals about the writing process.

WRITING AND SPORTS ARE BOTH PERFORMANCE SKILLS. You may know who won every Wimbledon since 1980, but if you don't actually play tennis, you're not a tennis player—just somebody who knows a lot about tennis. Similarly, you can know a lot about writing, but to demonstrate (and improve) your skills, you must *write.*

WRITING AND SPORTS BOTH REQUIRE INDIVIDUALS TO MASTER COMPLEX SKILLS AND TO PERFORM THESE SKILLS IN AN ALMOST INFINITE NUMBER OF SITUATIONS. Athletes must learn specific skills, plays, or maneuvers, but they can never execute them routinely or thoughtlessly. Writers must be similarly resourceful and flexible. You can learn the principles of effective essay organization, for instance, and you may write a number of essays that are well organized. Nevertheless, each time you sit down to write a new essay, you have to consider your options and make new choices. This is a primary reason that smart writers don't rely on formulas or rules but instead use rhetorical sensitivity to analyze and respond to each situation.

thinking rhetorically

EXPERIENCED ATHLETES AND WRITERS KNOW THAT A POSITIVE ATTITUDE IS ESSENTIAL. Some athletes psych themselves up before a game or competition, often using music, meditation, or other personal routines. But any serious athlete knows that's only part of what having a positive attitude means. It also means running five miles when you're already tired at three, or doing twelve repetitions during weight training when you're exhausted and no one else would know if you did only eight. A positive attitude is equally important in writing. If you approach a writing task with a negative attitude ("I never was good at writing"), you create obstacles for yourself. Having a positive, open attitude is essential in tennis, skiing—and writing.

TO MAINTAIN A HIGH LEVEL OF SKILL, BOTH ATHLETES AND WRITERS NEED FREQUENT PRACTICE AND EFFECTIVE COACHING. "In sports," a coach once said, "you're either getting better or getting worse." Without practice—which for a writer means both reading and writing—your writing skills will slip (as will your confidence). Likewise, coaching is essential in writing because it's hard to distance yourself from your own work. Coaches—your writing instructor, a tutor (or writing assistant) at a writing center, or a fellow student—can help you gain a fresh perspective on your writing and make useful suggestions about revision as well.

EXPERIENCED ATHLETES AND WRITERS CONTINUALLY SET NEW GOALS FOR THEMSELVES. Athletes continually set new challenges for themselves and analyze their performance. They know that coaches can help but that *they* are ultimately the ones performing. Experienced writers know this too, so they look for opportunities to practice their writing. And they don't measure their success simply by a grade. They see their writing always as work in progress. Successful athletes, like successful writers, know that they must *commit* to a process that will enable them to perform at the highest possible level.

> For a case study of student Daniel Stiepleman's process of interacting with a text, exploring ideas, and developing an essay for a first-year writing class, see "Composing an Academic Argument: A Case Study of One Student's Writing Process" (Chapter 5, pp. 137–53).

Writing Communities

Finding a Community

For many people, one big difference between writing and sports is that athletes often belong to teams. Writers, they think, work in lonely isolation. In fact, this romanticized image of the writer struggling alone until inspiration strikes is both inaccurate and unhelpful. If you take a careful look at the day-to-day writing that people do, you quickly recognize that many people in business, industry, academia, and other professions work as part of one or more teams to produce written texts. In many cases, these individuals' ability to work effectively with others is key to a successful career. Those who write for school, community-based projects, or even for personal enrichment also often turn to others for ideas and advice.

Even when writers do a good deal of their composing alone, they often find it helpful to talk with others before and while writing. A group of neighbors writing a petition to their city council requesting that a speed bump be installed on their street might well ask one person to compose the petition. In order to do a good job, the writer would have to talk extensively with her neighbors to generate the strongest ideas possible. She would probably also present drafts of the petition for her neighbors' review and approval.

Most writers alternate between periods of independent activity, composing alone at a computer or desk, and periods of social interaction—meeting with friends, colleagues, or team members for information, advice, or responses to drafts. They may also correspond with others in their field, or they may get in touch with people doing similar work through reading, research, or online technologies. These relationships will help them learn new ideas, improve their skills, and share their interest and enthusiasm.

Sometimes these relationships are formal and relatively permanent. Many poets and fiction writers, for instance, meet regularly to discuss work in progress. Perhaps more commonly, writers' networks are informal and shifting, though no less vital. A new manager in a corporation, for instance, may find one or two people with sound judgment and good writing skills to review important letters and reports. Similarly, students working on a major project for a class may meet informally but regularly to compare notes and provide mutual support.

Online technologies and the Web have increased the opportunity for writers to work collaboratively. Using online spaces, from course Web sites to blogs and public writing communities such as Writing.com ("for writers and readers of all interests and skill levels"), writers everywhere are sharing their writing and getting responses to works in progress.

Working Collaboratively

Because you're in the same class and share the same assignments and concerns, you and your classmates constitute a natural community of writers. Whether your instructor makes it a requirement or not, you should explore the possibility of forming a peer group or joining one that already exists. In order to work effectively, however, you and your peers need to develop or strengthen the skills that will contribute to effective group work.

As you prepare to work collaboratively, remember that people have different styles of learning and interacting. Some of these differences represent individual preferences: Some students work out their ideas as they talk, for instance, while others prefer to think through their ideas before speaking. Other differences are primarily cultural and thus reflect deeply embedded social practices and preferences. Effective groups are pragmatic and task-oriented, but they balance a commitment to getting the job done with patience and flexibility. They value diversity and find ways to ensure that *all* members can comfortably participate in and benefit from group activities.

Effective groups also take care to articulate group goals and monitor group processes. Sometimes this monitoring is intuitive and informal. But sometimes a more formal process is helpful. If you're part of a group that meets regularly, you might begin meetings by having each person state one way in which the group is working well and one way in which it could be improved. If a problem such as a dominating or nonparticipating member is raised, deal with it immediately. The time spent responding to these comments and suggestions will ensure that your group is working effectively.

Group activities such as peer response and collaborative troubleshooting can help improve your writing ability and prepare you for on-the-job teamwork. Remember, though, that groups are a bit like friendships or marriages. They develop and change, and they require care and attention. You have to be committed to keeping the group going, being alert to signs of potential trouble, and willing to talk problems out in order to benefit from them.

Students juggling coursework, jobs, families, and other activities can sometimes find it difficult to get together or to take the time to read and respond to one another's writing. Getting together with classmates to share your writing is well worth the effort it takes. If it proves impossible, however, you may have one important alternative: a campus writing center. Many colleges and universities have established writing centers as places where you can go to talk with others about your writing, get help with specific writing problems, or find answers to questions you may have. If your campus does have a writing center, take advantage of the opportunity to get an informed response to your work.

|||||||||||||||||||||||||||||||||||||||||||||||||||||||||||||||||||||||||||||||||||||||

FOR COLLABORATION

Meet with your group to discuss how you can most effectively work together. Begin by exchanging names, phone numbers, and email addresses, and take time just to get to know each other. You might also see if your group can formulate some friendly rules to guide group activities. (You might all agree, for instance, to notify at least one member if you can't make a meeting.) Be sure to write these rules down and consult them as you work together. Try to anticipate problems, such as coordinating schedules, and discuss how to resolve them.

FOR EXPLORATION

If your campus has a writing center, make an appointment to interview a tutor (sometimes also called a writing assistant or peer consultant) about the services the center provides. You may also want to ask the tutor about his or her own experiences as a writer. Your instructor may ask you to present the results of your interview orally or to write a summary of your discussion.

Guidelines for Group Work

1. Review your assignment and agree on goals and procedures.

Doing a brief activity in class? Limit yourselves to a few minutes to set goals.

Doing an extended project with meetings outside of class? Take ten to fifteen minutes to set goals.

2. Assign roles, but be flexible.
Effective group members are willing to assume multiple roles as needed.

■ *Group leaders* assign tasks, set priorities, and take responsibility for progress.

■ *Consensus builders* facilitate communication and mediate conflicts.

■ *Task masters* try to keep everyone focused and productive.

3. Encourage productive conflict.
Capitalize on the diverse perspectives and strategies that people bring to a problem.

■ *Encourage the discussion of new ideas.*

■ *Consider alternative approaches to your subject.*

■ *Don't be afraid to disagree.* Just be sure that the discussion remains friendly and focused on the task at hand.

FOR THOUGHT, DISCUSSION, AND WRITING

1. Now that you have read this chapter, set some goals for yourself as a writer. Make a list of several goals you'd like to accomplish in your composition class this term. What would you most like to learn or improve? What would you like to change about your writing process? Then write a paragraph or two discussing how you plan to achieve these goals.

2. You can learn a great deal about your own composing process by observing yourself as you write. To do so, follow these steps:

   ■ Choose an upcoming writing project to study. Before beginning this project, reflect on its demands. How much time do you expect to spend working on this project, and how do you anticipate allocating your time? What challenges does this project hold for you? What strengths and resources do you bring to this project?

   ■ As you work on the project, keep track of how you spend your time. Include a record in this log of when you started and ended each work session, as well as a description of your activities and notes commenting on your process. What went well? What surprised you? What gave you problems? What might you do differently next time?

   ■ After you have completed the project, draw on your prewriting analysis and process log to write a case study of this project. As you do so, consider questions such as these: To what extent was your prewriting analysis of your project accurate? How did you actually allocate your time when working on this project? What strategies did you rely on most heavily? What went well with your writing? What was difficult? Conclude by reflecting about what you have learned from this case study about yourself as a writer.

3. All writers procrastinate occasionally—some just procrastinate more effectively than others. After brainstorming or freewriting about your favorite ways of procrastinating, write a humorous or serious essay on procrastination.

4. The Exploration activities on pp. 20 and 21 encouraged you to reflect on your assumptions about writing and your experiences as a writer. Drawing on these activities and on the rest of the chapter, write an essay in which you reflect on this subject. You may choose to write about pivotal incidents in your experiences as a writer, using particular occasions to support the general statements you make about your experiences.

CHAPTER 3

Analyzing Rhetorical Situations

Whenever you write—whether you're word processing an essay or designing a brochure for a student organization—you are writing in the context of a specific rhetorical situation involving you as the writer, who you're writing for, what you're writing, and the medium you use to share what you have written. Each rhetorical situation comes with unique opportunities and demands: A management trainee writing a memo to her supervisor, for example, faces different challenges than an investigative journalist working on a story for the *New York Times* or a student writing an essay for a history class. Successful writers know that they need to exhibit rhetorical sensitivity—an understanding of the relationships among writer, reader, text, and medium—to help them make decisions as they write and revise.

In this chapter of *The Academic Writer,* you will learn how to ask questions about your rhetorical situation—questions that will enable you to determine the most fruitful way of approaching your topic and of responding to the needs and expectations of your readers. You will also learn how to recognize the textual conventions that characterize different communities of language users. This kind of rhetorically sensitive reading is particularly helpful when you are learning new forms of writing—which is the case, for example, when you enter college or begin a new job.

Learning to Analyze Your Rhetorical Situation

thinking
rhetorically

Rhetoric involves four key elements: writer, reader, text, and medium. When you think about these elements and pose questions about the options available to you as a writer, you are analyzing your rhetorical situation.

The process of analyzing your rhetorical situation challenges you to look both within and without. Your intended meaning—what you want to communicate—is certainly important, as is your purpose for writing. But unless you're writing solely for yourself in a journal or notebook, you can't ignore

The Rhetorical Situation

your readers or your situation. You also need to consider which medium will best convey your ideas. Both at school and on the job, sometimes your medium will be predetermined; at other times, however, you will have options. Analyzing your rhetorical situation helps you respond creatively as a writer and yet keeps you aware of limits on your freedom.

In your daily life, you regularly analyze your rhetorical situation when you communicate with others—though you most often do this unconsciously and intuitively. Imagine, for instance, that you've been meaning to contact a close friend. Should you call, email, text, instant message, send a handwritten note, or contact him some other way? The answer depends on your situation. If you just want to let your friend know that you're thinking of him, you might choose text, instant message, or email because their ease and informality suit this purpose well. If your friend maintains a Facebook page, you might visit his wall, read some posts to see what he's been up to, and then leave a greeting. But what if you're writing because you've just learned of a death in your friend's family? The seriousness of this situation and its personal nature might prompt you to send a handwritten note instead.

NOTE FOR MULTILINGUAL WRITERS

This chapter's approach to rhetoric and rhetorical sensitivity is grounded in the Western rhetorical tradition. Other traditions hold different values and assumptions about communication. For example, if part of your education took place in a non-Western culture, you may have learned an approach to communication that values maintaining communal harmony as much as (or more than) individual self-expression, which is highly valued in Western cultures. For some raised in non-Western cultures, English as it is written in school, business, and everyday contexts may seem abrupt and even rude. As a writer learning to communicate in different languages and communities, you need to understand the assumptions held by writers who are grounded in the Western rhetorical tradition — but you do not need to abandon your own culture's values. Your writing (and your thinking) will be enriched when you learn how to draw on *all* the rhetorical sensitivity that you have gained as a speaker, listener, writer, and reader.

Using Your Rhetorical Analysis to Guide Your Writing

Effective writers draw on their rhetorical sensitivity to determine the most effective ways to communicate with readers. Often, writers do this without thinking: The student deciding how best to get in touch with a friend didn't consciously run through a mental checklist but rather drew on his intuitive understanding of his situation. When you face the challenge of new and more difficult kinds of writing, however, as you do in college, it helps to analyze your rhetorical situation consciously.

|||||||||||||||||||||||||||||||||||||||||||||||||||||||||||||||||||||||||||||||||||

FOR EXPLORATION

Imagine that you need to compose the following texts:

- An application for an internship in your major
- A flyer for a march you are organizing to protest a tuition increase
- Your response to a film that you viewed in class, posted to an online discussion board
- A substantial research-based essay for a class you are taking

Spend a few minutes thinking about how you would approach these different writing situations, and write a brief description of each, using the following questions:

- What is your role as writer? Your purpose for writing?
- What image of yourself do you wish to present? How will you create this image?
- How will your readers influence your writing?
- How will the medium you use affect your communication?
- What role, if any, should images, graphics, and multimedia play?

|||||||||||||||||||||||||||||||||||||||||||||||||||||||||||||||||||||||||||||||||||

Questions for Analyzing Your Rhetorical Situation

Writer

1. Why are you writing?

- to convey information?
- to change the reader's mind?
- to entertain the reader?
- to move the reader to action?

2. How will your goals affect the form, content, and medium of your text?

3. Is the role you will play in the text . . .

- fixed (e.g., essay exam)? or flexible (e.g., narrative)?

4. What image of yourself do you want to convey to your readers? Will you write as . . .

- a serious student?
- a concerned citizen?
- something else?

How will you use language to achieve this effect?

Reader

1. Who is your intended audience?

- a specific audience (e.g., readers of a particular magazine)?
- a general audience?
- a specific reader (e.g., your teacher)?

Do you need to consider demographics, such as age, gender, religion, income, occupation, education, or political preference?

2. What role do you want readers to adopt as they read?

What cues will you use to signal this role?

3. How will your writing appeal to your readers' interests, values, and beliefs?

Will they be interested from the outset, or do you need to create and maintain their interest?

4. How might your readers' needs and expectations influence the form, content, and style of your writing?

Questions for Analyzing Your Rhetorical Situation

Text

1. How much freedom do you have in deciding on form and content?

Are you responding to an *assignment*?

If so, does it dictate form and/or content?

What *genre* are you writing in? Are its styles and conventions . . .

rigidly defined (as in lab reports)? or *flexible (as in a narrative or profile)?*

Does your subject require certain kinds of evidence or exploration of certain issues?

2. Would it help you to look at examples of this kind of writing written by other people?

Medium

1. How much freedom do you have in deciding what medium to use?

Are you responding to an *assignment*?

If so, does it limit your choice of media?

Do you face *practical constraints*—such as time, expertise, and expense—that might affect your choice of medium?

Does the *kind* of text you're writing make some media more appropriate than others?

2. What expectations might your audience have in terms of medium?

Might some media be more *accessible* to your audience than others?

Might your audience be more *comfortable* with some media than with others?

Setting Preliminary Goals

Before beginning a major writing project, you may find it helpful to write a brief analysis of your rhetorical situation, or you may simply review these questions mentally. Doing so can help you determine your preliminary intentions or goals as a writer. (Your intentions will often shift as you write. That's fine. As you write, you'll naturally revise your understanding of your rhetorical situation.) Despite its tentativeness, however, your analysis of your situation will give you a sense of direction and purpose.

In Chapter 2, you saw Mirlandra Ebert's response to the Exploration activity on p. 21. Rather than writing a letter about her experience as a writer, Mirlandra created a collage (see p. 22). Here is the analysis of her rhetorical situation that Mirlandra composed before creating her visually rich text.

Mirlandra Ebert's Analysis

Writer: The poster I will create is about who I am as a writer. There are many experiences that have shaped me and that will continue to shape me, but I don't have to cover all of them. I just need to decide which are the most important and focus on them. I need content that's understandable, but I don't just want to say "I am _____." I don't think I know what goes in the blank. As a person, sometimes I feel like I reinvent myself every day, almost as if I see myself from a different angle and then I interpret myself differently. I feel the same way as a writer. This poster assignment is an opportunity to express that aspect of my life. The most important role I see for myself as a writer here is to have a voice in this piece. It should be a contradictory, busy, and chaotic voice (busy in the sense of visually rich and active), but still convey strength and fluidity.

Reader: My intended audience is my professor and my classmates. I want to create a text that everybody in my class can connect with in some way. Most of our class is just out of high school, but there are also nontraditional students who may engage differently with my work. I also need to be aware of gender issues. I need to think about how some aspects of my project, such as the flowered background, will come across. Although my audience is diverse, I think I can hold their interest because there will be so much going on in my poster.

thinking
rhetorically

Text: In terms of my text, I have a lot of freedom in this assignment as long as I stay focused on the main topic. The only conventions I need to address are issues of size and readability. I want to be careful to reflect my busy and varied "writing self" but in a way that's not too cluttered to make sense. I don't have to be logical, as I have to be in an essay, so I've got lots of flexibility here. I know I want to express what I've learned from teachers and then engage many smaller ideas about who I am as a writer that have to do with other parts of my life. Before I started on this project, I looked at other posters that students had created. This was helpful, but I want to express my own ideas in my own way. Many examples I looked at used only words and images. I want to move beyond that and include physical objects that represent me.

Medium: In terms of medium, I'm working with the advantages and limitations of posterboard and collage. If I can attach something to posterboard, then it's OK. My audience may expect a basic 2-D poster with pictures and graphics, but I don't think it will create confusion or discomfort if I include other objects. So far I intend to attach a pen I like to write notes with, sticky notes of all sizes, some push pins, my favorite outlining paper, and a hair tie because I'm always messing with my hair when I write. I think these personal objects will make for a more interesting medium.

thinking rhetorically

Here is another analysis of a rhetorical situation, this one by student Alia Sands, whose essay appears on pp. 47–50. Alia analyzed her situation as a writer by using the questions provided on pp. 41–42. She begins with some general reflections about her assignment.

Alia Sands's Analysis

I am writing an essay for my first-year writing class. The assignment asked us to read an essay by Richard Rodriguez titled "Aria." This essay is included in Rodriguez's literacy narrative *Hunger of Memory*. The assignment asked us to respond personally to Rodriguez's text but also to engage with and synthesize his assertions about bilingual education.

Writer: I am writing a personal narrative regarding my experiences as a half-Hispanic, half-Caucasian middle-school student in Marshalltown, Iowa. This narrative will engage with and respond to Richard Rodriguez's chapter "Aria" from *Hunger of Memory*. I hope that by using my own experience I can show how special programs for bilingual students, however well-intentioned, raise complicated questions and may have multiple (and unintended) consequences. My purpose in writing this piece is to engage with Rodriguez's text while also conveying my own story. As I am not an expert on bilingual education, my goal is to situate my experience in its particular context, demonstrating the effect Marshalltown's separation of Hispanic students from the general school population had on my sense of identity.

The image I wish to present of myself is of particular concern to me. I am not the child of immigrants. Unlike Rodriguez, I have not felt that I had to choose between a public and private language in order to succeed in school and work. I wish to portray my experiences as unique to myself and decidedly *not* indicative of all or even most Hispanic students, as many have struggled in ways I have not.

I will use language that is academic while appropriate to a general audience who may not be familiar with issues faced by Hispanic students in public schools in the United States. I do not wish to convey anger or bitterness for what I feel was an error on the part of the school, but I do wish to use language that emphasizes the gravity of the situation and how important I feel it is for schools to recognize how much is denied to students and how their sense of identity is affected when they are not included in mainstream instruction.

Reader: I am assuming that my readers are my instructor as well as my fellow students at Oregon State University. I assume that they are from diverse backgrounds; some of them may have had experiences similar to my own and some of them may be unfamiliar with issues of bilingual education or the feeling of not having a public language or identity. As issues pertaining to race and education are often sensitive ones, I'm hoping to communicate in a way that acknowledges differences in opinion while still taking a clear stance based upon my own experience and my understanding of Rodriguez's text. I am trying not to be reductive when it comes to complicated situations. I don't want to imply that I know what kind of education will be beneficial to everyone. I do hope to show how my experiences overlap with the ideas discussed by Rodriguez and how those experiences have led me to conclusions about what can happen when students are excluded, rather than included, in the use of public language.

Text: I only have a few pages to do the following: summarize Rodriguez's text; convey a meaningful story about my own experiences; and discuss the connections between the two. The length of the paper, then, will be a significant constraint. I will have to carefully edit my narrative, deciding on the most essential details to include, and also figure out what elements (examples, quotes, ideas) of Rodriguez's text I need to discuss. I will not be using multimedia or images, so I must engage my readers through my prose — I'll have to write clearly and succinctly because I have so little space, but I'll also need to use vivid language that will bring my experiences and other examples to life. (For example, I will be mentioning a movie, *Stand and Deliver*, which I was required to watch repeatedly in middle school. I will need to summarize its plot in order to convey its significance, but I'll also want to give readers a clear sense of what watching it felt like — the impression it made on me when I saw it for the first, second, third, etc., time.)

Medium: I currently am not choosing to include any images, graphics, or multimedia in my essay. If I were writing a research paper on this topic, I would probably include graphics or images that would help readers better understand the information I am presenting. As most of my paper will respond to and synthesize Rodriguez's work, I do not feel that images or graphs are necessary to help readers better understand my own experiences or those of Rodriguez.

Here is Alia's essay. As you read it, keep her analysis of her rhetorical situation clearly in mind. In what ways did her analysis inform the essay that she wrote?

Sands 1

Alia Sands
Professor Rhoads
Writing I
May 1, 2010

A Separate Education

Bilingual education and support for nonnative English speakers in classrooms are widely debated topics in academia today. While some argue that students benefit from learning in their native languages, others, like writer Richard Rodriguez, argue that bilingual education deprives students of a shared public identity, which is critical to their full participation in civic life. In middle school, as a half-Hispanic student who only spoke English, I was surprised to find myself in a special class for Hispanic students. My experience in the class brought Rodriguez's misgivings about the effects of separate education vividly to life: Being excluded from mainstream instruction even for a few class periods a week caused me to reevaluate my identity and question whether or not I was actually a member of the broader community.

In the chapter "Aria" from *Hunger of Memory: The Education of Richard Rodriguez,* Richard Rodriguez discusses his own experience of second-language acquisition. Rodriguez, who describes himself as "socially disadvantaged—the son of working-class parents, both Mexican immigrants" (10), did not receive bilingual instruction and was actively discouraged by the nuns running his school from speaking Spanish at home. Though at first Rodriguez was reluctant to embrace English as his primary language because he could not believe "that English was [his] to use" (18), he grew increasingly comfortable with it. His experience learning English led him to believe that the common practice of separating students from mainstream classroom instruction and from that public language "dangerously . . . romanticize[s] public separateness and . . . trivialize[s] the dilemma of the socially disadvantaged" (27).

My story is different from Rodriguez's. My sister Hannah and I grew up in Marshalltown, Iowa, the children of a Hispanic mother and an Anglo father,

Sands 2

both college-educated. In school, I remember at some point checking off a box identifying myself as "Hispanic." In sixth grade, I received a small slip of paper instructing me to go to a basement classroom after lunch rather than to math class. When I arrived at the classroom, my older sister, Hannah, and about ten other students—all of whom were Hispanic—were already there.

There was a large Hispanic population in Marshalltown; many recent immigrants were employed in farming as well as in a local meat-packing plant. While there weren't many Hispanic students in my middle school, there were enough for the district to feel it necessary to send an instructor who said she would help us "integrate" more fully into the general school population. We were "at risk," she said. She promised to help us to learn English and to value our home culture while also becoming meaningful parts of American culture.

Unfortunately, our instructor did not speak Spanish and assumed that none of us spoke English. In fact, more than three-fourths of the students in the class were bilingual, and those who weren't bilingual only spoke English. None of them spoke *only* Spanish. My older sister and I had never spoken Spanish; many of the other students were from Mexico and had only recently come to the United States, but they had improved their English throughout the school year attending regular classes and spoke enough English to understand what was said in classrooms. It was clear we were all being singled out based solely upon ethnicity. We had no idea that we were "at risk" until the instructor told us we were.

Statistics showed, she said, that most of us would not go to college. Many of us would drop out of school. She told us she sympathized with how uncomfortable we must be in class, not understanding English. Her first act as instructor was to go around the room pointing to objects and saying their names, drawing out the vowels slowly. Oooverhead projeeectoor. Blaaackboard. Liiight. She stopped in front of me and held up a pencil. My blank expression must have confirmed her suspicions about our substandard English skills, so she said "pencil" over and over again until I replied,

Sands 3

"Uh, pencil?" hoping she would go away. One of the boys across the room laughed loudly and said something in Spanish.

When our instructor moved to the next student to teach "notebook," I leaned over to a girl sitting at my table.

"What did he say?" I asked, pointing to the boy across the table.

"He said that stupid woman can't tell you don't speak Spanish."

He was right—but that was not the only thing she didn't seem to understand. We spent the next few weeks watching the movie *Stand and Deliver* over and over. *Stand and Deliver* is the story of how Jaime Escalante began teaching a remedial math class in East Los Angeles and developed a program that led his students to take and pass the AP calculus exam. Our teacher would beam happily after showing us the movie and would tell us that this movie was proof that we didn't need to cheat to excel. She told us we could stay in school, not join gangs, and not get pregnant. The implication, of course, was that because we were Hispanic, we were somehow more likely than others to cheat, to join gangs, and to have unprotected sex. The teacher, and the school, attempted to "empower" us by using stereotypical and racist assumptions about our knowledge of English and our abilities.

In "Aria," Rodriguez argues that his mastery of English represented a social change, not just a linguistic one: It made him a successful student and participant in the larger community (32). Rodriguez emphasizes the "public gain" that comes with language acquisition, advising that people be wary of those who "scorn assimilation" and discount the consequences of not having access to the public language of power and the public community (27). These consequences had most likely been considered at some point by the students in the Hispanic class I was a part of; the fact that the native Spanish speakers were all bilingual indicated their awareness of the importance of speaking English in order to function in and become part of the Marshalltown community. The instructor, however, continued to emphasize our difference from the larger community.

Sands 4

Unlike Rodriguez, before that class I had always had a sense of myself as part of the public community. I assumed I would go to college: If my family could not afford to send me, I would get scholarships and jobs to fund my education. I assumed that being a native speaker of English guaranteed me a place in the public community. Being put in the basement caused me to question these assumptions. I learned what I imagine other students in the classroom may have already known—that even if you were bilingual or spoke English perfectly, there was no guarantee that you would be considered part of the public community.

Richard Rodriguez describes how becoming part of public society is a process with both benefits and costs. He asserts that "while one suffers a diminished sense of *private* individuality by becoming assimilated into public society, such assimilation makes possible the achievement of *public* individuality" (26). This process of developing a public identity is not always a simple one, especially when it involves changes in language or in relationships. As my experience and Rodriguez's demonstrate, schools play an active role in shaping students' sense of themselves as individuals. With increasingly diverse student bodies like the one in my middle school, educators face the difficult question of how best to educate students from a variety of backgrounds, while at the same time helping all students become members of a broader public community.

I don't think my middle school had the answer. I don't, either, and I'm not sure there is a one-size-fits-all solution. What I am sure about is this: Educators in every community need to honestly evaluate what they're doing now, and then, working with students and their parents, find ways to help students realize their full potential, both as individuals *and* as members of the larger society.

Work Cited

Rodriguez, Richard. "Aria." *Hunger of Memory: The Education of Richard Rodriguez.* New York: Bantam, 1982. 9–41. Print.

Note: In an actual MLA-style paper, Works Cited entries start on a new page.

|||||||||||||||||||||||||||||||||||||||||||||||||||||||||||||||||||||||||||||||

FOR EXPLORATION

To what extent does Alia Sands's essay achieve the goals she established for herself in her analysis of her rhetorical situation? Reread Alia's analysis, and then reread her essay. Keeping her analysis in mind, list three or four reasons that you believe Alia does or does not achieve her goals, and then find at least one passage in the essay that illustrates each of these statements. Finally, identify at least one way that Alia might strengthen her essay were she to revise it.

|||||||||||||||||||||||||||||||||||||||||||||||||||||||||||||||||||||||||||||||

Using Aristotle's Three Appeals

Analyzing your rhetorical situation can provide information that will enable you to make crucial strategic, structural, and stylistic decisions about your writing. In considering how to use this information, you may find it helpful to employ what Aristotle (384–322 B.C.E.) characterized as the three appeals. According to Aristotle, when speakers and writers communicate with others, they draw on these three general appeals:

Logos, the appeal to reason

Pathos, the appeal to emotion, values, and beliefs

Ethos, the appeal to the credibility of the speaker or writer

As a writer, you appeal to *logos* when you focus on the logical presentation of your subject by providing evidence and examples in support of your ideas. You appeal to *pathos* when you use the resources of language to engage your readers emotionally with your subject or appeal to their values, beliefs, or needs. And you appeal to *ethos* when you create an image of yourself, a persona, that encourages readers to accept or act on your ideas.

These appeals correspond to three of the four basic elements of rhetoric (writer, reader, and text). In appealing to *ethos*, you focus on the writer's character as implied in the text; in appealing to *pathos*, on the interaction of writer and reader; and in appealing to *logos*, on the logical statements about the subject made in your particular text. In some instances, you may rely predominantly on one of these appeals. A student writing a technical report, for instance, will typically emphasize scientific or technical evidence (*logos*), not emotional or personal appeals. More often, however, you'll draw on all three appeals in order to create a fully persuasive document. A journalist writing a column on child abuse might open with several examples designed to gain her readers' attention and to convince them of the importance of this issue (*pathos*). Although she may rely primarily on information about the negative consequences of child abuse (*logos*), she will undoubtedly also endeavor

thinking
rhetorically

to create an image of herself as a caring, serious person (*ethos*), one whose analysis of a subject like child abuse should be trusted.

This journalist might also use images to help convey her point. One or more photographs of physically abused children would certainly appeal to *pathos*. To call attention to the large number of children who are physically abused (and thus bolster the *logos* of her argument), she might present important statistics in a chart or graph. She might also include photographs of well-known advocates for child protection to represent the trustworthiness of her report's insights (and contribute to *ethos*). In so doing, the journalist is combining words, images, and graphics to maximum effect.

In the following example, Brandon Barrett, a chemistry major at Oregon State University, uses Aristotle's three appeals to determine how best to approach an essay assignment for a first-year writing class that asks him to explain what his major is and why he chose it.

In presenting the assignment, Barrett's teacher informed students that their two- to three-page essays should include "information about your major that is new to your readers; in other words, it should not simply repeat the OSU catalog. Rather, it should be your unique perspective, written in clear, descriptive language." The teacher concluded with this advice: "Have fun with this assignment. Consider your audience (it should be this class unless you specify a different audience). And remember Aristotle's three appeals. How will your essay employ the appeals of *logos*, *pathos*, and *ethos*? As you write, keep these two questions in mind: What is your purpose? What do you hope to achieve with your audience?" Brandon's essay is preceded by his analysis of his rhetorical situation and of his essay's appeals to *logos*, *pathos*, and *ethos*.

Brandon Barrett's Analysis

thinking rhetorically

I'm writing this essay to explain how I made the most important decision in my life to date: what to major in while in college. I want to explain this not only to my audience but to myself as well, for bold decisions frequently need to be revisited in light of new evidence. There are those for whom the choice of major isn't much of a choice at all. For them, it's a *vocation*, in the strict Webster's definition of the word: a summons, a calling.

I'm not one of those people, and for me the decision was fraught with anxiety. Do I still believe that I made the right choice? Yes, I do, and I want my essay not only to reflect how serious I feel this issue to be but also to convey the confidence that I finally achieved.

Writer: I'm writing this as a student in a first-year writing class, so while the assignment gives me a lot of flexibility and room for creativity, I need to remember that finally this is an academic essay.

Reader: My primary reader is my teacher in the sense that she's the one who will grade my essay, but she has specified that I should consider the other students in the class as my audience. This tells me that I need to find ways to make the essay interesting to them and to find common ground with them.

Text: This assignment calls for me to write an academic essay. This assignment is different, though, from writing an essay in my history class or a lab report in my chemistry class. Since this is based on my personal experience, I have more freedom than I would in these other classes. One of the most challenging aspects of this essay is its limited page length. It would actually be easier to write a longer essay on why I chose chemistry as my major.

Medium: Our assignment is to write an academic essay. While I could potentially import graphics into my text, I should only do so if it will enrich the content of the essay.

After analyzing his rhetorical situation, Brandon decided to use Aristotle's three appeals to continue and extend his analysis.

Logos: This essay is about my own opinions and experiences and therefore contains no statistics and hard facts. What it should contain, though, are legitimate reasons for choosing the major I did. My choice should be shown as following a set of believable driving forces.

Pathos: Since my audience is composed of college students, I'll want to appeal to their own experiences regarding their choice of major and the sometimes conflicting emotions that accompany such a decision. Specifically, I want to focus on the confidence and relief that come when you've finally made up your mind. My audience will be able to relate to these feelings, and it will make the essay more relevant and real to them.

Ethos: The inherent danger in writing an essay about my desire to be a chemistry major is that I may be instantly labeled as boring or a grind. I want to dispel this image as quickly as possible, and humor is always a good way to counter such stereotypes. On the other hand, this is a serious subject, and the infusion of too much humor will portray me as somebody who hasn't given this too much thought. I want to strike a balance between being earnest and being human. I also need to write as clearly and confidently as I can manage. If I seem insincere or uncertain, then my audience may question the honesty of my essay.

Brandon Barrett
Professor Auston
Writing 101
Jan. 20, 2010

The All-Purpose Answer

When I was a small child, I would ask my parents, as children are apt to do,
questions concerning the important things in my life. "Why is the sky blue?"
"Why do my Cocoa Puffs turn the milk in my cereal bowl brown?" If I asked
my father questions such as these, he always provided detailed technical
answers that left me solemnly nodding my head in complete confusion.
But if I asked my mother, she would simply shrug her shoulders and reply,
"Something to do with chemistry, I guess." Needless to say, I grew up with
a healthy respect for the apparently boundless powers of chemistry. Its
responsibilities seemed staggeringly wide-ranging, and I figured that if there
was a God he was probably not an omnipotent deity but actually the Original
Chemist.

In my early years, I regarded chemistry as nothing less than magic
at work. So what is chemistry, if not magic—or a parent's response to a
curious child's persistent questions? Chemistry is the study of the elements,
how those elements combine, how they interact with one another, and how
all this affects Joe Average down the street. Chemists, then, study not magic
but microscopic bits of matter all busily doing their thing.

When all those bits of matter can be coerced into doing something
that humans find useful or interesting—like giving off massive quantities
of energy, providing lighting for our homes, or making Uncle Henry smell
a little better—then the chemists who produced the desired effect can pat
themselves on the back and maybe even feel just a little bit like God.

Chemists solve problems, whether the problem is a need for a new
medicine or a stronger plastic bowl to pour our Wheaties into. They develop
new materials and study existing ones through a variety of techniques that
have been refined over the decades. Chemists also struggle to keep the
powers of chemistry in check by finding ways to reduce pollution that can

Barrett 2

be a by-product of chemical processes, to curb the dangers of nuclear waste, and to recycle used materials.

Chemistry is a dynamic field, constantly experiencing new discoveries and applications — heady stuff, to be sure, but heady stuff with a purpose.

Chemistry isn't a static, sleepy field of dusty textbooks, nor does it — forgive me, geologists — revolve around issues of questionable importance, such as deviations in the slope of rock strata. Those who know little about chemistry sometimes view it as dull, but I am proud to say that I plan to earn my B.S. in chemistry. And from there, who knows? That's part of the beauty of chemistry. After graduating from college, I could do any number of things, from research to medical school. The study of chemistry is useful in its own right, but it is also great preparation for advanced study in other fields since it encourages the development of logical thought and reasoning. In one sense, logical thought (not to mention research and medical school) may seem a giant step away from a child's idle questions. But as chemistry demonstrates, perhaps those questions weren't so childish after all.

||||||||||||||||||||||||||||||||||||||||||||||||||||||||||||||||||||||||||||||||||||||

FOR EXPLORATION
Where can you see evidence of Brandon's attention to Aristotle's three appeals? Write one or two paragraphs responding to this question. Be sure to include examples in your analysis.

||||||||||||||||||||||||||||||||||||||||||||||||||||||||||||||||||||||||||||||||||||||

Analyzing Textual Conventions

When you analyze your rhetorical situation, you ask commonsense questions about your writing purpose and situation. As you do so, you draw on your previous experiences as a writer, reader, speaker, and listener to make judgments about the text's purpose, subject matter, and form. For familiar kinds of texts, these judgments occur almost automatically. No one had to teach you, for instance, that a letter applying for a job should be written differently than an instant message asking a friend to drop by for pizza: Your social and cultural understanding of job-hunting would cause you to write a formal letter. You make similar judgments as a reader. When you glance through your mail,
thinking
rhetorically

tossing aside ads while eagerly searching for a letter notifying you about a financial aid package, your actions are the result of an implicit rhetorical judgment you're making about the nature and value of these texts.

When faced with less familiar kinds of texts, you may have to work harder to make judgments about purpose, subject matter, and form. I recently received a letter from a former student, Monica Molina, who now works at a community health center, where one of her responsibilities is to write grant proposals. In her letter, she commented:

> It took quite a while before I could feel comfortable even thinking about trying to write my first grant proposal. Most of the ones at our center run 50 to 100 pages and seem so intimidating—full of strange subheadings, technical language, complicated explanations. I had to force myself to calm down and get into them. First I read some recent proposals, trying to figure out how they worked. Luckily, my boss is friendly and supportive, so she sat down with me and talked about her experiences writing proposals. We looked at some proposals together, and she told me about how proposals are reviewed by agencies. Now we're working together on my first proposal. I'm still nervous, but I'm beginning to feel more comfortable.

Like Monica, those entering new professions often must learn new forms of writing. Similarly, students entering a new discipline will often have to work hard to master unfamiliar language or writing styles. Chapter 7, "Writing in the Disciplines: Making Choices as You Write," will help you as you write your way across the curriculum.

Indeed, writers who wish to participate in any new community must strive to understand its reading and writing practices—to learn how to enter its conversation, as the rhetorician Kenneth Burke might say. The forms of writing practiced in different communities reflect important shared assumptions. These shared assumptions—sometimes referred to as *textual conventions*—represent agreements between writers and readers about how to construct and interpret texts. As such, they are an important component of any rhetorical situation.

The term *textual convention* may be new to you, but you can understand it easily if you think about other uses of the word *convention*. For example, social conventions are behaviors that reflect implicit agreement among the members of a community or culture about how to act in particular situations. At one time in the United States, for example, it was acceptable for persons who chewed tobacco to spit tobacco juice into spittoons in restaurants and hotel lobbies. (In fact, the use of spittoons was at one time considered refined, compared to the frequently employed alternative of spitting directly on the ground, indoors or out.) This particular social convention has changed over time and is no longer acceptable.

If social conventions represent agreements among individuals about how to act, textual conventions represent similar agreements about how to write and read texts. Just as we often take our own social conventions for granted, so too do we take for granted those textual conventions most familiar to us as readers and writers. When we begin a card or letter to our parents by writing "Dear Mom and Dad," for instance, we don't stop to wonder if this greeting is appropriate; we know from our experience as writers and readers that it is.

Textual conventions are dynamic, changing over time as the assumptions, values, and practices of writers and readers change. Consider some of the textual conventions of email and other online writing. If we're writing our parents an email, many of us will not start it with "Dear Mom and Dad." Instead, we'll begin with something like "Hi there—" or we'll just jump into our message with no greeting. (Note: While leaving out an email salutation is considered acceptable in less formal contexts—possibly because the name of the recipient is built into email systems—rhetorically savvy writers of email know that when they're writing a work- or school-related email to a superior or teacher, they should include both a salutation and a clear statement of their subject.)

Emoticons—symbols such as :-) to indicate happiness, :-(to indicate sadness, or :-O to indicate shock or surprise—provide another example of changing textual conventions. These symbols were developed by online writers as a kind of shorthand for the kind of emotion conveyed by voice, gesture, and facial expression in face-to-face communication. Not all who use email use emoticons, and those who do use them know they're more appropriate in some situations than others. But as a textual convention, emoticons clearly respond to the needs of online writers and readers.

When you think about the kind of writing that you are being asked to do, you are thinking in part about the textual conventions that may limit your options as a writer in a specific situation. Textual conventions bring constraints, but they also increase the likelihood that readers will respond appropriately to your ideas.

The relationship between textual conventions and medium can be critical. Students organizing a protest against increased tuition, for example, would probably not try to get the word out by writing an essay on the subject. In order to get as many students as possible to participate in the protest, they would more likely put together an inexpensive, attention-getting flyer and post it around campus. After the protest march, they might draft a letter to the editor to summarize the speakers' most important points; they might set up a blog to post announcements and to encourage student participation; they might even post a manifesto with many of the characteristic features of an analytical essay.

Some textual conventions are specific. Lab reports, for example, usually include the following elements: title page, abstract, introduction, experimental design and methods, results, discussion, and references. Someone

thinking rhetorically

writing a lab report can deviate from this textual convention, but in doing so runs the risk of confusing or irritating readers.

Other textual conventions are more general. Consider, for instance, the conventions of an effective academic essay:

An effective academic essay is . . .

well organized

well developed

— that is, it . . .

- establishes its subject or main idea in the *introduction*.
- develops that idea in a coherent manner in the *body*.
- summarizes or completes the discussion in the *conclusion*.

logical

— that is, it . . .

supports its main points with appropriate *evidence*, *illustrations*, and *details*.

clear

readable

— that is, it . . .

uses words, sentences, and paragraphs that are *carefully crafted*, *appropriate* for the writer's purpose and subject, and *free of errors* of usage, grammar, and punctuation.

In writing an academic essay, you usually have more freedom in deciding how to apply the conventions than you do, say, when writing a lab report. For example, an introduction is called for, but its specific form is not prescribed: how you begin depends largely on who your audience is, why you're writing, the disciplinary context in which you're writing, your chosen medium, and other factors. As a result, deciding how to introduce your material can be challenging (though, with practice and effort, it *can* be mastered).

Observing a Professional Writer at Work: Comparing and Contrasting Textual Conventions

One way to strengthen your own writing skills is to observe successful writers in action. Let's look at three articles by linguist Deborah Tannen to see how one writer tackles the problem of creating an effective and appropriate introduction. Each article is based on Tannen's research into the limitations of what she describes as America's "argument culture," a subject she investigated in her book *The Argument Culture: Stopping America's War of Words*, but they are addressed to quite different audiences. Tannen is not only a pro-lific and best-selling writer — she has published 21 books and more than 100 articles — but she also writes for unusually diverse audiences. As a student writing in college, you probably won't face Tannen's specific task: writing about the same general topic for multiple audiences. You can nevertheless learn a good deal about what it means to be a rhetorically sensitive and intel-lectually agile writer by studying Tannen's introductions.

The first article excerpted here — "For Argument's Sake: Why Do We Feel Compelled to Fight about Everything?" (pp. 60–61) — appeared in the Sunday edition of the *Washington Post*, a major newspaper with a large na-tional distribution. The second article — "Agonism in the Academy: Surviv-ing Higher Learning's Argument Culture" (pp. 62–63) — appeared in the *Chronicle of Higher Education*, a weekly newspaper read by faculty, staff, and administrators in community colleges, colleges, and universities. The final section of each issue of the *Chronicle* concludes with a one-page opinion col-umn. Tannen's article appeared as such a column. The final article excerpted here — "Agonism in Academic Discourse" (pp. 64–65) — was published in the *Journal of Pragmatics*, a British publication aimed primarily at scholars interested in such topics as pragmatics (the study of language as it is used in a social context), semantics, language acquisition, and so on. Those who read this journal work in academic disciplines such as linguistics, sociology, psychology, anthropology, and philosophy. (Note that the article follows the British style of punctuation.)

| | | | | | | | | | | | | | | | | | | | | | | | | | | | | | | | | | | | | | | | | | | | | | | | | | | | | | | | | | | | | | | | | | | | | | | | | | | | | | | | | | | | | | |

FOR EXPLORATION

Read the introductions to Tannen's three articles (pp. 60–65) carefully, and write three paragraphs characterizing their approaches—one paragraph for each article. (Be sure to read the abstract and the footnote on the first page of the article from the *Journal of Pragmatics*, which provides important cues about Tannen's rhetorical situation and the interests and expectations of her scholarly readers.) Here are some questions for you to keep in mind as you read.

■ How would you describe Tannen's tone in each article?

■ What kinds of examples are used in each article, and what function do they serve?

■ What relationship is established in each article between writer and reader, and what cues signal this relationship?

■ What assumptions does Tannen make in each article about what readers already know?

■ How would you describe the persona, or image of the writer, in each article?

| | | | | | | | | | | | | | | | | | | | | | | | | | | | | | | | | | | | | | | | | | | | | | | | | | | | | | | | | | | | | | | | | | | | | | | | | | | | | | | | | | | | | | | | |

𝕿𝖍𝖊 𝖂𝖆𝖘𝖍𝖎𝖓𝖌𝖙𝖔𝖓 𝕻𝖔𝖘𝖙 MARCH 15, 1998

For Argument's Sake

Why Do We Feel Compelled to Fight About Everything?

By DEBORAH TANNEN

I was waiting to go on a television talk show a few years ago for a discussion about how men and women communicate, when a man walked in wearing a shirt and tie and a floor-length skirt, the top of which was brushed by his waist-length red hair. He politely introduced himself and told me that he'd read and liked my book *You Just Don't Understand*, which had just been published. Then he added, "When I get out there, I'm going to attack you. But don't take it personally. That's why they invite me on, so that's what I'm going to do."

We went on the set and the show began. I had hardly managed to finish a sentence or two before the man threw his arms out in gestures of anger, and began shrieking— briefly hurling accusations at me, and then railing at length against women. The strangest thing about his hysterical outburst was how the studio audience reacted: They turned vicious—not attacking me (I hadn't said anything substantive yet) or him (who wants to tangle with someone who screams at you?) but the other guests: women who had come to talk about problems they had communicating with their spouses.

My antagonist was nothing more than a dependable provocateur, brought on to ensure a lively show. The incident has stayed with me not because it was typical of the talk shows I have appeared on—it wasn't, I'm happy to say—but because it exemplifies the ritual nature of much of the opposition that pervades our public dialogue.

Everywhere we turn, there is evidence that, in public discourse, we prize contentiousness and aggression more than cooperation and conciliation. Headlines blare about the Starr Wars, the Mommy Wars, the Baby Wars, the Mammography Wars; everything is posed in terms of battles and duels, winners and losers, conflicts and disputes. Biographies have metamorphosed into demonographies whose authors don't just portray their subjects warts and all, but set out to dig up as much dirt as possible, as if the story of a person's life is contained in the warts, only the warts, and nothing but the warts.

It's all part of what I call the argument culture, which rests on the assumption that opposition is the best way to get anything done: The best way to discuss an idea is to set up a debate. The best way to cover news is to find people who express the most extreme views and present them as "both sides." The best way to begin an essay is to attack someone. The best way to show you're really thoughtful is to criticize. The best way to settle disputes is to litigate them.

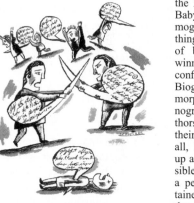

Robert Neubecker for The Washington Post

The Washington Post MARCH 15, 1998

It is the automatic nature of this response that I am calling into question. This is not to say that passionate opposition and strong verbal attacks are never appropriate. In the words of the Yugoslavian-born poet Charles Simic, "There are moments in life when true invective is called for, when it becomes an absolute necessity, out of a deep sense of justice, to denounce, mock, vituperate, lash out, in the strongest possible language." What I'm questioning is the ubiquity, the knee-jerk nature of approaching almost any issue, problem or public person in an adversarial way.

Smashing heads does not open minds. In this as in so many things, results are also causes, looping back and entrapping us. The pervasiveness of warlike formats and language grows out of, but also gives rise to, an ethic of aggression: We come to value aggressive tactics for their own sake—for the sake of argument. Compromise becomes a dirty word, and we often feel guilty if we are conciliatory rather than confrontational—even if we achieve the result we're seeking.

Here's one example. A woman called another talk show on which I was a guest. She told the following story: "I was in a place where a man was smoking, and there was a no-smoking sign. Instead of saying 'You aren't allowed to smoke in here. Put that out!' I said, 'I'm awfully sorry, but I have asthma, so your smoking makes it hard for me to breathe. Would you mind terribly not smoking?' When I said this, the man was extremely polite and solicitous, and he put his cigarette out, and I said, 'Oh, thank you, thank you!' as if he'd done a wonderful thing for me. Why did I do that?"

I think this woman expected me—the communications expert—to say she needs assertiveness training to confront smokers in a more aggressive manner. Instead, I told her that her approach was just fine. If she had tried to alter his behavior by reminding him of the rules, he might well have re-belled: "Who made you the enforcer? Mind your own business!" She had given the smoker a face-saving way of doing what she wanted, one that allowed him to feel chivalrous rather than chastised. This was kinder to him, but it was also kinder to herself, since it was more likely to lead to the result she desired.

Another caller disagreed with me, saying the first caller's style was "self-abasing." I persisted: There was nothing necessarily destructive about the way the woman handled the smoker. The mistake the second caller was making—a mistake many of us make—was to confuse ritual self-effacement with the literal kind. All human relations require us to find ways to get what we want from others without seeming to dominate them.

The opinions expressed by the two callers encapsulate the ethic of aggression that has us by our throats, particularly in public arenas such as politics and law. Issues are routinely approached by having two sides stake out opposing positions and do battle. This sometimes drives people to take positions that are more adversarial than they feel—and can get in the way of reaching a possible resolution. I have experienced this firsthand.

For my book about the work-place, "Talking from 9 to 5," I spent time in companies, shadowing people, interviewing them and having individuals tape conversations when I wasn't there. Most companies were happy to proceed on a verbal agreement setting forth certain ground rules: Individuals would control the taping, identifying names would be changed, I would show them what I wrote about their company and change or delete anything they did not approve. I also signed confidentiality agreements promising not to reveal anything I learned about the company's business.

Some companies, however, referred the matter to their attorneys so a contract could be written. In no case where attor-

Agonism in the Academy: Surviving Higher Learning's Argument Culture

By Deborah Tannen

A reading group that I belong to, composed of professors, recently discussed a memoir by an academic. I came to the group's meeting full of anticipation, eager to examine the insights I'd gained from the book and to be enlightened by those that had intrigued my fellow group members. As the meeting began, one member announced that she hadn't read the book; four, including me, said they'd read and enjoyed it; and one said she hadn't liked it because she does not like academic memoirs. She energetically criticized the book. "It's written in two voices," she said, "and the voices don't interrogate each other."

Quickly, two other members joined her critique, their point of view becoming a chorus. They sounded smarter, seeing faults that the rest of us had missed, making us look naive. We credulous three tried in vain to get the group talking about what we had found interesting or important in the book, but

our suggestions were dull compared to the game of critique.

I left the meeting disappointed because I had learned nothing new about the book or its subject. All I had learned about was the acumen of the critics. I was especially struck by the fact that one of the most talkative and influential critics was the member who had

> **I remain convinced that agonism is endemic in academe — and bad for it.**

not read the book. Her unfamiliarity with the work had not hindered her, because the critics had focused more on what they saw as faults of the genre than on faults of the particular book.

The turn that the discussion had taken reminded me of the subject of my most recent book, *The Argument Culture.* The phenomenon I'd observed at the book-group meeting was an example of what the cultural linguist

Walter Ong calls "agonism," which he defines in *Fighting for Life* as "programmed contentiousness" or "ceremonial combat." Agonism does not refer to disagreement, conflict, or vigorous dispute. It refers to ritualized opposition—for instance, a debate in which the contestants are assigned opposing positions and one party wins, rather than an argument that arises naturally when two parties disagree.

In *The Argument Culture,* I explored the role and effects of agonism in three domains of public discourse: journalism, politics, and the law. But the domain in which I first identified the phenomenon and began thinking about it is the academic world. I remain convinced that agonism is endemic in academe—and bad for it.

The way we train our students, conduct our classes and our research, and exchange ideas at meetings and in print are all driven by our ideological assumption that intellectual inquiry is a metaphorical battle. Following from that is a second assumption, that the best way to demonstrate intellectual prowess is to criticize, find fault, and attack.

Many aspects of our academic lives can be described as agonistic. For example, in our scholarly papers, most of us follow a conventional framework that requires us to position our work in opposition to someone else's, which we prove wrong. The framework tempts—almost requires—us to oversimplify or even misrepresent others' positions; cite the weakest example to make a generally reasonable work appear less so; and ignore facts that support others' views, citing only evidence that support our own positions.

The way we train our students frequently reflects the battle metaphor as well. We assign scholarly work for them to read, then invite them to tear it apart. That is helpful to an extent, but it often means that they don't learn to do the harder work of integrating ideas, or of considering the work's historical and disciplinary context. Moreover, it fosters in students a stance of arrogance and narrow-mindedness, qualities that do not serve the fundamental goals of education.

In the classroom, if students are engaged in heated debate, we believe that education is taking place. But in a 1993 article in *The History Teacher*, Patricia Rosof, who teaches at Hunter College High School in New York City, advises us to look more closely at what's really happening. If we do, she says, we will probably find that only a few students are participating; some other students may be paying attention, but many may be turned off. Furthermore, the students who are arguing generally simplify the points they are making or disputing. To win the argument, they ignore complexity and nuance. They refuse to concede a point raised by their opponents, even if they can see that it is valid, because such a concession would weaken their position. Nobody tries to synthesize the various views, because that would look indecisive, or weak.

If the class engages in discussion rather than debate—adding such intellectual activities as exploring ideas, uncovering nuances, comparing and contrasting different interpretations of a work—more students take part, and more of them gain a deeper, and more accurate, understanding of the material. Most important, the students learn a stance of respect and open-minded inquiry.

Academic rewards—good grades and good jobs—typically go to students and scholars who learn to tear down others' work, not to those who learn to build on the work of their colleagues. In *The Argument Culture*, I cited a study in which communications researchers Karen Tracy and Sheryl Baratz examined weekly colloquia attended by faculty members and graduate students at a large university. As the authors reported in a 1993 article in *Communication Monographs*, although most people said the purpose of the colloquia was to "trade ideas" and "learn things," faculty members in fact were judging the students' competence based on their participation in the colloquia. And the professors didn't admire students who asked "a nice little supportive question," as one put it—they valued "tough and challenging questions."

One problem with the agonistic culture of graduate training is that potential scholars who are not comfortable with that kind of interaction are likely to drop out. As a result, many talented and creative minds are lost to academe. And, with fewer colleagues who prefer different approaches, those who remain are more likely to egg each other on to even greater adversarial heights. Some scholars who do stay in academe are reluctant to present their work at conferences or submit it for publication because of their reluctance to take part in adversarial discourse. The cumulative effect is that nearly everyone feels vulnerable and defensive, and

ELSEVIER

Journal of Pragmatics 34 (2002) 1651–1669

journal of
PRAGMATICS

www.elsevier.com/locate/pragma

Agonism in academic discourse[☆]

Deborah Tannen

Linguistics Department, Georgetown University, Box 571051, Washington DC 20057-1051, USA

Abstract

The pervasiveness of agonism, that is, ritualized adversativeness, in contemporary western academic discourse is the source of both obfuscation of knowledge and personal suffering in academia. Framing academic discourse as a metaphorical battle leads to a variety of negative consequences, many of which have ethical as well as personal dimensions. Among these consequences is a widespread assumption that critical dialogue is synonymous with negative critique, at the expense of other types of 'critical thinking'. Another is the requirement that scholars search for weaknesses in others' work at the expense of seeking strengths, understanding the roots of theoretical differences, or integrating disparate but related ideas. Agonism also encourages the conceptualization of complex and subtle work as falling into two simplified warring camps. Finally, it leads to the exclusion or marginalization of those who lack a taste for agonistic interchange. Alternative approaches to intellectual interchange need not entirely replace agonistic ones but should be accommodated alongside them. © 2002 Elsevier Science B.V. All rights reserved.

Keywords: Academic discourse; Agonism; Disagreement; Ritualized opposition; Exclusion

---

☆ Varying versions of this paper were delivered at the Georgetown Linguistics Society 1995, Washington, DC; Georgetown University Round Table on Languages and Linguistics 1999, Washington, D.C.; Pragma99, Tel Aviv, Israel, August 1999; and as the Hayward Keniston Lecture, University of Michigan, October 27, 1999. A briefer account, written for a more general audience, appears as "Agonism in the Academy: Surviving Higher Learning's Argument Culture", The Chronicle of Higher Education March 31, 2000, B7-8. Some sections of the present paper are based on material that appears in my book The Argument Culture; most, however, is new. I would like to thank Elizabeth Eisenstein, Shari Kendall, Joseph P. Newhouse, and Keli Yerian for leading me to sources that I cite here. For thoughtful comments on an earlier draft, I am grateful to A.L. Becker, Paul Friedrich, Susan Gal, Heidi Hamilton, Natalie Schilling-Estes, Ron Scollon, Malcah Yaeger-Dror, and three anonymous reviewers. This contribution is dedicated to the memory of Suzanne Fleischman, whose death which occurred while I was working on the paper cast a shadow of sadness, and whose own work, like her article cited here, made such an enormous contribution to restoring the person of the scholar to scholarship.
    E-mail address: tannend@georgetown.edu (D. Tannen).

0378-2166/02/$ - see front matter © 2002 Elsevier Science B.V. All rights reserved.
PII: S0378-2166(02)00079-6

1652   *D. Tannen / Journal of Pragmatics 34 (2002) 1651–1669*

1. Introduction and overview

In doing discourse analysis, we use discourse to do our analysis, yet we seldom examine the discourse we use. There are, of course, important exceptions, such as Tracy (1997) on departmental colloquia, Fleischman (1998) on the erasure of the personal in academic writing, Goffman (1981) on "The Lecture", Herring (1996) on e-mail lists, Chafe and Danielewicz (1987) who include "academic speaking" and "academic writing" in their comparison of spoken and written language, and Swales' (1990) study of academic writing as well as his recent examination of the physical and interactional contexts that give rise to it (1998). Perhaps most closely related to my topic is Hunston (1993), who examines oppositional argumentation in biology, history, and sociolinguistics articles (two each), and concludes that the less empirical disciplines are more 'argumentative'. Here I turn my attention to an aspect of academic discourse that, as far I know, has not previously been examined: what I call "agonism".

Ong (1981: 24), from whom I borrow the term, defines agonism as "programmed contentiousness", "ceremonial combat". I use the term to refer not to conflict, disagreement, or disputes per se, but rather to *ritualized* adversativeness. In academic discourse, this means conventionalized oppositional formats that result from an underlying ideology by which intellectual interchange is conceptualized as a metaphorical battle. In a recent book (Tannen, 1998), I explore the role and effects of agonism in three domains of public discourse: journalism, politics, and law. Here I turn to the discourse domain in which I first identified the phenomenon and began thinking about it: the academy.

My goal is to uncover agonistic elements in academic discourse and to examine their effects on our pursuit of knowledge and on the community of scholars engaged in that pursuit. In arguing that an ideology of agonism provides a usually unquestioned foundation for much of our oral and written interchange, I focus on exposing the destructive aspects of this ideology and its attendant practices. I do not, however, call for an end to agonism – a goal that would be unrealistic even if it were desirable, which I am not sure it is. Rather, I argue for a broadening of our modes of inquiry, so that agonism is, one might say, demoted from its place of ascendancy, and for a re-keying or 'toning down' of the more extreme incarnations of agonism in academic discourse.

In what follows, I begin by sketching my own early interest in agonism in conversational discourse. Then I briefly present some historical background, tracing the seeds of agonism in academic discourse to classical Greek philosophy and the medieval university. Against this backdrop, I move to examining agonistic elements as well as the cultural and ideological assumptions that underlie them in academic discourse: both spoken (at conferences, in classrooms, and in intellectual discussions) and written (in grant proposals, journal articles, books, and reviews of all of these). I demonstrate some unfortunate consequences of the agonistic character of these discourse types, both for the pursuit of knowledge and for the community of scholars and others who hope to gain from our knowledge. I then suggest that the existence and perpetuation of agonistic elements in academic discourse depends on

By glancing at the first pages of Tannen's three articles, you'll notice some important clues about these three publications and about Tannen's expectations about their readers.

thinking rhetorically

For example, the first page of "For Argument's Sake: Why Do We Feel Compelled to Fight about Everything?" (p. 60), has a good deal of white space and large illustrations. This layout is designed to draw readers into Tannen's text. After all, the *Washington Post* is a large multisection newspaper, and the Sunday edition is much larger than the daily edition. People who read the *Post* often don't have a specific purpose when they read: They browse, reading whatever catches their eye.

Tannen has likewise tailored her material to gain these readers' attention. The colloquial title ("For Argument's Sake"), for example, is meant to assure people that the content is accessible and interesting, and the incident that Tannen describes at the start of her article is dramatic: She recalls her encounter with an unusually dressed man with waist-length red hair who, like her, is waiting to appear on a television show. After he praises her book *You Just Don't Understand*, the man announces, "When I get out there, I'm going to attack you. But don't take it personally." After describing the rest of this incident and reflecting on her antagonist, Tannen moves quickly to the major assertion of her article, which she expresses in plain language and addresses to a "we" that encompasses every potential reader: "Everywhere we turn, there is evidence that, in public discourse, we prize contentiousness and aggression more than cooperation and conciliation." The rest of her article provides examples of a widespread argument culture in America and suggests some of that culture's limitations.

The second article, from the *Chronicle of Higher Education* (p. 62), is somewhat more visually dense than the first—though it does have some white space and a drawing of stylized boxers at the top of the page. Subscribers to the weekly *Chronicle of Higher Education* represent a more specialized readership than that of the *Post*: They either work in or are interested in higher education. Still, the diversity within this readership—which includes everyone from faculty across the disciplines to administrators and staff in various offices on campus—means that just as readers skim daily newspapers like the *Washington Post,* so, too, do many readers skim the *Chronicle*. As a consequence, the *Chronicle* article also competes for readers' attention with an inviting layout.

Rather than using an attention-getting title, however, in this article Tannen uses the scholarly term *agonism* to identify her subject. Given the diverse readership of the *Chronicle*, this might be an unfamiliar term for some readers. Tannen addresses this potential problem by using a catchy subtitle—"Surviving Higher Learning's Argument Culture"—that would appeal to nearly anyone involved in the famously argumentative world of higher education.

In the *Chronicle* article, as in the *Post* article, Tannen begins by recounting an incident that suggests a culture of argument. Rather than referring to the conventions of television talk shows, which the average reader is likely to recognize, she focuses on an experience her audience of educators might share—participating in a reading group whose members find it easier to criticize than praise a book (even when they haven't read it). Next, she mentions her recently published book, *The Argument Culture*; clarifies what she means by *agonism*; and, after briefly describing her book, sets out the thesis of her article: "The way we train our students, conduct our classes and our research, and exchange ideas at meetings and in print are all driven by our ideological assumption that intellectual inquiry is a metaphorical battle. Following from that is a second assumption, that the best way to demonstrate intellectual prowess is to criticize, find fault, and attack." The "we" in this thesis sentence is a different "we" from the one addressed in the *Post* article: She has narrowed the scope of her audience to include those who work in education and place high value on intellectual activity. In the remainder of this article, Tannen provides evidence to support her assertions, considers some of the negative consequences of agonism in the academy, and affirms the benefits of changing the culture of the academy.

An important difference between the *Washington Post* article and the *Chronicle of Higher Education* article involves the examples and evidence that Tannen provides. In the *Post* article, Tannen focuses on examples that a broad range of readers can identify with, such as a phone call to a call-in talk show, the adversarial nature of the legal process, and the ritual attacks on politicians that often appear in the popular press. However, in the *Chronicle* article, she provides a limited range of examples that involve academic life. She also supports her position by citing other scholars whose research supports her position. In these and other ways, Tannen adjusts her argument to address her particular rhetorical situation.

Tannen's third article (p. 64) appeared in the *Journal of Pragmatics*, a specialized publication that has the most cramped and least inviting first page. Rather than using an attention-getting title, Tannen simply announces her subject: "Agonism in Academic Discourse." The article begins with a full page of prefatory material: the article title, the author's name and university address, an abstract, keywords, and a lengthy footnote that mentions previous versions of the article and acknowledges the many people who played important roles in her writing process.

The article itself is divided into sections with numbered headings. The first section, "Introduction and overview," begins with a dense and heavily referenced discussion of the fact that "In doing discourse analysis, we [scholars] use discourse to do our analysis, yet we seldom examine the discourse we use." After acknowledging exceptions to this statement, Tannen stakes out a major claim for her article: "Here I turn my attention to an aspect of academic discourse that, as far [as] I know, has not previously been examined: what I call 'agonism.'" (Because originality is highly prized in the academy, Tannen's claim that her subject "has not previously been examined" is particularly important.) After providing further information about this term, Tannen establishes the framework for her article: "My goal is to uncover agonistic elements in academic discourse and to examine their effects on our pursuit of knowledge and on the community of scholars engaged in that pursuit."

Unlike the *Post* and *Chronicle* articles, which are relatively brief, Tannen's article in the *Journal of Pragmatics* is eighteen densely argued pages long. In subsequent sections, she covers such topics as the roots of agonism in ancient Greek and medieval church discourse. Clearly, Tannen expects much more of readers of this scholarly article than she does of readers of the previous two articles. She assumes that readers will be familiar with the many references she cites or will at least appreciate their inclusion. She also assumes that readers will have considerable prior knowledge of her topic and will care deeply about it.

Tannen faces a different rhetorical situation in addressing readers of the scholarly *Journal of Pragmatics*. Like readers of the *Post* and the *Chronicle*, subscribers to the *Journal of Pragmatics* don't have the time to read every article, but they don't make their choices based on inviting titles, illustrations, or opening anecdotes. Instead, they skim the tables of contents, noting articles that affect their own research or have broad significance for their field. The prefatory material in Tannen's third article matters very much to them; they can review the abstract to determine not only *if* but also *how* they will read the article. Some will read only an article's abstract, others will skim the major points, and others will read the article with great care, returning to it as they conduct their own research. Readers of the *Journal* wouldn't want an engaging introduction like the ones Tannen includes in the *Post* and the *Chronicle* articles. Instead, they value clear, specific headings and scholarly citations over inviting titles, illustrations, and opening anecdotes.

Although these three articles are grounded in the same research project, they differ dramatically in structure, tone, language, and approach to readers. Textual conventions play an important role in these differences. As shared agreements about the construction and interpretation of texts, textual conventions enable readers and writers to communicate successfully in different rhetorical situations.

| | | | | | | | | | | | | | | | | | | | | | | | | | | | | | | | | | | | | | | | | | | | | | | | | | | | | | | | | | | | | | | | | | | | | | | | | | | | | | | | | | | | | | | |

FOR EXPLORATION

Take five to ten minutes to freewrite about your experience of reading the introductions to Tannen's three articles, as well as the subsequent analysis of them. What has this experience helped you better understand about the role that textual conventions—and rhetorical sensitivity—play in writing? If this experience has raised questions for you as a writer, be sure to note them as well. Be prepared to share your response to this exploration with your classmates.

||||||||||||||||||||||||||||||||||||||||||||||||||||||||||||||||||||||||||||||||||

NOTE FOR MULTILINGUAL WRITERS

The conventions of academic writing vary from culture to culture. If you were educated in another country or language, you may have written successful academic texts that followed textual conventions that differ from those you have to follow now. Conventions that can differ in various cultures include the rhetorical strategies that introduce essay topics, the presence and placement of thesis statements, the kinds of information that qualify as objective evidence in argumentation, the use (or absence) of explicit transitions, and the use (or absence) of first-person pronouns.

Given these and other potential differences, you may find it helpful to compare the conventions of academic writing in North America with those of your home culture.

Using Textual Conventions

You already know enough about rhetoric and the rhetorical situation to realize that there can be no one-size-fits-all approach to every academic writing situation.

What can you do when you are unfamiliar with the textual conventions of a particular discipline or of academic writing in general? A rhetorical approach suggests that one solution is to read examples of the kind of writing you wish to do. Deborah Tannen, whose introductions you read earlier in this chapter, undoubtedly drew upon her experience reading the publications in which her work appeared as she wrote her texts. Discussing these models with an insider—your teacher, perhaps, or an advanced student in the field—can help you understand why these conventions work for such readers and writers. Forming a study group or meeting with a tutor can also increase your rhetorical sensitivity to your teachers' expectations and the conventions of academic writing.

thinking rhetorically

Finally, a rhetorical approach to communication encourages you to think strategically about writing—whether personal, professional, or academic—and to respond creatively to the challenges of each situation. As a writer, you have much to consider: your own goals as a writer, the nature of your subject and writing task, the expectations of your readers, the textual conventions your particular situation requires or allows, the medium in which to express your ideas. The rhetorical sensitivity that you have already developed can help you respond appropriately to these and other concerns. But you can also draw on other resources — on textual examples and on discussions with teachers, tutors, and other students. As a writer, you are not alone. By reaching out to other writers, in person or by reading their work, you can become a fully participating member of the academic community.

|||||||||||||||||||||||||||||||||||||||||||||||||||||||||||||||||||||||||||||||||||||

FOR THOUGHT, DISCUSSION, AND WRITING

1. From a newspaper or a magazine, choose an essay, an editorial, or a column that you think succeeds in its purpose. Now turn back to the Questions for Analyzing Your Rhetorical Situation on pp. 41–42, and answer the questions as if you were the writer of the text you have chosen. To answer the questions, look for evidence of the writer's intentions in the writing itself. (To determine what image or persona the writer wanted to portray, for instance, look at the kind of language the writer uses. Is it formal or conversational? Full of interesting images and vivid details or serious examples and statistics?) Answer each of the questions suggested by the guidelines. Then write a paragraph or more reflecting on what you have learned from this analysis.

2. Alia Sands and Brandon Barrett did a good job in anticipating their readers' expectations and interests. In writing their essays, they focused not just on content (what they wanted to say) but also on strategy (how they might convey their ideas to their readers). Not all interactions between writer and reader are as successful. You may have read textbooks that seemed more concerned with the subject matter than with readers' needs and expectations. Or you may have received direct-mail advertising or other business communications that irritated or offended you. Find an example of writing that in your view fails to anticipate the expectations and needs of the reader, and write one or two paragraphs explaining your reasons. Your teacher may ask you to share your example and written explanation with your classmates.

3. Analyze the ways in which one or more of the following print advertisements (pp. 71–74) draw on Aristotle's three appeals: logos, pathos, and ethos.

|||||||||||||||||||||||||||||||||||||||||||||||||||||||||||||||||||||||||||||||||||||

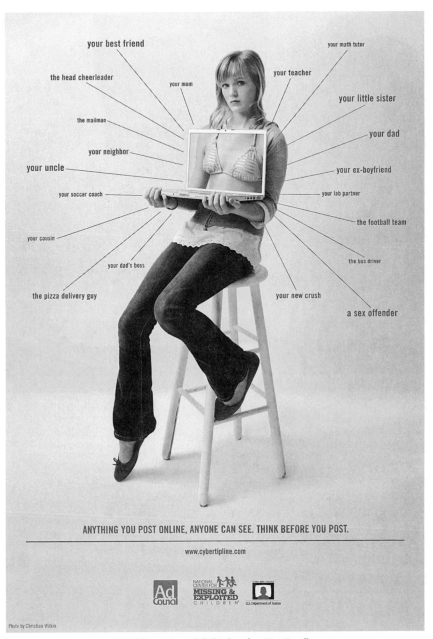

Public Service Ad: "Think Before You Post"

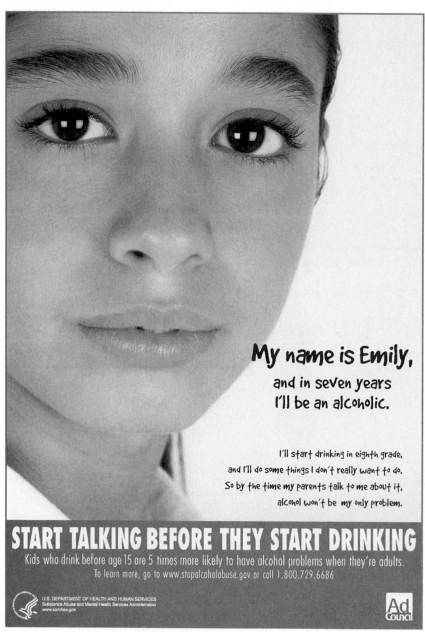

Public Service Ad: "My Name Is Emily"

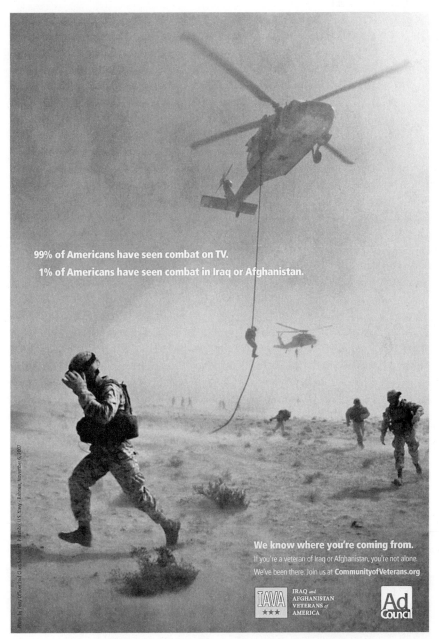

Public Service Ad: "We Know Where You're Coming From"

Public Service Ad: "Ignoring Global Warming Won't Make It Go Away"

Analyzing Texts and Contexts

A rhetorical approach to writing looks at the various contexts in which you write. Even if you are writing alone at your computer, you are writing in the context of a specific rhetorical situation. By analyzing that situation, you can identify your purpose and goals as a writer, develop an appropriate persona or voice, and respond to the expectations of your readers. You also can understand and implement the appropriate textual conventions for courses across the curriculum.

thinking rhetorically

Gaining an understanding of context is particularly important when you enter a new community of writers and readers. Accordingly, as you enter the academic community, you need to develop an insider's understanding of the conventions that characterize academic writing. Some of these conventions apply across the disciplines; for example, a successful academic argument must reflect an open, unbiased intellectual engagement with the subject, whether that subject is a Renaissance painting or the Federal Reserve System. Moreover, whatever your subject, the logic behind your conclusions and the evidence for them play a key role in any academic argument.

Most college instructors believe that *all* academic writing involves argument. But the model of argument they have in mind isn't about winning or losing a debate; it involves using evidence and reasoning to discover a version of truth about a particular subject. I use the words *a version* here to emphasize that in academic writing, what constitutes the "truth" is always open to further discussion. A political scientist or economist who makes a convincing argument about federal policy on harvesting timber in national forests knows that others will add to, challenge, or refine that argument. In fact, having others respond to an observation is a sign that the writing has successfully raised questions that others consider important. In this sense, the scholarly work of the academy is a conversation, rather than a debate.

Understanding Your Audience

Because your instructors are the primary readers of your college writing, you need to understand their values and their goals for you and other students. They all share a commitment to the ideal of education as inquiry. Whether they teach in business, liberal arts, agriculture, engineering, or other fields, your instructors want to foster your ability to think, write, and speak well. When they read your papers and exams, they're looking for evidence of both your knowledge of a subject and your ability to think and write clearly and effectively.

But your instructors will not necessarily bring identical expectations to your writing. Methods of inquiry and research questions vary from discipline to discipline, and textual conventions reflect these differences. A lab report for a chemistry class will use different kinds of evidence and organizational patterns than an essay for an American literature class. Stylistic expectations also vary among disciplines. Passive voice (as in *It was discovered . . .*) is more common in the sciences than in the humanities, for instance.

Despite these disciplinary differences, college instructors generally agree that educated, thoughtful, and knowledgeable college graduates share certain characteristics. They believe, for instance, that perhaps the worst intellectual error is oversimplifying. They want their students to go beyond simplistic analysis and arguments to deeper and more complex understandings. Thus a historian might urge students to recognize that more was at stake in the American Civil War than freeing the slaves, and an engineer might encourage students to realize that the most obvious way to resolve a design problem isn't necessarily the best way.

Most college instructors want students to be able to do more than memorize or summarize information. Indeed, they strive to develop students' abilities to analyze, apply, question, and evaluate information. They also want students to consider multiple perspectives, to recognize that nearly every issue has at least two sides. Because most intellectual issues are complex, instructors often teach students to limit the issue, question, or problem under discussion. They also believe that arguments should be supported by substantial and appropriate evidence, not logical fallacies.

Such habits of mind bring tangible rewards: According to experts in business and industry, they are precisely the habits of mind that lead to success in the world of work.[1] More importantly, however, these habits of mind are intrinsically rewarding. Being able to analyze a complex issue or problem, work through an argument, and develop your own position on a subject brings intellectual satisfaction and confidence. It also enables you to participate effectively as a citizen in an increasingly complex world.

What do instructors look for in students' writing? Most broadly, they want evidence of learning and a real commitment to and engagement with the subject. Particularly in the humanities, they want to see that you are mak-

---

[1]See, for example, *Are They Really Ready to Work?* (http://www.21stcenturyskills.org/documents/FINAL_REPORT_PDF09-29-06.pdf).

ing connections between the issues discussed in class and your own life and personal values. And they always want you to adhere to academic standards of clear thinking and effective communication. More specifically, most instructors hope to find the following characteristics in student writing:

- A limited but significant topic
- A meaningful context for discussion of the topic
- A sustained and full development of ideas, given the limitations of the topic, time, and length
- A clear pattern of organization
- Fair and effective use of sources (both print and online)
- Adequate detail and evidence as support for generalizations
- Appropriate, concise language
- Conventional grammar, punctuation, and usage

The essay on pages 78–79, written by student Hope Leman for a class on politics and the media, meets these criteria. The essay was a response to the following assignment for a take-home midterm exam:

> Journalists often suggest that they simply mirror reality. Some political scientists argue, however, that rather than mirroring reality journalists make judgments that subtly but significantly shape their resulting news reports. In so doing, scholars argue, journalists function more like flashlights than like mirrors. Write an essay in which you contrast the "mirror" and "flashlight" models of the role of journalists in American society.
>
> Successful essays will not only compare these two models but will also provide examples supporting their claims.

Since Hope was writing a take-home midterm essay, she didn't have time to do a formal written analysis of her rhetorical situation. Still, her essay demonstrates considerable rhetorical sensitivity. Hope understands, for instance, that given her situation she should emphasize content rather than employ a dramatic or highly personal style. Hope's essay is, above all, clearly written. Even though it has moments of quiet humor (as when she comments on funhouses at the end of paragraph 2), the focus is on articulating the reasons why the "flashlight" model of media theory is the most valid and helpful for political scientists. Hope knows that her teacher will be reading a stack of midterms under time pressure, so she makes sure that her own writing is carefully organized and to the point.

thinking rhetorically

Hope Leman
Professor Roberts
Composition 101
April 20, 2010

The Role of Journalists in American Society: A Comparison
of the "Mirror" and "Flashlight" Models

The "mirror" model of media theory holds that through their writing and
news broadcasts journalists are an objective source of information for the
public. This model assumes that journalists are free of bias and can be relied
on to provide accurate information about the true state of affairs in the world.
Advocates of the "flashlight" model disagree, believing that a journalist
is like a person in a dark room holding a flashlight. The light from the
flashlight falls briefly on various objects in the room, revealing part — but
not all — of the room at any one time. This model assumes that journalists
cannot possibly provide an objective view of reality but, at best, can convey
only a partial understanding of a situation or an event.

In this essay, I will argue that the "flashlight" model provides a more
accurate and complex understanding of the role of journalists in America
than the "mirror" model does. This model recognizes, for instance, that
journalists are shaped by their personal backgrounds and experiences and by
the pressures, mores, and customs of their profession. It also recognizes that
journalists are under commercial pressure to sell their stories. Newspapers
and commercial networks are run on a for-profit basis. Thus reporters have
to "sell" their stories to readers. The easiest way to do that is to fit a given
news event into a "story" framework. Human beings generally relate well
to easily digestible stories, as opposed to more complex analyses, which
require more thought and concentration. Reporters assigned to cover a given
situation are likely to ask "What is the story?" and then to force events into
that framework. Reality is seldom as neat as a story, however, with neat

Leman 2

compartments of "Once upon a time . . ." "and then . . ." and "The End."
But the story framework dominates news coverage of events; thus the media
cannot function as a mirror since mirrors reflect rather than distort reality
(except in funhouses).

The "mirror" model also fails to acknowledge that journalists make
choices, including decisions about what stories to cover. These choices can
be based on personal preference, but usually they are determined by editors,
who respond to publishers, who, in turn, are eager to sell their product to the
widest possible audiences. Most people prefer not to read about seemingly
insoluble social problems like poverty or homelessness. As a result,
journalists often choose not to cover social issues unless they fit a particular
"story" format.

In addition to deciding what to cover, journalists must determine the
tone they will take in their reporting. If the "mirror" model of media theory
were accurate, journalists wouldn't make implicit or explicit judgments in
their reporting. But they do. They are only human, after all, and they will
inevitably be influenced by their admiration or dislike for a person about
whom they are writing, or by their belief about the significance of an event.

From start to finish, journalists must make a series of choices. They first
make choices about what to cover; then they make choices about whether
their tone will be positive or negative, which facts to include or omit, what
adjectives to use, and so on. Mirrors do not make choices—but a person
holding a flashlight does. The latter can decide where to let the light drop,
how long to leave it on that spot, and when to shift the light to something
else. Journalists make these kinds of choices every day. Consequently, the
"flashlight" model provides the more accurate understanding of the role that
journalists play in American society, for the "mirror" model fails to take into
account the many factors shaping even the simplest news story.

|||||||||||||||||||||||||||||||||||||||||||||||||||||||||||||||||||||||||||||||||||||||||||

FOR COLLABORATION

Working with a group of classmates, respond to these questions about Hope Leman's essay. Appoint a recorder to write down the results of your discussion, which your instructor may ask you to present to the class.

1. Hope begins her essay not by attempting to interest readers in her subject but by defining the "mirror" and "flashlight" models of media theory. Why might this be an effective way to begin her essay?

2. Writers need to have a working thesis, or controlling purpose, when they write. ✳ Sometimes they signal this purpose by articulating an explicit thesis statement. Sometimes only subtle cues are necessary. (Students writing a personal essay might not want, for instance, to state their controlling purpose explicitly at the start of their essay but rather let readers discover it as they read.) In her essay, Hope includes an explicit thesis statement. Identify this statement, and then discuss the reasons that it is necessary in her particular situation.

3. Academic writing is sometimes viewed as dull and lifeless—as, well, *academic*. Yet even in this essay written under time pressure, Hope's writing is not stuffy, dull, or pompous. Examine her essay to identify passages where a personal voice contributes to the overall effectiveness of her essay. How does Hope blend this personal voice with the objective and distanced approach of her essay?

|||||||||||||||||||||||||||||||||||||||||||||||||||||||||||||||||||||||||||||||||||||||||||

Understanding How Analysis Works

As a student, you must respond to a wide range of writing assignments. For an American literature class, you may have to analyze the significance of the whiteness of the whale in *Moby Dick*, whereas a business management class may require a collaboratively written case study; you may need to write a lab report for a chemistry class and critique a qualitative research report for sociology. Although these assignments vary considerably, they all draw on two related skills: analysis and argument. The remainder of this chapter will help you strengthen the first of these two important academic skills—analysis.

Analysis involves separating something into parts and determining how these parts function to create the whole. When you analyze, you examine a text, an object, or a body of data to understand how it is structured or organized and to assess its effectiveness or validity. Most academic writing, thinking, and reading involve analysis. Literature students analyze how a play is structured or how a poem achieves its effect; economics students analyze the major causes of inflation; biology students analyze the enzymatic reactions that comprise the Krebs cycle; and art history students analyze how line, color, and texture come together in a painting.

· · · · · · · · · · ✳   See also Chapter 10, pp. 290–91.
:
:
:

As these examples indicate, analysis is not a single skill but a group of related skills. An art history student might explore how a painting by Michelangelo achieves its effect, for instance, by comparing it with a similar work by Raphael. A biology student might discuss future acid-rain damage to forests in Canada and the United States by first defining acid rain and then using cause-and-effect reasoning to predict worsening conditions. A student in economics might estimate the likelihood of severe inflation in the coming year by categorizing or classifying the major causes of previous inflationary periods and then evaluating the likelihood that such factors will influence the current economic situation.

Analysis often is connected with and leads to *synthesis*. When you analyze something, you examine it critically to better understand how it is structured and how the parts contribute to the overall meaning. In much academic writing, *synthesis* is an important counterpart to analysis, for it enables you to understand (and often argue for) connections and contradictions within a text or among groups of texts that you have analyzed. For a good example of synthesis, take a look at Alletta Brenner's research paper in Chapter 6 (pp. 205–15). In this paper, Alletta synthesizes a number of sources as part of her analysis of the role that human trafficking plays in the American garment-manufacturing industry.

Different disciplines emphasize different analytic skills. (For more on what's required in different disciplines, see Chapter 7.) But regardless of your major, you need to understand and practice these crucial academic skills. You will do so most successfully if you establish a purpose and develop an appropriate framework or method for your analysis.

Establishing a Purpose for Your Analysis

Your instructors will often ask you to analyze a fairly limited subject, problem, or process: Mrs. Ramsey's role in Virginia Woolf's *To the Lighthouse*, feminists' criticisms of Freud's psychoanalytical theories, Mendel's third law of genetics. Such limited tasks are necessary because of the complexity of the material, but the larger purpose of your analysis is to better understand your topic's role within a larger context—for example, a literary work that you are analyzing, or a political or philosophical theory. When you analyze a limited topic, you're like a person holding a flashlight in the dark: The beam of light that you project is narrow and focused, but it illuminates a much larger area.

Even though the purpose of your analysis is to understand the larger subject, you still need to establish a more specific purpose for your analysis. Imagine, for instance, that your Shakespeare instructor has asked you to write an essay on the fool in *King Lear*. You might establish one of several purposes for your analysis:

thinking
rhetorically

■ To explain how the fool contributes to the development of a major theme in *King Lear*

■ To discuss the effectiveness or plausibility of Shakespeare's characterization of the fool

■ To define the role the fool plays in the plot

■ To agree or disagree with a particular critical perspective on the fool's role and significance

Establishing a specific purpose helps you define how your analysis should proceed. It enables you to determine the important issues to address or the questions to answer.

There are no one-size-fits-all procedures for establishing a purpose for your analysis. Sometimes your purpose will develop naturally as a result of reading, reflection, and discussion with others. In other instances, it may help to draw on the invention strategies described in Chapter 9; these strategies help you explore your subject and discover questions to guide your analysis. Since writing and thinking are dynamically interwoven processes, you may at times need to *write* your way into an understanding of your purpose by composing a rough draft and seeing, in effect, what you think about your topic.

Developing an Appropriate Method for Your Analysis

Once you have a purpose, how do you actually analyze something? The answer depends on the subject, process, or problem being analyzed. In general, however, you should consider the methods of inquiry characteristic of the discipline in which you're writing. While students studying *To the Lighthouse* or Mendel's third law may use the same fundamental analytic *processes* — for example, definition, causal analysis, classification, and comparison — the relative weight they give to these different processes and the way they shape and present their final analyses may well differ.

The following questions can help you develop an appropriate method for your analysis. If, after considering these questions and reflecting on your experiences in a class, you continue to have difficulty settling on an appropriate method, meet with your instructor to get help. You might ask him or her to recommend student essays or professional articles that clearly model the analytical methods used in the field.

thinking
rhetorically

Questions for Developing an Appropriate Method for Analysis

1. Have your instructors approached analysis in class . . .

systematically, using methodologies like case study or problem solving?

or

on a case-by-case basis, depending on the subject?

2. What kinds of evidence and examples do they draw on?

3. What kinds of questions do your instructors typically ask in class discussions?

Why might people in the discipline view these as important questions?

4. What kinds of answers to these questions do your instructors favor?

Why might people in this discipline value such responses?

Understanding the Relationship between Analysis and Argument

All academic writing has an argumentative edge, and sometimes that edge is obvious. If a student writes a political science essay arguing that the government should follow a particular environmental policy, that student is explicitly arguing that the government should do something. Essays that discuss whether something should or should not be done are easily recognizable as arguments—probably because they follow the debate format that many associate with argumentation.

But writers can express judgments—can present good reasons for their beliefs and actions—without explicitly endorsing a course of action. For example, a music theory student analyzing the score of a Beethoven sonata may argue that the second movement of the particular sonata is more daring or innovative than music historians have acknowledged. To do so, she must convince her reader, in this case her teacher, that she has a sophisticated understanding of the structure of the sonata. Analysis will play a particularly central role in this student's writing: By identifying specific features of the score and positing relationships among these features, she will demonstrate her understanding of Beethoven's use of the sonata form.

thinking rhetorically

As this example demonstrates, analysis and argument are interdependent. Argumentation depends on analysis, for through analysis writers clarify the logic of their thinking and provide evidence for their judgments. The student arguing that the government should follow a particular environmental policy, for example, would have to analyze the potential benefits and disadvantages of that policy and demonstrate that it's workable in order for his argument to be convincing. Similarly, analysis always carries an implicit argumentative burden, for when you analyze something, you are in effect asserting "This is how I believe X works" or "This is what I believe X means."

Academic analysis and argument call for similar habits of mind. Both encourage writers to suspend personal biases. This is not to say that academic writers are expected to be absolutely objective. Your gut feeling that "workfare" programs may not provide single parents with adequate support for their children may cause you to investigate this topic for a political science or economics class. This gut feeling is a strength, not a weakness, for it enables you to find a topic that interests you. Once you begin to explore your topic, however, you need to engage it dispassionately. You need, in other words, to be open to changing your mind.

If you do change your mind about the consequences of workfare programs, the reading and writing you have done probably have given you a more detailed understanding of the issues at stake. To write a successful essay about this topic, you will have to describe these issues and analyze their relationships and implications, developing logical connections that make your reasoning explicit. Such a process naturally engages you in both analysis and synthesis. In these and other ways, you will demonstrate to readers that you have indeed understood your subject.

The essay by Hope Leman that begins on p. 78 is a good example of academic analysis. In this essay, Hope is not arguing that something should or should not be done. Rather, she is attempting to understand whether the "mirror" or "flashlight" model best describes the role of journalists in American society.

Analyzing Academic Arguments

Analysis plays a key role in all academic writing. It helps readers and writers understand the texts they encounter as they move across the disciplines, and recognize, examine, and formulate arguments about them. In the world of academia, written works, visual works, and even events or behaviors can be considered "texts" susceptible to analysis. While written texts are still most fundamental to academic study, the ability to analyze texts that depend heavily on images and graphics—whether they are television ads, multimedia presentations, or Web sites—has become increasingly important in our media-saturated culture. For advice on analyzing visuals, see the discussion that concludes this chapter (pp. 106–14), as well as pp. 138–53 of Chapter 5, for a case study of student Daniel Stiepleman's analysis of a public service ad for the National Center for Family Literacy.

The analysis of any complex text will feel less intimidating if you address three basic questions:

thinking
rhetorically

- What question is at issue?

- What position does the author take?

- Do the author's reasons justify your acceptance of his or her argument?

The remainder of this chapter provides strategies that you can use to become a more sophisticated and critical reader of texts of all kinds.

|||||||||||||||||||||||||||||||||||||||||||||||||||||||||||||||||||||||||||||||||||||

FOR EXPLORATION
Take a few moments to freewrite about your previous experiences in analyzing academic arguments. Have you been more interested in some kinds of arguments than others? (You might enjoy analyzing political and historical texts, for instance, but find arguments in other areas less interesting.) Do these differences reflect personal preferences, cultural norms, or some other factors? What was your most positive experience with academic analysis, and what factors made it positive? What was your most negative experience, and what factors made it negative? What questions and concerns do you have regarding the analysis of academic arguments? Be prepared to share what you have written with your classmates.

|||||||||||||||||||||||||||||||||||||||||||||||||||||||||||||||||||||||||||||||||||||

Determining the Question at Issue

thinking
rhetorically

When you determine the question at issue, you get to the heart of any argument and distinguish major claims from minor elements of support. You can then identify the author's position and evaluate whether he or she has provided good reasons for you to agree with this position.

Greek and Roman rhetoricians developed a method called *stasis theory* for determining the questions at issue in any argument. Stasis theory encourages readers to identify the major point on which a particular controversy rests. This method presents six basic questions at issue in argumentative writing.[2]

Stasis Questions

QUESTIONS OF FACT arise from the reader's need to know
"Does _____ exist?"

QUESTIONS OF DEFINITION arise from the reader's need to know
"What is it?"

QUESTIONS OF INTERPRETATION arise from the reader's need to know
"What does it mean?"

QUESTIONS OF VALUE arise from the reader's need to know
"Is it good?"

QUESTIONS OF CONSEQUENCE arise from the reader's need to know
"Will _____ cause _____ to happen?"

QUESTIONS OF POLICY arise from the reader's need to know
"What should be done about it?"

As you determine the kinds of issues addressed in a particular argument, you will draw on your rhetorical sensitivity. You do this naturally in your everyday life. Imagine that a friend has urged you to drive with her to a concert in a city an hour away. You'd like to attend the concert, but it's on a midweek work night. Depending on your situation, the primary question at issue may be one of *value*. If you value the concert enough, then you can justify the time, expense, and late-night bedtime involved in attending the concert. On

---

[2]In this discussion of stasis theory, I employ the categories presented in John Gage, *The Shape of Reason: Argumentative Writing in College*, 3rd ed. (Needham Heights, MA: Allyn and Bacon, 1991), 40.

the other hand, the primary question at issue for you may be one of *consequence*: This would be the case if you couldn't justify time away from study, work, and family, especially on a weeknight.

Here is an argument by Amitai Etzioni about the advantages and disadvantages of traditional protections of privacy in North America. Etzioni is a professor at George Washington University and former senior adviser to the White House (1979–1980). He has written over a dozen books, including *The Limits of Privacy* (1999), from which this excerpt is taken. As you read his analysis, consider which of the six Stasis Questions—fact, definition, interpretation, value, consequence, and policy—are most clearly at stake in his argument.

Less Privacy Is Good for Us (and You)

AMITAI ETZIONI

Despite the fact that privacy is not so much as mentioned in the Constitution and that it was only shoehorned in some thirty-four years ago, it is viewed by most Americans as a profound, inalienable right.

The media is loaded with horror stories about the ways privacy is not so much nibbled away as it is stripped away by bosses who read your e-mail, neighbors who listen in on your cell phones, and E-Z passes that allow tollbooth operators to keep track of your movements. A typical headline decries the "End of Privacy" (Richard A. Spinello, in an issue of *America*, a Catholic weekly) or "The Death of Privacy" (Joshua Quittner, in *Time*).

It is time to pay attention to the other half of the equation that defines a good society: concerns for public health and safety that entail some rather justifiable diminution of privacy.

Take the HIV testing of infants. New medical data—for instance, evidence recently published by the prestigious *New England Journal of Medicine*—show that a significant proportion of children born to mothers who have HIV can ward off this horrible disease but only on two conditions: that their mothers not breastfeed them and that they immediately be given AZT. For this to happen, mothers must be informed that they have HIV. An estimated two-thirds of infected mothers are unaware. However, various civil libertarians and some gay activists vehemently oppose such disclosure on the grounds that when infants are tested for HIV, in effect one finds out if the mother is a carrier, and thus her privacy is violated. While New York State in 1996, after a very acrimonious debate, enacted a law that requires infant testing and disclosure of the findings to the mother, most other states have so far avoided dealing with this issue.

Congress passed the buck by asking the Institute of Medicine (IOM) to conduct a study of the matter. The IOM committee, dominated by politically correct people, just reported its recommendations. It suggested that all pregnant women be asked to consent to HIV testing as part of routine prenatal care. There is little wrong with such a recommendation other than it does not deal with many of the mothers who are drug addicts or otherwise live at society's margins. Many of these women do not show up for prenatal care, and they are particularly prone to HIV, according to a study published in the American Health Association's *Journal of School Health*. To save the lives of their children, they must be tested at delivery and treated even if this entails a violation of mothers' privacy.

Recently a suggestion to use driver's licenses to curb illegal immigration has sent the Coalition for Constitutional Liberties, a large group of libertarians, civil libertarians, and privacy advocates, into higher orbit than John Glenn ever traversed. The coalition wrote:

> This plan pushed us to the brink of tyranny, where citizens will not be allowed to travel, open bank accounts, obtain health care, get a job, or purchase firearms without first presenting the proper government papers.
>
> The authorizing section of the law . . . is reminiscent of the totalitarian dictates by Politburo members in the former Soviet Union, not the Congress of the United States of America.

Meanwhile, Wells Fargo is introducing a new device that allows a person to cash checks at its ATM machines because the machines recognize faces. Rapidly coming is a whole new industry of so-called biometrics that uses natural features such as voice, hand design, and eye pattern to recognize a person with the same extremely high reliability provided by the new DNA tests.

It's true that as biometrics catches on, it will practically strip Americans of anonymity, an important part of privacy. In the near future, a person who acquired a poor reputation in one part of the country will find it much more difficult to move to another part, change his name, and gain a whole fresh start. Biometrics see right through such assumed identities. One may hope that future communities will become more tolerant of such people, especially if they openly acknowledge the mistakes of their past and truly seek to lead a more prosocial life. But they will no longer be able to hide their pasts.

Above all, while biometrics clearly undermines privacy, the social benefits it promises are very substantial. Specifically, each year at least half a million criminals become fugitives, avoiding trial, incarceration, or serving their full sentences, often committing additional crimes while on the lam. People who fraudulently file for multiple income tax refunds using fake identities and multiple Social Security numbers cost the nation between $1 billion and $5 billion per year. Numerous divorced parents escape their financial obligations to their children by avoiding detection when they move or change jobs. (The sums owed to children are variously estimated as running between $18 billion to $23 billion a year.) Professional and amateur criminals, employing fraudulent identification documentation to make phony credit card purchases, cost credit card companies and retail businesses an indeterminate number of billions of dollars each year. The United States loses an estimated $18 billion a year to benefit fraud committed by illegal aliens using false IDs. A 1998 General Accounting Office report estimates identity fraud to cost $10 billion annually in entitlement programs alone.

People hired to work in child care centers, kindergartens, and schools cannot be effectively screened to keep out child abusers and sex offenders, largely because when background checks are conducted, convicted criminals escape detection by using false identification and aliases. Biometrics would sharply curtail all these crimes, although far from wipe them out single-handedly.

The courts have recognized that privacy must be weighed against considerations of public interest but have tended to privilege privacy and make claims for public health or safety clear several high hurdles. In recent years these barriers have been somewhat lowered as courts have become more concerned with public safety and health. Given that these often are matters of state law and that neither legislatures nor courts act in unison, the details are complex and far from all pointing in one direction. But, by and large, courts have allowed mandatory drug testing of those who directly have the lives of others in their hands, including pilots, train engineers, drivers of school buses, and air traffic controllers, even though such testing violates their privacy. In case after case, the courts have disregarded objections to such tests by civil libertarians who argue that such tests constitute "suspicionless" searches, grossly violate privacy, and—as the ACLU puts it—"condition Americans to a police state."

All this points to a need to recast privacy in our civic culture, public policies, and legal doctrines. We should cease to treat it as an unmitigated good, a sacred right (the way Warren and Brandeis referred to in their famous article and many since) or one that courts automatically privilege.

Instead, privacy should rely squarely on the Fourth Amendment, the only one that has a balance built right into its text. It recognizes both searches that wantonly violate privacy ("unreasonable" ones) and those that enhance the common good to such an extent that they are justified, even if they intrude into one's privacy. Moreover, it provides a mechanism to sort out which searches are in the public interest and which violate privacy without sufficient cause, by introducing the concept of warrants issued by a "neutral magistrate" presented with "probable cause." Warrants also limit the invasion of privacy "by specification of the person to be seized, the place to be searched, and the evidence to be sought." The Fourth may have become the Constitutional Foundation of privacy a long time ago if it was not for the fact that *Roe v. Wade* is construed as a privacy right, and touching it provokes fierce opposition. The good news, though, is that even the advocates of choice in this area are now looking to base their position on some other legal grounds, especially the Fourteenth Amendment.

We might be ready to treat privacy for what it is: one very important right but not one that trumps most other considerations, especially of public safety and health.

||||||||||||||||||||||||||||||||||||||||||||||||||||||||||||||||||||||||||||||||||||||||

FOR COLLABORATION

After you have read Etzioni's argument, list the two most significant Stasis Questions (see p. 86) at stake in his argument. Find at least one passage that you believe relates to each question. Then meet with a group of classmates, and share your responses to this assignment. (Appoint a timekeeper to ensure that all members of your group have a chance to share their responses.) To what extent did you agree or disagree with other group members on the stasis questions at stake in Etzioni's analysis? As a group, choose the two questions that best apply to Etzioni's argument, and agree on two or three reasons why each question is central to his argument. Be prepared to share the results of your discussion with your class.

||||||||||||||||||||||||||||||||||||||||||||||||||||||||||||||||||||||||||||||||||||||||

Identifying an Author's Position on a Question

You may find it helpful to identify an author's position in two stages: *First, read the text carefully to determine the main question that the author has presented.* If you review the first three paragraphs of Etzioni's argument beginning on p. 87, for instance, you'll note that he observes in paragraph 1 that privacy "is viewed by most Americans as a profound, inalienable right" and goes on to argue in paragraph 3 that "It is time to pay attention to the other half of the equation that defines a good society: concerns for public health and safety that entail some rather justifiable diminution of privacy." The remainder of the excerpt clarifies and supports his position on this issue.

After you have identified the author's position, you can read his or her argument critically. Reading critically doesn't mean simply looking for logical flaws, poor evidence, and so on. Rather, critical readers shift stances as they read to develop a complex understanding of the issues at hand. In this sense, critical readers know how to play what Peter Elbow calls the believing and doubting game.[3] When you play the believing game, you attempt to believe the author's arguments by engaging these arguments sympathetically. You put yourself in the position of the author or of someone who supports the author's position. You ask yourself what interests and experiences might cause the author to take this position. Similarly, when you play the doubting game, you ask what objections someone with different interests and experiences might make. Other ways of doubting an argument include examining the claims and considering the evidence that supports each claim.

The Questions for Critical Reading on pp. 92–93 can help you become a more active and critical reader who reads both with and against the grain of an author's argument.

|||||||||||||||||||||||||||||||||||||||||||||||||||||||||||||||||||||||||||||||||||||||

FOR EXPLORATION

Reread the excerpt from Amitai Etzioni's *The Limits of Privacy* (pp. 87–90). After doing so, respond to each of the Questions for Critical Reading on pp. 92–93. What did this guided rereading of Etzioni's text help you to better understand about it?

FOR COLLABORATION

After you have analyzed Etzioni's argument with the help of the Questions for Critical Reading, meet with a group of classmates to share the results of your analysis. Appoint a timekeeper so that all group members have an opportunity to share their results. To what extent did other group members agree in their responses to the questions for critical reading? To what extent did they disagree? What did you learn as a result of this experience? Be prepared to share your responses with the rest of the class.

|||||||||||||||||||||||||||||||||||||||||||||||||||||||||||||||||||||||||||||||||||||||

Using Aristotle's Three Appeals

As the Questions for Critical Reading on pp. 92–93 suggest, you may agree with a writer's position on a subject but nevertheless question the support that he or she provides. One of the hallmarks of a critical reader, in fact, is the ability to maintain a critical distance from an argument, even when you have strong feelings for or against the author's position.

Two analytical frameworks—one ancient and one contemporary—can help you evaluate the strengths and limitations of academic arguments. The first of these systems, Aristotle's three appeals, is introduced on p. 51 in Chapter 3.

thinking rhetorically

---

[3] Peter Elbow, *Writing without Teachers* (New York: Oxford UP, 1973), 147–91.

Questions for Critical Reading

1. What is the author's purpose or agenda?

(*Note: This may or may not be identical to the position that the author takes in his or her argument.*)

2. How much do you know about the author's assumptions, beliefs, and experiences?

3. What are the author's qualifications to discuss the topic?

4. What unstated assumptions or underlying values and commitments does the author seem to hold?

How might these influence his or her position?

5. What does the author want readers to *do* as a result of reading this text?

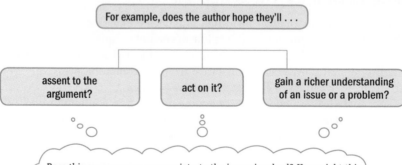

For example, does the author hope they'll . . .

assent to the argument?

act on it?

gain a richer understanding of an issue or a problem?

Does this purpose seem appropriate to the issues involved? How might this purpose influence the form and content of the author's argument?

6. **What reasons does the author offer in support of his or her ideas?**

(Are they good reasons?)

7. **What kinds of sources does the author rely on?**

How current and reliable are they? Are any perspectives left out?

8. **What objections might be raised to this argument?**

9. **Does this argument include images, graphics, or media?**

If so, how do they appeal to readers or listeners? Does their appeal seem appropriate or questionable?

10. **How open to persuasion are you with this particular topic?**

How willing are you to listen to another point of view?

If you agree with the author, can you maintain a critical distance so that you can examine the claims and support that the writer provides?

In his *Rhetoric*, Aristotle determined that speakers and writers draw on three general appeals when they attempt to persuade others:

- *Logos*, the appeal to reason

- *Pathos*, the appeal to emotion, values, and beliefs

- *Ethos*, the appeal to the credibility of the speaker or writer

One way to analyze an argument is to determine which type of appeal the author draws on most heavily and his or her effectiveness in using it. When you consider appeals to *logos*, ask yourself if the author has articulated clear and reasonable major claims and supported them with appropriate evidence. Appeals to *pathos* raise different issues: Here you identify the strategies that the author has employed to appeal to readers' values and interests. Finally, appeals to *ethos* encourage you to consider the author's credibility and trustworthiness as demonstrated in his or her argument.

Appeals to *logos* are often considered especially trustworthy by North American readers, particularly in academic contexts. Logical appeals include firsthand evidence drawn from observations, interviews, surveys and questionnaires, experiments, and personal experience; and secondhand evidence drawn from print and online sources. Critical readers do not automatically assume that support drawn from logical appeals is valid. After all, not all sources are equally valid, and facts can be out-of-date or taken out of context. (For a discussion of how to evaluate print and online sources, see pp. 186–92.)

Critical readers look at all three of Aristotle's appeals in context. Appeals to *pathos* — to readers' emotions, values, and beliefs — can certainly be manipulative and inappropriate. We've all seen ads that seem to promise one thing (youth, beauty, fitness) to sell another. Nevertheless, emotional appeals play key roles in many kinds of arguments, including academic arguments. A student writing about humanitarian issues growing out of the Iraq War might begin her essay by describing the loss of life, order, and basic material necessities that have resulted from the war. In so doing, she would be appealing to readers' emotions and emphasizing the importance of her topic. The same is true for appeals to *ethos*. While we might be skeptical when we see an ad where a movie star or sports hero praises a product, this doesn't mean that all appeals to *ethos* are suspect.

In this regard, let's return to the excerpt from Etzioni's *The Limits of Privacy* (pp. 87–90). The biographical information that accompanies this excerpt provides information about Etzioni's experience and qualifications that can help readers determine whether Etzioni is an authority on issues of privacy. Critical readers will keep this knowledge in mind as they read his argument, but they'll also consider the credibility with which he makes his case. Does he use examples that are fair and reasonable? Does he develop a balanced, thoughtful argument? Does he seem to have society's best interest at heart, or is he pushing an agenda of his own personal assumptions and beliefs? By asking questions such as these, readers can determine whether they should trust Etzioni's credibility as a thinker and writer. In short, critical readers respect relevant experiences and qualifications that authors bring to various issues, but they focus primarily on what the author does and says in the text that they are currently reading.

|||||||||||||||||||||||||||||||||||||||||||||||||||||||||||||||||||||||||||||||||||||||

FOR EXPLORATION

Drawing on your understanding of Aristotle's three appeals, analyze the excerpt from Etzioni's *The Limits of Privacy* (pp. 87–90). What appeals does he draw on most heavily? How effective is he in using these appeals? (Be sure to comment on each of the three appeals.)

FOR COLLABORATION

Meet with a group of classmates to share your responses to the previous Exploration. Appoint both a timekeeper and a recorder to summarize your group's responses. Begin by addressing this question: To what extent did members of your group agree about Etzioni's effectiveness in his use of Aristotle's three appeals?

After responding, develop a group position on Etzioni's use of Aristotle's three appeals. To do so, first agree on a statement that conveys your group's sense of how Etzioni employed each appeal. Then find one or two examples from his text that support your analysis. Be prepared to share the results of your discussion with the class.

|||||||||||||||||||||||||||||||||||||||||||||||||||||||||||||||||||||||||||||||||||||||

Using Toulmin's Framework

Aristotle's framework for analyzing academic arguments encourages you to step back from your commonsense understandings of — and immediate responses to — an argument. In other words, it enables you to gain critical distance on your reading. A second framework that serves this purpose was developed by the British philosopher Stephen Toulmin; it is sometimes referred to simply as Toulmin argument or the Toulmin system. According to Toulmin, most arguments contain the following common features:

- *Claims* are statements of fact, opinion, or belief that provide the fundamental structure for arguments.

- *Qualifiers* are one or more statements that limit or clarify the claim in some way.

■ *Warrants* are links from the claim to reasons and evidence. Warrants often take the form of assumptions and beliefs that may or may not be explicitly stated.

■ *Reasons* are smaller assertions that support claims. They often begin with the word *because*.

■ *Evidence* includes examples, facts, statistics, statements by authorities, and personal experience used to back up reasons (and sometimes warrants).

Toulmin's framework encourages readers to consider every link in an argument's chain—including those aspects of the argument, such as warrants, that might be left unstated. Sometimes a warrant is so self-evident that writers don't state it explicitly. Few readers, for example, would object to the assertion that "Sylvia should make an excellent lawyer because she excelled in her classes in law school and in her early years of legal practice," even though the warrant for this claim ("Excelling in law school and in the early years of legal practice are good predictors of a person's success after law school") is missing. On other occasions, the absence of a warrant is a major flaw in the development of an argument. Many arguments about controversial subjects flounder because the writers incorrectly assume that their audience will accept their unstated warrants.

With Toulmin's system in mind, consider Etzioni's discussion of HIV testing of infants. This discussion appears in paragraphs 4 and 5 of his excerpt (pp. 87–88). Etzioni's main claim here (a subclaim of his larger argument) is clear. In the last sentence of paragraph 5, he argues that "To save the lives of . . . children . . . [of women who have HIV, these children] must be tested at delivery and treated even if this entails a violation of mothers' privacy." Note that Etzioni's claim is qualified by his recognition that violating the mother's privacy is a serious matter. To meet his burden of proof, Etzioni must demonstrate that the benefits of testing infants for HIV outweigh the costs to new mothers, whose privacy rights will be violated.

Etzioni provides several reasons in support of his argument. He points out, for instance, that recent research by the *New England Journal of Medicine* shows that infants born with HIV can ward off the disease if they are tested at birth and treated immediately. As evidence of the need for such testing, he adds that "An estimated two-thirds of infected mothers are unaware" that they have HIV. Etzioni undertakes a second and related line of reasoning when he argues that efforts to address this problem without requiring the mandatory testing of all newborn infants have failed.

Etzioni's argument about HIV testing can be analyzed as follows:

Claim: Testing newborn infants for HIV should be mandatory.

Qualifier: Testing newborn infants for HIV should be mandatory, even though this represents a violation of mothers' privacy.

Warrant: (Concerns for the health of newborn infants should take precedence over the need to maintain the privacy of their mothers.)

Reasons: Testing newborn infants for HIV should be mandatory, because (1) with testing and treatment, the lives of most infants who are born with HIV could be saved; (2) high-risk mothers who are particularly at risk of having infants with HIV are least likely to be aware that they have the disease and least likely to agree to voluntary testing; and (3) efforts to increase the number of infants who are tested for HIV without requiring mandatory testing have failed.

Evidence: (1) Authoritative medical data emphasize the benefits that can be gained by testing and treatment. (2) Data from such sources as the *Journal of School Health* confirm that high-risk mothers are particularly prone to HIV. (3) Unnamed sources estimate that two-thirds of infected mothers are unaware they have HIV.

This analysis outlines the basic structure of Etzioni's argument, but it still leaves room for readers to disagree about whether testing should be mandatory. Those who hold strong civil libertarian views may disagree with Etzioni's warrant, while others may question the reliability of the estimate that "two-thirds of infected mothers are unaware" that they have HIV. Etzioni's failure to provide evidence for this estimate—when he does provide evidence for other reasons that support his claim—might reasonably make some readers skeptical. They might argue that the number of women who are unlikely to know they have HIV and unlikely to be tested is much smaller than Etzioni suggests, and that given this fact the need to protect mothers' privacy should take precedence.

Finally, some readers might point out that Etzioni doesn't specify who should require mandatory testing (the federal government? the states?) or how it might best be carried out. Since Etzioni's discussion of mandatory HIV testing is part of a larger argument about privacy, it may be unrealistic to expect him to discuss issues of implementation, but critical readers would nevertheless note that these issues are unaddressed in Etzioni's text.

||||||||||||||||||||||||||||||||||||||||||||||||||||||||||||||||||||||||||||||||||||||

FOR EXPLORATION

Choose another section of Etzioni's argument (pp. 87–90), such as his discussion of biometrics, and analyze it according to Toulmin's system. What does this analysis reveal that you did not notice in earlier readings of the excerpt?

||||||||||||||||||||||||||||||||||||||||||||||||||||||||||||||||||||||||||||||||||||||

Recognizing Fallacies

thinking
rhetorically
○○

When you analyze an argument, you should be aware of *fallacies* that may be at work. Fallacies are faults in an argument's structure that may call into question the argument's evidence or conclusions. Some fallacies are easy to recognize. If someone told you that Bono's position on global warming is ridiculous because he's just a celebrity, you would probably recognize that this assertion is illogical and unfair. Such a statement is an example of an *ad hominem* fallacy, in which an attack on someone's character or actions masquerades as a critique of his or her position. This fallacy, like all fallacies, tends to shut down, rather than encourage, communication.

To determine whether an argument is grounded in a fallacy, you need to consider it in the context of its specific rhetorical situation, including the place and time in which the argument was or is being made. Sometimes judgments about a person's character or actions are relevant to an argument, for instance. In other words, just because a writer or speaker grounds part of an argument in such a judgment doesn't mean that he or she is committing an *ad hominem* fallacy.

Since the time of Aristotle, rhetoricians have developed diverse ways of naming, describing, and categorizing various fallacies. Often the fallacies are categorized according to Aristotle's three major appeals of argument — ethical appeals (appeals to *ethos*), emotional appeals (appeals to *pathos*), and logical appeals (appeals to *logos*).

The following guidelines list some of the most significant fallacies that appear in arguments. As you read the brief descriptions, remember that the point of studying fallacies is not to discredit the ideas of others, but rather to thoughtfully evaluate the arguments of others and to develop fair, well-reasoned arguments of your own.

Guidelines for Identifying Fallacies

Ethical Fallacies

Writers who employ ethical fallacies attempt to destroy the credibility of those who disagree with them. Examples of ethical fallacies include the following:

AN AD HOMINEM attack is an unfair attack on a person's character or actions, one that diverts attention from the issue at hand.

"Any American who opposes the war in Iraq is unpatriotic."

(A person's position on a war does not necessarily reflect his or her patriotism.)

GUILT BY ASSOCIATION is an effort to damage a person's credibility by associating him or her with an unpopular or discredited activity or person.

"Hip-hop is bad because some hip-hop musicians have been involved in criminal activities."

(Some—but not all—hip-hop musicians have engaged in criminal activities, but their personal behavior is separate from the music that they create.)

Emotional Fallacies

Emotional appeals can play a valid and important role in argumentation, but when these appeals are overblown or unfair, they distract readers from attending to the point that is being argued. Examples of emotional fallacies include the following:

A BANDWAGON APPEAL argues that readers should support a person, an activity, a product, or a movement because it is popular. This appeal is particularly common in advertising:

"Frosty Puffs™ is the best-selling cereal in America!"

A SLIPPERY SLOPE fallacy occurs when writers exaggerate the future consequences of an event or action, usually with an intent to frighten readers into agreeing with their argument.

"If we ban *Beloved* from our school library, the next thing you know, we'll be burning books!"

Logical Fallacies

Logical fallacies are arguments in which the claims, warrants, or evidence are invalid, insufficient, or disconnected. Examples of logical fallacies include the following:

BEGGING THE QUESTION involves stating a claim that depends on circular reasoning for justification.

"Abortion is murder because it involves the intentional killing of an unborn human being."

(This is tantamount to saying that "Abortion is murder because it is murder." This fallacy often detracts attention from the real issues at hand, for the question of whether a fetus should be considered a human being is complex.)

A HASTY GENERALIZATION is drawn from insufficient evidence.

"Last week I attended a poetry reading supported by the National Endowment for the Arts, and several of the speakers used profanity. Maybe the people who want to stop government funding for the NEA are right."

(One performance doesn't constitute a large enough sample for such a generalization.)

A NON SEQUITUR is an argument that attempts to connect two or more logically unrelated ideas.

"I hate it when people smoke in restaurants; there ought to be a law against cigarettes."

(Eliminating smoking in restaurants and the negative effects of secondhand smoke do not require the elimination of legal tobacco sales.)

Putting Theory into Practice: Academic Analysis in Action

Readers engage in academic analysis not to criticize or dissect another's argument but rather to understand that argument as fully as possible. When you analyze an academic argument, you attempt to go beyond your immediate response — which often takes the form of binary-driven observations ("I agree/don't agree, like/don't like, am interested/not interested in X") — to achieve a fuller, more complex understanding of it.

Here is an example of a successful analysis of an academic argument. This essay by Stevon Roberts, a student at Oregon State University, analyzes the excerpt from Etzioni's *The Limits of Privacy* presented earlier in this chapter (pp. 87–90).

Roberts 1

Stevon Roberts
Dr. Mallon
Composition 101
Oct. 10, 2010

The Price of Public Safety

As a former senior adviser to the White House and author of *The Limits
of Privacy*, Amitai Etzioni is a formidable advocate for revision of one of
America's most cherished luxuries: protection of personal privacy. In "Less
Privacy Is Good for Us (and You)," an argument excerpted from the above
volume, Etzioni urges Americans to look critically at traditional expectations
for personal privacy and to be prepared to sacrifice those expectations for
increased public health and safety. Although the volume was published
before the terrorist attacks on September 11, 2001, the events of that day
give an increased sense of urgency to Etzioni's message and consequently
might make Americans more receptive to protocols that afford protection
from public risks in general.

> Roberts identifies the argument he's discussing and suggests that its author is a credible authority.

> Roberts identifies Etzioni's position.

> Roberts contrasts the rhetorical situations of the writing of the piece and his reading of it.

Etzioni opens his argument by discussing recent HIV testing procedures
in hospitals that may infringe on the rights of pregnant women. He then
shifts gears and takes a brief look at public outrage from the Coalition for
Constitutional Liberties regarding driver's license availability. Next, he
gives us a crash course in "biometrics," a controversial new technology
that could save billions of dollars lost to fraud every year. Finally, Etzioni
addresses our fears (and those of other civil libertarians) that these and other
procedures that are designed to increase our public health and safety will not
be implemented justly and ethically. Etzioni admits, however, that a growing
number of people and interest groups are not convinced that old laws—such
as the Fourth Amendment, which protects the United States from becoming a
military state—can protect us from new technology. We are left to wonder:
Is Etzioni justified in making his unconventional claims despite such well-
founded opposition?

> In this paragraph, Roberts summarizes Etzioni's argument fairly, and closes by introducing his main question: Is Etzioni's argument legitimate?

After some brief media references, Etzioni's first substantial argument
involves a real-world privacy dilemma facing pregnant women as well as

Roberts 2

various health and legal groups. Specifically, he focuses on HIV testing of newborns. This is an excellent place to start because the reactions of these groups help to shed light on our current attitudes toward privacy. Etzioni refers to the *New England Journal of Medicine*, which published evidence suggesting that infants born to HIV-infected women could ward off the disease with early diagnosis and treatment with AZT. In order for the infants to be treated, they must be tested. This becomes a privacy issue because testing infants for HIV also reveals whether "the mother is a carrier, and thus her privacy is violated" (91).

> In this paragraph and the next, Roberts notes the major evidence Etzioni provides in support of his claim.

As Etzioni acknowledges, arguments in favor of required HIV testing of infants have met strong—and even "vehement"—opposition from civil libertarians, as well as from some gay activists. Indeed, the question of whether to test infants for HIV has been so contentious that most states, as well as the federal government, have avoided taking it on. In this regard, Etzioni chastises Congress for "pass[ing] the buck by asking the Institute of Medicine (IOM) to conduct a study of the matter" (92). This effectively illustrates Congress's lack of willingness to become involved. IOM's solution suggests that all pregnant women should consent to HIV testing as part of their routine prenatal care. However, Etzioni feels this would leave out many women who "are drug addicts or otherwise live at society's margins" (92). Such women, he argues, "do not show up for prenatal care, and they are particularly prone to HIV, according to a study published in the American Health Association's *Journal of School Health*" (92). A succinct sentence sums up his solution: "To save the lives of their children, they [infants] must be tested at delivery and treated even if this entails a violation of mothers' privacy" (92).

This is a well-documented and compelling argument. Other parts of Etzioni's text, however, are not so well rounded. Instead of taking seriously the arguments forwarded by civil libertarians and others who raise concerns about privacy, Etzioni focuses on the media, which he believes tell "horror stories" about "The Death of Privacy" (91). When he does address the views of other groups, he represents their concerns by an inflammatory statement

> Roberts establishes his own *ethos* by signalling that he's providing a balanced assessment of Etzioni's argument.

Roberts 3

from the Coalition for Constitutional Liberties, which accuses those in favor of the plan of pushing the country "to the brink of tyranny" (92).

With this brief (and wholly unsuccessful) transition, Etzioni moves from the Coalition's alarmist complaints to Wells Fargo's introduction of "a new device that allows a person to cash checks at its ATM machines because the machines recognize faces" (92). These machines rely upon a new technology called biometrics, which, Etzioni explains, can use "natural features such as voice, hand design, and eye pattern to recognize a person with the same extremely high reliability provided by the new DNA tests" (92). Etzioni acknowledges that biometrics is a controversial technology, and he concedes that "it will practically strip Americans of anonymity, an important part of privacy" (92). With this new technology, people would find it difficult to change their names, move to another part of the country, and gain a fresh start in life. His solution is a hope that "future communities will become more tolerant of such people, especially if they openly acknowledge the mistakes of their past and truly seek to lead a more prosocial life" (92).

To his credit, Etzioni is quick to follow up the drawbacks of biometrics with compelling statistics about the potential benefits. He says, "Above all, while biometrics clearly undermines privacy, the social benefits it promises are very substantial" (92). He refers to the $1 billion to $5 billion lost annually to tax fraud, $18 billion to $23 billion annually in lost child support, and $18 billion a year lost to fraud committed by illegal aliens with false IDs. In addition to the potential economic benefits, he says sex offenders who use false IDs would be more effectively screened and would less easily find work at child-care centers or schools (93).

Etzioni's presentation of biometrics is, ironically, both calculated and lacking in logic. His predominantly economic appeal doesn't mention the cost associated with Wells Fargo's new face-recognizing ATM machines. Because he makes no attempt, even hypothetically, to weigh the cost of biometrics implementation against the savings from fraud protection or other liabilities, readers are left to assume that the overall results are beneficial, when that might not, in fact, be the case. For example, although

Margin notes:

Roberts asserts his first criticism of Etzioni's argument: He contends that Etzioni's representation of opposing viewpoints is not balanced.

Roberts again balances criticism of Etzioni's argument with praise.

Roberts presents another major criticism of Etzioni's use of evidence ("calculated and lacking in logic").

Roberts 4

he discusses credit card fraud, there is no mention of Internet credit card fraud. Biometrics countermeasures to combat this threat are likely to manifest as computer hardware add-ons, putting an unfair financial burden on lower-level consumers while taking the liability away from the credit card companies. It seems reasonable that while calculating the potential benefits, Etzioni should also calculate potential losses or system limitations, as he does when admitting that biometrics would not singlehandedly wipe out abusers from child-care centers.

Additionally, the author's appeals to *pathos* lack substance. In fact, his only olive branch to the human condition is a concession that biometrics may make it difficult for criminals seeking a new life. His solution to this problem is a touchy-feely dream in which everyone magically becomes more tolerant of criminals that repent and sin no more. Further, he makes no mention at all of persons seeking new lives for reasons other than legal trouble, such as women who have fled abusive husbands.

Roberts raises questions about Etzioni's appeals to *pathos* and points out that Etzioni does not anticipate a potential limitation to his argument.

Etzioni concludes his argument by considering court trends in balancing the need to protect personal privacy with concerns about public health and safety. Etzioni observes that courts have tended to "privilege privacy and make claims for public health or safety clear several high hurdles" (93). More recently, however, the courts are lowering these barriers with growing concern for public interest. For example, the courts have mandated drug testing for those who "directly have the lives of others in their hands, including pilots, train engineers, drivers of school buses, and air traffic controllers, even though such testing violates their privacy" (93). Etzioni reports that the ACLU feels these new laws "condition Americans to a police state" (93).

"All this," according to Etzioni, "points to a need to recast privacy in our civic culture, public policies, and legal doctrines. We should cease to treat it as an unmitigated good, a sacred right (the way Warren and Brandeis referred to in their famous article and many [other legal theorists have] since) or one that courts automatically privilege" (93). He feels that we should instead rely on the Fourth Amendment, which has built into its text

Roberts 5

safeguards that balance privacy and public security. His interpretation of
the document's reference to "unreasonable" search protocols recognizes the
difference between searches that "wantonly violate privacy" and those that
"enhance the common good to such an extent that they are justified, even if
they intrude into one's privacy" (93). Additionally, the amendment addresses
sufficient cause by introducing warrants "issued by a 'neutral magistrate'
presented with 'probable cause'" (93–4). Etzioni apparently believes
interpretation of this document will be uniform from one court to the next.
This assumption is problematic at best.

> Roberts challenges one of Etzioni's key assumptions.

The author leaves us with a new vision of privacy as a "very important
right but not one that trumps most other considerations, especially of public
safety and health" (94). With this parting thought, the author packages
a difficult and complex concept into a pill that is not terribly difficult to
swallow. By the same token, however, his oversimplification may leave
some readers feeling like something is missing.

Indeed, something is missing—the rest of Etzioni's book, from which
this excerpt originates. Readers of this argument can only hope that Etzioni
deals carefully and respectfully with the arguments of civil libertarians in
other parts of his work, for he certainly does not do so here. His tendency to
use only the most inflammatory statements from his opponents suggests he
has no interest in fully addressing their respective concerns.

> Roberts adds to his own *ethos* by acknowledging the limitations of his perspective, as a reader not of the book but the excerpt.

All things considered, Etzioni begins his essay with a clear purpose and
a logical, tangible starting point. Through the inclusion of several diverse
public-interest groups, health organizations, courts, and governmental
bodies, he initially appears to address all aspects of the moral dilemma.
This is especially true in the obvious benefit to newborns with HIV who
are diagnosed early. But in this excerpt, he distracts readers from the true
opposition by focusing primarily on the media, while turning the Coalition
for Constitutional Liberties and the ACLU into radical doomsayers that
jeopardize public welfare. He marginalizes their concerns, argues for
increased biometrics applications on the chance that billions of dollars might
potentially be protected from fraud, and opposes legislation that would

> Roberts closes his essay with a careful summary of his major points in examining Etzioni's argument.

Roberts 6

protect potential victims because society potentially could be more forgiving. Consequently, his venture into the hypothetical realm leaves opponents (and critical readers) unsatisfied.

Work Cited

Etzioni, Amitai. "Less Privacy is Good for Us (and You)." *The Academic Writer: A Brief Guide.* Ed. Lisa Ede. 1ˢᵗ ed. Boston: Bedford, 2008. 91–94. Print.

Note: In an actual MLA-style paper, Works Cited entries start on a new page.

||||||||||||||||||||||||||||||||||||||||||||||||||||||||||||||||||||||||||||||||

FOR EXPLORATION

Now that you have read Etzioni's argument several times and have also read Stevon Roberts's analysis of it, reread Stevon's essay to determine its strengths and limitations. Identify two or three passages from the essay that struck you as particularly significant and helpful, and write several sentences of explanation for each passage. Next, identify one or more ways this essay might be even more successful.

FOR COLLABORATION

Bring your response to the previous Exploration to class to share with a group of peers. Appoint a timekeeper and a recorder. After all group members have shared their responses, answer these questions: (1) To what extent did other members of your group agree in their evaluation of Stevon Roberts's analysis? To what extent did they disagree? (2) Now that you have heard everyone's responses, what two or three passages does your group feel best demonstrate Stevon's analytical skills? (3) How might Stevon's essay be further strengthened? Be prepared to share the results of your discussion with the class.

||||||||||||||||||||||||||||||||||||||||||||||||||||||||||||||||||||||||||||||||

Reading Visual Texts

Why is it important to be able to read visual images and to understand the role that design and visual elements can play in written texts? Perhaps the most important reason has to do with the increasingly pervasive role that images have come to play in modern life. Driving down the street, watching television, skimming a magazine, reading online: In these and other situations, we're continually presented with images and visual texts, many of which are designed to persuade us to purchase, believe, or do certain things. Often these images can be a source of pleasure and entertainment. But given the persuasive intent of many images, critical readers need to develop ways to read visual texts with the same insight they bring to written texts—at least if they want to be informed consumers and engaged citizens.

As an academic writer, you will frequently be asked to analyze traditional print texts. Increasingly, however, the ability to analyze *visual* texts—that is, texts that rely partly or completely on illustrations, photos, and visual design to convey their meanings—is gaining importance in academic writing.

If you haven't done so before, writing about visual texts can seem intimidating at first: How can you "get enough out of" a simple photograph, for example, to write about it? How do you go about understanding the relationship between text and image? The guidelines on pp. 111–12 will give you a place to start.

thinking rhetorically

Even apparently simple visual texts can have rich cultural histories. Here, for instance, is a well-known photograph of the Marxist revolutionary Che Guevara.

Ernesto "Che" Guevara, Photographed by Alberto Korda on March 5, 1960

An Argentinian by birth, Ernesto "Che" Guevara played a key role in the Cuban revolution. This photo of Guevara was taken by photographer Alberto Korda on March 5, 1960, in Havana, Cuba. Korda recognized the power of the photo, but it was not distributed broadly until after Guevara's October 9, 1967, execution. After Guevara's death, this photograph quickly achieved near mythic status. Today, this image—and manipulations of it—persist in global culture as a powerful symbol of countercultural and political resistance. Below, for instance, is a stylized version of the original photograph available as public domain clip art via www.wpclipart.com.

In this rendering, the historical Guevara has become, literally, an icon, which appears today in countless reproductions in every imaginable context, adorning posters, T-shirts, bumper stickers, Cuban currency, and even ice cream wrappers, wine labels, and condoms.[4] Guevara's image has also become a popular tattoo, sported by Angelina Jolie and Mike Tyson, among many, many others. (For an entertaining sampling, try searching Google images for "Che tattoo.")

"Che" Clip Art

---

[4]For additional examples accompanied by intelligent discussion, see author Michael Casey's Web site companion to his book *Che's Afterlife* at http://www.chesafterlife.com/images/.

"LiberaChe," by Artist Christopher Nash

Some uses of the image employ irreverence or outright mockery to resist the heroic image of Guevara promoted by his admirers. For example, "LiberaChe" by artist Christopher Nash morphs Guevara, usually the epitome of machismo, into a likeness of the flamboyant, rhinestone-bedecked entertainer Liberace, who was especially popular in the mid-twentieth century.

The widespread use of Guevara's image has also given rise recently to "meta-" references to its popularity—that is, to uses of the image that make tongue-in-cheek reference to how frequently the image is used. For instance, a T-shirt sold online by the *Onion* depicts Guevara wearing a T-shirt with his own image. In a similar vein, the cartoon from the *New Yorker* on p. 110 depends upon readers recognizing not only Che Guevara's iconic image but also that of Bart Simpson (an image that vies with Guevara's image in terms of its ubiquity).

As "meta-" references, these uses of Guevara's image call into question the ways in which the image has been and continues to be used. Rather than invoking Guevara as a symbol of countercultural and political resistance, they seem to be suggesting something about the image's commercialization—about its (mis)appropriation as a fashion statement and a means of perpetuating a consumer culture that the historical Guevara rejected.

Cartoon: Che and Bart

Chapter 5 presents an extended case study of one student's analysis of a visual text, a public service ad (PSA) for the National Center for Family Literacy. ✳ This case study shows student Daniel Stiepleman moving from his early explorations of this PSA through planning, drafting, and revision. Daniel struggled at times with his analysis, as is clear from the two rough drafts included in the chapter. But his effort more than paid off; his final essay, presented on pages 150–53, represents a thought-provoking and engaging analysis of a visual text.

✳ bedfordstmartins.com/academicwriter
For more advice and practice analyzing visual texts, go to **Re:Writing** *and then click on* **Visual Analysis**.

Guidelines for Analyzing Visual Texts

1. What is your general impression of the design and presentation of words and images in this text? **For example, is it . . .**

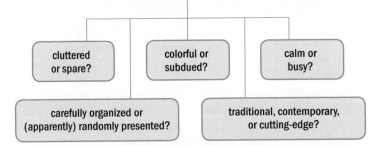

cluttered or spare?

colorful or subdued?

calm or busy?

carefully organized or (apparently) randomly presented?

traditional, contemporary, or cutting-edge?

2. What design elements are important in this text? **For example, does it present . . .**

a single dominant image?

a variety of images?

If so, how are the images related? What is your eye drawn to first? Why?

3. What is the relationship between image and text? Does the text function primarily to . . .

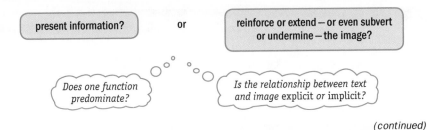

present information?

or

reinforce or extend — or even subvert or undermine — the image?

Does one function predominate?

Is the relationship between text and image explicit or implicit?

(continued)

4. In what ways does the design appeal to logic and to reason? to emotion?

5. What role (if any) does the credibility of a company or an individual play in this text?

Does the text assume that readers would recognize a trademark or corporate name, for instance, or a photograph or drawing of a well-known figure?

6. Does the text assume prior knowledge about an image?

If so, what sort of knowledge?

historical?   artistic?   cultural?   political?

What role does this prior knowledge play in helping the visual text achieve its impact?

Does it work differently depending on the extent of the reader's prior knowledge?

7. How would you describe the impact or message of the text?

8. Does it achieve its *intended* impact?

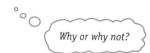

Why or why not?

||||||||||||||||||||||||||||||||||||||||||||||||||||||||||||||||||||||||||||||||||||

FOR EXPLORATION

Take a look at the public service announcement on p. 114 on the topic of treatment for drug addiction.

Using the Guidelines for Analyzing Visual Texts presented on pp. 111–112, write your responses to each question. Finally, write one or two paragraphs about what you have learned as a result of this analysis.

FOR THOUGHT, DISCUSSION, AND WRITING

1. Interview an instructor who teaches a class you are taking this term or a class in your major area of study. Ask this person to describe his or her understanding of the goals of undergraduate education and the role that your particular class or field of study plays in achieving these goals. Discuss the special analytic skills required to succeed in this course or field. Ask this person what advice he or she would give to someone, like yourself, who is taking a class in this field or planning to major in it. Be prepared to report the results of this interview to the class. Your instructor may also ask you to write an essay summarizing and commenting on the results of your interview.

2. Find an editorial or opinion column that interests you in a newspaper or general news magazine, such as *Newsweek* or *Time*.

   ■ Using stasis theory as described on p. 86, determine the most important questions at issue in this editorial or column. Then use the Questions for Critical Reading on pp. 92–93 to analyze the text you have chosen. Write a brief summary of what these activities have helped you understand about your reading. If your analysis has raised questions for you as a reader, articulate them as well.

   ■ Use either Aristotle's three appeals (pp. 91–95) or Toulmin's framework for analyzing arguments (pp. 95–97) to further analyze the text you have chosen. After doing so, reread the summary you wrote earlier. What has this additional analysis helped you to better understand about your reading?

   Your teacher may ask you to write an essay analyzing the editorial or opinion column you have chosen.

||||||||||||||||||||||||||||||||||||||||||||||||||||||||||||||||||||||||||||||||||||

Are we making strides in the fight against meth? **Absolutely.**

Law enforcement officials, professionals in drug prevention and treatment, and many others have been working hard to eliminate meth from people's lives. And it's working—meth use has declined among young adults since 2002.[1]

There is still much work to be done, however. In areas across the country where meth use and production continue, this drug leaves a path of destruction that rips apart communities and families, endangers children and overburdens police forces.

Left untreated, drug addiction costs communities millions of dollars and places untold burdens on families. But treatment for addiction, including for meth, works.[2] Not only does it work, but it's a no-nonsense way to fight the disease of addiction and break the cycle of drug abuse and crime often associated with meth.

Just ask Josh.

Josh's first encounter with meth at the age of 17 spiraled into a full-blown addiction. It cost him his job at a car dealership, his house, and the trust of his family. Soon after, Josh was arrested for meth possession. Through a drug court in Dunklin County, MO, Josh was provided the treatment, structure and accountability he needed to turn his life around. His recovery is an ongoing process that continues today; Josh now works as a junior drug counselor and lives with his wife and kids.

DRUG ADDICTION TREATMENT IS COST-EFFECTIVE
For every $1 invested in drug treatment programs there's a $12 savings in crime and health care costs.[3]

People can—and do—recover from meth addiction.
Find out about substance abuse treatment, and support meth treatment in your community.

National Association of Drug Court Professionals
National Association of Attorneys General
Major Cities Chiefs Association
Community Anti-Drug Coalitions of America (CADCA)
Partnership for a Drug-Free America

Visit methresources.gov
or call 1-800-662-HELP

Office of National Drug Control Policy

Making and Supporting Claims

As Chapter 4 emphasizes, analysis and argument are linked in powerful ways. To write an effective argument, you must analyze both your own ideas and those of others. But academic argument requires more than strong analytical skills. A successful academic argument also requires careful, well-supported reasoning that anticipates your readers' interests and concerns.

Understanding — and Designing — Academic Arguments

The first step in writing a successful academic argument is to understand the ways in which academic arguments are similar to and different from other kinds of arguments. Viewed from one perspective, all language use is argumentative. If you say to a friend, "You *have* to hear Coldplay's new CD!" you're making an implicit argument that it's important (in order to be in the know, for sheer pleasure, or some other reason) to listen to that particular music. A sign that advertises the "Best Deep-Dish Pizza in Chicago" is also making an argumentative claim about the quality of the pizza relative to the competition. Even prayers can be viewed as arguments: Some prayers represent direct appeals to God; others function as meditations directed toward self-understanding. In either case, those who pray are engaged in an argument for change — either in themselves or in the world around them.

As these examples suggest, arguments serve many purposes beyond confrontation or debate. Sometimes the purpose is to change minds and hearts or to win a decision; this is particularly true in politics, business, and law. But winning isn't always the goal of argument — especially in the academy, where writers focus on contributing to the scholarly conversation in their fields. Given this focus, students who bring a debate model of argumentation to academic writing often encounter problems. Think about the terminology used in debate: Debaters *attack* their *adversaries,* hoping to *demolish* their *opponents'* arguments so that they can *win* the judge's approval and claim *victory* in the contest. In academic arguments, the goal is inquiry and not conquest. Your teachers aren't interested in whether you can attack or demolish your opponents. Rather, they value your ability to examine an issue or problem from multiple perspectives. They want you to make a commitment not to "winning," but to using clear reasoning and presenting substantial evidence.

Not all scholarly arguments are identical, however. Because they reflect the aims and methods of specific disciplines, they can vary in significant ways. For example, interpretation—whether of literary texts, artwork, or historical data—is central to arguments in the humanities. Scholars in the social sciences often argue about issues of policy; they also undertake studies that attempt to help readers better understand—and respond to—current issues and events. For instance, a sociologist might review and evaluate recent research on the effects of children's gender on parents' child-rearing practices and then present conclusions based on her own quantitative or qualitative study. Argument is also central to research in the natural sciences and applied sciences: Engineers who argue about how best to design and build trusses for a bridge, or chemists who present new information about a particular chemical reaction, are making claims that they must support with evidence and reasons.

Although scholarly arguments reflect disciplinary concerns, all scholars agree that the best arguments (1) explore relevant ideas as fully as possible and from as many perspectives as possible, (2) present their claims logically, and (3) include appropriate support for all significant claims. These preferences distinguish academic arguments from other kinds of arguments. You and your friend might spend an hour on a Saturday night arguing about the merits of Coldplay's new album, but your discussion would undoubtedly be fluid and improvisational, with many digressions. In academic argument, great value is placed on the careful, consistent, and logical exploration of ideas.

In a way, what is true of design is also true of academic arguments. (See the discussion of writing as design in Chapter 1.) Most academic arguments are open-ended and cannot be solved once and for all. Philosophers have been arguing for centuries, for instance, about whether it is possible to justify warfare, just as historians continue to argue about the significance and consequences of specific wars. In this sense, academic argument is endless: No important topic or issue is ever resolved once and for all. Similarly, there is no one correct process of composing or designing arguments. Some scholars who study what philosophers term *just war theory* take a historical approach; others emphasize ethical arguments. In this sense, those writing academic essays are participating in an ongoing scholarly conversation.

The process of identifying problems is central to writers of academic arguments, just as it is for designers. A literary scholar who believes that other critics of Toni Morrison's *Beloved* have inadequately recognized the importance of religious imagery in that novel is describing a problem. Since literary texts—like other complex data sets—are open to multiple interpretations, this critic's argument—her response to the problem—will depend in part on subjective value judgments. The same occurs when a historian argues that previous accounts of the fall of Saigon near the end of the Vietnam War overemphasize the Western media's role in this event, or when an economist argues that current theories of macroeconomics cannot account for the development of e-commerce on the Internet.

Perhaps most important, those composing academic arguments are, like designers, concerned with what might, could, and should be. A biologist proposing a new method for protecting wetlands, a sociologist reporting the results of a new study on children in foster care, a communication scholar analyzing the effect of *The Da Vinci Code* on public perceptions about Catholicism, and a historian reconsidering previous studies of the spread of the Black Plague in medieval Europe are all composing writing that *matters*—writing that addresses complex problems, expands the scholarly conversation, and makes a difference.

Exploring Aristotle's Three Appeals

Academic writing places a high premium on the quality of ideas, evidence, and organization—that is, on logical appeals, or *logos*. This doesn't mean, however, that as a writer you should avoid emotional appeals (*pathos*) and ethical appeals (*ethos*). All writers—whether they're composing a letter to a friend, an editorial for the student newspaper, or an essay for a history class—need to establish their *ethos*, or credibility. Academic writers generally do so by demonstrating knowledge of their subject and of the methodologies that others in their field use to explore it. They reinforce their credibility when they explore their subject evenhandedly and show respect for their readers. Writers demonstrate this respect, for instance, when they anticipate readers' concerns and address possible counterarguments. In these and other ways, academic writers demonstrate *rhetorical sensitivity*. (For more on analyzing rhetorical situations and on Aristotle's three appeals, see Chapter 3.)

Just as all writers appeal to *ethos*, so too do they appeal to *pathos*—to emotions and shared values. Sometimes this type of appeal is obvious, as in requests for charitable contributions that feature heart-wrenching stories and images. Even texts that are relatively objective and that emphasize appeals to *logos*, as much academic writing does, nevertheless draw on and convey emotional appeals. An academic argument that uses formal diction and presents good reasons and evidence is sending readers a message based on

thinking rhetorically

pathos: "This subject is much too important for me to treat it frivolously. It requires the attention that only reasoned argument can give."

In academic writing, appeals to *pathos* can also emphasize just how much is at stake in understanding and addressing a problem or an event. Scholars writing about the Holocaust, for instance, often use vivid descriptions to encourage readers to connect personally with their text. Moreover, to bring immediacy and impact to an argument, writers often employ figurative language, such as metaphors, similes, and analogies. (For example, some scholars who have written about the massacre that occurred when Nanking, China, fell to the Japanese on December 13, 1937, refer to this event as the Rape of Nanking.) They also may use images and graphics to lend visceral impact to their point.

Understanding the Role of Values and Beliefs in Argument

When you write an academic argument, you give reasons and evidence for your assertions. A student arguing against a Forest Service plan for a national forest might warn that increased timber harvesting will reduce access to the forest for campers and backpackers or that building more roads will adversely affect wildlife. This writer might also show that the Forest Service has failed to anticipate some problems with the plan and that cost-benefit calculations unfairly reflect logging and economic-development interests. These are all potentially good reasons for questioning the plan. Notice that these reasons necessarily imply certain values or beliefs. The argument against increasing the timber harvest and building more roads, for instance, reflects the belief that preserving wildlife habitats and wilderness lands is more important than the economic development of the resources.

Is this argument flawed because it appeals to values and beliefs? Of course not. When you argue, you can't suppress your own values and beliefs. After all, they provide links between yourself and the world you observe and experience. In Toulmin's terms, these links are warrants: They thus play an important role in any argument. ✳

Suppose that you and a friend are getting ready to go out for breakfast. You look out the window and notice some threatening clouds. You say, "Looks like rain. We'd better take umbrellas since we're walking. I hate getting soaked." "Oh, I don't know," your friend replies. "I don't think it looks so bad. I heard on the radio that it wasn't going to start raining until the afternoon. I think we're okay." Brief and informal as this exchange is, it constitutes an argument. Both you and your friend have observed something, analyzed it, and drawn conclusions—conclusions backed by reasons. Although you each cite different reasons, your conclusions reflect your different personal preferences. You're generally cautious, and you don't like getting caught unpre-

✳ To review Toulmin's system for analyzing arguments, see pp. 95–97.

pared in a downpour, so you opt for an umbrella. Your friend relies on expert opinion and might be more of a risk-taker.

If your individual preferences, values, and beliefs shape a situation like this where only getting wet is at stake, imagine how crucial they are in more complicated situations, such as determining whether a controversial government proposal is right or wrong, just or unjust, effective or ineffective. Argument necessarily involves values and beliefs, held by both writer and reader, that cannot be denied or excluded—even in academic argument, with its emphasis on evidence and reasoned inquiry. The student arguing against the Forest Service plan can't avoid using values and beliefs as bridges between reasons and conclusions. And not all of these bridges can be explicitly stated; that would lead to an endless chain of reasons. The standards of academic argument require, however, that writers explicitly state and defend the most important values and beliefs undergirding their argument. In this case, then, the student opposing the Forest Service plan should at some point state and support the belief that preserving wildlife habitats and wilderness lands should take priority over economic development.

It's not easy to identify and analyze your own values and beliefs, but doing so is essential in academic argument. Values and beliefs are often held unconsciously, and they function as part of a larger network of assumptions and practices. Your opinions about the best way for the government to respond to unemployed individuals reflect your values and beliefs about family, the proper role of government, the nature of individual responsibility, and the importance of economic security. Thus if a political science instructor asks you to argue for or against programs requiring welfare recipients to work at state-mandated jobs in exchange for economic support, you need to analyze not just these workfare programs but also the role your values and beliefs play in your analysis. The guidelines on pp. 120–21 will help you do so, thus enabling you to respond more effectively to the demands of academic argument.

thinking rhetorically

At the same time, when you argue, you must consider not only your own values and beliefs but also those of your readers. The student writing about the Forest Service plan would present one argument to a local branch of the Sierra Club (an organization that advocates for protecting the environment) and a very different argument to representatives of the Forest Service. In arguing to the Sierra Club, the student would expect readers to agree with his major warrants and therefore might focus on how the group could best oppose the plan and why members should devote time and energy to this particular project.

His argument to the Forest Service would be designed quite differently. Recognizing that members of the Forest Service would know the plan very well, would have spent a great deal of time working on it, and would be strongly committed to it, the student might focus on a limited number of points, especially those that the Forest Service might be willing to modify. The student

Guidelines for Analyzing Your Own Values and Beliefs

1. Use informal invention methods to explore your values and beliefs about a subject.

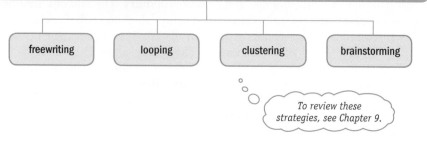

| freewriting | looping | clustering | brainstorming |

To review these strategies, see Chapter 9.

2. Avoid subjects about which you feel so strongly that you can't understand opposing points of view.

Freewriting about gun control, for example, may help you realize that your convictions about this issue are so deeply rooted in your beliefs, values, and experiences as to be unchangeable.

3. Pay attention to links (called *warrants* in the Toulmin system) between a claim and its support.

For example, most arguments in favor of environmental protection are grounded in the warrant that preserving the environment is more important than such goals as growing the economy.

Remember that these warrants are often unstated and audience specific.

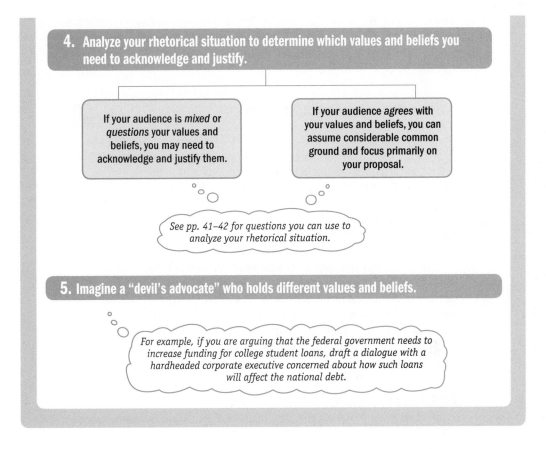

4. **Analyze your rhetorical situation to determine which values and beliefs you need to acknowledge and justify.**

If your audience is *mixed* or *questions* your values and beliefs, you may need to acknowledge and justify them.

If your audience *agrees* with your values and beliefs, you can assume considerable common ground and focus primarily on your proposal.

See pp. 41–42 for questions you can use to analyze your rhetorical situation.

5. **Imagine a "devil's advocate" who holds different values and beliefs.**

For example, if you are arguing that the federal government needs to increase funding for college student loans, draft a dialogue with a hardheaded corporate executive concerned about how such loans will affect the national debt.

would be wise to assume a tone that isn't aggressive or strident to avoid alienating his audience. He would articulate his most important warrants and align them whenever possible with the beliefs and values of those who work for the Forest Service.

In the case of the academic arguments you'll write as an undergraduate, of course, your reader is generally your instructor. In this rhetorical situation, the most useful approach is to consider values and beliefs that your instructor holds as a member of the academic community. In writing for an economics or a political science instructor, the student arguing against the Forest Service plan should provide logical, accurate, and appropriate evidence. He should avoid strong emotional appeals and harsh expressions of outrage or bitterness, focusing instead on developing a succinct, clearly organized, carefully reasoned essay.

The essays by Hope Leman (pp. 78–79) and Stevon Roberts (pp. 101–6) that appear in Chapter 4 are excellent examples of arguments that respect the values and beliefs that instructors hold as members of the academic community.

NOTE FOR MULTILINGUAL WRITERS

The standards of academic argument that are discussed in this book reflect the Western rhetorical tradition as it is taught in the United States—a tradition that you are learning if you are new to this country. This tradition encourages writers to clearly articulate and directly defend their values and beliefs. Other rhetorical traditions, including your own, may be different. Some traditions, for instance, encourage writers to convey their assumptions and values *indirectly*.

Try to identify any differences between the ways in which writers are encouraged to address their values and beliefs in your home culture and in the Western rhetorical tradition. If you discuss these differences with your teacher and classmates, you will enrich everyone's understanding of the way rhetorical practices differ in various contexts.

FOR EXPLORATION

Think of an issue that concerns you, such as a campus controversy, a recent decision by your city council, or a broad national movement (e.g., to provide on-campus child-care facilities, house the homeless, or improve public transportation). After reflecting on this issue, use the guidelines presented on pp. 120–21 to analyze your values and beliefs. Then respond to the following questions.

1. Given your values and beliefs, what challenges would writing an academic essay on this subject pose for you?

2. To what extent did your analysis help you understand that others might reasonably hold different views on this subject? Make a list of the possible opposing arguments. Then briefly describe the values and beliefs that underlie these counterarguments. How might you respond to these arguments?

3. Now write the major assertions or arguments that you would use to support your controlling idea, or thesis. Below each assertion, list the values or beliefs that your readers must share with you to accept that assertion.

4. How have the Guidelines on pp. pp. 120–21 and this Exploration helped you understand how to write an effective academic argument? If you were to write an academic argument on this issue, how would you now

organize and develop your ideas? What strategies would you use to respond to your readers' values and beliefs?

||||||||||||||||||||||||||||||||||||||||||||||||||||||||||||||||||||||||||||||||||||

Mastering the Essential Moves in Academic Writing

Appeals to *ethos* and *pathos* play important roles in academic argument. For an academic argument to be effective, however, it must be firmly grounded in *logos*. The remainder of this chapter presents strategies that you can follow to meet the demands of academic writing. These strategies will help you to (1) determine whether a claim can be argued, (2) develop a working thesis (an appropriately limited claim), (3) provide good reasons and sound evidence for your argument, (4) acknowledge possible counterarguments, (5) frame your argument as part of the scholarly conversation, and (6) consider whether visuals would strengthen your argument.

Determining Whether a Claim Can Be Argued

You can't argue by yourself. If you disagree with a decision to increase school activity fees, you may mumble angry words to yourself, but you'd know that you're not arguing. To argue, you must argue *with* someone. Furthermore, the person must agree with you that an assertion raises an arguable issue. If you like hip-hop music, for example, and your friend, who prefers jazz, refuses to listen to (much less discuss) your favorite CD, you can hardly argue about her preferences. You'll both probably just wonder at the peculiarities of taste.

Similarly, in academic argument you and your reader (most often your instructor) must agree that an issue is worth arguing about if you're to argue successfully. Often this agreement involves sharing a common understanding of a problem, process, or idea. A student who writes an argument on the symbolism of Hester Prynne's scarlet *A* in *The Scarlet Letter*, for example, begins from a premise that she believes the teacher will share—that Hester's *A* has significance for the impact and significance of the novel.

The Guidelines on p. 124 can help you compose an effective and arguable claim.

Developing a Working Thesis

Arguable claims must meet an additional criterion: They must be sufficiently limited so that both writer and reader can determine the major issues at stake and the lines of argument that best address them. In a late-night discussion with friends, you may easily slip from a heated exchange over the causes of the

Guidelines for Developing an Arguable Claim

1. Choose an issue that has no easily identifiable solution and that has something significant at stake.

An arguable claim presents a position (for example, "Financial institutions have a responsibility to safeguard their databases to deter identity fraud.")

Facts that can be verified—for example, "Identity theft costs consumers huge amounts of time and money"—are not arguable claims.

2. Choose an issue or a problem on which readers might have varying perspectives.

3. Attempt to persuade readers to believe or do something.

Some arguments attempt to *convince* readers that an act or a belief is right or wrong, helpful or unhelpful.

Other arguments explore deeply complex issues or problems with a goal of *understanding*, not persuasion.

current unrest in world affairs to a friendly debate about whether Kris Allen or Adam Lambert deserved to win the *American Idol* competition in 2009.

In an academic argument, however, you must limit the discussion not just to a single issue but to a single thesis—a claim you will argue for. It's not enough, in other words, to decide that you want to write about nuclear energy or the need to protect the wilderness. Even limiting these subjects—writing about the Three Mile Island nuclear reactor or the Forest Service's Land Management Plan for the White Mountain National Forest—wouldn't help much. That's because your thesis must be an *assertion*—something, in other words, to argue about.

An appropriately limited thesis makes it clear (for you and for your reader) what's at stake in your argument. For this reason, many instructors and writers suggest that academic arguments should contain an explicit thesis statement—a single declarative sentence that asserts or denies something about the topic. The assertion "The U.S. Forest Service's Land Management Plan for the White Mountain National Forest fails adequately to protect New Hampshire's wilderness areas" is an example of a thesis statement.

Developing a clear, limited thesis statement can help you as a writer stay on track and include evidence or details relevant to the main point rather than extraneous or loosely related information. Readers—especially busy readers like your college instructors—also find thesis statements helpful. A clearly worded thesis statement helps instructors read your writing more efficiently and critically.

Here is the first paragraph of an essay written for a class on Latin American history. The thesis statement is italicized. Notice how it clearly articulates the student's position on the topic, the role of multinational and transnational corporations in Central America.

Over the past fifty years, Latin American countries have worked hard to gain economic strength and well-being. To survive, however, these countries have been forced to rely on multinational and transnational corporations for money, jobs, and technological expertise. *In doing so, they have lost needed economic independence and have left themselves vulnerable to exploitation by foreign financiers.*

A clear thesis statement can help both writer and reader stay on track as they "compose" an essay.

Often, thesis statements appear early in an essay. In her analysis of the "mirror" and "flashlight" models of the role of journalists in American society that appears in Chapter 4, Hope Leman articulates an explicit thesis statement at the beginning of the second paragraph of her essay: "In this essay, I will argue that the 'flashlight' model provides a more accurate and complex understanding of the role of journalists in America than the 'mirror' model does" (p. 78).

Stevon Roberts takes a different tack in his analysis of an excerpt from Etzioni's *The Limits of Privacy* in that same chapter. Roberts begins his essay by commenting on Etzioni's strong credibility as a writer and follows this by summarizing Etzioni's argument. Rather than introducing a thesis statement, Roberts concludes his second paragraph by raising the question that motivates and guides his analysis: ". . . Is Etzioni justified in making his unconventional claims despite . . . [the] well-founded opposition" of civil libertarians and others concerned with privacy issues (p. 101)? As will be discussed more fully later in this chapter, Roberts spends the bulk of his essay carefully analyzing Etzioni's text, reserving final judgment until his concluding sentence, where he summarizes his analysis by arguing that ultimately the excerpt from Etzioni's text "leaves opponents (and critical readers) unsatisfied" (p. 106).

Both approaches represent thoughtful and effective responses to the writers' specific assignments. Hope Leman's assignment required her to take a stand on her topic, so it made sense for her to present her thesis statement early on. (Hope was also writing under time pressure since she was completing a take-home midterm.) Stevon Roberts's assignment was more general—to respond to and evaluate the excerpt from Etzioni's book. It thus made equally good sense for him to defer his final judgment until he completed this analysis and demonstrated his ability to engage Etzioni's ideas via his own critique.

Sometimes you may develop a working thesis early in your writing process. This is especially likely if your assignment requires you to take a stand and specifies the options available to you, as Hope Leman's assignment did. At times, however, you may have to think—and write—your way to a thesis. In situations like this, you'll develop your thesis and gather evidence recursively as you deepen your understanding of your topic and your rhetorical situation. This chapter concludes with a case study of one student writer, Daniel Stiepleman, whose argument evolved in this way. Reading Daniel's prewriting and drafts will help you better understand how to work through the process of making and supporting claims in academic arguments. Often you will discover, as Daniel did, that you need to explore your ideas at considerable length before determining your thesis.

Providing Good Reasons and Supporting Them with Evidence

To support a claim in a way that readers will find truly persuasive, you'll need to provide good reasons. Chapter 4 discusses three tools for analyzing and evaluating arguments: stasis theory, Aristotle's three appeals, and the

Toulmin system. You can use the same analytical tools to construct and revise your own arguments.

Let's say that you've drafted an argument challenging increased standardized testing in public schools. You're majoring in education, and you have strong feelings about federally mandated assessments, such as the No Child Left Behind legislation. Your draft explores your ideas as freely and fully as possible. Now it's two days later—time to step back and evaluate the draft's effectiveness. So you turn to Aristotle's three appeals.

As you reread your draft with the appeals of *ethos*, *pathos*, and *logos* in mind, you realize that you've gathered a lot of evidence about the limitations of standardized testing—and thus made good use of appeals to *logos*. Your argument is much less successful in employing the appeals of *ethos* and *pathos*, however. Your rereading has helped you realize that the passion you bring to this subject caused you to write in a strident tone, which might make readers distrust your credibility and sense of fairness. You also haven't considered the advantages of standardized testing or the reasons that some people find it helpful and even necessary. Critical readers might well suspect that you've stacked the deck against standardized testing.

Clearly, you need to strengthen your argument's appeal to *ethos*. You revise your tone so that it's more evenhanded; you also consider multiple points of view by presenting and evaluating possible counterarguments. Perhaps in the process you'll discover some shared values and beliefs that can strengthen your argument. (You could acknowledge your opponents, for instance, for recognizing the importance of education as a national, and not just a local, concern.) You'll want to find as many ways as possible to demonstrate that you realize your subject is complex and that reasonable people might have different ideas on the best way to address it.

What about *pathos*? In rereading your essay, you realize that in gathering strong evidence to support your claim, you've failed to give your subject a human face. You've got plenty of statistics and expert testimony but little that demonstrates how standardized testing affects real students and teachers. Based on your own experiences and those of peers, you have good examples of how standardized testing can have a negative impact, so you write yourself a reminder to include at least one such example in your revised draft. You also look for other ways to remind readers that national debates over standardized assessment aren't about impersonal test scores but about the real-life learning and teaching experiences of students and teachers across America.

As this example suggests, such analytical tools as Aristotle's three appeals, stasis theory, and the Toulmin system can play a key role in the construction of arguments. You may not use these tools to write the first draft of your argument (after all, your initial flow of ideas might be limited if you constantly asked yourself, "Does Toulmin's system call this point a claim, reason, warrant, qualifier, or evidence?"), but once you have a rough draft you can use these tools to test your ideas and identify problems that need

thinking
rhetorically

to be addressed and areas that need to be strengthened. The student who's arguing that recent increases in standardized testing threaten the quality of students' education, for instance, might find it helpful to identify the most important stasis questions at issue in her argument. Are they questions of fact? Definition? Interpretation? Value? Consequence? Policy?

In addition to using analytical tools, you can ask commonsense questions about the evidence that you include to support your claims. (See Questions for Evaluating Evidence, p. 129.)

|||||||||||||||||||||||||||||||||||||||||||||||||||||||||||||||||||||||||||||||||||||||

FOR EXPLORATION

Think again about the issue you analyzed in response to the Exploration on pp. 122–23. Formulate a tentative, or working, thesis statement that reflects your current position on this issue. Articulate two or three reasons or claims that support your thesis, and then list the major evidence you would use to support these claims. Finally, write a brief statement explaining why this evidence is appropriate, given your thesis statement, the reasons or claims that you have written, and your intended audience.

|||||||||||||||||||||||||||||||||||||||||||||||||||||||||||||||||||||||||||||||||||||||

Acknowledging Possible Counterarguments

Since academic argument is modeled on inquiry and dialogue rather than debate, as a writer you must consider multiple sides of an issue. Responding to counterarguments demonstrates that you've seriously analyzed an issue from a number of perspectives, rather than simply marshalling evidence to support your predetermined position.

There are a number of ways to discover counterarguments. You could imagine dialogues with one or more "devil's advocates," or you could discuss your subject with a group of classmates. You might even interview someone who holds a different position. Being aware of your own values and beliefs can also help you identify counterarguments. The student arguing against the Forest Service plan might consider the views of someone with different values, perhaps a person who believes in the importance of economic development, such as the owner of a lumber company or individuals living in towns supported by the timber industry. Finally, reading and research can expose you to the ideas and arguments of others.

How you use counterarguments will depend on your subject and rhetorical situation. In some instances, counterarguments can play an important structural role in your essay. After introducing your topic and indicating your thesis, for example, you might present the major counterarguments to your position, refuting each in turn. You might also group the counterarguments, responding to them all at once or throughout your essay.

Questions for Evaluating Evidence

1. How *representative* are my examples?

> *Will readers find these examples relevant to my argument?*

2. Do I provide *enough* examples to make my point? (Do I provide too *many*, and risk overwhelming my audience?)

3. Is the *significance* of my examples clear? Are they clearly related to my key points?

4. If I have used statistical evidence, was this evidence compiled by a *disinterested* source?

If *not*, do I have a good reason for presenting statistics from a source with an established position on my topic?

> *Such sources can play a helpful role in your argument as long as you make it clear that the source is a stakeholder with a clearly established position on your topic.*

Are the statistics based on an *adequate sample*, and have I drawn *appropriate inferences* from them, given the sample size?

Have I considered *multiple interpretations* of this statistical evidence?

5. What *authorities*, if any, do I draw upon to support my argument?

Are these authorities *qualified* to comment on my topic?

> *Why?*

Are any of them likely to be *biased*?

Are their comments *timely*?

> *If they are not — if I am citing an ancient authority on a contemporary topic, for instance — do I have a clear reason for why this authority's comment is relevant?*

Do I need to share the authorities' *credentials* with readers, or can I assume that readers already know and respect these sources?

In his essay in Chapter 4 (pp. 101–6), which is organized around a point-by-point analysis of Amitai Etzioni's text, Stevon Roberts acknowledges counterarguments to many of the issues raised in his analysis. He is careful from the beginning to affirm the strong credibility that Etzioni, a former senior advisor to the White House, brings to his subject. He takes care, as well, to identify those elements of Etzioni's argument with which he is in agreement. On p. 102, for instance, Roberts comments that Etzioni's position on prenatal HIV testing represents "a well-documented and compelling argument." Although Roberts is critical of Etzioni's discussion of biometrics, he acknowledges that "to his credit, Etzioni is quick to follow up the drawbacks of biometrics with compelling statistics about the potential benefits" (p. 103). In these and other ways, Roberts makes it clear that rather than simply looking for reasons to disagree with Etzioni he is working hard to engage his ideas seriously and respectfully. The effect is to strengthen the presentation of his own position.

||||||||||||||||||||||||||||||||||||||||||||||||||||||||||||||||||||||||||||||||

FOR COLLABORATION

This activity will help you recognize possible counterarguments to the thesis that you have been developing in this chapter. To prepare, be sure that you have a clear, easy-to-read statement of your working thesis and of the major evidence you would use to support it. Now spend five to ten minutes brainstorming a list of possible counterarguments.

Bring these written materials to your group's meeting. Determine how much time the group can spend per person if each student is to get help. Appoint a timekeeper. Then have each writer read his or her working thesis, evidence, and possible counterarguments. Members of the group should then suggest additional counterarguments that the writer has not considered. As you proceed, avoid getting bogged down in specific arguments; instead, focus on generating as many additional counterarguments as possible. Continue this procedure until your group has discussed each student's work.

||||||||||||||||||||||||||||||||||||||||||||||||||||||||||||||||||||||||||||||||

Framing Your Argument as Part of the Scholarly Conversation

The previous discussion has emphasized the basic elements you need to understand in order to compose an effective academic argument. Whatever your topic or discipline, to argue effectively you need to understand the role of values and beliefs in argument, determine whether a claim can be argued, develop a working thesis, provide good reasons and supporting evidence, and acknowledge possible counterarguments. This section will discuss additional essential rhetorical "moves" that successful academic writers regularly employ—moves that signal to readers that the writers are familiar with the scholarly conversation of which their essays are a part.

In one way or another, for instance, most academic writers must find a meaningful way to *enter the conversation* that grounds or motivates their topic. In her essay in Chapter 4, for instance, Hope Leman begins her discussion by contrasting the "mirror" and "flashlight" models of media theory, making it clear that her essay will represent her own take on this ongoing controversy (p. 78). Stevon Roberts takes a different approach in his essay that appears in that same chapter. He enters the conversation that Etzioni has begun with his book on privacy by acknowledging Etzioni's expertise and pointing out that the terrorist attacks of September 11, 2001, might "make Americans more receptive to protocols that afford protection from public risks in general" (p. 101) despite a potential loss of privacy. In so doing, Roberts demonstrates that he is aware of the context of Etzioni's original publication and of how subsequent events might strengthen Etzioni's arguments for some readers. Throughout his essay, Roberts demonstrates that he is informed and knowledgeable about his topic—and thus well qualified to enter the ongoing conversation surrounding issues of privacy.

Another essential "move" in academic writing—one that may seem simple but is not—is the ability to concisely and fairly *summarize* the words and positions of others. When you summarize the words and thoughts of others, you indicate to readers that you are familiar with the scholarly conversation on your topic. In the case of Hope Leman's essay in Chapter 4, her summaries require broad strokes: She is writing a take-home exam and is responding to general theories of media rather than one or more texts. Stevon Roberts's summaries play an even more important role in his analysis, given the fact that he is responding to a specific text, and doing so in a fairly detailed manner. Roberts devotes the first half of the second paragraph of his essay to a detailed point-by-point summary of Etzioni's text; as he analyzes this text, he stops periodically to summarize specific elements of Etzioni's argument; finally, he summarizes Etzioni again in his concluding paragraph. Roberts's summaries make it clear, first of all, that he is fairly representing Etzioni's text. They also serve as important signposts or structuring elements for his analysis.

Another important argumentive "move" in academic writing is the ability to effectively *quote and interpret* the words of those with whom you are in conversation. Quoting, like summarizing, is one way that writers can show that they are fairly representing the thoughts and ideas of those whose ideas and arguments they are discussing. You probably already understand that choosing the best passages to quote is essential, but it is equally important to explain why this or that quotation is relevant and, especially, how it links to the major lines of your argument.

If you turn again to Stevon Roberts's essay in Chapter 4 (pp. 101–6), you'll notice that he is quite strategic in quoting Etzioni's text. Sometimes Roberts's quotations demonstrate his willingness to grant Etzioni his due. This occurs when he quotes Etzioni's proposal to require prenatal HIV testing, which Roberts praises as a "well-documented and compelling argument" (p. 102). At other times Roberts's purpose in quoting Etzioni is to call attention to limitations in his argument, as when he suggests that Etzioni's inclusion of an inflammatory statement from the Coalition for Constitutional Liberties represents a "brief (and wholly unsuccessful) transition" in his argument (p. 103).

When you are writing an academic argument, sometimes your own contribution and thoughts can become lost in the larger discussion. Your essay can focus too much on what *others* have to say about your topic, in other words, and not enough on what *you* have to say in response. In situations like this, you need to find ways to *make your own contributions to the conversation clear*. One way of doing this is to introduce new information that you have acquired through experience or research. Sometimes you will do this explicitly, as Stevon Roberts does in his analysis of Etzioni's text. When Stevon points out that Etzioni fails to mention the costs associated with employing biometric technology, for example, he is contributing to the conversation on privacy by identifying a flaw in Etzioni's argument and by introducing relevant new data.

Similarly, in her essay in Chapter 4, Hope Leman draws upon her general understanding of how the media work. Here is the second paragraph of Hope's essay, with explanations of the moves she's making there:

In this essay, I will argue that the "flashlight" model provides a more accurate and complex understanding of the role of journalists in America than the "mirror" model does. This model recognizes, for instance, that journalists are shaped by their personal backgrounds and experiences and by the pressures, mores, and customs of their profession. It also recognizes that journalists are under commercial pressure to sell their stories. Newspapers and commercial networks are run on a for-profit basis. Thus reporters have to "sell" their stories to readers. **The easiest way to do that is to fit a given news event into a "story" framework. Human beings generally relate well to easily digestible stories, as opposed to more complex analyses, which require more thought and concentration. Reporters assigned to cover a given situation are likely to ask "What is the story?" and then to force events into that framework. Reality is seldom as neat as a story, however, with neat compartments of "Once upon a time . . ." "and then . . ." and "the End." But the story framework dominates news coverage of events; thus the media cannot function as a mirror since mirrors reflect rather than distort reality (except in fun houses).**

In her first sentence, Hope **enters the conversation** on the "flashlight" vs. "mirror" model.

Hope **summarizes** the "flashlight" model in her second and third sentences.

In the remaining (**boldface**) section, Hope makes *her* contribution to the conversation.

A final essential move in academic writing involves *showing what's at stake in your argument* — explaining why the issue you are discussing is important and why readers should care about it. In her essay on the "mirror" and "flashlight" models of the role of journalists in Chapter 4, for instance, Hope Leman closes her essay by emphasizing that the power of the media makes it important for readers to have the richest possible understanding of the kinds of choices journalists make.

Whereas Hope makes this move at the end of her essay, Stevon Roberts emphasizes the significance of his argument early in his essay, when he comments that the events of September 11, 2001, "give an increased sense of urgency to Etzioni's message and consequently might make Americans more receptive to protocols that afford protection from public risks in general" (p. 101). Given this situation, this statement by Roberts suggests, it is all the more important to analyze clearly and carefully Etzioni's proposals to curtail protections of personal privacy.

This chapter began by discussing the model of argument that informs academic writing and emphasized that this model is based much more on inquiry than on debate: Rather than defeating opponents, the goal of academic argument is to enter the many rich scholarly conversations that occur in all the disciplines. The "moves" described in this chapter can help you enter these conversations in productive and rewarding ways.

|||||||||||||||||||||||||||||||||||||||||||||||||||||||||||||||||||||||||||||||||||||

FOR EXPLORATION

In Chapter 3 you read Alia Sands's essay "A Separate Education" (pp. 47–50). This essay responds to a chapter in Richard Rodriguez's book *Hunger of Memory*. Reread Alia's essay, with an eye toward identifying the "moves" discussed in this section. How does Alia employ each of these "moves" and frame her argument as part of the scholarly conversation? Try to identify at least one example of each "move."

|||||||||||||||||||||||||||||||||||||||||||||||||||||||||||||||||||||||||||||||||||||

Using Visuals to Strengthen Your Argument

Images and graphics play an increasingly important role in communication today. Everywhere we turn — when we walk down the street, watch television, or surf the Web — images and graphics compete for our attention (and, often, for our money — think of the power of such logos as Target's red-and-white bull's-eye or McDonald's golden arches). Most news media rely heavily on photographs, audio clips, video clips, interactive graphics, and other, emerging technologies (like CNN's holograms) to heighten the impact of their stories.

The use of multimedia and visually rich texts is not limited to professionals, though: Thanks to user-friendly software technologies, all of us can

Behind the Scenes at CNN.com

create texts that mix words, images, and graphics. But what role should such texts play in the academic writing you do as a student? Because academic argument typically emphasizes *logos* over *ethos* and *pathos*, rhetorical common sense suggests that you should use visuals when they strengthen the substance of your argument. Tables, charts, graphs, maps, and photographs can usefully present factual information that appeals to *logos* and helps the writer build credibility as well.

In writing about the collapse of the Tacoma Narrows Bridge in Tacoma, Washington, on November 7, 1940, for example, engineering student Brenda Shonkwiler used a number of images and graphics to good effect. In her essay, Brenda argued that engineers learned a number of key lessons from the bridge's failure, and that engineering students should continue to study this dramatic event. Over the course of her argument, Brenda emphasized that there had been many indications of a potential bridge failure: Indeed, the bridge had such a strong tendency to twist and turn in the wind that it earned the nickname "Galloping Gertie." To help readers visualize the bridge's failure, Brenda included three film stills of the bridge twisting and, ultimately, collapsing. One of these photos, which shows the center of the bridge undulating moments before the bridge collapsed, is presented on p. 135.

* bedfordstmartins.com/rewriting

For several additional model essays incorporating research, click on **ModelDoc Central.**

Shonkwiler 4

Fig. 2. Film still of the Tacoma Narrows Bridge twisting, 7 Nov. 1940, Tacoma Narrows Collection. Twisting just before failure.

Suspension bridges, in general, are more flexible than other types of bridges. To decrease the flexibility, suspension bridges are typically stabilized with stiffening trusses. Such stiffening trusses are frameworks consisting of many interconnected braces that allow wind to flow through them with relatively little resistance, while diminishing (dampening) vertical and torsional motions. The Tacoma Narrows Bridge had been stiffened with solid girders (horizontal beams) instead of trusses. (See Fig. 4.) Koughan says that the girders "were unusually shallow, only [eight feet] deep, in comparison

Student Essay Using Image for Evidence

expect the bridge to fail catastrophically the way it
did. (161)

    <u>Actions Taken</u>. According to Koughan, engineers
tried several methods to minimize or eliminate the
motion of the Tacoma Narrows Bridge, without success. First, they had tie-down cables strung from
the plate girders to fifty-ton concrete blocks on
the shore, but the cables soon snapped. They then
installed inclined cables to attach the main cables
to the bridge deck in the middle of the long span,
but these cables failed to prevent the bridge from

Table 1
Suspension Bridge Failure Due to Wind

Bridge (location)	Span (ft.)	Failure Date
Dryburgh Abbey (Scotland)	260	1818
Union (England)	449	1821
Nassau (Germany)	245	1834
Brighton Chain Pier (England)	255	1836
Montrose (Scotland)	432	1838
Menai Strait (Wales)	580	1839
Roche-Bernard (France)	641	1852
Wheeling (United States)	1,010	1854
Niagara-Lewiston (USA--Canada)	1,041	1864
Niagara-Clifton (USA--Canada)	1,260	1889
Tacoma Narrows Bridge	2,800	1940

Source: Petroski 160.

Student Essay Using Table for Evidence

Brenda also included a diagram identifying the major features of a suspension bridge, as well as other charts, graphs, and tables. For example, her table on p. 136 provides basic information about suspension bridge failures throughout the world due to wind. Through use of these visual elements, Brenda strengthened the substance of her argument. The guidelines on p. 138 will help you make the most effective use of images and graphics in your academic writing.

COMPOSING AN ACADEMIC ARGUMENT:
A Case Study of One Student's Writing Process

One of the major themes of this textbook is that written communication is situated within a particular context; therefore, there is no one-size-fits-all form of writing. Instead, just as designers must respond to the specifics of their situation, so too must writers respond to the specifics of their rhetorical situation. ✳ This book also emphasizes that writing is a *process*, one that often requires time and multiple iterations. This final section of Chapter 5 provides an extended case study of the process that one student, Daniel Stiepleman, followed in writing an academic argument.

When Daniel composed this essay, he was a student in a first-year writing class. Here is the assignment given to him and other students in the class:

> Write a two- to three-page analytical essay responding to an image of your choice. Be sure to choose an image that involves significant interaction between the text and graphics. Your essay should focus on how the words and graphics work together to generate the image's meaning and impact. Consider your instructor and your classmates to be the primary readers of your essay.

Daniel's first step after receiving his assignment was to look for an image that interested him. While he was flipping through the *The Atlantic* magazine, a public service announcement (PSA) for the National Center for Family Literacy (NCFL) caught his eye. An aspiring English teacher, Daniel found the message of the PSA to be powerful, yet something about it that he couldn't quite put his finger on troubled him. In order to explore his initial response to the PSA, Daniel decided to annotate the text and image, using the Questions for Analyzing Visual Texts on pp. 111–12 as a guide. You can see the PSA with Daniel's annotations on p. 139.

When he first encountered the PSA, Daniel thought that the text's argument was easy to summarize: Literacy improves lives. While annotating, Daniel noticed some details that he didn't catch at first, such as the way

To review the concept of the rhetorical situation, see Chapter 3. ✳

Guidelines for Using Visuals in Academic Writing

1.   Consider both the conventions of the discipline and your specific assignment.

What use of visuals is typical in your discipline?

What are your teacher's expectations and the constraints of your assignment?

Can you find *examples* of similar arguments?

For example, the social sciences and natural sciences have a tradition of using images and graphics to present and organize information; the humanities rely more upon the written word.

When in doubt, consult your teacher.

2.   Use charts, graphs, tables, and illustrations to organize information.

A simple chart or table can present information that would take several paragraphs to describe—thus freeing up space for analysis.

(See Chapter 11 for suggestions for creating and using visuals.)

3.   Use photographs and illustrations to bring a text to life or to portray experiences that are difficult to imagine.

An art history student might include a reproduction of a work she's discussing.

An anthropology student describing her research on life in rural trailer parks might include photos of such parks.

4.   Avoid using visuals as decorations.

Images and graphics can enrich your writing. But substance should always come first; visuals, second.

the layout and type style underscore the simplicity of the PSA's message. The more he looked at his notes and re-examined the image and words, the more he wondered *why* simplicity was such a central part of the message. He also started to think about what the NCFL was trying to accomplish with the PSA, and how other readers of *The Atlantic* might respond to it. And he still wasn't sure what it was about the message as a whole that troubled him.

Daniel Stiepleman's Annotation of the Public Service Announcement

At this point in his writing process, Daniel's primary purpose was to engage as fully and critically as he possibly could with the PSA that he had chosen to analyze. In order to explore his ideas more fully, Daniel decided to create a cluster on the word *illiteracy* to explore his response. ✱ After evaluating his cluster, Daniel realized that the causes and effects of illiteracy are more complicated than the PSA acknowledges – and that he had a promising topic for an essay.

Daniel's Cluster

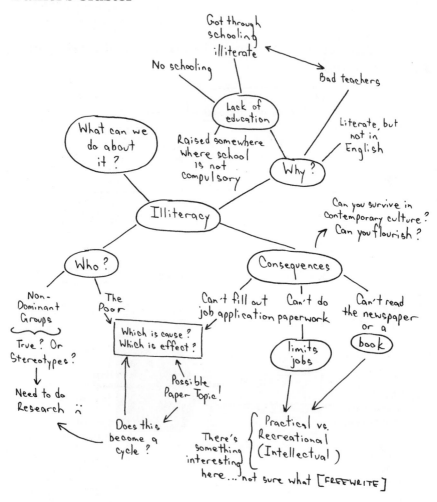

Thanks to these prewriting activities, Daniel had significantly deepened his understanding of the issues the PSA raised for him. He still did not feel ready to do a formal analysis of his rhetorical situation or to attempt a carefully structured first draft, so he decided to write a discovery draft.

✱ For more on invention strategies, see Chapter 9.

Daniel's Discovery Draft

Literacy, often taken for granted, is a gift. The ability to read text not only offers opportunities for escape and entertainment but gives access to ideas that challenge our own limited worldviews, thus allowing each of us to expand our understandings of our lives on our own terms, at our own pace. The generation of text allows for the further development and sharing of our own ideas with others, at a time when much of the world has lost reverence for oral traditions. Literacy is a gift.

Several organizations exist to help share this gift, but they are underfunded and need help from the public. It is for this reason that groups like the National Center for Family Literacy (NCFL) print public service announcements (PSAs). Obviously these announcements, which appear in magazines and newspapers, are directed toward an educated and literate audience. The task of the men and women who design these advertisements is to convince readers to donate time and/or money toward the cause of literacy training.

In my essay, I want to analyze a PSA that appeared in the April 2006 issue of *The Atlantic* magazine. This PSA uses both text and an image to affect the emotions of the reader. The PSA consists of a series of "Because I can read" statements. The "I" is presumably the woman pictured with a young girl who seems to be the daughter mentioned in the advertisement, though they don't look that much alike. The woman pictured in the PSA stares directly at readers and explains some of the many real-world ways her life has improved because of literacy: "I can fill out a job application . . . I can help my daughter with her homework . . . I can be a role model." By using a first-person narrator, the advertisement is, I think, very successful at adding an emotional element that can inspire people to want to help more illiterate Americans improve their lives. Even though some of the things that are stated in the PSA may not be necessarily linked with literacy, such as when she says, "I can contribute" (certainly there are ways she could contribute to society even without being literate), I think this flaw in the logic of the PSA is subtle enough that an American who is flipping through his or her magazine would probably not notice it.

After reviewing his discovery draft, Daniel realized that while it represented a good start on his essay, he still had considerable work ahead of him. Here's what Daniel wrote about this draft in his journal.

Daniel's Journal Entry

Now that I've got some distance from this draft, I can see that it really is just a starting point. Right at the end something clicked with me: a flaw in the logic of the PSA. I tried to dismiss it; I even thought about deleting it because it would be easier for me to write about the value of literacy. But the fact of the matter is that the logic behind this ad really is problematic. This is going to be harder to write about, but it's also a more interesting and provocative idea. I think that I need to rewrite with this idea (or something like it) as my thesis. I'm a little frustrated at having to start over, but the truth is that I probably wouldn't have noticed this problem with the PSA if I hadn't written this draft.

Thanks to the preceding activities, which encouraged him to explore his response to the PSA, Daniel now felt ready to undertake a more formal exploration of his situation and goals as a writer. This was the moment, he decided, when it made sense for him to consider his controlling purpose and rhetorical situation, and to do so in writing. Here is Daniel's analysis.

Daniel's Rhetorical Analysis

thinking
rhetorically

I am writing an analytical essay for my composition class. I want to persuade my readers — my instructor and my classmates — that there are some disturbing assumptions behind the National Center for Family Literacy's public service advertisement. If my readers are anything like I am, their first impressions will be that the ad must be good because it promotes literacy. I'm worried this will lead them to resist my argument that literacy isn't, as the ad implies, an easy solution to the problem of inequity. I've got to be convincing by using evidence, both from the text and from other sources.

How will I persuade them to accept my argument? After all, I had to write my way to seeing it. What tone should I adopt — an objective tone or a passionate one? I'm inclined to try the latter, but I know our instructor said that being objective is usually a more effective strategy. Plus that may help it sound less like I'm arguing that the PSA's negative consequences are on purpose. I'll need to be careful in my analysis of the PSA.

Daniel also decided to develop a plan for his essay. As Daniel noted in his journal, he is a visual thinker, and so traditional outlines don't work well for him. So he came up with a visual map that helped him imagine how his essay

might be organized (see below). It includes several questions he thought
he should address, reminders to himself, definitions of terms, and general
comments. He used his plan to further explore his ideas and to determine the
best organization for his essay. Although probably no one but Daniel could
develop an essay from the diagrams and notes he created, the plan fulfilled
his needs—and that's what counts.

Daniel's Plan for His Essay

Daniel was now ready to write a formal draft. He had a clear controlling purpose: He wanted to critically examine the logic and design of the NCFL PSA and to convince his readers that although the ability to read and write is valuable, literacy cannot by itself solve the problem of poverty. Here is Daniel's first formal draft of his essay. (Note that for Daniel's first draft, he has not yet created the necessary works cited page and his in-text citations are incomplete.)

Daniel's First Draft

Literacy, often taken for granted, is a gift. The ability to read text not only offers opportunities for escape and entertainment, but gives access to ideas that challenge our own limited worldviews, thus allowing each of us to expand our understandings of our lives on our own terms, at our own pace. The generation of text allows for the further development and sharing of our own ideas with others, at a time when much of the world has lost reverence for oral traditions. Literacy is a gift.

In recent years educational and other foundations have, in the print media especially, run literacy campaigns designed to persuade literate Americans to donate their time and/or money to the worthwhile cause of literacy education. These campaigns frequently create public service announcements (PSAs) to convey their message to the general public. One such PSA is produced by the National Center for Family Literacy (NCFL). Published in the April 2006 edition of *The Atlantic* magazine, the full-page advertisement essentially sets up a series of linked statements. It begins, "Because I can read," which is followed by a series of "I can . . ." statements, such as, "I can understand. I can write a letter. I can fill out a job application. I can finally get off welfare." At the bottom of the page is an invitation to help the person presented in this PSA and others like her get out of poverty by supporting the NCFL.

When I first read this PSA, I found it persuasive. But the more I thought about it, the more problematic the series of "I can" statements became. By asserting that the ability to read and write is tantamount to the ability to learn, be a role model, and contribute, the text also implies that people who are illiterate cannot learn, cannot be role models, and, worst of all, have nothing to contribute. Such persons, it seems, are utterly worthless without literacy.

The people reading *The Atlantic* are not illiterate. In fact, according to the magazine's Web site, the average reader of *The Atlantic* is a man in his early fifties with a college degree and a median household income of over $150,000. The image incorporated into the NCFL's "Because I can read" PSA is certainly not that of the typical reader of *The Atlantic*. The image is of a woman with an approximately ten-year-old girl, presumably her daughter, who is significantly darker skinned. What's more, the woman is not wearing a wedding ring. The image of illiteracy, then, is a single mother with a mixed-race child.

Can literacy solve this woman's problems? American society is immensely stratified; 58 percent of black and 62 percent of Hispanic children live in low-income households, as opposed to only 25 percent of white children (NCCP). According to the 1999 U.S. Census data, black and Hispanic Americans ("Hispanic" was still classified as a race in the 1999 census data) are twice as likely as European Americans to be unemployed. Those who work have a weekly income far less than whites — over $100 a week less for blacks, and almost $200 a week less for Hispanics (United States Census Bureau).

The NCFL PSA suggests that being able to read will magically get the woman portrayed in the ad off welfare. In reality, more highly educated black and Hispanic people are only slightly more likely to find work (as compared with equally educated whites) than their less-educated counterparts (United States Dept. of Education). Literacy does not equal social equality. Yet that is precisely what this PSA implies.

This PSA presents illiteracy as a problem of others who have not had the same advantages (role models, educational opportunities, membership in a dominant class or sex) as the readers. In so doing, it displays the inherent inequalities of our culture, but also offers an unrealistically simple solution to the problem — literacy. Given its purpose, the PSA is effective — but it is also a lie because it ignores the root causes of illiteracy. Granted, helping more Americans to become literate could be one step toward greater equality. So the question remains: Is the cumulative effect of this PSA harmful or good?

After writing this draft, Daniel knew that he would benefit from setting it aside for a while. After a day had passed, he decided to use the Questions for Evaluating Focus, Content, and Organization to analyze what he had written. ✱ Here is his analysis.

Focus: I think I do a good job of raising questions about the PSA. I wonder if I come on too strong, however. I also wonder if my focus is narrow and clear enough. I see that I don't write much about how the graphics and text interact. Our instructor specifically mentioned this in the assignment, so I need to pay more attention to that.

See Chapter 12, pp. 324–25. ✱ · · · · · · · · · · ·

Content: I talk about how literacy affects income, and I think that's important. But looking back at the draft, I see that I don't really explain what other factors might cause a person to be poor. I definitely need to do some more research. I wonder, too, if I should include the PSA or describe it more thoroughly so that I can focus readers' attention on the parts of the PSA that are most important. I'd better go back to the PSA to decide which are the most important parts.

Organization: I'm not happy with my intro and conclusion. I kept the same introduction from my discovery draft mainly because I didn't want to worry about it. I'll need to change that. I like how I conclude with a question, but I wonder if it isn't more important to answer that question instead. There's still lots to do, but at least I can see that my ideas are taking shape.

When Daniel analyzed the first draft of his essay, he realized that while he had done a good job of exploring and raising questions about the PSA, his essay wasn't as effective as it could be. He worried that he didn't provide enough evidence to convince readers that his argument was valid, and he was unhappy with his introduction and conclusion. He also realized that he didn't analyze how the words and graphics worked together to create meaning in the PSA.

Fortunately for Daniel, his teacher included in-class peer response sessions for all major writing assignments in their class, so Daniel was able to revise his essay and share it with members of his writing group for feedback. His second draft is presented here, with some of the group members' comments. (Notice that his essay now has a title and that he has revised it in significant ways. This early draft includes some source citations, not yet in final MLA form.)

Daniel's Second Draft with Peer Comments

Daniel's second draft had many strengths, which members of his writing group acknowledge. But they had suggestions for improvement as well. A number of them commented on the evidence in paragraph 3, asking for more background on what Daniel meant by "the systematic stratification of American society." Several readers wanted to know more about the PSA's goals and suggested that Daniel's negative tone made his overall argument less convincing than it could be.

Literacy in America: Reading between the Lines

Daniel Stiepleman

A woman and girl look straight at us. Their relationship to one another is unclear, but the girl, maybe ten, stands over the woman with a hand on her shoulder—she seems, unexpectedly perhaps, almost maternal. Huddled together in the lower right-hand corner, they are cradled between a thin border and text. A series of connecting statements takes up the bulk of the page. "Because I can read," it begins in the opposite corner in simple, black font, which is followed, in slightly indented grey, by a series of "I can" statements: "I can understand. I can write a letter. I can fill out a job application. I can finally get off welfare." The call and response repeats: "Because I can read . . . Because I can read . . . Because I can read." This page, a public service announcement (PSA) by the National Center for Family Literacy (NCFL), appears in *The Atlantic* magazine. From its short diction to its basic design to its three-color scheme, everything about this ad reinforces the simplicity of its logic: "Because I can read, I can succeed." This simplicity is reassuring and hopeful, but it's more than that; it's deceptive.

In order for the woman portrayed in this PSA to gain her worth through literacy, we are urged to accept that without reading and writing she is worthless. Asserting that once she learns to read, she can "learn . . . be a role model . . . [and] contribute," the PSA implies that people who cannot read or write cannot learn, cannot be a role model, and, worst of all, have nothing to contribute. It is here where both the simplicity and the logic of the NCFL's message begin to fall apart. The message becomes that people who are illiterate are worthless, and that must be why she is still on welfare. But perhaps even more astonishingly, literacy is supposed to magically solve her problems.

This assertion ignores the systematic stratification of American society. Is illiteracy alone the reason why 58 percent of all black children and 62 percent of all Hispanic children in America currently live in poverty, while only 25 percent of white children do (National Center for Children in Poverty)? Will literacy training change the fact that, according to the 1999 U.S. Census data, black and Hispanic Americans are twice as likely as white Americans to be unemployed? Or that those who do work make an average of over $100 a week less than whites if they're black and almost $200 a week less if they're Hispanic? It seems unlikely that simply

Great opening!
–Parvin

Really compelling description. I like the idea that the simplicity of the design reflects the simplicity of the logic. But I'm having trouble imagining the design: Can you show a picture of it?
–Eric

It sounds like you're saying the NCFL is deliberately insulting the people they help, but I don't think that's what you mean. Maybe you could start by explaining what they're trying to do with the ad?
–Kyong

Good evidence. Are there similar statistics for women?
–Parvin

Where does this information come from?
–Kyong

I'm not sure I follow you.What are the other reasons? Why wouldn't being able to read help a person succeed? Maybe you could answer the questions that start the paragraph.
　　　　–Eric

This sounds a little harsh.
　　　　–Eric

This is a strong conclusion. But your overall argument might be more ef-fective if you acknowledged the positive aspects of the ad—maybe in the introduction?
　　　　–Parvin

I love how you circle back to the image in your conclusion.
　　　　–Kyong

"Because I [or any illiterate person] can read . . . I can succeed." The NCFL's suggestion otherwise is an unfortunate confirmation of the great American myth that anyone can pull him- or herself up by the bootstraps through simple, concerted effort, with only his or her ability and desire standing as obstacles in the way.

This PSA's potential for success relates directly to the degree to which it does not depict reality. The ad suggests that all the illiterate people in America need to achieve worth — based on its assumption that they are, without literacy, worthless — is to gain the ability to read and write; and it counts upon the readers' inexperience with both poverty and illiteracy to maintain its fiction. This is a safe bet as, according to *The Atlantic's* Web site, the magazine's average reader is a man in his early fifties with a college degree and a median household income of over $150,000.

But the Census statistics portray a different image of America; it is a country in which the woman portrayed in the PSA will not so easily change her stake in the American dream. The injustice done by maintaining the myth of equal opportunity outweighs any good the NCFL can hope to accomplish with its ad. Looking at the woman more closely now, she seems somehow to know this. The girl is beaming, but there is a hesitance I see in the woman's smile. Am I projecting upon the image, or is there, in her face, concern? Her concern would be apt; she is shoved into the corner, held there, like so many Americans, beneath the weight of a text that would take the rich and daunting complexity of our multicultural society and give it short diction, basic design, and a three-color scheme. The illusion of simplicity.

After Daniel contemplated his readers' responses, he recorded his reac-tions and ideas in his journal.

Daniel's Response to Peer Comments

At first, I had some resistance to my writing group's comments. I've worked hard on this essay and taken it quite far, given my first draft. But after reading their comments and taking some time to think, I can see that they pointed out problems that I was just too close to my essay to see. Most important, I think I need to work some more on my tone so readers understand that I'm questioning the PSA's assumptions, not the value of literacy itself.

Several readers suggested that I include a new introductory paragraph that sets up the situation and explains what the PSA is trying to do. I thought quite a bit about this and tried out a few new paragraphs, but I kept coming back to the paragraph as it was. I really like this paragraph, so I decided to try to address their concerns by writing a new second paragraph.

Parvin commented that while I have evidence to support my claims, none of it cites the situation of women. Now that I think about it, this is very odd, given the nature of the PSA. I'll check additional sources of information so I can include that.

The rest of the comments seem relatively minor — less revision than editing. I need to fix citations in the text and prepare the Works Cited page. Then I'll be really close to a final draft!

In reflecting on his group's responses, Daniel does a good job of taking their comments seriously while also holding to his own vision of his essay. It's not possible to show all the stages that Daniel's draft went through, for this process includes many scribbles, inserts, and crumpled papers. But the final draft demonstrates that his analysis of his readers' responses enabled him to truly revise his essay, to "see again" how he could most effectively make his point. Daniel's final draft begins on p. 150.

Daniel's Final Draft

In the process of writing his essay, Daniel was able to articulate what was at first only a vague sense of unease about the National Center for Family Literacy PSA. As he moved from his first draft to the second, Daniel was able to identify why the ad concerned him. He clarified the problems with the PSA's logic in his third draft, while also attending more carefully to the interplay of words and graphics in the PSA.

Daniel's final draft, you will probably agree, develops an argument that is not only persuasive but also stylish. His tone is more even-handed, his paragraphs are more coherent, and his language is more polished. The effort that Daniel put into his essay more than paid off. This effort required planning: Daniel knew that he would have to work his way to a clear sense of purpose, audience, and organization, so he built in the necessary time for prewriting, drafting, and revising. The result is an engaged, persuasive analysis, and a good demonstration of the inseparable nature of academic analysis and argument.

Stiepleman 1

Daniel Stiepleman
Professor Chang
English 100
20 March 2010

Literacy in America: Reading between the Lines

A woman and girl look straight at us. Though they look nothing alike, they are apparently mother and daughter. The girl, maybe ten, stands over the woman with a hand on her shoulder; it is she who seems maternal. Huddled together in the lower, right-hand corner of the page, they are cradled between a thin border and text. This text, presumably the words of the woman pictured, takes up the bulk of the page. "Because I can read" begins in the upper left-hand corner in simple, black font. This is followed, in slightly indented grey, by a series of "I can" statements: "I can understand. I can write a letter. I can fill out a job application. I can finally get off welfare." The call and response repeats: "Because I can read . . . Because I can read . . . Because I can read."

When I came across this page in *The Atlantic* magazine (see Fig. 1), the image of the girl and the woman was what first caught my eye, but it was the repeated statement "Because I can read" that captured my imagination. Its plainness was alluring. But as I read and reread the page, a public service announcement (PSA) designed to solicit donations of time and money for the National Center for Family Literacy (NCFL), I grew uncomfortable. The PSA, with its short diction, basic design, and black-and-white color scheme, reinforces the simplicity of its logic: "Because I can read, I can succeed." This simple message, though it promotes a mission I believe in, I fear does more harm than good.

The problem is with the underlying logic of this PSA. If we as readers believe the "Because I can read" statements, we must also believe that without literacy the woman in the PSA is worthless. Asserting that because a person can read, she "can learn . . . be a role model . . . [and] contribute," the PSA implies that people who cannot read or write cannot learn, cannot be role models, and, worst of all, have nothing to contribute to society. This is

Stronger intro-
duction focuses
readers on the
image being
analyzed

New paragraph
extends context

Copy of PSA
included so
readers can
judge for
themselves

Revised thesis
statement is
more balanced

Stiepleman 2

Because I can read,
    I can understand. I can write a letter.
    I can fill out a job application.
    I can finally get off welfare.

Because I can read,
    I can learn. I can help my daughter
    with her homework,
    I can inspire her to be better.
    I can be a role model.

Because I can read,
    I can succeed, I can
    contribute. I can live
    my life without fear,
    without shame.
    I can be whatever
    I want to be.

Because I can read.

National Center for Family Literacy

Literacy can make the difference between poverty and progress.
Visit www.famlit.org to help us write more success stories.

TOYOTA Proud Sponsor

Fig. 1. NCFL Public Service Announcement. *The Atlantic*, April 2006. Print.

the real reason, the PSA suggests, why the woman portrayed in the photograph is still on welfare. But perhaps even more astonishing, literacy is supposed to be a quick fix to her problems.

This assertion ignores the systematic stratification of American society. Is illiteracy alone the reason why 60 percent of all black children and 61 percent of all Hispanic children in America currently live in poverty, while only 26 percent of white children do (National Center for Children in Poverty)? Will literacy training change the fact that, according to 1999 United States Census data, black and Hispanic Americans are twice as likely as white Americans to be unemployed? Or that those who do work make, on average, between $100 and 200 a week less than whites (406)? In the case of the woman pictured in the PSA, should literacy indeed lead her to a job, she is likely to make half as much money as a man with the same demographics

New evidence added to strengthen argument

Sources are cited

Stiepleman 3

Less accusing
tone wins
readers over

who works in the same position (United States Dept. of Education). It is not my intent to undermine the value of being able to read and write, but given the other obstacles facing the disadvantaged in America, it seems unlikely that simply because someone learns to read, he or she "can succeed."

New paragraph
provides
examples of
obstacles that
could prevent a
literate person
from succeeding
The benefits and opportunities for success extend well beyond a person's ability to fill out a job application. Race, class, and gender are powerful forces in our society, and the obstacles they present are self-perpetuating (Rothenberg 11–12). Even a well-educated person, if she is from a minority or low-income group, can find it overwhelmingly difficult to land a well-paying job with possibilities for advancement. The lack of simple things that middle-class readers of *The Atlantic* take for granted — the social connections of a network, the money for a professional wardrobe, a shared background with an interviewer — can cripple a job search. The NCFL's suggestion otherwise is an unfortunate reinforcement of the great American myth that anyone can pull him- or herself up by the bootstraps, with only his or her ability and desire standing as obstacles in the way.

Language is
more balanced
The PSA suggests that all the illiterate people in America need to achieve worth is the ability to read and write. But Americans disadvantaged by race, class, or gender will not so easily alter their position in our stratified culture. As long as we continue to pretend otherwise, we have no hope of changing the inequities that continue to be an inherent part of our society. For this reason, as much as I value this PSA's emphasis on the importance of literacy, I question its underlying logic.

Looking at the woman portrayed in the PSA more closely now, she seems somehow to know that her and her daughter's lives cannot improve so easily. Though the girl is beaming, there is a hesitance I see in the woman's smile and concern in her face. And it is apt; she is shoved into the corner, held there, like so many Americans, beneath the weight of a text that would take the rich and daunting complexity of our multicultural society and give it the illusion of simplicity.

Stiepleman 4

Works Cited

National Center for Children in Poverty. *Low-Income Children in the United States*. New York: Columbia, Mailman School of Public Health, September 2006. Web. 27 Feb. 2007.

National Center for Family Literacy. Advertisement. *The Atlantic*. Apr. 2006: 59. Print.

Rothenberg, Paula S. *Race, Class, and Gender in the United States: An Integrated Study*. 2nd ed. New York: St. Martin's, 1992. Print.

United States. Census Bureau. "Labor Force, Employment, and Earnings." *Statistical Abstract of the United States: 1999*. Census Bureau, 1999. Web. 5 Mar. 2007.

———. Dept. of Education. Inst. of Education Science. Natl. Center for Education Statistics. *1992 National Adult Literacy Survey*. NCES, 1992. Web. 2 Mar. 2007.

||||||||||||||||||||||||||||||||||||||||||||||||||||||||||||||||||||||||||||||||||||||

FOR THOUGHT, DISCUSSION, AND WRITING

1. This chapter has presented activities designed to improve your understanding of academic argument. The Exploration on pp. 122–23, for instance, asks you to identify the values and beliefs that have led you to hold strong views on an issue. The one on p. 128 asks you to formulate a working thesis and to list the major evidence you would use to support it. Finally, the group activity on p. 130 encourages you to acknowledge possible counterarguments to your thesis. Drawing on these activities, write an essay directed to an academic reader on the topic you have explored, revising your working thesis if necessary.

2. This chapter focuses on argumentative strategies that apply across the academic curriculum. While scholars in all disciplines would probably agree with this discussion, they might add that arguments in their own disciplines have unique features. Interview a teacher whose course you are currently taking in one of the following areas: the humanities, the social sciences, the natural and applied sciences, or business. Ask this teacher what characteristics he or she looks for in a

successful academic argument in this discipline. Also ask what kinds of visuals are appropriate. Then write a brief summary describing what the interview helped you understand about argument in this discipline.

3. Newspaper editorials and opinion columns represent one common form of argument. If your college or university publishes a newspaper, read several issues in sequence, paying particular attention to the editorials and opinion columns. (If your school doesn't publish a newspaper, choose a local newspaper instead.) Choose one editorial or opinion column that you believe represents a successful argument; choose another that strikes you as suspect. Bring these texts to class, and be prepared to share your evaluations of them with your classmates.

Doing Research: Joining the Scholarly Conversation

When you hear the word *research*, you probably think of looking for articles in the library or surfing the Web to find quotes to finish a paper or project. But, in fact, you are doing research any time you consult a source to answer a question or solve a problem. If you check reviews on a site like TripAdvisor before booking a hotel, look up the correct spelling of a new word in the dictionary, or ask a group of friends on Facebook for restaurant recommendations, you are conducting research.

In some important ways, however, college-level research is a whole new ball game. You have probably been taught before how to do academic research, and some of the things you have learned and the habits you have developed will serve you well as you do research in college. Others will not. Earlier chapters in this book have emphasized that writing for academic audiences means understanding how academics think about issues. It also means understanding how they think about evidence, and what types of sources they will expect you to use. The tools for finding those sources discussed in this chapter can help you meet those expectations.

You are becoming an academic researcher at a very exciting time. Old ways of doing research are shifting and becoming more powerful, and new pathways to information are opening up every day. The technological innovations and seemingly ever-expanding field of resources also present a challenge, however: To do academic research well, you must learn to sort efficiently through vast amounts of material in order to find what you need.

You need to learn more than how to use article databases or check off items on a list for evaluating sources. You need an understanding of how knowledge is created and distributed in our world, and of how to leverage that understanding to find, use, evaluate, and manage information with purpose and intent. With today's tools, anyone can find sources to support a paper

Note: Oregon State University Librarian Anne-Marie Deitering played a key role in the development and drafting of this significantly revised and expanded chapter. I am extremely grateful for her expertise and for her commitment to this project.—L.E.

with little effort. It is up to you to decide if you want to distinguish your work from the rest, to go beyond the obvious and find unique, interesting, compelling sources that will push you, and your audience, to think in new ways.

As an academic researcher, you play a number of different roles, and each one has its own set of choices. As a researcher, you need to learn to explore multiple perspectives, consider a variety of sources, cope with uncertainty, and keep an open mind. You must become an expert at gathering, organizing, and managing multiple information streams. You need to become a keen judge of what you find, effectively evaluating both information and the research processes that helped you find that information. Finally, as you become a creator as well as a consumer of information, you must come to understand the processes of scholarly knowledge construction and decide how you want what you create to be used and by whom. The strategies presented in this chapter aim to help you effectively manage all of these roles.

The lessons you have learned about thinking rhetorically are central to the research process. In Chapter 1, rhetoric was defined as "a practical art that helps writers make effective choices within specific rhetorical situations"; subsequent chapters helped you learn how to think rhetorically as a writer, and to use your rhetorical understanding to make appropriate choices as you navigate the writing process. Thinking rhetorically also makes you a better researcher and can help you make good choices throughout the research process.

The Questions for Analyzing Your Rhetorical Situation as a Researcher on p. 157 will guide you as you embark on any research project, so be sure to refer to them frequently.

||||||||||||||||||||||||||||||||||||||||||||||||||||||||||||||||||||||||||||||||||||||||||

FOR EXPLORATION

Think back to some academic research you've done in the past. First identify a positive research experience, and write several paragraphs about it. What made this research satisfying and productive? Now write a few paragraphs about a research experience that was frustrating, unproductive, or in other ways difficult. Why do you think it went the way it did? Finally, consider what you have learned by thinking and writing about these two experiences. Jot down a few pointers you should follow to improve your future research efforts.

||||||||||||||||||||||||||||||||||||||||||||||||||||||||||||||||||||||||||||||||||||||||||

Questions for Analyzing Your Rhetorical Situation as a Researcher

1. **Think about what you are trying to accomplish in your research project. How do these goals affect your source selection?**

2. **What role does this rhetorical situation invite you, as a researcher, to play? Is it . . .**

   fixed by the requirements of the assignment (engaging with the scholarly literature, demonstrating original research)?

   or

   more open?

3. **Could you benefit from looking at examples of this kind of writing?**

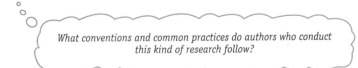

   What conventions and common practices do authors who conduct this kind of research follow?

4. **What image of yourself do you want to present in your final project?**

   How will the sources you use help you present yourself in this way?

EXPLORING

The researcher-explorer is . . .

- Interested in learning new things
- Ready to think about a question from multiple perspectives
- Familiar with lots of different sources
- Comfortable with uncertainty
- Open-minded

For any research project, you need to search for sources. *How* you search, though, varies depending on the type of research you need to do. It's useful to think about two kinds of searching: *exploratory searching* and *lookup searching*. You probably do dozens of lookup searches every day. If you want to know a movie time, how to spell a word, what the average temperature is for your city, or how much caffeine there is in green tea, a lookup search will get you the information you need. Lookup searching is about defining exactly what you need to know so that you can find the one source you need to get your question answered.

You may have had teachers who encouraged you to approach academic research as you would approach a lookup search—to think about your topic, define your argument, and narrow your focus as quickly as possible so that you can look for sources that match that focus. With deadlines looming and other classes demanding your attention, you, too, might be tempted to define a narrow, specific research question as quickly as possible. Try to resist this urge.

As discussed in Chapter 5, academic arguments are based on an open-minded exploration of the issues and a willingness to consider multiple perspectives. *Exploratory search*—not lookup search—will help you meet these goals. The process of conducting exploratory search can be demanding, but your gains in productivity will be significant.

You may think of exploration as something you do to prepare for research. Exploration, though, is not a preliminary stage of the writing process: It is an essential part of researching a complex topic for a scholarly audience. When you do academic research, you should expect to do several exploratory searches. For example, during an exploratory search on a topic like alternative fuels, you could come across a fascinating article on biodiesel, which might lead you to explore the conversation on that topic. You might then learn that many people make a connection between the production of alternative fuels like biodiesel and shortages in the global food supply. This could

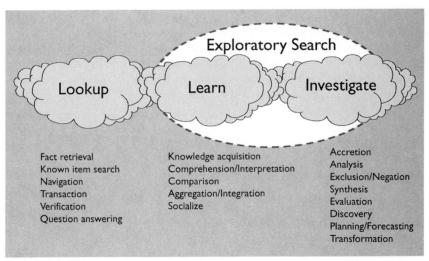

Diagram of Exploratory Search[1]

lead you into another exploratory search, this time on how energy production and use affect hunger. As this example shows, academic research is a process of inquiry, which means exploring different bodies of literature and multiple points of view.

Considering Multiple Perspectives

Doing an exploratory search requires that you think rhetorically about your project. This means reflecting on your own needs and situation as a writer, considering your readers' perspectives, *and* recognizing the different points of view expressed by the authors who have written about your topic.

In Chapter 5, you learned that when you construct academic arguments, you must consider your own values and beliefs, as well as those of your readers. Exploration helps you understand multiple perspectives. Academic research is not a matter of identifying "both sides of the story": It is a rare topic that only has two sides. Instead, think about your topic as a continuum of ideas: There may be two extremes that are easy to define, but there are also a whole variety of different positions that fall into the middle ground. Most academic writers position themselves in that middle ground, synthesizing ideas from many places.

[1] Gary Marchionini, "Exploratory Search, from Finding to Understanding," *Communications of the ACM* 49, no. 4 (2006): 420.

Think about the types of topics academic writers address, big questions like "Should the government regulate hate speech?" or "Should there be cooperative international action against global warming?" People who answer "yes" to either of those big questions can have *very* different reasons for doing so. As an academic writer, you want to explore all of these reasons in order to develop your own perspective. There will be gaps in your argument if you maintain a narrow focus, based on what you already know, throughout your research process.

Looking at a Variety of Sources

You can also expect gaps in your arguments when you only look at one *type* of source. Sources are created for different reasons, and different types of sources do different things for you as a researcher.

Using Reference Works

ENCYCLOPEDIAS.   Reference works like encyclopedias are a good place to get an overview of the issues related to a topic. An article from an encyclopedia like the *Encyclopedia Britannica*, which is intended for a general audience, will provide a broad, objective overview of a topic. An article from a scholarly encyclopedia, like the *Encyclopedia of Science, Technology and Ethics*, or the *Encyclopedia of Domestic Violence*, will provide a somewhat more detailed overview, and it may also outline the most common scholarly opinions or schools of thought on it. As an academic researcher, you may start here, but you will want to move beyond the neutral summaries these tools provide as you develop a deeper understanding of your topic.

WIKIPEDIA.   You are probably familiar with the online encyclopedia Wikipedia (http://wikipedia.org). You might also have been warned never to use Wikipedia in an academic project. Many instructors do forbid its use as a source in research projects because Wikipedia is a *wiki*, which is a Web site that anyone can edit. This makes it a very dynamic and comprehensive reference source — it tends to include articles on topics that are extremely current, and also on topics that are extremely esoteric — while at the same time making it unreliable in some instructors' eyes, since virtually anyone, expert or not, can change the content.

Wikipedia can nevertheless be an excellent place to explore a topic for researchers who are aware of how it works, and who understand that they will use different types of sources at different stages in their research process. Imagine, for example, that you are taking a class on technology and new media. Your instructor has assigned a research paper for the class, but

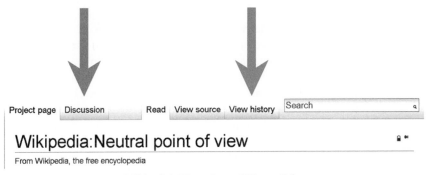

Wikipedia's Discussion and History Tabs

the topic is open. You've always wondered about the history of typewriters. Might this be a good topic? Consulting Wikipedia's article on typewriters could help you answer this question. If you determine that you do have a viable topic, you would then turn to additional sources (some of which will be recommended on the Wikipedia entry).

The *History* tab at the top of every Wikipedia article gives you access to every version of the article that has ever existed, so you can see how the argument on a page changes over time. Every Wikipedia article also has a Discussion page, which is like a backchannel where the people writing the main article can talk about it. Sometimes, these discussions are pretty dull, focused on formatting or punctuation. In other cases they are very useful, showing how people with different values, beliefs, or points of view differ in their interpretation of the same facts. Unlike an article in a traditional encyclopedia, the Wikipedia articles allow you to discover which claims in the article were divisive and which claims had wide agreement.

Browsing the Scholarly Literature

Reference sources like print encyclopedias and Wikipedia can be useful for gaining a general overview of your topic, but they are not the types of sources you will rely on to build your own academic arguments. In order to find the kinds of in-depth treatments that will be useful, expert researchers spend a fair amount of time browsing through scholarly articles and books on their topics, knowing that they will revisit these same sources later in their research process. As you explore such sources, keep your mind open to new ideas and new connections. One way to do this is to use broad keywords in your initial searches. For example, if you are interested in researching breast cancer, you could search Medline, a database of scholarly articles about health, using a broad keyword phrase like "breast cancer" early in your process. Later, you decide that your real interest is in the effectiveness of screening methods for breast cancer. To find articles related to that interest, you could search the same database, using more specific phrases like "mass screening methods" or "early detection."

Most scholarly articles and the databases that index them include *abstracts*, short summaries where the author(s) briefly describe their research, their results, and their conclusions. While you are browsing, use these abstracts to see whether a particular article is likely to help you in further exploring your topic. Online catalogs for books, too, provide some information on what's covered through tables of contents, subject headings, and, in some cases, summary descriptions. When you locate a book on your topic, browse the table of contents, introduction and/or preface, and subject index to see whether it's worth a closer look. Take notes as you explore, recording specific terms scholarly authors use to talk about your topic and identifying the types of research studies commonly done on your topic. If certain authors or titles are mentioned frequently in the works you consult, make a note of them for future investigations.

Using Review Articles and Scholarly Anthologies

Some fields, particularly the biomedical sciences and social sciences such as psychology or social work, encourage the publication of *review articles*, in which the author analyzes the body of published research on a topic. An up-to-date review article is a gold mine for the researcher. Review articles not only list the most important and influential articles on a topic, but they also explain how those articles connect to each other.

Another useful tool is the *scholarly anthology*, which is a collection of influential articles on a topic published in book form. The editor of a scholarly anthology will usually include an introduction placing all of the work in the book in context. Like review articles, scholarly anthologies can provide a valuable shortcut to assembling the most important sources on a given topic.

Exploring the Social Web

Social media like blogs, Facebook, and Twitter might not seem relevant to an academic research process, but they can be. Many scholars maintain their own blogs, where they talk about their research and developments in their field. Some blogs are specifically devoted to discussions of peer-reviewed or scholarly research. Academic researchers who attend conferences and professional meetings often use Twitter to report on interesting papers and discussions. Finally, Facebook groups on special interests can provide you with contacts who share similar interests and with information on meetings, lectures, and other events that might be of interest to you in exploring your topic.

Coping with Uncertainty

Research can be a stressful process, especially in the early stages. At different points in your research process, you will not know for sure what your topic is going to be; what you are going to say about it; what sources are available; and whether you will be able to complete everything you have to do in time. In this context, with deadlines looming, it can be difficult to take the time to explore and think about your topic before you start writing. The time you spend exploring, however, is anything but wasted. Identifying a focus that is truly yours eliminates a lot of the uncertainty from your process. It lets you separate relevant sources and lines of inquiry from those that are related, but tangential. And when your focus is connected to the larger conversation on your topic, you know that the sources that you need are there for you to find.

Keeping an Open Mind

Think back to Aristotle's three appeals. Because the idea of research is so tied up with evidence, it may seem as if the only one of Aristotle's appeals that could have any relevance here is *logos*. ✳ In fact, thinking about *ethos* is just as helpful in this early, exploratory stage of the research process.

thinking rhetorically

As you learned in Chapter 5, your ethos as a writer is connected to the image of yourself that you want to present to the reader. One of the most important elements of *ethos* in academic writing is the idea of open- or fair-mindedness: You want to present yourself as the type of thinker who has carefully considered multiple perspectives on a topic, and who is able to refine, revise, and expand her thinking about a topic as she encounters new ideas and evidence. In the exploration phase of the academic research process, you are gathering the information you need to build your *ethos* as an academic writer.

This isn't always easy. It takes conscious effort to make sure that you give information that *challenges* your beliefs the attention it deserves. Research shows that the human brain tends to focus on information that is consistent with its previously held beliefs. To effectively explore, therefore, you need to take the time to think about what you are reading in your sources, and you also need to take some time for reflection. Be proactive about identifying areas where your beliefs are strong and difficult to change. Ask yourself frequently whether your own values and beliefs are preventing you from seeing the value of new information. (See pp. 120-21 for a summary of techniques you can use to examine your own values and beliefs in argument.)

For more on Aristotle's appeals, see pp. 51-52. ✳

Finding a Focus

Your main goal when you explore is to find a *focus* for your research—that is, to figure out what you think, and what you want to argue. This is not a matter of finding one or more sources that you agree with, so that you can adopt those authors' points of view as your own. It is not a matter of finding the "truth" about your topic in your sources (at least not finding a truth that has been articulated by someone else). Academic writers *construct* their arguments: that is, they build them out of the facts, figures, theories, concepts, ideas, and arguments that have been developed by a community of thinkers over the years. These arguments are original and creative in that they build on what has come before, drawing new connections among ideas, but they do not come out of nowhere.

Finding a focus helps you determine which sources are relevant and which are not, making it easier for you to leave aside things that are interesting but not helpful. This is not to say that your academic research process will be simple or linear. As you read and write about new ideas, your thinking on your topic will evolve. You may need to go back and explore again as you find new issues related to your topic, and you will probably keep looking for sources throughout your writing process.

Studies of how students do research suggest that finding a meaningful focus for a project is the most important thing a student can do to feel happy with the project's outcome. You may not find a good focus for every research project you do, but taking the time to try is well worth it. Effective academic writers develop strategies for finding a focus or at least for recognizing one when it appears. One third-year business major who does a lot of presentations, for example, hones her focus by creating and refining PowerPoints: When her slides begin to tell a coherent story, she knows she is focused enough to move forward in her research process. Another student, a senior history major, uses note cards to keep track of interesting ideas. He sorts and resorts the cards on a big table until an interesting connection jumps out and grabs him. Then, he can focus his information-gathering on developing that connection.

||||||||||||||||||||||||||||||||||||||||||||||||||||||||||||||||||||||||||||||||||||||||||||||||

FOR EXPLORATION

Think back about a research project that you really feel good about. This might be a project you did for school, or it might be a time when you had to answer an important question for yourself. Reflect on your process, and write several paragraphs about this experience. What made this project really "yours"? What was your focus, or your answer? How did you put your answer or solution together? When did you feel like you knew what you wanted to say? While you were gathering sources? During the writing process? At some other point?

||||||||||||||||||||||||||||||||||||||||||||||||||||||||||||||||||||||||||||||||||||||||||||||||

GATHERING INFORMATION

The researcher-gatherer . . .

- Finds an individual focus and point of view on a topic
- Plans an efficient research process
- Finds and participates in communities and conversations about a topic
- Thinks rhetorically about keywords
- Uses the right research tools for the job

Planning Your Research Process

The first step in planning your research process is understanding your assignment's requirements: The best clue to how much and what kind of effort your project will take is there. Sometimes, the assignment will define everything you need to do, from the documentation style you must use for your citations, to the number of sources you need, to the databases and research tools you must use to find those sources. Sometimes, of course, those variables are up to you. Either way, it's critical to know from the outset what is in store, and what you can hope to achieve in the time you have.

Equally important are considerations of audience; the extent of research necessary (depending both on what you already know and what you want to find out); the specific type(s) of research called for (dependent on the topic and the discipline in which you are writing); and the amount of time you have to complete the project.

For questions that will help you start your research, see p. 166.

Managing Your Time

It should be obvious by now that academic research is a process that cannot, or at least should not, be done in one sitting or one session. Some sources are more accessible than others: You might be able to do all of your research at your computer, or you might have to go to the library, your professor's office, or an archive. You may also find sources that you want that are not accessible on your campus—for these sources, you will need to budget extra time. There are many useful online tools designed to help you manage your time, for instance the Assignment Calculator from the University of Minnesota Libraries (http://www.lib.umn.edu/help/calculator/).

Questions to Help You Start Your Research

1. Do you have a clear sense of your assignment?

Do you need to explain something, compare one idea to another, or argue a particular point of view?

Will you need to turn in anything — such as a first draft — before the final due date?

2. Who is your audience?

Will your readers already know something about the topic?

Will your readers have strong feelings or opinions about your topic?

3. What role will research play in this writing project?

What do you need to learn about your topic?

What knowledge do you already have about your project? Do you already have opinions about your topic?

How will you ensure that those opinions do not keep you from approaching your topic with an open mind?

4. Does the topic require particular research strategies or sources?

Many health topics, for example, call for up-to-date sources. For an essay on the evolution of rock 'n' roll, though, you would need to consult historical material and listen to some early recordings.

5. Given the due date for your final project, how should you allocate your time?

In a paper on corporate fraud for a business course, for instance, you might want to interview the CEO of a local company, so you would need to build in the time for this activity — along with time for print and online research.

There is another level of accessibility you should consider while planning your project: intellectual accessibility. Some research projects will ask you to stretch yourself and use sources that are difficult to digest. Even experts in a field will read scholarly sources multiple times to understand them: As a student, you will frequently do research in fields where you are not an expert. You should accordingly budget more time than you think you will need to read and understand your sources. You should also expect that you may need to do additional research to clarify new concepts and ideas that you find in your sources.

Staying Organized

Once you start gathering sources, you will need a plan for how to manage them. As your argument evolves, sources that seemed irrelevant early on might become essential. You don't want to spend your valuable writing time relocating an article you already found once. Many expert researchers use low-tech tools like note cards for this purpose (often with great success), but there are also some powerful online tools you can use to keep track of what you are finding.

Saving What You Find Online

Online article databases like Academic Search Premier and ProQuest come loaded with tools that will help you stay organized. Most will allow you to sort articles into folders, and to save or email those folders to yourself. Some allow you to create an account where you can store useful articles permanently. With these accounts, you can also save your searches so that you can revisit a set of results later, when and if your focus shifts.

If you are using many different research tools, you may want to keep track of what you find in a single place. Online spreadsheet tools like those found in Google Documents (http://docs.google.com) or Zoho (http://sheet.zoho.com) allow you to create a spreadsheet of sources that can be accessed from any computer with an Internet connection. These tools are free, but they do require you to create an account.

Online bookmarking tools such as Delicious (http://delicious.com), Connotea (http://connotea.org), and CiteULike (http://citeulike.org) are also extremely useful. These tools also require you to create an account. Once you have done so, you can save useful sources to the Web and then access your library of materials from any computer with an Internet connection. (Just be aware that the default setting for these tools is public, meaning that the sources are visible to anyone browsing the service.) ✳

See also "Using the Social Web," p. 179. ✳ · · · · · · · · · · ·
· · · ·

Citation Managers

Citation management tools including Refworks, Endnote, and Zotero allow you to build a personal library of sources and also help you format your citations and build bibliographies. All of these tools integrate with word processing programs, allowing you to cite items in your library as you write. With the notable exception of Zotero (http://zotero.org), most of these tools are proprietary, meaning you need to purchase a license to use them; however, some colleges provide campus-wide licenses for their students and faculty. Check with your institution's library to see if you have access.

You should try a variety of these tools to see what works for you. An important part of being an effective academic researcher is managing all of the information you come across so that you can access it again later when you need it. Remember, one of the primary goals of academic research writing is to learn something new and then communicate that learning to other people. You don't want to lose your new understanding as soon as you turn the paper in: You want to make it part of your personal knowledge base.

The guidelines on p. 169 can help you manage a research project effectively.

NOTE FOR MULTILINGUAL WRITERS

If much of your research experience has been in a language other than English, when you start a research project you may want to work closely with general reference librarians and other librarians who specialize in your subject area. (Most university libraries have staff who specialize in areas such as the humanities, social sciences, biological sciences, or education.) If possible, meet weekly with a tutor in your writing center as well. At these meetings, you can review your ongoing work as well as your research timetable.

Finding and Participating in the Conversations about Your Topic

thinking rhetorically

To academic writers, books, articles, and presentations on a topic function as a kind of ongoing conversation. Participants in these conversations exchange ideas, build on them, challenge them, and reshape them into new questions. Like any conversation, these scholarly conversations have a set of (sometimes unwritten) rules that make them work. The people who participate in them may never engage with each other face-to-face, but in their scholarly

Guidelines for Managing a Research Project

1. Check the basics.

Make sure you have a solid understanding of the assignment, your audience, and your deadlines.

2. Take the time to explore the literature on your topic with an open mind.

Be open to new ideas and new information.

Think critically about how to integrate new information into what you already know and believe.

3. Develop a preliminary search strategy.

Decide which kinds of sources are likely to be the most helpful, and whether time constraints might be a problem with any of them.

4. Establish a timetable for the project, and review it often.

List the activities you need to complete, along with tentative due dates.

Schedules may vary quite a bit from one research project to another.

5. Expect the unexpected.

Build in enough time to give you flexibility to revisit sources and rerun searches as your thinking evolves.

As you learn about your topic, resources that seemed irrelevant at first might become valuable.

work they share certain assumptions about how ideas should be presented, about the kinds of evidence they should use, and about the types of questions they should address.

In order to participate in these conversations, you'll need to know first, how to find them, and, second, how to contribute to them once you do. Thinking rhetorically about your project can help you figure out how to do both, whether you are writing for the academic community in general, or for a specific disciplinary community.

The Basics of Online Searches

Most research today starts at the computer, with a keyword search. Though you will in most cases eventually need to consult printed books or primary documents for your research project, you will probably start your research online. In order to do so efficiently, you'll need to know a few basics.

DATABASES. Different online research tools contain different types of sources, but in all of them the computer stores information in a structured way. For example, in Academic Search Premier, a database of articles from journals, newspapers, and magazines (also called a *periodical database*) the computer stores the article *titles* in one category, or *field,* and the *authors* in another. The easiest way to visualize a database is as a simple table:

Title	Author	Source	Volume	Date
Habitat mapping of the Atlantic bluefin tuna derived from satellite data: Its potential as a tool for the sustainable management of pelagic fisheries	Druon, J-N	Marine Policy	34	March 2010
Pretty Good Yield and exploited fishes	Hilborn, R	Marine Policy	34	January 2010

The fields in a database vary depending on the type of information that is being collected. The Internet Movie Database (www.imdb.com) would look more like the following:

Title	Director	Writer	Release Date	Rating
School of Rock	Linklater, R.	White, M.	2003	PG-13
Across the Universe	Taymor, J.	Clement, D. La Frenais, I.	2007	PG-13

KEYWORD SEARCHES.   *Keyword searches* are usually the best way to start searching a database. Used as search terms, keywords are the words you choose to describe your topic. The database or search engine you are using will scan its contents for your keywords, and give you a list of results that contain them.

It is important to understand, though, when you do a keyword search you are probably not searching every field in the database. For example, most article databases will look for your keywords in the title, abstract, and subject heading fields, but not in the text of the article itself. Why? Because if your keywords appear in one of the first three fields, the chances are good that the article will be relevant to your research. On the other hand, if your keywords appear just once in the text of a thirty-page article, it might be only tangentially related to your topic.

The searches that you do in academic databases and library catalogs are not as broad as those you do in search engines. They will retrieve fewer results, but because your results have your keywords in prominent places, they can be more relevant—once you figure out what the best keywords are. This might take some trial and error. Start with some broad keywords, and take note of the terms that are used to describe your topic in the articles you find. For example, searching a scholarly article database for articles about "animal testing," you may notice that the term "vivisection" appears frequently. You will probably want to try another set of searches that use that term.

The process of choosing keywords is, of course, a rhetorical process. Thinking rhetorically about your keywords will help you choose terms that are meaningful within a particular discourse. A part of this rhetorical process is also thinking about your audience: What terms will they expect you to use to talk about your topic? At the same time, you must also think about the people who have produced the sources you want to use, and identify the terms and words they might use in their work. The best keywords will be those that are important (and that mean the same thing) to people in both groups.

thinking rhetorically

SEARCHING THE INTERNET AND SEARCHING SPECIALIZED DATABASES.   When searching for information on the Internet, most users turn to an Internet search engine like Google. These can be understood as extremely large databases. Computer programs called *Web crawlers* (or *spiders*) visit Web pages and pull data about the pages into a database. When you type keywords into Google's search engine, it doesn't search for your keywords everywhere on the Web; instead, it searches for them in its own huge database (see p. 172).

Internet search engines are becoming ever more sophisticated, but they index literally billions of Web pages. They are a powerful tool to use, especially when you are initially scanning to find out what is out there about your topic. Because they initially pull in information from all over the Web, they can help you find resources in places you would never think to search. At the

How Keywords Work in a Search Engine

same time, searches with one or two keywords in Google tend to return results that range widely—sometimes so widely as to be virtually useless. At some point in your academic research process, you will need to search more precisely. One strategy at that point is to use keywords effectively; another is to think about using a different kind of research tool. In most cases, this means turning to a *specialized database*.

Specialized databases like EBSCO's Academic Search Premier include far less material than do Internet databases, so searching them will yield significantly fewer results, but the results you do get will be more relevant for academic research. If you type "Hawthorne Scarlet Letter" into Google, for example, you will receive upwards of 800,000 returns, many of which are only tangentially related to the classic novel. If you type "Hawthorne" and "Scarlet Letter" as keywords into the first two search fields in Academic Search Premier, by contrast, you'll receive 160 or so returns, virtually all of which discuss the novel. When you make the shift from exploring to gathering sources, this is a critical difference.

If your first search in a specialized database returns little or nothing of use, don't assume that there are no articles about your topic. It may be that your specific keywords are in the full text of the article but not in the title or abstract, so you'll need to change the default so that your search includes

Keyword Searches via Google and Academic Search Premier

full text. On the other hand, it may be that your keywords are not widely used in academic books and articles. In your initial searches in article databases, then, your best strategy is frequently to start with a very broad search, using only one or two key terms. Once you have scanned enough results to get a sense of what is available on your topic, you can narrow your results by adding keywords that frequently appear in the titles and abstracts of relevant articles.

Keep in mind that the keywords that will be effective for one project may be entirely ineffective for another project, even if both projects are on the same topic. This concept is simple, but it can be hard to remember when you are immersed in the process of trying to find sources. Also, keep in mind that you are unlikely to craft a keyword search that will only retrieve relevant articles. You may well use some of the sources you find on your initial search, but you will most likely not use *all* of them. You will need to do additional searches as you develop your understanding of your topic.

ALTERNATIVES TO KEYWORD SEARCHING.   Keywords will usually be your first entry point into a database, but they're not the only option you have. There are alternatives that offer you more precision and accuracy in your searching, as for example when you want to find a specific book or article. With most tools, you can specify particular fields to search. Choosing the "author" field to search for a specific author is an obvious way to use field searching. You can also use fields to narrow your keyword searching. For example, say that a default keyword search in your database matches your keywords against the article title, journal title, abstract, and subject headings. If you specify that your keywords must appear in an article title, you will get fewer results, but those results are more likely to focus on your specific topic.

CONTROLLED VOCABULARY AND THESAURI. Another way to increase the precision of your searches is to find out if your research tool gives you access to any kind of *controlled vocabulary*. Keywords are essentially uncontrolled vocabulary. If you prefer the term "film" to "cinema," you can use "film" as much as you want; if the authors who produce the texts you want to find use "cinema" exclusively, however, you'll have difficulty finding their work. This is why thinking rhetorically about your keywords is so important.

To ease some of these potential difficulties, some databases establish what is known as a controlled vocabulary. Authors can use "film" or "cinema"—whichever they prefer—but when their articles go into a database, the agreed-upon label "film" is attached to their article. Researchers then just have to find out what the agreed-upon, or controlled, term is for their topic.

The research tools you will use for academic writing usually have some kind of controlled vocabulary available. Some specialized databases like ERIC (for sources in education) or PsycINFO (for sources in psychology) provide searchers with powerful thesauri to help them refine their searches. Searchers can identify key terms, and the thesaurus will point them to related terms, both broader and narrower. By browsing these related terms, searchers can find additional sources that might provide interesting new perspectives on their initial query.

Research Tools

There are many different ways to do research today, and many different research tools to choose from. Some tools, like Internet search engines, provide access to a vast number of resources on every conceivable topic. Others are more specialized, like PsycINFO, providing you access to one type of resource or resources on a specific topic. Some are freely available online. Others are only available by subscription, and some of these subscriptions are so expensive that only large institutions can afford them. Luckily for you, as a part of your college or university community, you have access to many such resources.

In an academic research process, you can expect to use many different types of research tools as you gather your sources. You might use your library's catalog to track down a book you saw referenced in an article; you might run across an article on a scholarly journal's Web site and then use your library's

APA PsycNET™ American Psychological Association

| SEARCH | BROWSE | TERM FINDER |

Thesaurus of Psychological Index Terms

| term begins with | term contains | term hierarchy |

Look up term perfectionism **GO**

Browse Terms A B C D E F G H I J K L M N O **P** Q R S T U V W X Y Z

Select Matching Terms Perceptual Sty ◀ **Previous** | **Next** ▶ Permissiveness **Explode**

☐ Select All on Page

⊟ ☐ **Perfectionism** (1009)

> **Year Introduced:**
> 1988
>
> **PsycINFO Posting Notes:**
> 1009
>
> **Broader Term(s):**
> ☐ **Personality Traits**
>
> **Related Term(s):**
> ☐ **Compulsions**
> ☐ **Conscientiousness**
> ☐ **Self Criticism**

"Term Finder" Thesaurus (PsycINFO)

article databases to find the full text of the article; you might find a person with research interests similar to yours through a social bookmarking site like Delicious and visit some Web sites that person recommends. There are too many research tools available to discuss them all, and what you need for your project is always going to be specific to your particular rhetorical situation. Nevertheless, this section will give you a sense of what is possible using different types of research tools.

ARTICLE (OR PERIODICAL) DATABASES. Most article databases (also sometimes called *periodical databases*) are proprietary, meaning that they are only accessible if you are a subscriber, or if you are part of an institution that subscribes. As a college student you probably have access to a good number of proprietary article databases at your college library. Some databases are available through public libraries. You may also have access to article databases at your place of employment.

Some article databases store only descriptions of the articles using standard bibliographic information (author, title, subject, page length, etc.): They let you know that an article exists, but require you to go elsewhere to find the actual text. Other databases include the full text of the article along with the bibliographic information. A third category provides full-text access to some articles and only bibliographic information about the others.

When you find a description of an article in a database that does not offer full text, you have several options for finding the article itself. First, you need to check whether your library subscribes to the journal in which the article appeared. (Some libraries provide a link to the article databases that lets you check automatically; otherwise, you'll have to do a separate search in the library's catalog.) If your college does not have a subscription to the journal you want, you can usually request a copy of the article you need from another library: Ask your college librarian for help.

Some databases focus on a particular type of article, like newspaper articles, magazine articles, or journal articles. General-purpose databases include all types of articles and cover a variety of disciplines. They are often a good starting point for an academic research project. Examples include EBSCO's *Academic Search Premier*, Gale's *InfoTrac College Edition*, and the *ProQuest Research Library*. Other databases provide in-depth coverage of a particular discipline. If you have already chosen a major, it is an excellent idea to find out what the important databases are in your discipline. (Your instructors will expect you to consult these when you do research in your major, but they may not think to mention them specifically to you.)

A NOTE ON NUMBERS.   You are no doubt familiar with typing keywords into an Internet search engine and getting back huge numbers of hits, many of which won't be credible, or even relevant. You probably look at only a small fraction of hits that appear on the first few pages of results. Your expectations for how many results you will get on *any* search, though, may be shaped by these experiences with Internet search engines. Some research shows that when students don't see large numbers of hits on a search, they worry about the quality of their search or the viability of their research topic, even when the number of hits is perfectly adequate to support their specific research needs.

Be realistic about the number of sources you really need to write your paper or fulfill your assignment. It may be tempting to throw a topic out when your initial searches on a scholarly periodical database like PsycINFO only retrieve twenty articles, but twenty scholarly articles is plenty to support a typical college research paper. For many papers you only need a few articles that really dig into your topic to generate enough ideas to build your own argument. Choosing a topic that is less well represented in the literature can be a great way to make your research stand out.

Questions to Consider When Choosing an Article Database

1. Is it a full-text database, or an index?

2. What are its dates of coverage?

3. How current is the content in the database?

4. Does the database focus on the literature in a particular field?

5. What are the most important databases for research in my discipline?

6. Is there an easy way to identify peer-reviewed or scholarly articles in this database?

7. Does the database offer special tools, like citation formatting, of particular interest to academic writers?

LIBRARY CATALOGS. Library catalogs are databases that let you search everything in a library's collection. Every library tries to tailor its collection to the needs of its students and faculty, and, at almost all academic libraries, this means lots of books and journals. At a school with a strong film studies program, though, you could expect to find a large film collection in the library. At a school with a strong natural resources curriculum the library would likely house an extensive map collection. At a chiropractic college, you could even expect to find bones and skeletons available for checkout.

For questions to consider when using a library catalog, see p. 178.

SEARCHING THE INTERNET. While there are some challengers, Google remains dominant in the area of Internet searches because of the huge amount of data it has indexed, and because its ranking algorithm continues to

Questions to Consider When Using Library Catalogs

1. If your institution has multiple libraries, can you limit your search to the specific library you want to use?

2. If your institution has multiple campuses, can you search the holdings of all campus libraries at the same time?

3. If your institution belongs to a regional consortium of libraries, can you easily search all of the libraries where you have borrowing privileges at the same time?

4. If you find a book or other item that is available on another campus, in another branch, or at another university, how easily and quickly can you expect to receive the book?

5. Can you easily limit your search to a particular type of information source (books, videos, maps, etc.)?

deliver results that are perceived to be highly relevant by its users. In addition to Google Search (its standard search engine), Google has two related search engines of particular interest to you as an academic researcher: Google Books and Google Scholar.

Google Books (http://books.google.com) is a large, searchable database of digitized books. In some cases, you can download the full text of the books; in others, you can only access a snippet that includes your keywords. Google Scholar (http://scholar.google.com) is Google's attempt to provide a targeted search of scholarly information. With this tool, you can quickly scan the scholarly literature on a topic across a variety of disciplines. You can set your preferences in Google Scholar so that your results will be connected to the holdings of your college library. This allows you to search broadly in Google Scholar, and then get the articles at no cost to you through your library's subscriptions.

Google's dominance does not mean that it is the only Internet search option. There are a variety of alternatives available. Some of these will disappear quickly, and no doubt others will emerge. Some search engines try to control Web searches by limiting the pool of sites being searched to those that have been selected by human editors: Two examples are Sweet Search (http://www.sweetsearch.com/), where students are the target audience, and the Librarians Index to the Internet (http://lii.org), which points users to Web sites that have been selected and reviewed by librarians.

Search tools also exist that are available by subscription only and provide you with easy ways to pay for the content you find. A good example of this is DeepDvye (http://www.deepdyve.com), a scholarly search engine that includes an option to "rent" articles. These services can be useful to you if your school's subscriptions are limited and after you leave school, but remember that while you are in school you should always make use first of the services and collections your tuition has already paid for.

There are also tools that try to look at searching in an entirely new way. WolframAlpha (http://www.wolframalpha.com/), for example, calls itself a "computational knowledge engine": Instead of providing links to Web sites, this tool makes assumptions about what you're looking for and compiles information about your search terms. (See p. 180 for a screenshot of a Wolfram Alpha search.)

USING THE SOCIAL WEB. So-called social Web tools like Delicious and CiteULike (discussed on p. 167) provide you with a powerful way to find sources. When people use these tools to bookmark sites they find online, their bookmarks are usually public and searchable; searching with Delicious and CiteULike, then, allows you to search thousands of people's bookmarks at once. While you have no guarantees about any individual site, you do know that for every source you find, some person thought it was worth the effort to save. Also, if you really like the sources one person has saved, you can browse the rest of the items that person has saved in that category, and find new things that might interest you.

Finding sources in this way requires a shift in thinking: Instead of finding sources, you are finding people, people who are sharing their work and research on a topic of interest to you. You cannot control what they will find for you, or when, but you may well end up finding sources and ideas that you would not have found without joining that particular online community.

Conducting Field Research

Sometimes, instead of sifting through the research others have done, you will want to conduct some research yourself: You might want to interview an expert on your topic, obtain an array of opinions on a topic by means of a questionnaire, or observe an interaction or event firsthand. These kinds of activities are known as *field research*. Many students find that field research

WolframAlpha Search

helps them build enthusiasm for their learning because they are uncovering information that no one before has compiled in exactly the same way.

A note of caution is appropriate here. Any time you do research on other people, you must treat your research subjects ethically and with respect. You will have a great deal of latitude in interpreting what your subjects say in interviews, for example, or a particular behavior that they exhibit, so you must do so fairly and thoughtfully. For your field research to be valued by an academic audience, you must show that you have drawn your conclusions from your research, not from preconceived conclusions. Your campus may have training or guidelines for students engaged in primary research. Talk to your instructor, or investigate your school's Web site, to find out more.

Interviews

Interviews often provide information that is unavailable through other kinds of research. For a psychology paper about child abuse, for example, you might interview a local caseworker who works with abused children. For a

Guidelines for Conducting Interviews

1. Request an interview in advance.

Explain why you want the interview, how long it will take, and what you hope to accomplish.

On the day of the interview, show up on time.

2. Bring a list of written questions, but be flexible.

If the interviewee focuses on one question or moves to a related issue, just accept this change in plans and return to your own questions when appropriate.

If the interviewee doesn't want to answer a direct question, try asking about the subject in a less direct fashion.

3. If you wish to tape-record the interview, remember to ask permission first.

4. Take notes during the interview, even if you use a tape recorder.

Your notes will refresh your memory later on, when you don't have time to review the entire tape; they can also help you identify the most important points of the discussion.

political science paper on the Iraq War, you might consult a veteran of the war. If you do conduct interviews, keep in mind that a good interviewer is first of all a good listener—someone who is able to draw out the person being interviewed. Since interviews are more formal than most conversations, be sure to prepare carefully for them by doing some background research on the interviewee and by preparing a list of questions.

See p. 181 for guidelines on conducting interviews.

Questionnaires

Questionnaires can provide information about the attitudes and experiences of a large number of people. You might, for instance, survey your fellow students about their views on college sports or your school's policy on hate speech. Some disciplines, such as sociology and political science, use questionnaire and polling data extensively as scientific measurements of the general population's views. In introductory classes, though, students generally use questionnaires to get a rough idea of broad trends or differing perspectives on a topic. The information you gather from such questionnaires can serve only as anecdotal evidence; it cannot, in other words, play a primary role in supporting an argument.

See the guidelines for designing and using questionnaires on pp. 183–84.

Observation

Sociologists and anthropologists have rich traditions in firsthand observation. They often do research as participant-observers, living in and moving among various communities to observe social customs and patterns of behavior. Scholars using this approach have gathered data on many kinds of groups, from day-care centers to crack houses to corporate boardrooms.

Although you most likely won't be doing such full-scale research, you can still generate stimulating material by closely observing various activities or groups. If you're writing a paper on the effectiveness of your local city council, for example, you might attend several meetings and take the role of participant-observer during question-and-answer sessions. You might also consider observing groups you already belong to: If you're writing about gender differences and work as a restaurant waitperson, for instance, you might study the tipping practices of men versus those of women. As with other forms of field research, observation can bring interesting new perspectives to a subject.

Guidelines for Designing and Using Questionnaires

1. Determine the purpose of the questionnaire and explain your purpose briefly at the top.

Consider: How will the results tie in to the rest of your research project?

2. Decide who will receive the questionnaire.

For a business paper, you might want to survey an entire small company, or a representative sample — say, every fifth employee from an alphabetized list — at a larger company.

3. Decide how you will distribute the questionnaire and obtain responses.

Will you email it, send it by regular mail, or hand it out in person?

Make sure the questionnaire states clearly how respondents should return it: Via your email address? By using the postage-paid reply envelope you've enclosed? Some other way?

4. Consider whether you need any "personal characteristics" questions such as gender, income, marital status, age, or education.

If, for example, you were gathering opinions about the homeless in your community for a sociology paper, the respondents' income levels may be relevant.

continued

5. Write questions that are clear and to the point.

It's usually best to ask questions with yes-or-no or multiple-choice answers, or to ask people to rank things on a scale (say, from 1 to 5). If a questionnaire is too long or complicated, few people will fill it out.

6. Show a draft of your questionnaire to some friends before copying and distributing it.

Seek feedback on the clarity, fairness, and user friendliness of your questions.

7. Give respondents a deadline for returning the questionnaire.

8. Analyze the questionnaire results carefully.

Look for trends, major points of agreement and disagreement, and so forth.

Try to summarize what you have learned before incorporating the results into your paper.

EVALUATING

The researcher-evaluator . . .

- Makes rhetorical choices about sources throughout the research process
- Knows the value of many types of information sources
- Understands how scholarly information is created and communicated
- Uses a variety of tools to evaluate sources
- Looks beyond the text itself when evaluating sources

Evaluation is a process of making rhetorical choices about your sources, choosing sources based on what you need both as a student and as a writer who wants to communicate with, and convince, an audience. As you have already learned, academic writers do not expect to produce the last word on a topic, but to contribute to an ongoing scholarly conversation. You are not trying to find someone else's version of the truth and report it; you are responsible for constructing your own perspective on the "truth" of your topic. This means that you cannot evaluate sources without reading them, thinking about them, and sometimes even writing about them.

A common tool used to evaluate information sources is a checklist of criteria. Checklists *can* help you identify some important information to keep in mind as you read and evaluate a source. It *is* useful, for example, to know whether a source is biased — that is, whether it is trying to promote an agenda or to advocate a particular position. Such checklists can be problematic, however, because they suggest that you can evaluate sources before you read them, and without considering your particular rhetorical situation. For example, finding out that a source is biased is not necessarily a reason to reject it. As an academic writer, you will frequently find that authors who articulate a point of view are more useful to you as you construct your own arguments than are those who remain determinedly "neutral." In order to fairly and usefully evaluate your source's appropriateness for your project, you have to identify the nature of the bias, weigh it against the source's factual accuracy, and decide what the bias will mean, in the end, for your project's purpose and audience.

The guidelines we present on pp. 191–92, following the discussion of Understanding and Evaluating Sources on pp. 186–90, will help you evaluate your sources with more precision than a simple checklist will allow.

Understanding and Evaluating Sources

In Chapter 3, you learned about writing for different audiences and within different discourses. Like your choice of language, medium, and writing strategies, your choice of sources will depend to some extent on your purpose, your project, and your audience. For most papers you'll write in college, your primary audience will be your instructor. While you may not know enough about your instructors as individuals to tailor your sources to their expectations, you *can* write to meet their expectations as members of the academic community.

In most cases, this will mean at a minimum using sources that are reputable and relevant to your topic. In many cases, this will also mean using a significant number of scholarly, or peer-reviewed, sources. In fact, the requirement to use a specific number of "scholarly," "refereed," or "peer-reviewed" sources is one of the most common requirements you will see in academic research paper assignments.

The sections that follow will help you understand how peer-reviewed sources differ from other types of sources and how to evaluate them.

Choosing Different Types of Sources

Newspaper and magazine articles are usually written for a general audience, so they are accessible to anyone with a standard level of education. They are intended to be current and up-to-date, though they may provide historical perspective as well. Magazine and newspaper journalists place a high value on objectivity, but you will also find opinion pieces and editorials in most newspapers and magazines. Newspaper and magazine articles usually do not provide a bibliography or list of sources, even though they are frequently based on a reporter's research. (See Jamais Cascio's article from *The Atlantic* on pp. 261–62 for an example.)

Scholarly journal articles are called peer-reviewed articles, or refereed articles, because unlike magazine articles, journal articles have been critiqued by experts. These are discussed in more detail on pp. 187–88.

Books are written for both expert and general audiences. They give an author room to provide an in-depth overview of a topic. They are a good place to go to find a broader context for your topic. Academic books are usually thoroughly researched, with extensive bibliographies, making them an excellent tool for finding additional sources as well as useful and informative in their own right. Remember that sometimes only a part of a book will be useful to you; you do not need to read and use the entire thing.

Primary sources are different in different disciplines. A primary source is a source of original information, such as an eyewitness account of a historical event, data from experiments, novels, diaries, and more. Primary sources are called "primary" to distinguish them from *secondary sources*, or sources that provide synthesis or analysis of the information in primary sources.

Whether a source is primary or secondary depends in part on your research question. A history textbook, for example, would be a secondary source if you wanted to learn about the causes of the Civil War, and a primary source if you were interested in examining how history textbooks have changed over time.

Peer-Reviewed (Scholarly) Articles

Even when you are not required to use scholarly articles, they are useful sources when you are writing for academic audiences. *Peer review* is a collaborative process of quality control that is used by most academic journals to determine which articles should be published and which should not.

Here is a quick overview of a typical review process. An author or group of authors does a research study and writes the results of that study in the form of an article submitted to the editors of a journal in their discipline. The editors send the article to be reviewed by the author's peers—experts in the author's field of study. These reviewers examine the manuscript and write reviews in which they recommend one of these options: *publish*, *publish with revisions*, or *reject*. The reviews are sent back to the editor, who gives them to the author along with final decision. If the decision is *publish with revisions*, the authors will review the reports and decide whether they want to revise as requested. If they do, the review process may be repeated. If they do not, they retain their manuscript and may submit it to another journal. The whole process can take anywhere from a few months to several years.

As you have learned throughout this text, different disciplines or knowledge communities have different ways of doing things. Usually (but not always) peer-reviewed articles report on original research that contributes to the development of new knowledge within a discipline. The peer-reviewers will examine the author's manuscript to determine whether it is a good example of research in their shared discipline.

Peer reviewers have the expertise to determine whether the research methods selected for a study were appropriate for the question being studied. They can tell if the method was applied correctly, based on the description in the paper. They should be able to identify results that are reasonable for the study, and to comment on whether the authors' conclusions about those results make sense. They cannot know for sure, however, whether the results reported are valid and accurate, or whether future researchers can replicate them. In recommending publication, they can only guarantee that, to the best of their abilities to judge, the research in the article will in some way inform or advance future research; in other words, it is worthy of further examination and discussion within the discipline.

What does this mean for you as you try to evaluate the scholarly articles you find? It means that you should not blindly accept their conclusions as "true," and that you should try to find out where they fit within the larger conversation in the discipline. Is an article responding to other researchers' findings? Does it fill a gap in knowledge within the discipline, examining a question that hadn't answered before? Does it provide additional evidence for a theory or model that is important in the field? These questions can help you understand how important a particular article is and how relevant it might be to your project.

Online Sources

At one time, the type of information that was available on the Web was different from the information published by traditional scholarly and media outlets. This is no longer the case: A digital analogue exists for almost anything you can find in the print world. These digital versions are not always available for free, and they are not always easy to find, but newspaper articles, historical artifacts, out-of-print books, and scholarly journal articles are all out there. In most cases, then, it no longer makes any sense to think about online sources as something separate from print sources: Most of the skills you need to evaluate online sources are the same skills you should be using to evaluate any source.

There is, however, one thing to keep in mind when you are working with digital sources: They are less permanent than their print counterparts. A mistake in an article in a print encyclopedia, for example, will stay there until a new, corrected edition is released. Even then, the mistake will be present in the physical copies of the older edition. In an online encyclopedia, mistakes can be corrected as soon as they are discovered, leaving no public (or at least easily accessible) evidence that the mistake ever occurred.

This is important for you to understand as an academic writer. The ability to quickly correct mistakes is a good thing. But what if you, as an academic writer, refer your readers to a source, not knowing that it changed or moved after you referenced it? Online media outlets frequently refresh their front pages with new, up-to-date content. What if you cite an article that is there one day, and gone the next? This affects your readers' ability to track down your sources, and affects your credibility as an academic writer. If you rely heavily on information from hyper-dynamic sources—sources that change daily or hourly—you will make it difficult for your readers to appreciate the connections between your ideas and other ideas in the field.

This is not to say that you should not use dynamic online sources, simply that you should use them carefully and deliberately. If you know that a post or an article is going to disappear from a Web site shortly, provide a citation to the print version, if there is one; to a "permalink" or stable link to that specific information, if you can find one; or at least to the URL of the home page of the organization that published the information. (MLA, APA, and other documentation styles have specific rules for what to include in citations for online sources, so if your instructor requires that you follow a specific style, be sure that you adhere to those rules. For details, see the MLA and APA Documentation Guidelines section at the back of this book.)

You should also develop some additional evaluation skills to help you navigate this dynamic landscape. For example, the success of Wikipedia has led to a number of similar reference sources powered by wiki software. One of the features of these sites is *versioning*, meaning that as a page is revised, older versions are still available. You can use this information to ensure that there is an active community of people monitoring the information on the page, which can give you confidence that if bad or misleading information is added, it will be quickly repaired.

This idea of community is extremely important whenever you are evaluating information sources on the social Web, from blogs to wikis to online listserv archives to discussion boards. In general, a site with an active community, generating comments, links, ratings, or reviews, is easier to evaluate than one without an active community. Not only is the content being generated by the members of the community likely to be helpful as you evaluate, but the presence of the community itself demonstrates something about the impact of the source.

Tools for Evaluating Scholarly Resources

The social Web (sometimes known as Web 2.0) is especially useful to you as an academic writer because it can help you evaluate scholarly sources. You can easily find conversations among scholars on the Web. If you tap into these conversations, you can find a wealth of information about the relative value of different sources.

Here are descriptions of some useful resources for evaluating scholarly information. Be aware, though, that this is a rapidly changing landscape — by the time this book is published, some of these resources may have changed or disappeared, and others will launch that may be equally useful.

SCHOLARLY BLOGS. Blogging may not seem very academic, but scholarly blogs can be a very important source of information for you in your evaluation process. ScienceBlogs (http://scienceblogs.com), for example, is a project that aggregates blogs written by scholars and experts for a general audience. Not only do the bloggers analyze and critique scholarly articles in their posts, but the posts also frequently spark lively discussions in the comments area. Another site, Research Blogging (http://researchblogging.org), will point you to individual blog posts on academic topics. When scholarly bloggers write posts about a peer-reviewed research article, they can mark the posts with a special icon. The post then appears on the Research Blogging site and becomes a part of the Research Blogging Twitter feed.

RATINGS AND REVIEWS ON THE SOCIAL WEB.   Too often, we try to evaluate sources just by examining them closely. You can obviously get useful information this way, and in fact this step is necessary, but in this age of networked information there is no reason to limit yourself to a solitary examination of a text. Social bookmarking sites like Delicious and CiteULike not only help you organize and find information, but they can also help you evaluate it: When you can see how many people have saved an article or a Web site, you gain some information about how important that source is in the larger conversation. CiteULike (http://citeulike.org) also provides users with the ability to rate and review sources directly. Similar services allow users to exchange information on books. These services, like Goodreads (http://goodreads.com) and Library Thing (http://librarything.com) also include rating and reviewing options. Some college library catalogs also include features that allow users to bookmark, rate, or review sources.

Going beyond the text will be especially useful as you navigate sources that advocate a particular point of view. Sometimes the quickest way to identify that point of view is to look up the author, site, or sponsoring organization online. The information you find may itself be biased, but you can still get a sense of whether there is controversy about the author, or whether the organization is associated with a particular point of view, which can provide helpful context for your independent evaluation process.

CITATION TRACKING.   One of the ways that scholars show that they found a source interesting or useful is to cite it in their own work, so this can be an important factor to consider when you are evaluating sources. Your college library may license access to citation indexes such as the *Social Science Citation Index*, the *Arts and Humanities Citation Index*, and the *Science Citation Index*. These tools allow you to search for an author or an article and then track how many times that source has been cited by others in subsequent years. Google Scholar provides a similar service, listing a "cited by" line for every result.

Guidelines for Evaluating Sources

1. Is the source useful to you?

Considering where you are in the research process, does the source provide the kind of information you need? If it is not useful to you now, might it be useful to you later?

Do you have specific assignment requirements to fulfill? Does this source meet these requirements?

Does the source get you thinking? Does it give you ideas for new lines of inquiry, or help you draw connections between ideas?

2. Is this the kind of source your audience expects you to use?

Is the information neither too easy nor too difficult for your audience?

Will the source give your argument more credibility with your audience?

If the source is *not* what your audience expects, what can you do as a writer to show your audience *why* they should pay attention to it?

3. Who created this source?

If an author is identified, is it someone you find credible? Have other sources referred favorably to the author's work?

If you know little or nothing about the author, use a reference source or search engine to find out more.

Use a specialized database that will let you do citation tracking, or try Google Scholar's cited by link to see if the work is cited by other authors in the discipline.

continued

If *no* author is identified, has a group or an institutional sponsor produced the source? Is it credible?

If no author *or* sponsor is identified, you should reconsider your use of the source.

If you know little or nothing about the sponsor, use a reference source or search engine to find out more about it.

4. What is the author's (or institution's or agency's) *purpose* in creating this source?

Is the author trying to persuade you to do something or think in a certain way? If so, has that affected the quality of the information he/she provides — say, to include irrelevant or misleading information, or to exclude information that is relevant?

In order to gauge the quality of the information provided, compare it to other sources on a similar topic.

Is the site selling anything? If so, how much does this potentially affect the kinds of information presented and the ways in which it is presented?

5. If the source is a scholarly one, is it a good example of research in the discipline?

Does the author use footnotes and other references, indicating that the author is connecting the work to the larger conversation in their discipline?

Is the source cited in other works you're evaluating?

Is the information as up-to-date as you need it to be?

If you need cutting-edge information, an article from a preprint server (one that lets you see articles before they are published) might be most appropriate. For other research questions, a significant article from decades ago might be fine.

Reading More Closely and Synthesizing Material

Once you find a potentially useful source, study it with care so you can zero in on the specific information you need. Look, for instance, at the different elements in a source, such as an abstract, preface, introduction, and conclusion. Skim subheadings as well. They may direct you to some essential data, to an expert's point of view, or to a useful quotation. Last but not least, be sure to check footnotes and bibliographies, which can often lead you to other good sources—and to new opinions on the topic.

As you dig more deeply into your sources, you may begin to feel as though you're having a conversation with some of the experts. And, indeed, this is the way good research works: You'll agree with some sources, disagree with others, and begin to see trends in the information you gather. In other words, you'll be *synthesizing* information and reaching your own conclusions as you go along. For example, when Alletta Brenner researched human trafficking in American garment manufacturing, she began to see some major factors underlying human trafficking. She thus decided to group her information into three main categories: violation by factory owners, available immigrant labor, and poor enforcement of laws (see paragraph 3 of Alletta's essay on p. 207).

WRITING

The researcher-writer/content creator . . .

- Communicates in a way appropriate for the audience and discipline
- Avoids plagiarism
- Uses appropriate citation styles
- Uses information ethically, respecting the rights of others
- Understands his or her rights as a content creator and exercises them

Using Sources: Quoting, Paraphrasing, and Summarizing

When you conduct research, you gather information from a number of sources. In many instances, you also come to know who the experts are on your topic, what issues they think are important, and whether you agree with them. How should you use these various types of information in your research paper?

You have three options for integrating sources into your writing. You can *quote* your source's words exactly. You can *paraphrase* them by explaining their meaning in your own words. Or you can *summarize* the source's information by significantly abbreviating a paragraph, a chapter, or even an entire book.

As you think about these options, keep in mind that many student writers tend to overquote material from their sources. In other words, they quote wording that isn't particularly striking rather than integrating the information by paraphrasing or summarizing. For example, if Report A says, "From the year 1990 up until the present time, we have seen some modest improvement in the rate of adult literacy in the United States," it's probably not necessary to quote this statement. Instead, you could paraphrase it: *According to Report A, the adult literacy rate in the United States has increased somewhat since 1990* (and end with an in-text citation of the source). As you go through your research material, how can you figure out whether it's better to quote a source or relay the information in some other way? The guidelines on p. 195 will help you answer this question.

Whether you quote, paraphrase, or summarize, it's essential to acknowledge sources accurately, both in the text of your paper and in the works cited list (or bibliography). Within the text itself, you'll often want to use a *signal phrase* to introduce a source. Such phrases not only mention the source but also may indicate—with an appropriate verb—your attitude toward it. For instance, the signal phrase *Although Chomsky claims* gives the distinct impression that you disagree with Chomsky. You could, however, create a different impression by saying, at the end of a sentence, *which is confirmed by noted linguist Noam Chomsky*. Or you might introduce this source in a more neutral fashion: *Chomsky believes,* or *As Chomsky points out,* or *Chomsky's research suggests.* Be careful to use appropriate signal phrases and to vary their location: They shouldn't always appear at the beginning of a sentence. Remember as well that the documentation style you're following (MLA, APA, or others) will generally specify what to include in a signal phrase or an in-text citation (see Writer's References, pp. 347–402).

Even when you understand *why* you're quoting, paraphrasing, or summarizing a passage, you may be unsure about *how* to do so. When is a paraphrase just a paraphrase—and not *plagiarism* (the inappropriate use of another

Guidelines for Determining When to Quote, Paraphrase, or Summarize

1. *Quote directly* when the exact wording of a source is crucial.

> When the language is especially powerful and memorable

> When the author is an authority whose expertise buttresses your own position

> When you disagree with the source but want to allow the author to speak in his or her own words

2. *Paraphrase* when you want to convey information in your own words.

> When the author's own words are not particularly memorable but the details in the source are important

> When you don't want to interrupt your discussion with a direct quotation

3. *Summarize* when you want to present only the main idea of a long passage.

> When the details of a paragraph, a chapter, or an entire book are not important

> When comparing two or more lengthy arguments or analyses (as in two books with opposing views)

person's words and ideas)? Is it permissible to omit or change words in a direct quotation? The following sections will shed some light on these issues.

Quoting Accurately

When you incorporate a quotation into your writing—for any reason—you must include the exact words from the source. The following original passage is from a classic essay about illiteracy in America. Read the original, and then see how one student used a short quotation from it in her research essay (following MLA style).

ORIGINAL PASSAGE

> Illiterates cannot travel freely. When they attempt to do so, they encounter risks that few of us can dream of. They cannot read traffic signs and, while they often learn to recognize and to decipher symbols, they cannot manage street names which they haven't seen before. The same is true for bus and subway stops. While ingenuity can sometimes help a man or woman to discern direction from familiar landmarks, buildings, cemeteries, churches, and the like, most illiterates are virtually immobilized. They seldom wander past the streets and neighborhoods they know. Geographical paralysis becomes a bitter metaphor for their entire existence. They are immobilized in almost every sense we can imagine. They can't move up. They can't move out. They cannot see beyond.
>
> —Jonathan Kozol, "The Human Cost of an Illiterate Society"

SHORT QUOTATION

> Kozol points out that people who are illiterate often can't leave their own neighborhoods, which is "a bitter metaphor for their entire existence" (256).

In this example, Kozol is mentioned in a signal phrase, quotation marks surround his exact words, and a page reference appears at the end in a parenthetical citation (before the period, per MLA's style).

LONG QUOTATION

If you want to quote a longer excerpt, set it off in block style with no quotation marks. Introduce the quotation with a sentence or a signal phrase, and include a page reference at the end, *following* the period.

> Although illiteracy creates serious problems in many aspect of a person's life, its effect on mobility is particularly devastating. Jonathan Kozol puts it this way:

Illiterates cannot travel freely. When they attempt to do so, they encounter risks that few of us can dream of. They cannot read traffic signs and, while they often learn to recognize and to decipher symbols, they cannot manage street names which they haven't seen before. The same is true for bus and subway stops. While ingenuity can sometimes help a man or woman to discern directions from familiar landmarks, buildings, cemeteries, churches, and the like, most illiterates are virtually immobilized. (256)

SQUARE BRACKETS AND ELLIPSES

Occasionally you may want to change a quotation to make it fit appropriately into your paper—or to eliminate some details in the original. Use square brackets ([ ]) to show changes and ellipses (. . .) to show deletions. Be careful to use both techniques sparingly and not to distort the meaning of the original source. Here's how a student used brackets and ellipses in the previous quotation.

Although illiteracy creates serious problems in many aspects of a person's life, its effect on mobility is particularly devastating. As Kozol puts it, "Illiterates cannot travel freely. . . . They cannot read traffic signs and . . . cannot manage street names which they haven't seen before. . . . [M]ost illiterates are virtually immobilized" (256).

Writing A Paraphrase

A paraphrase expresses an author's ideas in your own words. To write an acceptable paraphrase, you should use different sentence structures and language than the original, but keep the overall length about the same. Following is an acceptable paraphrase of the original passage on p. 196. Note that it begins by introducing the source and ends with a page reference in a parenthetical citation.

ACCEPTABLE PARAPHRASE

Jonathan Kozol, an expert on literacy, explains that illiterates are unable to travel on their own outside of their immediate neighborhoods—and that it is hazardous for them to do so. People who can't read can't figure out most signs—for traffic, unfamiliar streets, bus stops, and so on. Occasionally they might be able to determine where they're going by looking at a part of the landscape that they know, such as a church or building. But most of the time illiterates are unable to move very far from the area where they live. In a way, the inability to travel symbolizes the lives of illiterate people, who are frozen in their economic and social situation and thus lack hope about the future (256).

UNACCEPTABLE PARAPHRASE

An unacceptable paraphrase results from one or more of the following mistakes: using the author's own words (without putting quotation marks around them); following the author's sentence structure—and just substituting synonyms for some of the author's words; putting your own ideas into the paraphrase. Be on the lookout for such errors in your paraphrase so that you don't plagiarize someone's material inadvertently. Remember, too, that it's fine to include a quotation within a paraphrase. The unacceptable paraphrase below is based on Kozol's original passage on p. 196. As you read this paraphrase, try to pinpoint the mistakes in it.

> Jonathan Kozol, an expert on literacy, says that illiterate people cannot travel very easily. When they try to travel, they run into problems that most of us can't imagine. Illiterate people are unable to decipher traffic signs, unfamiliar street signs, and many other kinds of directional aids. Sometimes a familiar landmark or building may help an illiterate person figure out how to go somewhere, but most illiterate people remain immobilized in their own neighborhoods. They are, in a sense, geographically paralyzed. They can't move in any direction—or see the future. Because of these problems, the United States needs to take immediate steps to eliminate illiteracy in this country (256).

This paraphrase contains plagiarized material: Some words or phrases are identical to the original, and some sentence structures follow the original too closely. In addition, the writer has added her own opinion at the end—something Kozol didn't say in the original paragraph.

Writing a Summary

Unlike a paraphrase, a summary is a brief account of an original piece of writing, such as a paragraph, a chapter, or even an entire book. Always write a summary in your own words, and try to condense the source's most important ideas. Here is a summary of Jonathan Kozol's original paragraph on p. 196.

SUMMARY

> Because illiterates cannot read signs and other directional aids, they cannot travel far from where they live. In much the same sense, they cannot move socially or economically to improve their lives (Kozol 256).

Taking Notes

Quotations, paraphrases, and summaries all rely on notes taken while you're doing your research. It's essential, therefore, to take accurate notes and to recheck each one against the original source. For any source that you plan to use, its basic publication information should already be in your records (see "Staying Organized," pp. 167–68). On a note, then, include just enough data to identify the source (such as the author and a short title), give a page reference, and indicate what kind of note it is (e.g., *quotation or paraphrase*).

Most writers take notes on a computer, but some prefer to use note cards or a notebook. The choice is up to you. For online research, a good approach is simply to download the material you need — along with the pertinent publication data. Once you have a downloaded copy, you can mark it up for your own purposes, and you don't have to worry about introducing an error into your note.

Understanding and Avoiding Plagiarism

Plagiarism is, quite simply, the intentional or unintentional use of others' words, ideas, or visuals as if they were your own. Whether you are a student, a scientist, a historian, or a politician, charges of plagiarism can have serious consequences. At some colleges, for example, students who plagiarize fail not only the assignment but also the entire course; at colleges that have honor codes, students may even be expelled.

There are a variety of online tools that can help you keep organized as you work and generate appropriate citations as you write. Many article databases provided by your college library will allow you to create a permanent folder of sources, which you can easily access later as you write. Some databases will also generate citations for you, in a variety of documentation styles. Ask your librarian if you need help using these features.

Bibliographic management tools like Zotero, EndNote, and Refworks will allow you to save references to articles and other sources as you do your research, take brief notes on your sources, and export formatted citations as you write. You can embed plug-ins for these tools into some word processing programs, which will allow you to connect to your source library as you write, generating your in-text citations as well as your final bibliography or works cited list. The time it takes you to learn to use these tools is well worth the protection they afford from unintentional plagiarism.

See the guidelines on p. 200 for a summary of strategies for avoiding plagiarism.

Guidelines for Avoiding Plagiarism

1. Give yourself enough time to complete your paper without undue stress.

2. Develop a working bibliography that is complete and accurate.

3. Develop a note-taking system that clearly identifies direct quotations and *use* it.

4. Write paraphrases and summaries in your own words.

> Label them appropriately and include full citations.

> If you include an author's language, even if it is only one brief but memorable phrase, use quotation marks.

5. Include citations for all source materials — written works as well as visuals — within the text of your paper *and* in a works cited or reference list.

6. When in doubt, ask your teacher or a tutor in the writing center. If you don't have time to ask, include the citation.

NOTE FOR MULTILINGUAL WRITERS

The concept of plagiarism is central to the modern Western intellectual tradition. It rests on the notion of intellectual property—the belief that language can be "owned" by writers who create original ideas. This belief contradicts the beliefs and practices of some other intellectual traditions. Indeed, in some countries, students are taught that using the words of others without citing them is a sign of respect, and writers in some countries assume that readers will recognize cited passages that are interwoven with the writers' own words. As a student at a North American institution, however, you need to follow Western documentation and citation practices. If you have questions or concerns about how to apply them, ask your instructor or Writing Center tutor.

Using Appropriate Citation Styles

You probably are aware that different disciplines use different documentation styles for integrating source material. MLA (Modern Language Association) style and APA (American Psychological Association) style are two of the most frequently required styles for undergraduates: MLA style is typically used in English and other areas of the humanities, whereas APA style is common in the social sciences. At the end of this chapter, you'll find a sample student essay using MLA documentation style (pp. 205–15). The documentation guidelines at the back of this book provide examples and explanations for MLA rules on pp. 348–80 and for APA rules on pp. 381–402.

Another popular documentation style is *Chicago* style, which is used in some disciplines in the humanities, including history. *Chicago* style is based on the guidelines in *The Chicago Manual of Style*, which is published by the University of Chicago Press. The Council of Science Editors (CSE) also has its own style, one that's commonly used in mathematics and the physical sciences. As you begin your research, it's important to find out which documentation style your instructor expects you to follow. If an instructor doesn't specify, be sure to ask.

Understanding and Asserting Your Rights as a Content Creator

As you have seen, online communities can be useful to you as an academic writer. Participating in these communities can help you at every stage of your research process. Fully participating, however, means putting some content of your own online. As an academic writer in the twenty-first century, you need to think of yourself as a creator, not just a consumer, of information. If you stop and think about it, you'll probably find that you are already contributing some online content, whether it be Facebook status updates, photos, or videos; reviews of a recent online purchase; or bookmarks at a site like Delicious.

Copyright

As a content creator, you have to decide how much control you want to assert over the things you create. Whenever you create something—text, images, sounds, or all three—you own the copyright to the thing you create unless you specifically transfer that copyright to someone else. You do not need to ask for copyright, or to register your work anywhere: As the creator, it is your intellectual property. As you develop your skills as an academic writer, you may be in a position to publish your own research, even as an undergraduate. When that happens, you will usually be asked to sign an agreement turning over some, or all, of your copyright to a publisher.

Copyleft, Creative Commons, and Privacy

Most online services allow you to decide how public you want your contributions to be. If you save bookmarks to Delicious, for example, your bookmarks will be public unless you specifically decide to make them private. If you upload photographs to Facebook, they will also be publicly accessible by default unless you change your privacy settings. There is no right answer to the question "How public should my content be?" but you should always *make* the decision, actively, for any content you post.

One way that you can exert some control over content you do make public is by attaching a Creative Commons (http://creativecommons.org/) license to your work. These licenses allow you to define whether or not other people have permission to use your work, and under what conditions they may use it. There are a variety of licenses to choose from. These licenses do not eliminate your copyright, nor do they legally transfer ownership of your intellectual property to anyone else. They simply grant permission, in advance, to others who may want to use your work.

It is important that you, as an academic writer, understand when and where you need permission to use the work of others. For example, if you want to find some images to use in a presentation that will later be posted on the Web, you need to be very careful about the images you choose. You are, in effect, publishing your presentation by posting it to the Web, and if you use someone else's image without permission, you are violating their rights. One way that you can guarantee that you are legally and ethically using the content produced by others is to look for a creative commons license that defines your right to use the information. By using the Creative Commons searches available at Flickr (http://www.flickr.com/creativecommons/) or at the Creative Commons site, you can determine whether the photographer or artist has given you prior permission to use his or her work. If not, you will have to contact him or her before publishing the work online.

Using Visuals Effectively

As you collect your source materials and consider the permissions you need to use different sources, pay close attention to the visuals you plan to use — tables, photographs, figures, maps, and other kinds of illustrations. Keep in mind that visuals should always be used to support a point you are making, not just to dress up your paper. Remember, too, that you need to cite sources for visuals, as you do for written materials from others.

    Once you have chosen a visual that will enhance your essay, be sure to incorporate it into the written text appropriately. Here are a few tips to follow:

- Refer to the visual in your text, and explain its content if necessary.

- Position the visual close to where you mention it.

- Label the visual, and cite its source.

For more on using visuals in your own projects, see pp. 133–37 and 302–20.

Isn't There More to Say Here on Writing?

This final section might strike you as brief, when there's clearly so much to think about in writing with, and from, research. Yet the brevity of this section illustrates something important about the recursive nature of the writing process, and, indeed, of all rhetorical activities. While there's much to learn about ways of doing research, there's really no "research paper writing process" that's clearly distinct from the many other strategies for writing you've learned about in other chapters: Part I leads you to think about writing and rhetoric broadly; Part II helps you accomplish specific kinds of college writing; and Part III gives you practical strategies for reading and writing effectively. So the short answer to the question posed by the heading above is that there *is* more to say — and you'll find it in the rest of the book.

Sample Research Essay Using MLA Documentation Style

Here is a research essay by Alletta Brenner, a student at the University of Oregon.

✳ bedfordstmartins.com/rewriting
For additional sample research projects using MLA, APA, Chicago, or CSE documentation styles, go to **Re:Writing** *and click on* **ModelDoc Central.**

Brenner 1

Alletta Brenner
Professor Clark
WR 222
11 May 2007

Name, instructor,
course, and date
double-spaced
and aligned at
left margin

Sweatshop U.S.A.: Human Trafficking

in the American Garment-Manufacturing Industry

Title centered

In early 1999, Nguyen Thi Le, a Vietnamese mother of two, signed a four-
year contract to work for a garment factory in American Samoa. The island
is a U.S. territory with a low minimum wage where enterprises seeking to
benefit from cheap labor costs can produce items with a "Made in U.S.A."
label. Dazzled by the opportunity to live in America and earn American
wages, Nguyen eagerly looked forward to her new job, even though she
would have to move an ocean away from her family and take out high-
interest loans to cover the five thousand dollar fee for airfare and work
permits. Despite these hardships, the job seemed to offer her the chance to
earn wages more than twelve times those available at home. If she worked

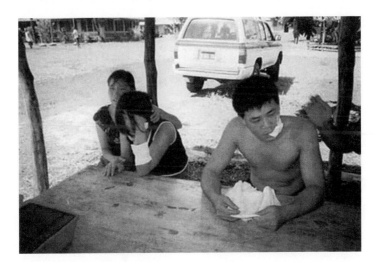

Fig. 1. Two Vietnamese workers after they were beaten at the Daewoosa
factory, American Samoa, 2000. National Labor Committee.

Brenner 2

abroad for just a few years, Nguyen believed, she could dramatically improve the quality of her family's life (Gittelsohn 16).

However, upon arrival, Nguyen found a situation radically different from what she had expected. She and the other Daewoosa workers were paid only a fraction of the wages the garment factory had promised. The factory owner deducted high fees—sometimes half their monthly paychecks—for room and board that the contract had indicated would be "free," and when orders were slow, the owner didn't pay them at all. Kept in a guarded compound, Nguyen and her fellow garments sewers had to work sixteen- to eighteen-hour days under deplorable conditions. When they complained, they were often punished with violence, intimidation, and starvation (see figs. 1 and 2). According to the *New York Times*, when word of these abuses surfaced and the factory finally shut down in 2001, the women were left out on the streets with no means to return home (Greenhouse). Stuck in Samoa, Nguyen learned that back home, loan sharks were hounding her family to repay the debt she had incurred. Though Nguyen eventually received U.S. government aid, which allowed her to move to the American mainland and

Opens with a narrative to engage readers' interest

Fig. 2. Daewoosa woman worker who lost her eye after being brutally beaten on November 28, 2000. National Labor Committee.

Brenner 3

acquire a new job, it will take many years for her to recover from the damage to her personal and financial life (*"Made in the U.S.A."?*).

Human Trafficking: An Overview

Though what happened to Nguyen and the other workers may seem unusual to you, such occurrences are common in the United States today. Every year thousands of persons fall victim to human trafficking: they are transported either against their will or under false pretenses for the purpose of economic or sexual exploitation. In recent years, politicians as well as the media have paid more attention to human trafficking. Movies, newspaper articles, presidential speeches, and United Nations resolutions portray human trafficking as a negative consequence of globalization, capitalism, and immigration. Yet rarely do such accounts analyze the larger questions of how and why human trafficking exists. This essay will address some of these larger questions. In the American garment-manufacturing industry, three forces fuel human trafficking: violations by factory owners, an available immigrant labor force, and poor enforcement of laws. Before analyzing these factors, this discussion will take a closer look at the term *human trafficking* and the scope of its practice.

The official definition of the term *human trafficking* evolved in 2001 as a part of a United Nations treaty on transnational crime. The UN's *Protocol to Prevent, Suppress and Punish Trafficking in Persons* defines human trafficking as the "recruitment, transportation, transfer, harboring or receipt of persons by means of threat or use of force or other means of coercion, abduction, fraud, deception, abuse of power or position of vulnerability . . . for the purpose of exploitation" (Article 3). According to this definition, human trafficking has three components: 1) movement over geographical space, either across or within national borders; 2) the extraction of profits by the exploitation of victims' bodies or skills; and 3) the coercion of victims, which may include a wide range of tactics and forms (Gallagher 986-87).

How, then, does human trafficking work in practice? It can occur both within and across national borders and may involve a single perpetrator

Main topic of human trafficking introduced

States thesis and key questions for essay

Definition and background information provided

Brenner 4

or an organized criminal network of recruiters, transporters, sellers, and buyers. The victims of human trafficking usually want to migrate and seek new employment. Van Impe reports that human traffickers typically pose as employers, employment agencies, or smugglers, offering to help victims by assisting them in entering a country or providing a job (114). Once an individual accepts this help, the trafficker may keep up the charade for quite some time, so when victims eventually realize what has happened, they may feel there is no choice but to submit to the trafficker's demands. After individuals have moved and started working, human traffickers use abusive and illegitimate tactics to force victims to work. They may, for example, threaten victims with physical violence, deportation, or debt bondage, wherein traffickers claim that a victim owes them money for transport or other services and then force him or her to work off the debt (U.S., Dept. of State, *Trafficking* 21).

How widespread is human trafficking in the United States? Both because of its relative wealth, and because it is a destination country for millions of migrant workers every year, the United States is one of the primary destinations for trafficked persons worldwide ("Country Report"). The U.S. Department of State estimates that between fourteen and eighteen thousand persons are trafficked in the United States each year (*Trafficking* 1-4); although the basis for these numbers is unclear, they appear to be consistent with global estimates on human trafficking. Not all victims are foreign-born, but immigrants are particularly vulnerable to such exploitation. In the United States, two-thirds of all human-trafficking cases investigated and brought to court since 2001 have involved foreign-born migrant workers, according to a recent report by the U.S. Department of Justice (75-91).

Signal phrase for source at end of sentence, before in-text citation

Human Trafficking in American Garment Manufacturing

Some of the largest human trafficking cases uncovered to date in the United States have occurred in the garment-manufacturing industry. In addition to the Daewoosa factory in American Samoa, investigators have found large

Brenner 5

sweatshops utilizing human trafficking in California, New York, and the Northern Mariana Islands. Police discovered one of the worst cases in El Monte, California, in 1995, where they found seventy-two Thai immigrants in an apartment complex surrounded by razor wire and armed guards. Trafficked from Thailand, the men and women had endured eighteen-hour workdays, seven days a week for seven years, sewing clothing for some of the nation's best-known clothing companies. Constantly threatened by violence to themselves and their families at home, the victims were forced to live in the same tiny, filthy apartments in which they worked. Grossly underpaid and forced to buy food and other necessities from their captors at inflated prices, the workers were in constant debt. To make matters worse, when police discovered and raided the compound, they arrested the workers for immigration violations and put them in jail. Only when local leaders and nongovernmental organizations spurred public outrage over the case were the workers released on bond and able to begin normal lives in the America they had once envisioned (Ross 143-47).

Violations by factory owners are one reason human trafficking such as that in El Monte occurs. Because most American clothing companies outsource the production of their garments to factories around the world, U.S. factories are under constant pressure to lower costs. Unfortunately, this pressure often translates into poorer wages and working conditions for those who produce clothing in this country and illegal activity on the part of their employers (Bonacich and Appelbaum 137). A common violation is the failure of factory owners to pay workers the legally mandated minimum wage. Unlike most U.S. workers, garment workers earn a piece-rate wage rather than an hourly wage. Because the amount of available work and the going rate for items sewed constantly fluctuates, the amount workers earn often reflects downward pressure. Employers, however, are supposed to make up the difference so that workers still make the minimum wage. When employers fail to do so or attempt to comply with the law by forcing workers to speed up production, the result is substandard pay. Some workers in the

First subtopic: violations by factory owners

Brenner 6

American garment-manufacturing industry earn less than four dollars an hour, and those who work from home make even less, sometimes as little as two dollars per hour.

Studies of garment manufacturers throughout the United States have found that violations of wage, hours, and safety laws are the rule, not the exception. For example, one study of textile-manufacturing operations in the New York City area found that seventy-five percent of them were operating in the informal sector—not legally licensed or monitored—with substandard wages and working conditions (*"Treated Like Slaves"* 5). A different study described in *Behind the Label* found that sixty-one percent of garment manufacturers in Los Angeles were violating wage and hours regulations, underpaying their workers by an estimated seventy-three million dollars every year. Yet another study found that in more than half of firms inspected, workers were in danger of serious injury or death as a result of health and safety law violations (Bonacich and Appelbaum 3).

Second subtopic: available immigrant labor force

Violations by factory owners, however, are only one part of the picture in the garment industry. Another factor is the availability of an immigrant labor force. Factories that produce clothing in the United States and its territories are heavily dependant upon immigrants to meet their labor needs. For example, Bonacich and Appelbaum report that in Los Angeles, which has the highest concentration of garment manufacturers in the nation, eighty-one percent of workers are Asian and Latino immigrants (171-75). In American territories, immigrant labor is even more prevalent. In Saipan, the U.S. territory with the largest number of garment factories, almost all garment workers are foreign-born. Because the indigenous populations of many territories are so small, most garment manufacturers could not survive without imported labor. For this reason, territories do not operate under the same immigration laws as the American mainland, where relatively few visas are available to low-skilled workers. Consequently, employers in U.S. territories are able to legally recruit and import thousands of employees from Asia and South America (Parks 19-22).

Brenner 7

For a number of reasons, the use of a predominantly immigrant workforce makes it easier for unscrupulous manufacturers to coerce and exploit workers. First, immigrant workers facing economic hardships often have no choice but to take risks and accept poor treatment and pay. A book published by Human Rights Watch quotes one Guatemalan woman who stayed with her abusive employers for many years:

> I am the single mother of two daughters. The salary there [in Guatemala] is not sufficient for their studies, their food, their clothes. I want them to get ahead in life. . . . Sometimes one is pressured by the economic situation. It's terrible what one suffers. . . . Sometimes I ask myself why I put up with so much. It's for this, for my mother and my daughters. (Pier 9-10)

A second reason is that those who enter the country illegally fear deportation. Indeed, as Lelio points out, because of their status, illegal immigrants often work in the informal sector "under the table" in order to avoid authorities, which makes it much easier for traffickers to exploit them (68-69). These jobs may be within individual homes, or at businesses owned by other immigrants within tightly knit ethnic communities. The strong fear of deportation that permeates many such communities enables factory owners to effectively enforce a code of silence on their employees, legal and illegal immigrants alike (Bonacich and Appelbaum 144-47).

A third reason is that many immigrants lack English language skills and knowledge of American laws and culture. Thus they find it difficult to do anything about the situation they're in.

Even though most immigrant workers at garment factories in American territories are there legally, they are just as vulnerable to human trafficking. Like immigrant workers in the mainland United States, they are often under a great deal of pressure to support families back at home. Because most immigrant workers in the territories take out high-interest loans simply to get

Brenner 8

their jobs, they are even more likely to accept deplorable working conditions than are illegal immigrants on the mainland. When employers fail to pay their workers appropriately (or sometimes at all), they can prevent workers from paying off their debts and thereby keep them as virtual prisoners. Indeed, human rights organizations have reported that thousands of garment workers live in severe debt bondage throughout American territories in the Pacific (Clarren 35-36).

The incidence of human trafficking gets further impetus from the "guest worker" immigration laws. Because such workers' visas depend on their employment with a particular firm, leaving the employer with whom they are contracted would break the terms of their visa. Ironically, this places legal guest workers in a more precarious position than those who immigrate illegally, for guest workers who violate the terms of their visas face deportation. Though some workers do leave and turn to prostitution or other forms of black market work to survive, the fear of being sent back home is a constant one. As a result, most stay with their abusive employers, hoping to someday pay off their debts and leave (Clarren 38-41).

Third subtopic: poor enforcement of laws

A final factor that contributes to human trafficking in the garment industry is that where protective labor laws and standards do exist, their enforcement tends to be lax (Branigin 21-28). Despite the rampant violation of labor and safety laws throughout the industry, most garment manufacturers are able to avoid legal repercussions. Even when human-trafficking cases in the garment industry do occur, they tend to run much longer than other trafficking cases, averaging over six years in duration (U.S., Dept. of State, *Matrix* 6-9). This occurs for several reasons. First of all, as noted previously, many garment factories operate illegally. Because the Department of Labor only investigates such operations when someone makes an official complaint, traffickers who can control their victims are able to avoid detection. This is generally not a difficult task because victims of trafficking often lack the skills and knowledge required to take such action.

Brenner 9

Second, inspectors from the Department of Labor and Occupational Safety and Health Administration rarely visit those factories that do operate legally. Even when workers complain, it can take up to a year for the government to open a case and make inspections. Moreover, when an investigation finally begins, owners often have advance warning, allowing them to conceal violations before the inspectors arrive. Some factory owners under investigation have been known to close up shop and disappear, leaving their employees out on the streets with months of back pay owed to them. These tendencies are especially prevalent in U.S. territories because of the geographic and bureaucratic distance between the islands and the governmental bodies that are supposed to regulate them. With the enforcement of most laws left up to local officials and agencies, many of whom stand to profit from arrangements with factory owners, human traffickers find it easy to avoid government interference. The risk for such activity is thus relatively low (Ross 210-11).

Conclusion

In 2001, the same year that Nguyen's case hit the American media, President Bush proclaimed that the United States has a special duty to fight against "the trade in human misery" that human trafficking represents today. Since then, the United States has created a wide range of anti-trafficking laws and measures, but little has changed in the lives of human-trafficking victims. Although the owner of the Daewoosa factory was eventually convicted of enslaving more than 250 workers in his factory, other garment manufacturers continue to operate much as they did a decade ago. Some high-profile American clothing companies, such as the Gap, have promised to stop contracting with factories that violate labor laws; however, the essential set-up of the industry remains fully intact. Until these problems are directly addressed, human trafficking will continue to be a blemish on the American dream and, as President Bush recognized in a 2004 speech, "a shame to our country."

Conclusion restates the problem

Brenner 10

Works Cited

Bonacich, Edna, and Richard Appelbaum. *Behind the Label: Inequality in the Los Angeles Apparel Industry*. Berkeley: U of California P, 2000. Print.

Branigin, William. "A Life of Exhaustion, Beating and Isolation." *Washington Post* 5 Jan. 1999: A6. Print.

Bush, George W. National Training Conference on Combating Human Trafficking. Tampa Marriott Waterside Hotel, Tampa, FL. 16 July 2004. Address.

Clarren, Rebecca. "Paradise Lost." *Ms.* Spring 2006: 35-41. Print.

"Country Report—The United States." *The Protection Project.* The Protection Project, 2002. Web. 28 Apr. 2007.

Gallagher, Anne. "Human Rights and the New UN Protocols on Trafficking and Migrant Smuggling: A Preliminary Analysis." *Human Rights Quarterly* 23 (2001): 986–87. Print.

Gittelsohn, John. "U.S. Sends Strong Message to Those Who Traffic in Human Lives." *Global Issues: Responses to Human Trafficking* 8.2 (2003): 14-17. Web. 2 Apr. 2007.

Greenhouse, Steven. "Beatings and Other Abuses Cited at Samoan Apparel Plant That Supplied U.S. Retailers." *New York Times* 6 Feb. 2001: A14. Print.

Lelio, Marmora. *International Migration Policies and Programmes.* Geneva: Intl. Organization for Migration, 1999. Print.

"Made in the U.S.A."? Clothing for J.C. Penney, Sears and Target Made by Women Held under Conditions of Indentured Servitude at the Daewoosa Factory in American Samoa. New York: Natl. Labor Committee, 2001. Web. 2 Apr. 2007.

National Labor Committee. "Photos Related to Daewoosa in American Samoa." National Labor Committee, n.d. Web. 30 Apr. 2007.

Parks, Virginia. *The Geography of Immigrant Labor Markets: Space, Networks, and Gender.* New York: LFB Scholarly Publishing, 2005. Print.

Pier, Carol. *Hidden in the Home: Abuse of Domestic Workers with Special Visas in the United States.* New York: Human Rights Watch, 2001. Print.

Ross, Andrew, ed. *No Sweat: Fashion, Free Trade and the Rights of Garment Workers.* New York: Verso, 1997. Print.

"Treated Like Slaves": Donna Karan, Inc., Violates Women Workers' Human Rights. New York: Center for Economic and Social Rights, 1999. Print.

Heading centered

First line of each entry flush left, subsequent lines indented

List doublespaced throughout

Photographs obtained from Web site

Brenner 11

United Nations. Office on Drugs and Crime. *Protocol to Prevent, Suppress and Punish Trafficking in Persons, Especially Women and Children, Supplementing the United Nations Convention against Transnational Organized Crime.* New York: United Nations, 2000. Print.

United States. Dept. of Justice. *Report on Activities to Combat Human Trafficking: Fiscal Years 2001-2005.* DOJ, 2006. Web. 24 Apr. 2007.

———. Dept. of State. *Matrix of Some of the Major Trafficking Cases in the United States of the Last Eight Years.* DOS, May 2003. Web. 4 May 2007.

———. *Trafficking in Persons Report.* DOS, June 2004. Web. 4 May 2007.

Van Impe, Kristof. "People for Sale: The Need for a Multidisciplinary Approach toward Human Trafficking." *International Migration* 1 (2000): 114. Print.

Three works from same government; hyphens substituted for name

||||||||||||||||||||||||||||||||||||||||||||||||||||||||||||||||||||||||||||||||||||||||

FOR THOUGHT, DISCUSSION, AND WRITING

1. After reviewing this chapter's discussion of paraphrasing and summarizing, select one of the sample essays that appear in Chapter 7, "Writing in the Disciplines: Making Choices as You Write." Choose a paragraph from the essay—one that strikes you as particularly interesting or informative. After reading this paragraph carefully, first write a paraphrase of it, and then summarize the same passage. Finally, write a paragraph explaining why your paraphrase and summary of this passage are effective.

2. Identify an important journal for scholars in your major. You will probably have to ask someone (a major advisor, a professor, or a librarian) to recommend a journal that is important and useful in your field. If you do not have a major yet, ask the person who teaches your favorite class to recommend a journal of interest to scholars in that field.

   Now, browse through a copy of that journal, taking note of the articles and the topics they cover. As you browse, ask yourself the following:

   ■ How did you gain access to the journal? You might have found the journal online, if access is open. More likely, you needed to access the journal via your library. Think about access as an issue: How easy or difficult is it for people to use the content in this journal? What would the advantages and disadvantages be of changing its level of accessibility?

◼ What do the articles tell you about how scholars in your field write? Do the articles have common characteristics (abstracts, section headings, citation styles)? Do the authors write in first person or third? Do they place their arguments into a context for you? What are some things they seem to assume you, as the reader, already know?

Write a paragraph reflecting on what you've learned.

3. Go to an academic social bookmarking Web site like CiteULike (http://citeulike.org) and do a simple search on a topic you recently discussed in one of your courses. The search results will represent articles or other sources that other scholars have saved to the site. Look at the tags these people used to identify the articles (if you are using CiteULike, there is a small "tags" link on the top of the results page), and look through at the abstracts and titles of the articles.

After doing this research, write out some of your thoughts about the social bookmarking process. Which concepts are tagged? How much variety did you find in the tags—that is, how many different terms do people use to refer to the same set of concepts? What does an examination of tagging tell you about how people in this field do research?

4. Go to ScienceBlogs (http://scienceblogs.com) or ResearchBlogging (http://researchblogging.org). Find a post about an article written by a scholar in your major discipline or a post about an article on a topic discussed in one of your classes. Read the blog post and any responses to it. Take note of important issues or any points of controversy, and try to determine where this scholarly discussion fits within the larger field.

Now, find and read the original article. (If the article is not available for free online—that is, if the link provided takes you to a fee-based site—search for the article through your library instead.) Compare the discussion on the blog about the article to the article itself. What information is available in both places? What information is available only in the post, or only in the article? How might each source be useful in an academic research process?

CHAPTER 7

Writing in the Disciplines: Making Choices as You Write

Part I of *The Academic Writer* began by asking this question: What does it mean to be a writer in the twenty-first century? Despite the increasing prevalence and power of visual and multimedia texts, writing does indeed still matter. In fact, those with access to computer and online technologies are writing more than ever before.

How can you negotiate the opportunities and challenges of twenty-first century communication? You can draw upon your understanding of the writing process and of the rhetorical situation. As Chapter 1 explains, when you analyze your rhetorical situation, you consider each of the four elements of rhetoric: writer, reader, text, and medium. In so doing, you approach writing as a problem-solving activity, with no one-size-fits-all solution. In each new situation, you draw on previous knowledge and experience and consider the needs and interests of your audience. You also address other aspects of your situation, such as the nature of the medium you're working in and the extent to which genres (or other elements of your situation) might limit or enable your work.

thinking rhetorically

Part II of *The Academic Writer* builds upon the rhetorical approach to writing conveyed in Part I. It applies this approach to the essential intellectual skills needed in college writing: the ability to analyze texts and contexts, make and support claims, and conduct research. One of the challenges you face as an academic writer is learning how to apply these skills in a wide range of courses—from philosophy to chemistry to psychology. You can use your knowledge of rhetoric and of the writing process to negotiate the demands of academic writing in a broad variety of disciplines. This chapter will help you do so, and it will introduce you to the expectations and conventions of these disciplines.

Meeting these expectations can be a significant challenge—especially when you take courses outside of your major. A student majoring in biology who is used to scientific writing may be unsure how to proceed when she has to write an essay interpreting a poem for her Introduction to Poetry class. By thinking rhetorically about the nature and purpose of writing in the humanities, this student can gain confidence, skill, and flexibility as a writer — attributes that will prove very useful when she graduates and begins a career. By learning how writing works in different fields, you can become a successful academic writer in *all* of the courses you take in college.

Thinking Rhetorically about Writing in the Disciplines

thinking
rhetorically

The conventions of academic writing in different disciplines have histories worth noting. For example, historians generally attribute the development of scientific writing to the rise of humanism and the scientific method during the Renaissance. Scientists such as Francis Bacon (1561–1626) emphasized the importance of reporting the results of experiments in clear and precise language so that experiments could be replicated. When in 1660 a group of scientists in Great Britain founded the Royal Society (a body that still exists), they worked to standardize methods for reporting scientific results. Practitioners refined these textual conventions over time, but, as David Porush notes in *A Short Guide to Writing about Science*, "the basic outline of the scientific report has changed little in over a century."[1] There is no need for it to change because the scientific report still meets the day-to-day needs of working scientists: It encourages effective and efficient communication among scientists.

Textual conventions in the humanities, too, have a history. One particularly important impetus for those conventions was the desire to interpret religious texts, which has been a strong tradition in most of the world's major religions: Christians have long studied the Bible; Muslims, the Koran; and Jews, the Torah. Over time, interpretive practices for reading religious texts were applied to secular works as well. This tradition of textual interpretation is particularly important to such disciplines in the humanities as literature, philosophy, religious studies, and rhetoric, but it has influenced such other areas as history, music, and art. In diverse ways, all of these disciplines explore what it means to be human, in part through analyzing or documenting human texts and experiences.

Whereas scientists work to achieve objective and reliable results that others can replicate, those in the humanities often study questions for which there is no definitive answer. What constitutes a just war? How can we best interpret Shakespeare's *The Tempest* or best understand the concept of free will? What were the most important causes of the Black Plague? Who is the better painter — Leonardo da Vinci or Michelangelo? Scholars in the humanities take it for granted that there are multiple ways to approach any topic.

---

[1]David Porush, *A Short Guide to Writing about Science* (New York: Harper, 1995), 8.

Though they hope that their writing will lead to a broader understanding of their subject, they don't expect that their research will result in the kind of knowledge generated by the scientific method. Indeed, in the humanities, originality is valued over replicability. Rather than relying on predetermined formats as scientific researchers do, scholars in the humanities structure their writing according to the nature and content of their analysis.

This brief discussion of the development of textual conventions in the humanities and sciences emphasizes that rather than being arbitrary forms to be filled in, the textual conventions that characterize different academic disciplines are deeply grounded in their history, nature, and goals. It is important to remember, however, that even though disciplines in these two broad areas share a number of general assumptions and practices, variations do exist. Moreover, disciplines in the social sciences, such as psychology, sociology, economics, anthropology, communication, and political science, include elements of both the sciences and the humanities, as does much writing in business.

As a college student, you can better understand your teachers' expectations as you move from, say, a chemistry class to a course in art appreciation by thinking rhetorically about the subject matter, methodology, and goals of the disciplines. The questions on p. 220 can guide this analysis.

* bedfordstmartins.com/rewriting

  For a collection of dozens of sample student projects written for courses across the disciplines, go to **Re:Writing** *and then click on* **ModelDoc Central**.

||||||||||||||||||||||||||||||||||||||||||||||||||||||||||||||||||||||||||||||||||||||

FOR EXPLORATION

Take five minutes to write freely about your experience of creating texts in various disciplines. Are you more confident writing for some disciplines than others? Why? What questions seem most important to you as you anticipate writing in courses across the curriculum?

FOR COLLABORATION

Bring your response to the previous Exploration to class, and share it with a group of students. After each person has summarized his or her ideas, spend a few minutes noting shared experiences and questions. Be prepared to report your results to the class.

||||||||||||||||||||||||||||||||||||||||||||||||||||||||||||||||||||||||||||||||||||||

Writing in the Humanities

In a general sense, those studying the humanities are attempting to determine what something means or how it can best be understood or evaluated. For this reason, textual interpretation is central to the humanities. Depending

Questions for Analyzing Writing in the Disciplines*

1. How would you characterize the overall style of writing in this discipline?

> somewhat formal?

> very formal?

2. What documentation style (such as MLA, APA, CSE, or *Chicago*) is used?

3. What constitutes appropriate and valid evidence in this discipline?

4. What role do quantitative and qualitative data play in this discipline?

> *Quantitative data include items that can be measured; qualitative data include items that can be systematically observed.*

5. What role does textual interpretation or other forms of interpretation (such as the interpretation of music or art) play in this discipline?

6. How does the writing use visual elements and formatting?

> Does it typically incorporate images, graphs, tables, charts, and maps?

> What role do headings and other elements of formatting play?

7. What types of texts do professionals in this discipline typically write?

8. What types of texts do students in this discipline typically write?

*In order to answer these questions, you'll need to read representative examples of writing from each field; your teacher or your own coursework can provide such examples, or you can look at samples in Bedford/St. Martin's Model Documents gallery (www.bedfordstmartins.com/modeldocs). You may also wish to interview instructors from each field.

upon their discipline, scholars in the humanities may read the same or similar texts for different analytical and interpretive purposes. An art critic may analyze paintings by the American folk artist Grandma Moses (1860–1961) to study her use of brush strokes and color, while a historian might study her work to learn more about life in rural America in the mid-twentieth century.

Given the importance that textual interpretation plays in the humanities, strong reading skills are essential. Chapter 8 provides strategies to strengthen your general critical reading skills (which will improve your performance in all the disciplines, not just the humanities).

Sample Student Essays in the Humanities

Here are two essays written by students in introductory humanities courses. The first one was written for an introductory philosophy class titled Great Ideas in Philosophy. The authors, Julie Baird and Stevon Roberts, were responding to the following questions on Descartes' *Meditations on First Philosophy*: *(1) What is Descartes' method of doubt, and how does he use it? (2) What kind of being is Descartes, and how does he establish his conclusion?* Note that this essay uses MLA documentation style, required for this course. (For details on this style, see the MLA Documentation Guidelines section at the back of this book.)

Julie and Stevon's teacher praised their writing, noting that they did an excellent job of addressing the questions he posed. In analyzing their rhetorical situation, Stevon and Julie realized that a careful reading of Descartes' work was essential, noting that:

> Our professor has emphasized the importance of our reading primary works in philosophy, rather than secondary textbooks. We realized that we needed to read Descartes' writing almost in the way we'd read a poem, looking carefully at what he says and doesn't say. Our assignment had a page limit, and our professor wanted us to focus more on analysis than on summary, so we picked only a few of the most important passages and gave a lot of attention to Descartes' style and meaning. In terms of our own writing, we focused mainly on being clear and concise. ✳

In keeping with conventions in the humanities, their essay employs minimal formatting: They use a clear, readable font, one-inch margins, and black type, and they double-space between lines.

thinking rhetorically

See Questions for Analyzing Your Rhetorical Situation, pp. 41–42. ✳

Baird and Roberts 1

Julie Baird and Stevon Roberts

Professor Campbell

PHL 150

24 April 2007

Name, instructor, course number, and date on left margin, double-spaced

I *Think* I Am, I *Think* I Am

Title centered

Introductory paragraph gives brief answer to assignment's questions

In *Meditations on First Philosophy,* Descartes introduces to us the concepts of being and existence. Through his documented rationale, we are able to share some conclusions about the kind of being that Descartes establishes that he is. In the first meditation, he proposes doubt as a key to decoding the mystery of truth. In his second meditation, he refutes doubt for the existence of thought and therefore concludes that he himself must exist in some form or other. It is then that he begins to explore the nature of that form, consequently giving us the opportunity to follow his logic and reach the same conclusion.

Addresses method of doubt—first part of assignment

Descartes first wets his philosophical feet (and ours) by creating a body of "knowledge" based on doubt. It is interesting to note that this knowledge is really derived from lack of knowledge since Descartes begins his meditations by discounting all of his previous knowledge as potentially untrue. Descartes claims, "Whatever I have up till now accepted as most true, I have acquired from either the senses or through the senses. But from time to time I have found that the senses deceive, and it is prudent never to trust completely those who have deceived us even once" (12). This suggests that Descartes is already preparing to divorce physical existence from a theoretical existence that is characterized by a thinking mind. But he's not certain of his existence at all up to this point.

Double-spaced throughout

Brief quotation supports answer to second part of assignment

In the second meditation, Descartes explores the possibility that there might exist a deceptive entity whose sole purpose is to deceive his senses. Descartes asserts that even if this were the case, the existence of the demon deceiving him necessarily requires his own existence. He says, "I too undoubtedly exist, if he is deceiving me; and let him deceive me as much as he can, he will never bring about that I am nothing so long as I think I am something" (17). This lays the foundation for Descartes' assertion that he is

Baird and Roberts 2

a thinking being because he persuades himself of, if nothing else, this one thing.

However, Descartes still believes he lacks a sufficient understanding of his existence. He uses his prior meditation on doubt to reason that he is not merely a human body or thin vapor. Instead, he is "a thing that thinks. . . . A thing that doubts, understands, affirms, denies, is willing, is unwilling, and also imagines and has sensory perceptions" (19). Descartes illustrates these qualities by explaining to us the physical characteristics of wax. Because these physical properties can be altered by exposure to different physical environments, he calls them "accidental" properties. But the wax remains. Even though characteristics that can be perceived by the senses are all altered, the essence of the wax is unchanged. He feels that he is just like the wax in that he has intrinsic properties that are not influenced by external forces: His core being (like that of the wax) remains, despite potentially false sensory perceptions.

In the sixth and final meditation, Descartes further separates the mind from the body and ultimately decides that he is a thinking being who exists apart from the corporeal but is still intimately tied with the physical body. He says that material things are capable of existing (in theory) since they can be perceived clearly and distinctly. Descartes illustrates this concept with mathematics. He distinguishes between a pentagon, which can be both imagined and understood in "the mind's eye," and a chiliagon (a polygon with 1,000 sides), which might be understood but not imagined. He uses this comparison to illustrate the difference between the mind and the imaginative effort, suggesting that corporeal math exists in our minds as physical law, while imagination predicates a superreal soul apart from the mind, which is where Descartes believes he exists. His final step is to completely divorce this soul from his body in saying he is "distinct from [his] body and can exist without it" (54).

In following Descartes' progression of logic, it is easy to arrive at the conclusion about what kind of being Descartes believes he is. Descartes first recognizes the limitations of his physical being and establishes a body of knowledge based on empirical evidence. In so doing, he offers a caveat:

Ellipses in quotation indicate omission

Quotation and examples answer question, What kind of being is Descartes?

Comparison example lays out Descartes' logic

Conclusion summarizes Descartes' steps, brings together answers to both parts of assignment

Baird and Roberts 3

There might exist a being whose purpose is to deceive his senses, in which case his own independent existence is unquestionably affirmed. With this confidence in his existence, he begins to explore the nature of that existence, explaining that any physical properties are merely "accidental" and that his true being exists apart from the physical world—but not completely. His core being (or soul) is still intimately tied with the physical body even though he can distinguish between them. Finally, Descartes arrives at the conclusion that he is a real, thinking being who exists apart from the entity that he had perceived via sensory experience.

Work Cited

Descartes, Rene. *Meditations on First Philosophy: With Selections from the Objections and Replies.* Trans. and ed. John Cottingham. Cambridge: Cambridge UP, 1996. Print.

Note: In an actual MLA-style paper, Works Cited entries start on a new page.

Here is another essay, written for an in-class exam in an American history course. The author, Elizabeth Ridlington, was responding to the following question: *During his presidency, did Lincoln primarily respond to public opinion, or did he shape public opinion more than he responded to it?* In analyzing her rhetorical situation, Elizabeth commented that:

thinking
rhetorically

My teacher phrased this as an either/or question, inviting a strong and clear position statement at the outset. Because this is a history class, I knew that I needed to provide evidence from primary documents we'd read, offering the kind of specific and concrete details that historians value. I also needed to incorporate material from the lectures. In thinking about how to present information, I knew it was important not just to provide evidence but also to explain the logic behind my choice of details. Doing this makes for a more coherent essay in which every paragraph supports my initial thesis statement. Finally, looking at events and actions from multiple perspectives is very important for historians, so I explained Lincoln's decisions in a variety of circumstances essentially as a series of mini case studies.

Elizabeth Ridlington

Lincoln's Presidency and Public Opinion

This essay argues that Lincoln shaped public opinion more than he responded to it and examines the issues of military recruitment, Northern war goals, and emancipation as examples of Lincoln's interaction with public opinion.

Introduction frames response, lists supporting points

At the start of the war, Lincoln needed men for the military. Because of this, he could hardly ignore public opinion. But even as he responded in various ways to public opinion, he did not significantly modify his policy goals. Lincoln's first call for seventy-five thousand soldiers was filled through militias that were under state rather than federal control. As the war progressed, the federal government took more control of military recruitment. The government set quotas for each state and permitted the enlistment of African American soldiers via the Militia Act. Kentucky, a slave state, protested, and Lincoln waived the requirement that blacks be enlisted so long as Kentucky still filled its quota. In so doing, Lincoln responded to public opinion without changing his policy goal. Another example of this strategy occurred when the first federal draft produced riots in New York City. When the riots occurred, Lincoln relented temporarily and waited for the unrest to quiet down. Then he reinstated the federal draft. Again, Lincoln responded to a volatile situation and even temporarily withdrew the federal draft. But he ultimately reinstated the draft.

Multiple examples for first supporting point

Lincoln's efforts to shape public opinion in the North in favor of the war provide another example of his proactive stance. Whenever he discussed the war, Lincoln equated it with freedom and democracy. Northerners linked democracy with their personal freedom and daily well-being, and therefore Lincoln's linkage of the Union with democracy fostered Northern support for the war even when the conflict was bloody and Northern victory was anything but guaranteed. After the emancipation, Lincoln continued his effort to influence public opinion by connecting the abolition of slavery with democracy. The image of a "new birth of freedom" that Lincoln painted in his Gettysburg Address was part of this effort to overcome Northern racism and a reluctance to fight for the freedom of blacks.

Second supporting point

The process that led to the emancipation provides perhaps the clearest example of Lincoln's determination to shape public opinion rather than simply respond to it. Lincoln's views on slavery were more progressive than those of many of his contemporaries. These views caused him personally to wish to abolish slavery. At the same time, Lincoln knew that winning the war was his highest priority. Consequently, retaining the border states early in the war was more important to Lincoln than emancipation, and for this reason he revoked Freemont's proclamation in the summer of 1861. In explaining this decision privately to Freemont, Lincoln admitted that he was concerned about public opinion in Kentucky since it would determine whether Kentucky stayed with the Union. However, in a letter that Lincoln knew might be made public, Lincoln denied that he had reacted to Kentucky's pressure and claimed that emancipation was not among his powers—a clear effort to gain public approval. Even when others such as Frederick Douglass (in a September 1861 speech) demanded emancipation, Lincoln did not change his policy. Not until July 1862 did Lincoln draft the preliminary emancipation proclamation. Rather than releasing it then, at the advice of his cabinet he waited for a time when it would have more positive impact on public opinion.

Lincoln realized that the timing of the Emancipation Proclamation was crucial. While he was waiting for an opportune time to release the document, Horace Greeley published his "Prayer of Twenty Million," calling on Lincoln to abolish slavery. Lincoln's response, a letter for publication, emphasized the importance of the Union and the secondary importance of the status of slavery. By taking this position, Lincoln hoped to shape public opinion. He wanted Northerners to believe that he saw the Union cause as foremost, so that the release of the proclamation would create as few racial concerns as possible. The Emancipation Proclamation was released on January 1, 1863. Once it was released, Lincoln stood by it despite strong public opposition. In 1864, when Democrats called for an armistice with the South, Lincoln stood by his decision to abolish slavery. He defended his position on military grounds, hoping voters would approve in the 1864 election.

As the examples I have just discussed indicate, Lincoln could not ignore public opinion, and at times he had to respond to it. But when Lincoln did so, this was always part of a larger effort to shape public opinion and to ensure Union victory.

Margin annotations:

Several primary sources cited to support third point

Final section cites primary sources, gives dates

Conclusion restates thesis

Instructor's Notes

The Academic Writer

Instructor's Notes

The Academic Writer

Second Edition

Lisa Ede

Prepared by

Sara Jameson
Oregon State University

and

Lisa Ede
Oregon State University

BEDFORD/ST. MARTIN'S
Boston ✦ New York

Copyright © 2011, 2009 by Bedford/St. Martin's

All rights reserved.
Instructors who have adopted *The Academic Writer: A Brief Guide,* Second
Edition, as a textbook for a course are authorized to duplicate portions of
this manual for their students.

Manufactured in the United States of America.

5 4 3 2 1 0
f e d c b a

For information, write: Bedford/St. Martin's, 75 Arlington Street, Boston,
MA 02116   (617-399-4000)

ISBN: 978-0-312-63090-4

CONTENTS

SECTION 1: HOW TO USE THESE INSTRUCTOR'S NOTES

These Instructor's Notes are designed to complement and support *The Academic Writer*. In writing these notes, we were particularly aware of the needs of beginning teachers of writing—teachers who bring many strengths to the classroom but who lack extensive pedagogical experience and who may be just becoming acquainted with research in composition studies. We hope to provide concrete suggestions that will enable beginning teachers to teach confidently and effectively—to embark successfully on the work in progress that teaching always comprises. In addition, we hope to provide some helpful and stimulating resources and suggestions for experienced teachers of writing who may already know *The Academic Writer*.

This manual is divided into the following seven sections:

- **Section 1: How to Use These Instructor's Notes** provides an overview of this resource, with advice for using it specially geared for new instructors, graduate teaching assistants, and writing program administrators. In addition, this section has a table showing how *The Academic Writer* supports the latest WPA Outcomes for student writing.

- **Section 2: Overview of *The Academic Writer*, Second Edition,** previews the text's distinctive features, including its focus on rhetorical situation, writing as design, twenty-first-century literacies, and a fresh and original look at information literacy and research.

- **Section 3: Sample Course Plans** suggests ways to use *The Academic Writer* for quarter and semester schedules, both with and without a supplemental reader. In addition to suggesting ways for using the chapters in their numerical order, Section 3 also offers suggestions for rearranging the chapters to meet other program goals and provides a fully developed syllabus showing how *The Academic Writer* can support courses in advanced composition.

- **Section 4: Meeting Classroom Challenges** includes ideas for fostering collaboration, supporting multilingual writers, assigning portfolios, managing the paper load, responding to students, helping students with time management, evaluating your own teaching, and integrating service learning.

- **Section 5: Teaching Key Concepts** offers practical advice for addressing in class some of the key concepts covered by *The Academic Writer*, including academic writing, information literacy and research, research writing, online writing, visual rhetoric, and writing as design. Also included is a section of suggested readings for these concepts.

- **Section 6: Chapter-by-Chapter Suggestions for Teaching from *The Academic Writer*** provides specific suggestions for teaching the concepts and activities presented in each chapter of *The Academic Writer*. Beginning instructors, in particular, should find this section helpful in preparing for class discussions and activities and in responding to students' writing.

• **Section 7: Sample Student Essays** presents nine complete samples of student writing that emerged from assignments in *The Academic Writer.*

Note that the entire contents of this manual may be downloaded from *The Academic Writer*'s catalog page at bedfordstmartins.com/catalog/academicwriter.

If you have suggestions about how this manual could be improved, please write to us in care of Bedford/St. Martin's, 33 Irving Place, 10th Floor, New York, NY 10003.

Note for New Instructors and Graduate Teaching Assistants

If you are a new teacher—especially if you are a TA who just received your BA a few months ago—you might feel underprepared to teach elements of rhetoric, composition, argument, and academic writing to students who may be only a few years younger than you are—or, for that matter, to some who may be quite a bit older. This sense of being underprepared can be especially acute if you have not taken a composition course yourself.

These Instructor's Notes are designed to help you move smoothly into your first terms or semesters of teaching composition with *The Academic Writer.* Of course, a great deal of the support you'll need is built into the text itself: *The Academic Writer*'s clear presentation of the elements of academic writing will extend your intuitive knowledge of academic writing and writing processes, and the Instructor's Notes will give you practical strategies for applying it.

It will help to read all of *The Academic Writer* along with at least Sections 2 and 5 of these Notes before the term or semester starts to orient yourself to the textbook's organization and its key concepts, and then review relevant portions of Section 4 on classroom challenges and Section 6 for chapter-by-chapter ideas to prepare for each class. Ultimately, you will want to be so familiar with the book that you can direct students' attention in class as needed. Rereading the relevant portions of the Instructor's Notes before each class will give you ideas for discussion and activities.

As a new teacher, you may be using syllabi and standard assignments provided by your writing program. If this is the case, ask how experienced instructors have found it best to work with them in conjunction with *The Academic Writer.* If your program does not provide standard syllabi and assignments, you can modify the sample course plans in Section 3 and assignments from these Notes to suit your philosophy and/or that of your program. For some programs, working through *The Academic Writer* chapters from start to finish is viable; for others, of course, creative reorganization will be necessary. (See pp. 28–30 for tips on using *The Academic Writer* chapters out of numerical sequence.)

The following pointers are meant to give you some idea of how different chapters in *The Academic Writer* address common classroom challenges.

The number and type of writing assignments in first-year writing programs varies quite a bit. The following broad categories of writing assignment occur in many programs, however, and are particularly well supported by *The Academic Writer*:

- A **rhetorical analysis** of one or more written or visual texts requires close reading, and allows students to advance their critical thinking, which will not only help them in other classes but also in reconsidering their own writing. See the student case study by Daniel Stiepleman in *The Academic Writer*, Chapter 5, pp. 137–53, for a step-by-step model of this kind of work. Chapters 1–5 in *The Academic Writer* and the critical reviews and analyses in the sample student essays at the end of these Notes (pp. 127–53) will be especially helpful for you as you plan an assignment to analyze a text.
- Among the other kinds of essays you will likely assign is a **research-based argument**. Students often think that academic writing consists of dry, scientific facts and a stiff tone; to head off this erroneous impression, you might refer them early on to "An Effective Academic Essay Is . . . " (p. 58). For the researched assignment, you can draw heavily on Chapters 4–7 of *The Academic Writer*. You can also look at the student sample by Todd Carpenter included in these notes on pp. 132–34.

For programs that emphasize **writing in the disciplines**, Chapter 7 covers a range of material, from lab reports to case studies to analyses or even essay exams. It's important, of course, for all students to understand the **conventions of academic writing** in their future field so they can design their work effectively. Use Chapter 4 to teach students how to analyze what particular academic audiences expect, what questions might bear exploring, and what counts as evidence in various academic communities. You can use the excerpts of Deborah Tannen's writing in Chapter 3 on pp. 60–65 to show how the same issue can be addressed to a range of audiences with appropriate adjustments in evidence and tone. See also "Teaching Academic Writing" in Section 5: Teaching Key Concepts in these Notes.

Questions of reading are addressed directly in Chapter 8, which teaches students key skills for situating and previewing texts.

Many students arrive in a college lacking a **rhetorical understanding of texts**. Many first-year students, for example, may not be familiar with genres, calling any book a "novel" and any article a "story." One way you can help students understand genres is to point out the samples of Deborah Tannen's arguments on pp. 60–65 to show how a writer meets three different audiences appropriately using the same topic. Your students may be surprised to notice how Tannen redesigns her argument for each rhetorical situation. Chapters 2–4 and 8 all help students understand the concept of the *rhetorical situation* of texts—both the ones they are reading and the ones they are writing.

As you plan the formal essays and informal class activities, it will help if you find out the typical **classroom demographics** in your program and what typical students arrive knowing. Get a sense of how many multicultural and multilingual students there will be and, if appropriate, use the "Notes for Multilingual Writers" in each chapter.

Ask about the ways in which your program expects you to focus on **grammar**, especially if the course you teach is designed for freshmen. If your school has a writing center or other resources for students, be sure that your students know about them: they can help your students now and for the rest of their college career.

For **other resources**, check to see whether your program maintains hard copy or online files where you may find helpful activities from colleagues that you can borrow and adapt for your class as well as professional development ideas to expand your teaching techniques. Also be sure to check out Bedford/St. Martin's many resources, including CD tutorials and online Web site support. Contact Bedford or your school's rep for more information.

Just as students sometimes struggle to imagine themselves as real writers, you might also struggle at first to imagine yourself as a real teacher. One general word of advice: Remember your own experience as a student. If you're a traditional-age TA, being close in age to most of your students and relatively recently in their shoes can actually be an advantage. Did you ever procrastinate? If you did, then you might be a little less frustrated if your students do—and you might gain some authority in the classroom by admitting that you procrastinated once, too, but you eventually learned not to. (Explaining why and how wouldn't hurt here, either.)

It's probably reassuring to know that even experienced instructors sometimes feel unprepared and uncertain about the best way to address some classroom challenges. Like writing, teaching is a lifelong work in progress. Just as *The Academic Writer* invites students to see themselves belonging to a supportive community of writers, so, too, these Instructor's Notes are a reminder that new instructors are part of a supportive community of writing instructors. We're here to help if you need it.

Note for Writing Program Administrators

These updated Instructor's Notes are designed in large part to help new instructors move smoothly into their first terms or semesters of teaching. Selecting *The Academic Writer* for your program will provide your TAs, adjuncts, and other less-experienced instructors with valuable tools to expand their rhetorical understanding and, therefore, their confidence in teaching.

Both *The Academic Writer* and these Instructor's Notes supplement teacher training and orientation—*The Academic Writer* by clearly presenting the elements of academic writing, reading, and rhetorical thinking, and the Instructor's Notes by providing strategies for teaching them. As a WPA, you can rely on *The Academic Writer*'s coverage of material that's critical in helping new instructors reinforce their own understanding of rhetoric and argument, so that they can guide their students in analyzing readings and designing their writing.

- **Aristotle's appeals** are represented in various contexts throughout the text—introduced in Chapter 3 (p. 51), returned to in Chapter 4 (p. 91) with material on using the appeals for analyzing arguments, and raised again in Chapter 5 in exploring how students can use the appeals in designing arguments (p. 117).
- *The Academic Writer* introduces the **Toulmin system** in Chapter 4 for analysis and again in Chapter 5 for writing, which will help new

instructors guide students to see how arguments use claims, supports, and warrants.

- The explanation of **stasis theory** on p. 86 gives new instructors language to discuss claims, both for analysis and for writing. New TAs who are recent undergrads will gain understanding and confidence from these explanations when teaching these concepts.
- New instructors can understand and teach **discourse communities** using the samples of Deborah Tannen's arguments on pp. 60–65 to show a writer designing her argument on the same topic for three different rhetorical situations.

Section 5 of these Notes, "Teaching Key Concepts" (p. 44), also will help your new instructors with more background on Aristotle, Toulmin, and stasis theory.

The Academic Writer works well with various approaches, including cultural studies, thematic, writing across the curriculum, or even modes-based. These Instructor's Notes provide your program with a variety of sample syllabi to suit these approaches and more. (See pp. 28–30 for using *The Academic Writer* out of numerical sequence.)

How *The Academic Writer* Supports the WPA Outcomes

As the tables below show, *The Academic Writer* helps programs meet the WPA Outcomes for college writing as adopted by the Council of Writing Program Administrators in April 2000.[1] WPAs, faculty, and composition scholars largely agree that these outcomes represent factors that are highly relevant for student success; in supporting these outcomes, *The Academic Writer* provides an opportunity for you to introduce new instructors to the consensus about the goals of the composition course.

Rhetorical Knowledge:
By the end of first-year composition, students should

Outcome	The Academic Writer
• Focus on a purpose • Respond to the needs of different audiences • Respond appropriately to different kinds of rhetorical situations • Use conventions of format and structure appropriate to the rhetorical situation	Part I overview on understanding rhetorical situations helps achieve these outcomes, with attention to writing as design and focus on audience, purpose, text (genre and content), and medium (print, online, etc.).

Continued

---

[1]http://www.wpacouncil.org/positions/outcomes.html

• Adopt appropriate voice, tone, and level of formality • Understand how genres shape reading and writing • Write in several genres	Part II provides specific overview and activities to achieve college writing.

Faculty in all programs and departments can build on this preparation by helping students learn

• The main features of writing in their fields • The main uses of writing in their fields • The expectation of readers in their fields	In addition to the overall information about understanding one's rhetorical situation, *The Academic Writer*'s Chapter 7 relates directly to writing in different disciplines.

Critical Thinking, Reading, and Writing:
By the end of first-year composition, students should

• Use writing and reading for inquiry, learning, thinking, and communicating • Understand a writing assignment as a series of tasks, including finding, evaluating, analyzing, and synthesizing appropriate primary and secondary sources • Integrate their own ideas with those of others • Understand the relationships among language, knowledge, and power	Chapter 8's extensive reading strategies directly address this outcome. Chapters 3 and 4 especially focus on the role of inquiry in academic writing. Chapter 6 in particular focuses on ways to find, evaluate, analyze, synthesize, integrate, and document the ideas of others. Part I especially attends to the questions of language, knowledge, and rhetorical thinking.

Faculty in all programs and departments can build on this preparation by helping students learn

• The use of writing as a critical thinking method • The interactions among critical thinking, critical reading, and critical writing • The relationships among language, knowledge, and power in their fields	Chapter 6 on inquiry and Chapter 7 on writing in the disciplines directly engage writing as a method of critical thinking via writing and how that leads to knowledge and power

Processes:

By the end of first-year composition, students should

• Be aware that it usually takes multiple drafts to create and complete a successful text • Develop flexible strategies for generating, revising, editing, and proofreading • Understand writing as an open process that permits writers to use later invention and rethinking to revise their work • Understand the collaborative and social aspects of writing processes • Learn to critique their own and others' works • Learn to balance the advantages of relying on others with the responsibility of doing their part • Use a variety of technologies to address a range of audiences	Chapter 2 plus Chapters 9–12 provide explanations and activities to guide students through multiple drafts, from invention to planning, drafting, and revision in a recursive manner, including collaboration, group work, peer review, and so forth. Chapter 5 provides an extended, in-depth sequential case study of a student's essay from brainstorming through revisions and reflection. Part I and Chapter 11 relate especially to writing for a broad range of audiences via a variety of print and online technologies and genres.

Faculty in all programs and departments can build on this preparation by helping students learn

• To build final results in stages • To review work-in-progress in collaborative peer groups for purposes other than editing • To save extensive editing for later parts of the writing process • To apply the technologies commonly used to research and communicate within their fields	WAC/WID programs can use *The Academic Writer* to see how educators can structure assignments to enhance the writing their students do. Section 2 of these Notes offers suggestions for using technologies for teaching and for students.

Knowledge of Conventions:

By the end of first-year composition, students should

• Learn common formats for different kinds of texts	In particular, Chapters 7, 10, 12, and samples throughout the book show various college writing assignments. *Continued*

- Develop knowledge of genre conventions ranging from structure and paragraphing to tone and mechanics
- Practice appropriate means of documenting their work
- Control such surface features as syntax, grammar, punctuation, and spelling

Chapter 6 discusses documentation.

Chapter 12 covers revision for conventions.

Faculty in all programs and departments can build on this preparation by helping students learn

- The conventions of usage, specialized vocabulary, format, and documentation in their fields
- Strategies through which better control of conventions can be achieved

Faculty can use Chapters 7 and 10 in particular to guide their students in appropriate writing for their field.

SECTION 2: OVERVIEW OF *THE ACADEMIC WRITER*

The Academic Writer draws on Kenneth Burke's idea of rhetoric as a conversation:

> *Imagine that you enter a parlor. You come late. When you arrive, others have long preceded you, and they are engaged in a heated discussion, a discussion too heated for them to pause and tell you exactly what it is about. In fact, the discussion had already begun long before any of them got there, so that no one present is qualified to retrace for you all the steps that had gone before. You listen for a while, until you decide that you have caught the tenor of the argument; then you put in your oar. Someone answers; you answer him; another comes to your defense; another aligns himself against you, to either the embarrassment or gratification of your opponent, depending upon the quality of your ally's assistance. However, the discussion is interminable. The hour grows late, you must depart. And you do depart, with the discussion still vigorously in progress.*
> —Kenneth Burke, *The Philosophy of Literary Form*

Students coming into academic settings are often asked to begin writing about controversial social issues such as abortion, gay marriage, or intelligent design before they have a deep understanding of the ongoing conversations surrounding these topics; as a result, they often write as if they are the first ones to discuss them. One of our first actions as instructors is therefore to help them find out about these conversations right off the bat—who is talking, who cares, and what's at stake. This is why *The Academic Writer* is organized to help students begin to think rhetorically *before* they start composing.

The Academic Writer addresses college students as writers in a rhetorical situation. Instead of assuming that they must learn to write only by following directions from teacher and text, this approach locates students in the spheres where they are writing, which empowers them to understand the decisions they need to make. They are apprentice writers, to be sure, but nonetheless fellow writers, who need to keep expanding their complex craft, with all its insights and ambiguity, as well as its power for learning, thinking, and transforming.

As teachers of writing, we always want our students to take themselves seriously as writers and to become active problem solvers. In that sense, this text has familiar goals. What may seem new is the way in which *The Academic Writer* asks students to undertake their composition studies in the role of writers. The goal of becoming a better writer is approached by completing papers, but it is inherently a work in progress. Such a goal is dynamic, not final.

As in the first edition, this second edition of *The Academic Writer* continues to ask students to see their writing as work in progress from the beginning. They are led to investigate, describe, plan, and question the rhetorical situation of their writing by using new samples and graphic demonstrations of the processes. They are encouraged to see themselves as part of a community of writers—to read each other's work and exchange serious suggestions. The emphasis on reading is essential for students to understand the rhetorical situation of any text and how various conventions affect their own writing. They are encouraged to become aware of and respond to their intellectual and cultural circumstances, in particular their situation as students writing in an academic environment. Their rhetorical situations may include various uses of electronic technologies and may open out to analyses of cultural context. They learn to take charge of their own writing processes, including evaluating and revising. Multilingual students are guided to consider cultural differences as part of the rhetorical situation.

The Academic Writer can have important consequences for you and for your students. Worried students will discover that their college writing projects become more manageable, which makes your job easier. In the process of learning to be proactive, students will be better able to guide their own writing progress, just as their instructors must be.

The Academic Writer invites students into the collaborative circle of writers that we, as more experienced writers, know to be a place where writing is often risky but also a rewarding and highly social activity. This text teaches principles of writing not as certainties, but as strategies, ways of going on despite encountering the inevitable problems. By changing the approach from having to be an expert to presenting yourself as an advanced fellow participant, you will gain more credibility with your students.

Importantly, *The Academic Writer* will help you establish your class as a community of writers. We believe that writing is a powerful component in the work of both individuals and groups. This text accordingly demonstrates not only how to write, but how to make writing an instrument of learning.

We proceed, however, with a certain humility. Since teaching, like writing, is always a work in progress and classrooms present widely differing rhetorical situations, the possibilities for using this text are multiple and complex. Our aim in writing these Instructor's Notes is to give you as much help as we can through suggested workable plans for teaching and sharing our experiences. As fellow teachers, we offer strategies, not certainties; we offer these Instructor's Notes as an act of collaboration.

Distinctive Features of *The Academic Writer*

The Academic Writer aims to provide a framework that can stimulate effective classroom interaction while at the same time offering instructors considerable autonomy and flexibility. This approach reflects the author's belief that composition texts should support and enrich, but not dominate, the life of the classroom.

The Academic Writer reflects recent research in composition and rhetoric, and yet as a practical textbook, it attempts to convey complex ideas without being intimidating to students. Its most distinctive features include the following:

• **A rhetorical approach to the processes of reading, writing, and research,** with an emphasis on strategies students can use to decide how to approach any writing task

- **Complete coverage of argument,** with a focus on mastering the essential moves: determining whether a claim can be argued, developing a thesis, providing reasons and support, acknowledging counterarguments, framing arguments as part of the scholarly conversation, and using visuals
- **A twenty-first-century approach to research,** which reframes it as a recursive process of exploration, information-gathering, evaluation, and composition and covers the "new basics" of online research
- Abundant examples of **student writing** from across the disciplines
- Thoughtful attention to **reading visual texts** and **using document design**
- **"Easy-reference" features,** such as the **"Guidelines"** and **"Questions"** boxes that summarize essential concepts, **"Thinking Rhetorically"** icons that flag key rhetorical advice, and a **"Writers' References" section** that illustrates MLA and APA documentation guidelines
- **"For Exploration"** and **"For Thought, Discussion, and Writing" activities** that encourage students to apply the concepts and strategies discussed in the text
- Attention in every chapter to the perspectives of **multilingual writers** and to strategies for **successful collaboration**

How *The Academic Writer* Is Organized

The Academic Writer is divided into three major parts.

Part I: "Writing Matters: Writing and Rhetoric in the Twenty-First Century"

Part I consists of three chapters that establish the conceptual and pedagogical framework for the text, enabling students to develop a sophisticated understanding of writing, reading, and research as fundamental, and fundamentally interconnected, processes. The discussion and activities in these chapters also encourage students to think of themselves as writers and participants in communities of writers, particularly in an academic community.

- **Chapter 1: Rethinking Writing: A Rhetorical Process for Composing Texts** introduces the concept of the rhetorical situation, in part as a bridge to a discussion of the concept of **writing as design,** which is emerging as the major metaphor for writing in the twenty-first century.
- **Chapter 2: Academic Writing: Committing to the Process** helps students gain insight into their own preferences as writers, enabling them to commit to a writing process that works for them and that results in successful academic writing. This chapter also encourages students to find a writing community and to productively engage in collaborative writing.
- **Chapter 3: Analyzing Rhetorical Situations** shows students how to use **rhetorical analysis**—a reading of audience and texts—to understand the framework for their own writing. The discussion in this chapter

includes the cross-cultural situation of multilingual writers as part of the rhetorical situation.

Part II: "Writing in College"

Part II consists of four chapters that speak to students about the reading and writing they do as members of the academic community. Students learn approaches to analyzing texts and writing arguments that will help them read and write more effectively in the disciplines.

- **Chapter 4: Analyzing Texts and Contexts** offers suggestions for analyzing **disciplinary conventions** and for **analyzing arguments**, with discussions of Aristotle's appeals, Toulmin's framework for argument, and logical fallacies.

- **Chapter 5: Making and Supporting Claims** helps students master the essential moves in academic argument; in doing so, it focuses on academic argument as **inquiry** rather than as debate. This chapter concludes with a case study that presents student writer Daniel Stiepleman's writing process, from invention and discovery through revision, as he develops an analysis of a public service advertisement.

- **Chapter 6: Doing Research: Joining the Scholarly Conversation** reframes research as a recursive process of exploration, information-gathering, evaluation, and composition. This radical revision of the previous edition's chapter, written in close collaboration with Oregon State University librarian Anne-Marie Deitering, covers the "new basics" of the online research process. It explains, for example, the use of online bookmarking tools and citation managers—as well current topics most textbooks don't even address, such as copyright and "copyleft" (the principle granting the public limited rights to distribute and modify an author's intellectual property), and how students can understand and assert their rights as content creators. To foster deep, transferrable learning, the chapter emphasizes the rationale behind the rules.

- **Chapter 7: Writing in the Disciplines: Making Choices As You Write** introduces students to the kinds of writing they can expect to do after they complete first-year writing courses and demonstrates how they can draw on their understanding of the rhetorical situation as they do so.

Part III: "Practical Strategies for Reading and Writing"

As the title suggests, Part III introduces students to a variety of practical strategies they can use as they read, plan, draft, design, and revise. In these five chapters, the text emphasizes not a prescribed series of steps that students must follow but a repertory of strategies they can draw on, working alone and with others, depending on their purpose and situation.

- **Chapter 8: Strategies for Reading** discusses **rhetorical sensitivity** in reading, the importance of **genre**, and strategies for **reading critically**.

- **Chapter 9: Strategies for Invention** covers strategies for discovering and exploring ideas.

- Chapter 10: **Strategies for Planning and Drafting** addresses strategies for planning, drafting, developing, and organizing ideas.
- Chapter 11: **Strategies for Designing Pages and Screens** discusses design in the context of the rhetorical situation, explains basic design principles, and provides numerous strategies for using layout, formatting, and visuals effectively.
- Chapter 12: **Strategies for Revision** emphasizes revising for focus, content, organization, and style, independently and with the benefit of peer feedback.

Following Part III is **"Writers' References,"** an easy-to-use reference section with fully up-to-date MLA and APA documentation guidelines. The MLA guidelines include visual "source maps" that annotate sample sources, giving step-by-step guidelines to help students evaluate and cite print and electronic materials.

Guidelines, Activities, and Other Pedagogical Features

Newly designed **"Guidelines"** and **"Questions" boxes** throughout the chapters summarize key concepts. Where appropriate, these boxes present decision-making and other processes in flowchart format, reinforcing the importance of decision making and active engagement in the processes of writing, thinking, and reading, and helping students find what they need more easily than ever before.

- **"Thinking Rhetorically"** icons flag passages where strategies are offered for understanding texts in context and for making decisions about constructing them.
- Activities in every chapter help students understand and apply the ideas presented in the text:
  - **"For Exploration"** activities are designed primarily to stimulate students' understanding of and response to the text; many also ask students to reflect on previous writing experiences or to brainstorm, freewrite, or talk with others in response to discussions in the text or to apply concepts or strategies presented in the text.
  - **"For Collaboration"** activities involve students in carefully designed collaborative learning and writing experiences. In general, assignments lead students to reflect on writing and the rhetorical situation of learning to write as the subject of a critical inquiry as well as the process they are undergoing.
  - **"For Thought, Discussion, and Writing"** activities at the end of every chapter encourage students to work in writing with concepts presented in the text.

Using the Writing Assignments and Activities in *The Academic Writer*

The Academic Writer contains several kinds of assignments and activities. Following is some advice about how to work with these suggestions as you plan your course.

1. *Freewriting:* Freewriting has "use" value rather than "exchange" value: It doesn't count in the same way that final drafts count. When you have students do freewriting assignments, therefore, be sure to keep the assignments "free." The basic idea is that writers will not be held accountable for the kinds of problems or errors that would ordinarily discount the value of their efforts.

With freewriting assignments, it helps to specify how much time students shouls take. Ask students to write for five, ten, or fifteen minutes. You'll often find that in the first four or five minutes they write down everything that they are used to thinking or saying to themselves and that the next few sentences come more slowly. You might want to structure your freewriting assignments accordingly, asking students to spend at least seven to ten minutes on topics that they probably have rehearsed quite a bit already. Or have them freewrite for five minutes, pause, read some responses, and then go back for a second time to write for another five to ten minutes.

Some multilingual students have difficulty with freewriting, especially in English. Suggest freewriting in the home language, and suggest other methods as well, such as making lists.

2. *Brainstorming:* Brainstorming is a form of listing that may be done by a group or an individual. Given a topic or problem, students are to write down every idea that comes to mind, as quickly as possible. We like to tell our classes that it's not a real brainstorming session unless they produce at least some ideas that are exotic, crazy, terrible, ridiculous, or reprehensible. The only rules are (a) don't stop to elaborate and (b) don't censor the list.

3. *Interviewing:* A number of the exercises in this book ask students to interview others—peers, family members, tutors, older students, instructors—for information about writing. These interviews serve collectively to help students construct a realistic idea of the rhetorical context within which they write. The interviews also help students step out of their isolated writing habits and think about asking others for information and help as a natural part of the writing process. Classes will benefit from the advice on interviewing in Chapter 6 as well as from your guidance.

To give students direction for and a sense of the possibilities of the interviewing assignment, have them role-play the interview first. For example, ask one student to play the role of an instructor in his field and ask another student in the same field to interview him. List on the board or an overhead additional ideas for questions submitted by other class members. Ask all students to take notes during the interview and to check them against one another for the accuracy of their understanding.

Through checking their notes, the major hidden problem of interviewing can usually become evident—that students often hear what they *expect* to hear rather than what is said (just as they may also misinterpret what they read when they do research). Finding this out during a practice interview helps students address this problem.

4. *Essays:* Most writing classes base final grades on essays that have been developed into final drafts. But you do not need to ask students to write only finished essays. You may want your students to try out many of the essay ideas prompted by assignments in the text and to choose just a few of the most promising to work into final draft form. Many instructors have students submit a *portfolio* of drafts and choose a certain number of essays for them to revise as the basis for evaluation at the end of the term.

When you decide on the essays you would like students to write, whether you use suggestions from the text or other assignments, you can develop a more elaborate explanation of the essay assignment to help your students and also use samples of student work to serve as models. (Sample essay assignments and student essays are collected in Section 7 of these Instructor's Notes.)

5. *Research: The Academic Writer* provides a strong foundation to help students master the research process, both in their writing classes and in classes across the disciplines, not only through Chapter 6, "Doing Research," and Chapter 7, "Writing in the Disciplines," but also through its emphasis on analyzing the rhetorical situation, its careful articulation of bridges between oral discussion and written projects, its attention to the place of conventions, and its opportunities for considering the differences and possible relationships between informal and formal writing.

How to Take Advantage of the Flexibility of *The Academic Writer*

One memorable discussion on a listserv related to writing pedagogy included the complaint that composition textbooks too often straitjacket instructors, limiting their options. Unlike some of these texts, *The Academic Writer* gives you the rhetorical support you need without insisting on any method or program, so it can be used effectively by teachers employing diverse approaches to the teaching of writing. In addition, students have consistently praised the text as both easy and interesting to read, so instructors are not required to spend large amounts of class time explaining the basic concepts in the text. Instead, instructors using *The Academic Writer* are able to engage the class in discussions of substantial rhetorical issues or of the diverse examples of student and professional writing.

Below are some specifics on how instructors who favor different approaches can use *The Academic Writer*.

For Use in Courses Emphasizing Electronic Technologies

Instructors who are introducing increased use of electronic technologies to their writing classes, including those teaching hybrid and online classes, will find suggestions throughout *The Academic Writer* for applying this rhetorical approach to writing and reading online. Chapters 1, 2, and 6 in particular focus on helping students to think rhetorically about the writing that they publish online, whether within a class Course Management System (CMS) such as Blackboard or WebCT or on a class blog, and about the Internet sources they might use for research.

In addition, *The Academic Writer*'s rhetorical approach to document design, most in evidence in Chapter 11, allows students to apply basic principles to any and all of their written work.

Because it explicitly teaches students to approach online writing with the knowledge gained from a rhetorical perspective—analyzing purpose, conventions, and audience—you will find that *The Academic Writer* can be used effectively for classes meeting in computer classrooms as well as for those with more limited access to the Internet.

Section 5 of these Instructor's Notes, "Teaching Key Concepts," offers more tips on online teaching (pp. 44–59).

For Use in Courses Emphasizing Collaborative Learning

Those who wish to engage students with collaborative learning activities will find substantial support for these approaches in this text, based on the idea of writing as an interactive or dialogic process. Part I of *The Academic Writer*, "Writing Matters: Writing and Rhetoric in the Twenty-First Century," devotes considerable attention to composing processes, including those that occur within communities and in specifically designated collaborative arrangements. The discussion is reinforced in Part III, "Practical Strategies for Reading and Writing." Furthermore, the "For Exploration," "For Collaboration," and "Thought, Discussion, and Writing" activities interspersed throughout the chapters all reinforce a process-centered, collaborative emphasis.

For Use in Courses Emphasizing Cultural Studies

The Academic Writer lends itself very well to the cultural studies approach used by some institutions where it has been adopted. The emphasis on students and the rhetorical situation throughout the text shows students how to include cultural analysis in their approach to writing and reading. As students learn to think in more complicated ways about how audiences interact with writing and about how cultural conventions define what can be said, they will come to understand how writing must negotiate its claims and how readers' interpretations arise out of specific cultural contexts that require analysis.

Interspersed throughout the text are notes and exercises designed to support multilingual and multicultural writers. These address the special concerns of such students, but they also assume that cultural differences can become resources for understanding a rhetorical and situated approach to writing.

For Use in Courses Emphasizing Modes of Discourse, WAC, or Thematic Approaches

Instructors who favor using the modes of discourse, WAC, or thematic approaches to the teaching of writing can also use *The Academic Writer* effectively. (Of course, these approaches are often used in conjunction with collaborative, process-oriented teaching practices.) Like many traditional rhetorics, *The Academic Writer* suggests topics, but does not require their assignment. Thus, instructors wishing to base class discussions and topic assignments on the modes, specific disciplinary conventions, or specific themes or subjects can easily do so.

For Use with Other Texts

Although *The Academic Writer* contains a number of essays by students and professionals and thus can be used as the sole text for a course, it can be combined with other texts as well. Like most rhetorics, *The Academic Writer* can be supplemented by a handbook that serves as a reference on grammar and usage for students.

In addition, the *The Academic Writer*'s approach to reading and academic writing more directly supports and reinforces the use of a reader than do many traditional rhetorics, which often contain brief examples of professional or academic writing but lack explicit commentary on the reading process or the nature of academic writing. *The Academic Writer* can thus be assigned very effectively with a traditional reader, a collection of readings exploring a particular theme or subject, a reader focusing on writing across the curriculum, or even a novel, a nonfiction work, or literacy narratives such as Richard Rodriguez's *Hunger of Memory*, Mike Rose's *Lives on the Boundary*, Keith Gilyard's *Voices of the Self*, Victor Villanueva's *Bootstraps*, or Natasha Lvovich's *The Multilingual Self*.

For Use in Courses *Other* Than Composition

Finally, we would like to note that while *The Academic Writer* is intended for use in first-year writing courses, it has also been used successfully with intermediate and advanced composition students or in courses on the teaching of writing.

Because we believe that *The Academic Writer* can be used successfully with quite diverse approaches to the teaching of writing, as well as with different levels of students, we would appreciate hearing from instructors who have used the text in their composition classes, and we would particularly appreciate receiving copies of syllabi, assignments, or other handouts that indicate how teachers have integrated the text into their classroom practices.

SECTION 3: SAMPLE COURSE PLANS

In the following syllabi, we present several possible ways of organizing your quarter or semester course using *The Academic Writer* with or without an accompanying reader. Some of these plans follow the sequence of the chapters in the textbook; you should, of course, feel free to vary the order of the chapters in ways that best suit your classroom and your program. For some ideas on doing so, see also the "Suggestions for Assigning Chapters Out of Numerical Sequence" (pp. 28–30).

Using *The Academic Writer* without an Accompanying Reader

Sample Eleven-Week Term/Quarter Schedule

Major Assignments: Four essays, developed from invention through rough and final drafts, plus an in-class final essay.

Week 1
- *The Academic Writer*, Preface and Chapter 1
- Assign essay 1

Week 2
- *The Academic Writer*, Chapters 2 and 3
- Rough draft of essay 1 due: in-class peer response

Week 3
- *The Academic Writer*, Chapters 4 and 5
- Final draft of essay 1 due
- Assign essay 2

Week 4
- *The Academic Writer*, Chapter 6
- Return graded essay 1
- Rough draft of essay 2 due: in-class peer response
- Additional online peer response by email

Week 5
- *The Academic Writer*, Chapter 7
- Final draft of essay 2 due
- Assign essay 3

Turn in all work to date (draft and final versions of essays 1 and 2)
Midterm course evaluation

Week 6
- *The Academic Writer*, Chapter 8
- Class meetings canceled: conferences (may be with individuals or with groups)

Week 7
- *The Academic Writer*, Chapters 9 and 10
- Return graded essay 2
- Rough draft of essay 3 due: in-class peer response
- Collaborative exercise

Week 8
- *The Academic Writer*, Chapter 11
- Final draft of essay 3 due
- Assign essay 4

Week 9
- *The Academic Writer*, Chapter 12
- Return graded essay 3
- Rough draft of essay 4 due

Week 10
- Final draft of essay 4 due in folder with all written work from the quarter
- Prepare students to write final essay in class

Finals Week
- Return graded essay 4
- In-class final essay 5

Sample Sixteen-Week Semester Schedule

Major Assignments: Seven essays, developed from invention through rough and final drafts, plus an in-class final essay

Week 1
- *The Academic Writer*, Preface and Chapter 1
- Assign essay 1

Week 2
- *The Academic Writer*, Chapter 2
- Rough draft of essay 1 due: in-class peer response

Week 3
- *The Academic Writer*, Chapter 3
- Final draft of essay 1 due
- Assign essay 2

Week 4
- *The Academic Writer*, Chapter 4
- Rough draft of essay 2 due: in-class peer response

Week 5
- *The Academic Writer*, Chapter 5

- Final draft of essay 2 due
- Assign essay 3

Turn in all work to date in a folder
Midterm course evaluation

Week 6
- *The Academic Writer*, Chapter 6
- Class meetings canceled: conferences (individual or group)
- Discussion of revision in conferences

Week 7
- *The Academic Writer*, Chapter 7
- Rough draft of essay 3 due: in-class peer response
- Discussion of revision

Week 8
- *The Academic Writer*, Chapter 8
- Final draft of essay 3 due
- Assign essay 4

Week 9
- *The Academic Writer*, Chapter 9
- Rough draft of essay 4 due: in-class peer response

Week 10
- *The Academic Writer*, Chapter 10
- Final draft of essay 4 due
- Assign essay 5

Week 11
- *The Academic Writer*, Chapter 11
- Rough draft of essay 5 due: in-class peer response
- Turn in all work to date in a folder

Week 12
- *The Academic Writer*, Chapter 12
- Discuss revision
- Final draft of essay 5 due
- Assign essay 6

Week 13
- *The Academic Writer*, Review "Writers' References" section
- Rough draft of essay 6 due: in-class peer response
- Assign essay 7

Week 14
- Review and practice

- Final draft of essay 6 due
- Rough draft of essay 7 due

Week 15
- Completion of activities, reflections on writing and group procedures
- Final draft of essay 7 due in folder with all written work from the semester
- Prepare students to write essay 8 as a final examination

Finals Week
- Essay written in class as final examination

Using *The Academic Writer* with a Reader

When you construct your course schedule, you might want to alternate days when students respond to readings with days when they write and work in groups. This pattern is especially useful during the beginning weeks of the class when students are reflecting about their own histories as writers and the kinds of writing processes they might use. Consider regularly using writing as a way to help students respond to their reading and learn the material it covers. For example, have students write opening and closing summaries of class discussions, responses to discussions, and questions or issues they wish to raise.

Sample Eleven-Week Quarter Schedule with a Reader

Major Assignments: Eight reading assignments, plus four formal essays from invention through rough and final drafts, and a fifth essay as an in-class final exam

Week 1
- *The Academic Writer*, Preface and Chapter 1
- Read and discuss assignment A from reader
- Assign activities from *The Academic Writer*

Week 2
- *The Academic Writer*, Chapter 2
- Read and discuss assignment B from reader
- Assign essay 1

Week 3
- *The Academic Writer*, Chapter 3
- Read and discuss assignment C from reader
- Rough draft of essay 1 due

Week 4
- *The Academic Writer*, Chapters 4 and 5
- Read and discuss assignment D from reader
- Final draft of essay 1 due
- Assign essay 2

Week 5
- *The Academic Writer*, Chapter 6
- Read and discuss assignment E from reader
- Rough draft of essay 2 due

Turn in all work completed to date
Midterm evaluation of the course

Week 6
- *The Academic Writer*, Chapter 7
- Class meetings canceled: conferences (with individuals or groups)
- Final draft of essay 2 due
- Assign essay 3

Week 7
- *The Academic Writer*, Chapter 8
- Read and discuss assignment F from reader
- Rough draft of essay 3 due

Week 8
- *The Academic Writer*, Chapters 9 and 10
- Read and discuss assignment G from reader
- Final draft of essay 3 due
- Assign essay 4

Week 9
- *The Academic Writer*, Chapter 11
- Read and discuss assignment H from reader
- Rough draft of essay 4 due

Week 10
- *The Academic Writer*, Chapter 12
- Completion of activities
- Reflections on writing and group processes
- Final draft of essay 4 due

Finals Week
- Essay 5 written in class as final examination

Sample Sixteen-Week Semester Schedule with Readings

Major Assignments: Thirteen readings, plus six essays, from invention through rough and final drafts, and a seventh essay as an in-class final exam

Week 1
- *The Academic Writer*, Preface and Chapter 1
- Read and discuss assignment A from reader
- Assign activities from *The Academic Writer*

Week 2
- *The Academic Writer*, Chapter 2
- Read and discuss assignment B from reader
- Assign essay 1

Week 3
- *The Academic Writer*, Chapter 3
- Read and discuss assignment C from reader
- Rough draft of essay 1 due

Week 4
- *The Academic Writer*, Chapter 4
- Read and discuss assignment D from reader
- Final draft of essay 1 due
- Assign essay 2

Week 5
- *The Academic Writer*, Chapter 5
- Read and discuss assignment E from reader
- Rough draft of essay 2 due

Week 6
- *The Academic Writer*, Chapter 6
- Class meeting canceled: conferences (with individuals or groups)

Week 7
- *The Academic Writer*, Chapter 7
- Read and discuss assignment F from reader
- Final draft of essay 2 due
- Assign essay 3

Week 8
- *The Academic Writer*, Chapter 8
- Read and discuss assignment G from reader
- Rough draft of essay 3 due

Midterm course evaluation

Week 9
- *The Academic Writer*, Chapter 9
- Read and discuss assignment H from reader
- Final draft of essay 3 due
- Assign essay 4

Week 10
- *The Academic Writer*, Chapter 10
- Read and discuss assignment I from reader

• Rough draft of essay 4 due

Week 11
- • *The Academic Writer*, Chapter 11
- • Read and discuss assignment J from reader
- • Final draft of essay 4 due
- • Assign essay 5

Week 12
- • *The Academic Writer*, Chapter 12
- • Read and discuss assignment K from reader
- • Rough draft of essay 5 due

Week 13
- • Discuss "Writers' References"
- • Read and discuss assignment L from reader
- • Final draft of essay 5 due
- • Assign essay 6

Week 14
- • Read and discuss assignment M from reader
- • Rough draft of essay 6 due

Week 15
- • Completion of activities
- • Reflections on writing and group processes
- • Final draft of essay 6 due
- • Prepare for essay 7

Finals Week
- • Essay 7 (final draft) written in class as final examination

Sample Full Syllabus for Using *The Academic Writer* for Advanced Courses

The Academic Writer also lends itself to use in upper-division advanced courses. More advanced students can usually make a much more extensive commitment to analyzing and exploring the rhetorical situation of their writing. Here is the syllabus constructed by Lisa Ede for one such class, a workshop in advanced composition taught at the senior level.

WR 416/516: ADVANCED COMPOSITION: FALL TERM

DR. LISA EDE
ENGLISH OFFICE: Moreland Hall 236, 737-1636
CWL OFFICE: Waldo 125B, 737-3710
EMAIL: LEde@orst.edu

OFFICE HOURS (Moreland Hall 236)
Monday & Wednesday, 3–4 P.M.
Tuesday, 3:30–4 P.M.

I'm generally on campus all day Monday through Thursday. Students are my highest priority, so I'd be happy to meet with you outside my scheduled office hours. Feel free to drop by my CWL office or to call or email me for an appointment. I spend most of my on-campus time at the CWL, so that's the best number to call if you're trying to reach me. I check my email regularly when I'm on campus. I don't have email at home, however, so keep that in mind if you're emailing me on a Friday, Saturday, or Sunday.

TEXTS
- Lisa Ede, *The Academic Writer: A Brief Guide*
- Photocopied professional and student essays. I will provide copies of the professional essays as a "payback" for my *The Academic Writer* royalty; you will provide copies of your own writing for group and/or class members, as indicated on the syllabus.

COURSE OVERVIEW

This class provides an opportunity for students to refine their writing skills while also exploring a number of important questions about writing: What does it mean to be a writer? How do writers learn to negotiate the diverse (and sometimes conflicting) expectations of different discourse communities? What role do textual conventions, and the assumptions underlying them, play in this process? What options do writers have if they wish to resist these conventions? How can writers know when it's safe to compose alternate or experimental forms—and how can they learn the conventions that underlie these (seemingly conventionless) texts? In this class we'll consider questions such as these as we work together on a series of writing projects.

COURSE POLICIES

Attendance: Since WR 416/516 is a writing workshop, attendance and participation are essential. More than two unexcused absences provides grounds for lowering your final course grade.

Due dates: Reading and writing assignments are due on the date indicated on the syllabus. Unless I have granted you an extension, I cannot accept late assignments.

Errors: As its title indicates, Advanced Composition is an advanced writing course. Students entering the class should thus have mastered the conventions of standard written English (SWE). As a consequence, I expect all drafts submitted for evaluation—as opposed to in-class or other informal writing—to be relatively free of major errors. I'm aware that even good writers can benefit from reviewing the conventions of SWE, so I've devoted a class to this topic. I'll also be happy to work with you individually on grammar, punctuation, and usage—and of course you can meet with a writing assistant at the CWL's Writing Center.

By the end of the term, students who wish to do well in this course should be submitting essays that are free of significant errors.

Revision: You may revise any of the essays for this class. To submit a revision, however, you must

- Provide evidence that you have met with either a peer or a writing assistant to work on your essay after I returned it to you. If you meet with a writing assistant, ask him or her to give you a blue slip, which you can attach to your essay. If you meet with one or more peers, either include a copy of their comments or a signed statement written by the student(s) with whom you met. This statement should provide basic information about your meeting—such as date, time, length of meeting—and summarize your work together.

- Write a two- to three-paragraph statement describing the major revisions you made and commenting on the reasons that you made these changes. You should also include a brief reflection about what you learned as a result of the process of revising.

- Include all previous drafts of your essay with your revised draft, clearly indicating the order in which they were composed.

COURSE REQUIREMENTS

Essay 1: Literacy narrative, 1 single-spaced page (10 percent of grade)
Essay 2: Response essay, 2 to 4 double-spaced pages undergraduate/ 4 to 6 pages graduate (20 percent of grade)

The worksheet for essay 2 addresses these questions:

- Which of the literacy narratives do you plan to respond to?

- Why did you choose this literacy narrative? Emotional engagement or dislike? Strong agreement or disagreement with the author? Some other reason?

- How do you plan to focus your response?

- What concerns do you bring to this assignment? Groups will have the last 10 minutes of the class to arrange for out-of-class responses to essay 2; these responses should occur during the fourth week of class.

Essay 3: Open topic, 3 to 5 pages double-spaced undergraduate/5 to 8 pages graduate (30 percent of grade)
Essay 4: Open topic, 3 to 5 pages undergraduate/5 to 8 pages graduate (30 percent of grade)

Final examination: Essay reflecting on what you have learned about writing—and about yourself as a writer (10 percent of grade)

A FEW MISCELLANEOUS COMMENTS AND SUGGESTIONS

Any of the four major essays may be written collaboratively. I strongly encourage you to take advantage of this opportunity to experience the satisfactions, and the challenges, of collaborative writing.

I encourage you to follow the practice of professional writers and acknowledge the contributions of others to your writing process. You can include a brief statement of acknowledgments at the bottom of the final page of your essay.

When you turn in formal writing assignments, please use a pocket folder to organize your materials. Put all notes, rough drafts, and peer responses in one pocket of the folder and your draft in the other. Please also include a writing process analysis for each essay. This analysis should (1) briefly describe how you wrote the essay (how long you worked, how difficult or easy you found the process, etc.), (2) characterize the strengths and weaknesses of your current draft as you perceive them, and (3) indicate several issues or questions you'd particularly like me to consider as I read your essay.

OSU's Writing Center, located in Waldo Hall, represents an important resource for writers of all levels. I urge you to take advantage of this important resource. In the past, many WR 416/516 students have set up weekly appointments with a writing assistant and have found this ongoing collaboration to be tremendously helpful. To make a half-hour appointment, call 737-5640.

COURSE SCHEDULE OVERVIEW: MAJOR DUE DATES

Week 3
- Essay 1 due

Week 4
- Essay 2 due

Week 5

During week 5, I will meet individually with students. We will discuss your general progress in the course and any other concerns you may have. In preparation for our conference, please write a proposal for your third essay, using the "Questions for Analyzing Your Rhetorical Situation" listed on pp. 41–42 of *The Academic Writer*. Bring this proposal to our conference. We should also have time to work on individual essays, so be sure to bring drafts (a revision of your first essay? a draft of your third essay?) that you'd like me to look at.

Week 6
- Essay 3 due

Week 7

Group workshops for essay 4. In preparation for this workshop, please write a proposal for your essay, using the "Questions for Analyzing Your Rhetorical Situation" listed in *The Academic Writer*. In addition, respond to these questions: What strengths do you bring to this writing project as you currently visualize it? What challenges does it pose for you? Finally, pose three troubleshooting questions you would like your group to address. Be sure to bring a copy for me.

Week 8

Group workshop for essay 4. Bring two copies of no more than two double-spaced pages of your essay—the first two pages might be logical— to class for response. In looking at the essays, you will be focusing primarily on style. Your purpose is to apply our recent discussions of style to your writing.

Week 11 (Finals Week)
- Essay 4 due

Suggestions for Assigning Chapters out of Numerical Sequence

The Academic Writer has twelve chapters, arranged in three parts, which you can use in various sequences to suit the aims of your course. When you follow the order given in the book, you begin by orienting students to writing, to their own composing processes, to reading as a writer, and to research as a process. The second part introduces students to the rhetorical situation in greater depth, extending it to writing and reading online. The third part introduces students to strategies for writing, moving from invention and planning through drafting to revision, and including collaboration.

Many instructors will find that proceeding through the text as it is organized supplies the logical order that they wish. However, *The Academic Writer* has worked well for instructors using other kinds of orders, including the following three examples.

For Use in Courses Emphasizing Writing Strategies First, Rhetorical Concepts Second

Beginning with Part III makes sense if you wish your students to start thinking about and experimenting with writing strategies immediately, reserving reflection on concepts such as the rhetorical situation and the writing process until later in the term. An assignment sequence with this emphasis would look like this:

- Chapter 9: Strategies for Invention
- Chapter 10: Strategies for Planning and Drafting
- Chapter 11: Strategies for Designing Pages and Screens
- Chapter 12: Strategies for Revision
- Chapter 8: Strategies for Reading
- Chapter 1: Rethinking Writing
- Chapter 2: Academic Writing
- Chapter 3: Analyzing Rhetorical Situations
- Chapter 4: Analyzing Texts and Contexts
- Chapter 5: Making and Supporting Claims
- Chapter 6: Doing Research: Joining the Scholarly Conversation
- Chapter 7: Writing in the Disciplines: Making Choices As You Write

For Use in Courses Emphasizing the Reading-Writing Connection

Particularly if you wish students to think in terms of academic writing in their first assignments, you might begin the class with Chapters 8 and 5, so that students understand the concept of the rhetorical situation, and then go to Chapters 4, 6, and 7. Chapters 1, 2, and 9 through 12 can follow, as shown:

- Chapter 8: Strategies for Reading
- Chapter 5: Making and Supporting Claims
- Chapter 4: Analyzing Texts and Contexts
- Chapter 6: Doing Research: Joining the Scholarly Conversation
- Chapter 7: Writing in the Disciplines: Making Choices As You Write
- Chapter 1: Rethinking Writing
- Chapter 2: Academic Writing
- Chapter 9: Strategies for Invention
- Chapter 10: Strategies for Planning and Drafting

- Chapter 11: Strategies for Designing Pages and Screens
- Chapter 12: Strategies for Revision

For Use in Two-Term/Two-Semester Composition Sequences

A logical arrangement for two-term sequences would be to choose for the first term a reader that emphasizes either individual or cultural narrative and analysis or writing that reflects the students' situation and community. One of the many multicultural readers available would be very suitable. Accompany reading assignments with Parts I, II, and III of *The Academic Writer*. In the second term, choose a different reader organized around issues or themes, or select a collection of academic essays and arguments. Begin by having students review Part III of *The Academic Writer* on reading and writing strategies.

Term One
- Chapter 1: Rethinking Writing
- Chapter 2: Academic Writing
- Chapter 3: Analyzing Rhetorical Situations
- Chapter 4: Analyzing Texts and Contexts
- Chapter 5: Making and Supporting Claims
- Chapter 6: Doing Research: Joining the Scholarly Conversation
- Chapter 7: Writing in the Disciplines: Making Choices As You Write
- Chapter 8: Strategies for Reading
- Chapter 9: Strategies for Invention
- Chapter 10: Strategies for Planning and Drafting
- Chapter 11: Strategies for Designing Pages and Screens

Term Two

Review *The Academic Writer*, Chapters 1 through 11, and ask students to use the chapters on strategies as a reference for this term. Focus especially on the revision process in Chapter 12.
- Chapter 12: Strategies for Revision
- Writers' References

SECTION 4: MEETING CLASSROOM CHALLENGES

This section of the Instructor's Notes offers practical advice for meeting some classroom challenges common to instructors of composition. Topics addressed include collaboration, support for multilingual writers, assigning portfolios, paper load, responding to students, helping students with time management, evaluating your own teaching, and suggestions for service learning opportunities.

Introducing Collaborative Practices

Writing classes increasingly make use of collaborative practices, some as supplements to a traditional, instructor-centered classroom and others as the informing principle of the course. Chapter 2 of *The Academic Writer* contains specific guidelines for helping students write collaboratively, and throughout the text, collaboration activities focus on group writing experiences. In this section of the Instructor's Notes, we try to help you discover the collaborative practices that are most appropriate to your situation.

To ensure effective collaborative learning experiences, instructors must pay as much attention to group dynamics as to content. Though the role of the instructor moves out of the spotlight, your *collaborative* role as structurer, responder, consultant, and facilitator demands great skill and may be crucial to the success or failure of the class. In the final part of this section, we provide some ways of evaluating your success in such a classroom. First, though, we address some specific tips for teaching such classes.

Suggestions for Using Collaborative Learning Groups in Classes

1. *Recognize the extent to which collaborative learning challenges both you and your students.* In a course grounded in a collaborative pedagogy, instructors and students need to learn new roles. Instructors need to learn to trust the collaborative learning process—to be able to exchange the certainty of a well-prepared lecture for the uncertainty of peer interactions. You must be able to put aside the hierarchies of expertise to make time for apprentice writers to talk about their craft. As a teacher, you need to recognize that students are more accustomed to competition, not cooperation, so they may be suspicious of group activities. Some may have no experience with collaborative groups, while others may imagine that working in groups is interesting but doesn't really count. Many will be used to focusing on short-term assignments rather than the long-term goal of a group writing project. *The Academic Writer* mediates this problem by integrating group activities (in the collaboration exercises) with the topics of each chapter.

2. *Acknowledge the importance of resistance.* Resistance to collaboration may reflect ongoing problems in relations among students that they are reluctant to address. Since the institution defines the instructor as an authority who insists on certain points of view or procedures or due dates or standards, you may find

resistance to all of these appearing as resistance to you. You will make such resistance more productive if you ensure that students understand that you want diverse responses and expect the assertion of differences. You can ask your students to write about resistance to discover the forms it takes in your class.

3. *Remember that collaborative learning extends beyond using peer-response groups.* Many instructors use peer-response groups in their writing classes. Such groups enable students to read and respond to work in progress, and we strongly recommend their use. Collaborative learning groups can function in other ways, however. Group activities suggested in *The Academic Writer* utilize a number of approaches. Students brainstorm together, compare responses to checklists and guidelines, analyze responses to readings, and write and revise together.

Keep in mind that collaborative learning activities need not be time-consuming. An instructor might want to have students spend ten minutes in groups discussing a question generated by a reading, for instance, before leading a full class discussion on the same issue.

4. *Develop ways to foster students' collaborative learning skills.* Instructors can improve students' ability to work collaboratively in the following ways:

- Use collaborative practices from the very first day of the term.
- Observe and interact with groups as they work together.
- Demonstrate through grades and other means that collaborative learning counts in your class.
- Take class time to discuss effective group dynamics and to respond to students' questions about group work.
- Encourage students to monitor their group's effectiveness through self-evaluations and peer evaluations.
- Recognize that the best collaborative assignments—whether brief and informal or extensive and formal—are those that benefit from the collaborative effort. The surest way to "kill" a collaborative assignment is to force students to work together on a project they could just as or more easily work on individually.

5. *Start early.* You may find it helpful to allocate time during the first two or three classes to help students learn to work collaboratively with each other. Students need to develop a willingness to explore a topic, to discover disagreements, and to negotiate the making of meaning. Beginning groups will benefit from heterogeneity and from assignments that encourage diverse responses, since the greatest threat to effective collaboration is a premature shutting down of differing perspectives.

- It is especially important to start with what students know. On the first day students can freewrite their responses to a question like "How can writing help you succeed in college?" and collect their responses in small groups. Encouraging students to come up with unpredictable answers will set another, more productive kind of standard for group activities.
- Next, the groups could write a collaborative answer to the question "Why write?" taking the various individual responses into account, and then report to the class as a whole. Such a sequence establishes on the

first day that group work is work, not a break. If students go on to do the activities in Chapters 1 and 2, they may compare responses to the questions about the kinds of writing they do and their writing experiences.

Through the acts of talking about writing and writing about talking, many students begin to think differently about the connections between speech and written language—connections that for many students have been hard to make or nonexistent. Talking makes the community of student writers literate about their shared experiences. Talking also leads students to collaborate with one another, to be excited about one another's work, and to see writing as a social act rather than a solitary one.

After students finish talking, of course, they should return to writing. *The Academic Writer* has a number of suggestions about essays students might write as the result of their inquiries. These essay assignments require students to synthesize what they have learned through writing exercises, exploration, reflection, and discussion.

6. *Structure groups and collaborative activities carefully.* There is no single ideal way to structure groups. There are some advantages to allowing students to form their own groups. There are also advantages to structuring groups yourself, especially once you know your students well. In either case, remember that groups work most effectively when members bring a variety of strengths and experiences to group activities. Remember as well that you have options: You could form groups for informal brief activities randomly (counting off students in groups of three or four, for instance) but allow students to choose long-term peer-response groups of five.

When you assign groups to collaborate on substantial projects (activities that involve more, for instance, than responding to a reading or a series of questions and then reporting back to the class), you should structure your assignments with particular care.

Effective collaborative learning assignments share the following characteristics:

- They require collaboration for the project to be completed successfully. Otherwise, they may seem like a waste of time to some students.
- They are explained in writing so students don't have to begin by arguing about the assignment.
- They suggest how the group should approach each stage of the assignment. They may also suggest possible roles for group members (recorder, timekeeper, reporter, and so on).
- They build opportunities for self-evaluation and peer evaluation into the assignment.
- They encourage group members to negotiate issues of authority and responsibility; they also encourage creative conflict while protecting minority views.

How can collaboration be graded? Simple check-off systems can provide the basis for a grade on collaborative work, using records submitted by groups at the end of each class.

For important, lengthy projects, students can receive a group grade. You can incorporate the feedback generated by troubleshooting and self-analysis in the determination of this grade. Students can submit individual portfolios reflecting their participation in a group project to help demonstrate excellence in leadership and good citizenship. Finally, students can submit peer evaluations in the form of letters assessing the contributions of other group members.

7. *Take advantage of the differences among students.* Working together requires careful leadership by the teacher to successfully organize group work, to initiate dialogue and provide a model of interaction, to keep the class as a learning community focused on its specific goals of studying writing, and, finally, to establish the basis for a sense of community and for good citizenship within that community.

What worries some instructors are the problems students might encounter while working together. What about the moments when students encounter conflict?

Some would say that one of the reasons a teacher-centered classroom limits the possibilities for learning is precisely that it avoids or even represses conflict. When it occurs, you as the instructor can help, not by lecturing, but by showing students how to engage in a dialectical exchange, which takes the other person's point of view into account without abandoning one's own.

8. *Assign multivocal collaborative essays.* Highlighting rather than smoothing over the differences in voices, styles, and perspectives has been an increasingly popular practice among feminists and others who want to honor differences as well as to suggest the collective mode of some groups' decision making. Rather than trying to produce a seamless document projecting agreement, then, your groups might try a collage or collection of their various texts, simply juxtaposed or else assembled with connecting explanations and transitions. Collage-type projects allow groups to realize how differences in language and culture may enhance knowledge.

This discussion of collaborative writing and learning is necessarily brief. For further information, see the suggested readings for collaborative practices at the end of Section 5 (pp. 55–56).

Working with Multilingual and Multicultural Writers

While multilingual writers may encounter some disadvantages in the classroom, they also possess an advantage: Students who do not share majority assumptions, perspectives, and habits of mind—as well as the majority language itself—may be very much aware that knowledge is "situated." If you can develop a classroom in which differences can be talked about and integrated into discussions, the awareness that results will increase all students' critical thinking about writing and the rhetorical situation. This attitude will also likely enlarge the perspectives of some students who have limited experience with other cultures and languages.

This does not mean that the academic writing you teach will be equally understandable to all students. In some instances, cultural assumptions prevent students from recognizing what they ought to do. For example, those who are taught to imitate rather than be independent may feel confused by the very idea of speaking out or being critical.

You may also discover that the difficulties some multilingual students have are shared by students who have grown up speaking English. For example, so-called "Generation 1.5" students are U.S.-educated English-language learners whose parents may speak little or no English at home. Generation 1.5 students often appear in conversation to be native English speakers; however, they are usually less skilled in the academic language associated with school achievement, especially in the area of writing.

If cultural differences of any kind pose difficulties, try to use them as part of the fabric of the class. We view the classroom as a kind of "contact zone" where various languages and cultures of the world meet, mix, and perhaps reshape each other. If you use this contact zone effectively, you can encourage students to think flexibly about their strategies for writing, to take an experimental and pragmatic perspective, and to try more than one approach to see what works best for them. You can also help students not just to learn the rules of a new language and culture but also to think critically about writing options. For example, it may sometimes be best for students to write first in their home language and translate into English later as needed. At other times, they may find it preferable to compose directly in English, which helps them learn how to think in another language. Students need to make such decisions themselves, but you can provide guidance.

Here, then, are some general guidelines for adapting your teaching of writing to a classroom with multilingual and multicultural students. (In Section 6 of these Instructor's Notes, we provide suggestions specific to *The Academic Writer* chapters.)

- *Make good use of differences in language and culture.* Instruction should respect—and take advantage of—the students' knowledge about their own language and culture. The "Notes for Multilingual Writers" that appear throughout the text encourage this kind of discussion.

- *Foster a nonthreatening environment for class participation.* For example, in the early days of the term, ask all students to hand in questions they'd like to discuss, and read them yourself rather than having students ask those questions orally. If students who might have been reluctant to speak see that their questions are fine and prompt discussion, they may begin to speak up themselves.

- *Offer multilingual students options.* Even though the students integrated into your writing class usually will have demonstrated a certain level of mastery in English, using standard English will not always be easy for them. For this reason, you might want to allow multilingual students options to work in their first language, where appropriate. The "For Exploration" activities in *The Academic Writer* could be written in a native or home language first, and most would not need to be translated. For example, students could work through the "For Exploration" activities on looping, brainstorming, and clustering in Chapter 9, experimenting with invention strategies in their first language, but then draft an essay in English.

- *Recognize problems associated with multiculturalism.* Problems can occur even with students who speak English and seem to have "mainstream" cultural understandings. Social-class differences, for example, can sometimes create misunderstandings and differing expectations similar to those that international students experience in our classrooms.

- *Take the initiative to understand multilingual and multicultural differences.* Don't make it the students' job to educate you about multilingual differences or the problems of multiculturalism. You can demonstrate that you are open to learn more, however, and invite all students to keep you informed about issues generated by their diversity.

For further information, see the suggested readings for multilingual and multicultural writers at the end of Section 5 (p. 57).

Using Portfolios

If you have assigned portfolios for your class, you will need to define the portfolio's purpose, contents, format, due dates, and criteria for evaluation. If other students or other evaluators outside the class will be judging the portfolio, inform students how that will work. When you have students doing a great deal of writing that is ungraded—freewriting, drafts, lists, reflections, group work, and other activities—it makes sense to have them keep a portfolio of their work for review at the end of the term. Direct students to the text's companion Web site for help with portfolios: **bedfordstmartins.com/ academicwriter**. And see the suggested readings on portfolios at the end of Section 5 (p. 57).

Handling the Paper Load

We've all been there: Too many papers, too little time. This section offers some advice on coping by controlling what's submitted in the first place.

A portfolio can be a way to help students manage the paper load by letting them gather all of their work in one place for a final assessment. Course Management Systems allow for the creation of online portfolios, which can provide good practice for your students for workplace writing. For more ideas about teaching online, see "Teaching Online Writing" in Section 5 (pp. 50–52).

Alternatively, some instructors reduce the number of finished essays they require students to complete in a single term, while increasing the number of revisions and drafts. Although one aspect of the paper load is perhaps improved, other problems quickly appear. How can instructors keep track of and give credit for the prewriting, drafting, and revising they require or encourage students to complete?

We suggest that instructors cope with the paper load created by multiple drafts by detailing in the clearest, most straightforward terms what they expect of students. A handout like "A Note to Students about Writing Assignments"

(p. 38) specifies what students are to turn in for writing assignments and thus will help both you and your students organize their work more efficiently. (Note that you will need to provide a lengthier handout if you assign portfolios. See *The Academic Writer*'s companion Web site for information on student portfolios: **bedfordstmartins.com/academicwriter**.)

You will discover that your students' responses to the questions at the end of the handout will help increase their efficiency and effectiveness as writers. We have found that even relatively unskilled writers have a good sense of their essay's strengths and limitations. Having students articulate this means that you can begin feedback with comments such as the following: "As you suggested, Stephanie, your introduction sets your essay up nicely, but after a paragraph or so your writing does indeed lose focus."

A final note: Students do need wide-ranging responses to their writing, but the fact is that students need to write much, much more than writing instructors can reasonably hope to evaluate. You can greatly increase the focus and effectiveness of their evaluations by pressing students to draw on other resources such as writing centers for help.

Responding to Student Writing

The dialogue you establish with students through your responses to their writing plays a crucial role in determining your effectiveness as an instructor—and their success as students. Much has been written about instructors' comments on students' writing. Here we limit our discussion to several important principles:

1. *Mark, but do not correct, errors.* Research suggests that it is not helpful to provide detailed corrections of student errors or to line-edit their writing. Scholars have known for some time that many student errors are errors of performance (sloppy errors) rather than errors of competence (errors where the student truly does not know the correct form or rule). Accordingly, we suggest that when you read students' writing, you just put a checkmark next to any line with an error. (If there are multiple errors in a line, put multiple checkmarks—one for each error.)

Tell students that you will be happy to identify errors if they're unable to do so, but encourage them to attempt to identify and correct errors first. Point out that if they read papers aloud—even tape-record them—they will rapidly improve their ability to correct many problems of voice, syntax, style, diction, and even punctuation.

On days that essays are due, give students ten minutes or so to reread their essays and to correct any errors that they recognize. This practice helps students develop stronger editing skills and reduces some of your work as reader of student writing.

Errors that seem to be the result of widespread misunderstandings in your class can be the topic of an illustrated mini-lecture. Writing mechanics can also be explained in an attachment or link to a Web page student reference for your class or your writing program.

A Note to Students about Writing Assignments

Because I want to provide numerous opportunities for you to revise your writing, I have limited your assignments to [insert # of major assignments here] essays—roughly one essay [every other/every third] week. You will thus have time to plan and draft each essay, participate in peer-response groups, and revise your writing. All of these activities are important to your improvement as a writer. Consequently, when you turn in each draft of an essay, I want to examine not just your current typed draft but also any drafts or other work that preceded it. I can study the process you used to write an essay only if you organize your work carefully. (Doing so will also help you keep track of your progress and return to wording in earlier drafts, should you decide you'd like to do this.) Whenever you hand in an assignment, please be sure to include all of the following items that are relevant, arranged in the order listed below. Please arrange related items together, such as invention and other planning materials. Turn in all material for an essay in a file folder, a pocket folder, or electronically as indicated in each essay assignment.

1. Invention and other planning materials—all the notes, diagrams, random jottings, lists, or other things that you wrote down to stimulate or collect your thinking before and during drafting

2. Rough drafts—all working drafts, numbered in order of completion (and with pages numbered in each draft and in legible handwriting)

3. Peer-response forms—indicating the names of the students who responded to your work

4. Your revision—with each page numbered

5. Statement from you that answers the following questions:
   a. How did you write this essay? What was hard? Easier? How long (roughly) did you work on it, etc.?
   b. What aspect or aspects of this paper are you most satisfied with, and why?
   c. What aspect or aspects of this paper are you least satisfied with, and why?
   d. What did you learn about yourself as a writer by working on this essay?

2. *Make your comments to students count.* Remember that your job is not to comment on every strength or weakness in a student's essay but to provide advice that students can use as they write and revise. It is better to concentrate on a few salient points than to overwhelm the student with a multitude of suggestions and corrections. Brief, focused reading of certain sections can at times be more helpful than global responses.

3. *Make comments that reflect your reading process.* Indicate when you're intrigued, confused, or puzzled. Ask questions. Respond to the content of the essay. Let students know that a person (not a grading machine) is reading their work.

4. *Be sure to find ways to tell students what they are doing well.* Write summarizing statements that say what worked, what was persuasive, what was accomplished.

5. *Comment on the rhetorical situation of the essay.* Frequently, an early draft of an essay will suffer from an incomplete or poorly developed sense of situation. Your comments about the situation that the paper implies can help the student think more clearly about this aspect of writing.

6. *When you make suggestions for revision, focus on strategies rather than on specific content.* For example, if a draft is rambling or incoherent, you might ask the student to write a descriptive outline or to summarize the essay and then to reflect on the degree to which it fulfills his or her controlling purpose. Be especially attentive to the need for multilingual students to fully understand the concept of revision.

7. *Help students understand your comments by giving a public reading of one or more student papers, commenting as you go.* By showing students how you read their writing, you can demythologize the process and help students better interpret your comments. To engage in this process of commentary in class, you can make a transparency of a student paper (with permission) or provide copies of student papers for comment via email.

8. *Publish their writing.* In order to motivate students and give them a sense of audience, you might want to consider producing a class publication of students' writing. Sometimes we make such a publication the first assignment in the class. You might ask students, for instance, to write a brief essay on who they are as writers. After compiling students' essays, this publication could become a collection of readings for the class. On other occasions, we have made a class publication the culminating class activity. In this case, students would have the option of choosing their strongest essay and providing copies. Students may offer to contribute artwork, lettering, or a computer graphic for the cover, or you could collaborate on a design for a Web site.

Publishing a collection of essays gives students a sense of accomplishment. It also gives them a reason to take the last step of editing seriously. Some instructors have classes buy packets of selected examples of student writing drawn from past terms. Some programs, such as the Composition Program at the University of Arizona, publish books of essays selected from student submissions, together with comments and questions.

9. *Encourage multiple responses.* Students benefit from multiple responses. You can help them find other readers through peer-response groups, writing centers, and sharing their work with friends, family, roommates, and others.

For further resources on responding to student writing, see the reading suggestions at the end of Section 5 (p. 58).

Helping Students Plan and Manage Writing Time

Your syllabus will define the general schedule for the term, so students will know when assignments of reading and writing are due. However, you may find that many students lack a clear idea of how to plan their writing time effectively when they work on assignments outside of class. You might want to provide class time for groups to share advice about scheduling and completing writing projects; you can also have students interview others about how much time writing takes (something they are not often realistic about). You may want your students to return to the "Guidelines for Managing a Research Project" (p. 169) in Chapter 6 each time they begin a writing project. If your students continue to have trouble scheduling their writing as the course progresses, refer them to Chapter 10, "Strategies for Planning and Drafting," as needed.

Don't be afraid to talk with your students about your own writing habits and rituals and what works for you. The testimony of many professional writers suggests that a regular turn at the writing desk is essential, whether one feels productive or not. Surprisingly, some of the students who have the most trouble with blocks and procrastination are people who don't allow themselves to stop writing once they have started. This kind of "must work until death" attitude leads them to put off writing. Sometimes it helps to suggest that such students keep *both ends* of a schedule—sticking to their planned quitting time even though they can imagine writing more.

Evaluating Your Teaching

And finally, after grading your students' work, you may wonder how well you are doing. Teaching, like writing, takes place within a rhetorical situation. You will surely wish to assess your own progress in reaching your class and to make adjustments to improve instruction during the term.

The frequent sampling of students' experiences, ideas, drafts, and reflections that *The Academic Writer* suggests will serve as an important means of keeping in touch with your class, so that these informal moments of evaluation can take place with no special structure beyond the dialogic form of instruction. Informal write-to-learn activities can also provide useful feedback. You might end a class period, for instance, by asking students to (1) write one thing they've learned as a result of class discussion or activities or (2) write one question they have or one difficulty they're experiencing. Such comments can give you a good sense of students' progress.

Still, you will probably wish to provide for some more formalized kinds of evaluation. Your students may have plenty of opportunities to give you feedback about how they are doing and yet not take full advantage of the possibility. There may be misunderstandings about your aims and procedures that you need to address straightforwardly; students may believe that you expect them to be good students in terms defined by teacher-centered or lecture-dominated classrooms, for example. They may also expect you to be a good teacher according to such norms. Thus you may wish to take time periodically to explicitly evaluate the progress of the class. You can do this yourself by asking students for anonymous comments or soliciting comments and suggestions in an ongoing way—perhaps with a suggestion box or an email location. If your class has a Course Management System such as Blackboard, you can set up an anonymous quiz.

You can also benefit from bringing others into your classroom to observe and comment. If your institution provides the opportunity, try midterm evaluation visits from an instructional center or from colleagues, whose interviews with your students can reveal trends you had not noticed and whose observations of the class can give you the benefit of a disengaged opinion. The benefits of such visits depend on collegiality and a shared understanding of your writing program. They should be "formative" rather than "summative" evaluations—that is, directed toward improving instruction rather than making judgments about your teaching ability. Such evaluations should begin with a conference before the visit when you discuss your goals and your concerns and also include a postvisit conference when you can hear the views of the evaluator and explore any changes in your teaching that you want to make.

In most colleges and universities your teaching will be evaluated in a more formal way when the class has finished. Perhaps students will be asked to fill out an evaluation form or write brief comments. Many institutions that are paying more careful attention to teaching are asking for teaching portfolios. Your own notes and reflections about the class, together with the syllabus, sample papers, handouts, and even letters from students, are items that may eventually contribute to a portfolio representing your teaching of that class in a final evaluation.

The following questions are often included in institutional evaluations. Although teaching evaluations may seem to assume a teacher-centered classroom, they are also useful for teachers of classrooms using response groups and collaborative activities. Think about ways to determine how well your class is doing—and how well your students understand your approach.

1. *Did the instructor make this class interesting? The Academic Writer* tries to show students how to build their own sense of commitment to writing assignments rather than depend on teachers or on the content of assignments. The frequent responses to their concerns and to their work that are a part of a collaborative classroom do, however, form a major component in generating interest. You can improve students' engagement in your writing class through the quality of their interactions with you and with other students. And you can teach them how to improve the quality of their interactions in other classes and with other instructors by thinking in terms of building engagement rather than depending on instructors to make the course interesting.

2. *Is the instructor well organized?* When you teach a writing course, all the recommendations made for organizing collaborative writing groups are appropriate. That is, it's important to make goals clear, timelines definite, agreements explicit—and it's important to attend to group process, to make sure everyone understands and has a chance to contribute, to ensure that disagreement has a place, and to communicate students' responsibilities.

Unlike lecture-centered classrooms, whose success may seem to depend on the teacher's preparation alone, writing classrooms depend for their success on students' participation as well. In particular, this may mean thoughtful attention to the organization of response groups and collaborative assignments. It also means finding ways to keep track of the many kinds of writing and reading you ask students to do, whether graded or not.

3. *Did the teacher give clear assignments?* Were expectations clear? Our experience suggests that students greatly appreciate explicit guidelines. The many Guidelines and Questions features included in *The Academic Writer* should help students know what to do step by step as they work through the writing process. They will also appreciate explicit assignments from you and help with understanding the grading system you will use. Students generally find essay writing and essay exams much less "clear" than "objective'" measures. If you find this to be true for your students, you might want to talk with them about ways of evaluating the complexities of writing and collaborative work.

4. *Have you learned significantly from this course?* For a writing class, this question should not be translated as "Have you learned to write yet?" As we who are professionals in the field know well, writing is not a skill that can be mastered once and for all. Your class ought to help students plan and critically assess their own writing projects within a rhetorical situation that is appropriate. This sense of critical authority, this increasing self-confidence in learning more about how to write—and not learning to write in any final way— may be their most significant achievement in your class.

Incorporating Community Service and Writing

Many writing programs have added a service learning component to their classes. *The Academic Writer* is ideally suited for community service writing projects, which typically take one of two forms:

1. Students may write assignments—such as brochures, newsletters, posters, or Web sites—for a specific community organization.
2. Students may work as interns or volunteers in a community organization and write reflectively about their experiences.

To include a community service assignment in your class, you need to work out an arrangement between a local organization and your students. Doing so will be easier if you have a list of contacts with telephone numbers and email addresses. (Such a list may already be available on your campus or at your community chamber of commerce.) Following is a brief list of steps you might have students follow. (Modify this list accordingly if your students will work as interns or volunteers.)

Guidelines for Organizing Community Service Assignments

1. Contact and interview a representative of the community organization for which you will write.

2. Develop a written proposal—or work schedule—for your project that states clearly what you will do and how long you believe it will take.

3. Develop a brief checklist that can serve as a basis for evaluation by the organization's representative, and leave some space for his or her comments.

4. Complete the project, and submit a copy to the instructor as well as to the organization, together with the signed evaluation.

For information on setting up your writing class to include community service as a component, see the suggested readings at the end of Section 5 (p. 56).

SECTION 5: TEACHING KEY CONCEPTS

This section of the Instructor's Notes offers practical advice for addressing in class some of the key concepts covered by *The Academic Writer*, including academic writing, information literacy and research, research writing, online writing, visual rhetoric, and writing as design. Also included is a section of suggested readings for these concepts and for the challenges discussed in Section 4.

Teaching Academic Writing

Argument and/as Inquiry

Chapter 4, "Analyzing Texts and Contexts," and Chapter 5, "Making and Supporting Claims," help students understand that academic argument is active inquiry that is dependent on reason and analysis. These chapters draw on several theories of argument: Aristotle's analysis of rhetorical appeals, stasis theory, and Stephen Toulmin's descriptions of the elements of argument.

The text explains that there is, in fact, a continuum of "argument" in academic writing, and that from one perspective, everything written is an argument. However, some kinds of writing call for more structured argument, with a recognizable thesis, a "question at issue," and careful articulation of reasons and evidence. Such reasoned and supported argument enjoys a privileged status in academia because Western culture endorses it.

Some students in your classes may come from cultures that prefer less pointed forms of reasoning. You should point out that they may need to master Western approaches in order to write successfully in current and future courses. Toward that end, they may find it useful to think in terms of switching genres. If poets can learn to write sonnets as well as haiku, students can learn to write arguments that will earn them success and a hearing for their ideas.

At the same time, we cannot totally separate academic argument from the open-ended processes of inquiry—from the pursuit of knowledge rather than persuasion, from evaluating counterarguments, and from admitting uncertainty. The need for this connection may not always be apparent to students. One of our students, deeply involved in animal rights activities, explained that she composed her arguments by beginning with the conclusion she wanted her readers to arrive at, trying out all the ways she could to persuade them to agree with her, and refuting any possible rebuttal they could find. Because she failed to include the possibility of changing her own mind or of discovering knowledge that would modify her ideas, this student pursued an idea of argument contrary to the kind of academic inquiry presented in *The Academic Writer*. She did not realize that her work would actually be stronger by incorporating and respecting naysayers and by setting up her position as entering an ongoing conversation by acknowledging alternatives while presenting her own views.

One way you can help your students transition to more sophisticated college writing is to have your class and your classroom serve as a model of effective and engaged inquiry. The careful processes of reflection, analysis, searching for evidence, and weighing of reasons, as well as the effort to be understood clearly, will help them better understand the values and expectations that inform academic writing. You can help them by repeatedly calling attention to these processes and by monitoring students' understanding.

For additional discussions of argument, see the selected readings at the end of this section (p. 55).

Tone

Your students still may have difficulty understanding—or they may be intimidated by—academic writing. Many think that academic writing requires a stuffy formal tone and were taught to avoid the use of first-person pronouns at all costs. Others come into class writing in a casual and conversational style they might use when talking to friends. The challenge, then, is to teach an appropriate academic language and tone.

As *The Academic Writer* shows, many disciplines in the humanities use the first-person, but for students whose disciplines generally do *not* favor the personal pronoun, you can help them see how they can take a position without using "I" by making moves such as "although formerly it was thought that . . . , newer data suggest . . . ."

Some students may find it especially difficult to write in ways that seem overly formal or distant from their cultural traditions. Indeed, you may be sympathetic to these students. International students testify that academic writing in North America sometimes seems to them "rude" or insulting to the reader because of what seems to be an abrupt statement of thesis at the beginning of a traditional academic essay. It's helpful for all students in your class to know about these differences, since they may inadvertently violate cultural sensibilities when they are writing for international readers (a common occurrence on the Internet).

What Counts As Evidence

Another distinction you can help your students with is "what counts as evidence" in a particular discipline or assignment. Many students assume that academic discourse tries to avoid personal preferences. However, much contemporary composition scholarship has challenged the very idea that such purity is possible; accordingly, many professors in the humanities encourage their students to intertwine the personal with course content and to argue from their own sense of values. Most scholars in rhetoric and composition agree that the purpose of academic writing is to engage students with important ideas so they can become not only successful students but also active critical thinkers and citizens. In this regard, an abstract situation of argument is less important than whether the argument matters to the writer and the reader. For example, Patricia Bizzell says, "What I really care about is what my students believe, how they will conduct their lives, and not just whether they have learned to analyze beliefs or lives in correct postmodern fashion" (*Academic Discourse and Critical Consciousness* 279).

In other disciplines and for certain types of writing, such as a lab report, for example, students will be expected to be as objective and impersonal as possible. Therefore, in order to become successful academic writers, your students will have to learn how to differentiate between genres in disciplines as well as how to distinguish opinions from reasoned, well-supported arguments. You can point out that opinions have value, particularly when they establish a helpful context and clarify a rhetorical situation, but that for opinions to "count" in the academy they must become part of a process of inquiry rather than a conversation-ending generalization. You can also emphasize that in academic writing (and in classroom discussions), evidence and reasons are as important as conclusions. You may find it helpful to contrast academic writing and inquiry with discussions and debates students may have heard on television, where an attitude of conclusiveness trumps the search for knowledge. Just as we need to suspend a "rush to judgment" when researching and follow our inquiry where it leads us, so students need to learn to be open minded about evidence and about decisions they make in their writing processes.

Teaching Information Literacy and Research

Whether a new graduate teaching assistant (TA) or an experienced tenure-line faculty member, writing instructors these days are expected to keep up to date with constant advances in information literacy (IL). This section aims to help with some ways to think about and teach information literacy in the writing classroom. There is also a list of suggested reading about information literacy at the end of this section (p. 57).

As writing instructors, we have probably all written research-based arguments. Some of us remember using card catalogs and index cards, while others cannot remember searching without Google Scholar and Zotero to record our sources. New technologies ease and speed the process of finding information, but the same challenges remain of finding the relevant conversations to enter and the evidence we need for our writing.

It is commonly said that recent high school graduates are digital natives, having grown up using computers. However, many instructors encounter surprising variations in students' information literacy skills. Although they may be proficient at social networking, for example, they often need help with information technologies, and many of them find the wealth of resources offered by libraries to be overwhelming.

Perhaps most significantly, many first-year students struggle to understand effective search concepts and techniques. Many students arrive in classes with little significant experience doing research and still thinking in terms of the old-fashioned, five-paragraph essay. For these students, IL may be a new and unfamiliar concept. It's your job to help them gain a much broader and more sophisticated view of what IL means so they can become effective and, hopefully, eager learners. Chapter 6 provides students with a fresh way to think about research and gives you a framework for helping them move forward.

The Academic Writer's emphasis on starting by analyzing the rhetorical situation for any writing project guides students to search out which conversations they could listen to and enter. Chapters 5 and 6 help students understand that the expectations of academic writing go well beyond a hunt for a handful of sources to support their predetermined thesis statements. Students will discover how writing that acknowledges and engages with other speakers on their topic will be more interesting and more persuasive than the kinds of writing projects they're used to composing.

Some Background on Information Literacy (IL)

Although term papers have been assigned in writing classes since the 1940s or even earlier, the explicit emphasis on the concept of IL dates to the early 1990s. According to NCTE's policy statement "Literacy Learning in the 21st Century,"

> **Twenty-first century students need to gather information from multiple sources, evaluate their reliability, and apply their findings effectively.** *Most students like to use the Web, but often lack skills necessary to find information or to use that information effectively. Teachers need to provide explicit instruction on strategies such as formulating a research question, evaluating information, evaluating the search process, and assimilating information[1] . . . Therefore, professional development about information literacy is crucial.[2]*

While this NCTE statement relates to K–12 instruction, its claim about twenty-first-century literacies applies equally to college writing classes because of what students may or may not have learned before arriving at college.

Further, WPA Outcomes[3] for college writing classes clearly overlap with the Information Literacy Competencies of the Association of College and Research Libraries (ACRL). (For a detailed comparison, see the analysis by Barbara D'Angelo of Arizona State University at **http://knol.google.com/k/information-literacy-and-wpa-outcomes-statement#**.) These intertwined goals can help you plan writing assignments and lesson plans. The close connections between writing and IL have engendered productive collaborations between composition and library faculty for expanding IL learning in writing classes.

Assessing Your Students' Information Literacy

Asking students to complete a short questionnaire in class on their previous research and library experience can help you assess their current knowledge and prepare what they need next. You may notice that quite a few students suffer from "library anxiety," a concept described by librarian Constance Mellon over twenty years ago for the resistance students exhibit—"research-phobia"—when feeling overwhelmed by searching in libraries (which of course now includes searching via library web pages and databases). The

---

[1]Footnote from the NCTE policy statement Kulper, E., Colman, M., & Terwel, J. (2005). The web as an information resource in K–12 education: Strategies for supporting students in searching and processing information. *Review of Educational Research* 75(3), 283–328.

[2]**http://www.ncte.org/library/NCTEFiles/Resources/Magazine/CC0183_Brief_Literacy.pdf**

[3]See the section "Note for Writing Program Administrators" in these Instructor's Notes (pp. 4–5).

"too-much-information" syndrome remains, coupled with insecurity about using new tools. In addition, as reluctant as students can be to ask their writing instructors for help and information, they can be even more reluctant to ask for help from an unknown librarian. That's why many libraries now have a "live chat" tool to encourage students to seek help. You can help them enormously if you can show them how much they're missing if they rely solely on Google. Such humorous YouTube clips as "Help Me, Ninja Librarian" (**www.youtube.com/watch?v=rYDb4fzowB8**) can also help students overcome their reluctance to enter the library (even virtually).

Note: Instructors are not immune to library anxiety, and even some writing instructors dread required research paper assignments. This can explain why faculty are sometimes reluctant to consult librarians for help teaching or to invite librarians into their classes. When instructors are less than eager about an assignment, students pick up the attitude too. Your job, then, is to embrace the excitement of research and share that with students.

What Resources Are Available at Your School?

Wherever you are teaching, you should make an effort to find out your institutions' resources for teaching information literacy. Ask whether librarians can come to your classroom or whether the library sponsors workshops for an introduction/review of the library databases and research skills. Some librarians are able and willing to make an interactive library page for your class and assignments, with links to online course pages and tutorials at your library and at other universities. For example, check out the CLIP (Collaborative Library Instruction Project) tutorials at **http://clip-il.wetpaint.com/page/Tutorials**, which demonstrate such topics as evaluating Internet sources and incorporating sources into research papers.

Teaching Research Writing

Many students assume that all writing is creative or personal unless research is specifically assigned. Most writing, however, requires knowledge about context, other debates, audience, evidence, and details. In other words, much of what we write is based on the knowledge that research—formal or informal—provides. As Oregon State University graduate student Travis Margoni pointed out at a presentation at the 4th Annual Oregon Information Literacy Summit, instructors can even assign research for a personal literacy narrative as students fill in details to bring the scenes alive for readers. Chapter 6 of *The Academic Writer* provides research techniques that students can use to effectively join the scholarly conversation on a variety of topics.

Ideally, students will come to view research as a natural part of the writing process and will recognize that ethical standards govern research. For example, when you point out to students that interviewing other class members about their views is a form of research, you help them see the need for conducting such inquiries responsibly and carefully. You also help them understand that informal research is a part of their everyday lives.

Evaluating Sources

Evaluating Web sites in particular is a key issue to work on with your students. In Chapter 6 of *The Academic Writer*, the "Guidelines for Evaluating Sources" (pp. 191–92) help students assess the rhetorical situation of a site and determine how credible it is and how it might best be used. The assignments in Chapter 6 will help students expand their ability to conduct effective Web searches and critically evaluate all sources. For an additional overview and discussion of evaluation criteria, see the CLIP tutorial at **http://clip-il.wetpaint .com/page/Tutorials** and Elizabeth Kirk's "Evaluating Information Found on the Internet" at **www.library.jhu.edu/researchhelp/general/evaluating**.

Documentation and Plagiarism

Documentation and plagiarism are also key issues for writing courses that incorporate research. Students frequently turn to the Web for answers to questions, but they are not in the habit of documenting such research. Some think they only have to cite actual quotes. To help students acknowledge their debts to others, refer them to Chapter 6 of *The Academic Writer*, which covers the documentation of written material (quotations, paraphrases, summaries) as well as visuals. "Guidelines for Avoiding Plagiarism" (p. 200) provides students with a clear view of their responsibilities. Other sections of Chapter 6, along with the "Writers' References" section at the back of the book, will help students integrate and document source material appropriately.

Assigning this material for students' careful review is, therefore, essential. Because reinforcement of the principles explained there is almost always necessary, however, it helps to be prepared. Here are some common problems you may encounter:

- *Understanding when to credit a source.* Students may not understand that slightly changing the original words of a source does not eliminate the necessity of documenting it. In addition, many students don't understand that they have to not only change the words but also the sentence structure of a passage for an ethical paraphrase. The section on plagiarism in Chapter 6 emphasizes ways you can structure assignments in order to help students avoid unintentional plagiarism. Such plagiarism is partly a problem of sloppy note taking or a lack of knowledge about documentation conventions. One useful outside resource for introducing students to the practice of acknowledging sources is Referen©ite from the University of Aukland (**http://cite.auckland.ac.nz/**), which features a series of video clips of international students talking about citation.

- *Using sources to gain credibility.* Sometimes students do not realize that they gain credibility by using quotations and other sources only when such source material is relevant and appropriate. While all of *The Academic Writer* provides support for such inquiry, Chapter 6 discusses the evaluation and use of sources in depth.

- *Integrating quotations successfully.* Most students do not know how to integrate quotations into their own text gracefully. *The Academic Writer* provides some help with this, particularly on pp. 194–200, but your students will benefit from some class time spent on the mechanics of this. Working on paraphrasing, summarizing, and so forth can help eliminate the common practice of patch-writing, using large chunks of quoted texts.

- *Encountering several levels of plagiarism.* It is clearly academic dishonesty when students simply copy someone else's work and call it their own—downloading a paper from the Internet, copying a paper written by another student, reusing their own paper from another class, or copying from printed works, perhaps from more than one—and most students recognize this. They may not understand, however, that pasting together quotations from a number of sources without acknowledgment also constitutes plagiarism. They are also often unsure as to what counts as "common knowledge" that does not need to be cited. You may want to supplement your discussion of plagiarism with the Bedford/St.Martin's CD-ROM "i-cite visualizing sources" at **bedfordstmartins.com/icite**.

- *Curbing plagiarism in your course.* A clear announcement on your syllabus and in your class, some time spent in explanation, and follow-up detection work on multiple drafts will help ensure that your students do not practice plagiarism in your class. Engaging students fully in the writing process and asking them to save print or online copies of work in progress also discourages plagiarism. Some instructors ask for photocopies or printouts of all work that has been cited.

- *Addressing cultural differences and plagiarism.* Be ready to spend extra time explaining documentation to multicultural writers. There are cultural differences in how sources are used in texts, and these students may not be familiar with Western conventions of intellectual property and documentation practices.

Teaching Online Writing

Whether you teach in a computer lab; a classroom with a computer, projector, and document camera; or a traditional classroom that is not yet wired (and that does not have wireless), you can use electronic technologies to enrich your teaching.

In many colleges and universities, both instructors and students have access to Course Management Systems (CMS) such as Blackboard. The use of such systems can help you achieve efficiencies in your teaching—by posting course materials and PowerPoint presentations, sending email to your students, conducting peer review online, and extending classroom discussions via a discussion board or list. Your CMS may offer podcasting of lectures and Virtual Office Hour features. We encourage you to become familiar with these ways of extending your teaching and the classroom experience.

If your classroom has an Internet connection and you have access to a projector, you may use the Internet as a basis for class discussions and analyses and for teaching information literacy. You may, for example, analyze several Web sites in class, using the "Guidelines for Evaluating Sources" in Chapter 6 (pp. 191–92). Even without an Internet connection, if you have access to a laptop computer and a projector, you can bring examples into class to demonstrate.

Students' Expertise in Online Writing

Students arrive with varying experience and expertise in online writing. Many students text regularly and maintain social network sites. You can draw on these experiences to help them build bridges between their self-sponsored writing and their academic writing. A surprising number may arrive not knowing the basics of how to format an academic essay using a word processing program (e.g., putting in headers or footnotes) or how to do effective keyword searching in an academic database. Be prepared to help some catch up.

Helping Students Understand Online Writing Rhetorically

Although many students are experienced online communicators, they still need to learn how to think rhetorically about the online writing they do and about the public nature of the Internet. Students need to be aware that some people have failed to get positions for which they have applied because employers have checked their MySpace or Facebook sites (and not much liked what they found there). Emails that are too informal may cause professors to decline giving a recommendation.

You can generate interesting and informative class discussion by asking students about differences in the way they compose text messages to friends versus email messages to teachers and supervisors. (Many current students view email as an old-fashioned and somewhat cumbersome technology in comparison to texting, IMing, and tweeting.) Most students have a good deal to say about this and related issues.

Using Online Writing in Your Classroom

The following suggestions will help you integrate online writing in a way that makes sense for you, and for your students:

- *Assess the knowledge and access your students have as soon as possible.* It is always good to talk with your students to determine if any have limited access to computers and the Internet. It is equally helpful to inquire about their technological expertise. Some distance-learning programs require students to complete a survey to assure that they have sufficient technology and technology skills to complete the class successfully. If you make assumptions without checking, you may waste class time explaining what everyone knows. Or you may face a class of frustrated and demoralized students who have not been able to follow your instructions.
- *Highlight resources such as computer labs and workshops.* Check the resources of your institution for both hardware (laptops and computer labs) and software training. Workshops offered by the computer center, the library, the teaching resources center, or the writing program itself

may range from basic uses of email and Web browsers to more advanced Web publishing, discussion groups, and collaborative writing programs.

• *Realize that using electronic technologies requires extra time.* Be sure to plan accordingly. We estimate that adding significant amounts of online writing, particularly if you meet in a computer classroom, may cut your time for class activities by as much as one-third—even though your reading and writing assignments have not increased.

• *Give your students explicit directions about using email to interact with you.* Don't forget to include your email address on your syllabus. Then specify: What kinds of email do you want? Will you comment on drafts and papers? What turnaround time should students expect when they email you?

• *Plan how you will organize the submission of online assignments.* The more work you accept online, the more critical it becomes to think about how you will keep track of it and ensure access when you need it. You should also consider whether you will comment electronically (perhaps with Track Changes?) or print their work to add handwritten comments.

• *Remember that you are teaching writing, not technology.* You are not expected to be a technology expert, although you should not ask students to do what you do not understand well enough to explain briefly. The simplest functions (use of email, CMS, and Web sites) have interesting and extensive rhetorical implications; there's no need to add technological complexity to the coursework. Above all, keep in view your central purpose. *The Academic Writer* emphasizes the rhetorical situation of online writing, not the technology needed to do it.

Teaching Visual Rhetoric

The concept of visual rhetoric is integrated throughout *The Academic Writer*. Chapter 4, "Analyzing Texts and Contexts," and Chapter 8, "Strategies for Reading," lead students carefully through strategies for reading visual texts. Chapter 5, "Making and Supporting Claims," and Chapter 11, "Strategies for Designing Pages and Screens," discuss appropriate and effective uses of visuals in academic writing. You can take advantage of this attention to using visuals and document design by including visual texts in your assignments for both reading and writing.

If you encourage or assign the composition of Web-based texts, attention to design elements will be crucial. Of course, visual elements can also significantly strengthen conventional text-based assignments, and writing in many disciplines includes the use of maps, charts, graphs, and tables. For examples, refer students to the student texts by Daniel Stiepleman in Chapter 5 and Alletta Brenner in Chapter 6 of *The Academic Writer*. You may wish to help students make this connection by having them describe what the visual elements contribute to these essays.

For an approach to visual rhetoric online, see "Visual Rhetoric," available at **www.sla.purdue.edu/dblakesley/visual**. For exercises offering practice with visual analysis, go to **bedfordstmartins.com/rewriting** and click on Visual Analysis. For further reading, see the Visual Texts list at the end of this section (p. 58).

Teaching Writing as Design

Drawing on cutting-edge composition theory, Chapter 1, "Rethinking Writing," introduces the concept of writing as design. The design concept as explained on page 9 through the work of Bryan Lawson helps students see that the writing situation is complex.

For some students, the idea that writing may be open-ended rather than clearly formulaic can be liberating, while other students, used to Scantron graded tests with right answers, may find this frustrating. This frustration can also affect students' reactions to holistic essay grading, when they get a B and wonder what mistakes they made or where points were taken off. Explaining the idea of writing as design helps you show students that grades reflect general overall quality of writing, not just lack of errors. Working with this concept will also help students value revision and collaboration more highly.

Further Reading in Composition Studies

The following bibliography does not attempt to list all the works that might be included in a basic bibliography of works on composition. Rather, we have included here those works that, by their broad scope or bibliographic emphasis, provide useful introductions to different areas.

Should you wish to know more about the theoretical and research basis of *The Academic Writer*, you may find useful the following essays on the teaching of writing by Lisa Ede: "Teaching Writing" in Lindemann and Tate's *Introduction to Composition Studies*, cited below, and "Methods, Methodologies, and the Politics of Knowledge" in Kirsch and Sullivan's *Methods and Methodologies in Composition Studies*, cited below.

General

Bartholomae, David. "Writing with Teachers: A Conversation with Peter Elbow." *CCC* 46 (Feb. 1995): 62–71. Print.

Bartholomae, David, and Anthony Petrosky, eds. *Ways of Reading: An Anthology for Writers*. 4th ed. New York: St. Martin's, 1996. Print.

Beaufort, Anne. *College Writing and Beyond: A New Framework for University Writing Instruction*. Logan: Utah State UP, 2007. Print.

Berlin, James. *Rhetorics, Poetics, and Cultures: Refiguring College English Studies*. Urbana: NCTE, 1996. Print.

Berlin, James, and Michael J. Vivion, eds. *Cultural Studies in the English Classroom*. Portsmouth: Boynton/Cook, 1992. Print.

Bloom, Lynn Z., Donald A. Daiker, and Edward M. White, eds. *Composition Studies in the New Millenium: Reading the Past, Rewriting the Future*. Carbondale: Southern Illinois UP, 2003. Print.

Brandt, Deborah. *Literacy as Involvement: The Acts of Writers, Readers, and Texts*. Carbondale: Southern Illinois UP, 1990. Print.

Bullock, Richard, and John Trimbur. *The Politics of Writing Instruction: Post-secondary*. Portsmouth: Boynton/Cook, Heinemann, 1991. Print.

Clifford, John, and John Schilb. *Writing Theory and Critical Theory*. New York: Modern Language Association of America, 1994. Print.

Corbett, Edward P. J., Nancy Myers, and Gary Tate, eds. *The Writing Teacher's Sourcebook*. 4th ed. New York: Oxford UP, 2000. Print.

Durst, Russel K. *Collision Course: Conflict, Negotiation, and Learning in College Composition*. Urbana: NCTE, 1999. Print.

Eagleton, Terry. *Literary Theory: An Introduction*. Oxford: Blackwell, 1983. Print.

Elbow, Peter. *Writing with Power: Techniques for Mastering the Writing Process*. New York: Oxford UP, 1981. Print.

Enos, Theresa. *A Sourcebook for Basic Writing Teachers*. New York: Random, 1987. Print.

Faigley, Lester. *Fragments of Rationality: Postmodernity and the Subject of Composition*. Pittsburgh: U of Pittsburgh P, 1992. Print.

Flower, Linda. *The Construction of Negotiated Meaning: A Social Cognitive Theory of Writing*. Carbondale: Southern Illinois UP, 1994. Print.

Geertz, Clifford. *Local Knowledge: Further Essays in Interpretive Anthropology*. New York: Basic Books, 1983. Print.

———. *Works and Lives: The Anthropologist as Author*. Stanford, CA: Stanford UP, 1988. Print.

Gould, Stephen Jay. "Evolution as Fact and Theory." *Discover* May 1981: 34–37. Print.

Harkin, Patricia, and John Schilb. *Contending with Words: Composition and Rhetoric in a Postmodern Age*. New York: Modern Language Association of America, 1991. Print.

Heilker, Paul, and Peter Vandenberg, eds. *Keywords in Composition Studies*. Portsmouth: Boynton/Cook, 1996. Print.

Jarratt, Susan, and Lynn Worsham, eds. *Feminism and Composition Studies: In Other Words*. New York: Modern Language Association of America, 1998. Print.

Keller, Evelyn Fox. *Reflections on Gender and Science*. New Haven: Yale UP, 1985. Print.

Kirsch, Geza, and Patricia Sullivan. *Methods and Methodologies in Composition Studies*. Carbondale: Southern Illinois UP, 1992. Print.

Lindemann, Erika, and Gary Tate. *An Introduction to Composition Studies*. New York: Oxford UP, 1991. Print.

Lunsford, Andrea. *The St. Martin's Handbook*. 6th ed. Boston: Bedford/St. Martin's, 2007. Print.

McClelland, Ben W., and Timothy R. Donovan. *Perspectives on Research and Scholarship in Composition*. New York: Modern Language Association of America, 1985. Print.

Reynolds, Nedra, Patricia Bizzell, and Bruce Herzberg, eds. *The Bedford Bibliography for Teachers of Writing*. 6th ed. Boston: Bedford/St. Martin's, 2004. Print.

Rottenberg, Annette T. *Elements of Argument: A Text and Reader*. 8th ed. Boston: Bedford/St. Martin's, 2006. Print.

Spellmeyer, Kurt. *Common Ground: Dialogue, Understanding, and the Teaching of Composition*. Englewood Cliffs: Prentice, 1993. Print.

White, Edward M. *Assigning, Responding, Evaluating: A Writing Teacher's Guide*. 4th ed. Boston: Bedford/St.Martin's, 2007. Print.

Academic Writing

Bartholomae, David. "Writing with Teachers: A Conversation with Peter Elbow." *CCC* 46 (Feb. 1995): 62–71. Print.

——. "Inventing the University." *When a Writer Can't Write*. Ed. Michael Rose. New York: Guilford, 1985. 134–65. Print.

Bizzell, Patricia. *Academic Discourse and Critical Consciousness*. Pittsburgh: U of Pittsburgh P, 1992. Print.

Chiseri-Strater, Elizabeth. *Academic Literacies: The Public and Private Discourse of University Students*. Portsmouth: Boynton/Cook, 1992. Print.

Elbow, Peter. "Being a Writer vs. Being an Academic: A Conflict in Goals." *CCC* 46 (Feb. 1995): 72–83. Print.

——. "Reflections on Academic Discourse: How It Relates to Freshmen and Colleagues," *College English* 53.2 (Feb. 1991): 135–55. Print.

——. "Voice in Writing Again: Embracing Contraries." *College English* 70.2 (2007): 168–88. Print.

Fox, Helen. *Listening to the World: Cultural Issues in Academic Writing*. Urbana, IL: NCTE, 1994. Print.

Geisler, Cheryl. *Academic Literacy and the Nature of Expertise*. Hillsdale: Erlbaum, 1994. Print.

LeCourt, Donna. *Identity Matters: Schooling the Student Body in Academic Discourse*. Albany: SUNY UP, 2004. Print.

Weisser, Christian R. *Moving Beyond Academic Discourse: Composition and the Public Sphere*. Carbondale: Southern Illinois UP, 2002. Print.

Argument

Barnett, Timothy. *Teaching Argument in the Composition Course: Background Readings*. Boston: Bedford/St. Martin's, 2002. Print.

Emmel, Barbara, Paula Resch, and Deborah Tenney, eds. *Argument Revisited, Argument Redefined: Negotiating Meaning in the Composition Classroom*. Thousand Oaks: Sage, 1996. Print.

Fulkerson, Richard. *Teaching the Argument in Writing*. Urbana: NCTE, 1996. Print.

Collaborative Practices

Brooke, Robert, Ruth Mirtz, and Rick Evans. *Small Groups in Writing Workshops: Invitations to a Writer's Life*. Urbana: NCTE, 1994. Print.

Clark, Suzanne, and Lisa Ede. "Collaboration and Resistance." *The Right to Literacy*. Ed. Andrea A. Lunsford, Helene Moglen, and James Slevin. New York: MLA, 1990. 276–85. Print.

"Collaborative Writing." Special issue of *Technical Communication: The Journal of the Society for Technical Communication* 38.4 (1991). Print.

"Collaborative Writing in Business Communication." Special issue of *The Bulletin of the Association for Business Communication* 53.2 (1990). Print.

Ede, Lisa, and Andrea Lunsford. "Collaboration and Concepts of Authorship." *PMLA* 116.2 (Mar. 2001): 354. Print.

——. *Singular Texts/Plural Authors: Perspectives on Collaborative Writing*. Carbondale: Southern Illinois UP, 1990. Print.

Forman, Janis, ed. *New Visions of Collaborative Writing*. Portsmouth: Boynton/Cook, Heinemann, 1992. Print.

LeFevre, Karen Burke. *Invention as a Social Act*. Carbondale: Southern Illinois UP for the Conference on College Composition and Communication, 1987. Print.

Reagan, Sally Barr, Thomas Fox, and David Bleich. *Writing With: New Directions in Collaborative Teaching, Learning, and Research*. Albany: SUNY UP, 1994. Print.

Semones, Lara. "Collaboration, Computer Mediation, and the Foreign Language Writer." *Clearing House* 74.6 (July/Aug. 2001): 308–13. Print.

Spears, Karen. *Sharing Writing: Peer Response Groups in English Classes*. Portsmouth: Boynton/Cook, Heinemann, 1988. Print.

Speck, Bruce W. *Facilitating Students' Collaborative Writing*. San Francisco: Jossey-Bass, 2002. Print.

Spigelman, Candace. *Across Property Lines: Textual Ownership in Writing Groups*. Carbondale: Southern Illinois UP, 2000. Print.

Community Service

Adler-Kassner, Linda, Robert Crooks, and Ann Watters. *Writing the Community*. Urbana: AAHE/NCTE, 1997. Print.

Eyler, Janet, Dwight Giles, and Angela Schmiede. *A Practitioner's Guide to Reflection in Service-Learning: Student Voices and Reflections*. Nashville: Vanderbilt UP, 1996. Print. Note: The National Service-Learning Clearinghouse in Minnesota will provide copies of the guide at cost. Contact: glass007@tc.umn.edu.

Klooster, David, and Patricia Bloem. *The Writer's Community*. New York: St. Martin's, 1995. Print.

Watters, Ann, and Marjorie Ford. *A Guide for Change: Resources for Implementing Community Service Writing*. New York: McGraw-Hill, 1995. Print.

——. *Writing for Change: A Community Reader*. New York: McGraw-Hill, 1995. Print.

Design (Writing as)

Lawson, Bryan, *How Designers Think: The Design Process Demystified*. 4th ed. London: Architectural Press, 2006. Print.

Marback, Richard. "Embracing Wicked Problems: The Turn to Design in Composition Studies." *CCC* 61.2 (2009): 397–419. Print.

Documentation and Plagiarism

Howard, Rebecca Moore. "Sexuality, Textuality: The Cultural Work of Plagiarism." *College English* 62.4 (2000): 473–92. Print.

Porter, James. "Intertextuality and the Discourse Community." *Rhetoric Review* 5.1 (1986): 34–47. Print.

Evaluating Your Teaching

Bramblett, Anne, and Alison Knoblauch, eds. *What to Expect When You're Expected to Teach: The Anxious Craft of Teaching Composition*. Portsmouth: Heinemann, 2002. Print.

Dethier, Brock. *First Time Up: An Insider's Guide for New Composition Teachers*. Logan: Utah State UP, 2006. Print.

Wilhoit, Steven. *The Longman Teaching Assistant's Handbook*. New York: Pearson, 2008. Print.

Handling the Paper Load

Bean, John C. *Engaging Ideas: The Professor's Guide to Integrating Writing, Critical Thinking, and Active Learning in the Classroom*. Hoboken: Jossey-Bass, 1996. Print.

Sommers, Nancy. "Across the Drafts." *CCC* 58.2 (2006): 248–56. Print.

Information Literacy

Ballenger, Bruce. "Rethinking the Research Paper." Paper presented at CCCC, March 1992. Print.

Deitering, Anne-Marie, and Sara Jameson. "Step by Step through the Scholarly Conversation: A Collaborative Library/Writing Faculty Project to Embed Information Literacy and Promote Critical Thinking in First-Year Composition at Oregon State University." *College & Undergraduate Libraries* 15.1–2 (2008): 57–79. Print.

Mellon, Constance. "Attitudes: The Forgotten Dimension in Library Instruction." *Library Journal* 113.14 (1998): 137–40. Print.

Nutefall, Jennifer, and Phyllis Ryder. "Teaching Research Rhetorically." *Academic Exchange Quarterly* 9.4 (Fall 2005): 307–11. Print.

Multilingual and Multicultural Writers

Ballister, Valerie M. *Cultural Divide: A Study of African-American College-Level Writers*. Portsmouth: Boynton/Cook, 1993. Print.

Bizzell, Patricia. "'Contact Zones' and English Studies." *College English* 56.2 (Feb. 1994): 163–69. Print.

Cushman, Ellen. *The Struggle and the Tools: Oral and Literate Strategies in an Inner City Community*. Albany: SUNY UP, 1998. Print.

Dubin, Fraida, and Natalie A. Kuhlman, eds. *Cross-Cultural Literacy: Global Perspectives on Reading and Writing*. Englewood Cliffs: Prentice Hall, 1992. Print.

Durgunoglu, Aydin Yucesan, and Ludo Verhoeven, eds. *Literacy Development in a Multilingual Context: Cross-Cultural Perspectives*. Mahwah: Erlbaum, 1998. Print.

Fox, Helen. *Listening to the World: Cultural Issues in Academic Writing*. Urbana: NCTE, 1994. Print.

Frière, Paolo. *Education for Critical Consciousness*. New York: Continuum, 1973. Print.

——. *Pedagogy of the Oppressed*. New York: Seabury Press, 1970. Print.

Gilyard, Keith. *Let's Flip the Scrip: An African American Discourse on Language and Learning*. Detroit: Wayne State UP, 1996. Print.

Labov, William. *Language in the Inner City*. Philadelphia: U of Pennsylvania P, 1972. Print.

Schaafsma, David. *Eating on the Street: Teaching Literacy in a Multicultural Society*. Pittsburgh: U of Pittsburgh P, 1993. Print.

Schor, Ira, and Caroline Pari, eds. *Critical Literacy in Action: Writing Words, Changing Worlds*. Portsmouth: Boynton/Cook, 1999. Print.

Portfolios

Belanoff, Pat, and Marcia Dickson, eds. *Portfolios: Process and Product*. Portsmouth: Heinemann-Boynton/Cook, 1991. Print.

Yancey, Kathleen Blake. *Portfolios in the Writing Classroom: An Introduction*. Urbana: NCTE, 1992. Print.

Yancey, Kathleen Blake, and Irwin Weiser, eds. *Situating Portfolios: Four Perspectives*. Logan: Utah State UP, 1997. Print.

Reader and Audience

Ede, Lisa. "Audience: An Introduction to Research." *CCC* 35.2 (1984): 140–54. Print.

Ede, Lisa, and Andrea Lunsford. "Audience Addressed/Audience Invoked: The Role of Audience in Composition Theory and Pedagogy." *CCC* 35.2 (1984): 155–70. Print.

——. "Representing Audience: 'Successful' Discourse and Disciplinary Critique." *CCC* 47.2 (1996): 167–79. Print.

Murray, Donald. "All Writing Is Autobiography." *CCC* 42.1 (1991): 66–74. Print.

Responding to Student Writing

Haswell, Richard H. "Minimal Marking." *CE* 45.4 (1983): 600–4. Print.

Horvath, Brooke K. "The Components of Written Response: A Practical Synthesis of Current Views." *Rhetoric Review* 2.1 (1985): 136–56. Print.

Smith, Summer. "The Genre of the End Comment: Conventions in Teacher Responses to Student Writing." *CCC* 48.2 (1997): 249–68. Print.

Sommers, Nancy. "Responding to Student Writing." *CCC* 32.2 (1982): 148–56. Print.

Straub, Richard, ed. *A Sourcebook for Responding to Student Writing*. Creskill: Hamptom P, 1999. Print.

Rhetorical Situation

Grant-Davie, Keith. "Rhetorical Situations and Their Constituents." *Rhetoric Review* 15.2 (1997): 264–79. Print.

The articles below are listed in chronological order because each represents a response to the previous arguments:

Bitzer, Lloyd F. "The Rhetorical Situation." *Philosophy and Rhetoric* 1 (1968): 1–14. Print.

Vatz, Richard E. "The Myth of the Rhetorical Situation." *Philosophy and Rhetoric* 6 (1973): 154–61. Print.

Consigny, Scott. "Rhetoric and Its Situations." *Philosophy and Rhetoric* 7 (1974): 175–86. Print.

Jamieson, Kathleen M. Hall. "Generic Constraints and the Rhetorical Situation." *Philosophy and Rhetoric* 7 (1974): 162–70. Print.

Brinton, Alan. "Situation in the Theory of Rhetoric." *Philosophy and Rhetoric* 14 (1981): 234–48. Print.

Biesecker, Barbara A. "Rethinking the Rhetorical Situation from within the Thematic of Difference." *Philosophy and Rhetoric* 22 (1989): 110–30. Print.

Visual Texts

McQuade, Donald, and Christine McQuade. *Seeing and Writing*. 3rd ed. Boston: Bedford/St. Martin's, 2006. Print.

Odell, Lee, and Susan M. Katz. *Writing in a Visual Age*. Boston: Bedford/St. Martin's, 2006. Print.

Writing Online

Hewett, Beth, and Christa Ehmann. *Preparing Educators for Online Writing Instruction: Principles and Processes*. Urbana: NCTE, 2004. Print.

Warnock, Scott. *Teaching Online, How and Why*. Urbana: NCTE, 2009. Print.

Writing Process

Berkenkotter, Carol. "Decisions and Revisions: The Planning Strategies of a Publishing Writer." *CCC* 34 (1983): 156–69. Print.

Harris, Muriel. "Composing Behaviors of One- and Multi-Draft Writers," *College English* 51.2 (1984): 174–91. Print.

Lamott, Anne. *Bird by Bird: Some Instructions on Writing and Life.* New York: Anchor Books, 1995. Print.

Murray, Donald M. "The Maker's Eye." *Writer* 111.10 (1998): 20–24. Print.

——. "Response of a Laboratory Rat—or, Being Protocoled." *CCC* 34.2 (1983): 169–72. Print.

Osborn, A.F. *Applied Imagination: Principles and Procedures of Creative Problem Solving.* Third Rev. Ed. New York: Scribner's, 1963. Print.

Perl, Sondra. "The Composing Processes of Unskilled College Writers." *Research in the Teaching of English* 13 (1979): 317–36. Print.

Tomlinson, Barbara. "Tuning, Tying, and Training Texts: Metaphors for Revision." *Written Communication* 5 (1988): 58–81. Print.

SECTION 6: CHAPTER-BY-CHAPTER SUGGESTIONS FOR TEACHING FROM *THE ACADEMIC WRITER*

Part I: Writing Matters: Writing and Rhetoric in the Twenty-First Century

In Part I of *The Academic Writer* students are asked to consider what it means to be a writer in the twenty-first century. In order to help them negotiate the communication and writing challenges of this century, Part I leads students from consideration of personal, self-sponsored writing situations to consideration of academic discourse.

Chapter 1: Rethinking Writing: A Rhetorical Process for Composing Texts

Chapter 1 of *The Academic Writer* orients students to their rhetorical situation as writers and readers in the twenty-first century. Changes in technology have created new communication opportunities and challenges for students, and many students will at some point have jobs for which they will have to create a variety of texts. In order to help your students negotiate this terrain, Chapter 1 stresses a commonsense approach to writing, giving students credit for what they already know and forecasting the factors and choices that may enter into learning to improve their writing.

This chapter also counters some of the expectations about a writing class that many students bring with them. It stresses the interactive nature of writing, its complexity, and the need for students to use their judgment in making decisions. The chapter speaks of writing as a process and focuses attention on that process as it is situated in cultures and in specific contexts. It includes discussion of online writing and visual texts as rhetorical issues from the beginning, encouraging students to draw similarities between the principles and characteristics of design and the writing process.

Concepts

1. *Writing in the twenty-first century and the impact of communication technologies:* Chapter 1 begins by asking students to think about the importance of writing in the twenty-first century. Words still play a role in how we communicate, of course, but computers and online technologies allow for the more prominent integration of the visual with the verbal. This chapter helps students think about the impact of technologies on writing and understand how these changes affect how they read texts and approach writing in print and online.

2. *Rhetoric:* Students often have no idea what *rhetoric* means. They may have heard the expression "that's just rhetoric" used to complain about a

political speech or an advertisement, and so they may think of writing as rhetorical when it wrongly values form over content.

You might want to point out to your students that rhetoric does not inherently necessitate this kind of imbalance. Instead, rhetoric is persuasive discourse. Understanding rhetoric requires taking into account the four key elements of the rhetorical situation: the role of the writer, the expectations of readers, the text created to convey ideas, and the medium used to make the communication possible.

You may need to remind your students that there is nothing magical about a rhetorical approach to writing—it is a practical art and offers concrete ways to think about their situations as writers. You can show them that they actually already unconsciously understand the elements of the rhetorical situation—who's speaking, to whom, how, and when—even if they have never studied rhetoric. For example, they already know what's involved in composing the most effective request for borrowing money, in terms of what to say and when, and how this must vary when asking a parent, a close friend, or an acquaintance.

The analogy of writing to design is a key aspect of Chapter 1. Reviewing the material in *The Academic Writer* on Bryan Lawson's book *How Designers Think* (pp. 9–10) will help students understand writing as problem solving for a particular situation. Students often hope that there is a single "right" way to write— "just tell me how to do it"—but can come to appreciate the critical thinking that designing writing for a particular rhetorical situation asks them to do.

You will find that *The Academic Writer*'s rhetorical approach allows you to easily integrate other cultural texts into your writing classes. You will also find that the rhetorical approach helps students see the continuity between their own writing and the writing produced around them. Rhetorical study can apply equally to everything students read and write—freewriting, a formal essay turned in for a grade, an article in Wired, the textbook for a psychology class, emails, Web sites, and so on.

You can begin right away to encourage your students to adopt a rhetorical way of thinking about all the texts they encounter. One way to do that is by asking students to consider how the various elements of rhetoric interact whenever they are looking at any piece of writing. Who is the writer? What is the writer's persona? Who is the reader? What cultures and languages are involved? What is the context? When was it written and how is that significant? Why was a particular medium chosen, and is it effective? How does the text reflect these elements?

3. *Composing as design:* Your students, and perhaps some colleagues, might resist the idea that images and design elements should be given more relevancy in academic writing. However, the ongoing developments in communication technologies are shortening the gap between writing and design. Words are still important, but writers are effectively integrating both visual and verbal elements in texts with increasing frequency. This may be particularly important for students in sciences and business where the use of exhibits (graphs, charts, photographs, etc.) is important. Our contention is that *all* students these days need to know how to find, select, integrate, discuss, and ethically document images in

their writing. And of course the design of pages in business and technical writing projects is very important for the ways that information is packaged and presented for a certain purpose and audience.

When your students review Bryan Lawson's list from his book *How Designers Think* (p. 9) and read about the similarities between writing and design, they will begin to understand how they can apply the creative process of design to the process of academic writing. Both writers and designers, they will understand, are problem solvers who must draw on their experience and their knowledge of their rhetorical situation to make effective choices about content, writing, and the appearance of their work. This understanding is particularly helpful for students who have mistakenly viewed writing as either filling in forms that others have devised (for reasons that students don't understand) or as psyching out the teacher. It's especially important for students to accept that writing and design and even research can be called "processes" because there is no one single right approach.

4. *Rhetorical sensitivity:* Students acquire rhetorical sensitivity just as they acquire language—through experience. Of course, students in your classes may vary widely in the amount of previous experience with written texts that they bring to your writing courses, and you will want to take their different degrees of rhetorical sensitivity into account. What kinds of things have they read and written before? What experience have they had with academic writing specifically? Are any of your students better attuned to oral presentations than to written texts? You can refer to the example in Chapter 1 of the roommates trying to solve the problem of their messy room. Do you have students who feel so uncertain about every detail of written language that they must approach it as a foreign discourse—who are, in fact, nonnative speakers in the world of academic discourse?

You can help students translate some parts of their "rhetorical sensitivity" into their written work by asking them to explicitly identify what they know—not necessarily in particularly sophisticated vocabularies. When they explain what works, to you or to other students, they are making their knowledge conscious and accessible.

Most students, for example, know quite a bit, perhaps even from watching television, about how a story should be structured, and they can apply that knowledge to narrative passages in each other's compositions. Most understand, tacitly, how devices that frame and structure a text help orient the reader: They can point out that they don't understand what an essay is about and that the writer needs to beef up the opening without needing much formal instruction on the topic of introductions.

On the other hand, students who have never read a persuasive essay or a critical review cannot understand what it should be like from a series of rules. If they have no prior experience with the kinds of texts you want them to write, students need plenty of examples and models to follow. You can provide the samples found in *The Academic Writer* and in the back of these Instructor's Notes.

5. *Cultural and linguistic differences:* Point out the "Notes for Multilingual Writers" boxes in this chapter and in each of the following chapters. You

may wish as well to pay specific attention to the relations of rhetoric and culture that are foregrounded by a diversity of linguistic backgrounds. Cultural ideas about who should speak and how, and cultural ideas about audience may affect the interactions of your students. If you are encouraging students to write drafts in their native or home language, you may choose to introduce the idea of "code switching" at this point.

To some degree, most students, not only multilingual students, may not yet feel at home in academic writing and must learn, to some extent, how to "code switch" from the vernacular, or the less formal English they may have used in earlier school experiences. Part of rhetorical sensitivity involves learning when and how to code-switch so that writing becomes appropriate to the rhetorical situation.

Some notes and activities in this chapter ask multilingual writers to think about translation, or else about composing in English from the start. Some composition scholars, including Peter Elbow, have urged instructors to let students write first drafts in whatever vernacular seems most apt to free their expression and then change subsequent drafts to fit the academic occasion. Such issues of translation and interpretation are very interesting and rhetorically complex—well worth ongoing discussion in your class.

Activities

(pp. 4–5) *For Exploration:* This Exploration asks students to list the kinds of writing they do and the media they use to write. You might want to start this exercise on the first day of class because it immediately moves students into the writing process, it affords an opportunity for students to share writing experiences, and it establishes the fact that students are already writers.

If you want to help class members get to know one another and begin to establish the class as a community, put the responses up on the board or on an overhead projector. The result will be an informal survey of the kinds of writing the students have done and their reasons for writing.

You will establish the first evidence that you take them seriously as writers simply by the act of listening to their responses, some of which will probably be "I never write unless I have to" and other expressions of duress. Press them to define for themselves what they consider to be productive and satisfying writing experiences. Finally, if you collect or record the responses, you have an informal inventory of your class to help with planning lessons. This can be part of a "getting to know you" activity.

(p. 12) *For Exploration:* After considering the discussion of the relationship between writing and design in this chapter, this Exploration asks students to freewrite in class or as homework about what connections discussed in the chapter might help them better understand written communication. You could ask them to add sketches or graphical elements such as flow charts or clustering. Their answers will help you see where they may still be confused.

(p. 14) *For Collaboration:* After completing the previous Exploration, this activity asks students to share their findings in small groups and then to share ideas with the class. You may want to direct each group to come up with one or two connections to write down on large poster paper, overhead projector paper, or the chalkboard. You can have the class as a whole review each group's suggestions for similarities and differences in their conclusions.

(pp. 16–18) *For Exploration:* This exercise asks students to review two promotional pieces, an ad and a Web page for Levi's, and to respond to several questions about design elements, persuasiveness, and rhetorical sensitivity. To extend this analysis, you may want to have your students meet in groups to discuss their responses. In connection with question #3 about subjective value judgments and cultural stereotypes, one important aspect always is to ask students what prior knowledge is needed to "get it" for any text (which also connects to the Multilingual Writers notes).

(pp. 18–19) *Note for Multilingual Writers:* You might ask your multilingual students or students who have spent time in different cultures to bring in a sample visual text from another culture to show how the connections between written word and visual elements are similar and different.

(p. 19) *For Thought, Discussion, and Writing:* You may wish to assign some or all of these activities as entries in a writer's notebook or journal that you might collect from time to time. A blue book can work well for a journal, being light and of standard size. Additionally, the second activity under this heading is a good starting point for an essay assignment for a literacy narrative.

1. This activity asks students to reflect on their understanding of the terms *rhetoric* and *rhetorical sensitivity*. You may want your students to share their paragraphs and questions about *rhetoric* and *rhetorical sensitivity* with you so you can address questions in class, especially if you find several students have the same questions or are misunderstanding these terms.

2. This activity builds on the first "For Exploration" activity and uses that list as a start for a literacy narrative essay about the kinds of writing students do and how they incorporate visual and design elements in their writing. After completing their essay, students make this analysis of their writing and design habits by creating a visual text using words, images, and graphics to convey the ideas discussed in their essay. You may find it useful to have your students share their visual texts with each other, asking them to compare and contrast each other's work.

3. Students are often curious about how much writing their current or prospective field requires. However, other than adding up the total page counts for assignments they are required to write, many students do not stop to consider the kinds of writing done in their field, the role of images or other multimedia elements, how professors evaluate writing assignments, and whether students might have useful advice for others taking classes in the field. You may want to ask your students to complete a short essay that summarizes their interview findings and includes their reflections on what they found. An assignment like this is often used to create reports for professional and technical writing classes for upper division students, so this activity would be a good start. See Section 2 of these Instructor's Notes for further discussion on interviewing (pp. 14–15) and

Chapter 7 in *The Academic Writer* for a discussion about writing in various disciplines. You could also use this as an exercise to practice citation.

Chapter 2: Academic Writing: Committing to the Process

Chapter 2 introduces your students to the concept that writing—especially academic writing—is a process as much as a product. Depending on their prior writing experiences, they may have ideas about writing that can block their progress. This chapter seeks to demystify the rituals of writing and the sense of isolation so that students will learn to regard their own writing practices as open to interaction, analysis, and change. In particular, the chapter emphasizes ways that expert as well as beginning writers can improve on raw inspiration.

The text presents some of the different forms that planning, drafting, and revising can take and helps students develop confidence in adapting processes in their own ways. Through exercises and activities, the text shows them how to develop more flexibility and more conscious decision making about writing habits. Many students begin to see how they can change their writing processes for various writing situations. Under the pressure of deadlines, for example, they may sometimes have to shorten their planning or revising. The writing strategies presented here and in your classroom will help them make wiser choices about how to approach planning, drafting, and revising in changing circumstances as well as how to take responsibility for their composing decisions.

One composing strategy discussed in this chapter is *collaborative writing*. While most students will have had a certain amount of experience working in groups, they often have no idea how widespread the necessity of writing with others could be. They will probably not have carried collaborative writing all the way through a project to final publication for a single shared grade, yet many will move into disciplines that make extensive use of team projects or into careers that ask employees to write jointly. Many will also find themselves working collaboratively in their communities. This chapter helps students address ways to improve group functioning as well as ways to adapt the writing processes they have been developing to the special demands of collaborative planning, drafting, and revising.

Concepts

1. *Magical thinking:* Many students believe writing requires a natural talent, genius, or inspiration—"I'm just not good at writing"—and that hard work does not make much difference in how well one can write. Such a belief greatly influences their writing habits and discourages them from making much effort to change the way they write. Chapter 2 is structured to interrupt the automatic and unconscious writing habits of your students.

Students often have even more superstitions about revision and procrastination. Many students remember an essay they wrote at the last minute that received an A, while another essay was revised and revised but received only a C. Of course, frequently those last-minute A papers worked well because the students tried nothing new and just repeated what they'd already mastered, whereas the much-revised papers may have represented some genuine learning, not yet fully articulated or polished enough for an A. To encourage the hard work of significant revision and deep thinking, students need rewards such as portfolio evaluation, low-risk early assignments, or ways to let later drafts and papers compensate for early poorer grades.

You may want to take time to talk with your students about how they think about writing and how those thoughts affect their results. A useful technique is to ask them to brainstorm associations with the word *writer*. Typical responses include the following: genius, glasses, dead, brilliant, reclusive, creative, eccentric. You could also ask them to freewrite beginning with "A writer is someone who . . . ." Many teachers also find it productive to share some of their own writing processes with students.

2. *Composing strategies and literacy narratives:* To help students understand their strategies in order to change them, Chapter 2 asks students to identify the composing strategies that work best for them for different assignments and to recognize differences among what works for different people. Students who can see the writing process as strategies they can try will be more likely to try new ones.

Along with understanding their own strategies and how well these might or might not work, this chapter also encourages students to examine the ways writing connects to their history and sense of identity. They can see how they came to be the writers they are today, and this will help them feel empowered to make decisions and develop an *ethos*, a sense of writing authority and power to cope with various rhetorical situations.

Asking students to write a history of their experiences writing in school and out can enlighten them on the evolution of their strategies and empower them to see how they could take charge to change their habits.

The two "For Exploration" activities and a "For Collaboration" activity at the beginning of the chapter (pp. 20–23, discussed below) help with understanding these concepts.

3. *Managing the writing process and identifying composing styles:* In addition to learning about their own preferred or habitual writing processes, students who share their literacy narratives can learn a lot from seeing how differently others compose.

This chapter identifies three composing processes and helps students understand the traits of each: **heavy planning, heavy revising,** and **sequential composing**. You can use the three student responses by Sara Steinman, Eduardo Alvarez, and Wei Liao (pp. 23–24) to help your students analyze how they manage the planning, drafting, and revising processes of writing. Once students understand that all of these can be effective strategies, you can create assignments to experiment with new approaches. Try an assignment that asks them to write in a new way or to deliberately exaggerate the opposite of their usual manner to develop flexibility.

Although students have often learned some planning skills, such as outlining, they often resist revising skills. In many cases, their high school papers were written in a single draft, graded, and abandoned for the next paper. Revision may have been seen only as correcting a few surface errors. Showing them manuscript pages that are marked up heavily—your own or the examples in Donald Murray's "The Maker's Eye," *Writer* 111.10 (1998): 20–24—can help students believe that writers really do this.

To help students practice extensive revision, try asking them to cut a 1,500-word draft in half or shift the focus radically—typical tasks for professional writers. Or cut apart an essay and ask student teams to try arranging the paragraphs in ways that make sense, then to discuss their reasons and evaluate the results. You can also combine freewriting with heavy revising to good effect. For further information, see Muriel Harris, "Composing Behaviors of One- and Multi-Draft Writers," *College English* 51.2 (1984): 174–91.

The notion of writing as recursive—the sequential style of planning, revising, and more writing; followed by planning, revising (with frequent returns to research—see Chapter 6), and more writing—baffles students who imagine a linear, unidirectional process. You can help them experience this method and see how it might help them by crafting a series of intermediate stages for an essay from freewrite to first draft, second draft, adding new material, and so on.

4. *Procrastination:* Students wait until the deadline to write for a variety of reasons, including writer's block, a belief that they work best under pressure, and the pressing demand of other classes. Designing multipart sequential assignments can help students overcome procrastination. As you help them learn some new and effective strategies, you can also discuss the question of time management.

Some students who procrastinate are avoiding anxiety. A writing assignment can often seem too monumental to begin. You can lower the anxiety barrier by encouraging students to write uncritically at first. Most of your students will identify with Holly Hardin's appraisal of the role of procrastination in her writing process (pp. 28–29). Holly understands that she needs to better distinguish between activities that help her plan her writing and those that help her avoid writing at all costs.

Another motive for procrastination is simply that most college students see other classes as more important than a required writing class. We hear them say, "This class has too much writing." You might want to discuss this frankly, letting students talk about their frustrations with university requirements while pointing out that a writing course realistically requires rather large amounts of time. This can help reduce resistance and build a happier writing community.

5. *Analyzing one's composing process:* The "Quiz: Analyzing Your Composing Process" (pp. 30–31) will help students reflect on what they just read about various composing styles and apply that to themselves, not only seeing their previous habits but also evaluating how effective those habits might be and what changes might make them more productive writers. You can also have students write a process memo in class when final drafts are being collected, asking them to think back and record all the steps for completing that paper, saying what helped them most, what they might have done differently if they had more time, or what new ideas they could carry forward for another

assignment. You can specifically ask how their composing process on this paper differed from past processes. This can help you encourage students to become more flexible, practicing explorers and designers.

6. *Collaboration:* As this chapter explains, collaboration in college and the outside world can take many forms, and students may work together at several stages of their writing process. Many people first set about a collaborative writing task from necessity or because it is required. But often they discover unforeseen benefits from writing with others. Not only can it be easier to come up with more and better ideas for writing and revising when several writers are brainstorming, but it can also be easier to negotiate blocks and do research. Designing collaborative tasks also forces the heavy planners to start writing sooner than they might otherwise.

Whatever else happens, collaboration requires an explicit, commonly understood set of plans and schedules for writing and an investment from you to make the process real and useful in your classroom. Collaboration also requires students to address differences of opinion and perhaps discover what's at stake in their own perspectives. If you specifically discuss the significance of such exchanges, students will increase their understanding of the interaction between author and audiences in any rhetorical situation. You can use the several "For Collaboration" exercises in this chapter (pp. 23, 32, 35) to discuss this concept.

Working collaboratively gives students less individual flexibility in exchange for the added power of group work. The "Guidelines for Group Work" (p. 36) provide specific suggestions for groups to use to open up discussion, emphasize the importance of articulating and communicating shared understandings, advocate taking advantage of electronic technologies, and warn against using a cut-and-paste method. Collaborative writing works best, in other words, when the writers work on group processes as they go, and is likely to run into trouble if writers simply split up the duties and go their separate ways.

As you assign collaborative projects, build in time and space for these group exchanges, and check to make sure that students are genuinely collaborating on their effort. Work to avoid the frequent frustration that the weaker writers will just hamper the stronger ones and get a better grade than they deserve. Consider whether you will assign a group grade for all to share or individual grades to reflect the amount of time each student invests. Also consider how you might use online spaces for asynchronous group work.

You can also connect the concept of collaboration to the sports model of teamwork, emphasizing that you are the writing coach, not the opposing team, and your goal is to help them write as well as they can and continually set new writing "personal best" goals. In addition to the single-player sports models decribed in Chapter 2—tennis and skiing—you can bring in other activities popular at your school and in your community to help students connect the many similarities to practicing and improving their writing with practicing and improving athletic and artistic skills (piano, dance, drama).

Of course the sports model leads to discussions of winning, which you can productively relate to coaching versus grading. Emphasizing your coaching role helps students focus on their real audience—whether it is the scholarly community in their discipline or a citizen group in their community. (If you are not familiar with Peter Elbow's *Embracing Contraries: Explorations in Learning and Teaching* [Oxford University Press, 1987], we highly recommend it.)

Activities

The first three activities in this chapter are coordinated to lead students from their response to reading to a collaborative task growing out of their own writing. It is a model as well, then, of ways you can integrate informal, personal writing with reading, collaboration, and discussion.

(p. 20) *For Exploration:* This first exploration asks students to describe their earliest memories of learning to write and read. Question 7 asks them about what images come to mind. One activity you can do early in the term to help students understand their styles and also get acquainted is to post around the room pictures of animals—such as an eagle, otter, lion, or octopus—and ask students to stand by the picture that best represents their writing personality. Then discuss with the others grouped there what characteristics they share and report back to the class. Are they playful writers? Hawkeyed critics? Connected to and grasping everything?

(p. 21) *For Exploration:* This second exploration exercise draws on the previous Exploration, asking students to create portraits of themselves as writers. These could be letters, poems, songs, or multimodal texts. The image of Mirlandra Ebert's collage (p. 22) shows one example that is creative and personal. With students' permission, you might post or photocopy the texts and create a class book or online posting. The experience of reading other students' writing—especially writing about how they write—early in the term can be very powerful and build community. These literacy narratives usefully connect personal history to community as well as to writing.

(p. 23) *For Collaboration:* This activity uses student letters and other texts about writing experiences created in the previous Exploration as the basis for group discussion. You can keep the students' exchange focused by asking them to report to the whole class after a certain amount of time.

This discussion can be an important source of information for you as well as for your students about the general profile of the class. You might give groups twenty to twenty-five minutes to answer the questions and then take another ten minutes to hear reports of the results.

Notice that students are asked to work toward a sense of group cohesiveness by identifying commonalities, then by noting differences, and finally by reporting common goals. Differences will often reflect context and situation. Multilingual students may be able to add cultural differences to the discussion.

Many students have histories as writers that are really histories of the teachers they had—good and bad—and chronologies of grading dramas. Consider making time to discuss the experience of evaluation here—of being graded, and more generally, of having writing evaluated by others.

How are your groups doing at this point? Do they feel reasonably comfortable with each other and with the idea of group tasks? If some are working with a great deal of awkwardness and inhibition, you might want to give some attention to group processes.

(p. 30) *Quiz: Analyzing Your Composing Process:* This activity directs students to think and write (if you decide to make this a written activity). You can have students focus on *all* the writing they do, or narrow their responses to their process for academic writing.

(p. 32) *For Collaboration:* Students discuss the previous "Quiz: Analyzing Your Composing Process" in order to identify and describe their own characteristic style of composing. Students usually enjoy figuring out their composing style. Many students start to experiment with writing processes and timing as they see composing increasingly as a matter of making design choices that they can control. This assignment asks your students to decide for themselves which writing practices work well and to decide on ways to do better.

You might have to limit time for talking about individual responses to the questions to get groups to move firmly toward making some statements about writing. Then, although it takes an extra ten to fifteen minutes, it is worth having groups report on the results of their thinking. Doing so can move the class from thinking mostly about their own work to making generalizations about the nature of the writing process that they can pursue.

(p. 35) *For Collaboration:* This activity instructs students to meet with their writing group (created by you or formed on their own) and discuss how the group can most effectively work as a team. By exchanging contact information, getting to know each other a little, and drawing up some friendly rules to help guide the group's activities, your students will be more likely to give and receive useful collaborative feedback in their writing groups.

Even if you do not wish to establish ongoing groups in your class, you might want to help students form collaborative support groups to meet outside of class. Usually at least some students in a class will be interested in such a voluntary group. Once they get together and organize, they might meet once or twice a week to read and respond to each other's work, exchange ideas and discoveries, and make suggestions to each other. Be aware, though, that without your help and modeling, groups sometimes have difficulty staying on task and finding meeting time. You can help with the time issue if you have an online Course Management System such as Blackboard (or an open-source CMS such as Moodle) to create online groups for students to share work such as proposals and drafts and to facilitate peer-review workshops.

(p. 35) *For Exploration:* This assignment asks your students to make an appointment with a writing tutor and conduct an interview about the services the writing center provides. Assigning an interview has the advantage of removing any imagined stigma about going to the writing center. First-year students in particular are often surprisingly shy about seeking out help, so it makes sense to encourage them to become familiar with what is available in a low-stakes way, especially if they have no other introduction to the services.

You may want students to report their findings to the class or write a summary of their discussion as an assignment. You may also want to offer extra credit for writing center visits.

Note that if you assign students to interview a writing assistant at the writing center, you might forewarn the center about the date you choose.

(p. 37) *For Thought, Discussion, and Writing:* These activities can be used for homework or small assignments to help reflect and solidify the concepts students have learned in this chapter.

1. This activity asks students to write down concrete goals for themselves as writers. This paragraph can help show you how well students' expectations for the class align with your expectations. However, when you look at the goals your students write down, you may find that some students still have little conscious understanding of their writing and little knowledge of what a writing goal might be. Their goals may be vague rephrasings of something a former teacher told them they should do or guesses about what you want them to have as goals rather than anything they have a deep commitment to accomplish.

   You might want to have students record these goals in a writing notebook where they can use them to assess their writing progress, modifying them or adding other goals as needed.

2. This assignment encourages students to learn more about their own composing process by conducting a brief case study of themselves as they work on a writing project. Keeping a detailed process log is essential to the success of this assignment, for the process log enables students to get beyond vague generalities about their writing—generalities such as "coming up with ideas is hard" or "revising makes me nervous"—to more specific understandings of the strategies they employ (and the habits they draw on) when they write.

   Students are often surprised by what they discover when they analyze their process logs recording their steps. Students sometimes overestimate how long they typically work on their writing, for instance. Recording when they start and end each work session helps them become more aware of the amount of time it can take to make significant progress in writing.

   Depending on the nature and goals of your course, you can use this assignment in various ways. You may have students keep process logs and write an informal analysis of what they have learned by studying their own writing as a prelude to a class discussion of this activity. You can use step 3 as the process memo for students to complete when they submit formal essay assignments. Or you may make the case study one of your course's major writing assignments.

3. This assignment asks your students to write about procrastinating—whether as a freewrite, formal essay, or multimodal text. It's a subject that releases a great deal of pent-up energy. It's also a topic that allows most students to draw on extensive personal experience. I like to encourage students to take the fun seriously—that is, to imagine some attitude toward procrastination besides automatic responses of guilt and pleasure, to rethink and revise their first impressions. Procrastination is an especially important problem for your class because it forecloses the possibility of learning to revise. In other words, it may be a way of not learning much of what there is to be taught in a writing class.

4. This assignment puts students to work on a systematic ongoing project of self-examination and self-consciousness about their experiences as a writer. You can assign this meta-analysis together with another writing assignment, and you can go on to use a version of such analysis for each assignment the student turns in for evaluation.

Chapter 3: Analyzing Rhetorical Situations

Chapter 3 provides students with a framework for understanding the concept of "rhetorical situation," showing students how to analyze it and how a more acute sense of the relations among the elements of rhetoric will enable them to write more effectively.

The "Questions for Analyzing Your Rhetorical Situation" (pp. 41–42) help students grasp how writers think their way through each of the four elements as they compose and revise. To help your students gain confidence in making design decisions when composing, you might stress that, just as the rules for writing are not absolute, there are no magic or mathematical formulas for figuring out what the rhetorical situation is or how to address readers. Students often want simple, clear answers so they can solve their writing problems quickly. Some say they feel blocked when there's too much to take into account. And of course most of us as teachers are used to hearing students say plaintively, "I don't know what you want," even when we think we've made an assignment crystal clear. Working students through the steps of "Questions for Analyzing" will help.

Analyzing rhetorical situations may seem fascinating for students when they can see that this activity is genuinely practical—but they may be frustrated if they see it as just an abstract exercise. Later in this section we offer some possible activities you can use to analyze texts. Of course you also need to help students think concretely about their actual rhetorical situations as writers in college and in their various communities.

One such community is your own classroom, which is also likely to provide a multitude of examples of cultural diversity, whether economic, regional, linguistic, gendered, or other. Cultural assumptions, of course, are an often unspoken source of students' difficulties with understanding and accommodating to a specific rhetorical situation. Multicultural students are probably more conscious of differing cultural influences than most, and can perhaps help all your students become more conscious about the cultural assumptions they are making. And, of course, all of your students share to some degree the experience of entering into the new subculture of the academy and trying to understand its traditions and conventions. The inevitable complexity and newness in an academic situation can be very disorienting to all students, so help from you and perhaps from writing tutors will be important.

Concepts

1. *Rhetorical situation:* This chapter defines the concept of rhetorical situation in terms of the writer, the reader, the text, and the medium. If your course structure permits it, you may want to discuss the rhetorical situation more

broadly as well. Critical theory has led many in English departments to conclude, along with Terry Eagleton, that the discipline might best be described as rhetorical studies. Furthermore, much recent work in sociology, anthropology, psychology, political science, and philosophy has also demonstrated a turn to rhetoric, a sense that culture itself might be defined in terms of rhetorical situations. Inquiry like that of Clifford Geertz shows how rhetorical analysis could involve everything we know—our knowledge of culture (the way it works, its codes and conventions), our grammatical competence, our vocabulary, and our knowledge about the world (what it is and what it ought to be).

Cultural studies are inherently rhetorical. The idea of the rhetorical situation explained in this chapter reflects a cultural tradition that comes down to us from Aristotle, through numerous interpretations. Although students from non-Western cultures may not think easily in terms of three separate appeals to *ethos*, *logos*, and *pathos*, you can still teach the usefulness of these categories. For a contemporary understanding of the rhetorical situation, together with debates about how its cultural context might be addressed, see the "Further Reading in Composition Studies" bibliography at the end of Section 5 (pp. 53–59).

Chapter 3 asks students to think about writing projects in several different situations. Using the idea of contacting a friend, the text begins by asking students to consider the rhetorical differences between, for example, email, texting, or a handwritten note.

This chapter helps students connect analyzing the rhetorical situation with planning to write, establishing intentions and goals. The flowcharts within "Questions for Analyzing Your Rhetorical Situation" (pp. 41–42) help students turn analysis into strategy.

2. *The writer:* Students usully identify so closely with the *I* of their writing that they tend to believe that they always write simply as themselves. In portraying the writer in terms of *persona, voice*, and *ethos*, this chapter suggests instead that, to some extent, we choose an appropriate image of self and of character when we write. In other words, the writer is rhetorical, produced by the text, and writers need to change the persona representing themselves to suit different rhetorical situations.

Students may not notice how naturally they adapt when they move from informal to formal situations, for example, or from a written medium to one dominated by images. Try explaining this with an analogy: People change their *personas* in response to a situation, just as they change clothes—wearing jeans for one occasion and formal dress for another, one outfit for work, and another for play. You can probably help most students improve their control of the rhetorical situation by asking them to think about just how the writer needs to "sound" or "look" to be convincing. Students who have already internalized a good repertoire of successful approaches to writing will be able to write un-self-consciously, to simply feel "sincere" and also write well, but other students will be liberated if you encourage them to write parodies or play roles.

This analogy to theatricality has, of course, some limitations: Good writers seldom adopt more than a few roles or "personae" for different circumstances. Instead, they gradually develop authority, a "voice," made up of knowledge, experience, character, and understanding of appropriate conventions. Writers who haven't done this yet can struggle. Reminding students to think about "who is the writer here" will help them acquire strategies and devices that work for them.

The "Questions for Analyzing Your Rhetorical Situation" (pp. 41–42) lead students through a consideration of purpose, goals, roles, and images. You can help students understand "fixed" versus "flexible" in terms of how much latitude they have in determining their purpose, goals, role, and image. A researched argument or lab report, for example, usually requires a fairly fixed role for the writer, whereas a narrative essay may allow more latitude for a personal voice and self-expression.

3. *The reader:* Your students have perhaps already learned to think about their readers when they write. But they need to understand that the "reader" is both more and less specific than they might think. Unlike an audience physically present at an oral presentation or performance, the rhetorical reader in a writing situation does not necessarily correspond to a single person or group of people. Instead, the reader holds a role in the discourse that the writer and the situation both help to define.

In addition to having a sense of typical readers, writers have an obligation not just to appeal to the reader but to create the reader as a participant or interlocutor, someone who might talk back or engage in the conversation. In a sense, then, the reader is anyone who might respond to the text's message. The writer develops a relationship with the reader, cuing the reader about the role to take. This idea of "reader invoked" is explained more in Lisa Ede and Andrea Lunsford's essay "Audience Addressed/Audience Invoked." (See the "Further Reading in Composition Studies" bibliography at the end of Section 5.)

For these reasons, students need to imagine their readers clearly and sympathetically, not to view them as the blank unknown "general public" or as judges hunting for every error, and not to limit them to knowable persons such as instructors or the other members of their writing groups.

You can productively use the three samples of Deborah Tannen's arguments from the *Washington Post,* the *Chronicle of Higher Education,* and the *Journal of Pragmatics* (pp. 60–65) to discuss readers, as well as the concept of overlapping discourse communities. Another effective activity is to bring (or ask students to bring) to class a range of popular and scholarly magazines in order to deduce from the advertisements and articles the needs and values of the readers being addressed.

4. *The text:* It's helpful to remind students that the word text in this book and in many academic disciplines refers to all examples of writing, including visual texts in print, online, and in multimedia, and not just to a book required for a class. When students analyze a text, they need to consider the conventions of form, style, and logic that govern its presentation.

Although rhetoric evolved from the study of speeches, and students can benefit from analyzing the rhetorical situations of oral presentations on television and in classrooms, a written text differs from spoken language in ways that sometimes create opportunities and difficulties for students. Texts operate according to conventions and codes of written language—and genres—that students frequently don't know or haven't yet mastered.

Students often have very limited genre sense, calling any book a "novel" and any shorter piece a "story," whether it is an article, editorial, or essay. To help students expand their repertoire of genre conventions, you might explore rhetorical conventions that they do know well, such as the various lists and quizzes available on Facebook, so they can see what kinds of tacit understandings might be included. This chapter offers a variety of texts for students to explore as well.

5. *The medium:* Even though they are bombarded daily by visual images, many students think of a writing assignment only in terms of words put to paper. Encourage them to consider various kinds of media and whether a particular medium is appropriate in a specific rhetorical situation. Should they create a PowerPoint presentation, a blog posting, a brochure, or a more traditional essay? You might ask the class to discuss Mirlandra Ebert's decision to create a poster for her writing assignment (see pp. 43–44). Do your students agree with Mirlandra's decision? What are the advantages and disadvantages of different media? How often do they even consider "medium" when they begin an assignment? Also talk to them about using visuals that support the points in the text—such as graphs, charts, and photographs, which they will see later in Brenda Shonkwiler's essay in Chapter 5 (pp. 135–136), where the visual display of evidence augments the argument.

6. *Aristotle's appeals:* This chapter introduces the traditional Aristotelian categories for persuasive appeals: *logos, pathos,* and *ethos.* Your students may not be used to thinking about writing as an act of persuasion (or, indeed, as practical in any respect whatsoever), so you might want to take some time in class to point out the persuasive component of all writing.

Brandon Barrett's analysis of how he will appeal to *logos, pathos,* and *ethos* as he plans his class essay (pp. 52–53) should provide a helpful example. Doing an in-class exercise with advertisements (either those included in *The Academic Writer* or others you bring in to class) is a great way to teach the appeals.

Later, when students look at academic writing, you can point out how more subtle forms of the same appeals work to make a text authoritative and convincing. Scholarly work in fields like women's studies often points out the persuasive aspect of even the most objective-seeming writing. See, for example, Evelyn Fox Keller's *Gender and Science.*

The appeal to *logos* is based on evidence and reasoning, so it is the most powerful appeal in most academic writing. Remind your students to consider the appeal to reason even in texts that they do not regard as objective. You can explain the difference between what is called artistic reasoning (a courtroom debate) and inartistic reasoning (examples, facts, and figures) and show how both are used. For example, their analyses of their own writing histories or processes provide examples that go beyond an appeal to *pathos* or *ethos,* even though those are the primary appeals.

Many students have studied persuasion as part of units on propaganda and logical fallacies. Sometimes they have translated the idea of logical fallacy into a rule banning everything that is not *logos.* They may think you want them to write dry-as-dust informational prose, appealing to evidence alone.

You can point out that sometimes a heavy emphasis on *logos* is inappropriate. Further, writers who rigorously segregate *pathos* from *logos* are apt to produce unmitigated sentiment or unmitigated fact. If students are encouraged to consider all three appeals carefully, they will find it easier to plan balanced papers that are well adapted to their purposes.

The appeal to *pathos* is based on emotion, or on values, beliefs, and desires. When students think about how to effectively address readers, they need to think about readers' values and attitudes as well as more obvious kinds of feelings. What assumptions are readers likely to accept? Aristotle lists certain commonplaces that human beings are likely to share or that apply commonsensically to large groups of people. For example, the old are likely to respond to appeals for greater security, the young to appeals for change. Through class discussions, you can elicit your students' contemporary understanding of what might seem commonsense knowledge. You can help students distinguish between more or less universal appeals such as those Aristotle describes and appeals that are culture specific: for example, the appeal to explore new frontiers that is so familiar to North American audiences.

The third appeal, to *ethos*, turns to the good character of the writer—to the audience's willingness to believe what the writer says. The *persona* adopted by the writer helps convey the appeal to *ethos*. Because students are particularly vulnerable, writing from a position of little authority, they often struggle with *ethos*. This is not a problem that finding a personal voice can fully solve, and it is not easily resolved by imitating the *ethos* of someone else (including the teacher). Since *ethos* is deeply involved with the interaction of individual, ethics, and rhetorical situation, it is an especially difficult but fruitful starting point for discussion. You can help students see that logical writing, sufficient and suitable evidence (depending on the paper), and strong, error-free writing create a sense of good character.

7. *Academic discourse:* Most rhetoric and composition theorists agree that the academic reading and writing tasks students encounter in their classes belong to a rather specialized discourse. Part of what we are teaching is how to succeed in this academic discourse community, which may be alien indeed to some students and questionable to others.

The Academic Writer does not ask your students to master a specific form of writing; rather, it encourages them to develop a readerly, rhetorical approach to writing that will enable them to assess any discourse's possibilities and limits. You may wish to help them analyze, for example, the rather strict set of methods represented in scientific writing. You may also wish to help them look for the cultural and social implications of discourses. Your students should learn not only to emulate but also to critique certain examples of academic writing. "An Effective Academic Essay Is . . . " (p. 58) helps students to think about academic writing in broader terms than lab reports and reviews of the literature.

8. *Textual conventions:* This chapter directs students to pay attention to the functions of conventions, ranging from the general to the specific: persona, genre, style, organization, and diction, among others. Rather than looking at these conventions formally, out of context, this chapter shows students how

to analyze the ways the rhetorical situation might condition the choice of form and the ways that conventions shape reading. A letter from Monica Molina (p. 56) tells of her process learning to write grant proposals at work, using models of former proposals and consultation with her boss. Introductions to three different reports of research on argument by Deborah Tannen (pp. 60–65) show how textual conventions shape the reader's experience and how some conventions—understood in the context of a professional journal—can even limit the ability of the uninitiated to understand at all.

These textual conventions, bound to the rhetorical situation, are part of what students will learn about their disciplines. Students will improve their reading if they understand that they need to look for such conventions, and they will improve their writing if they understand that textual conventions can give them accepted ways of organizing material. This understanding, in other words, will help demystify the processes of reading as well as writing and alert students to recognize the role that textual conventions play in our construction and interpretation of texts. As students begin to look for such conventions, reading like writers, they become "noticing" readers, newly aware of what works and how it works.

Activities

(p. 40) *For Exploration:* This activity asks students to apply their understanding of the elements of rhetoric to four writing situations:

- The first, an application for an internship in the student's major field, requires an academic/professional role and a limited purpose. Students should be asking themselves questions such as these: Will they need to follow a set of specific forms or guidelines? Who could they ask about the requirements of such an application?

- The second, a flyer for a student march protesting a tuition increase, has a persuasive purpose. Ask students how they might incorporate Aristotle's three appeals into the flyer. Why is a flyer an effective medium in this instance? How might visuals be used?

- The third, a posting to the class's online discussion board, asks students to integrate personal and academic roles in a quasi-public voice. Ask students to consider how their language changes when they know that numerous classmates will be reading their comments about the film.

- The fourth, a research-based essay, requires students to consider seriously all the elements of rhetoric. Ask them to take a close look at their topic and evaluate it in terms of their role and purpose as writers, the language they will use, the effect of their readers on what they write, and any images they might include.

Most students will find that they already have a considerable amount of tacit knowledge about rhetorical situations. Some students have difficulty doing this analysis, but that difficulty may not always be a symptom of ineptitude. (At least one good student wished we would just get to the point and tell him the right way to do the internship letters.) These are students who need to understand that rhetorical reasoning doesn't involve a single right solution but requires them to make decisions based on ways of thinking about rhetorical situations.

It may help in such cases to give students sample materials by someone else to read and discuss first the kinds of choices other writers have made. If they are working in groups and exchanging the answers to this question, members of the group will be helped by hearing the variety of acceptable ways that others might handle the situation.

(p. 51) *For Exploration:* This activity asks students to analyze Alia Sands's essay to decide whether it achieves the goals she has set for herself in her analysis of her rhetorical situation. This work allows them to rehearse the kind of careful analysis they should apply to each other's papers when they function as readers.

(p. 55) *For Exploration:* This activity asks students to apply their understanding of appeals—*logos, pathos,* and *ethos*—to Brandon Barrett's student essay. Like the earlier analysis of a student essay, this practice will help students not only with their own writing but also with giving helpful responses to each other's papers.

(p. 59) *For Exploration:* This exercise asks your students to write a paragraph about each introduction to the three articles by Deborah Tannen. These analyses should reveal some of students' tacit assumptions about the meanings of forms, connecting conventions of writing with readers' assumptions about an article's intention or purpose. Your students will probably vary widely in their ability to decode the formats of these introductions. Some will simply get stuck at saying the first one is easier than the others. To help improve their ability to analyze and decode conventions, discuss the results of the critical reading together with the comparison of these introductions before students do the next exercise.

(p. 68) *For Exploration:* The questions in this exercise lead students to examine further the differences and similarities among Deborah Tannen's three introductions via a freewrite.

(p. 70) *For Thought, Discussion, and Writing:*

1. This activity takes yet another step toward establishing connections between reading and writing, asking students to apply the "Questions for Analyzing Your Rhetorical Situation" to a newspaper or magazine selection they view as successful.

   Be sure to make their selection process a part of the discussion: They may choose pieces that they actually prefer, or they may choose pieces that represent what they imagine as excellence, perhaps far from their private choices of reading. What do you want them to analyze? Here is an opportunity to discuss the differences between the reading intended for college classes (such as a textbook or selected reading) and reading aimed at a different audience. You can also talk about overlapping audiences.

2. This exercise asks students to find an example of writing that fails to address the reader effectively and to write an explanation of why they think it fails. If you have students bring their examples to class for group discussion, you can ask them to find out whether other readers might be

more responsive than they were, and then to add a few sentences about how this extended inquiry did or did not change their minds about the rhetorical effectiveness of their examples.

3. The chapter ends with four public-service advertisements for students to analyze rhetorically.

Part II: Writing in College

Part II of *The Academic Writer* helps students to build on the rhetorical approach to writing across a wide range of discourses, applying this approach to analyzing texts and contexts, making and supporting claims, and conducting research. They should become familiar with writing in different fields and begin to see how they can use their knowledge of rhetoric and the writing process to become successful writers in all of the courses they take in college, as well as in their careers and in their everyday lives.

Chapter 4: Analyzing Texts and Contexts

Chapter 4 discusses the expectations students need to consider when their audience is academic, pointing out that academic discourse depends on reason, analysis, and argument. Chapter 4 includes material on analyzing academic arguments: discussions of the questions at issue, critical reading, good reasons, Aristotle's appeals, Toulmin's framework, and fallacies. Finally, this chapter helps students read and analyze visual texts.

At the beginning of the chapter, your students will find a list of characteristics of effective student writing (p. 77), which will help you answer their recurrent question: "What do instructors want?" They will also find specific suggestions about academic writing assignments and how to develop plans to complete them successfully. Multilingual students should be invited to discuss with the instructor and fellow students the differences they observe between expectations for American academic assignments and any they may be familiar with from their culture.

As they work through this chapter, students will find it helpful to have a current writing project in mind so they can put the suggestions into practice. If your students are not already working on an assignment, you might choose one of the sample assignments at the very end of the chapter in the "For Thought, Discussion, and Writing" section.

Concepts

1. *Understanding the academic audience:* What do members of an academic community look for, as readers of their students' writing? Not, perhaps, what some of your students may expect—that is, not just evidence that students have done the assignment or even that they have learned what was expected. Students may improve their ability to assess academic writing situations if they see their instructors as people thinking about a certain body of knowledge, rather than just as evaluators of student papers. That means that individual instructors evaluate papers within a set of disciplinary standards, and students

will have to learn something about the discipline, not just about general writing, to succeed.

Fortunately, the work on rhetorical situation that students have done will help them analyze academic assignments and understand how much deeper thinking is needed to get the job done. By approaching their writing assignments as an opportunity to take on the role of practitioner in a field, using typical inquiry and thinking, students will be more successful at giving instructors what they really do want in their students' papers: evidence of thought. Take some time to go over the characteristics of effective student writing on p. 77 to help students understand. You can also use the sample essay by Hope Leman (pp. 78–79) to discuss how her essay demonstrates each of these characteristics.

2. *Analyzing academic writing assignments:* Although assignments range from the broad and general to the limited and specific, keywords such as *define* or *evaluate* point to appropriate strategies. Help students see that these keywords suggest varying levels of complexity: An evaluation may include definition, analysis, and summary, for example. Students may respond with a simpler mode than the assignment requires or oversimplify its complexity. For example, in critical reviews students may simply write a summary instead of also including an evaluation. Or they may include nothing but evaluative conclusions with no summaries of the content or definitions of criteria. A key point to emphasize to students is the need to not oversimplify despite a temptation and a frustration when faculty seem to be "complicating" ideas.

3. *Identifying the assumptions inherent in a writing assignment:* Identifying assumptions requires students to ask: What is the rhetorical situation of this class? What are the learning outcomes and criteria? Even when extensive outcomes and objectives are listed on a syllabus, students may read them as a list of disconnected tasks. And worse, they may fail to think further about what purposes a class may have.

Since students need to learn what kinds of connections might be made in a given discipline and how assumptions might be examined critically, they should be encouraged to formulate and reformulate for themselves what they see as the direction and purpose of each of their classes. The flowchart demonstrating the "Questions for Developing an Appropriate Method for Analysis" (p. 83) will help students focus their thinking so that they can revise their own writing assignments or lead a discussion.

4. *Analysis is a group of skills:* In academic discourse or inquiry, analysis and argument are intimately related. When your students understand that they need to include analysis to develop their responses, they will not feel so frustrated about the problem of including evidence to support a position. They will see that comparing, defining, categorizing, showing cause and effect, and evaluating are the work of reasoned inquiry and that this work supports argument. Students need to realize that even or especially in disciplines such as literary criticism, which students sometimes imagine as a matter of personal taste, unsupported appeals to emotions or beliefs (or both) are not acceptable. Students may be confused by needing to "support" a response like "This poem seems sort of depressed"; they may think they need "facts" to but-

tress their conclusion, instead of having to articulate their process of analytic thinking.

You may also find that your students have trouble seeing how analysis and argument connect. A journal article on population growth, defining and explaining causes and effects, might seem purely factual with no argument. Pointing out where an author has used analysis will help make the structure of reasoned argument visible to students.

5. *Purpose and significance:* Knowing what is significant and interesting in a field is part of what it means to be an expert, and of course our students are not yet experts. Nevertheless, students can learn to develop a feeling for the significance of an argument in a particular field by focusing on a manageable purpose for their analysis and recognizing how it might fit into a wider context. For instance, an essay on the plausibility of the fool in *King Lear* can not only provide a discussion of the fool that the assignment evokes but also address a larger point about characterization in drama. Point out to students that one way to discover a worthwhile analytical approach is to relate two elements. In the case of Hope Leman's essay on the role of journalists in American society, she is trying to determine if the "mirror" or "flashlight" model best describes this role, juxtaposing two metaphors to analyze a phenomenon.

6. *Methods for analysis:* Students must figure out the preferred methods of analysis for the disciplines they study. The "Questions for Developing an Appropriate Method for Analysis" (p. 83) recommend that they first use the instructor's classroom presentations as a model, analyzing his or her methods, and noticing what counts as evidence and what kinds of questions are asked. In addition, the sample student analysis essays in this chapter—especially Stevon Roberts's evaluation analysis—can be used to model helpful approaches. You can help further by pointing out the methods of analysis you yourself use or would use if you were approaching a topic they are discussing.

7. *Questions at issue:* Using John Gage's description of stasis theory, the chapter lists six types of questions at issue that students may find in their analysis of arguments: questions of fact, definition, interpretation, value, consequence, and policy. You might also be familiar with these as "claims of fact or claims of definition," which is how they connect to Toulmin's framework (described in #10 on p. 83).

Help your students see why it is important to determine the question at issue in order to see whether the author has used effective approaches. For a question of fact, specific evidence is essential, but a question of consequence might call for causal analysis. As your students think more carefully about the kinds of arguments they are reading and writing, they will learn to sort through evidence in terms of its relationship to their point—that is, the question at issue or claim they are making.

While commenting on student drafts, you can help students understand that "what counts as evidence" depends on their purpose and the question at issue, as well as on their discipline. They may assume that facts speak for themselves and that their task is to accumulate a great many. They may tell you that because science is based on fact, it is not arguable, overlooking the many vigorous arguments about scientific interpretation. So, you need to help them understand that selecting and interpreting facts actually makes an argument.

For questions of evaluation, students may not yet see the differences between judgments, criteria, and examples. For instance, in a critical review, students may say that a film was "well done," without explaining their standards for good films or listing examples. Students may not know how to negotiate the difference between popular standards and personal preferences, especially because entertainment values have encouraged them to think that raw response is enough. You might ask your class, for example, whether they think the judges on *American Idol* provide good evidence for a question of value—that is, for saying whether a singer is good or not.

Class discussion will also reveal interesting differences of opinion as to what topics of argument seem acceptable or taboo in society or their discipline. See if your class feels that these different opinions are based on gender, ethnicity, race, religion, politics, region, family conventions, or other factors. Does your class agree as to what is the touchiest subject, the argument everyone would like to avoid? This is a discussion to which multicultural and multilingual students may have especially valuable contributions.

Students may have problems with advocacy, perhaps in part because they think "everyone has the right to their own opinion" or because they were raised not to question authority at home or in school. As a result, they are apt to separate problem solving from a reasoned consideration of values. A student may, for example, examine a hot topic such as child abuse or drugs or teen pregnancy by collecting quotes as if they were facts, submitting a collage of problems and solutions rather than thinking through the various positions and their relative merit.

When students submit position papers, taking a stand against abortion or in favor of rain forest protection, they may mistake passionate opinions for a solid argument. You may want to address directly the forms of public debate your students are used to hearing and reading and ask them to look at them critically. What models have influenced students' ideas of good arguments? Can they bring some examples to class? Should they be relying on these models? Do they differ from the models they are seeing in the academic world?

You can return to the Deborah Tannen examples on pp. 60–65 for her discussion of American attitudes toward argument and how these attitudes differ from academic argument. Because students seem drawn to questions of policy, you may find it helpful to assign different types of questions at issue to expand their critical thinking. This chapter invites the class to discuss these concepts in relation to "Less Privacy Is Good for Us (and You)" by Amitai Etzioni (pp. 87–90).

8. *The author's position and critical reading:* The chapter suggests that students engage in a "two-step" process of reading—first to understand what the author's position is, and then to engage that position critically.

You may find it helpful to work with the class as a whole on the "believing and doubting" game suggested by Peter Elbow. How does Etzioni's essay look from a sympathetic reading, from the perspective of agreeing with the writer? What happens when you read more skeptically—which of his strategies seem vulnerable, less persuasive? If this is a kind of Burkean "conversation," who else might be participating, as sources or context for the writer and as sources and contexts for your students? What do they bring to this reading? How hard is it to agree? How hard it is to read critically? Why? The "Questions for Critical Reading" (pp. 92–93) will help students analyze the reading systematically.

9. *Aristotle's appeals:* This chapter returns to the three appeals of Aristotle first discussed in Chapter 3, this time in order to help students evaluate arguments. The point is not only to decide which appeals the writer uses, but also to determine how effectively each appeal is used.

Appeals to *logos* rest on a structure of reason that includes not only evidence drawn from facts, from primary and secondary sources, but also on methods of analysis. The chapter urges a certain skepticism, since academic arguments rely so heavily on the appeal to *logos.* It may be helpful to distinguish between what is called "artistic" (or reasoning) *logos* from "inartistic" (facts and statistics) *logos* and to discuss which kind seems to be preferred in certain disciplines and why.

Pathos, the appeal to emotion, values, and beliefs, depends very much on the writer's knowledge of the readers, both as individuals and in a cultural context. A writer choosing a vocabulary drawn from hip-hop might appeal to a young audience but such an appeal could suffer from the problems often encountered by *pathos* — that is, its effectiveness is limited to a certain group in a particular time and place. Help your students see that academic argument often strives for a more general, or even universal, audience.

Finally, *ethos* is an appeal that depends on how the writer represents herself. What goes into creating the reader's confidence that the writer is sincere, truthful, reliable, equitable, knowledgeable, thorough, and balanced? Why are these important qualities for the *ethos* of an academic argument? If students worry that they are not yet credible experts on a topic, show them that the way they assemble materials builds their credibility. Are there other qualities in a writer that students like? How might the question of *ethos* be culturally determined or even belong to a specific discourse community? Here you can use the "For Collaboration" activity on p. 95 to analyze Etzioni's essay in terms of Aristotle's appeals.

10. *Toulmin's framework:* This chapter summarizes the features of argument identified by Stephen Toulmin: claims, qualifiers, warrants, reasons, and evidence. The identification of *warrants* is particularly important because students can learn to trace the chain of reasoning in an argument even where it is not explicit by describing the warrants—unstated assumptions and premises—that are invoked. The personal, political, and cultural "unconscious" of an argument will rest in its warrants.

To illustrate how audience-specific warrants are, it can be effective to briefly discuss the Declaration of Independence's "self-evident truths" and ask for which audiences these would have been self-evident. Students quickly realize that for some, including King George III, they would not have been.

Toulmin's framework is a reworking of the classic syllogism, which he found unhelpful for real-world problems. Similarly, John Gage has argued that reasoned inquiry proceeds not through syllogisms or formal logic but through the informal logic of *enthymemes,* similar to the idea of warrants in that the third premise in a syllogism is not expressed but rather assumed. So, for example, an argument takes on the form of **x because y**—"The war was not justified because no weapons of mass destruction were found." The assumption here is that the only justification for the Iraq war was Iraq's possession of weapons of mass destruction. The response to this argument might not be direct—"Such weapons will be found"—but might rather reflect an unstated warrant: "There were many other reasons that the war was justified."

Students can use Toulmin's framework to analyze Etzioni's argument (see "For Exploration," p. 97) as well as to build and analyze their own arguments. Use Stevon Roberts's essay "The Price of Public Safety" (pp. 101–6) to demonstrate ways to approach analysis through Aristotle and Toulmin.

11. *Fallacies in argument:* Fallacies represent shortcuts that seem obviously unfair, unjustified, and invalid if the underlying claims and warrants are analyzed and made explicit. However, since most argument rests on informal logic, such fallacies are a matter of degree. Rather than listing prohibited strategies, the description of fallacy presented here is based on the rhetorical situation, and the fallacies are grouped around Aristotle's appeals.

This chapter describes the following: **ethical fallacies** (*ad hominem, guilt by association*); **emotional fallacies** (*bandwagon appeal, slippery slope*); and **logical fallacies** (*begging the question, hasty generalization,* and *non sequitur*). This is not an exhaustive list, of course. (You can easily find lists of additional fallacies online.) Your students may enjoy thinking about other traditional fallacies or making up names for new varieties—for example, *reality show appeal.*

12. *Visual texts:* With the explosion of visual texts online, the improved technology permitting students to use visual elements in their work, and expectations by faculty that students know how to integrate and discuss appropriate images or exhibits for their work, writing instructors need to help students locate, evaluate, and ethically and effectively use images. This chapter helps students think about the rhetoric of visual texts by discussing the iconic image of Che Guevara and various ways the image has been repurposed. Equally effective for discussion is the public service advertisement about crystal meth use.

The "Guidelines for Analyzing Visual Texts" (pp. 111–12) begin with a formal or aesthetic reading and continue into a rhetorical analysis via the appeals to *logos, ethos,* and *pathos.* The point is to emphasize the rhetorical and persuasive aspect of visual texts as well as their interaction with written texts.

Have students refer to the "Guidelines for Using Visuals in Academic Writing" (p. 138) in Chapter 5 to show them how Alletta Brenner's use of images in her sweatshop essay (pp. 205–15) and Brenda Shonkwiler's use of photos and charts in her analysis of the Tacoma Bridge failure (pp. 135–36) make appropriate academic appeals.

Activities

(p. 80) *For Collaboration:* This exercise has students work together on three discussion points about Hope Leman's essay. If you wish, ask them to report the results of their discussion to the class.

1. The first discussion question asks students to think about the **abrupt beginning** of the essay, which was written for a midterm. They can focus on the question of how and when to take wider audiences into account in academic writing. For an exam, there is no need to interest the reader/grader—but this may also be true of other kinds of academic writing.
2. The second item brings up the question of the **controlling purpose and the thesis**. Students are asked to identify the thesis and then discuss why it is important to be explicit in this context.
3. The third question points to the use of a **personal voice** in Leman's essay—while not dominant, voice is nevertheless an effective part of an objective academic answer. After discussing these points, ask students if they have changed their minds about the standards instructors might use to grade midterm essays. If they were to construct a grading rubric, what elements would they include?

(p. 85) *For Exploration:* This activity asks students to freewrite about their previous experiences reading and analyzing academic arguments. By asking them to think about the articles that have interested (or bored?) them, you can validate their reactions while showing the importance of a fair analysis. Multilingual and multicultural writers can usefully explore how language differences might have affected their experience with analyzing academic arguments and how cultural differences might have entered into their responses. You can make use of these responses to prompt class discussion or set up an analysis assignment.

(p. 90) *For Collaboration:* This group activity asks each student to identify two of the questions at issue in Etzioni's argument, along with passages that illuminate the questions, and then to discuss their answers with other students. In particular, they should explore the agreements and disagreements they found among themselves, perhaps with an eye to the assumptions they reveal. Then they are asked to agree on two stasis questions and present reasons why these are central. This offers an opportunity to think about differences in readings. Multicultural students may have some very interesting things to say about differences in cultural assumptions about privacy, and so they may also offer some interesting perspectives on Etzioni's argument. Is Etzioni culturally limited in his assumptions?

(p. 91) *For Exploration:* This exercise asks students to apply the "Questions for Critical Reading" (pp. 92–93) to the excerpt from Etzioni's *The Limits of Privacy* after rereading critically. The first question asks what they think the purpose or agenda of the author might be. Ask how their beliefs about privacy changed as they read. How much does Etzioni's introduction about the Constitution match the students' final assessment of his purpose? You could encourage them to do a little research to find out more about Etzioni, in connection with the second question for critical reading. See the related "For Collaboration" below.

(p. 91) *For Collaboration:* This exercise connects with the "For Exploration" above, asking students to discuss their answers in a group. They may have gathered a considerable amount of material, so give them adequate time for an exchange. They may need to select and/or summarize in order to present their findings to the entire class.

(p. 95) *For Exploration:* This activity asks students to analyze where and how Etzioni uses each of Aristotle's three appeals and whether they are effective for his purpose.

(p. 95) *For Collaboration:* After the previous Exploration, students can work together to discuss their responses about appeals in Etzioni's argument and create an evaluation of examples from the Etzioni essay. Help your students see that they can admire an author's appeal even if they disagree with his purpose, and vice versa.

(p. 97) *For Exploration:* In this activity, students are asked to choose one part of Etzioni's argument and use Toulmin's system to analyze it. Since they have already worked on this argument, they may very well imagine they have been thorough. Their reports of what they have found that they did not see earlier may demonstrate the "microscope" effect of a Toulmin analysis. You can point out that such a detailed close reading of a text is an important method of analysis and can reveal significant evidence in arguments of many kinds.

(p. 106) *For Exploration:* In this activity, students read the analysis of Etzioni's argument by Stevon Roberts. By now, they should be very familiar with Etzioni's essay, yet likely they will find in Roberts's essay critical readings they had not considered. Students are asked to identify and explain two or three examples of critical thinking in Roberts's essay, then to do a critical reading that suggests improvements to his essay, drawing on their own analyses of Etzioni.

(p. 106) *For Collaboration:* The process of critical reading continues in this activity, as students bring the previous individual analyses together to discuss Roberts and Etzioni. At this point, they should write about the extent of their agreements and disagreements with Roberts and choose the best passage from the essay, together with their recommendations for improvement, to share with the class. Many students could greatly improve their performance in academic writing through this kind of patient close and critical rereading. Showing them that their first reading cannot generate the kind of precise understanding that further analysis will reveal can be a powerful help in their future work on their own academic arguments.

(p. 113) *For Exploration:* This exercise asks students to apply the "Guidelines for Analyzing Visual Texts" (pp. 111–12) to the public service advertisement about crystal meth use on the following page and then to reflect in writing on what they learned. To help students develop a vocabulary for the analysis of visual texts, you may wish to work through advertisements in class first or to ask for students to report their conclusions after they write them.

(p. 113) *For Thought, Discussion, and Writing*

1. Interviewing instructors can give students a chance to find out more about their classes and their major, and it can give them crucial practice in learning how to discuss assignments with faculty. Sharing their findings in class or writing an essay based on their interview notes can provide a helpful learning experience.

Instead of sending students to interview individual faculty, you could invite a panel of instructors to your class for questions in situations when individual interviews may not work or may overload colleagues.

Be alert to possible confusions, such as students being intimidated or having difficulty understanding their instructors. In addition, some faculty may not have experience explaining assumptions about disciplinary writing for beginners. In any event, this assignment can help students better understand their academic writing tasks, and any confusion they have provides you with an opportunity to clarify.

The text suggests an essay as the final step. If there is still confusion, students could benefit from writing about why they still do not understand the goals of undergraduate education or of a particular class or why they feel anxious or frustrated about the analytic and argumentative skills required.

2. This second activity using an editorial or opinion column asks your students to put the suggestions from the chapter into practice by analyzing the appeals, questions at issue, claims, and warrants used in arguments. The objective is not to find airtight distinctions among arguments, because most editorials will, in fact, mix questions of fact, value, policy, and so forth. Furthermore, your students, like all audiences, will read for the appeals that seem persuasive to them and will tend to give those appeals priority. Students may disagree about what the major questions of editorials might be, so the exercise provides practice in identifying claims of different kinds.

If their discussion reveals different readings, this opens an opportunity to discuss the task of a reader in arguments. You might ask students what this discovery suggests for their own arguments. Ask them to consider how editorials work effectively—how claims prove anything—in spite of their various readers. Resist letting the discussion resort to the conclusion of "everyone has his or her own opinion," since that does not solve the puzzle of effective argument. As an alternative, use arguments from such online publications as *Slate*, *Salon*, *Wired*, *Undercurrent*, and *Bad Subjects*. English-edition newspapers from non-English-speaking countries provide further interesting material for analysis.

Chapter 5: Making and Supporting Claims

This chapter addresses the contexts for academic argument and how academic argument differs from other kinds of argument, particularly debate. It points out the chief characteristic of academic discourse: that argument serves as a method of inquiry, not as a process of taking sides. The chapter reviews Aristotle's appeals and discusses why it is worthwhile to make an argument in academic disciplines and how to determine what's at stake in order to form a thesis. In addition, the chapter provides guidance for using visuals appropriately and effectively in academic arguments (as a precursor to Chapter 11). The chapter concludes with an extended case study of a student's composing process from beginning to final draft.

Concepts

1. *Academic argument:* This chapter presents academic argument as a method of inquiry and a means of discovering knowledge by participating in an ongoing scholarly conversation. This view of argument, and its refutation of the view of argument as a raw win-lose power struggle between opposing views, might surprise students new to the academy.

Using the concept of "design" may help students grasp the various elements of academic arguments, especially because there is no single right way to design an argument nor any easy "once and for all" solution for these ongoing conversations. The more you can help students accept this uncertainty, the less they will expect you to "show me how to do it" as if writing an argument were a math problem with a right solution.

2. *Aristotle's three appeals in academic argument:* This chapter emphasizes that academic argument does not rest solely on an appeal to *logos*. The appeals to *ethos* and *pathos* may include such matters as the style of presentation and visual aspects, choice of vocabulary, and the judicious use of figurative language. Note, though, that students who seek to use figurative language in their arguments should exercise caution (unless the metaphor is taken from a source text).

As for *ethos*, remind students that despite their novice understanding in a field, they can build credibility by being thorough, using the accepted methodologies of the field, and respecting other positions. Appeals to *logos* in academic argument usually appear, however, as the logical and evidentiary requirements of disciplines—good reasons (artistic *logos*), acceptable evidence (inartistic *logos*), and the inclusion of counterarguments.

3. *The role of values, assumptions, and beliefs:* Even academic arguments depend on a number of assumptions that remain unexamined, the warrants in Toulmin's framework, which may puzzle students. Use the "Guidelines for Analyzing Your Own Values and Beliefs" (pp. 120–21) to help students understand warrants.

We sometimes talk with our students about the "duh" factor, the warrant that is obvious for a particular audience. An easy activity is to ask students to recommend a film and a reason to view it: An argument that "We should see the film *Avatar* because of the great special effects" is built on the warrant that the audience admires special effects. Alternatively, maybe "We should see *Avatar* because of the social message"? A very different warrant is invoked, one that might be more effective with different people. Consider how you will work with students who say that adjusting an argument and its warrants for the values and beliefs of different audiences might be considered manipulative.

You might also want to talk about why assumptions and warrants often remain unexamined. Show students how disciplines as interpretive communities have patterns of shared assumptions, values, and beliefs. A challenge to these assumptions is generally a major enterprise, a disciplinary revolution. For example, a basic assumption in writing about literature has been the idea that literary texts are different from—and better than—other kinds of writing. Feminism, cultural studies, and poststructuralism have all challenged this assumption, generating considerable theoretical controversy. Scientific discourse also undergoes changes, but effective challenges to widely accepted theories—such as the theory of evolution—might be too major an enterprise for a successful student paper in your class. (See Stephen Jay Gould's essay "Evolution as Fact and Theory" as a useful resource.) Students often raise very interesting questions about disciplines because they do not know what is taken for granted. However, the truth is that students will seldom succeed in revolutionizing a discipline—their argument will instead fail to seem effective. Students need to be aware of these regular patterns of disciplinary assumptions in order to write successfully.

Students also need to think about what warrants and assumptions their own arguments depend on and how they might be challenged. Do your students write about something as if everyone agreed with or shared the experience? Peer groups can help with this, pointing out assumptions that someone might challenge, though sometimes students prefer to agree to avoid uncomfortable confrontation or admitting to divergent beliefs. Cultural diversity in your class may help ensure that provincialism will be challenged. You can show that such questioning is valuable. The "For Exploration" activity on p. 122 helps students work through their own warrants.

4. *Can this claim be argued?* As the three sets of Guidelines in this chapter suggest, arguments need to be about something that is at issue, and they need to persuade readers to believe in their claims or to do something. Frequently students have a hard time understanding what the thesis of an essay ought to be because they are thinking more of reporting than of taking a position on a topic. Instead, they need to address an audience and array of positions. But the academic audience is unfamiliar. And student peer-response groups do not automatically provide a good sense of an audience that is committed to the ideas of a certain discipline.

Ask group members to imagine what convictions might be unsettled or overthrown if the writer proves a certain point. In academic argument, "what's at stake" points not only to opposing sides of an issue, but more to the significance of the argument in the larger (perhaps disciplinary) conversation. The argument must be stated as a thesis, meaning that the student must take a limited position.

Even when students understand the idea of a thesis and can identify it in the papers of others, some do not like asserting themselves in a position-taking stance. This resistance can stem from their experience in what Tannen calls "the argument culture," a desire not to offend others; or they may lack confidence in their ideas or believe that "everyone is entitled to their opinion." Multicultural writers may find North American position taking rude. Urge students to locate examples of theses that both state a position and avoid engaging in a confrontational *ethos*.

Another challenge is to help students see that just because an issue is important that does not make the claim arguable. Students who wish to argue that people should quit smoking may be baffled when told that is not really arguable. Instead suggest an arguable thesis that makes the warrants explicit: "Anti-smoking ads will not significantly reduce the number of teens who start smoking unless they can convince teens to value long-term health over short-term rebellion and peer pressure."

Finally, students need help in understanding how important it is to limit claims. For example, one student starting out to write about the causes and effects of the Vietnam War was surprised to discover that he could be more successful narrowing his thesis to the health effects of Agent Orange.

5. *Good reasons and evidence:* The analysis in this chapter demonstrates how the rhetorical situation might enter into students' reviews of their arguments as they use the tools discussed in Chapter 4: Aristotle's appeals, the questions at issue, and Toulmin's framework. Students should not begin this review too early in the process of generating their arguments—rather, their critical analysis should take place after they have gone through the process of writing a first draft.

You can talk to them about their use of sources at this point. Perhaps you will want to introduce the problem of choosing secondary sources with these questions in mind. What about using a source that is out of date, unacceptable within a discipline, biased, or that merely produces useful background? Use Chapter 7 as well to help students see what counts as evidence in a particular field. The "For Exploration" activity on p. 128 asks students to consider the appropriateness of the evidence they have selected.

6. *Counterarguments:* Students need to understand the importance of considering and including counterarguments in academic writing. In fact, counterarguments may provide the stimulus for writing about a topic in the first place. Thinking of counterarguments will help students recognize and answer possible challenges to their assumptions. Considering counterarguments also will shift their reasoning from diatribe to dialogue. Counterarguments can also serve as an important way of organizing an essay.

You can encourage students to assume critical roles even when they have limited knowledge or do not feel confident in their ability to be critical. Use group work to dramatize the practice with the "For Collaboration" activity on p. 130. Students need to learn to play the devil's advocate, raising counterarguments for themselves. You can have them argue one side and then the other without asking them to take up an *ethos* that could cynically argue both sides. Or take a few topics for general discussion, and pass out pieces of paper assigning positions ("You are a logger in favor of cutting old-growth timber." "You are an environmentalist against cutting old-growth timber.") Ask students to write out slips of paper representing various positions on their topics to perform this exercise in groups. Point out how learning to reason from the standpoint of the other is also an exercise in empathy, a recognition of the complexity of most arguments. Show them how taking counterarguments into account can help them develop balanced theses.

Martin Luther King Jr.'s "Letter from Birmingham Jail" is a useful text for showing how to respectfully engage counterarguments with his sophisticated use of "you say this but here's why you are wrong" moves, using each of the charges against him to structure his response.

7. *Using visuals in academic arguments:* Have students use the "Guidelines for Using Visuals in Academic Writing" (p. 138), and caution them about

two things: The visuals should be appropriate for the academic discipline in which students are writing, and the visuals must support the points students are making in the text. It may help if you discuss the appeal to *logos* (rather than *ethos* and *pathos*) in the visuals that Brenda Shonkwiler chose for her essay on the Tacoma Narrows Bridge. For example, how are the graphs, charts, and photographs part of her evidence? In what ways, if at all, are they a more effective kind of evidence than written text? In other words, did she choose a good medium in this instance? Would visuals that appeal to *pathos* be appropriate for this essay as well?

In addition to discussing how to select visuals, it's helpful to show students how to find, insert, and correctly and ethically cite them. When integrating any visuals, students should learn how to include a reference and should be able to demonstrate their relevance, just as they should with quotes.

Composing an Academic Argument: A Case Study

This extended case study provides a chance to follow student Daniel Stiepleman's entire thinking process for a writing project from the original assignment to final draft. By seeing how Daniel thought his way through the steps from reading the sample text and annotating it as part of the reading process, to a discovery draft, a prewriting journal entry, a rhetorical analysis, first draft, revision, revised second draft with peer comments and response, to finished essay, students can see how a piece of writing evolves and how analysis and argument constantly interact.

You might consider asking your students to discuss this entire case study and freewrite about it. How can they learn from the techniques Daniel uses? For students used to writing a single draft the night before it is due, this case study can be an effective argument for the value of the writing process.

Activities

(p. 122) *For Exploration:* This exercise asks students to analyze their own values, assumptions, and beliefs about a possible writing topic. They are to list opposing arguments as part of their analysis. This will not only help them imagine counterarguments they might address; it also will reveal much about their own commitments. Those in danger of being overinvolved with an issue are encouraged to think about their unexamined assumptions and whether they want to examine them. Those who habitually choose topics because they seem obvious or workable begin instead with a sense of commitment to an issue. Ask your students to repeat this "For Exploration" for each essay topic they consider.

(p. 128) *For Exploration:* This exercise asks each student to think about appropriate and effective reasons and evidence supporting a tentative thesis on a particular question at issue for a particular audience.

Use this activity to show students how they may need to rewrite a thesis statement after thinking about evidence and claims and to help them see how they might address claims in hierarchical order to organize their evidence. For example, does a writer on teen pregnancy think that the most important claim is one of fact—arguing that teen pregnancy is a problem connected with poverty, disproportionately affecting girls from low-income families? Or is the most important a claim of policy—that the government ought to fund programs to prevent teen pregnancy because it increases poverty and all its accompanying problems?

Often the emotions associated with a much-discussed public issue make the issue seem self-evident. Refusing to take the self-evident for granted can sometimes give a student a lead for his or her thesis. For example, the writer could observe that teen pregnancy seems a persistent problem despite mass education about sex and birth control, and ask if there are other reasons why teens keep getting pregnant.

(p. 130) *For Collaboration:* This exercise asks your students to think of as many counterarguments to a thesis as possible, without pausing at this point to develop any of them. You may need to practice this assignment several times when you first assign it so that everyone gets a feeling for what counterarguments might be like. You might also bring a couple of statements to class on each of the next two or three days and challenge students to produce counterstatements, writing them down as a list or brainstorming aloud.

(p. 133) *For Exploration:* This activity returns to the essay "A Separate Education" by student Alia Sands seen in Chapter 3 (pp. 47–50). The exercise asks students to identify the rhetorical moves she makes, in terms of claims and questions at issue, use of Aristotle's appeals, evidence and reasons, underlying warrants, and addressing of possible counterarguments.

(p. 153) *For Thought, Discussion, and Writing*

1. This essay assignment pulls together the separate steps in preparing an argument that students have worked on throughout the chapter. Encourage students to refine their ideas as they develop their essays. If they have, indeed, worked their topic through the various exercises and followed the case study, they have probably found themselves with considerable written material and perhaps a few visuals. The complexity now revealed will, in fact, make it a less familiar essay assignment. Most students have developed shortcuts that allow them to write but also reduce their effectiveness in the long run. You may find yourself at this point needing to reassure your students that the more sophisticated essay they are about to write will serve them better in their academic careers—and that such writing also takes practice to master.

2. This activity asks students to interview a teacher about the characteristics of a successful argument in his or her discipline and to write an interview summary. If they return to the same teacher they have interviewed before, they might think about how the idea of a successful argument is related to the disciplinary conventions and methods they have previously asked about. You can see the possibility of an interview essay here: Using all the material they have gathered over the term, students can discuss writing practices, visuals, and what makes a good argument in a particular discipline.

3. This activity asks students to select and bring to class two editorials or opinion columns from the school newspaper (or other source you specify)—one that seems successful and one that seems "suspect." If you collect these

ahead of time, you can share and discuss them with the whole class. You might also select the most interesting for smaller groups of students to analyze and evaluate. As a final step, you might want to have them specify the ways these arguments do and do not work as "academic" arguments, and why.

Suggestions for Further Activities

1. Using the "Guidelines for Using Visuals in Academic Writing" (p. 138), have your students come up with some possible visuals for the argument they have been working on throughout this chapter. Since they should by now have a thesis and preliminary evidence, they may already have in mind some photographs or tables that would enhance their essays.

Many students "stick in" visuals because they are striking or handy (easy to find online) even though the visuals may be only marginally related to their topic, so it's a good idea to warn students about this tendency. You might remind them that for some topics, such as a local government or campus issue, they may want to create their own visual—a graph from the data of others (with the source cited, of course), their own map, or a pertinent photograph. If they do field research (see Chapter 6), which is not unusual in an academic argument about a local issue, they could put questionnaire results in a table.

2. To help students get a feel for the kind of topics about which they can effectively argue, ask them to make a list of possible topics under the following headings: a) topics I'm passionate about, but about which I am unwilling to change my mind; b) topics I care about but about which I am still open to multiple points of view; and c) topics about which I don't care enough to spend time analyzing and arguing. You might encourage students to discuss their responses in groups. They may discover that one student's passionate topic is of little interest to another student.

Chapter 6: Doing Research: Joining the Scholarly Conversation

Chapter 6 takes a fresh broad look at research and information literacy from a rhetorical perspective—an integral part of the reading and writing relationship—in academic settings as well as in students' everyday lives.

We want students to go beyond finding sources to support the thesis of a research paper and to see that they are always researching—whether for a paper or to find the best DVD player. We want them to think of information in a new way and learn more effective "look up" search strategies, but more importantly we want them to explore new terrain from multiple perspectives to engage with interesting material and especially others talking about issues. This chapter helps your students step-by-step through the process of thinking rhetorically about an assignment to creating effective research questions and developing strategies that will enable them to join the scholarly conversation on their chosen topic.

The guidelines in this chapter give students new ways to think about research and their roles as writers, as explorers, and as gatherers of information before moving into practical new search strategies as part of managing a research project. The chapter also offers some of the latest ways to think about the material they find, how to save it, and how to use it. Seen this way, research is "creative" invention as it generates content that shapes a line of argument. Research can also stimulate new essay topics.

In addition to material to guide secondary research, the chapter provides guidelines for primary research: conducting interviews and using questionnaires. The chapter also discusses tools for understanding and using these sources, including visuals. Finally, there is material on effectively quoting, paraphrasing, and summarizing, leading to a useful discussion of plagiarism. This chapter closes with an annotated research essay with a complete Works Cited page.

A Note on Getting Help: With today's rapidly emerging technologies, it can be difficult for instructors to stay current with the new search tools. Consider collaborating with your librarian for a refresher and resources you can share with students. Many libraries now have tutorials or interactive sessions to familiarize students with search tools for the wide range of sources they may be using. For more on this and on information literacy generally, see pp. 46–48 of these Instructor's Notes.

Concepts

1. *Exploring, gathering, evaluating, writing:* This chapter shows students a different way to think about the various roles they take on as they work on any project that requires information. Gathering and evaluating information are probably familiar concepts, but the willingness to retain an open mind to keep exploring a topic may be new. Students coming from a "get it done" approach may take a while to realize the value of investing time in inquiry, exploring a topic before settling on a focus. This approach changes the research perspective from "look it up" to "let's see what's out there."

You can help students experiment with the inquiry approach by structuring both small informal assignments as well as larger papers toward finding an ongoing conversation to enter, starting by finding what others are saying. Use the "Questions to Help You Start Your Research" on p. 166 to help students move forward.

2. *Academic searching and researching:* This chapter defines academic research as entering the conversation on a particular topic. The chapter shows students how to effectively use keyword searching and various search tools, catalogs, and databases to find material online and in print. In addition to teaching up-to-date skills for secondary research, the chapter overviews primary field research strategies such as interviews or questionnaires.

This chapter emphasizes the variability of the research process, making a number of suggestions to enhance the exploration, discovery, and elaboration of ideas. This reflects the principle that research is also invention, not merely a matter of locating authorities to back up one's predetermined point. Students must still behave as writers and designers, actively shaping their purpose.

3. *Managing a research project:* No matter how large or small the research project, students struggle with meeting deadlines. This chapter helps them plan and carry out a project, skills they can take forward to future writing

projects. The "Guidelines for Managing a Research Project" (p. 169) help students develop a timeline and plan search strategies that will be most effective given their project and topic.

One exercise that can help is to ask students to predict each phase of a project, and then note the actual date they reached this point. After the research project is completed, have students reflect on their *tentative* versus *actual* timelines. This activity will help students better determine more accurate timelines for future research projects.

4. *Starting with secondary sources:* Because a key component of "entering the conversation" is finding the thread of the conversation, which is often evolving asynchronously in various media, writing assignments frequently require a variety of source types. Students need to understand why assignments require these different sources, and they need to learn ways to explore, interpret, and select them.

You can help students understand the relevance of certain aspects of sources, such as timeliness, peer review, and audience. Students also need to understand that most newspapers, magazines, and scholarly journals (even many books) now exist in both print and digital form, blurring old distinctions of print vs. online sources.

Have students check your library's databases for free subscriptions to online material, or do so yourself and communicate the information to students. If your library offers interlibrary loans or materials from a multilibrary consortium, show students how to access that material and explain likely timeliness (for project management). If your students are not familiar with finding library material, you might explain how to read call numbers and show the benefits of finding helpful materials in the vicinity of the item sought. Students also often enjoy source scavenger hunts where pairs or small groups are tasked to find various sources in different sections of the library.

One key point to emphasize is that there is often no best or perfect source. Students should learn to build from what they find, not search for the one source that backs them up. Rather, it is their job to synthesize what they find and make the new knowledge themselves.

5. *Conducting interviews, using questionnaires, and recording observations:* In addition to requiring information from secondary sources, many assignments require field research. While disciplines that use these primary research methods extensively (such as sociology, political science, and anthropology) have well-established protocols, students can also use these methods less formally for various projects (of course without scientific validity).

The text provides a set of "Guidelines for Conducting Interviews" (p. 181) and "Guidelines for Designing and Using Questionnaires" (pp. 183–84), as well as some suggestions for using close observation as a research tool. Ethnographic and auto-ethnographic observations are popular research methods that aid critical understanding of cultures. As anthropologists remind us, however, the study of other people's behavior and values always needs to take account of the beholder's perspective as well, to make explicit the inevitable ethnocentrism and bias and correct it to the maximum extent possible.

6. *Understanding and evaluating sources:* Once students begin to gather material, they must evaluate it using rhetorical sensitivity. The "Guidelines for Evaluating Sources" (pp. 191–92) provide a series of specific questions to guide thinking. You may want to have students bring sources to class so you can address these questions directly. Issues of credibility, writing quality (or even correctness), bias, timeliness, and context become acute with Web pages, and students can bring printouts of the pages for discussion. Asking questions about a source's purpose and sponsor may help students consider whether and how to use material. Help students understand that even if a source has a clear agenda or bias, the material might still be useful for contextualizing the argument if the agenda is made explicit in their paper. You can also help students by discussing sponsorship—whose work gets published, where, and why. This will prepare students for the later discussion of differing discourse communities and what counts as evidence in Chapter 7, "Writing in the Disciplines."

7. *Determining when to quote, paraphrase, or summarize:* Most students can benefit from a clearer understanding of the three ways of integrating source material into a piece of writing and how to choose which method to use when. The most common error is to quote too often, rather than saving quotations for the "gems." A paper patched together from blocks of quotations has probably not integrated the material into the argument very well and may not contain enough of the student's own writing. Another common student problem is using the quotation to make the argument, rather than putting their claim in their own words. The chapter shows students how to avoid "drop quoting" by setting up quoted material with a significant signal phrase (with citation) followed by an exit comment on how the quote amplifies the student's argument.

In addition to quoting, paraphrasing and summarizing are essential and often misunderstood tools for incorporating material. Students need practice writing concise summaries rather than listing ("and then; and then . . . "). Being able to identify and articulate the main claim in a text is part of critical thinking. See also the useful material on summarizing in Chapter 8 (pp. 267–68).

Paraphrase poses a different challenge—staying true to the original while changing the words and sentence structure. This difficulty often spurs students to quote, as the easier way out. Practice with paraphrase and summary can help. Depending on classroom technology, you can put sources on a screen and talk through summary and paraphrase or have students use sources from their research project to paraphrase and summarize, and share for discussion in a small group.

8. *Avoiding plagiarism:* Students may think that plagiarism only means intentionally using another student's paper or downloading a paper from the Internet. Help them understand the need to cite everything they use, especially the text they copy/paste. Following through their drafts and being familiar with your students' writing style can help you notice these problems. Encourage students to build their Works Cited page from the start, listing every source as they add it, as this can help later if they need to return to a

source. Too often students leave the citations until after they write and end up forgetting sources. Your school may have resources for academic honesty that can help you teach avoiding plagiarism.

Activities

(p. 156) *For Exploration:* This activity asks students to reflect on previous experiences with research, identifying one that was satisfying and one that was difficult, and to write a few paragraphs about each, along with two or three suggestions for making research more satisfying in the future. This can help alleviate "library anxiety" and the resistance to searching. Reading their freewrites can help you plan activities to expand information literacy as well as help with their projects. Encouraging students to discuss their freewrites in small groups may provide fresh perspectives. International students can share differences in research methods from their cultures.

(p. 164) *For Exploration:* This activity asks students to reflect on a research project they really felt good about and to write a few paragraphs about the experience. As with the previous activity, this may help alleviate the all-too-common resistance to doing research if students can realize that it is not always just for school, the teacher, or someone else, but that it can be self-sponsored and satisfying. The other big part of this exploration is the question about when students "knew" what they wanted to say, which will help them realize that the "answers" are not always "out there" to be found but are synthesized from students' interpretations of their findings. This second part may puzzle some students, but it provides a good opening for you to discuss concepts of knowledge and their role as creators of knowledge. Reading students' responses can help you strategize on ways to make their research projects more their own and more meaningful. Encouraging students to discuss their responses in small groups may provide fresh perspectives.

Suggested Additional Activities

1. Ask students to bring magazines to class, and pair them with scholarly journals you may have so that they can compare their articles, evidence, language, and audiences. Show them how looking at the advertisements gives clues to the audience, the typical readers. The language and topics provide more clues. Remind students of the three selections by Deborah Tannen on pages 60–65, which show her argument in a general newspaper, a newspaper aimed at academics, and a scholarly journal. Point out the features of each of these genres.

2. Using a sample research topic, ask your students to develop a short questionnaire for the class to identify trends or differing perspectives, and then have them answer the questionnaire themselves and discuss the results. Did the questionnaire offer clear, fair, and user-friendly questions? Do the questions help identify major points of agreement and disagreement, trends, and so forth?

3. To show the difference between primary and secondary sources, you can bring in some actual primary sources along with the secondary sources

about them. Mixing a variety of primary and secondary sources in a box and asking students to identify which category they would fall into—and in which context(s)—can be a useful, hands-on learning activity for students.

4. Have students search terms in Google Scholar and write a paragraph or two on the variety of findings. Ask them to notice author/researcher names that appear frequently and then try different searches using those names to see how the search evolves. Ask them to think about the "scholarly conversation" their project might imply. You could have them try two or three searches to find out what, in fact, the conversation seems to be. They could try these terms in a regular Web browser, and then use an image search to explore results. (Often visuals are attached to useful material that did not turn up immediately in regular searches.) Then ask students to reflect on and compare these various searches.

(pp. 215–16) *For Thought, Discussion, and Writing*

1. This exercise asks students to paraphrase and summarize a paragraph and then to reflect in writing on why their paraphrase and summary are (or are not) effective, and on the distinctions between summaries and paraphrase. If your class emphasizes a research paper, you will find this writing of summaries an especially important process, one to come back to later. Remind students that summaries and paraphrases as well as quotes need to be cited. You can ask for documentation and works cited as part of this exercise.

2. This exercise asks students to identify an important journal for scholars in their major. Be ready to help them locate the journal, especially if they are not sure how or whom to ask. You may need to help them locate a journal that is not too advanced for them. If you have a librarian who works with you, you could ask for some sample listings.

   a. If they can get the journal in print, they can browse through the pages easily. If they need to find the journal online, browsing through a single issue may not be as easy. Using Google Scholar, they may find the journal's main site, and might find some open articles. If they use your library databases, they may encounter some new search challenges. Be ready to show them how to use databases, such as EBSCOhost, which have "search within this publication" tools that show the entire table of contents for an issue and allow browsing.

   b. If you can get some sample articles, you can help students identify significant components of them. You can also use the scholarly article by Deborah Tannen on p. 64 to give them examples of such things as an abstract, keywords, and so on, and to help students become familiar with scholarly conventions and language.

   c. When they write the paragraph reflecting on what they have learned, you will get a better sense of how much they now understand and what you may need to review.

3. This exercise asks students to go to an academic social bookmarking Web site like CiteULike (**http://citeulike.com**) and do a simple search on a

topic they recently discussed in one of their courses. The search results will represent articles or other sources that other scholars have saved to the site. When students look at the tags these people used to identify the articles (if they are using CiteULike, there is a small "tags" link on the top of the results page), and then look at the abstracts and titles of the articles, they should find many interesting items. You might want to search CiteULike yourself first to become familiar with it so that you can demonstrate in class if need be.

This activity helps you teach the concepts of keywords and of socially constructed knowledge. You can compare the "folksonomies" (the ways that people think critically and categorize information) in evidence on CiteULike to Library of Congress (LC) subject terms.

When you see what your students have written about the concepts of tagging and categorizing, you may want to discuss these issues in class. Students need lots of help with the concepts of keywords so that they can become efficient and effective searchers and browsers for information.

4. This exercise asks students to go to ScienceBlogs (**http://scienceblogs .com**) or ResearchBlogging (**http://researchblogging.org**), which feature posts by scientists about new research in various fields. When they find a post about an article written by a scholar in their major discipline or a post about an article on a topic discussed in one of their classes, they can read the blog post and any responses to it. They may question whether they can use these blog posts as evidence, so you may want to talk about that. The posts are especially useful for showing students where the "conversations" are and who some of the major players are. Then, too, the posts will point to some useful articles and research. If students start research projects with what others are saying first and respond to the positions, rather than trying to start from a preconceived thesis statement looking for backers, they will learn to be more successful thinkers and scholars.

As students try to find and read the original articles underlying the blog posts, they get good practice understanding both how conversations are carried out in different genres and for different audiences as well as how information or knowledge is shared and used, and what they can then use for their own writing. In addition, they can see more ways to find issues, clues to more information, and evidence they can use.

Chapter 7: Writing in the Disciplines: Making Choices As You Write

Chapter 7 presents the concept of thinking rhetorically in the disciplines and introduces students to the textual conventions of a variety of disciplines. The chapter poses questions to help guide students through analyzing texts in the disciplines and presents sample essays in the humanities, the natural and applied sciences, the social sciences, and business. For first-year students, especially those who have not yet declared a major, understanding that writing expectations vary by discipline will be very helpful.

Concepts

1. *Thinking rhetorically about writing in the disciplines:* It is important for students to realize that the differing textual conventions of various disciplines have evolved to meet the needs, interests, and goals of those who work within them. When students understand these textual conventions and traditions, they can draw on this knowledge to make better rhetorical decisions as they prepare to write.

2. *Writing in the humanities:* Textual interpretation is central to those working in the humanities, and students should understand that sometimes scholars in the humanities may read the same or similar texts for different analytical and interpretive purposes. You can help your students think rhetorically about writing in the humanities by having them work through the two sample humanities essays included in this chapter. Both examples demonstrate how strong reading skills (discussed further in Chapter 8) and careful analysis of the rhetorical situation helped each author effectively meet assignment requirements and instructor expectations. You can ask your students if they are currently taking courses in the humanities and discuss how assignments in those classes differ from this writing class.

3. *Writing in the natural and applied sciences:* Most students assume that writing plays a key role only in the humanities. However, scientists writing in the natural and applied sciences spend considerable time writing research reports, journal articles, and grant proposals. By reviewing the sample essay in this section, you can show your students how the established formats in this discipline promote efficient communication and facilitate exact replication of experiments. Ask your students to bring samples from their science classes to share and discuss.

4. *Writing in the social sciences:* Scholars in the social sciences use many textual conventions from the humanities and the sciences. Writing in this group of disciplines may involve exploring questions through controlled methods of qualitative research such as surveys and questionnaires, experiments, observations, interviews, case studies, and ethnographic field work. The work by student Tawnya Redding in this section is an example of just one kind of writing in the social sciences, the review of the literature. You may want to use a sample essay from another social science, especially from a course that students are currently taking, and have students discuss how the writing reflects communication tasks required in jobs in each discipline. You can also point out how literature reviews are used in the humanities and sciences.

5. *Writing in business:* Business writers need to communicate with both internal and external audiences. The textual conventions of writing in business have evolved along with developments in the technologies of communication. In the twenty-first century, business writers must be able to communicate effectively in both print and online environments, thinking rhetorically about the differing needs and situations of their readers. This section includes a sample business memo. You may want your students to review the memo and the authors' comments about how they analyzed the information they were given for this assignment and their rhetorical situation. This

assignment may be similar to one they will have in a future business writing class. You could have your students respond from the position of Rosa Donahue in a rhetorically appropriate way.

Activities

(p. 219) *For Exploration:* This exercise asks students to freewrite about their experience of creating texts in various disciplines. Use this exercise to find out if your students are more confident in writing for some disciplines than others.

(p. 219) *For Collaboration:* This activity uses the previous Exploration and asks students to share their experiences with a group of students. Often students will find they have shared experiences and fears about writing in some disciplines.

(p. 248) *For Thought, Discussion, and Writing*

1. This exercise requires students to meet with a group of classmates who share the same interest in a major area of study. What kinds of writing will they need to do in this discipline? How well are they prepared to write in this discipline? Ask students to create a list of writing challenges and to brainstorm productive ways to overcome these challenges.

2. This exercise asks students to write an essay about why they are drawn to a particular discipline or general area of study. This assignment can help students determine why they want to pursue an area of study or career, requiring them to think critically about their interests and goals as well as the challenges and rewards associated with their choice.

3. This activity asks students to study either a student essay in this chapter or one of their own pieces of writing, focusing on its vocabulary, style, evidence, and use of conventional formats. In studying their own work and working with the "Questions for Analyzing Writing in the Disciplines" (p. 220), students can become more comfortable at analyzing their work objectively and thinking rhetorically about their writing situation and the textual conventions of the discipline. They could also practice "translating" their writing from one discipline to another.

Suggestions for Further Activities

1. Use the "Questions for Analyzing Writing in the Disciplines" (p. 220) to better understand the expectations of members of a particular discipline in the humanities, the natural and applied sciences, or the social sciences. Students can meet in groups (either mixed groups or groups focused on the same discipline) to discuss the results of their analysis. Students can follow this activity by writing an informal analysis or a formal essay.

2. With the help of a librarian or an instructor in the field, identify a respected journal in one of the disciplines in the humanities, the natural and applied sciences, or the social sciences. Choose one or two articles in the journal, and analyze them using the questions on p. 220. What additional insights into the expectations of those in this field does this activity generate?

Part III: Practical Strategies for Reading and Writing

Chapter 8: Strategies for Reading

This chapter turns to the complexities of reading and shows how reading is a process of analysis and interpretation that applies to visual as well as to written texts. Even though reading and writing are fundamentals of literacy, their apparent simplicity is deceptive. Just as students take beginning, intermediate, and advanced writing classes, so they also need to keep advancing their reading skills. Both reading and writing are active rhetorical processes.

In Chapter 8, *The Academic Writer* pays special attention to the kind of critical reading skills students need in college and to the rhetorical analysis that will help them make connections between their reading and writing. The focus on genres will help students understand differences in texts, for example, how a magazine article such as Jamais Cascio's "Filtering Reality" from *The Atlantic* differs from an editorial or e-zine posting, and how these are different from scholarly and academic writing, which also varies importantly by discipline. Here again you can turn back to Tannen's three samples on pages 60–65 to discuss genres.

In this chapter, you will find a number of specific suggestions and examples to help students read a text more effectively. In particular, "Guidelines for Strong Reading" and "Questions for Previewing a Text" provide questions for analyzing the reading process and considering texts within a rhetorical situation. This chapter also provides help for previewing, annotating, outlining, summarizing, and analyzing different types of texts. It connects well with Chapter 4, "Analyzing Texts and Contexts," so a refresher might be effective.

Concepts

1. *Critical, active, strong reading:* Whether your students are first-year students or more advanced, you may find you need to emphasize to them the idea that critical does not mean "finding something wrong," a widespread misunderstanding that can turn a rhetorical analysis of a text into a mere list of faults. Most students recognize that poetry and fiction require interpretation, and they may even see literary interpretation as a practice that requires a lengthy apprenticeship. But they generally have not extended the practice of critical reading to other kinds of texts, including visual texts. Given tools for reading analytically, students can consciously improve their critical thinking.

Furthermore, students frequently assume that reading is a passive activity—no more than decoding and retaining information for a test. But as we know, reading, like writing, involves problem-solving strategies as students engage with various genres that assume different background knowledge and that occur within specific rhetorical situations. This process of active engagement is *strong* reading, a concept urged by David Bartholomae and Anthony Petrosky in *Ways of Reading*. As *strong* readers, students are reading critically, engaging in active dialogue with the author by asking questions and posing counterarguments. Connecting critical reading with the idea of a conversation may prove especially helpful. If the written text is an author's monologue, then active, strong, critical reading is the way readers analyze, evaluate, agree, and disagree. Annotating (see #5, p. 104) comes in as another way of "talking back/talking with" authors. Strong reading can help students select more effective material for their research projects and strengthen their overall writing skills, enabling them to better participate in the scholarly conversation on their research topics (see Chapter 6).

The "Guidelines for Strong Reading" (pp. 255–57) will help your students with the variety of written and visual texts, whether hard copy or online, that they will encounter in their classes and their lives. As the chapter points out, we read different texts in different ways for different purposes. The graphic flow chart will help your students visualize this process.

2. *Genres:* "Genre" is a familiar idea in literature. Your students probably know that a poem, novel, short story, and play follow certain conventions, and these expectations shape their reading; at the same time, students may call any piece of prose a "story" and any book a "novel," without being sensitive to the differences in the meanings of those terms. It is helpful to sharpen their sensitivity to genre by discussing with them the conventions that govern written texts—academic, literary, and popular—as well as visual texts such as Web sites and television commercials. This will help them complete research assignments that require specific genres of sources (see Chapter 6).

To help students understand mixed genres, you might wish to discuss *The Atlantic* article by Jamais Cascio (pp. 261–62). If students wish to use the Cascio article for a research assignment, they must understand that it is a magazine article that won't count as a scholarly or book source requirement even though they found it in a textbook. Show them how to cite it using the "work in an anthology" format. Be sure to point out to students that two pieces of about the same length—one a stand-alone essay and one an excerpt from a book—may show very different genre structures (see #7, "Analyzing Lines of Argument" on p. 105). Also consider having them do in class the "For Exploration" activity on p. 252, which asks students to list the different genres they read on a daily basis and how they read them.

3. *Previewing:* The "Questions for Previewing a Text" (p. 259) ask students to notice the publishing history of a hard copy or online text (written or visual); to find the author, title, format, and organization; and then to survey the text quickly to predict what it will include and what response the reader might have to it. Depending on the genre, clues about the usefulness of a text can be found in the abstract, the entry in the library catalog, or even an Amazon customer review. Previewing helps students decide whether or not to read the article or book at all and how to read with appropriate questions. Previewing is an important tool for the research strategies introduced in Chapter 6. The "For Exploration" activity on p. 260 asks students to use these tools to preview Cascio's article.

4. *Analyzing visual elements:* This chapter introduces students to the powerful rhetoric of visual texts. Critical readers must be aware of the persuasive intent of visual elements and be able to "read into" them. You can work through the ways that visuals appeal to *logos*, *pathos*, and *ethos* along with the symbolism

of various colors. Remind students about Chapter 4's "Guidelines for Analyzing Visual Texts" (pp. 111–12). Note, too, that an extended discussion on creating visual texts and document design can be found in Chapter 11.

5. *Annotating:* Annotating is helpful when critically reading a text. Students usually have a variety of annotation habits, though some of their techniques may actually hinder their analysis. Suggestions for more active ways of interacting with the text than simply underlining or highlighting include the following:

- Asking questions about the material
- Noting terms and vocabulary; identifying keywords students could use
- Noting main ideas, passages, thesis statements, and points brought up in class
- Responding to ideas by talking back to the author—agreeing, disagreeing, or both
- Responding to style and technique, noticing "what it does" as well as "what it says"
- Using a reading journal for notes and comments

Be sure to point out that students are not exempt from annotating if they don't want to write in their textbooks because they intend to sell them back. If this is the case, they need to make their notes in a journal or in an electronic format.

Visual maps, from outlining to clustering, may also help students annotate and respond to a reading. Note that using a reverse or scratch outline to reveal the structure of a reading can help students learn the logic of outlining, which will be useful when they're starting their own preliminary drafts. Some students may benefit from other methods of visualizing the structure of readings. In addition to mapping or clustering, they may find a visual diagram or a "what it says/what it does" chart easier than an outline for thinking about their main points. See the example of clustering in Chapter 9 (p. 279) for another use of visual representations.

To help your students annotate more effectively, ask them to briefly summarize their favorite annotating technique and then review the "Questions for Annotating a Text" (p. 265). Do they annotate all texts in the same way? Are there other choices your students can make when annotating different kinds of texts that will be more helpful to them? The "For Exploration" activity on p. 266 asks students to practice annotating on Cascio's article.

6. *Summarizing:* As mentioned in Chapter 6, students often need help grasping the main points of what they read. The "Guidelines for Summarizing a Text" on pp. 267–68 give students tools for understanding how to be concise and avoid the "and then" list. You might also consider showing them the classic four-sentence rhetorical précis format as a handy critical-thinking guide for summary. (See **http://oregonstate.edu/instruct/phl201/modules /rhetorical-precis/sample/peirce_sample_precis_click.html** for a great demonstration of the format.) You might want to use the article by Jamais Cascio (pp. 261–62) for summary practice and compare and discuss the versions students generate.

7. *Analyzing lines of argument:* Students often are asked to analyze and evaluate material that does not appear to be an argument in the conventional sense, perhaps because it is presented as a reasoned analysis or appears in a source they consider so authoritative that there seems no question that it is fact (rather than claim). For example, students may tell us that there is no debate about nuclear power because it is science, and science is fact. What they sometimes fail to see is that science constantly advances understanding, and research overturns old ideas.

The questions in this chapter help make a text's structure and its elements of argument visible for students, beginning with the major claim or thesis (whether explicit or implicit) and the appeals used—*logos*, *ethos*, and *pathos*. When students are asked to research, read, and report on material, instructors expect them to get at the significance of what they have read. Yet frequently students do not yet know enough about a field or topic to recognize what's at stake, or they do not read material as if it were an argument at all. Accustomed to reading for facts in a text (what it says), students may fail to notice its effects (what it does). Students usually also assume that their professor knows what's significant; they often write a response assuming the reader knows the material, rather than including a summary. They don't realize that the summary they make is part of their own argument.

Students can learn how to be critically self-conscious about their reading. They need to know if they have gotten the point—and why or why not. When they reflect on their reading processes, they can better assess their reading skills and their limits. They learn to consider whether they know enough about psychology or computers to read the samples in the text. Some find it an enormous relief to realize that reading skill is not a matter of natural talent but something they can and should constantly improve as they take an active role in their education.

As Chapter 8 points out, multilingual writers may find Western argument style different from what they are used to. While the idea of argument implied by a straightforward organization (a claim or thesis plus support) seems clear and obvious, many cultures consider such a direct approach unsubtle, rude, or unpersuasive. For an extensive discussion of how cultural traditions of indirect argument can create student resistance to North American English conventions, see Helen Fox, *Listening to the World: Cultural Issues in Academic Writing.*

Activities

(p. 252) *For Exploration:* In this exercise, students are asked to make a list of the different kinds of texts they read, and to explore how they change their approach to these texts depending on what the texts are and why they are reading them. Then students are asked to freewrite for five minutes about what strategies they already use when reading these texts. If you have students discuss their findings in groups or as a class, you can obtain a general understanding of the reading strategies your students use.

(p. 260) *For Exploration:* In this exercise, students use the "Questions for Previewing a Text" (p. 259) to practice how to quickly clarify their purpose and the context for reading Cascio's "Filtering Reality."

(p. 266) *For Exploration:* This exercise helps students annotate a variety of materials. Students are asked to use the Cascio article to work through the "Questions for Annotating a Text" (p. 265) and should become more comfortable with annotating texts as part of their own critical reading process. You might want to have them jot their annotations on a sheet to collect and review.

(p. 266) *For Exploration:* Using the Cascio article again as their main text, students are asked to follow the "Guidelines for Summarizing a Text" (pp. 267–68) to create a brief one-paragraph summary about the article. Ask students to share and compare.

(p. 269) *For Exploration:* Identifying and analyzing lines of argument can be tough. Returning to the now-familiar Cascio article, students are asked to use all the "Questions for Analyzing a Text's Argument" (pp. 270–71) to analyze Cascio's major claim, assumptions, appeals, evidence, and credibility.

(p. 269) *For Collaboration:* This activity helps students gain perspective on their critical-reading strategies. By completing and reviewing their responses to the chapter's "For Exploration" activities, students can work together to better understand how their critical-reading strategies are similar or dissimilar and what changes they could make to help them be more effective critical readers.

(p. 272) *For Thought, Discussion, and Writing*

1. This exercise asks students to analyze the first chapters of two textbooks they are using for other classes. You may want to have students do this either as a single writing assignment or as ongoing part of their reading journals. Then, you could have them share their results as a group activity.

2. This exercise asks students to freewrite for five minutes after selecting a text they have read recently, focusing on how their expectations and previous experiences influenced their reading of the text. Consider how you can use these freewrites to elicit cultural, social, and rhetorical judgments they have made before and after reading this text and apply them to the assignments you are giving them in class.

3. If students haven't already done the "For Exploration" activities above on Cascio's "Filtering Reality," then consider assigning them now to preview, annotate, summarize, and analyze the argument. After completing these tasks, students are asked to answer a series of questions that help them focus on strong reading strategies.

4. This exercise challenges students to select one or two reading strategies that they have not used in the past and to try them as they work on a current reading assignment. The reading could be a text you select for the class or a source for a research paper. Students could work in groups and discuss their reactions and the effectiveness of trying different reading skills. After discussing this experiment, each student can write a brief analysis about which strategies worked better for them and why. This works well as an extra-credit assignment.

Suggestions for Further Activities

1. Ask students to interview an expert or a more advanced student in their area about their reading and report the results in class. Interview questions could include:

- What do they typically read in classes in their field?
- Are they assigned online reading?
- How much reading is generally assigned?
- How difficult do they find this reading?
- Do their instructors discuss these readings extensively in class, or do they assume that students have read assigned materials and instead discuss other subjects?
- What role do the readings typically play in these courses as a whole?
- Is there a difference between reading from their textbook and outside reading?
- What advice would upper-class students give to new students about the best way to approach required readings in this field?

If you are teaching lower-division students, you might ask them to consult with upper-division students in their major; if your students are undergraduates, ask them to interview graduate students or other knowledgeable sources. Multilingual students may benefit from interviewing a student who speaks their language. (You can refer students to Chapter 6 in the textbook for a discussion of interviewing.)

Like most inquiry that aims to investigate genuinely interesting questions, your students' work will encounter real-life difficulties. When they report their findings in groups and the class as a whole, they may have wildly varying information. Some of their interviews may not be very reliable, either because the answers are superficial or because the interviewees don't know everything they should about the reading they are expected to do. For example, even juniors and seniors do not always know systematic ways to review the literature for a research project or what "the literature" might include in their discipline. Since this exercise explores the realities of the academic writing and reading situation, you can usefully move to discussions that compare and contrast the ways you are handling reading material in this class to the various practices in other classes on campus. Because this exercise offers the opportunity for students to research and describe the contribution of reading to their rhetorical situation in college, it is well worth going on to assign an essay that summarizes their results.

2. After students review the extended case study in Chapter 5 of Daniel Stiepleman's writing assignment about the public service announcement (PSA) for the National Center for Family Literacy (pp. 137–53), have your students search for other PSAs in print or online. Select two or three examples that include persuasive text and visual elements for your class to analyze. Working as a class or in groups, have students use Chapter 4's "Guidelines for Analyzing Visual Texts" (pp. 111–112) and this chapter's "Guidelines for Summarizing a Text" (pp. 267–68) to create a summary analyzing the PSA's argument and detailing how the layout, word selection, images, and so on influence their response to the text. Do your students have different reactions? What elements in each of the PSAs influence their reactions? You might have students work in groups to develop their own PSAs and compose one or two paragraphs explaining how and why they selected specific words, images, layouts, and the like to develop their argument.

Chapter 9: Strategies for Invention

Chapter 9 presents a number of strategies for invention. If you have students go through this chapter with a particular assignment in mind, you may want to have them be selective about the methods of invention they try—and ask them to come back to this chapter several times during the term with other assignments in mind. Or your students can experiment with all of the techniques, returning to use the most appropriate ones more extensively with future assignments.

Note that the process of research, which they should have already encountered in Chapter 6, can be thought of as a strategy of invention as well, and that the journalist's questions (see p. 110 of these notes) can spur further research.

Concepts

1. *Strategies for invention:* The strategies and approaches in this chapter will help students both before they really have a topic and once they have settled on their topic. Students often struggle to find a topic they want to write about. As a result, they sometimes end up with tired topics such as "baseball and steroids" that are rarely well presented and that we often ban (partly because they so often lead to plagiarism). Although we know that students who enjoy their topics will likely be more engaged, we also know students who bog down by refusing to choose a topic and move forward. Sometimes students cannot imagine that a favorite topic—European soccer or *The Simpsons*—could be suitable for a paper. Further, some students imagine that narrowing a topic might restrict sources to the point that a paper will be too short, whereas narrowing the topic would actually make the paper more manageable. For example, one student who wanted to write about the causes and effects of the Vietnam War (in five pages) was afraid to narrow his topic, until he realized he would find enough on just the effects of Agent Orange.

This chapter also presents invention as both an individual and a collaborative process, giving students ways to tap into what they already know and suggesting ways they can work together. As you work through the strategies presented in the text, you may find it especially helpful to frame these tasks in two ways, as both an individual and a group effort.

Some students may assume that "real" writers know how to generate information "from the air" and feel that they themselves are stuck. This chapter helps students realize that invention methods can help them discover what they already know and what they still need to find out about a topic. Students who are overly formulaic about invention may be freed to see new connections by informal processes like clustering. On the other hand, students who do not have much experience with North American English academic discourse may not think of using very common patterns like cause and effect, or comparison and contrast. They may be especially helped by these traditional approaches if they do not know the kinds of questions that might typically be asked, or answered, in an argument.

2. *Discovering ideas:* Reading and experimenting with various invention strategies will help students find ideas and better explore those ideas in their writing. Students, especially multilingual students, need to understand that different invention approaches can be used depending on the writing assignment and that they should not rely on just one or two invention strategies for all of their assignments.

3. *Freewriting:* This chapter introduces freewriting as an informal and powerful invention strategy. Freewriting can help students, especially those nervous about writing, explore various ideas about a topic in a short period of time without the fear of having their thoughts judged or censored by others and themselves. Having students freewrite for five to ten minutes about a topic is a great way to begin class discussion or help students identify possible research questions. You can start with a prompt such as "List five things that you would like to change" and then have them pick one to freewrite about.

Students working on a research project can collaborate with a partner to develop research questions. First have your students freewrite for five minutes about their individual topic, and then ask them to swap their freewrites. After they review their partner's freewriting results, have each student compose different research questions about their partner's topic. Finally, students can review the suggested research questions and discuss with their partner how they can further explore and focus their research ideas. Help students craft research questions that are exploratory, not "look-up" questions requiring merely factual answers.

4. *Looping:* As an extended or directed form of freewriting, looping helps students focus their ideas through analysis and reflection. By selecting or composing a sentence that summarizes the most intriguing, compelling, or productive issue, detail, or image about the subject of their freewriting, students can start writing a second loop and subsequent loops by repeating this process until they have exhausted the subject and narrowed their ideas.

After completing several rounds of looping about a topic, have students review and analyze the results of each loop: Can they identify possible essay ideas? Does each subsequent loop narrow or expand the focus of their research? Have students compare freewriting and looping: Is one process more effective than the other? Can they think of different writing activities where looping might help them more than freewriting?

You can also loop with a group: Have students freewrite for five or ten minutes, and then ask them to write brief responses to each other's work. This exercise creates a certain intensity and focus that may be especially helpful to get students started on a project.

5. *Brainstorming:* Individual and group brainstorming can help students generate a variety of ideas on any topic. Alex Osborn, credited with naming this technique, believed that brainstorming should be a group rather than an individual activity. The enthusiasm created by a group collaborating on a topic could help improve the quality of ideas and generate more promising topic leads. See the "Guidelines for Group Brainstorming" (p. 277).

You might want to have your students test individual and group brainstorming to see which session generates the most viable ideas. Have students brainstorm individually for three minutes on a topic, writing down everything from facts to images, memories, and other responses. Then have students form groups and brainstorm aloud on the same topic for two minutes. When they are done, have them compare the results from each session: How did their individual results vary from their group results? Did having more or less time affect the quantity and quality of their results? Did one session seem more effective than the other? Are there certain topics where students could benefit from collaborative brainstorming?

6. *Clustering:* Using a visual invention technique such as clustering can be a good tool for most students. Clustering enables students to explore topic ideas in a more in-depth, creative, and visual way. Many students prefer visual mapping of some kind, substituting the cluster for an outline and developing more and more elaborate graphics and figures as they continue planning their research projects. Most students find that the center of their cluster and the resulting branches contain preliminary ideas for the main argument, supporting claims, and counterargument of their research project.

After your students have selected their research topic, have them write down the first word that comes to mind when they think about their topic and use that word as the starting point for a cluster. Then have students work on their clusters for twenty seconds before passing the cluster to another student to work on for twenty more seconds. Have students continue passing each cluster to a different student every twenty seconds until you reach two minutes. Then have students return the cluster to the original owner. Give students some time to review their now collaborative cluster, identifying the most compelling and key ideas. Finally, ask each student to write a paragraph about what ideas from the collaborative cluster they might use to help plan their research project.

7. *Asking the journalist's questions:* This chapter details the six questions often taught in journalism class: *who, what, when, where, why,* and *how.* Since these questions consider several aspects of a topic, they can readily point to what students do and do not know about a topic. Students can get at the stakes of an issue by shaping the "What?" to include "So what?" and the "Who?" to focus on the stakeholders by asking "Who cares?". Identifying possible stakeholders can help with research if students can think *where* these groups of people are likely to discuss the topic. For example, the question of adding new bike paths downtown might affect local businesses whose discussion may be reported in the local newspaper or on the television news, whereas environmental advocates may note their support in magazine articles or Web pages.

When you are first teaching these questions, you might want to bring in several newspaper articles on a particular topic and have your students work through each article identifying how the author does or does not answer each question. Then ask your students to use these six questions to explore their own research topic, focusing on how this strategy can help them organize their ideas and identify areas they may need to explore further.

8. *Asking topical questions:* Many students like working with the journalist's questions and the topical perspectives adapted from Aristotle's *Rhetoric*. The systematic and comprehensive quality of these questions and Aristotle's topics can prompt useful lines of thinking. A few enthusiasts may actually answer each of the "Questions for Exploring a Topic" (pp. 283–84), perhaps putting their subjects diligently through all (or a number of) the topical places with the hope of making a paper that is truly encyclopedic. Answering the questions doesn't solve the problem of organization, as you might want to point out, though the topics do suggest possibilities for organization.

9. *Writing a discovery draft:* At some point during any writing assignment, there comes a time when students just need to start writing. A discovery or "zero" draft can help students begin writing about their topic without having to worry about producing a polished paper. It is important to emphasize that a discovery draft will allow students to start organizing their ideas on paper as well as to objectively evaluate and fine-tune their research ideas and writing goals. Remind students to resist the urge to stop to correct their grammar, vocabulary, or punctuation mistakes at this stage and give themselves permission to write what Anne Lamott calls a "shitty first draft."

10. *Inventing collaboratively and troubleshooting:* This chapter's strategies for inventing collaboratively emphasize the social components of invention and show students that they can reach out to others for help to generate ideas and develop their research project. Both the "Guidelines for Group Brainstorming" (p. 277) and "Guidelines for Troubleshooting" (pp. 286–87) facilitate collaborative invention strategies.

If your students have not had much experience working in groups, you may want to pay special attention to troubleshooting. Hold a group troubleshooting session, and then have students freewrite for five to ten minutes about the experience. Have groups list strengths and weaknesses and make some decisions about how to improve on problem areas. You may want to discuss common findings with the class as a whole. Work as a consultant with groups that seem to need further help—most frequently because members are reluctant to give firm advice. You should also be sure to protect students against the coercive potential of group consensus-making by encouraging diversity and divergent reasoning.

Activities

(p. 276) *For Exploration:* This activity asks students to use the freewriting process with a question, idea, or topic of interest, helping them both to generate material and to focus on what is significant about it and then loop back. Many students will find strong subjects for writing through freewriting and looping, and some will be enchanted when they discover their unknown resourcefulness.

(p. 278) *For Exploration:* Using their earlier freewriting from the preceding "For Exploration" activity, students are asked to create a single sentence summarizing the issue or question raised in their freewriting. Students are asked to brainstorm and then mark the new ideas or images that did not appear in their earlier freewriting exercise, considering how these new ideas help their understanding of the question or topic. Students sometimes use brainstorming and listing as an opening shotgun approach and then have trouble elaborating and developing their subject. Here they are integrating brainstorming with other modes of invention.

(p. 280) *For Exploration:* This exercise adds clustering to the methods of invention used in the previous "For Exploration" activities in this chapter. If you have students who have not tried clustering before, you may be amazed at how liberating it seems for many of them. Students who respond well to visual representations may also want to try out more elaborate graphic schemes or maps for arranging their ideas. This technique can also point out unexpected connections between aspects of the topic.

(p. 281) *For Exploration:* Students are asked to work with a familiar subject or a new topic to answer the six journalist's questions and to consider whether this strategy helps them determine what information they know and what information they need to find out about their topic.

(p. 282) *For Exploration:* Using the topic from the previous "For Exploration" activity, students are asked to apply the topical questions to further explore their topic, uncovering new research ideas and developing research goals. After completing this task, students are asked to compare and contrast the journalist's questions and topical questions methods of invention. Notice that the topics work as methods of discovery; they will also work to suggest ways of arranging and developing the subject so that invention overlaps with drafting.

(p. 287) *For Collaboration:* This exercise asks students to meet in groups to analyze the advantages and disadvantages of the different invention strategies introduced in this chapter. After working through a series of questions and considering their learning, composing, and cultural preferences, students are asked to evaluate how these preferences as well as situational differences in each assignment might influence which invention strategies they choose for particular writing assignments.

(p. 287–88) *For Thought, Discussion, and Writing*

1. This activity puts to use the invention work completed in this chapter. Students develop a discovery draft by continuing to explore a topic, conducting some informal research and working through a few of the topical questions. Topics that draw on students' personal experiences help them make bridges from the familiar writing to the academic. But there is a danger: Such topics also tap a formidable store of stereotypes, clichés, and automatic responses. The invention methods help bypass this ready banality, partly by generating so much material that students can get beyond it and partly by allowing contradictions and complexities to be described before they are hidden by premature explanations. When used together, these methods will press the student to engage topics critically and place them in larger cultural and historical context.

2. Watching and evaluating a group brainstorming or troubleshooting session has the merit of grounding the observer empirically. Because it connects to improving a real-world activity, with consequences, it short-circuits the often hidden rhetorical situation of the classroom. If you decide to give

your whole class the assignment, perhaps you will want to have groups exchange task and observer roles. Group members can also collaborate on notes, brainstorm results, and discuss recommendations as a group.

3. This assignment asks students to experiment with and evaluate a strategy not used before. It encourages students to use the strategies from this chapter again and again during the term and with various writing assignments. You might assign a new strategy of invention whenever the group seems to be lapsing into hasty invention or when individual students need extra work.

Suggestion for Further Activities

Research may be seen as one aspect of invention. Draw research into these strategies for invention by making it part of the exercise. For example, you can add the extra step of searching online with a browser or library database to freewriting and looping. More formal invention methods can include surveying sources or summarizing a reading. Integrating research into an essay topic inserts it more persuasively into academic writing.

Chapter 10: Strategies for Planning and Drafting

Expanding on Chapter 9, this chapter emphasizes different ways and strategies for planning and drafting and grounds the concept of the controlling purpose with its working thesis in the rhetorical situation. The chapter also suggests procedures for overcoming writer's block and includes a sample student writing plan for an essay comparing three pizza parlors.

Concepts

1. *Working thesis:* If writing is social and not the act of a solitary individual writing alone, then the goals of the writer develop out of a discursive community. The individual writer's purpose arises in a particular rhetorical situation that consists of the potential readers, their concerns, the conventions of their discourse, and the additions the writer wants to make to the communal and scholarly conversation. However, choosing an appropriate controlling purpose isn't always a conscious, carefully articulated process. For students in a writing class, finding a writing purpose can seem mysterious, especially when the assignments do not arise from a personally felt need to express something. This chapter suggests ways to help students determine and shape their purpose through a working thesis.

Some assignments explicitly state the purpose. For example, an assignment to choose two essays and synthesize a conversation about a question at issue gives a lot of direction for a suitable working thesis. On the other hand, despite assignment directions, some students are so wedded to a purpose they may have—for example, to argue for or against a social issue they care deeply about—that you may need to work hard to redirect them to meet the assignment's purpose. For many students, their purpose is mainly to get a good grade. You can help them see that there are usually several good ways to fulfill the assignment successfully and simultaneously be authentic to their own purposes.

This chapter defines an effective working thesis as one that "narrows your topic, helps you organize your ideas, enables you to determine what you want to say and *can* say, helps you decide if you have enough information to support your assertions, and points to the most effective way to present your ideas" (p. 290), especially for a specific audience and a specific genre. When you have students think about their goals for a particular assignment, ask them to define their purpose in just this way—analyzing the rhetorical situation, describing it succinctly, and stating what they want to accomplish.

The chapter's "Questions for Establishing a Working Thesis" (p. 291) provide a useful checklist for current and future projects. Help students see that a good deal of preliminary invention and even drafting may take place before writers have a clear idea of their thesis. This "thesis-seeking" time can generate material that clarifies their direction. Starting with too rigid a purpose before drafting—"I'm going to prove XYZ"—may not succeed if the student doesn't have enough support for that audience. However, writers must start somewhere, so having students develop a tentative working thesis helps them focus on what they need to do next. You can also preview for them the later part of the chapter (p. 299) that discusses "Using a Thesis Statement" and show the difference between their working and final thesis statements, the various kinds of statements that can work, and where they might occur in an essay, depending on the genre or type of writing. You may need to help multicultural writers with the idea that North American academic writing typically expects a thesis statement in the introduction whereas popular magazine essays may delay the thesis until the end or even leave it implicit.

2. *Planning:* Students who write drafts without plans may waste a good deal of their time—and yours—because commenting helpfully on a loose collection of materials is an inefficient way to help students with the writing process. Help students see writing plans as helpful tools meant to be used and revised, especially since there is no one-size-fits-all plan. Students should view planning as a starting point. If students are having trouble developing a plan, a review of Chapters 3 and 9 on analyzing the rhetorical situation and on invention strategies can help.

It can be useful to find out what kinds of planning students have done in previous classes. Many are used to the classic outline for a research paper—often with annotated bibliography—which has the advantage of previewing the entire paper, but the disadvantage of locking points into place that revision (see Chapter 12) may indicate would be more effective elsewhere. You may want to assign outlines as one kind of planning, along with another kind, such as proposals, in which students list a working thesis, the research they need to do, their intended audience, any challenges they foresee, and so on. If you need proposals before students start drafting, you can see who is on the right track and who may have misunderstood the assignment. Students who are be reluctant to change a draft once the words are on the page may be much more willing to change plans from a proposal before they start writing.

Organizational plans can arise from typical "topics" or approaches or from textual conventions. For example, Lisa DeArmand's pizza essay fits the compare/contrast approach and can be effectively treated in a few ways—all about each restaurant sequentially, for example, or comparing by categories such as taste, price, and convenience. The plan, the working thesis, and her organizational structure may depend on the class she is in. The approach she takes for her business class would change if she were writing her pizza comparison for a class in food science.

Sketching typical structures for students can help them see options for the broad shape of their paper. You can also try a "what it says/what it does" outline to help students notice what they already have for some parts—introduction, body, conclusion—and what they need. As their paper evolves, that may require changes in the working thesis. Reassure them that changing their plan and their thesis is natural and necessary at times.

Sometimes students have trouble planning because they are still exploring their topics, and they imagine that they need to have reached conclusions or taken a stand before they can go on. Help students see that a plan can also consist of a series of questions, issues, or problems. Many kinds of writing projects do not require conclusiveness.

Also, rhetorical planning is itself a form of inquiry and invention. Thinking about *how* to write is intimately connected with thinking about *what* to write. For this reason, multilingual writers may want to explore the advantages of planning either in English or in their home language.

Many students do very well using looping, freewriting, or discovery drafts to discover what a topic has to offer. Such processes combine invention and drafting. You can help direct your students by marking passages you find especially effective or interesting and pointing out connections in these early stages. Also have students mark passages they find promising to help you focus your comments, or have them ask questions based on such a draft. Their plan may emerge inductively. If the whole draft seems coherent, you can summarize what it is about and make a scratch or reverse outline showing them what they have done so far.

3. *Drafting:* Even with a plan, many students struggle with starting and managing the actual drafting process. The drafting strategies discussed in this chapter can help your students build momentum and overcome various writing hurdles. It may be useful for you to talk with students about your own practices here—emphasizing differing practices for different kinds of writing. You might also want to address the tremendous gap students often experience between the ideal and the real situation of their writing. You may have students who procrastinate or resist writing because they don't have much time, their writing is not a high priority, their ideas are not yet clear, or they believe their writing is not good enough. The "Guidelines for Overcoming Writer's Block" (p. 295) and the "Guidelines for Drafting on a Computer" (p. 297) offer suggestions for working through writing roadblocks and moving forward. These strategies include using rituals, getting started without trying for perfection, and talking to others.

You might want to set aside some time in class for students to freewrite about their resistance, allowing volunteers to read their results to the class. As you discuss resistance, acknowledge that most writers experience it sooner or later. Many students have unrealistic ideas about how long it takes to write, and they will not schedule enough time. Try suggesting writing smaller chunks that can be arranged later, as this may seem less intimidating than drafting a whole paper. As students begin to take ownership of their writing, you may see the cycles of writing, incubation, and reflection showing results. Assigning multiple rough drafts can help students keep up the momentum on a project rather than leaving it for the last minute. And, if your institution has a writing center, remind students how helpful it can be to plan or brainstorm a draft with a writing tutor.

4. *Developing and organizing:* Some students think of drafting as nothing but articulating and organizing their ideas, with little additional discovery or research involved. The more conventional and well rehearsed the topic, the more this is apt to be true. But we know that drafting involves ongoing invention and arrangement decisions. Help students see how focusing on building strong connections between questions of content and questions of form and between the writer's ideas and the reader's expectations will help. As their working thesis evolves into a thesis statement, as they unpack abstractions and make ideas explicit, as they craft transitions between ideas, sentences, and paragraphs, they can see whether and how conventional formats can help with organization. At this stage you might again remind students of organizational formulas—problem solving, cause and effect, definition, and comparison and contrast—that can be effective.

Activities

(p. 293) *For Exploration:* Students are asked to use the questions included in this "For Exploration" activity to explore their past methods of making plans and to think of ways to improve planning. Since some students seem especially resistant to planning, the questions may help them start thinking purposefully about their usual strategies. You may be able to use the results of this "For Exploration" activity to lead into a discussion of various planning methods. Putting the practice into words makes it available for monitoring and changing.

(p. 298) *For Exploration:* This Exploration asks students to think about and articulate their typical drafting habits and drafting sessions to identify common problems and see whether they can try some new strategies. You could use their results as a springboard for discussing a variety of drafting strategies.

(p. 301) *For Thought, Discussion, and Writing*

1. This activity asks students to select a writing assignment they are working on and develop a workable plan for it. As they draft, students keep a record of their activities and then reflect on the extent to which their initial plan was helpful and realistic. Comparing proposed and actual planning and drafting activities helps students take a more extensive look at their actual writing processes. You might ask them to compare the results with the earlier descriptions of themselves they have written. Multilingual writers can keep this record either in their home language or in English, but note that it will prepare them better to discuss plans with the instructor and in groups if they write in English.

2. This assignment asks students to interview someone who works in the field they hope to enter. Students are to ask how their subjects plan writing, how they draft, whether they work collaboratively or alone, what electronic or other technologies influence their planning and drafting strategies, what aids they use, and how they overcome writing hurdles. Then students write an essay about their findings. This interview can serve not only to gather information but also to get advice—on how the interviewee deals with writing blocks, for example. Students can then share and discuss their findings. They may discover that writers in different disciplines tend to plan in certain ways.

3. Writing an essay about writer's block offers students a chance to have some fun, perhaps to make impassioned descriptions about the crisis they've been in because of writing blocks or the extreme measures taken for a "cure." You might share Anne Lamott's humorous "cure" of imagining the negative voices as mice that she puts into a sealed jar: Inside they might be hollering, but she no longer hears them. The activity encourages students to become analytical about resistance as well. This assignment lends itself to collaboration; students can describe their experiences with the problem and conclude with group recommendations for overcoming writer's block.

Suggestions for Further Activities

1. As a variation on the second activity in the previous section, have students work in pairs to interview each other about their composing processes. Ask them to share the results of their interview with the class, either orally or in writing.

2. Instead of asking students to collaborate on an essay on writer's block, ask them to work together to develop an essay called "Ten Tips for Writers." As is the case with the third "For Thought, Discussion, and Writing" activity, this is an opportunity for students to have fun even as they share interesting and helpful ideas.

Chapter 11: Strategies for Designing Pages and Screens

Chapter 11 helps students use a rhetorical perspective when designing documents and shows them that document design is fundamental to creating clear, concise, and engaging texts. The chapter integrates visual features into the rhetorical analysis of planning.

Students have many choices available for how they will "publish" their papers, and even the most conservative presentation is likely to use some of the principles of design covered in this chapter: alignment, proximity, repetition, contrast, formatting, layout, color, fonts, typefaces, spacing, pagination, and visuals. Some writing assignments require illustrations; others may be enhanced by using photographs or artwork; and it is becoming increasingly easy to access such elements. Web design, of course, depends more heavily than print on the visual and has little allegiance to traditional print formats. The influence of Web design on print texts may show up in your students' work as illustrations printed from the Web for papers.

The "Guidelines for Thinking Rhetorically about Document Design" (pp. 305–6) in this chapter provide questions to prompt a rhetorical analysis. To help your students better understand the purpose of different types of visuals and make more effective design decisions, this chapter includes various visual examples ranging from tables and diagrams to such documents as a brochure, a Web text, and a flyer.

Concepts

1. *Looking at document design and the rhetorical situation:* Your students may have thought about document design as part of the requirements for an assignment rather than as a rhetorical element over which they have a degree of strategic control. For any writing assignment, it is important for students to consider the rhetorical situation and make informed decisions about document design and other visual elements. Academic essay assignments require students to select design elements that reflect the seriousness and formality of the rhetorical situation.

The "Guidelines for Thinking Rhetorically about Document Design" will help students determine their writing goals and strengths, the reader's expectations, textual conventions, and the requirements and limitations of their medium. You can have students return to these guidelines for each new assignment to help them ground document design decisions in the particular rhetorical situation. If your assignments are conducive to the inclusion of a table or graph, that would provide an opportunity to show students how to find, select, integrate, position, and ethically cite the images they have used or generated. Help students see how to refer to and discuss the images included, rather than just dropping them in. You may also want to discuss how visuals advance the Aristotelian appeals: the *logos* of graphs and charts, the *pathos* of images, and the *ethos* of organizational symbols.

2. *Document design and cultural differences:* Conventions of document design may vary, sometimes considerably, across cultures. These differences play a role in rhetorical sensitivity and in the often unconscious judgments your students make. You might find it interesting to compare the design elements in documents from several cultures in class. If your classroom includes multilingual and multicultural students, you will have an even better reason for paying attention to these differences, and these students may have easy access to documents and publications from other languages and cultures that they can share in class.

3. *Basic principles of design:* This chapter discusses the principles of alignment, proximity, repetition, and contrast as applied to many basic design decisions. Your students may want to experiment with such elements as font, color, visuals, and illustrations. A rhetorical approach to visual design helps them analyze whether these elements are necessary and integral to the overall purpose or simply distracting. The chapter includes "Guidelines for Using Color Effectively" (pp. 309–10) and "Guidelines for Using Visuals Effectively" (pp. 313–14) in addition to several document design examples. You can use these resources to help students recognize effective design features and use design strategies in their own document design decision-making process. A

basic understanding of how these principles work will help students in their "reading" of a text as well.

4. *Using visuals ethically:* Just as students must document carefully the sources of citations, they should note sources of illustrations and photographs and pay careful attention to the question of copyright. When they are using this material in a print document submitted for class, they are, under "fair use," less likely to violate copyright law than when they use visuals on Web sites. The "Guidelines for Using Visuals Effectively" cover documenting visual sources and using visuals responsibly and ethically. Help students see how to add captions and cite sources properly on their Works Cited page. Some sites, such as Flickr, label images that are in the Creative Commons and available for free use as long as credit is given.

You may want to have your students practice composing written requests for permission to use visuals from online sources. Figure 11.1 on p. 314 shows students one example of an email permission request.

Activities

(p. 303) *For Exploration:* This activity asks students to freewrite about their responses to visual elements in all their reading—not just academic reading. You might prompt them to be specific or to look first at some of the material they read and then freewrite. You can bring a variety of materials to class yourself, as an alternative, and have them respond to the various design elements. If you have Internet access and a projector in your classroom, you can examine some Web sites as a group. The responses can be used to start discussion and will help you plan further.

(p. 316) *For Exploration:* This exercise asks students to consider how visual elements contribute to the effectiveness of Alletta Brenner's research essay in Chapter 6. You can have students write two or three paragraphs about the effectiveness of this essay's design for the assignment; then ask them to discuss their findings in groups to see if there is agreement on Brenner's use of design principles. In addition, you can ask students to review how Brenner observes the conventions of copyright law and to bring in examples of unethical uses of visuals and copyright law; then discuss as a class how each instance is unethical and what could be done to make the use ethical.

(p. 319) *For Thought, Discussion, and Writing*

1. This exercise asks students to analyze the design elements of the articles by Deborah Tannen presented in Chapter 3, using the guidelines presented in Chapter 11. Students can draw on their earlier work analyzing the changing rhetorical situation in the introductions to Deborah Tannen's argument, but this time to see how visual and design elements interact with those rhetorical situations, particularly with the various audiences. Is it always the case that visual elements are used to address the broadest audiences? Can your students think of instances in which the visual elements of a text are narrowly directed to an expert audience? It may be helpful to point out that most likely a graphic designer on staff added the visuals and page design, not Tannen herself, whereas students most likely are both writer and designer.

2. This activity asks students to evaluate the design of *The Academic Writer* using the design principles they have learned in Chapter 11. Then they are asked to offer suggestions for improvement, drawing on the principles of design and their own design preferences. (Collect their suggestions and send them to us c/o Bedford/St. Martin's, 33 Irving Place, 10th Floor, New York, NY 10003; we are interested in what your students have to say. You can honestly tell them they could have an effect on future editions of the book.)

3. This activity suggests a community-based writing project—a flyer, brochure, newsletter, or Web page. You can develop this as a major assignment for the term, if such community-based learning interests you. Many students are already involved in volunteer work or internships that might lend themselves to such a project. For suggestions about including community service in your class, see Section 4 of these notes.

4. This exercise asks students to evaluate a visual from *Wired*, which represents results from a study on Americans' knowledge of current events. The analysis can serve as the basis of an essay if you choose to assign it. This is a particularly rich example of how to use the principles of design to present information. You might also think about using it as the basis for class analysis and asking students to locate their own examples for an essay.

Suggestions for Further Activities

1. After working through the various exercises on visual elements and design, ask students to analyze their own writing practices: What examples of visual design appear in your own writing, and how do they vary with the audience? in online writing? personal writing? diaries, journals, memoirs? academic work? How do visual elements help or hinder your writing? You can also talk with students about your own writing: about the assignment pages, syllabi, and so on that you create for their classes. If you also create a Web site for the class, such as with Blackboard, WebCT, or another online CMS, you can discuss the design decisions you made and ask for feedback.

2. Chapter 2 includes a collage on "Who I Am as a Writer" by Mirlandra Ebert (p. 22). Ask your students to analyze the effectiveness of its design elements. You might also ask them to construct their own collages and to discuss why they designed them as they did.

Chapter 12: Strategies for Revision

Chapter 12 addresses the larger questions of revision, asking students to think about revision as an opportunity to look at their work as readers. Students are encouraged to approach the revision process by considering the meaning of the word *revision*. When they revise, students should "see again" their essay's logic and organization, looking beyond simple, small-scale edits. The chapter moves on to cover the big issues—focus, content, and organization—and provides suggestions for using feedback from various sources including friends, family, classroom groups, writing tutors, and instructors. Then the chapter introduces students to revision strategies pertaining to matters of structure, coherence, and style. A sample paper by student Stevon Roberts showing his planning, first draft, analysis based on peer feedback, and final draft helps you show students the extent of significant revision you expect and how beneficial it is.

By now your students have probably accumulated a great deal of material to work on—and perhaps they have written much longer rough drafts than they are used to revising. Many of your students have probably been amazed and gratified by the sheer number of pages of writing they can produce when they do freewriting and loops or apply Aristotle's topics. For the first time, they may have too much, their drafts approach or exceed the page limits, and they must make choices about what to include. The new experience of having enough and cutting out paragraphs and sentences is so wonderful for some students that we frequently encourage them to overwrite their drafts for the first assignment that focuses on revising—that is, to make the rough draft perhaps twice as long as the final paper might be. Many students can hardly believe that they could easily write more than needed and are ready to enter a new economy of "re-vision" based not on scarcity but on abundance.

Revising sometimes poses some difficult issues, nevertheless. For example, if students come to class with the kind of draft that we associate with automatic writing—something facile that they've learned to produce without much risk—they may find it very hard to open the draft to inspection. Some work sounds good and says little. Revising may just make that more obvious. On the other hand, if students bring work that has come out of freewriting, that has rough edges but also a lot of character, they sometimes seem prone to revise it into more stereotypical, less-exciting forms. There's as much art to revising as to inventing, and perhaps as little guarantee that the result will be wonderful. But you can increase your students' chances of success by multiplying their options. If students know a number of people from whom to seek responses and a number of ways to try revising, they can develop a sense of agency to take control of their work in progress. Once they see revising as part of a process they understand and can freely tap, they may expand their process to add productive revision, maybe even as the most rewarding part of a project. Finally, as they learn to use a growing sense of audience, they can revise more firmly within a well-conceived rhetorical situation. This chapter shows them how to tap the resources of several audiences: family, friends, writing-group members, writing assistants, and, of course, instructors.

Concepts

1. *Revising objectively through "re-vision":* This chapter emphasizes the larger dimensions of revision, giving examples of genuinely new visions or approaches to rough drafts that allow students to write more successful versions of their papers. This kind of global revision requires that the writers take readers seriously. The chapter points out how this differs from editing, with its concern for correctness. By following the "Guidelines for Revising

Objectively" (p. 322), your students can "see again" their essay and develop a new vision for their revision plan. Without claiming to rid themselves of all bias, they can still take on the analytic and critical attitude toward their own work that they have been adopting as a rhetorical reader of others' work.

To show your students the difference between revising and editing, you might ask them to work in pairs to read each other's drafts through quickly to determine the main point of what is said. The problems they encounter getting this main point and the differences of opinion about what it is and whether it suits the author's intention are matters for global revision. By contrast, if you want them to experience proofreading, have them read the last paragraph of the paper, word by word, backwards from the end, checking for errors in spelling. Contrasting these two activities clarifies the point: Revision is concerned with the production of meaning. Since meaning, forms, and style are not separable, however, revision also pushes students beyond the safe boundaries of what they already know how to say.

Using new writing approaches may very well cause a momentary regression in the writer's mastery. As you press students to use conventions they have not practiced before and to use forms of academic discourse that do not yet seem integrated into their habitual ethos, part of their revising will be learning to integrate these new languages with their old successes. This happens at the level of revision rather than at the level of invention, where students' first drafts have stayed on familiar ground. Multilingual writers should be encouraged to attend to global issues first, rather than attend to correctness. However, they may need to revise for correctness as well before they submit drafts to readers.

2. *Evaluating focus, content, and organization:* The controlling purpose or thesis gives *focus*, which grows out of the rhetorical situation and the writer's clarity about what's at stake. A lack of focus shows up as a mismatch between the essay intended by the writer and the essay interpreted by various readers. Focus, therefore, depends heavily on the relationship between the writer's goals and his or her understanding of the rhetorical situation, conventions, and expectations. Students might be surprised to know that they can and should revise a thesis statement to reflect where the essay actually did go, rather than trying to force an essay to fit a narrow thesis they might have started with.

Content develops and elaborates the writer's controlling purpose. Most students hear a good deal about the need for more specifics and greater detail in their writing. In order to know what kind of elaboration is needed, they need to have a clear purpose, which helps them determine what additional details, supporting evidence, or counterarguments they should include to sharpen an essay.

As students revise their drafts, they need to adjust the *organization* to accommodate their readers. Students seem clearer on what is needed for introductions and conclusions, but they often bog down in the middle. We can suggest various organizational schemes that may help them shape material to support a clear line of argument. Some genres, such as a literature review, have highly conventionalized formats students need to learn. But for any writing, students need to constantly rethink (with the reader, their assignment, and rhetorical situation in mind) how much evidence, definition, elaboration, and reasoning are needed; how many other perspectives or other arguments they need to acknowledge; how much background or context must be included; and how much detail is too much. And then they need help knowing what goes where.

Working with students on a reverse or scratch outline of Roberts's sample essay in this chapter can help them see his organizational scheme and how it varied during revision. This can make for helpful discussion. A "what it says/what it does" outline is a great tool to help students understand the roles of various parts of an essay.

3. *Benefiting from responses:* This chapter provides several sets of guidelines for getting and using responses to a rough draft. You might want to ask the whole class to try some of them, for example, listening to a paper read aloud by someone else or asking every student to meet with a writing assistant at the writing center (and perhaps giving extra credit for the visit). Note: If you plan to require your entire class to visit the writing center, you should check first as to their schedule.

The chapter also makes important, specific suggestions for using peer-response groups as an integral part of revising. Many writing-across-the-curriculum programs have found that such response groups are helpful to students writing papers in content-area classes.

Responses from peer groups and from the instructor are, of course, examples of variations in interpretation. Frequently, however, students regard these different perspectives as some kind of error, either in the readers or in the writer, rather than as the inevitable differences that need to be negotiated to improve communication. Teaching your students how to use a response group productively will help them greatly in the future.

4. *Coherence:* Coherence arises from the reader's ability to follow the connections between ideas, between sentences, and between paragraphs in a piece of writing, connections that the writer should provide. Students ask if their paper "flows," yet often need practice seeing where awkward jumps occur or how to fix them. Students can learn specific techniques to improve coherence, including using transitions, pronouns, and repeated key words and sentence structures, all cuing devices writers can consciously add to their work without changing it much, sometimes with a great increase in clarity.

You can use the introductory paragraph to Ian Frazier's "Home Town" (p. 341) to discuss the methods Frazier uses to maintain coherence. Then ask students to review two paragraphs of an essay they are working on, keeping in mind the "Guidelines for Revising for Coherence" (p. 342). Do they notice places where their draft is less coherent? What are two suggestions they could follow to help maintain or strengthen coherence in their writing?

5. *Appropriate voice:* Effective writers vary their writing persona, or voice, depending on the rhetorical situation. Although we use the term *voice* to talk about the sense of personal presence created by the writer, it's misleading and perhaps a bit mystifying to talk as if a writer has only a single way of sounding that is authentically the writer's own. A few students regard stylistic flexibility as hypocritical or unfaithful to their true selves, but students need to develop

several modes of personal and impersonal address for varying writing occasions because there are academic, political, and cultural implications in the voice a writer adopts. Some students begin our classes using a voice that is much too casual for academic writing, while others bring an overly formal or stilted voice.

It's helpful to admit how challenging it is to switch voices. If students cannot reconcile their sense of personal voice with the kind of objectivity demanded in academic writing, they will face continuing problems with their writing. To help your students determine an appropriate voice for any writing assignment, you may want to review the discussion of Aristotle's three appeals—*logos, pathos,* and *ethos*—in Chapter 3 and encourage students to consult the "Guidelines for Effective Prose Style" (pp. 345–46) when they begin to work on their first and subsequent drafts.

For students who are having trouble imagining themselves taking on a persona that seems alien, ask them to write a parody of the voice they find most difficult to imitate. Exaggerating or making fun of the voice can remove objections. When they don't have to be successful in the pretense, students can gain some experience practicing the persona. This issue of voice is a different matter for multilingual students, some of whom may have a sense of voice only when they write in their home language. Reading in English will help.

6. *Style:* While style reflects all the choices the writer makes about syntax, order, and diction, some basic guidelines may help students develop a more effective style. This chapter analyzes some examples and explains some of the elements of *good* style, with advice on how to work on sentence structure and variety, use concrete language, and reduce wordiness. The "Guidelines for Effective Prose Style" (pp. 345–46) can help. Also see Edward P. J. Corbett's useful discussion of style and guidelines for analyzing style in *Classical Rhetoric for the Modern Student,* 4th ed. (New York: Oxford UP, 1998), 380–426.

Activities

(p. 323) *For Exploration:* This assignment asks students to reflect on their earlier experiences with revision, distinguishing it carefully from editing. Encourage them to share stories of disaster, triumph, and mistaken opinion, and try to get some sense of how much and what kind of revision your class has done in the past, either by asking students to turn in written responses or by holding a class discussion. Don't be surprised if you have several students report that they ruin everything they revise: It's a common, self-serving superstition. Sometimes it may even be true. If they use all the writing skills they have mastered in the first draft, a revision can plunge students into new problems they haven't yet solved. Try to establish an atmosphere in which taking a risk is worthwhile and leads to growth as a writer. Here's an analogy we have found useful with students: When remodeling a house, a room does become worse as the old is torn out, before it gets better. That intermittent mess of revision is normal.

(p. 325) *For Exploration:* Students are asked to use the "Questions for Evaluating Focus, Content, and Organization" (pp. 324–25), to put these strategies to work in their own drafts. First they are to answer each question with respect to their draft, as fully as possible. Then they are to list their goals for revision. This will be an extremely comprehensive analysis if carried through carefully. It might, for example, lead to their seeking out additional counterarguments and details, perhaps through research, or trying a test outline or summary to judge their effectiveness with organization. It is, in other words, a time-consuming exercise, worth giving as much importance as you might give to peer revision. You can productively use the case study of Robert's revision of his essay (pp. 330–34) as a model for the deep thinking you expect your students to carry out.

You might consider adding to this activity by asking students to freewrite on Roberts's revision process. What do they think of all the work he did here? What surprised them?

(p. 336) *For Collaboration:* This activity asks students to think about how they perceive peer response and to consider the kinds of responses they find most helpful. Since this isn't always easy to articulate, the collaborative part of the exercise helps students adapt or add to what they might have simply borrowed from the chapter. More important, it helps the group function more effectively. Often students say they want "tough" or "critical" responses and don't get enough of them, though they also admit that they don't know how to give good responses. This is where you can remind them of the analytical skills from Chapters 3 and 4, especially. The kinds of analysis they can perform on other texts, they can learn to use with their classmates. Also they may fear suggesting changes that would require the classmate to do a lot of work or make major changes. As group members come to trust each other more, they will be more willing to risk a critique that would entail substantial revision. You can help each group draw up their own individualized "peer-review" checklist for their drafts, which gives them more agency in the process.

(pp. 344, 346) *For Thought, Discussion, and Writing*

1. This assignment asks students to reflect on their revision by numbering their drafts and then looking back at the pile. You can ask them to include all the drafts in their portfolio as a demonstration of their progress. Then, as they look back—as on an archeological dig—they can learn the steps that were easier and come up with more efficient plans for revision on their next essay.

2. This assignment asks students to interview others about their revision. They may be surprised to discover the variety of revision strategies and develop further understanding about the relationship between revising strategies and the kinds of writing that result. If this is a class assignment or option, it makes sense to have all students do the interviewing work to-gether in groups of three. Perhaps this is a good opportunity for them to talk with people not in their usual response group. The resulting essays could be developed individually, or each group could collaborate on a single essay or report that summarizes the group's experiences. Or this can be done casually with a response to the class from each group.

3. This exercise asks students to put into practice on their own draft the chapter's suggestions for improving coherence. After they have tried out the suggestions, you can ask students to discuss the results. Remind them

that coherence depends on the ability of the reader to follow their logic. Adding extra transitional words and phrases can help. You may want to make such intensive checks a regular part of the classroom routine for a while, at least until you think students are beginning to resolve their questions about coherence.

4. This exercise asks students to revisit Jamais Cascio's essay in Chapter 8 on pp. 261–62 to answer a series of questions on style, voice, prose style, and structure.

Suggestions for Further Activities

1. Ask students to write their own personal guidelines for revision. Such an effort enables students to internalize what has been presented to them. They can draw on Reberts's revision plans. Since revision concepts take time for assimilation, you may want to ask them to update their revising guidelines periodically or whenever they start to revise a new assignment. Don't judge their understanding of revision by their ability to produce guidelines. Just because they have a clear sense of what they should do, doesn't mean that they are actually able to do it yet.

2. You might want to apply revision to composing online. Emails are notoriously not revised. You could ask the class to brainstorm a list of ten situations when one should revise an email.

SECTION 7: SAMPLE STUDENT ESSAYS

On the following pages are sample essays written by students for courses using *The Academic Writer*. The examples of successful student writing include the following:

Personal essay: Kira Wennstrom, "The Boys of Summer" (pp. 128–30)

Reflective personal essay: Monica Molina, "Between Cultures" (pp. 130–32)

Argument essay: Todd Carpenter, "Why Isn't There a National Bottle Law?" (pp. 133–34)

Critical review of a reading from an academic area: Hannah Grubb, "Everyday Exposure to Toxic Pollutants" (pp. 134–35)

Critical review of a book: Chris Bowman, "Laying It on the Lines" (pp. 136–38)

Analysis of a play: Jacob Agatucci, "Dialogue as Image in *King Lear*" (pp. 138–40)

Analysis of a poem: Beth Runciman:

- "An Analysis of Emily Dickinson's Poem #48" (First Draft) (pp. 141–43)
- "An Exploration of Emily Dickinson's Poem #48" (Second Draft) (pp. 143–45)
- "The Matriarch's Bird" (Final Draft) (pp. 147–49)

Analysis of a visual text: Michelle Fuller, "Faculty Show Critique" (pp. 150–51)

Essay exam response: Eric Hill, "The Hopi Worldview: A Cyclical Model of Balance and Duality" (pp. 152–53)

Sample Personal Essay

Kira Wennstrom, a first-year biology major, responded to this relatively open-ended assignment: Write an essay describing a personal experience and explaining the significance of that experience. Wennstrom had few problems coming up with a topic. During the previous summer she had cared for two children while their mother was in the hospital. The experience had taught her a great deal about herself and about the bond between parents and children. She wanted to explore her experience further and to share with others what she had learned.

The Boys of Summer

Kira Wennstrom

Few teenagers get the chance to be parents, and for those who do, it's usually too late to change their minds. One summer, though, I was given the opportunity to play the role of mother — without the lifetime commitment.

When Josh and Timmy's mother had to go to the hospital, she asked me if I would be willing to stay with them until she could return home. I quickly accepted, envisioning a few days of playing "mommy" to the kids whose babysitter I had been for about two years. However, my visions of happy homemaking paled when the few days became two weeks and the trouble and responsibility of being a parent began to hit home.

Since the children were only five and eight, I couldn't leave them alone in the house; I had to be with them twenty-four hours a day. While my friends swam and tanned at the lake, I spent my days as a "housewife": planning meals, doing laundry, cleaning house. I handled all the minor emergencies that seem to follow little boys around like shadows. There were fights to be settled, Kool-Aid to be cleaned out of the carpet, and once or twice pots and pans to be rescued from the sandbox to cook dinner.

My days were whittled away with meals, dishes, and mountains of laundry. I did a load of wash almost every other day and just barely kept up. I was also amazed by the complexities of working out a simple dinner schedule. There was no single entrée that both boys approved of, and it was like walking hot coals to try to serve anything new. They would sooner have starved, I think, than eat anything that didn't come out of a wrapper, box, or can. Most of all, though, I missed my privacy. Because the children were so dependent on me, I never had a moment to myself. I sometimes found it very difficult to force a smile when one of the boys interrupted a quiet moment with yet another demand on my time.

As the days passed and I became more proficient at running my little household, I began to realize a very surprising thing. Despite the trouble they caused, despite the demands they made, my two charges were becoming very special people to me — people who needed me. I remember taking the boys to the beach one afternoon and buying them a corn dog and soda lunch with Gummi worms for dessert. Josh, who was older than Timmy, loved the lake and delighted in swimming out just past the dock where the water was especially cool. Timmy was afraid to follow his brother and sat beside me on the sand, sucking on his last Gummi worm and looking wistfully out to where Josh was laughing and diving. After half an hour of this, Timmy touched me on the arm and said, "Take me to Josh, Kira."

"Are you sure, Timmy?"

"Mm-hm. But hold on tight to me."

So I held on tight to him, and we waded into Rainy Lake's cool green water. When we got out past the point where Timmy could touch bottom, he locked his arms around my neck and pressed his face against my shoulder, but he didn't ask me to take him back. As we neared the spot where Josh was playing, I called, and he swam over to us. We splashed each other and giggled, and Timmy clutched me with one hand and Josh with the other. Their bodies were slick like seals, warm against me in the chill lake water. Together we swam along the shore, and they held on to me to keep afloat. They trusted me to keep them safe, and I would have drowned before I broke that trust. I loved them.

Because I loved them, the children had a hold on me like nothing else I know. Simply by going out to play each day, they gave me more hours of worry than I like to admit. Every time one of them was late coming home, I imagined all the dreadful things that might be happening — an angry dog, a child molester, a car accident — until he walked through the door, perfectly safe and wanting supper. When one of them was angry or hurt, I hurt. They were children, and it's so hard to be a child sometimes, almost as hard as being a mother.

My own mother, whom I telephoned with great regularity, seemed to find enormous delight in the fact that I was going through the same things she had been trying (and failing) to explain to me for seventeen-odd years. She gave me marvelous suggestions on how to cope with the demands of my new family and then, I am sure, hung up the phone and laughed her socks off in utter vindictiveness. But I can forgive her this because, although I didn't know it then, what I was experiencing was invaluable.

I look at mothers, especially my own, with better understanding now and with less scorn. I look at children with a little more appreciation.

I use my time alone more carefully now; I spend it wisely, now that I know how crucial it is. Most of all, I value my freedom more highly than ever because I know what it is to give up that freedom. As much as I cared about those children, it's not time yet to let others make such claims on my life. I understand now how important it is to live for yourself before you live for anyone else.

Sample Reflective Personal Essay

The personal essay is a common form of academic writing, particularly in the humanities. This personal essay by Monica Molina, a student at Oregon State University, was written for an ethnic studies class in response to an assignment to reflect on ethnic heritage.

Between Cultures

Monica Molina

Opening the door and peering curiously around the room full of brown faces, I felt nervous and awkward. My fears were soon eased, however, as cheerful voices welcomed me to an Oregon State University Hispanic Student Union meeting. Although I wasn't sure what the meeting would be about, I felt suddenly comfortable — almost like I was among family. But then some students in the corner began speaking in Spanish, their crescendo building with excitement as they shared a story. Soon it seemed that everyone was adding bits of information. I sat quietly, just getting the gist of what they were saying. Then everyone broke into laughter. Everyone but me, that is; I had missed the punchline.

Spanish sounds like a song to me, one that is beautiful and rich, but one I can't quite catch the words to. I ache for the foreign sounds to roll off my tongue, but instead only a few words stumble out, flat and anglicized. I studied Spanish for three years in high school, and for one year in college, but learning a language in a classroom from textbooks is different from hearing it spoken by your parents at home. My father is Mexican, and his native language is Spanish. But he has never spoken anything other than English with my mother, sisters, and me.

I was surrounded by Anglo culture as I grew up, and I assimilated easily, not even knowing what I was missing. Educated in mainstream schools and raised in a predominantly white neighborhood, I accepted the images I saw on television and in the movies. Most of the time, I took for granted that we would speak English at home. When my friends learned that my father was Mexican and asked me if I spoke Spanish, or if we spoke it at home, I always answered "no," feeling a sudden sense of confusion and loss.

At times as I was growing up, I wondered why my father never spoke Spanish with us. Recently, I decided to ask him about it. My dad seemed surprised by my question and replied that he didn't know; perhaps it was because he was too busy to teach us. He didn't seem to want to talk about this subject. I could tell that he didn't understand why I asked the question or what it might mean to me. I didn't push my question, for I realized that it really doesn't matter why my father didn't speak Spanish with us. What matters is how I feel about this now — now that I realize I know only the Anglo side of my heritage and not the Mexican side. What matters is my desire to connect with my father's culture, with the Mexican heritage that has been ignored and silenced.

When I was a child, I asked innocent questions about life in Mexico that annoyed my father, questions like "Do they have ice cream in Mexico?" My dad would shake his head in disbelief at these questions and not even answer. Now I realize that the questions reminded him too much of snobby Anglos asking if the water was safe to drink in Mexico. My father must have found it hard to realize how little I knew about Mexican culture. Moreover, he probably felt there was no point in teaching us about a culture we would never embrace as our own.

My father struggled to learn to speak English and to make a place for himself in this country. But my father's English reminds my mom, sisters, and me that he is different from us. Dad's English is distinct in that he has created his own pronunciations and vocabulary. His words and phrases have become part of our family language, and we sometimes tease him about them. One of his favorite phrases is "You crazy!"; now we all say that to each other. We also mimic the exasperated way he says "What?!" Sometimes my father realizes that we are teasing him and laughs, but other times he gets angry. His anger reminds me how easy it is to forget his struggles with English and with Anglo culture, just as it is hard for my father to sense my need to connect with his Mexican way of life.

When I was a fifth grader, I remember my father coming to me with business letters to check for grammar and spelling. As I gently explained to my dad why a tense was wrong or a word misspelled, I knew it must have been hard for him to ask his daughter for help. My father's lack of English skills coupled with my limited knowledge of Spanish highlighted the gap between our Anglo and Mexican cultures. I felt this gap most strongly when my dad called his family in Mexico. Calling home was a pretty big event, and Mom would tell us to be quiet so Dad could hear. We would sit listening to the unfamiliar language, fascinated with the quick sounds and changes in expression. After my father hung up, we would rush to him and ask what he had said.

As a teenager, and now as a college student, I have made attempts to learn about my father's culture. Sometimes I try to explain my longing to connect with my Mexican heritage to my father, but he doesn't seem to understand why this is important to me. He also doesn't understand why some people would question my identification with Mexico and its cultural heritage. When I told my dad that people sometimes ask whether I am Mexican and are surprised when I say "yes" since I can't speak Spanish very well, he says it's none of their business and "to hell with them." Lately I'm beginning to think that my father may be right. Other people may worry if I don't fit into predetermined ethnic categories. But I think I can identify with both Mexican and Anglo cultures as long as I define what that means for me.

I come home from another Hispanic Student Union meeting, excited about the possibility of attending my first MECHA (Movimiento Estudiantil Chicano de Azatlan) conference. Entering my house, I notice that the answering machine light is on and push the button. My father begins the message he has left for me. Because his voice is so familiar, I don't usually hear my father's accent. But today it rings out as a reminder of the ways in which we're both similar and different. As I listen to my dad telling me what time he'll pick me up for a quick trip home, I think of how different my world is from his. My father came to a new country and had to work hard to support a family; he had to believe that he was gaining more than he was giving up. Because my father has struggled, I have more opportunities. In some ways, my success will be his. But unlike my father, I may not have to choose between two cultures. For me, gaining something new may not have to mean leaving something else behind.

Sample Argument Essay

Todd Carpenter wrote the following essay in response to this assignment: "Write a two- to three-page argumentative essay on a subject of your own choice. Consider your instructor and your classmates the primary readers of your essay." Carpenter described his rhetorical situation in these terms:

> *I am writing an argumentative essay for my composition class. I want to convince my readers—my instructor and my classmates—that our government should institute a national bottle law. Oregon is one of the eleven states that currently have bottle laws, so most students in the class may already agree with me about this law's importance. (Because Oregon's bottle bill has been implemented since 1972, students may not realize how important it is.) But because this essay is for my writing class, I've got to present an unbiased view. Even if my instructor agrees that there should be a national bottle law, I still must present an effective argument. In class, my instructor has stressed the importance of looking at both sides of an issue and presenting evidence for my views on it, so I'll try to do that here.*

Why Isn't There a National Bottle Law?
Todd Carpenter

What do you do with your empty cans and bottles? There are two choices: throwing them away or recycling. Throwing away an aluminum beverage container wastes as much energy as filling a can with gasoline and pouring half out. Besides wasting energy, throwing away bottles and cans causes pollution, increases the volume of solid wastes, and uses up natural resources. To control these problems, only eleven states have adopted bottle laws. The U.S. government should require every state to have a bottle law or institute a national bottle law.

To understand how a bottle law can help, you must know how it works. When consumers buy canned or bottled beverages at the store, they pay deposits. This deposit can range from five to twenty cents per bottle or can. In order to get this deposit back, the bottles and cans must be returned to a supermarket after they are emptied. The supermarkets then return the bottles and cans to their manufacturers for either reuse or recycling.

Recycling plays a significant role in reducing pollution and solid waste. Recycling aluminum reduces air emissions associated with aluminum production by 96 percent. Solid waste is also reduced as aluminum and glass are eliminated from landfills. Finally, a large percentage of the pollution on and around the streets and highways is bottles and cans. If these could be returned to supermarkets for cash, people would be less likely to throw them away. Extracting aluminum ore requires twenty times as much electricity as recycling the metal. Therefore, if we recycled more aluminum, less aluminum ore would have to be extracted. This could save enough energy to provide electrical power for at least two million people annually.

Bottle laws are currently in effect in Oregon, Vermont, Maine, Michigan, Iowa, Connecticut, Delaware, Massachusetts, New York, California, and Hawaii. These laws work largely because the general public supports them. A recent poll of Americans revealed that 73 percent support bottle laws. This support undoubtedly results from people's concern about pollution and our planet's limited resources.

Given the large number of people in favor of bottle laws, you might expect that we would already have a national bottle law. But a vocal minority of people don't want to bother with saving their containers, so they oppose such legislation. Some supermarket chains also lobby against bottle laws; they don't want to have to deal with all the cans that people would bring to them. I understand these individuals' concerns; recycling bottles and cans does require extra effort from consumers and distributors. The larger economic and ecological issues indicate that this extra effort is worthwhile.

Finally, steel and aluminum companies and metal workers' unions oppose bottle laws because they fear they would cause cuts in their production and therefore affect jobs and wages. EPA and General Accounting studies estimate, however, that a national bottle law would produce a net increase of eighty thousand to one hundred thousand jobs, so these fears are misplaced.

Although 54 percent of the aluminum beverage cans made and used in the United States are currently recycled at more than twenty-five hundred recycling centers, we could increase this to as much as 90 percent by requiring a national bottle law. Instead of worrying about the inconvenience and possible economic consequences of instituting a national bottle law, we should consider the ecological gains. In the future, a little time saved will mean nothing compared to a polluted and destroyed environment.

Sample Critical Review of a Reading from an Academic Area

The following essay was written by Hannah Grubb for an introductory chemistry class. The assignment involved selecting a chemistry-related article from a recent issue of *Scientific American,* and summarizing and responding to it in a critical review. Grubb chose "Everyday Exposure to Toxic Pollutants" by Wayne R. Ott and John W. Roberts, which appeared in the February 1998 issue of *Scientific American.*

"Everyday Exposure to Toxic Pollutants"
Hannah Grubb

Pollutants are everywhere. Walking down a busy street, I inhale car exhaust, gas fumes, secondhand smoke, and other toxic substances. Flying into Los Angeles to visit friends, I notice that the sky over the city is a distinctly different color than the beautiful clean air over the Pacific Ocean. Opening the newspaper, I read debates about the use of pesticides and news of the war on pollution. Like many people, I worry about the effects of pollution on my health. But rarely have I thought about the toxins that I could be breathing in my very own home.

"Everyday Exposure to Toxic Pollutants" examines those toxins and considers their relative concentrations indoors and outdoors. After reading this article by Wayne R. Ott and John W. Roberts, I now know that I have more to worry about sitting in my own home than when I go jogging through city streets. Their study discusses the presence of volatile organic compounds, carbon monoxide, pesticides, and dangerous particles within and outside of homes across America. One surprising finding is that even in cities where industrial and chemical processing plants have a major presence, the air outside is generally cleaner than the air indoors. The source of this indoor pollution, according to Ott and Roberts, is ordinary consumer products, such as air fresheners and cleaning compounds, and various building materials. Another major pollutant, tetrachloroethylene, is found on clothes that have been dry cleaned. This chemical has been found to cause cancer in laboratory animals. Chloroform, a gas that also causes cancer in laboratory animals, is a by-product of showers, boiling water, and clothes washers.

Dust particles, which are continually around us (whether we can see them or not), also carry toxic particles into our lungs. I might pick up particles of insecticides on my shoes, for instance, and carry these particles into my home where they can settle and mix in with other dust. This is especially dangerous for small children, who spend most of their time on or near the ground and who are still developing. But adults are at risk as well. Ott and Roberts state that "pesticides and volatile organic compounds found indoors cause perhaps 3,000 cases of cancer a year in the U.S., making these substances just as threatening to nonsmokers as radon . . . and second-hand tobacco smoke" (90). Ott and Roberts conclude that the main sources of indoor pollution are such run-of-the-mill products that most people don't even think to question whether they should or shouldn't use them. Because the effect of indoor pollutants is not as noticeable as, say, the exhaust from an old car, few people are aware of their dangers. But they should be, as this analogy from Ott's and Roberts's article suggests: "If truckloads of dust with the same concentrations of toxic chemicals as is found in most carpets were deposited outside, these locations would be considered hazardous-waste dumps" (91).

"Everyday Exposure to Toxic Pollutants" by Ott and Roberts is a relevant and informative discussion of problems that many people don't even realize exist. It certainly puts general concerns about pollution in perspective. Recently there have been campaigns about the use of pesticides in our residence hall cafeterias. And as I went jogging the other day, I cringed as I passed a smoker, and I purposely ran through quiet neighborhoods to get away from cars and their pollution. Perhaps I should have been worrying about inhaling chloroform every time I make a cup of tea.

Sample Critical Review of a Book

College students are often asked to read and respond to one or more books. Chris Bowman, a student at Oregon State University, was asked to do just this in an ethnic studies course on narratives of Latino migration. Bowman chose to write a critical review essay about *Between the Lines: Letters between Undocumented Mexican and Central American Immigrants and Their Families and Friends,* a collection of letters edited by Larry Siems and published in 1992 by the University of Arizona Press.

Laying It on the Lines

Chris Bowman

To read *Between the Lines* is to begin to understand the lives of migrant Latinos in America. I emphasize the word *lives* because it is often automatic to think with singularity: *the* migrant worker. In this book, a collection of letters between immigrants to the United States and their families and friends in Mexico and Central America, multiple stories emerge. These stories provide powerful insights into the many complex relationships that are affected when Latinos come to the United States.

The letters collected in *Between the Lines* are from husbands and wives, daughters and sons, in-laws, nieces, uncles, sisters, fathers, and mothers. Friends write to friends. Priests write for those who cannot write themselves. Surprisingly, the letters from illiterate Latinos—letters that, in the case of those who speak indigenous languages, have been translated twice—have a refreshingly emotional style that feels like conversation. But whether the authors wrote or dictated their thoughts, through almost every letter there winds a thread of love and longing for those who are far away.

In many letters, writers implore their loved ones to write, send photos, send news. To encourage response, the writers send their own news— about health, children, finance. They also share gossip, advice, and hopes for the future. In this respect, these migrants and their families are like any other ordinary "American" family. And yet they are clearly not ordinary. These writers lead difficult lives, more difficult than those of many Americans.

In the very first letter, the writer tells of his deep sadness when he realized how much he would have to endure to get to America. Another letter writer describes her disappointment when friends give her a chilly reception when she comes to the United States. Worried that she has done something wrong, she discovers that her friends were both sad and angry that she would now be subjected to the hardships that they had endured.

As these examples indicate, the letters in *Between the Lines* are very powerful. And they are powerfully arranged by Larry Siems, the editor of this collection. Siems has organized the letters to suggest the process that migrants and their loved ones experience as the migrants acculturate. The first letters are from those who have recently arrived in this country, and while they speak of hardship, there is an underlying tone of hopefulness.

The next section is composed of letters from those who have been left behind. These letters convey faith in and encouragement for the migrants, as well as fears and advice about how to negotiate new situations. The next three sections are from close friends, spouses, and families. It is clear from the letters in these sections that the writers have been apart for some time—but that the letters continue to nurture their relationships. The final section includes a mix of letters that emphasize the complexity and difficulty of the lives of migrants. They also demonstrate the reasons that people continue to risk these difficulties to come to the United States.

Between the Lines contributes to an understanding of the lives of Latino migrants in America because it tells a different story than that portrayed in the media. The media often portray migrants as people who impulsively leave one country for another. As these letters reveal, the decision to leave family and friends is heart-wrenching. One man writes of how he hid when his friend came to tell him goodbye because he could not bear the parting. Many apologize to their families for leaving but state that this is the only way that they can help their families.

Between the Lines also corrects many popular misconceptions about the lives of Latino migrants. These are not people on public assistance. These are workers who are sending money home to loved ones and saving what little they can for their future. The letters tell stories of migrants who are exploited by employers who refuse to pay them after a job has been completed, knowing full well that the undocumented worker has no recourse in such a situation. Letters also tell (time and time again) of migrants being scorned because they do not speak English. One writer describes how "here one feels like a sad lost dog. . . . [In Mexico] one has freedom even to scream in his house and do in his house whatever he pleases, and here if you do all this the first to arrive are the police because the neighbors call them" (299).

For most who come, the United States is not like they thought it would be. So maintaining a link with their families and friends is vital to their existence. Not that they entirely leave their past behind. The letters in *Between the Lines* indicate that many migrants move to neighborhoods where they know at least one person from their home country—or even village. The letters that go back and forth from the United States to home thus participate in an ongoing neighborhood grapevine that discourages misbehavior.

Clearly, as Larry Siems indicates in his comments on the letters in this collection, these are individuals attempting to lead ordinary lives. They are also people who are deeply misunderstood and shamelessly abused. It's heartbreaking to read of vigilante groups who look on border crossings as opportunities for target practice. How ironic that many citizens in the

United States are concerned about such practices as bilingual education but can't see the many ways that Latino migrants are mistreated in our country.

Between the Lines tells the story of human beings who are striving to provide for themselves and for their families. This should be a familiar story—but in this case it is not. These people know what it's like for their families to go hungry. Many know the horrors of war. And all know what it's like to be forced to leave the ones they love in order for them (and often for their families) to survive. That's what this book is about.

Sample Analysis of a Play

The following essay by Jacob Agatucci is a model example of academic analysis. Here, Jacob does not argue that something should or should not be done; rather, he attempts to understand the roles that stage directions and cinematic technique play in helping contemporary audiences to better understand Shakespeare's plays. As a result, Jacob focuses on providing clear and specific examples as well as on analyzing the connections among and the implications of these examples.

Dialogue as Image in *King Lear*

Jacob Agatucci

What can theater and film directors do to help contemporary audiences appreciate the role of dialogue in Shakespeare's plays? What role can stage directions and cinematic technique play in helping audiences to understand the relationships among characters? These are important questions because contemporary audiences often find it difficult to follow the intricacies of Shakespearean dialogue. The language in which Shakespeare wrote is alien to many ears, and the lines are often delivered so quickly that the viewer finds it difficult to remember where a character stands in relation to other characters in a play. *King Lear* is a relevant example. Though the dialogue of the opening act defines the conflicts of the play—estranging loyal daughter from father and suggesting the deception of Goneril, Regan, and Edmund—important elements of this conflict could be lost to the untrained ear. The 1987 British Broadcasting Company (BBC) production of *King Lear* is a cinematic adaptation that honors Shakespeare's language and intentions but aids in its delivery through visual supplementation.

An example of this supplementation can be found during Act I, Scene 1, which occurs as *King Lear* derides Cordelia for not equaling her sisters' false expressions of love. The profiles of Lear and Cordelia, facing one another, fill the frame during the scene. Their faces are far enough apart to allow a space between them in which Kent is carefully framed—blurred and in the background. Thus the staging and cinematography, in addition to the dialogue, provide a visual representation of the disaffected parties (Lear and Cordelia) and the man (Kent) who seeks to alleviate their estrangement. This cinematic technique neatly encapsulates the relationship among these three characters and calls attention to an important feature of the plot.

A similar moment occurs when Scene 1 segues into Scene 2. Here, as in the earlier scene, essential characters in *King Lear* are brought together. In this case, however, it is the villains who are brought together. Here, the profiles of Regan and Goneril dominate the shot as they reflect on Lear's "long-ingraffed condition" (I.1.330). Like Kent, Edmund is framed between them and in the background. Just as the former scene linked the protagonists of the play, this scene links its antagonists. This scene also emphasizes Edmund's role in the various deceptions that are central to the plot of *King Lear*. As Regan and Goneril end their exchange, they pull out of the frame to the left and right, and the camera focuses on Edmund, who is in the background. Since the next scene (Act I, Scene 2) begins with Edmund's soliloquy, Edmund's destructive ambition is visually linked with Goneril's and Regan's deceit.

Both of these scenes could easily have been shot with Kent and Edmund absent — but then viewers would have had to rely solely on dialogue to link characters and motives. Fortunately, the director chose to structure the play along visual as well as auditory lines. To do so, the director had to go beyond the stage directions included in *King Lear*, which revolve around entrances and exits, to consider the ways in which staging and cinematography could help clarify both the immediate dialogue and future character relations. As a consequence, the BBC adaptation is especially sensitive to the needs of an audience that may not be familiar with Shakespearean dialogue.

Though Shakespeare's language is paramount within his plays, the BBC production of *King Lear* provides an innovative example of how the effective use of visual cues can supplement and clarify dialogue. Through both the physical placement of characters on the stage and careful cinematic technique, the BBC production uses visual cues to reinforce Shakespeare's dialogue. As a result, the experience of audience members is enriched, for they are left not simply with Shakespeare's words but with a synergistic combination of auditory and visual elements.

Works Cited

King Lear. Dir. Jonathan Miller. Prod. Shaun Sutton. BBC and Time-Life Films, 1987. Videocassette.

Shakespeare, William. *King Lear. The Complete Works of Shakespeare.* Ed.
David Bevington. 4th ed. New York: Longman, 1997. 1167–1218. Print.

Sample Analysis of a Poem (First, Second, and Final Drafts)

Beth Runciman, a student at Smith College in Northampton, Massachusetts,
wrote the following draft essays analyzing a poem by Emily Dickinson for an
American literature survey course. As a first step in her composing process,
Beth wrote an analysis of her rhetorical situation. Here is Beth's analysis:

> *This assignment calls for a formal argument, so I will need to follow the
> conventions of an academic essay, with a clear introduction and conclu-
> sion and a logical order to the organization. The assignment asks us to
> demonstrate that we understand what's going on in the poem we choose
> to write about—that we locate the poem in its historical context and that
> we talk about the literary techniques the author is using to make her point.
> I'll want to make sure that the argument I present is grounded in evidence
> from the poem itself and that I'm able to quote specific lines from the poem
> to support what I say. I'll also want to use the vocabulary we've studied in
> class—terms like image, metaphor, meter, and line break.*
>
> *The audience for this essay is my professor. I know that she appreciates
> Dickinson's poetry, but what she'll be looking for in my essay isn't so much
> appreciation as understanding. To help convey that understanding, I need
> to adopt a tone of objectivity and authority.*

Notice how in these comments Beth moves from a general assessment of her
assignment—"I need to follow the conventions of an academic essay, with a
clear introduction and conclusion and a logical order to the organization"—to
consideration of the conventions of the discipline for which she is writing—
literary criticism. Beth understands that when instructors read student
writing, they do so from the perspective of their disciplinary training. Given
this, Beth recognizes that her goal is to demonstrate her ability to analyze and
interpret Dickinson's poem and not to persuade her teacher to believe or do
something.

Beth's understanding of her rhetorical situation will influence the choices
she makes as a writer. To become more self-conscious about these choices,
Beth concluded her analysis by considering how her essay might best address
Aristotle's three appeals:

Logos: *"I'll appeal most strongly to* logos *(reason) when writing this essay.
To be successful, I've got to show my teacher that I can analyze the poem
in detail and draw conclusions from my analysis."*

Pathos: *"Emotional appeals won't play a strong role in my essay. Dickinson's poem is very emotional, but my analysis needs to focus on its technique and content. I do want to appeal to* pathos *in one way, though: I
want to encourage the reader to appreciate Dickinson's skill and daring."*

Ethos: *"I want my teacher to see me as being fully in control of my ideas and their presentation. If my analysis (logos) is effective, my teacher will view me as a credible writer."*

This analysis reminded Beth that even when an assignment is relatively broad and openended, as hers was, her teacher nevertheless had specific expectations about how students could best complete it. In this instance, Beth's teacher expected that successful students would write essays demonstrating their ability to "talk the talk and walk the walk" of literary criticism.

As mentioned earlier, Beth worked her way through three drafts before she arrived at an essay that satisfied her. According to Beth, each draft had a slightly different purpose. "In my first draft," she said, "I was trying to analyze the poem itself and understand how Dickinson's choices of meter, rhythm, imagery, and syntax made the poem what it was. I wrote this draft to talk to myself about all the ways the poem was working. I knew I would need to know it inside out to write a formal argument about it."

Beth wrote this comment, by the way, in a writing-process journal that she kept while working on her essay. Beth was taking a first-year writing class at the same time that she was enrolled in her American literature survey class, and her writing instructor had asked her students to choose a writing assignment from a different class and keep detailed notes about their writing process. You may find it helpful to undertake similar self-study.

Following the Emily Dickinson poem that Beth chose to analyze is her first draft essay.

An Analysis of Emily Dickinson's Poem #48 (First Draft)
Beth Runciman

Once more, my now bewildered Dove
Bestirs her puzzled wings
Once more her mistress, on the deep
Her troubled question flings —

Thrice to the floating casement
The Patriarch's bird returned,
Courage! My brave Columba!
There may yet be Land!

In poem #48 ("Once more, my now bewildered Dove"), Dickinson talks about feelings of hope and feelings of desperation, and she uses the story of Noah and the end of the flood as a metaphor to do so. In the story, Noah releases a dove from the ark three times near the end of the flood. He knows that if the bird cannot see land, it will return to the ark. If land is in sight, however, the bird will fly toward it, showing Noah the direction in which to sail. Dickinson builds the whole poem around this image. She replaces

"The Patriarch," Noah, with a female speaker; we know this from the word "mistress." This speaker's tone is desperate, as Noah's would be as well—an ark can hold only so much food, and if the bird does not direct Noah to land soon enough, all living creatures will perish.

Dickinson's rhythm and word choice create a frantic and desperate tone in the first stanza. We know this from the progression of the speaker's adjectives, from "bewildered" to "puzzled" to "troubled," in which each adjective is more severe than the preceding one. The verb "flings" at the end of the stanza is a desperate action as well, drawing attention to the speaker's urgency. Working against this urgency metaphorically, however, is the time the speaker has had to endure simply waiting. We get this sense in the poem's first phrase, "Once more," as well as in the stanza's rhythm. The speaker talks in iambs, making the reader wait for the stressed syllable. In this way, the speaker creates in the reader a feeling similar to what she is experiencing.

This desperation is not unchecked, however. The speaker's attention in the poem is focused on the dove, a symbol of hope. Here Dickinson uses the image of Noah releasing and waiting for the dove. From this image we infer that Noah is watching the bird carefully and earnestly as it flies. In the biblical story, if Noah loses sight of the bird and it does not return, he will not know which way to sail, and eventually everything on his boat will perish. The speaker in this poem is trying to ignore her own desperation and pay attention only to her hope, as symbolized by the bird. Dickinson's syntax as well as her imagery support this idea of hopeful attention. We know from the word "my" in the first line that this poem is written in the first person. In the second and third lines, however, the speaker refers to herself in the third person as "her mistress," the mistress of the dove. The speaker is so focused on the dove that the sense of the bird replaces the speaker's sense of self as a valid reference point. The bird is so important that it makes sense for the speaker to talk about herself only in relation to it.

The second stanza serves to clarify the speaker's imagery about the flood and to change the poem's tone. "Thrice to the floating casement / The Patriarch's bird returned," is a direct reference to Noah's experience as told in the Bible. In the last two lines of this stanza, the voice of the speaker and the voice of Noah merge together. Instead of desperation, both these voices encourage the dove in its search for land and thus encourage the spirit of hopefulness within themselves. By ending the poem with the assertion "There may yet be Land!" the speaker shows the reader that her circumstances have not gotten the better of her. In this way, Dickinson uses the poem as a way of presenting an emotional process or progression—in this case, from the heavy and urgent feelings of fear to the strong and self-assured experience of hope and faith.

*   *   *

Even in this early version, Beth's essay has a number of strengths. Perhaps most impressive is her ability to read Dickinson's poem with care and to make specific and detailed comments about the meaning of the poem and Dickinson's craft as a writer. Beth uses the vocabulary of literary criticism (terms like "stanza," "iambs," and "image") to good effect. And she draws on her previous knowledge of the Bible to clarify some of the references in the poem. Nevertheless, when Beth looked closely at her draft, she saw some limitations. "There's a lot of specific information in this draft," she wrote in her process journal. "But it doesn't add up. There's not a clear enough point. I end with a kind of assertion about how the poem works, but it's pretty general. It could probably apply to a number of other poems by Dickinson." Beth's last comment is particularly telling, for if her comments could apply to other Dickinson poems, then she is writing at a fairly general level and needs to sharpen both her analysis and her argument.

The next time Beth worked on her essay, she decided to begin by freewriting about her goals for this drafting session. Writing in her process journal, Beth commented, "I think I understand how this poem works, but I'm not doing enough with it. I've got to figure out exactly what I want to argue in my essay. I think that I could do more with the biblical references that Dickinson uses. In my first draft I talk about these references, but I don't really explain how important they are to the poem's meaning. I'll try to do that now." Here is the second draft that Beth wrote, in response to the goals set out in her freewriting.

An Exploration of Emily Dickinson's Poem #48 (Second Draft)
Beth Runciman

Poets often write for an audience that shares a certain background or knowledge base. They build their poems assuming that readers will be familiar enough with their references to understand the work. Writing in the late nineteenth century, Emily Dickinson frequently used biblical allusions in her poetry. In this essay, I explore how such an allusion works in Dickinson's poem #48 ("Once more, my now bewildered Dove"). I closely read the poem, describing the poetic techniques Dickinson uses, and I demonstrate that the reader's knowledge of the story of Noah and the Ark plays a crucial role in the poem's communication with the reader.

According to the biblical story, Noah released a dove from the ark three times near the end of the great flood. Noah knew that if the bird could not see land, it would return to the ark. If land were in sight, however, the bird would fly toward it, showing Noah the direction in which to sail. Dickinson builds her whole poem around the image of this third release. In poem #48, she writes:

> Once more, my now bewildered Dove
> Bestirs her puzzled wings
> Once more her mistress, on the deep
> Her troubled question flings —
>
> Thrice to the floating casement
> The Patriarch's bird returned,
> Courage! My brave Columba!
> There may yet be Land!

The first and second lines of the second stanza refer directly to Noah's experience as told in the Bible. However, in this poem Dickinson also selectively edits this biblical scene, making the story her own. She replaces "The Patriarch," Noah, with a female speaker; we know this from her choice of the word "mistress." Throughout the poem, Dickinson draws on her readers' knowledge of the end of the flood to talk about the feelings of hope and feelings of desperation that belong to her unique speaker.

Dickinson's rhythm and word choice create a frantic and desperate tone in the first stanza. We know this from the progression of the speaker's adjectives, from "bewildered" to "puzzled" to "troubled," in which each adjective is more severe than the preceding one. The verb "flings" at the end of the stanza is a desperate action as well, drawing attention to the speaker's urgency. These choices underscore the desperation implicit in the biblical story. Noah's ark can hold only so much food, and if the bird does not direct Noah to land soon enough, all living creatures will perish.

Working against this urgency metaphorically, however, is the time the speaker has had to endure simply waiting. We get this sense in the poem's first phrase, "Once more," as well as in the stanza's rhythm. The speaker talks in iambs, making the reader wait for the stressed syllable. In this way, Dickinson creates in the reader a feeling similar to what her speaker is experiencing, waiting and watching for the bird.

The speaker's desperation is not unchecked, however. Her attention throughout the poem is focused on the dove, a traditional symbol of hope. Here, Dickinson draws on the image of Noah releasing and waiting for the dove; in the story, we infer that Noah is watching the bird carefully and earnestly as it flies. If Noah loses sight of the bird and it does not return, he will not know which way to sail, and eventually everything on his boat will perish. By structuring her poem around this image, Dickinson suggests that her speaker is trying to ignore her own desperation and pay attention only to her hope, as symbolized by the bird. The syntax in the poem supports this idea of hopeful attention. We know from the word "my" in the first line that this poem is written in the first person. In the second and third lines, however, the speaker refers to herself in the third person as "her mistress," the mistress of the dove. The speaker is so focused on the dove that the sense of the bird replaces the speaker's sense of self as a valid reference point. The bird is so important that it makes sense for the speaker to talk about herself only in relation to it.

In the last two lines of this stanza, the voice of the speaker and the voice of Noah merge. Instead of desperation, both these voices seek to encourage the dove in its search for land and thus encourage the spirit of hopefulness within themselves. By ending the poem with the assertion "There may yet be Land!" the speaker shows the reader that her circumstances have not gotten the better of her.

In this poem, then, Dickinson uses the biblical image as a way of presenting an emotional progression within her speaker, from the heavy and urgent feelings of fear to the strong and self-assured experience of hope and faith. She draws on changes in tone, supported by her choices of rhythm and syntax, to support the emotional process the biblical scene suggests. She also edits the image to serve her purposes, and she depends on the reader's prior knowledge of the biblical version for her changes to be meaningful. Dickinson's poem is an excellent example of an author drawing on and interpreting a shared cultural story in a piece of poetry.

* * *

This second draft improves Beth's earlier effort in several important ways. The new introduction provides background information that leads directly to a statement of purpose: "In this essay, I explore how such an allusion works in Dickinson's poem #48 ('Once more, my now bewildered Dove'). I closely read the poem, describing the poetic techniques Dickinson uses, and I demonstrate that the reader's knowledge of the story of Noah and the Ark plays a crucial role in the poem's communication with the reader." Included in this statement of purpose is a thesis statement: "the reader's knowledge of the story of Noah and the Ark plays a crucial role in the poem's communication with the reader." Also helpful is Beth's comment that she will "closely read the poem"—for what those in the discipline of English studies call "close reading" is a specific way of reading texts. In using this term here, Beth is signaling to her teacher that she understands the importance of this method for analyzing literary texts and will employ it in her essay.

The next two paragraphs of Beth's second draft generally follow the lines of her first draft—but with one important difference. Beth revises the first draft's straightforward observation (that Dickinson "replaces 'The Patriarch,' Noah, with a female speaker") with the stronger and more pointed comment that "in this poem Dickinson also selectively edits this biblical scene, making the story her own." In addition to this change, Beth significantly develops the conclusion to her essay. Beth's first draft ended with the observation that "Dickinson uses the poem as a way of presenting an emotional process, or progression, in this case from the heavy and urgent feelings of fear to the strong and self-assured experience of hope and faith." This sentence now begins a new paragraph that builds on many of the observations Beth has made about how the poem achieves its effect. The final sentence of this draft— "Dickinson's poem is an excellent example of an author drawing on and interpreting a shared cultural story in a piece of poetry"—demonstrates that Beth not only understands the poem but can generalize from it to other literary efforts.

After completing the second draft of her essay, Beth waited a day before rereading it. "I need to have time between drafts," she wrote in her process journal. "I either love or hate my writing right after I've written something. Either way, there's no point in trying to work with it then." When Beth did return to her draft, she saw that she had improved her essay. But she was still dissatisfied with her overall argument. "What frustrates me," Beth wrote, "is that I haven't been able to convey how gutsy Dickinson is being in this poem." In an effort to clarify her ideas, Beth spent some time rereading Dickinson's poem and brainstorming and freewriting about it. She also reviewed notes she had taken during class discussions of Dickinson's poetry. Finally, she returned to her original analysis of her rhetorical situation. "There's nothing wrong with this analysis," Beth wrote in her process journal. "But it's pretty general. Maybe if I force myself to be more specific I can work out what I want to do." So Beth wrote a new second paragraph for her analysis:

> In class, we talked about how subversive Emily Dickinson's poetry was for her historical moment, and I remember being surprised at the critical edge that laced much of her work. For this assignment I want to explore not only how #48 works as a poem but also how it challenges certain norms of nineteenth-century New England society. I want my reader to come away from my essay with an appreciation of Dickinson's method for critiquing the culture in which she lived her life, as well as with an appreciation for her poetic skills and her use of biblical references.

As Beth noted in her process journal, this was a critical moment in her writing. She was finally able to see what she wanted to be at stake in her argument. She didn't want just to show that Dickinson was a good poet who knew how to use biblical allusions effectively. She wanted to demonstrate that Dickinson was a subversive poet. As Beth explained in her process journal, this insight was important in several ways. "I saw I had the hook that I needed to give my argument zip," she wrote. "But even better, I reconnected with my passion for Dickinson. I'm a rebel, and I was really drawn to the rebel in Dickinson—but I couldn't find a way to get that into my writing. Now I can."

The Matriarch's Bird (Final Draft)
Beth Runciman

Once more, my now bewildered Dove
Bestirs her puzzled wings
Once more her mistress, on the deep
Her troubled question flings —

Thrice to the floating casement
The Patriarch's bird returned,
Courage! My brave Columba!
There may yet be Land!

Poets often write for an audience that shares a certain background or knowledge base, and they build their poems assuming that readers will be familiar enough with their references to understand their work. Writing in the late nineteenth century, Emily Dickinson frequently used allusions to biblical stories in her poetry. In this essay, I explore how such an allusion works in Dickinson's poem #48 ("Once more, my now bewildered Dove"). I closely read the poem, describing the techniques Dickinson uses to communicate through it, and I argue that the reader's knowledge of the story of Noah and the Ark plays a crucial role in this communication.

More is going on in this poem, however, than a simple reference to a shared cultural story. Dickinson selectively edits the details of this tale, and she retells it with her own unique and, I would argue, subversive slant. Instead of calling to mind the familiar story of Noah and reinforcing traditional nineteenth-century values, Dickinson changes the tale to suggest a radical revision of nineteenth-century ideals. The fact that the text she revises is held sacred by most of her audience makes this revision all the more startling and gives the poem its subversive appeal.

According to the Bible, Noah released a dove from the ark three times near the end of the flood. He knew that if the bird could not see land, it would return to the ark. If land were in sight, however, the bird would fly toward it, demonstrating to Noah the direction in which to sail. In poem #48, Dickinson builds her entire poem around the image of this third release. "Thrice to the floating casement / The Patriarch's bird returned" is a direct reference to Noah's experience as told in the Bible. Dickinson's poem depends on her readers' recognition of the biblical story from these brief lines. The tone in both of her stanzas — the tone she sets up to match Noah's emotional state during the releasing of the dove — reinforces this recognition.

In the first stanza, her rhythm and word choice create a frantic and desperate tone. We know this from the progression of the speaker's adjectives. Each adjective — from "bewildered" to "puzzled" to "troubled" — is more emphatic than the preceding one. The verb "flings" at the end of the stanza is a desperate action as well, drawing attention to the speaker's urgency. These choices underscore the desperation implicit in the biblical story. Noah's ark can hold only so much food, and if the bird does not direct Noah to land soon enough, all living creatures will perish.

Working against this urgency metaphorically, however, is the time the speaker has had to endure waiting for the dove to return. We get this sense in the poem's first phrase, "Once more," as well as in the stanza's rhythm. The speaker talks in iambs, making the reader wait for the stressed syllable. In this way, Dickinson creates in the reader a feeling similar to what her speaker is experiencing.

There is something unexpected about this speaker, however. Dickinson replaces the figure of "The Patriarch," Noah, with a female speaker; we know this from her choice of the word "mistress" and by the female possessive pronoun that appears in "*her* troubled question." To Dickinson's contemporaries, this would have been a scandalous revision indeed. At that time in New England, biblical laws were invoked to uphold the father as the rightful ruler of the family and to maintain separate spheres of work for men and women. Women were expected to be obedient wives, to stay home, and to raise children, and stories from the Bible were frequently told to ensure that they did so. To suggest that a woman could have done the work that Noah did — responding to the very voice of God and saving all living creatures from certain death — would disrupt the assumptions on which society was built. Not only was Dickinson suggesting that women could do men's work; she was using the same text her contemporaries frequently called on to suggest exactly the opposite.

So, of course, Dickinson takes particular care to ground the reader in the biblical tale, despite the fact that the speaker is female. While the poem opens with a desperate and frantic tone, the speaker's desperation is not unchecked. Throughout the poem, her attention is focused on the dove, a traditional symbol of hope. If Noah loses sight of the bird and it does not return, he will not know which way to sail, and eventually all living creatures on his boat will perish. Drawing on this shared cultural knowledge, Dickinson suggests that her speaker, like Noah, is trying to ignore her own desperation and pay attention only to her hope, as symbolized by the bird. By structuring her poem around the exact emotional dimensions of this moment, Dickinson reinforces the idea that her speaker is, in fact, the same Noah as in the biblical story.

Dickinson's syntax works to communicate her speaker's hopeful attention. We know from the word "my" in the first line that this poem is written in the first person. In the second and third lines, however, the speaker
refers to herself in the third person as "her mistress," the mistress of the dove.
The speaker is so focused on the dove that the bird replaces the speaker's self
as a reference point. In the last two lines of this stanza, the voice of the
speaker and the voice of Noah merge. Instead of desperation, both these
voices seek to encourage the dove in its search for land and thus encourage the spirit of hopefulness within themselves. By ending the poem with
the assertion "There may yet be Land!" the speaker shows the reader that
her circumstances have not gotten the better of her. These are the most
subversive lines in the poem: In them, Dickinson's speaker becomes Noah
and speaks with his voice. There is no longer any room for doubt about who
this speaker is or about the fact of Dickinson's substitution of a female for
Noah. By speaking out in the voice of Noah, one of the most important men
in the sacred biblical text, Dickinson's female speaker becomes impossible
for her reader to dismiss.

Several things are going on in this poem, then. Dickinson presents her
readers with a poem that documents an emotional progression, from the
heavy and urgent feelings of fear to the strong and self-assured experience
of hope and faith. She draws on changes in tone, supported by the careful
use of rhythm and syntax, to support this progression. Dickinson builds
this progression around a well-known biblical tale and depends on her readers' shared cultural knowledge of the Bible. However, she edits the tale to
convey a more subversive message. By substituting a female speaker for
Noah, Dickinson challenges fundamental assumptions of sex-segregated,
nineteenth-century society; further, her challenge is based in the very text
on which those assumptions were thought to rest. Thus does Dickinson's
poem quietly — but effectively — challenge the cultural norms of her day.

*   *   *

The first thing you might have noticed about Beth's draft is that it now
has a title: "The Matriarch's Bird." This title provides important cues to the
reader about the focus of her essay, for "matriarch" calls to mind "patriarch."
This is a term used in the Hebrew Scripture to refer to such important male
figures as Adam and Noah. A "matriarch," then, is a female figure of great
importance in her society. Beth's title thus prepares readers for her discussion of Dickinson's subversion of the biblical story of Noah and the Ark.

There are other important additions to Beth's essay. After the introduction, which resembles that of the previous draft, Beth's new second paragraph
claims "More is going on in this poem, however, than a simple reference to a

shared cultural story." This paragraph adds complexity and significance to Beth's interpretation of Dickinson's poem. While her earlier drafts focused primarily on how Dickinson's poem works—how it is put together and achieves its effect—this final draft goes beyond analysis to argument. It demonstrates that Beth can read a poem with care, place that poem in its historical context, and make claims about its contemporary significance.

In the sixth paragraph, Beth further develops and supports her position. She does so by building on an observation that has appeared in all three drafts: that Dickinson replaces the figure of Noah with a female speaker. But here for the first time she considers the cultural context of this change and provides explicit links that connect evidence with larger generalizations:

> To Dickinson's contemporaries, this would have been a scandalous revision indeed. At that time in New England, biblical laws were invoked to uphold the father as the rightful ruler of the family and to maintain separate spheres of work for men and women. Women were expected to be obedient wives, to stay home, and to raise children, and stories from the Bible were frequently told to ensure that they did so. To suggest that a woman could have done the work that Noah did—responding to the very voice of God and saving all living creatures from certain death—would disrupt the assumptions on which society was built. Not only was Dickinson suggesting that women could do men's work; she was using the same text her contemporaries frequently called on to suggest exactly the opposite.

Here, and again in the closing paragraphs of her essay, Beth effectively argues that Dickinson not only grounds her poem in her readers' knowledge of the Bible but subverts the biblical story for her own purposes.

In three drafts, Beth was able to write her way to an effective academic argument. In her final process journal entry, Beth commented on this experience, observing, "In this essay, I didn't know exactly what I was going to argue until the final draft—but I wouldn't have been able to see that argument and make it work if I hadn't studied the poem by writing the other drafts first." With each draft, Beth's argument became clearer, and the links between her evidence and her generalizations became both more explicit and more fully developed.

Sample Analysis of a Visual Text

For an introductory art class, Michelle Fuller attended a show of artwork by faculty members at Oregon State University, where she chose a particular piece of art to analyze for this essay. Her assignment was to analyze the elements of composition in a painting, print, drawing, or sculpture.

Faculty Show Critique

Michelle Fuller

I viewed many diverse pieces of artwork at the Fairbanks Gallery Faculty show. I found the painting *Avocados and Parrot Tulips* by Shelley Jordan, a still life done in oil on canvas, particularly appealing. I enjoyed it not for what was painted but for how it is painted. Jordan employs an excellent use of composition, light, and brushwork.

One of the first things I noticed when viewing *Avocados* was that my eye continually moved around the canvas. I did not expect this to happen because I have seen many bland and static still lifes before. Items such as two vases with tulips, a glass plate, avocados, and fabric are arranged on a table in an almost circular composition. Not only does this motion lead the eye around the surface, but it also leads the eye to travel off the canvas and back on again. Lines created by the tulip stems aid this motion and draw the eye inward on the canvas. I also appreciated how the contrast between the straight tulip stems and the curving avocados and plates creates compositional movement.

Another thing that kept my eye moving is the excellent use of light throughout *Avocados*. Highlights are painted in small, incompletely blended dabs whose repetition across the canvas greatly contribute to the visual interest of the work. In some areas, such as the avocados, highlights also illustrate the texture of objects. In addition, Jordan uses color instead of relying on plain white highlights to create reflections and the appearance of falling light. These highlights reinforce the idea that objects like the vases and the glass plate have shiny, reflective surfaces. I felt the artist's use of light enliven what I often consider to be a dull subject matter.

When inspecting the brushwork of the highlights, I also noticed the mastery with which the work as a whole had been painted. The brushstrokes are confidently applied, and it seems as if no area needs reworking. This proficient application of paint is very important to the overall unity of the painting. Without it, the highlights and objects might seem disorganized — but the skillful painting technique helps unite the piece's different objects. Moreover, there is a pleasing variety of brushstrokes throughout the piece. The difference between the more softly blended background and the more impasto application of the highlights creates a needed sense of depth in the still life.

Avocados and Parrot Tulips is one of the best still lifes I have seen in a long time. It seems to me that Jordan did not intend this painting to be a political statement or some other kind of dramatic message. Instead, I think that *Avocados* was simply intended to be a beautiful piece of art—and that Jordan did an excellent job of fulfilling this intention.

Sample Essay Exam Response

Eric Hill was a student at the University of Southern California when he wrote this essay as a take-home midterm exam for an anthropology class. The essay was written in response to this assignment: "In a succinct and clearly organized essay, describe the Hopi worldview, and relate it to other cultural worldviews."

The Hopi Worldview: A Cyclical Model of Balance and Duality
Eric Hill

One of the most striking characteristics of Hopi myth and cosmography is the repetition of specific themes and metaphors. A theme that appears consistently throughout Hopi thought and that seems to be at the heart of their complex symbology is a cyclical view of the universe. This cyclical view is reflected not only in Hopi ceremonies and beliefs but also in their secular activities. It forms the basis of their culture and dictates much of their daily behavior—including rituals for birth and death.

The Hopi's cyclical view of the universe is both like and unlike Western views. It is like Western views in that it has a definite sense of duality. But it is not the kind of polarized duality found in most Western religious and cultural models, where body and soul, mind and spirit, are at odds. Reading about the Hopi, I was surprised to discover that much in Hopi thought seems essentially Taoist in nature. Like Taoists, the Hopi reconcile life and death by viewing them as two halves of the same whole. When a child is born into a Hopi household, a ritual is performed in which the infant is named and covered in cornmeal. The ritual for the dead is carried out in much the same manner: The deceased is given a new name, and the body is washed and then covered in cornmeal. In the Hopi's cyclical view of the universe, opposites exist to create a sense of balance *through* their polarization.

It is no coincidence that the Hopi view of life directly parallels the path of the sun across the sky. Just as the human emerges from the womb into this life, the sun emerges from the horizon in the East. Both the sun and human being enter this world via the navel or entrance from the underworld. Both must "set" at the end of their cycle and then enter once again into the underworld. This mythical image of emergence and reemergence gives Hopi thought a distinctly Eastern rather than Western flavor.

This cyclical dance of duality is made even more apparent by the significance of corn in Hopi life. Besides being the most important staple in their diet, corn is essential to their ceremonial life. In nature, corn must die to seed the ground so that more corn can be produced. With the growing of corn, as with other aspects of Hopi life and culture, the life-death-life cycle is clearly delineated. As this example indicates, corn is the embodiment of many symbols, concepts, and practices essential to Hopi thought. This is evident in their view of the corn mother, who is androgynous: The tassel or pollen stem is male, while the ear is female. Here, as elsewhere in Hopi thought, the necessity of coexisting opposites is emphasized. Male and female qualities share equal importance in the life cycle.

As these examples indicate, from the Hopi perspective, birth and death, male and female, are opposites (in the sense that they are two different ends or aspects of reality); yet they nevertheless emerge (and reemerge) together into life here, above, and below. The Hopi world view is unique; it reflects Hopi culture and history. But it also looks both to the East and the West. Like Western cosmographies, it is based on dualisms. But like Eastern cosmographies, it sees these dualisms as interdependent aspects of reality that emerge (and reemerge) as part of larger processes.

These two essays are excellent examples of writing in the humanities. Both take clear positions that are grounded in the careful reading and interpretation of sources. Both provide evidence for their positions, and both explain why this evidence is important. The writers establish their credibility primarily through the content of their ideas, although their ability to express these ideas clearly and concisely is also important to their overall success.

✱ bedfordstmartins.com/rewriting

For additional sample student projects written for the humanities, go to **Re:Writing** *and then click on* **ModelDoc Central**.

Writing in the Natural and Applied Sciences

Whatever their skill level, students in the humanities expect that writing will play a key role in their education. Those majoring in other areas, particularly the natural and applied sciences, sometimes assume otherwise. They're wrong. Here's what David Porush tells students to expect if they enter the sciences:

> You will write to report your research. You will write to communicate with colleagues at other institutions. You will write to request financial support for your work. You will write to colleagues, managers, and subordinates in your own institutional setting. You will write instructions and memos, and keep lab notebooks.[2]

Porush's argument is supported by other scientists. When faculty members in the department of chemistry at Oregon State University developed a writing guide for their students, they had this to say about the importance of writing in their field.

> Is writing important in chemistry? Don't chemists spend their time turning knobs, mixing reagents, and collecting data? They still get to do those things, but professional scientists also make presentations, prepare reports, publish results, and submit proposals. Each of these activities involves writing.[3]

---

[2]David Porush, *A Short Guide to Writing about Science* (New York: Harper, 1995), xxi–xxii.
[3]Oregon State University Department of Chemistry, "Writing Guide for Chemistry," http://www.chemistry .oregonstate.edu/writing/WritingGuide2000.htm.

Victoria McMillan, author of *Writing Papers in the Biological Sciences*, likewise points out that "no experiment, however brilliant, can contribute to the existing fund of scientific knowledge unless it has been described to others working in the same field."[4]

Because established formats for scientific writing encourage efficient communication and facilitate replication of experiments, scientists use them whenever possible. At the same time, they pay particular attention to the effective presentation of data, often using figures, tables, images, and models. This attention to format and document design is equally important in student writing in the sciences.

Scientists write a variety of kinds of texts. Since maintaining and operating labs can be costly, scientists spend considerable time writing proposals to fund research projects. Most research proposals follow this format: title page, introduction, purpose, significance of the study, methods, timeline, budget, and references. The format for research reports and journal articles is generally as follows: title, author(s), abstract, introduction, literature review, materials and methods, results, discussion, and references.

Sample Student Essay in the Natural and Applied Sciences

Scientists value precision, clarity, and objectivity. The following essay, an undergraduate research proposal by Tara Gupta, demonstrates these traits. Note that Tara uses headings to mark the various sections of her proposal. She also uses the documentation style required by the Council of Science Editors (CSE). For details on this reference style, consult its handbook, *Scientific Style and Format: The CSE Manual for Authors, Editors, and Publishers*, 7th ed. (2006).

---

[4]Victoria McMillan, *Writing Papers in the Biological Sciences*, 4th ed. (Boston: Bedford, 2006), 1.

Field Measurements of
Photosynthesis and Transpiration
Rates in Dwarf Snapdragon
(*Chaenorrhinum minus* Lange):
An Investigation of Water Stress
Adaptations

Complete title, specific and informative

Tara Gupta

Proposal for a
Summer Research
Fellowship
Colgate University
March 12, 2010

Shortened title and page number

Water Stress Adaptations 2

Headings throughout help organize the proposal

Introduction states scientific issue, gives background information, cites relevant studies

Introduction

Dwarf snapdragon (*Chaenorrhinum minus*) is a weedy pioneer plant found growing in central New York during spring and summer. The distribution of this species has been limited almost exclusively to the cinder ballast of railroad tracks,[1] a harsh environment characterized by intense sunlight and poor soil water retention. Given such environmental conditions, one would expect *C. minus* to exhibit anatomical features similar to those of xeromorphic plants (species adapted to arid habitats).

However, this is not the case. T. Gupta and R. Arnold (unpublished) have found that the leaves and stems of *C. minus* are not covered by a thick, waxy cuticle but rather with a thin cuticle that is less effective in inhibiting water loss through diffusion. The root system is not long and thick, capable of reaching deeper, moister soils; instead, it is thin and diffuse, permeating only the topmost (and driest) soil horizon. Moreover, in contrast to many xeromorphic plants, the stomata (pores regulating gas exchange) are not found in sunken crypts or cavities in the epidermis that retard water loss from transpiration.

Personal letter cited in parentheses, not included in references

Despite a lack of these morphological adaptations to water stress, *C. minus* continues to grow and reproduce when morning dew has been its only source of water for up to five weeks (R. Arnold, personal communication). Such growth involves fixation of carbon by photosynthesis and requires that the stomata be open to admit sufficient carbon dioxide. Given the dry, sunny environment, the time required for adequate carbon fixation must also mean a significant loss of water through transpiration as open stomata exchange carbon dioxide with water. How does *C. minus* balance the need for carbon with the need to conserve water?

Aims and scope of proposed study

Aims of the Proposed Study

The above observations have led me to an exploration of the extent to which *C. minus* is able to photosynthesize under conditions of low water availability. It is my hypothesis that *C. minus* adapts to these conditions by photosynthesizing in the early morning and late afternoon, when leaf and air temperatures are lower and transpirational water loss is reduced. I predict

Water Stress Adaptations 3

that its photosynthetic rate may be very low, perhaps even zero, on hot, sunny afternoons. Similar diurnal changes in photosynthetic rate in response to midday water deficits have been described in crop plants.[2,3] There is only one comparable study[4] on noncrop species in their natural habitats.

 Thus, the research proposed here aims to help explain the apparent paradox of an organism that thrives in water-stressed conditions despite a lack of morphological adaptations. This summer's work will also serve as a basis for controlled experiments in a plant growth chamber on the individual effects of temperature, light intensity, soil water availability, and other environmental factors on photosynthesis and transpiration rates. These experiments are planned for the coming fall semester.

Methods

Simultaneous measurements of photosynthesis and transpiration rates will indicate the balance *C. minus* has achieved in acquiring the energy it needs while retaining the water available to it. These measurements will be taken daily at field sites in the Hamilton, NY, area, using an LI-6220 portable photosynthesis system (LICOR, Inc., Lincoln, NE). Basic methodology and use of correction factors will be similar to that described in related studies.[5-7] Data will be collected at regular intervals throughout the daylight hours and will be related to measurements of ambient air temperature, leaf temperature, relative humidity, light intensity, wind velocity, and cloud cover.

Budget

1 kg soda lime	$53.90
(for absorption of CO_2 in photosynthesis analyzer)	
1 kg anhydrous magnesium perchlorate	$274.40
(used as desiccant for photosynthesis analyzer)	
Shipping of chemicals (estimate)	$12.00
Estimated 500 miles travel to field sites in own car	$202.50
@ $0.405/mile	
CO_2 cylinder, 80 days rental	$100.00
(for calibration of photosynthesis analyzer)	
TOTAL REQUEST	$642.80

Margin notes:

CSE documentation, citation-sequence format

States significance of study

Connects study to future research projects

Methodology described briefly

Itemized budget gives details

Water Stress Adaptations 4

References

Numbered references relate to citation order in text

1. Widrlechner MP. Historical and phenological observations of the spread of *Chaenorrhinum minus* across North America. Can J Bot 1983;61(1):179-87.

2. Manhas JG, Sukumaran NP. Diurnal changes in net photosynthetic rate in potato in two environments. Potato Res. 1988;31:375-8.

3. Yordanov I, Tsonev T, Velikova V, Georgieva K, Ivanov P, Tsenov N, Petrova T. Changes in CO_2 assimilation, transpiration and stomatal resistance in different wheat cultivars experiencing drought under field conditions. Bulg J Plant Physiol. 2001;27(3-4):20-33.

4. Chaves MM, Pereira JS, Maroco J, Rodrigues ML, Ricardo CP, Osório ML, Carvalho I, Faria T, Pinheiro C. How plants cope with water stress in the field: photosynthesis and growth. Ann Bot. 2002;89(Jun): 907-916.

5. Jarvis A, Davies W. The coupled response of stomatal conductance to photosynthesis and transpiration. J Exp Bot. 1998;49(Mar):399-406.

6. Kallarackal J, Milburn JA, Baker DA. Water relations of the banana. III. Effects of controlled water stress on water potential, transpiration, photosynthesis and leaf growth. Aust J Plant Physiol. 1990;17(1):79-90.

7. Idso SB, Allen SG, Kimball BA, Choudhury BJ. Problems with porometry: measuring net photosynthesis by leaf chamber techniques. Agron J. 1989;81(4):475-9.

Before embarking on her grant proposal, Tara spent time analyzing her rhetorical situation. Here is her analysis:

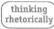

I am writing because I wish to persuade a committee to grant me funds for working on my scientific project. Because I want the readers (scientists) to notice my ideas and not the medium, and because I want to convince them of my scientific merit and training, I will use the traditional medium and style for scientists — a written research proposal. A research proposal follows a standard format. Hence, I would say that my role as a writer, and my product, is relatively fixed. In the end, I want readers to hear the voice of a fellow scientist who is hardworking, trustworthy, and a creative observer.

To be persuasive, I need to understand the behaviors, motivations, and values of scientists. I expect the readers, as scientists, to immediately begin formulating questions and hypotheses as I present the background information — scientists instinctively do this. My job is to give them the best information to help them form the questions I would like them to be thinking about. In addition, it is important to include all logical steps in proceeding with my idea and background knowledge, especially since the scientists reading my proposal are not all in my research field and cannot fill in the information gaps. Nothing is more boring or painful for a scientist than reading something that has flawed logic which they have trouble following or understanding. I also need credibility, so I will have references for all background information.

Scientists value communication that is succinct, concrete, logical, accurate, and above all, *objective*. For example, if I want to discuss the environmental conditions these plants live in, I will not write a subjective account of how I've grown up in this area and know how hot and dry it can be in the summer. Instead, I will present an objective account of the environmental conditions using specific language (location, temperatures, moisture). In science, the hardest information to write about is ambiguous information, since it can be difficult to be succinct, concrete, logical, accurate, or objective; though in the end, this ambiguity is where the next experiment is and where the real work is to be done.

In reading Tara's analysis, you might be surprised by how extensive and complex her thinking is. After all, scientists just follow the conventions of scientific writing, don't they? Tara's analysis is a powerful demonstration of the kind of rhetorical sensitivity that scientists draw upon when they write proposals, lab reports, and other scientific documents.

✳ bedfordstmartins.com/rewriting
For additional sample student projects written for the natural and applied sciences, go to **Re:Writing** *and then click on* **ModelDoc Central**.

Writing in the Social Sciences

The social sciences, disciplines such as sociology, psychology, anthropology, communications, political science, and economics, draw from both the sciences and the humanities. Many scholars in the social sciences address questions that interest humanities scholars, but their methods of investigating these questions differ. Consider the topic of aging. An English professor might study several novels with elderly characters to see how they are represented. A philosopher might consider the moral and political issues surrounding aging and longevity. A sociologist, on the other hand, might explore the ways in which the elderly are treated in a particular community and evaluate the impact such treatment has on elders' mood and activity level.

In general, social scientists explore questions through controlled methods, including (1) surveys and questionnaires, (2) experiments, (3) observation, (4) interviews, (5) case studies, and (6) ethnographic field work. Careful observation is central to all of these methods, for, like scientists, social scientists value the development of objective and reliable knowledge. As a result, they ground their arguments in quantitative data (data based on statistics) or qualitative data (data based on observations). An economist studying the effect of aging on earning power might gather statistics that enable him to generate a hypothesis about their relationship. A sociologist might use one or more surveys, interviews, and case studies to gain a nuanced understanding of the impact of aging on self-perception and self-esteem.

Writing is as important in the social sciences as it is in the natural and applied sciences and humanities. As Deidre McCloskey, internationally known economist and author of *Economical Writing*, points out, a person trained in economics "is likely to spend most of her working life writing papers, reports, memoranda, proposals, columns, and letters. Economics depends much more on writing (and on speaking, another neglected art) than on the statistics and mathematics usually touted as the tools of the trade."[5] In her book, McCloskey argues for the value of a rhetorical approach to writing in economics.

Because the social sciences look to both the sciences and the humanities, the forms of writing within the social sciences can be particularly varied. For example, a writing guide for political science students at Oregon State University lists the following types of assignments: summary, abstract, book report, reaction note, think piece, radio script, briefing note, journal, image analysis, agency analysis, book review, essay, essay-type exam, analytical case brief, research project for methodology, and research paper. A similar guide for sociology majors includes these assignments: theory paper, content paper, quantitative research paper, case study, and qualitative research paper.

---

[5] Deidre McCloskey, *Economical Writing,* 2nd ed. (Long Grove: Waveland Press, 2000), 5.

Sample Student Essay in the Social Sciences

Pages 236–44 present an example of effective writing in the social sciences. Tawnya Redding wrote this essay for an upper-level psychology class in clinical research methods. A major assignment for the class was to write a review of the literature on a possible theoretical experiment. Tawnya chose to write her review on music preference and the risk for depression and suicide in adolescents. Note that this essay uses APA documentation style, required for this course.[6] For details on this reference style, see the APA Documentation Guidelines section at the back of this book.

---

[6]The formatting shown in the sample paper that follows is consistent with typical APA requirements for undergraduate writing. Formatting guidelines for papers prepared for publication differ in some respects; see pp. 381–402.

Shortened
title and page
number appears
on each page

Mood Music 1

Title, double-
spaced

Mood Music:

Music Preference and the Risk for Depression and Suicide in Adolescents

Student name,
course title,
instructor name,
and date,
double-spaced

Tawnya Redding

Psychology 480

Professor Bernieri

February 23, 2009

Mood Music 2

Abstract

The last 20 years have shown a growing concern for the effects that certain genres of music (such as heavy metal and country) have on youth. While a correlational link between these problematic genres and increased risk for depression and suicide in adolescents has been established, researchers have been unable to pinpoint what is responsible for this link, and a causal relationship has not been determined. This paper will begin by discussing correlational literature concerning music preference and increased risk for depression and suicide, as well as the possible reasons for this link. Finally, studies concerning the effects of music on mood will be discussed. This examination of the literature on music and increased risk for depression and suicide points out the limitations of previous research and suggests the need for new research establishing a causal relationship for this link as well as research into the specific factors that may contribute to an increased risk for depression and suicide in adolescents.

Abstract heading, centered

Abstract content— a summary of Tawnya's review of the literature

Double-spaced and presented without indentation

Mood Music 3

Mood Music: Music Preference and

the Risk for Depression and Suicide in Adolescents

Music is a significant part of American culture. Since the explosion of rock 'n' roll in the 1950s there has been a concern for the effects that music may have on those who choose to listen, and especially for the youth of society. The genres most likely to come under suspicion in recent decades have included heavy metal, country, and even blues. These genres have been suspected of having adverse effects on the mood and behavior of young listeners. But can music really alter the disposition and create self-destructive behaviors in listeners? And if so, what genres and aspects of these genres are responsible?

The following review of the literature will establish the correlation between potentially problematic genres of music, such as heavy metal and country, and depression and suicide risk. First, correlational studies concerning music preference and suicide risk will be discussed, followed by a discussion of the literature concerning the possible reasons for this link. Finally, studies concerning the effects of music on mood will be discussed. Despite the link between genres such as heavy metal and country and suicide risk, previous research has been unable to establish the causal nature of this link.

The Correlation Between Music and Depression and Suicide Risk

Studies over the past two decades have set out to establish the causal nature of the link between music and mood by examining the correlation between youth music preference and risk for depression and suicide. A large number of these studies have focused on heavy metal and country music as the main genre culprits in association with youth suicidality and depression (Lacourse, Claes, & Villeneuve, 2001; Scheel & Westefeld, 1999; Stack & Gundlach, 1992). Stack and Gundlach (1992) examined the radio airtime devoted to country music in 49 metropolitan areas and found that the higher the percentages of country music airtime, the higher the incidence of suicides among whites. Stack and Gundlach (1992) hypothesized that themes in

---

Marginal annotations:

Full title, centered

Opening sentences set context for study, argue for significance

Questions frame focus of report

Second paragraph outlines paper's purpose, structure, and conclusion

Heading, centered and boldface

Opening sets chronological context

APA-style parenthetical citation to three studies

Source named in the body of the text

Mood Music 4

country music (such as alcohol abuse) promote audience identification and reinforce preexisting suicidal mood, and that the themes associated with country music were responsible for the elevated suicide rates. Similarly, Scheel and Westefeld (1999) found a correlation between heavy metal music listeners and an increased risk for suicide, as did Lacourse et al. (2001).

Reasons for the Link:
Characteristics of Those Who Listen to Problematic Music

Unfortunately, previous studies concerning music preference and suicide risk have been unable to determine a causal relationship and have focused mainly on establishing a correlation between suicide risk and music preference. This leaves the question open as to whether an individual at risk for depression and suicide is attracted to certain genres of music or whether the music helps induce the mood, or both.

Some studies have suggested that music preference may simply be a reflection of other underlying problems associated with increased risk for suicide (Lacourse et al., 2001; Scheel & Westefeld, 1999). For example, in research done by Scheel and Westefeld (1999), adolescents who listened to heavy metal were found to have lower scores on Linehan, Goodstein, Nielsen, and Chiles's Reasons for Living Inventory (1983) and several of its subscales, a self-report measure designed to assess potential reasons for not committing suicide. These adolescents were also found to have lower scores on several subscales of the Reason for Living Inventory, including responsibility to family along with survival and coping beliefs.

Other risk factors associated with suicide and suicidal behaviors include poor family relationships, depression, alienation, anomie, and drug and alcohol abuse (Lacourse et al., 2001). Lacourse et al. (2001) examined 275 adolescents in the Montreal region with a preference for heavy metal and found that this preference was not significantly related to suicide risk when other risk factors were controlled for. This was also the conclusion of Scheel et al. (1999), in which music preference for heavy metal was thought to be a

Headings organize a review of the literature; this section discusses studies that fail to establish music as a causal factor in suicide risk

Identifies an important psychological measurement tool

Mood Music 5

red flag for suicide vulnerability but which suggested that the source of the problem may lie more in personal and familial characteristics.

George, Stickle, Rachid and Wopnford (2007) further explored the correlation between suicide risk and music preference by attempting to identify the personality characteristics of those with a preference for different genres of music. A community sample of 358 individuals was assessed for preference of 30 different styles of music, along with a number of personality characteristics including self-esteem, intelligence, spirituality, social skills, locus of control, openness, conscientiousness, extraversion, agreeableness, emotional stability, hostility, and depression (George et al., 2007). The 30 styles of music were then sorted into eight categories: rebellious (for example, punk and heavy metal), classical, rhythmic and intense (including hip-hop, rap, pop), easy listening, fringe (for example, techno), contemporary Christian, jazz and blues, and traditional Christian. The results revealed an almost comprehensively negative personality profile for those who preferred to listen to the rebellious and rhythmic and intense categories, while those who preferred classical music tended to have a comprehensively positive profile. Like Scheel et al. (1999) and Lacourse et al. (2001), this study also supports the theory that youth are drawn to certain genres of music based on already existing factors, whether they be related to personality or situational variables.

Reasons for the Link:
Characteristics of Problematic Music

Another possible explanation for the correlation between suicide risk and music preference is that the lyrics and themes of the music have a negative effect on listeners. In this scenario, music is thought to exacerbate an already depressed mood and hence contribute to an increased risk for suicide. This was the proposed reasoning behind higher suicide rates in whites in Stack and Gundlach's (1992) study linking country music to suicide risk. In this case, the themes associated with country music were thought to promote

Transitional sentence announces discussion of a new group of studies

Mood Music 6

audience identification and reinforce preexisting behaviors associated with suicidality (such as alcohol consumption).

Stack (2000) also studied individuals with a musical preference for blues to determine whether the themes in blues music could increase the level of suicide acceptability. The results demonstrated that blues fans were no more accepting of suicide than nonfans, but that blues listeners were found to have lowered religiosity levels, an important factor for suicide acceptability (Stack, 2000). Despite this link between possible suicidal behavior and a preference for blues music, the actual suicide behavior of blues fans has not been explored, and thus no concrete associations can be made.

Distinguishes this study from previously cited study conducted by the same researcher

The Effect of Music on Mood

While studies examining the relationship between music genres such as heavy metal, country, and blues have been able to establish a correlation between music preference and suicide risk, it is still unclear from these studies what effect music has on the mood of the listener. Previous research has suggested that some forms of music can both improve and depress mood (Johnson, 2009; Lai, 1999; Siedliecki & Good, 2006; Smith & Noon, 1998).

Heading and transitional sentence identify problem not yet answered by the research

Lai (1999) found that changes in mood were more likely to be found in an experimental group of depressed women versus a control group. The physiological variables of heart rate, respiratory rate, blood pressure, and immediate mood state were measured before and after the experimental group had listened to music of their choice for 30 minutes and the control group had listened to pink sound (similar to white noise) for 30 minutes. It was found that music listening had a greater effect on participants' physiological conditions, as decreases in heart rate, blood pressure, and respiratory rate were greater in the experiment group than the control group (Lai, 1999). This study suggests that music can have a positive effect on depressed individuals when they are allowed to choose the music they are listening to.

Mood Music 7

In a similar study, Siedliecki and Good (2006) found that music can increase a listener's sense of power and decrease depression, pain, and disability. Researchers randomly assigned 60 African American and Caucasian participants with chronic nonmalignant pain to either a standard music group (offered a choice of instrumental music between piano, jazz, orchestra, harp, and synthesizer), a patterning music group (asked to choose between music to ease muscle tension, facilitate sleep, or decrease anxiety), or a control group. There were no statistically significant differences between the two music groups. However, the music groups had significantly less pain, depression, and disability than the control group.

On the other hand, Martin, Clark and Pearce (1993) identified a subgroup of heavy metal fans who reported feeling worse after listening to their music of choice. Although this subgroup did exist, there was also evidence that listening to heavy metal results in more positive affect for some, and it was hypothesized that those who experience negative affect after listening to their preferred genre of heavy metal may be most at risk for suicidal behaviors.

Smith and Noon (1998) also determined that music can have a negative effect on mood. Six songs were selected for the particular theme they embodied: (1) vigorous, (2) fatigued, (3) angry, (4) depressed, (5) tense, and (6) all moods. The results indicated that selections 3–6 had significant effects on the mood of participants, with selection 6 (all moods) resulting in the greatest positive change in mood while selection 5 (tense) resulted in the greatest negative change in mood. Selection 4 (depressed) was found to sap the vigor and increase anger/hostility in participants, while selection 5 (tense) significantly depressed participants and made them more anxious. Although this study did not specifically comment on the effects of different genres on mood, the results do indicate that certain themes can indeed depress mood. The participants for this study were undergraduate students who were not depressed, and thus it seems that certain types of music can have a negative effect on the mood of healthy individuals.

Mentions seemingly contradictory findings in the research

Mood Music 8

Is There Evidence for a Causal Relationship?

Despite the correlation between certain music genres and an increased risk for depression and suicidal behaviors in adolescents (especially that of heavy metal), it remains unclear whether these types of music can alter the mood of at-risk youth in a negative way. This view of the correlation between music and suicide risk is supported by a meta-analysis done by Baker and Bor (2008), in which the authors assert that most studies reject the notion that music is a causal factor and suggest that music preference is more indicative of emotional vulnerability. However, it is still unknown whether these genres can negatively alter mood at all, and if they can, whether it is the themes and lyrics associated with the music that are responsible. Clearly, more research is needed to further examine this correlation, as a causal link between these genres of music and suicide risk has yet to be shown. However, even if the theory put forth by Baker and Bor (2008) and other researchers is true, it is still important to investigate the effects that music can have on those who may be at risk for suicide and depression. Even if music is not the ultimate cause of suicidal behavior, it may act as a catalyst that further pushes individuals into a state of depression and increased risk for suicidal behavior.

Heading and transitional sentence emphasize inconclusive nature of studies

Emphasizes need for further research and suggests the direction research might take

References
begin new page;
double-space
throughout

First line of each
entry begins
at left margin;
subsequent
lines indent
1/2 inch

Online
document
identified with
URL

Citation follows
APA style for
print journal
article

Article from
a database
identified with
the article's doi
(Digital Object
Identifier)

Mood Music 9

References

Baker, F., & Bor, W. (2008). Can music preference indicate mental health status in young people? *Australasian Psychiatry, 16*, 284-288.

George, D., Stickle, K., Rachid, F., & Wopnford, A. (2007). The association between types of music enjoyed and cognitive, behavioral, and personality factors of those who listen. *Psychomusicology, 19*(2), 32-56.

Johnson, F. D. (2009). The effects of music on temporary disposition. Retrieved from http://clearinghouse.missouriwestern.edu/manuscripts/260.php

Lacourse, E., Claes, M., & Villeneuve, M. (2001). Heavy metal music and adolescent suicidal risk. *Journal of Youth and Adolescence, 30*, 321-332.

Lai, Y. (1999). Effects of music listening on depressed women in Taiwan. *Issues in Mental Health Nursing, 20*, 229-246. doi: 10.1080/016128499248637

Linehan, M. M., Goodstein, J. L., Nielsen, S. L., Chiles, J. A. (1983). Reasons for staying alive when you are thinking of killing yourself: The Reasons for Living Inventory. *Journal of Consulting and Clinical Psychology, 51*, 276-286. doi:10.1037/0022–006X.51.2.276

Martin, G., Clark, M., & Pearce, C. (1993). Adolescent suicide: Music preference as an indicator of vulnerability. *Journal of the American Academy of Child and Adolescent Psychiatry, 32*, 530-535.

Scheel, K., & Westefeld, J. (1999). Heavy metal music and adolescent suicidality: An empirical investigation. *Adolescence, 34*, 253-273.

Siedliecki, S., & Good, M. (2006). Effect of music on power, pain, depression and disability. *Journal of Advanced Nursing, 54*, 553-562. doi: 10.1111/j.1365-2648.2006.03860.x

Smith, J. L., & Noon, J. (1998). Objective measurement of mood change induced by contemporary music. *Journal of Psychiatric & Mental Health Nursing, 5*, 403-408.

Snipes, J., & Maguire, E. (1995). Country music, suicide, and spuriousness. *Social Forces, 74*, 327-329.

Stack, S. (2000). Blues fans and suicide acceptability. *Death Studies, 24*, 223-231. doi: 10.1080/074811800200559

Stack, S., & Gundlach, J. (1992). The effect of country music on suicide. *Social Forces, 71*, 211-218.

In reflecting on her experience writing this essay, Tawnya had this to say:

thinking
rhetorically

> My assignment was to write a literature review on a topic of my choice. Since the literature review is a fairly standard genre in psychology, my role as a writer was both fixed and flexible. It was fixed in that I had to follow the conventions for literature reviews; this includes conveying the tone of a serious scholar, in part by using the statement-oriented third person rather than the first person. But it was flexible in that I was able to determine what material to include in the review, the conclusions I drew from my analysis, and my suggestions for future research. My professor was the intended reader for this essay, but I also had a more general critical reader in mind as I wrote. I wanted to encourage readers to think critically about the studies being presented. What are the strengths and weaknesses of the studies? How might they be improved? What information is lacking in the current research? What problem has previous research not yet addressed, and how might future research do so? The constraints of the literature review were actually enabling in that I was able to build upon this foundation to go beyond simply conveying information to raising important questions about my topic and the research that has investigated it.

✱ bedfordstmartins.com/rewriting

For additional sample student projects written for the social sciences, go to **Re:Writing** *and then click on* **ModelDoc Central**.

Writing in Business

Historians of business writing emphasize the roles that the spread of literacy in the Middle Ages and the invention of the printing press in the Renaissance played in this history. According to Malcolm Richardson, a contributor to *Studies in the History of Business Writing*, even before capitalism developed in Europe there were scribes and scriveners, who played a key role in both government and private communication.[7] In the fourteenth century, what some historians believe to be the first business writing school opened in England, and in the sixteenth century, Angell Day's *The English Secretary or Method of Writing Epistles and Letters*, one of the earliest business communication texts (which at this time primarily took the form of letter writing), appeared.

---

[7]George H. Douglas and Herbert William Hildebrandt, eds., *Studies in the History of Business Writing* (Urbana, IL: Association for Business Communication, 1985).

The conventions that characterize modern business writing—particularly the preference for clear, concise, goal- and audience-oriented communication and an easy-to-read visual design—developed slowly but steadily. With the growth of the middle class and the increase of commerce, businesspersons needed to be able to communicate with both internal and external audiences. Basic forms of business writing, such as memos, letters, proposals, and reports, became more standard. As layers of management evolved and departments proliferated, written internal communication became increasingly important, as did changes in the technologies of communication. The typewriter and carbon paper (and, later, dictaphones and photocopiers) transformed the office through the mid-twentieth century.

Developments in online, electronic, and digital communication are once again effecting powerful changes in business writing. Today's business writers communicate online, as well as in traditional print environments. They must be able to work effectively in teams, and they need to be able to respond to the demands of working in a global environment. The essential characteristics of effective business writing, however, remain grounded in basic issues of rhetorical sensitivity. When writing for business, it's especially important to consider the differing needs—and situations—of your readers. You may need to consider readers spread geographically or across an organization chart, and, in some cases, you may even need to consider future readers.

Sample Student Memo for Business Writing

The memo shown on p. 247 was written by Michelle Rosowsky and Carina Abernathy, two students in a business class. Their memo presents an analysis and recommendation to help an employer make a decision. As you read, notice how the opening paragraph provides necessary background information and clearly states the memo's purpose. Even if this memo is forwarded to others, its purpose will be clear. Michelle and Carina are also careful to follow the traditional memo design format and to use bold type to emphasize the most important information.

This assignment took the form of a case study. The students' teacher provided them with a series of hypothetical facts about a potential business transaction. Their job was to analyze this information, determine their recommendations, and communicate them in the most effective form possible.

In reflecting on their memo, Michelle and Carina commented that the first and most important step in their writing process involved analyzing both the information that they were given and their rhetorical situation.

We had to first analyze the facts of the case to come up with an appropriate recommendation and then present the recommendation within the format of a typical business memo. Because it's written for a

❖ Jenco ❖

INTEROFFICE MEMORANDUM

To: ROSA DONAHUE, SALES MANAGER

From: MICHELLE ROSOWSKY & CARINA ABERNATHY, *MR CA*
SALES ASSOCIATES

Subject: TAYLOR NURSERY BID

Date: JANUARY 30, 2006

CC:

As you know, Taylor Nursery has requested bids on a 25,000-pound order of private-label fertilizer. Taylor Nursery is one of the largest distributors of our Fertikil product. The following is our analysis of Jenco's costs to fill this special order and a recommendation for the bidding price.

The total cost for manufacturing 25,000 pounds of the private-label brand for Taylor Nursery is $44,075. This cost includes direct material, direct labor, and variable manufacturing overhead. Although our current equipment and facilities provide adequate capacity for processing this special order, the job will involve an excess in labor hours. The overtime labor rate has been factored into our costs.

The absolute minimum price that Jenco could bid for this product without losing money is $44,075 (our cost). Applying our standard markup of 40% results in a price of $61,705. Thus, you could reasonably establish a price anywhere within that range.

In making the final assessment, we advise you to consider factors relevant to this decision. Taylor Nursery has stated that this is a one-time order. Therefore, the effort to fill this special order will not bring long-term benefits.

Finally, Taylor Nursery has requested bids from several competitors. One rival, Eclipse Fertilizers, is submitting a bid of $60,000 on this order. Therefore, our recommendation is to slightly underbid Eclipse with a price of $58,000, representing a markup of approximately 32%.

Please let us know if we can be of further assistance in your decision on the Taylor Nursery bid.

Margin annotations:

Authors initial next to their names

Paragraphs flush left

Bold type highlights the most important financial information

Double-spaced between paragraphs

Options presented and background given

Final recommendation

Closing offers further assistance

busy manager, we wrote the memo as concisely as possible so that the information would be available at a glance. We also put the most critical calculation, the manufacturing cost, at the beginning of the memo and in bold so that the manager could find it easily and refer back to it later if necessary. We go on to make a recommendation about a bidding price and then provide a few other relevant facts since the goal of the memo is to enable the manager to ultimately make her own decision. The succinctness of the memo also reflects our confidence in the analysis, which gives us a strong and positive *ethos* and helps establish our reliability and competence.

* bedfordstmartins.com/rewriting
   For additional student samples of business writing, go to **Re:Writing** *and then click on* **ModelDoc Central***.*

|||||||||||||||||||||||||||||||||||||||||||||||||||||||||||||||||||||||||||||||||||||||||||

FOR THOUGHT, DISCUSSION, AND WRITING

1. Although you may not have determined your major area of study yet, you probably have some idea of whether you want to major in the humanities, social sciences, or sciences. Meet with a group of classmates who share your general interests. Working together, first make a list of the reasons you all find this area interesting. Next, make a list of the writing challenges that students in this area face. Finally, choose two of these challenges and brainstorm productive ways that students can respond to them. Be prepared to share the results of your discussion with the entire class.

2. Write an essay in which you reflect on the reasons you are drawn to a particular discipline or general area of study. How long-standing is your interest in this discipline? What do you see as its challenges and rewards? (Before writing this essay, you might like to read Brandon Barrett's essay on his decision to major in chemistry, which appears on pp. 54–55.)

3. Choose one of the student essays presented in this chapter, and analyze it to determine what features reflect the disciplinary preferences described in this chapter. Alternatively, choose an essay you have written for a class in the sciences, social sciences, or humanities and similarly analyze it. In studying either your own essay or an essay that appears in this chapter, be sure to consider its vocabulary, style, method of proof, and use of conventional formats.

|||||||||||||||||||||||||||||||||||||||||||||||||||||||||||||||||||||||||||||||||||||||||||

Strategies for Reading

Why—and how—do people read? Not surprisingly, they read for as many different reasons and in as many different contexts as they write. They read to gain information—to learn how to program their DVR, to decide whether to attend a movie or purchase a new product, or to explore ideas for writing. They read for pleasure, whether by surfing the Web, browsing through a magazine, or enjoying a novel. They read to engage in extended conversations about issues of importance to them, such as ecology, U.S. foreign policy, or contemporary music. In all of these ways, people read to experience new ways of thinking, being, and acting.

Reading and writing are in some respects parallel processes. The process of reading a complex written work for the first time—of grappling with it to determine where the writer is going and why—is similar to the process of writing a rough draft. When you reread an essay to examine the strategies used or the arguments made, you're "revising" your original reading, much as you revise a written draft. Because writing requires the physical activity of drafting, you may be more aware of the active role you play as writer than as reader. Reading is, however, an equally active process. Like writing, it is an act of *composing*, of constructing meaning through language and images.

Applying Rhetorical Sensitivity to Your Reading

Reading, like writing, is a *situated* activity. When you read, whether you're reading traditional print or multimedia texts, you draw not only on the printed words and images but also on your own experiences to make cultural, social, and rhetorical judgments. The purposes you bring to your reading, the processes you use to scrutinize a text, your understanding of the significance of what you read—these and other aspects of your reading grow out of the relationships among writer, reader, text, and medium. ✱

thinking
rhetorically

To review the discussion of the rhetorical situation, see Chapter 3.

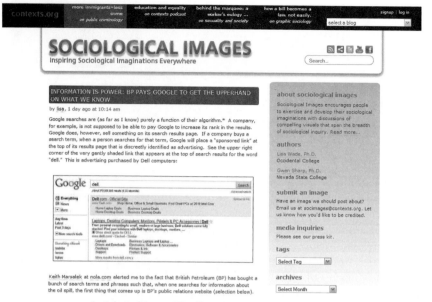

Sociological Images Blog (http://contexts.org/socimages)

An example might help to clarify this point. Imagine two people sitting in a café reading and drinking tea. One person is reading an accounting textbook for a course she's taking; the other is sitting with his laptop browsing blogs. Both individuals are reading texts—but they are undoubtedly reading them in quite different ways.

The accounting student has many reasons for believing her textbook is authoritative and therefore reads it slowly and with care. If asked what she's doing, she might say she's studying rather than reading. The person browsing blogs, on the other hand, knows that blogs, which can be put out by anyone with the time and inclination, range from well-written and thought-provoking reflections on contemporary issues to poorly written diatribes. Before diving in, then, he quickly skims various blogs to see if the topics are interesting and the writing worth reading. (He ends up spending a good deal of time on *Sociological Images*, a well-written blog that conducts in-depth explorations of culturally significant images.)

Recognizing the Importance of Genre

The differences between how these two people read reflect their purposes as well as their social and cultural understandings of the texts. These readers are also, however, influenced by the texts' *genre*—that is, by the kinds of text or the category to which they belong, such as textbook, blog, ezine, scholarly

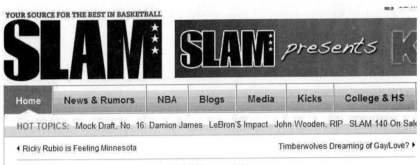

YOUR SOURCE FOR THE BEST IN BASKETBALL

SLAM | SLAM *presents* | K

| Home | News & Rumors | NBA | Blogs | Media | Kicks | College & HS |

HOT TOPICS: Mock Draft, No. 16: Damion James LeBron'$ Impact John Wooden, RIP SLAM 140 On Sale

◀ Ricky Rubio is Feeling Minnesota   Timberwolves Dreaming of Gay/Love? ▶

June 6, 2010 2:41 pm | 54 Comments

Kobe Bryant Doesn't Give a [Bleep] Where LeBron Goes

Admist accusations that LeBron James' media blitzkreig/upcoming free agent tour is upstaging the NBA Finals, Kobe Bryant was asked about the Chosen One's Choice and made his stance <u>quite clear</u>.

"You're asking me if LeBron is going to New York?" Bryant told The Post. "I'm trying to tell you in a polite way, I don't give a [bleep].

"As a fan, it's a big deal," Kobe added. "You're talking about LeBron and Dwyane Wade, it's two huge names changing cities. It alters things drastically in the NBA. But I really don't care about it."

Byron Scott, now an ESPN broadcaster, was standing with Bryant and cracked up.

"Why are people talking about LeBron anyway?" Scott said. "Let me tell you something. From me just knowing Kobe, he doesn't give a [bleep] what everyone is talking about anyway."

"I couldn't have said it better," Bryant piped in.

This is probably a testament to Bryant's focus on the task at hand, but rest assured, come July 1 Kobe Bryant will most definitely give a [bleep] about any threats to another Laker dynasty.

Screenshot from *Slam*

article or book chapter, short story, or newspaper article. When we recognize that a text belongs to a certain genre, we make assumptions about the form of the writing and about its purposes and subject matter.

For example, a businessperson reading a company's annual report understands that it is a serious document and that it must follow specific conventions, including those of standard written English. When the same person goes online to read *Slam*, a magazine for basketball insiders, he brings quite different expectations to his reading. *Slam* uses a good deal of specialized sports jargon, including some street and hip-hop language. The businessperson would obviously find this language inappropriate in business writing, but he not only accepts but enjoys its use in *Slam*.

As a student, and in your general reading, you will be a stronger, more effective reader if you are attentive to genre. The following are some common genres with selected examples:

Personal writing: letters, blogs, Facebook posts, personal essays

Academic writing: textbooks, scholarly articles and books, lab reports, essay exams, research papers

Popular writing: articles in mass-market magazines, reviews, fan publications

Civic writing: editorials, letters to the editor, advocacy Web sites

Professional writing: technical and scientific articles and books, job applications, business memos

Creative or literary writing: poetry, stories, novels

In thinking about genre, it's important to remember several important points. The first is that all genres have histories: They are not static forms but socially constructed responses to the specific needs of writers and readers. It is also important to note that while some genres, such as lab reports, have changed little over time, others are more fluid. Think, for instance, about the variety of blogs that exist today—everything from personal blogs read only by a limited number of the author's friends and family members to blogs such as *The Huffington Post* that circulate widely in ways similar to more traditional print media.

When we move through our daily lives, we intuitively understand many genre differences and respond appropriately as readers: For example, we read instructions for our new HD television differently from the ways in which we read a scholarly article for a class or the news feed on Facebook. As a college student, however, you need to develop a sophisticated response to an array of academic genres. A textbook written for students in an introduction to sociology course is very different from a scholarly article or book published in this same area.

Particularly as you take courses in various disciplines, you will find it helpful to ask yourself what the defining features are of the genre you are reading. The questions on p. 253 will help you.

||||||||||||||||||||||||||||||||||||||||||||||||||||||||||||||||||||||||||||||||||||||||

FOR EXPLORATION

Consider the different ways you read texts. Start by making a list of the different kinds of texts you read, such as textbooks, newspaper editorials, graphic novels, Facebook pages, and popular magazines. Then think about how your approach to these texts changes according to what they are and why you're reading them. For instance, do you read the introduction to a psychology text differently than you do your Facebook news feed or the sports page in your local newspaper? Freewrite for five minutes about the reading strategies you already use.

||||||||||||||||||||||||||||||||||||||||||||||||||||||||||||||||||||||||||||||||||||||||

Questions to Ask about Genres

1. What is the primary *purpose* of the text you are reading?

2. Who is the intended *audience* of the text?

| A general audience (for example, a newsstand magazine like *Time*) | A specialized audience (for example, a scholarly journal like *Adolescent Psychiatry*) | A student audience (for example, this textbook) |

3. Does the *genre* of the text fall into one of the categories below?*

| Writing in the humanities | Writing in the natural and applied sciences |

If so, what characteristics of this genre does the text exhibit?

| Writing in the social sciences | Business writing |

4. What level of *formality* does the text exhibit?

| Does the author use first person ("I"), as is characteristic of personal writing and some writing in the humanities? | or | Is the tone objective and impersonal? |

5. How are sources used and cited in the text?

Sources are neither formally cited nor explicitly mentioned (as, for example, in magazines like *People* or *Vogue*).

Sources are not formally cited, but sources are referred to and text appears to be fact-checked (as, for example, in some textbooks and some general interest magazines such as *The New Yorker*, *The Atlantic*, and *Harper's Magazine*).

Sources are formally cited (as, for example, in scholarly journals such as the *Publication of the Modern Language Association*).

*For descriptions of these broad generic categories, see Chapter 7, "Writing in the Disciplines."

NOTE FOR MULTILINGUAL WRITERS

If you have recently begun studying in the United States, it may be challenging to interpret texts that require extensive knowledge about American culture. You may also bring different rhetorical and cultural expectations to your reading than many of the other students in your classes. To better understand how you approach reading, reflect on how your background has influenced your expectations. It may be helpful to discuss these expectations with your teacher, your classmates, or a tutor in the writing center.

Becoming a Strong Reader

In their book *Ways of Reading,* David Bartholomae and Anthony Petrosky describe a kind of reading they call "strong reading":

> Reading involves a fair measure of push and shove. You make your mark on a book and it makes its mark on you. Reading is not simply a matter of hanging back and waiting for a piece, or its author, to tell you what the writing has to say. In fact, one of the difficult things about reading is that the pages before you will begin to speak only when the authors are silent and you begin to speak in their place, sometimes for them—doing their work, continuing their projects—and sometimes for yourself, following your own agenda.[1]

In other words, strong readers read not simply to gain information, but to engage in the process of inquiry. As they read, they engage in active dialogue with the author, posing questions and raising potential counterarguments.

If you're like many students, you may feel more confident reading for information than engaging in a strong reading of an essay, advertisement, poem, political treatise, engineering report, or Web site. Yet gaining the ability to make your mark on a verbal or visual text is one of the most important goals of a college education. In addition, strong reading leads to—and benefits—writing.

The guidelines on pp. 255–57 provide suggestions for practicing strong reading on a wide variety of print, online, and visual texts.

---

[1]David Bartholomae and Anthony Petrosky, *Ways of Reading,* 8th ed. (Boston: Bedford, 2008), 1.

Guidelines for Strong Reading

1. Be flexible.

Your purpose in reading should help you determine how to approach a text.

If you are researching an essay on urban homelessness, for instance, you might first skim a number of studies. Once you clearly defined your topic and purpose, you would begin reading in a more focused and critical manner.

2. Raise questions about the writer(s).

Who created this text?

What did this person (or persons) hope the text would accomplish?

To what extent does the text call attention to the role of its author, editor, designer, or Webmaster?

What social, historical, cultural, economic, or political factors might have influenced its composition?

How might those goals and factors have influenced the form, content, and look of the text?

3. Ask questions about the intended readers.

Are they a general audience? Specialists? Students?

What role does the text invite readers to adopt as they read (study, surf, scan, or otherwise engage with) this text?

Does the text assume considerable prior knowledge, or certain cultural or social understandings and preferences?

*Does it assume, for instance, that readers will expect images or other engaging design features?
...that readers will share certain values and beliefs?
...that readers will recognize a person whose photograph appears in an ad?*

continued

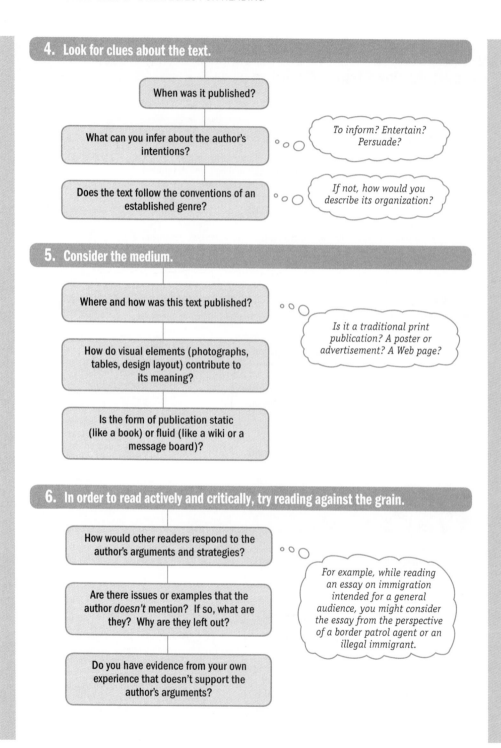

4. Look for clues about the text.

When was it published?

What can you infer about the author's intentions? — *To inform? Entertain? Persuade?*

Does the text follow the conventions of an established genre? — *If not, how would you describe its organization?*

5. Consider the medium.

Where and how was this text published? — *Is it a traditional print publication? A poster or advertisement? A Web page?*

How do visual elements (photographs, tables, design layout) contribute to its meaning?

Is the form of publication static (like a book) or fluid (like a wiki or a message board)?

6. In order to read actively and critically, try reading against the grain.

How would other readers respond to the author's arguments and strategies? — *For example, while reading an essay on immigration intended for a general audience, you might consider the essay from the perspective of a border patrol agent or an illegal immigrant.*

Are there issues or examples that the author *doesn't* mention? If so, what are they? Why are they left out?

Do you have evidence from your own experience that doesn't support the author's arguments?

7. Work through difficulties with a text.

Try identifying the reason(s) it seems difficult, and then turn these reasons into questions that you can use as you read.

Rather than becoming frustrated when a writer dwells on an issue that seems unimportant to you, for instance, ask yourself why scholars in this field might find the issue worthy of attention.

8. Interact with the text.

Pose questions.

Speculate about the implications of a line of argument.

Look for gaps in the presentation of evidence or ideas.

Use your personal experience to consider the issues raised by a text — and then imagine how someone different from you might approach these issues.

9. Be patient.

Read the text more than once, *especially* if it was rough going the first time around.

Just as the process of writing often requires rough drafts, so too can the process of reading require "rough readings." A text that on first reading seems difficult will often, on rereading, prove more engaging.

Developing Critical Reading Skills

The following discussion presents a number of strategies for critical reading and provides an opportunity for you to apply these strategies to a specific text, an article that appeared in the November 2009 issue of *The Atlantic*.

Previewing

When you preview a text, you survey it quickly to establish or clarify your purpose and context for reading, asking yourself questions such as those listed on p. 259. As you do so, recognize that print, online, and visual sources may call for different previewing strategies.

With print sources, for instance, it's easy to determine the author and publisher. To learn the author of a Web site, however, you need to know how to read Web addresses and drill through sites. Whereas such print texts as scholarly journals and books have generally undergone extensive review and editing to ensure their credibility, this may not be the case with online sources, which can appear and disappear with alarming frequency.

It may also be challenging to determine how accurate and trustworthy visually rich texts are. Many photographs, whether they appear online or in a national magazine, have been manipulated for effect (photographs in fashion magazines, for example, are routinely altered to hide cosmetic imperfections). In his blog for the *New York Times,* filmmaker and author Errol Morris presents a fascinating discussion of one (in)famous "fauxtograph" published on July 10, 2008, by many major newspapers, allegedly showing the firing of four Iranian missiles, at a time when tensions between the United States and Iran were at a historic high.[2] As this example shows, determining the accuracy, authority, and currency of online and visual resources can be of vital importance in the world beyond academia.

"Fauxtograph" Allegedly Showing the Firing of Four Iranian Missiles on July 10, 2008.
(The doctored photo is shown at right.)

---

[2]See Errol Morris, "Photography as a Weapon," August 11, 2008, http://opinionator.blogs.nytimes .com/2008/08/11/photography-as-a-weapon/.

Questions for Previewing a Text

1. Where and when was this text published?

If this text appears on the Web, how recently was it updated?

What do the place of publication and date suggest about the accuracy, authority, and currency of the text?

2. What, if anything, do you know about its author or creator?

3. What can you learn from the title?

4. How would you characterize the general design and presentation of words and images?

Cluttered or spare?

Colorful or subdued?

Calm or busy?

Carefully organized or (apparently) randomly presented?

Traditional, contemporary, or cutting edge?

5. What can you learn by skimming this text?

Is it divided into sections?

If so, how do they appear to be organized?

If the text is online, what embedded links does it provide?

How useful do these links seem to be?

What predictions about this text can you make on the basis of a quick survey? What questions can you formulate to guide your subsequent reading of the text?

6. What is your personal response to the text, based on this preview?

> ### NOTE FOR MULTILINGUAL WRITERS
>
> All readers benefit from previewing texts, but if you are a multilingual reader and writer, you will find previewing particularly helpful. It will give you valuable information that can help you read the text efficiently and effectively. As you preview a text, be sure to formulate questions about specialized terms or about the text's general approach.

| | | | | | | | | | | | | | | | | | | | | | | | | | | | | | | | | | | | | | | | | | | | | | | | | | | | | | | | | | | | | | | | | | | | | | | | | | | | | | | | | | |

FOR EXPLORATION

Using the Questions for Previewing a Text, preview "Filtering Reality," the article by Jamais Cascio reprinted on pp. 261–62.

| | | | | | | | | | | | | | | | | | | | | | | | | | | | | | | | | | | | | | | | | | | | | | | | | | | | | | | | | | | | | | | | | | | | | | | | | | | | | | | | | | |

Analyzing Visual Elements

When you read any kind of text, you need to be able to analyze its design and use of images and to understand the potentially powerful role that visual elements can play in written texts. Why? Perhaps the most important reason has to do with the increasingly pervasive role of images in modern life. Driving down the street, watching television, skimming a magazine—in these and other situations, we continually encounter images and texts—many of which are designed to persuade us to purchase, believe, or do certain things. Often these images can be a source of pleasure and entertainment. But given the persuasive intent of many images, critical readers will develop ways to not just "read" but "read into" them. The questions on pp. 111–12 can help you analyze visual texts. You might want to practice by answering the questions using the screenshot from *Slam* on p. 251, the article by Jamais Cascio reprinted on pp. 261–62, or another text your instructor assigns. ✳

> ✳ bedfordstmartins.com/rewriting
> *For more advice and practice in analyzing visuals, go to* **Re:Writing** *and then click on* **Visual Analysis**.

November 2009   Print | Close

Filtering Reality

HOW AN EMERGING TECHNOLOGY COULD THREATEN CIVILITY

By Jamais Cascio

IMAGE CREDIT: GLUEKIT

HERE'S A STARTLING vision for the next decade: two familiar online phenomena converge in an emerging technological arena to strike a fatal blow to American civil society.

The emerging technology, called "Augmented Reality," enables users to see location-specific data superimposed over their surroundings. Long a staple of science fiction, it's trickling into the real world through the iPhone and similar ultrasmart mobile phones. With AR applications such as Layar, the smart phone displays what its camera sees, with information about nearby buildings and shops, travel directions, even notes and "tags" left by other users in that location. Although AR now relies on handheld devices, electronics makers like Sony are working on systems that you wear like sunglasses, making augmented vision more immersive.

Here's where the first familiar online phenomenon shows up: spam. Nearly every communication method we invent eventually conveys unwanted commercial messages. AR systems will be used for spam too, whether via graffiti-like tags, ads that pop up when you look too long at a shop, or even abstract symbols stuck to a wall or worn on a shirt that, when viewed through an AR system, turn into 3-D animations.

Fortunately, just as Web browsers have pop-up blockers, AR systems will filter spam. Moreover, they'll likely be able to filter out *physical* ads, too, such as billboards—a capability that many opponents of visual clutter will find deliriously attractive.

This technology will have plenty of social uses, of course. Facial-recognition technology is improving, and would be a welcome addition to a personal AR system. Imagine never forgetting a face, and always being able to recognize a friend-of-a-friend on the street. And because the systems are linked to the Internet, once AR recognized someone, you could easily pull up his or her online footprint, such as a Facebook page.

This brings us to the second familiar online phenomenon: political polarization. On the Internet, the stark division between Red America and Blue America is reflected in the political information each side chooses to consume. The social-network analyst Valdis Krebs discovered that people who buy political books on Amazon.com cluster into divergent camps, with little overlap in the books they read. That dynamic also applies to political blogs and news sites.

Conceivably, users could set AR spam filters to block any kind of unpalatable visual information, from political campaign signs to book covers. Parents might want to block sexual or violent images from their kids' AR systems, and political activists and religious leaders might provide ideologically correct filters for their communities. The bad images get replaced by a red STOP, or perhaps by signs and pictures that reinforce the desired worldview.

Did I mention that the "wrong" people can get replaced too?

After California's Prop 8 ban on gay marriage passed, opponents of the measure dug up public records of donors supporting the ban, and linked that data to an online map. Suddenly, you could find out which of your neighbors (or the businesses you frequent) were so opposed to gay marriage that they donated to the cause. Now imagine that instead of a map, those records were combined with an AR system able to identify faces.

You don't want to see anybody who has donated to the Palin 2012 campaign? Gone, their faces covered up by black circles. You want to know who exactly gave money to the 2014 ban on SUVs? Easy—they now have green arrows pointing at their heads.

You want to block out any indication of viewpoints other than your own? Done.

This will not be a world conducive to political moderation, nor one where differing perspectives get along comfortably. It won't take a majority of people using these filters to poison public discourse; imagine this summer's town-hall screamers on constant alert, wherever they go. Yet this world will be the unintended consequence of otherwise desirable developments—spam filters, facial recognition, augmented reality—that many of us will find useful.

The knee-jerk answer would be to ban such reality filters, but a ban could be easily circumvented. The harder answer, but ultimately the correct one, would be to strengthen our society's ability to tolerate diverse viewpoints—to encourage not muddy centrism, but a basic ability to hear out, and to see, fellow citizens with a measure of respect.

Annotating

When you annotate a text, you highlight important words, passages, or images and write comments or questions that help you establish a dialogue with the text or remember important points. Some readers are heavy annotators, highlighting many passages and key words and filling the margins with comments and questions. Others annotate more selectively, preferring to write few comments and to highlight only the most important parts. In thinking about your own annotating strategies, remember that your purpose in reading should influence the way you annotate a text. You would annotate a text you're reading primarily for information differently than you would an essay you're reading for an assignment or a novel you're reading for a literature class.

Many readers annotate texts directly, either by writing on them or by "tagging" them electronically. If you're working with print and have borrowed the text or prefer not to mark up your own copy, you can use sticky notes, a separate piece of paper, a photocopy, or a computer file to copy or highlight important passages and to write questions and comments. (See p. 264 for an excerpt from student Stevon Roberts's annotated copy of Amitai Etzioni's essay "Less Privacy Is Good for Us (and You)," which appears on pp. 87–90. Roberts's essay responding to Etzioni's work can be read on pp. 101–6.)

How can you know the most effective way to annotate a text? The Questions for Annotating a Text on p. 265 can help you make appropriate choices as you read and respond to texts.

Congress passed the buck by asking the Institute of Medicine (IOM) to conduct a study of the matter. The IOM committee, dominated by politically correct people, just reported its recommendations. It suggested that all pregnant women be asked to consent to HIV testing as part of routine prenatal care. There is little wrong with such a recommendation other than it does not deal with many of the mothers who are drug addicts or otherwise live at society's margins. Many of these women do not show up for prenatal care, and they are particularly prone to HIV, according to a study published in the American Health Association's *Journal of School Health.* To save the lives of their children, they must be tested at delivery and treated even if this entails a violation of mothers' privacy.

Recently a suggestion to use driver's licenses to curb illegal immigration has sent the Coalition for Constitutional Liberties, a large group of libertarians, civil libertarians, and privacy advocates) into higher orbit than John Glenn ever traversed. The coalition wrote:

> This plan pushed us to the brink of tyranny, where citizens will not be allowed to travel, open bank accounts, obtain health care, get a job, or purchase firearms without first presenting the proper government papers.

The authorizing section of the law . . . is reminiscent of the totalitarian dictates by Politburo members in the former Soviet Union, not the Congress of the United States of America.

Meanwhile, Wells Fargo is introducing a new device that allows a person to cash checks at its ATM machines because the machines recognize faces. Rapidly coming is a whole new industry of so-called biometrics that uses natural features such as voice, hand design, and eye pattern to recognize a person with the same extremely high reliability provided by the new DNA tests.

It's true that as biometrics catches on, it will practically strip Americans of anonymity, an important part of privacy. In the near future, a person who acquired a poor reputation in one part of the country will find it much more difficult to move to another part, change his name, and gain a whole fresh start. Biometrics see right through such assumed identities. One may hope that future communities will become more tolerant of such people, especially if they openly acknowledge the mistakes of their past and truly seek to lead a more prosocial life. But they will no longer be able to hide their pasts.

Above all, while biometrics clearly undermines privacy, the social benefits it promises are very substantial. Specifically, each year at least half a million criminals become fugitives, avoiding trial, incarceration, or serving their full sentences, often committing additional crimes while on the lam. People who fraudulently file for multiple income tax refunds using fake identities and multiple Social Security numbers cost

handwritten annotations:

I wonder if these groups would put themselves into these categories

inflammatory & dismissive

maybe alarmist

what's the cost & who pays for it? Is it worth it?

not likely

This is a fantasy!

speculation — sounds like someone is trying to sell me on something... (oh right, they ARE !!)

Stevon Roberts's Annotations of "Less Privacy Is Good for Us (and You)"

Questions for Annotating a Text

1. What is your purpose in reading this text?

> *What do you need to annotate to accomplish this purpose?*

2. Where does the writer identify the text's purpose and thesis (or main idea)?

3. What are the main points, definitions, and examples?

> *Would it be useful to number the main points or make a scratch outline in the margin?*

4. What questions does this text suggest to you?

5. What key words play an important role in the discussion?

> *Does the text provide enough information so that you can understand these key words and appreciate their significance, or do you need further explanation?*

6. What passages seem particularly crucial?

> *What is your response to these passages?*

7. What role, if any, do images and graphics play?

> Are they primary or secondary in creating meaning?

> Do they reinforce, challenge, or in other ways complicate the written words?

8. Do your personal experience, values, or knowledge of the subject cause you to question the author's assertions, evidence, or method?

||||||||||||||||||||||||||||||||||||||||||||||||||||||||||||||||||||||||||||||||||||||||

FOR EXPLORATION

Annotate "Filtering Reality" by Jamais Cascio (pp. 261–62) as if you expected to write an essay responding to it for your composition class.

FOR COLLABORATION

Working in small groups, compare your annotations of the article. List all the various annotating strategies that group members used. To what extent did group members rely on similar strategies? What can individual differences tell you about your own strengths and limitations as an annotator?

||||||||||||||||||||||||||||||||||||||||||||||||||||||||||||||||||||||||||||||||||||||||

Summarizing

Never underestimate the usefulness of writing clear, concise summaries of texts. Writing a summary allows you to restate the major points of a book or an essay in your own words. Summarizing is a skill worth developing, for it requires you to master the material you're reading and make it your own. Summaries can vary in length, depending on the complexity and length of the text. Ideally, however, they should be as brief as possible, certainly no longer than a paragraph or two. The guidelines on pp. 267–68 offer suggestions for writing your own summaries.

||||||||||||||||||||||||||||||||||||||||||||||||||||||||||||||||||||||||||||||||||||||||

FOR EXPLORATION

Following the guidelines on pp. 267–68, write a one-paragraph summary of "Filtering Reality" (pp. 261–62).

||||||||||||||||||||||||||||||||||||||||||||||||||||||||||||||||||||||||||||||||||||||||

Analyzing Lines of Argument

Previewing, analyzing visuals, annotating, and summarizing can all help you determine the central points in a text. Sometimes the central argument is explicitly stated. In the final paragraph of "Filtering Reality," for instance, Jamais Cascio argues against banning such "reality filters" as "spam filters, facial recognition, augmented reality" and asserts instead that "The harder answer, but ultimately the correct one, would be to strengthen our society's ability to tolerate diverse viewpoints. . . ."

Not all authors are so direct. Someone writing about the role of feminism in contemporary North America may raise questions rather than provide answers or make strong assertions. Whether an author articulates a clear position on a subject or poses a question for consideration, critical readers

Guidelines for Summarizing a Text

1. Reread the material, trying to locate the main idea and the most important supporting points.

Start by skimming the text, focusing on the title, introduction, and conclusion.

Look for an explicit statement of the author's argument and purpose: If one exists, paraphrase it; if the main idea is implied but not stated, try to express it in a sentence or two of your own.

2. Highlight or number the major points the author uses to support the main idea.

To find these, look for topic sentences, call-outs (boldface or other design elements used for emphasis), and illustrations.

You might want to write those points down — in your own words — in a list or outline.

3. Identify how the major points relate to the main idea and to each other.

Before writing your summary, form a mental picture of how the author's argument is structured.

Examine the introduction and conclusion for clues, and consider how headings and lists signal the organization and relative importance of ideas.

continued

4. State the main idea and the major supporting points in your own words.

> Write your summary in paragraph form, as briefly and clearly as you can.

Stick to the main points and the most important ideas. Leave out examples and anecdotes, and don't try to mirror the author's organization.

5. Resist the urge to quote or paraphrase sentences or phrases from the original text.

It may help to put the original out of sight and work from memory and notes, referring back to the text for accuracy only after you have drafted the summary.

6. Be objective.

Your purpose is to distill the main idea and supporting points, not to record your reaction to the piece or to express your opinion of its merits.

attempt to determine if the author's analysis is valid—that is, if the author provides good reasons in support of a position or line of analysis.

The questions on pp. 270–71 provide an introduction to analyzing the argument of a text. For a fuller discussion of this and related issues, see Part II, "Writing in College."

NOTE FOR MULTILINGUAL WRITERS

The Questions for Analyzing a Text's Argument reflect one approach that you can use as you read. If your first experience of reading is grounded in a language and culture other than North American English, some of these questions may strike you as odd. In many cultures, for instance, writers do not announce the major claim or thesis of their text; doing so may seem overly obvious. As you read these questions, then, consider the extent to which they are culturally grounded. Remember, too, that everyone can learn from cultural differences, so think about the preferences in argumentation that you bring from your home (or parents') culture. You, your classmates, and your teacher will all benefit if you discuss these differences in class.

FOR EXPLORATION

Using the Questions for Analyzing a Text's Argument, analyze "Filtering Reality" (pp. 261–62). Be sure to answer all of the questions.

FOR COLLABORATION

By comparing your responses to this chapter's For Exploration questions with those of your peers, you can gain perspective on the effectiveness of your critical reading strategies. You can also better understand how different purposes and practices influence the reading of and responses to texts.

Bring your responses to the For Exploration questions in this chapter to class. Meeting with a group, compare your responses. After doing so, work together to describe briefly the extent to which your responses are similar or dissimilar. Then discuss what these similarities and differences have helped you understand about the process of critical reading, and try to come to two or three conclusions to share with your classmates.

Questions for Analyzing a Text's Argument

1. What is the major claim or thesis of this text?

Is it explicitly stated, or is it implicit, requiring you to read between the lines?

2. What interests or values may have caused the writer to develop this thesis?

Information about the writer from other sources, as well as clues from the writing itself, may help you determine this.

3. What values and beliefs about the subject do you bring to your reading of this text?

How might these values and beliefs affect your response to the writer's argument?

4. Does the writer define key terms?

If not, what role do these unstated definitions play in the argument?

5. What other assumptions does the writer rely on in setting up or working through the argument?

In texts on the Web, for instance, what choices and organizing principles do the links suggest?

6. What kinds of evidence does the writer present?

Is the evidence used logically and fairly?

Has the writer failed to consider any significant evidence, particularly evidence that might refute his or her claims?

7. What role, if any, do images and graphics play?

8. In what ways does the writer try to put the reader in a receptive frame of mind?

Does the writer attempt to persuade the reader through inappropriately manipulative emotional appeals?

9. How does the writer establish his or her credibility?*

What self-image does the writer create?

*For more on what makes a text credible, see Chapter 4, pp. 91–95, and Chapter 6, pp. 186–93.

| | | | | | | | | | | | | | | | | | | | | | | | | | | | | | | | | | | | | | | | | | | | | | | | | | | | | | | | | | | | | | | | | | | | | | | | | | | | | | | | | | | | | | | | | | | | | | | | |

FOR THOUGHT, DISCUSSION, AND WRITING

1. Analyze the first chapter of two textbooks you are reading this term (including this one, if you like). Do these textbooks share certain textual conventions? How do you think the writers of these textbooks have analyzed their rhetorical situation? These textbooks are written for you and other students. How effective are they in reaching you? How might they be more effective?

2. Pick a text that you have read recently (a traditional printed work, a visually rich text, or an electronic document of any length), and freewrite for five minutes about your experience of reading it. How did your rhetorical sensitivity affect the way you read it? To what extent did your expectations and previous experiences as a reader influence your interaction with the text? How would you approach it differently if you were to read it again?

3. Earlier in this chapter, you read "Filtering Reality" by Jamais Cascio (pp. 261–62). If you haven't already, use the questions and guidelines in this chapter to preview, annotate, summarize, and analyze Cascio's argument. Then answer the following questions.

   - As you skimmed this text, what were your expectations? To what extent did the form of the text and your knowledge of its original place of publication influence your expectations?

   - After reading the text more carefully, what was your response? To what extent did this response represent a deepening of or shift from your earlier expectations?

   - How did your own assumptions and values about current and developing digital and online technologies influence your reading?

   - How would you describe the author's stance or relationship with readers? What role does the text invite you to play as reader?

   - How did reading this text influence your own views about augmented reality?

   - What other observations about reading or about the subject of the potential challenges that new technologies pose for public discourse did this text stimulate in you?

4. Choose one or two of the critical reading skills discussed in this chapter that you haven't used in the past, and try them as you work on a current reading assignment. If you have time, discuss this experiment with some classmates. Then write a brief analysis of which skills work best for you and why.

| | | | | | | | | | | | | | | | | | | | | | | | | | | | | | | | | | | | | | | | | | | | | | | | | | | | | | | | | | | | | | | | | | | | | | | | | | | | | | | | | | | | | | | | | | | | | | | | |

Strategies for Invention

Like many writers, you may feel that finding ideas to write about is the most mysterious part of the writing process. Where do ideas come from? How can you draw a blank one minute and suddenly know the right way to support your argument or describe your experience the next? Is it possible to increase your ability to think and write creatively? Writers and speakers have been concerned with questions such as these for centuries. Ancient Greek and Roman rhetoricians, in fact, were among the first to investigate the process of discovering and exploring ideas. The classical Roman rhetoricians called this process *inventio*, for "invention" or "discovery." Contemporary writers, drawing on this Latin term, often refer to this process as *invention*.

In practice, invention usually involves both individual inquiry and dialogue with others. In working on a lab report, for example, you might spend most of your time writing alone, but the experiment you're writing about might have been undertaken by a group of students working together; you might look up some related research to be sure you understand the principles you're writing about; you might also ask other students or your instructor for advice in putting the report together. Every time you talk with others about ideas, or consult print or online materials for information, you're entering into a conversation with others about your topic, and, like all writers, you can benefit from their support and insights.

The strategies discussed in this chapter aim to help you invent successfully, whether you're having a conversation with yourself as you think through and write about ideas or working with classmates or friends. These methods can help you discover what you know—and don't know—about a subject. They also guide you as you plan, draft, and revise your writing.

Most writers find that some of the following methods work better for them than others. That's fine. Just be sure you give each method a fair chance before deciding which ones to rely on.

Discovering Ideas

Successful writers are pragmatists. Understanding that different writing tasks call for different approaches, they develop a repertoire of strategies to find ideas and explore those ideas in writing.

Read this section with a writer's eye. Which of these strategies do you already use? Which ones could you use more effectively? What other strategies might extend your range or strengthen your writing abilities? As you read about and experiment with these strategies, remember to assess their usefulness based on your own needs and preferences as a writer as well as on your particular writing situation.

> ### NOTE FOR MULTILINGUAL WRITERS
>
> When you practice the methods of invention, you're focusing on generating ideas — not on being perfectly correct. There's no need to interrupt the flow of your ideas by stopping to edit your grammar, spelling, vocabulary, or punctuation. Feel free, in fact, to invent in your first or home language — or even to mix languages — if it increases your fluency and helps you generate ideas.

Freewriting

Freewriting is the practice of writing as freely as possible without stopping. It's a simple but powerful strategy for exploring important issues and problems. Here is a description of freewriting by Peter Elbow, the professor who created this technique, as he describes it in his book *Writing with Power: Techniques for Mastering the Writing Process*:

> To do a freewriting exercise, simply force yourself to write without stopping for [a certain number] of minutes. . . . If you can't think of anything to write, write about how that feels or repeat over and over "I have nothing to write" or "Nonsense" or "No." If you get stuck in the middle of a sentence or thought, just repeat the last word or phrase till something comes along. The only point is to keep writing.[1]

Freewriting may at first seem *too* simple to achieve very powerful results, but in fact it can help you discover ideas that you couldn't reach through more

---

[1] Peter Elbow, *Writing with Power: Techniques for Mastering the Writing Process* (New York: Oxford University Press, 1981), 13.

conscious and logical means. Because it helps you generate a great deal of material, freewriting is also an excellent antidote for the anxiety many writers feel at the start of a project. It can also improve the speed and ease with which you write.

Freewriting is potentially powerful in a variety of writing situations. Writing quickly without censoring your thoughts can help you explore your personal experience, for example, by enabling you to gain access to images, events, and emotions that you've forgotten or suppressed. Freewriting can also help you experiment with more complex topics without having to assess the worthiness of individual ideas. The following shows how one student used five minutes of freewriting to explore and focus her ideas for a political science paper on low voter turnout:

> I just don't get it. As soon as I could register I did—it felt like a really important day. I'd watched my mother vote and my sisters vote and now it was my turn. But why do I vote; guess I should ask myself that question—and why don't other people? Do I feel that my vote makes a difference? There have been some close elections but not all that many, so my vote doesn't literally count, doesn't decide if we pay a new tax or elect a new senator. Part of it's the feeling I get. When I go to vote I know the people at the polling booth; they're my neighbors. I often know the people who are running for office in local elections, and for state and national elections—well, I just feel that I should. But the statistics on voter turnout tell me I'm unusual. I want to go beyond statistics. I want to understand *why* people don't vote. Seems like I need to look not only at research in political science, but also maybe in sociology. (Check journals in economics too?) I wonder if it'd be okay for me to interview some students, maybe some staff and faculty, about voting—better check. But wait a minute; this is a small college in a small town, like the town I'm from. I wonder if people in cities would feel differently—they might. Maybe what I need to look at in my paper is rural/small town versus urban voting patterns.

This student's freewriting not only helped her explore her ideas but also identified a possible question to address and sources she could draw on as she worked on her project.

Looping

Looping, an extended or directed form of freewriting, alternates freewriting with analysis and reflection. Begin looping by first establishing a subject for your freewriting, and then freewriting for five or ten minutes. This is your first loop. After completing this loop, reread what you have written and look for the center of gravity or "heart" of your ideas—the image, detail, issue, or problem that seems richest or most intriguing, compelling, or productive. Select or write a sentence that summarizes this understanding; this sentence will become the starting point of your second loop. The student who wrote about low voter turnout, for example, might decide to use looping to reflect on this sentence: "I want to understand *why* people don't vote."

There is no predetermined number of loops that will work: Keep looping as many times as you like, or until you feel you've exhausted a subject.

When you loop, you don't know where your freewriting and reflection will take you; you don't worry about the final product. Your final essay might not even discuss the ideas generated by your efforts. That's fine; the goal in freewriting and looping is not to produce a draft of an essay but to discover and explore ideas, images, and sometimes even words, phrases, and sentences that you can use in your writing.

|||||||||||||||||||||||||||||||||||||||||||||||||||||||||||||||||||||||||||||||||||||||||

FOR EXPLORATION

Choose a question, idea, or subject that interests you, and freewrite for five or ten minutes. Then stop and reread your freewriting. What comments most interest or surprise you? Write a statement that best expresses this center of gravity, or "heart," of your freewriting. Use this comment to begin a second loop by freewriting for five minutes more.

After completing the second freewriting, stop and reread both passages. What did you learn from your freewriting? Does your freewriting suggest possible ideas for an essay? Finally, reflect on the process itself. Did you find the experience of looping helpful? Would you use freewriting and looping in the future as a means of generating ideas and exploring your experiences?

|||||||||||||||||||||||||||||||||||||||||||||||||||||||||||||||||||||||||||||||||||||||||

Brainstorming

Like freewriting and looping, brainstorming is a simple but productive invention strategy. When you brainstorm, you list as quickly as possible all the thoughts about a subject that occur to you without censoring or stopping to reflect on them. Brainstorming can help you discover and explore a number of ideas in a short time. Not all of them will be worth using in a piece of writing, of course. The premise of brainstorming is that the more ideas you can generate, the better your chances will be of coming up with good ones.

Alex Osborn, the person generally credited with naming this technique, originally envisioned brainstorming as a group, not an individual, activity. Osborn believed that the enthusiasm generated by the group helped spark ideas. Group brainstorming can be used for a variety of purposes. If your class has just been assigned a broad topic, for instance, your group could brainstorm a list of ways to approach or limit this topic. Or the group could use email, an online discussion board, a wiki, or a blog to generate possible arguments in support of or in opposition to a specific thesis. (See the guidelines below for group brainstorming.)

There are also online resources available for brainstorming that you may find useful. Some software, including Thinkature and Bubbl.us, allows you to brainstorm and diagram relationships between ideas.

Those who regularly write with teams or groups cite increased intellectual stimulation and improved quality of ideas as major benefits of brainstorming together, but solitary brainstorming can be just as productive. To brainstorm alone, take a few moments at the start to formulate your goal, purpose, or problem. Then list your ideas as quickly as you can. Include everything that comes to mind, from facts to images, memories, fragments of conversations, and other general impressions and responses. (You are the only one who needs to be able to decipher what you've written, so your brainstorming can be as messy or as organized as you like.) Then review your brainstorming to identify the most promising or helpful ideas.

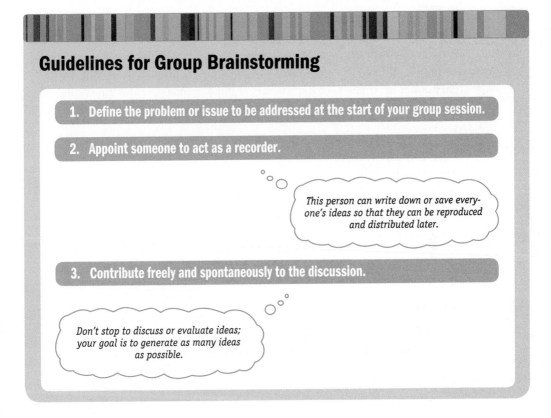

Guidelines for Group Brainstorming

1. Define the problem or issue to be addressed at the start of your group session.

2. Appoint someone to act as a recorder.

This person can write down or save everyone's ideas so that they can be reproduced and distributed later.

3. Contribute freely and spontaneously to the discussion.

Don't stop to discuss or evaluate ideas; your goal is to generate as many ideas as possible.

After freewriting about low voter turnout, for example, the student whose writing you read on p. 275 decided to brainstorm a possible list of reasons why people might not vote. Here is part of her list:

Some people (young people?) mistrust politicians

Alienated from the political process

Many political issues are highly polarized — abortion, research using stem cells, war, drugs, death penalty, health care, etc.

People in the middle may feel left out of the discussion

Don't know enough about the issues — or the candidates — to decide

"My vote won't make a difference"

Her brainstorming also raised several important questions:

What role does voter registration play?

Is the problem getting people to register — or getting registered voters to vote?

What's the connection between voting and other forms of community and civic engagement?

This student will need to explore her ideas further via both analysis and research, but her brainstormed list has raised important issues and questions for her to consider.

|||||||||||||||||||||||||||||||||||||||||||||||||||||||||||||||||||||||||||||||||||||||

FOR EXPLORATION
Reread the freewriting you did earlier, and then choose one issue or question you'd like to explore further. Write a single sentence summarizing this issue or question, and then brainstorm for five to ten minutes. After brainstorming, return to your list. Put an asterisk (*) beside those ideas or images that didn't appear in your earlier freewriting. How do these new ideas or images add to your understanding of your subject?

|||||||||||||||||||||||||||||||||||||||||||||||||||||||||||||||||||||||||||||||||||||||

Clustering

Like freewriting, looping, and brainstorming, clustering emphasizes spontaneity. The goal of all four strategies is to generate as many ideas as possible, but clustering differs in that it uses visual means to generate ideas. Some writers find that it enables them to explore their ideas more deeply and creatively.

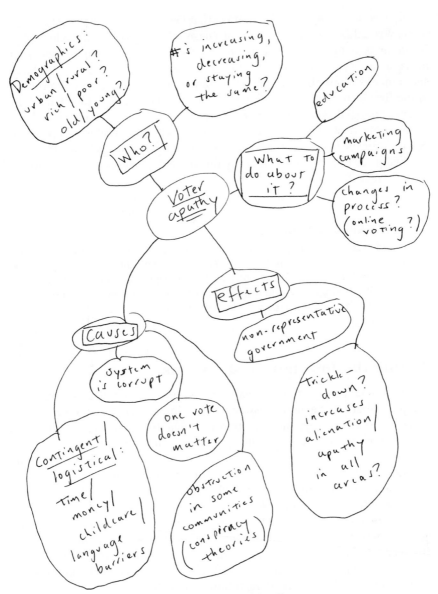

"Voter Apathy" Brainstorming Cluster

Start with a single word or phrase that best summarizes or evokes your topic. Write this word in the center of a page of blank paper and circle it. Now fill in the page by adding ideas connected with this word. Don't censor your ideas or force your cluster to assume a certain shape—your goal is to be as spontaneous as possible. Simply circle your key ideas and connect them either to the first word or to other related ideas. After clustering, put the material you've generated aside for a bit and then return to it so that you can evaluate it more objectively. When you do return to it, try to find the cluster's center of gravity—the idea or image that seems richest and most compelling. ✳

See p. 279 for a cluster done by the student whose writing appears on pp. 275 and 278.

|||||||||||||||||||||||||||||||||||||||||||||||||||||||||||||||||||||||||||||||||||||||||

FOR EXPLORATION

Reread the freewriting, looping, and brainstorming you have written thus far. Then choose one word that seems especially important for your subject, and use it as the center of a cluster. Without planning or worrying about what shape it's taking, fill in your cluster by branching out from this central word. Then take a moment to reflect on what you have learned.

|||||||||||||||||||||||||||||||||||||||||||||||||||||||||||||||||||||||||||||||||||||||||

Asking the Journalist's Questions

If you have taken a journalism class or written for a newspaper, you know that journalists are taught to answer six questions in articles they write: *who, what, when, where, why,* and *how.* By answering these questions, journalists can be sure that they have provided the most important information about an event, an issue, or a problem for their readers. And because they probe several aspects of a topic, the journalist's questions can help you discover not just what you know about it, but also what you *don't* know—and thus alert you to the need for additional research.

You may find these questions particularly useful when describing an event or writing an informative essay. Suppose that your political science instructor has assigned an essay on the political conflict in Darfur, Sudan. Using the journalist's questions as headings, you could begin working on this assignment by asking yourself the following questions:

■ *Who* is involved in this conflict?

■ *What* issues most clearly divide those engaged in this dispute?

■ *When* did the conflict begin, and how has it developed over the last few years?

✳ For another example of a cluster, see p. 140.

- *Where* does the conflict seem most heated or violent?

- *Why* have those living in this area found it so difficult to resolve the situation?

- *How* might this conflict be resolved?

Although you might discover much the same information by simply brainstorming, using the journalist's questions ensures that you have covered all the major points.

|||||||||||||||||||||||||||||||||||||||||||||||||||||||||||||||||||||||||||||||||||

FOR EXPLORATION

Using the journalist's questions, explore the subject that you have investigated in preceding Explorations in this chapter. (If you feel that you have exhausted this subject, feel free to choose a different topic.)

Once you have employed this method, take a few moments to reflect on this experience. To what extent did the strategy help you organize and review what you already know, and to what extent did it define what you still need to find out?

|||||||||||||||||||||||||||||||||||||||||||||||||||||||||||||||||||||||||||||||||||

Exploring Ideas

The previous invention strategies have a number of advantages. They're easy to use, and they can help you generate a reassuringly large volume of material when you're just beginning to work on an essay. Sometimes, however, you may want to use more systematic methods to explore a topic. This is especially true when you've identified a potential topic but aren't sure that you have enough to say about it.

Asking the Topical Questions

One of the most helpful methods for developing ideas is based on the topics of classical rhetoric. In his *Rhetoric*, Aristotle describes the topics as potential lines of argument, or places (*topos* means "place" in Greek) where speakers and writers can find evidence or arguments. Aristotle defined twenty-eight topics, but the list is generally abbreviated to five: *definition, comparison, relationship, circumstance,* and *testimony.*

The classical topics represent natural ways of thinking about ideas. When confronted by an intellectual problem, we all instinctively ask such questions as these:

- What is it? (*definition*)

- What is it like or unlike? (*comparison*)

- What caused it? (*relationship*)

- What is possible or impossible? (*circumstance*)

- What have others said about it? (*testimony*)

Aristotle's topics build on these natural mental habits. The topical questions can help you pinpoint alternative approaches to a subject or probe one subject systematically, organizing what you know already and identifying gaps that require additional reading or research. Simply pose each question in turn about your subject, writing down as many responses as possible. You might also try answering the expanded list of questions for exploring a topic on pp. 283–84.

|||||||||||||||||||||||||||||||||||||||||||||||||||||||||||||||||||||||||||||||||||||||

FOR EXPLORATION

Use the topical questions on pp. 283–84 to continue your investigation of the subject that you explored with the journalist's questions in the Exploration on pp. 280–81. What new information or ideas do the topical questions generate? How would you compare these methods?

|||||||||||||||||||||||||||||||||||||||||||||||||||||||||||||||||||||||||||||||||||||||

Researching

You're probably already aware that many writing projects are based on research. The formal research paper, however, is not the only kind of writing that can benefit from looking at how others have approached a topic. Whatever kind of writing you're doing, a quick survey of published materials can give you a sense of the issues surrounding a topic, fill gaps in your knowledge, and spark new ideas and questions.

Chapter 6 covers the formal research process in detail. At the invention stage, however, loose, informal research is generally more effective. If you're interested in writing about skydiving, for example, you could pick up a copy of *Skydiving* magazine or spend a half hour or so browsing Web sites devoted to the sport to get a better feel for current trends and issues.

To cite another example, imagine that you're writing about the Americans with Disabilities Act (ADA) for a political science assignment. After freewriting and asking yourself the journalist's questions, you find yourself wondering if the fact that President Franklin Delano Roosevelt was afflicted with polio had any influence on accessibility legislation. You type "FDR" and "disability" into a search engine, and, browsing the first few hits, you

Questions for Exploring a Topic

QUESTIONS ABOUT PHYSICAL OBJECTS

1. What are the physical characteristics of the object (shape, dimensions, materials, and so on)?

2. What sort of structure does it have?

3. What other object is it similar to?

4. How does it differ from things that resemble it?

5. Who or what produced it?

6. Who uses it? For what?

QUESTIONS ABOUT EVENTS

1. Exactly what happened? (who? what? when? where? why? how?)

2. What were its causes?

3. What were its consequences?

4. How was the event like or unlike similar events?

5. To what other events was it connected?

6. How might the event have been changed or avoided?

Note: These questions are based on those first proposed by Edward P. J. Corbett, *The Little Rhetoric and Handbook* (Glenview, IL: Scott, Foresman, 1982).

continued

QUESTIONS ABOUT ABSTRACT CONCEPTS (E.G., DEMOCRACY, JUSTICE)

1. How has the term been defined by others?

2. How do you define the term?

3. What other concepts have been associated with it?

4. What counterarguments must be confronted and refuted?

5. What are the practical consequences of the proposition?

QUESTIONS ABOUT PROPOSITIONS (STATEMENTS TO BE PROVED OR DISPROVED)

1. What must be established before the reader will believe it?

2. What are the meanings of key words in the proposition?

3. By what kind of evidence or argument can the proposition be proved or disproved?

4. What counterarguments must be confronted and refuted?

5. What are the practical consequences of the proposition?

learn that while FDR is now considered an inspiration for Americans with disabilities, he spent years trying to keep his wheelchair hidden from public view. Realizing that you're very interested in this shift in attitude, you decide to focus on the question of how the ADA has influenced public perceptions of disability. A few keystrokes have given you a valuable idea.

NOTE FOR MULTILINGUAL WRITERS

If you write in languages other than English, you may have learned ways of discovering and exploring ideas that are different from those discussed in this chapter. How are they different? If you have been educated in another culture, do the invention methods used in that culture reflect different rhetorical and cultural values? If there are significant differences, how have you dealt with them?

✴ bedfordstmartins.com/rewriting

For more advice and resources for beginning informal research, go to **Re:Writing** *and then click on* **The Bedford Research Room.**

Writing a Discovery Draft

Sometimes the best way to develop and explore ideas is to write a very rough draft and see, in effect, what you think about your topic. This strategy, which is sometimes called *discovery drafting*, can work well as long as you recognize that your draft will need extensive analysis and revision.

Writing a discovery draft is a lot like freewriting, although the process tends to be more focused and usually takes more time. As you write, stick to your topic as best you can, but expect that your thoughts may veer off in unexpected directions. The goal is not to produce a polished—or even a coherent—essay, but to put your ideas into written form so that you can evaluate them. Once you have completed a discovery draft, you can use it to identify and fine-tune your most promising ideas, to clarify your goals, and to determine what remains to be done. In order to do so, you will need to put your draft aside for a bit so you can look at it objectively. ✴

Troubleshooting

Troubleshooting is a simple but often productive means of identifying and resolving writing problems. It involves formally discussing work in progress with peers who respond with questions and advice—either in person or online. You will probably find group troubleshooting most productive in the early stages of writing, when you're still working out your ideas and determining your approach to your subject. For a list of guidelines for troubleshooting, see pp. 286–87.

For an example of one student's discovery draft, see p. 141. ✴ • • • • • • • • • •

Guidelines for Troubleshooting

1. Decide how much time to spend on each person's writing.

Appoint a timekeeper to enforce these limits.

If you're working online, establish a time frame for group members to respond to queries.

2. Begin by having the writer describe the issue or problem that he or she would like to discuss.

The writer should also identify questions for group response.

These questions may be general ("Do you have any suggestions about how I might develop my thesis?") or specific ("I like these four ideas, but I don't think they fit together very well. What could I do?").

3. Let the writer facilitate the resulting discussion.

If the writer needs a moment to write an idea down, he or she should ask the group to pause briefly.

The writer should also feel free to ask group members to clarify or elaborate on suggestions.

4. Respond to each writer's request for assistance as carefully and fully as possible.

Group members are helping you with your writing; you owe it to them to help with theirs.

5. Practice good "netiquette" if your group is chatting online or compiling ideas on a discussion board.

Use subject lines to help list members identify the purpose and content of your messages.

Keep your comments brief enough that they can be read on-screen easily.

Remember that electronic messages may circulate in unexpected ways; don't write anything in anger or make an attempt at humor that could cause you embarrassment later on.

FOR COLLABORATION

Meet with a group of classmates to discuss the methods of discovering and developing ideas. Begin by having group members briefly describe the advantages and disadvantages they experienced with these methods. (Appoint a recorder to summarize each person's statements.) Then, as a group, discuss your responses to these questions: (1) How might different students' preferences for one or more of these strategies be connected to different learning, composing, and cultural preferences? (2) What influence might situational factors (such as the nature of the assignment, or the amount of time available for working on an essay) have on the decision to use one or more of these strategies? Be prepared to discuss your conclusions with your classmates.

FOR THOUGHT, DISCUSSION, AND WRITING

1. Early in this chapter, you used freewriting, looping, brainstorming, clustering, and the journalist's questions to investigate a subject of interest to you. Continue your exploration of this topic by conducting some informal research and drawing on the topical questions. ✱ Then use the material you have gathered to write a discovery draft on your subject.

2. Observe a group of your classmates as they brainstorm (either in person or online), and make notes about what you see. It may be helpful to record how often each member of the group participates in the discussion, for example. Pay attention, too, to group dynamics. Is the group working effectively? Why or why not? What could group members do to interact more effectively? Summarize the results of your observations

See pp. 283–84. ✱

in a report addressed to the group. Be sure to suggest several ways that the group could work more effectively in the future.

3. Choose one of the strategies discussed in this chapter that you have not used in the past, and try it as you work on your current writing assignment. If you have time, discuss this experiment with some classmates. Then write a brief analysis of why this strategy did or did not work well.

|||||||||||||||||||||||||||||||||||||||||||||||||||||||||||||||||||||||||||||||||||||||||||

CHAPTER 10

Strategies for Planning and Drafting

Although it can be intensely rewarding, writing is not easy for anyone. Even professional writers struggle, but they are willing to work through moments of frustration to achieve the insights that make writing worthwhile. Writing is a complex, dynamic process that challenges you to draw on all your resources and to be open to change as your thoughts—and your drafts—take unpredictable twists and turns.

The processes of thinking and writing are too variable and too dependent on context to be reduced to rules or formulas. As Chapter 2 points out, different people have different composing styles, and many factors can affect the processes of planning and drafting, from the time available to the complexity of the writing task. ✳ No matter what your situation, however, the keys to successful writing are preparation and flexibility. There are also specific strategies you can learn that will make the challenge of composing a draft more manageable. You'll learn about those strategies in this chapter.

Understanding the Process of Planning

It may be helpful to think of planning as involving waves of play and work. When you're discovering and exploring ideas, for example, you're in a sense playing—pushing your ideas as far as you can without worrying about how useful they'll be later. Most people can't write an essay based on a brainstorming list or thirty minutes of freewriting, however. At some point, they need to settle down to work and formulate a plan for the project.

The planning activities described in this section generally require more discipline than the play of invention. Because much of the crafting of your essay occurs as a result of these activities, however, this work can be intensely rewarding.

For more on composing styles, see pp. 25–33. ✳

Establishing a Working Thesis

You can't establish a workable plan for your essay without having a tentative sense of the goals you hope to achieve by writing. These goals may change along the way, but they represent an important starting point for guiding your work in progress. Before you start to draft, then, try to establish a *working thesis* for your essay.

A working thesis reflects an essay's topic but also the point you wish to make and the effect you wish to have on your readers. An effective working thesis narrows your topic, helps you organize your ideas, enables you to determine what you want to say and *can* say, helps you decide if you have enough information to support your assertions, and points to the most effective way to present your ideas.

A few examples may help clarify this concept. Suppose that you're writing an editorial for your campus newspaper. "What are you going to write about?" a friend asks. "The library," you reply. You've just stated your topic, but this statement doesn't satisfy your friend. "What about the library? What's your point?" "Oh," you say, "I'm going to argue that students should petition library services to make more computers available to students. The current number can mean long waits at peak hours, and this is not only inconvenient, it's unfair to students who can't afford a personal computer." This second statement, which specifies both the point you want to make and its desired effect on readers, is a clearly defined working thesis. Further, because the newspaper editorial is an established genre with specific writing conventions, you know before you start that your argument will need to be brief, explicit, and backed up with concrete details.

You can best understand and establish a working thesis by analyzing the elements of your rhetorical situation: writer, reader, text, and medium. This process (which is described in detail in Chapter 3) should give you a clearer understanding of both your reasons for writing and also the most appropriate means to communicate your ideas. In some cases, you may be able to analyze your rhetorical situation and establish a working thesis early in the writing process by asking yourself the questions on p. 291. In many other instances, however, you'll have to think and write your way into understanding what you want to say.

A working thesis will help you structure your plan and guide your draft, but you should view it as preliminary, subject to revision. After you've worked on an essay for a while, your working thesis may evolve to reflect the understanding you gain through further planning and drafting. You may even discover that your working thesis isn't feasible. In either case, the time you spend thinking about your preliminary working thesis isn't wasted, for it enables you to begin the process of organizing and testing your ideas.

thinking rhetorically

Questions for Establishing a Working Thesis

1. **What main point do you want to make in this essay?**

   How does this main point relate to your purpose—to what you want your essay to do for readers?

2. **Who is the audience for this essay? Your teacher? A hypothetical or real nonacademic audience?**

   How might your audience's expectations influence your essay's form and content?

3. **If you are writing an academic essay, what disciplinary conventions do you need to consider in establishing a working thesis?**

4. **How can you structure your essay to communicate your ideas most effectively to readers?**

5. **What kinds of examples and details will best support your main point?**

6. **What kind of evidence will your readers find most persuasive?**

7. **How realistic are your intentions, given your rhetorical situation, the assignment, and your time and length limitations?**

8. **How will you accomplish your goals? Do you need to**

   - do additional reading or research?
   - talk with others?
   - spend more time discovering and exploring ideas?
   - write a discovery draft to see what you really think?

Formulating a Workable Plan

Once you have established a working thesis, you should be able to develop a plan that can guide you as you work. As the discussion of differing composing styles in Chapter 2 indicates, people plan in different ways. Some develop detailed written plans; others rely on mental plans; others might freewrite and determine their goals by reflecting on their own written text.

As a college student, you will often find written plans helpful. Some writers develop carefully structured, detailed outlines. Others find that quick notes and diagrams are equally effective. Developing a plan—whether a jotted list of notes or a formal outline—is an efficient way to try out ideas and engage your unconscious mind in the writing process. In fact, many students find that by articulating their goals on paper or on-screen, they can more effectively critique their own ideas—an important but often difficult part of the writing process.

There is no such thing as an ideal one-size-fits-all plan. An effective plan is one that works for you. Plans are utilitarian, meant to be used—and revised. In working on an essay, you may draw up a general plan only to revise it as you write. Nevertheless, if it helps you begin drafting, your first plan will fulfill its function well.

Consider, for example, one student's actual plan. Lisa DeArmand, a first-year student majoring in business, was writing an informal essay reviewing three popular pizza parlors near campus. She had already decided that the

	BOBBIE'S PIZZA	PIZZA-IN-A-HURRY	PIZZA ROMA
Cost for large pie (one topping)	$12.50	$13.50	$15.00
Positives	close to campus cheapest	coupons decent number of toppings	best pizza! two kinds of crust unusual toppings spicy and mild sauces
Negatives	limited hours delivery charge pizza OK but not great	crust thin and soggy tastes like frozen pizza	most expensive

Lisa DeArmand's Plan ✳

✳   For Daniel Stiepleman's plan for his essay on a public service announcement, see p. 143.

most effective way to approach her essay would be to compare the three restaurants, and she had detailed notes, including interviews with students, parts of which she planned to incorporate in her essay. Because Lisa had such a clear mental image of what she wanted to say and how she wanted to say it, she didn't need a highly detailed written plan—instead, she drafted a simple table.

NOTE FOR MULTILINGUAL WRITERS

You may find it helpful to consider how your knowledge of multiple languages or dialects affects the way you formulate plans. Is it easier and more productive to formulate plans in your first or home language and then translate these plans into English? Or is it more helpful to formulate plans in English because doing so encourages you to keep North American rules and expectations in mind? You may want to experiment with both approaches so that you can determine the planning process that works best for you.

FOR EXPLORATION

If you have ever created a plan for an essay or a school project, what kinds of plans have you typically drawn up? Do you formulate detailed, carefully structured plans, or do you prefer less structured ones? Do you use diagrams or other visuals? Or do you just start writing? Use these questions to think about the plans you have (or have not) used in the past; then spend ten minutes writing about how you might develop more useful plans in the future.

Developing Effective Strategies for Drafting

The British writer E. M. Forster once asked, "How can I know what I think until I see what I say?" You can see what he means if you take the writing process seriously: By working through drafts of your work, you gradually learn what you think about your subject. Although your process may begin with freewriting or brainstorming, drafting is the point in the process when you explore your ideas more fully and deeply, and it is through drafting that you create a text that embodies your preliminary goals.

Managing the Drafting Process

When you sit down to begin writing, it can be hard to imagine the satisfaction of completing a rough draft. Just picking up pen or pencil or turning on your computer can seem daunting. Once you pass the initial hurdle of getting started, you'll probably experience the drafting process as a series of ebbs and flows. You may write intensely for a short period, stop and review what you've written, make a few notes about how to proceed, and then draft again more slowly, pausing now and then to reread what you've written. It's important to keep your eye on the prize, though: Very few writers, if in fact any at all, can produce anything worth reading without going through this messy, sometimes painful, process.

While no two people approach drafting the same way—indeed, even a single person will take different approaches at different times—the strategies discussed in this section can help make your process more efficient and productive.

OVERCOMING RESISTANCE TO GETTING STARTED.   All writers experience some resistance to drafting; however, there are ways to overcome this resistance. Many writers rely on rituals to get started, such as clearing the writing space of clutter, gathering notes and other materials in a handy place, or queuing up a favorite song or playlist. Personal predispositions affect writing habits as well. Some people write best early in the morning; others, late at night. Some require a quiet atmosphere; others find the absence of noise distracting. Some find it easier to draft if they're doing something else at the same time; others shut down email and Facebook so they can focus. The trick is to figure out what works best for you.

Reading through early notes and plans is an effective way to begin a drafting session. It can be reassuring to remind yourself that you're not starting from scratch, and you may find yourself turning hasty notes and fragments into full sentences or grouping them into paragraphs—that is, drafting before you know it.

Perhaps the best motivation is to remind yourself that a draft doesn't have to be perfect. Your initial goal should simply be to *get something down* in writing. If you can't think of a way to open your essay, for instance, don't force yourself; just begin writing whatever you're ready to write and return to the introduction later.

BUILDING MOMENTUM.   While it might seem easier said than done, it's important to keep at it—to keep producing something, *anything*—so that the momentum can help you move steadily toward your goal. Accept that your draft will be imperfect, even incomplete, and just focus on putting your thoughts into words. By giving yourself permission to create a messy draft, you free yourself to explore ideas and discover what you want to say.

Guidelines for Overcoming Writer's Block

1. **Lower your standards. (If you can't find the right words, get them down in any form you can.)**

   Write enough to remind yourself of the point you want to make; then move on, and return to that section later.

2. **Change strategies. If you're stuck for ideas, take a break from drafting.**

   Revise your written plan.

   Spend ten minutes freewriting, brainstorming, diagramming, or clustering instead.

3. **Switch to a writing task that you can do.**

   If you can't determine how to make a particular point or explain an idea, turn to a different part of your essay.

   Review and annotate some background material.

   Switch to another project you need to complete.

4. **Talk out your ideas.**

   Find a friend or family member to talk with, and begin by saying, "I'm blocked. What I'm trying to say is . . ."

5. **Take a break.**

   Take a few minutes to describe in writing the difficulty you're experiencing; then put your writing aside and do something else—exercising, cooking, whatever.

Don't try to correct or polish your writing in the drafting stage: Stopping to check spelling or grammar can interrupt your momentum and throw you off balance. Furthermore, it's easier to delete unnecessary or repetitive material when you revise than it is to add new material. If you can't quite articulate an argument or formulate an example, write yourself a note and keep drafting. When you return to your draft, you can fill in these gaps.

Like most writers, you'll probably experience moments of writer's block when the words won't come. When this happens, try the block-busting strategies suggested on p. 295 to get back on track.

Finally, be aware that most word-processing programs offer a number of features that can make writing easier and more productive. If you're drafting quickly and wish to maintain your momentum but also remember a question or an idea, for example, you can insert comments as you write and return to them in a later drafting session. The guidelines on p. 297 offer tips on additional useful features. (Always be careful, of course, not to let your computer's capabilities distract you from the task of drafting itself.)

KEEPING IN TOUCH WITH YOUR "FELT SENSE." You attend to many things when you draft. You stop and reread; you reflect about your topic and assignment; you think about your readers. If you're an effective writer, you also look at what you've written not just to see what's on the page but also what *might* be there—that is, you take stock periodically and evaluate how what you've written so far measures up to the meaning you want to get across. Professor Sondra Perl calls this sort of awareness *felt sense*. This felt sense, Perl argues, encourages us to become aware "of what is just on the edge of our thinking but not yet articulated in words."[1]

The ability to develop and maintain felt sense doesn't require magical gifts. Rather, you need to draft for long enough periods so that you can become immersed in your writing. Additionally, as you write words, sentences, and paragraphs, you need to pause periodically to reflect on the extent to which your draft responds to readers' needs and expectations; it's also a good idea to jot down notes on these reflections.

ALLOWING TIME FOR INCUBATION. Ideally, you'll come to a natural stopping point, a moment when you feel that you've solved a problem you've been wrestling with or concluded a section you've been working on. At this point, take a few moments to jot down notes about what you've accomplished as well as about what you still need to do. You may also wish to ask yourself a few questions: "What's the best transition here?" "Which examples should I use next?" If you're like many writers, your subconscious mind will present appropriate answers when you next sit down to draft.

---

[1]Sondra Perl, *Felt Sense: Writing with the Body* (Portsmouth, NH: Boynton/Cook, 2004), xii.

Guidelines for Drafting on a Computer

1. *Use the* WINDOW *or* SPLIT BAR *function* to work on multiple documents (or multiple versions of a single document) at the same time.

> *You might, for example, place a freewrite, an outline, or a plan in one window and write your draft in the other, or you might keep your introduction in view as you write later sections.*

2. *Use* CUT *and* PASTE *functions* to move items from one file to another or to move sections of text within a draft.

3. *Use* TRACK CHANGES, COMMENT, *and* MARKUP *functions* to write notes or compare versions of a draft. ✳

> *These features allow you to interact with your own and others' writing without cluttering drafts with comments that need to be deleted later.*

4. *Use the* SAVE AS *function* to experiment without losing critical material.

> *Give each new attempt at a draft a different name or number, so all earlier versions will still be there if you change your mind.*

5. *Protect your work* by using the SAVE function frequently, making backup copies of your drafts, and printing hard copies.

For an example of markups made to this text while in manuscript stage, see p. 298. ✳ • • • • • • • • • •

How to share your purpose most effectively depends on a number of factors. If you're working on a take-home essay exam for a history class or an analytical essay for a mass media class, for example, you may wish to include in your introduction a *thesis statement,* usually a single sentence that states the main point of your essay.⌀ Your introduction may also preview the main lines of argument you'll use to support your position.

Much academic writing benefits from the inclusion of a thesis statement, but it is **not always** necessary or even desirable to include an explicit statement of your main point. If you're writing a personal essay **for your first-year writing class** about what the word *family* means to you, for example, you might decide that you don't want to articulate the main point of your essay in a single sentence. Instead, you might begin with an example that will create interest in your essay and show, rather than tell, what *family* means to you.

Comment [LE20]: I'm thinking that "usually" takes care of the "(though sometimes two or more)."

Deleted:

Deleted: (though sometimes two or more)

Deleted: Most readers expect to find a thesis statement in an academic essay, but in other kinds of writing

Deleted: situations

Deleted: , it may not be

Manuscript for p. 299 Showing Comments and Deletions

Sometimes it helps to *stop* thinking consciously about your ideas and just let them develop in your mind while you relax, sleep, or occupy yourself with other projects. After this period of incubation, you'll often spontaneously recognize how to resolve a problem or answer a question. (Don't confuse incubation with procrastination, however. *Procrastination* means avoiding the writing process; *incubation* means recognizing and using the fluctuations of the process to your advantage.)

|||||||||||||||||||||||||||||||||||||||||||||||||||||||||||||||||||||||||||||||||||||||||||||

FOR EXPLORATION

How do you typically draft an essay? How long do your drafting sessions usually last? What do you do when you run into problems? Could one or more of the suggestions presented here enable you to draft more productively? How might you best implement these suggestions? Spend five or ten minutes freewriting in response to these questions.

|||||||||||||||||||||||||||||||||||||||||||||||||||||||||||||||||||||||||||||||||||||||||||||

Developing and Organizing Your Ideas

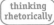

As you draft, you'll become more aware of what you have to say about a subject. Consequently, you'll also become increasingly engaged with issues of organization and structure. "What do I think about this subject?" becomes less important than "How can I best present my ideas to my readers?" This

section suggests strategies for responding to the second question. Keep in mind that these strategies are only suggestions; your use of them should be based on your understanding of your assignment, purpose, and rhetorical situation.

Using a Thesis Statement

North American readers quickly become irritated if writers violate their expectations about how certain kinds of writing should be organized. In general, readers expect writing that is straightforward and to the point. For this reason, sharing your working thesis with readers and providing cues about how you will achieve it are essential.

How to share your working thesis most effectively depends on a number of factors. If you're working on a take-home essay exam for a history class or an analytical essay for a mass media class, for example, you may wish to include in your introduction a *thesis statement*, usually a single sentence that states the main point of your essay. ✳ Your introduction may also preview the main lines of argument you'll use to support your position.

Much academic writing benefits from the inclusion of a thesis statement, but it is not always necessary or even desirable to include an explicit statement of your main point. If you're writing a personal essay for your first-year writing class about what the word *family* means to you, for example, you might decide that you don't want to articulate the main point of your essay in a single sentence. Instead, you might begin with an example that will create interest in your essay and show, rather than tell, what *family* means to you.

Whether or not you include a thesis statement, what's important is that you have a clear working thesis and that readers can figure it out easily. As you work on your draft, having a working thesis in mind—even if it's not expressed directly—will help you organize your thoughts; it will also help ensure that readers will stay with you.

> ✳ bedfordstmartins.com/rewriting
>
> *For more help developing a thesis statement for an academic project, go to* **Re:Writing** *and then click on* **The Bedford Research Room**.

Developing Ideas

It's a good idea to begin each new drafting session by reviewing the material you've already generated, looking for ideas and details to add or develop more fully. Often in rereading these explorations and early drafts, writers realize that they've relied on words that have meaning for themselves but not necessarily for their readers. Learning to recognize and expand or "unpack"

thinking rhetorically

For more on thesis statements, see Chapter 5, pp. 123–26. ✳

such words in your own writing can help you develop your ideas so that their significance is clear to readers.

Here is a paragraph from one student's freewriting about what the word *family* meant to her. While rereading her writing, she recognized a number of general and abstract words, which she underlined.

> When I think of the good things about my family, Christmas comes most quickly to mind. Our house was filled with such <u>warmth</u> and <u>joy</u>. Mom was busy, but she was <u>happy</u>. Dad seemed less absorbed in his work. In the weeks before Christmas he almost never worked late at the office, and he often arrived with brightly wrapped presents that he would tantalizingly show us—before whisking them off to their hiding place. And at night we did <u>fun</u> things together to prepare for the big day.

Words like *warmth* and *joy* undoubtedly have many strong connotations for the writer; most readers, however, would find these terms vague. This writer realized that in drafting she would have to provide plenty of concrete, specific details to enable readers to visualize what she means.

NOTE FOR MULTILINGUAL WRITERS

You may find it helpful to organize—and perhaps even develop—some of your thoughts in your first or home language.

Following Textual Conventions

When you draft, you don't have to come up with an organizational structure from scratch. Instead, you can draw on conventional methods of organization, methods that reflect common ways of analyzing and explaining information. Your subject may naturally lend itself to one or more methods of organization.

Suppose, for example, that you're writing an essay about political and economic changes in Eastern Europe in the 1990s. Perhaps in your reading you were struck by the different responses of Russian and Czech citizens to economic privatization. You might draw on conventional methods of *comparing and contrasting* to organize such an analysis. Or perhaps you wish to discuss the impact that severe industrial pollution in Russia could have on the development of a Western-style economy. After *classifying* the most prevalent forms of industrial pollution, you might discuss the consequences of this pollution for Russia's economy. In some cases, you may be able to use a single method of organization—such as *comparison*, *definition*, *cause and ef-*

fect, or *problem-solution* — to organize your entire essay. More often, however, you'll draw on several methods to present your ideas.

In considering how best to draw on conventional methods of organizing information, remember that you shouldn't impose them formulaically. Begin thinking about how to organize your writing by reflecting on your goals as a writer and on your rhetorical situation. If your analysis suggests that one or more methods of organizing information represent commonsensical, logical ways of approaching your subject, use them in drafting. But remember, the organization or structure you choose should complement your ideas, not be imposed on them.

thinking rhetorically

FOR THOUGHT, DISCUSSION, AND WRITING

1. Choose a writing assignment that you have just begun. After reflecting on your ideas, develop and write a workable plan. While drafting, keep a record of your activities. How helpful was your plan? Was it realistic? Did you revise your plan as you wrote? What can you learn about your writing process from this experience? Be prepared to discuss this experience with your class.

2. Interview someone who works in the field that you hope to enter after graduation, and ask the following questions about how he or she plans and drafts on-the-job writing.

    ■ What kinds of plans do you typically construct?

    ■ In what ways have new technologies influenced your planning and drafting strategies?

    ■ Do you experience writer's block? If the answer is yes, what block-busting strategies work best for you?

    ■ How do your profession and work schedule influence your planning and drafting?

    ■ How often do you write alone? As a member of a group or team?

    ■ What advice about writing would you give to a student who hopes to enter this field?

    Write an essay summarizing the results of your interview.

3. Think of a time when you simply couldn't get started writing. What did you do to move beyond this block? How well did your efforts work — and why? After reflecting on your experience, write an essay (humorous or serious) about how you cope with writer's block.

Strategies for Designing Pages and Screens

Until relatively recently, few academic writers concerned themselves with the visual look of a text. Although advertising copy, magazines and newspapers, and business and technical texts have long been influenced by design concerns, just twenty years ago most college writers produced simply formatted pages of straight prose, either in longhand or at the typewriter. Students were typically required to use specific margins, headings, blue or black ink, and appropriate paper, and to follow other basic formatting rules. But these were the only visual elements that students needed to be concerned about.

Today's digital technologies allow writers to make many more decisions about texts than they did in the past. Someone who wants to share her passion for black Labrador retrievers, for instance, could create a Web site, PowerPoint-based lecture, or a video about this popular breed. Each medium would require her to be as concerned with the visual as with the verbal, for in all of these media the verbal and visual are interdependent.

Even when writing more traditional text-based papers, writers have a staggering array of options, including the use of color, fonts, design templates, and software that allows them to create and incorporate drawings, photographs, charts, and graphs. With access to the Web, writers can also easily (if not always legally) download or create texts, images, and audio or video clips and integrate them into their writing. It is increasingly common for college students to develop texts that take full advantage of these options for document design.

In fact, document design is fundamental to creating readable, clearly organized, and engaging texts. Your goal for your academic projects should be an appropriate final design, one that creates a consistent overall impression and that is best suited to the kind of document you are creating.

This chapter will help you answer basic questions about designing effective texts, online and in print. (Note that your instructor may specify a particular document design or format. If you're unsure about instructors' preferences, don't hesitate to ask.)

Looking at Design and the Rhetorical Situation

Questions about document design are, in fact, *rhetorical* questions—questions, that is, that depend on your particular rhetorical situation, involving you as a writer, your audience, the ideas you want to convey, and the medium you use to deliver these ideas. * For any writing project, you should analyze your situation to make informed decisions about document design and other visual elements of communication.

thinking rhetorically

|||||||||||||||||||||||||||||||||||||||||||||||||||||||||||||||||||||||||||||||||||||||

FOR EXPLORATION

How attuned are you to the visual elements in texts you read in print and online? Take a few moments to think about the many different texts that you read—textbooks, magazines, newspapers, advertisements, Web sites, blog posts, Facebook, email, instant messages, just to name a few. Next, freewrite in response to these questions:

■ How much do design elements and images influence your response to and understanding of a text? Can you think of examples from a text you've read recently?

■ How does a magazine or Web site intended for twenty-somethings differentiate itself visually from one intended for a different readership? Try to provide examples, if possible from two texts that are similar in purpose but clearly intended for different audiences.

■ Do you have strong preferences about such visual features as type font, color, and images? If so, what are they?

|||||||||||||||||||||||||||||||||||||||||||||||||||||||||||||||||||||||||||||||||||||||

NOTE FOR MULTILINGUAL WRITERS

Most cultures have their own preferences about written texts, visual texts, and visual design principles. If you are an international student or come from a North American community that uses a language other than English, you may have noticed that newspapers in your home country or home community look considerably different from English-language North American newspapers. These differences reflect cultural preferences about visual design.

Take a few moments to consider these differences. How might such design preferences influence your decisions as a writer of academic texts? Which elements of your home community's or culture's visual design preferences might enrich your academic writing, and vice versa?

For more on rhetorical situation, see Chapter 3. *

thinking
rhetorically

Imagine two students who are working on different projects: One student is writing a twenty-page paper for an art history class on the nineteenth-century British artists called the Pre-Raphaelites; the other is writing a four-page analysis for an English class of a poem by the contemporary American poet Mary Oliver. Both have access to online content and images (such as reproductions of paintings by various Pre-Raphaelites or photographs of Mary Oliver). But should they use these images? If so, how?

A rhetorical response to these questions would consider the students' particular situations. Though they're writing different kinds of essays, both are writing *academic* essays, so any visual elements they use should reflect the seriousness and formality that characterize academic writing. Because ideas are central in academic writing, any image, chart, or other visual element should be essential to the intellectual richness and impact of the writing.

As you have perhaps already realized, both students do need to consider some visual elements. Because the paper about the Pre-Raphaelites is long, headings will help orient readers to critical divisions within the paper. Even more important, however, is the role that reproductions of art by the Pre-Raphaelites could play in this student's analysis. Such reproductions would enable readers to understand and evaluate the student's analysis of various paintings without having to refer to other sources. The student might also include photographs of the Pre-Raphaelites themselves if he's sure that the photos will enrich his analysis—for example, if he's discussing the historical, cultural, or social role of this movement in nineteenth-century England.

The student writing an analysis of one of Oliver's poems would need to attend to visual elements such as the use of white space, fonts, page numbers, and headings, which are important for any academic essay. But unless some aspect of the analysis specifically requires visual support, this student probably wouldn't include photographs or other visuals. They would add little to the development of her ideas and might even distract readers.

As these examples suggest, a rhetorical approach to document design encourages you to ask questions about your reader, your text, your medium, and yourself. (See the guidelines on pp. 305–6.)

* bedfordstmartins.com/rewriting
  For a tutorial on designing effective Web texts, go to **Re:Writing** *and then click on* **Tutorial Nation**.

Understanding the Basic Principles of Design

Once you know the basic principles of document design, you can create accessible, inviting texts that share information, lead readers smoothly through your presentation, and achieve your purpose. Whether you're creating a print text or a digital or online text, certain fundamental design principles are essential: these include *alignment*, *proximity*, *repetition*, and *contrast*.

Guidelines for Thinking Rhetorically about Document Design

1. Consider your topic, your time constraints, and your readers' needs and expectations.

> Add tables, graphs, and illustrations if they help you explain your ideas *and* if you have sufficient time to find and/or develop them.

> *For example, if you're writing an honors thesis on new techniques for groundwater purification, tables presenting data and illustrations explaining technicalities would likely be helpful. You should also have time and opportunity to talk about design and format requirements with your committee members.*

> Don't insert visuals arbitrarily when your topic doesn't require visual explanation, and don't struggle to find them for projects for which you have limited time.

> *For example, for a take-home midterm for a political science class, your instructor will expect you to focus on explaining your ideas, not hunting for images related to your topic.*

2. Reflect on your own goals and strengths as a writer, your role in this project, and your experience with design.

> How much authority do you have in this particular situation?

> How knowledgeable are you about the textual conventions that inform the kind of writing you're undertaking?

> How much do you know about various writing technologies that might visually enhance your text? (How much time do you have to take advantage of this knowledge?)

continued

3. Gather information about textual conventions.

Memos, for example, are formatted in certain ways, and they often include headings. ✳

In many of the sciences, tables and figures are common; other conventions include headings in lab reports and grant proposals.

In traditionally text-based disciplines such as English and philosophy, tables are rarely used, and figures — photographs, graphs, and other images — are used infrequently.

If you're unsure about the conventions for a particular discipline, take a conservative approach — or ask your instructor.

4. Consider the requirements and limitations of your medium.

If the assignment doesn't specify a medium, consider whether the one you've chosen will appeal to readers and effectively convey your intended meaning.

If the medium is assigned — text-based letter, research essay, Web site, PowerPoint slideshow, or poster, for example — pay careful attention to any requirements about size or format.

If the medium is online, consider the following:

- Will your text require updates?
- Will you need to request permission to publish online any sources or visuals you've used?
- Do you have access to — and skills for working with — the appropriate software?
- Do you need access to a high-speed Internet connection, color printer, scanner, or other hardware?

Alignment

This principle relates to the way words or visuals on a page or screen are lined up vertically and horizontally. Horizontally, the options are to present text as flush left, flush right, justified, or centered. (The text you're reading right

✳ For a sample memo, see p. 246.

now is horizontally justified—that is, the spacing between words and letters is adjusted so that each full line of text begins and ends precisely at the margins set for the page.) Vertically, text can be aligned with the top or bottom of the page, centered, or justified. (This text is vertically top-aligned, though in page layout, considerable effort is expended on filling out every page as fully as possible.) Your goal in designing your text should be to maintain a clear, consistent alignment so that readers can follow it without becoming distracted. You should be aware that lack of alignment is a very common Web design problem, so be sure that you don't mix alignments within a design.

Proximity

A page or screen makes effective use of the design principle of proximity when the relationships between text elements (such as headings, subheadings, captions, and items in a list) and visual elements (such as illustrations, charts, and tables) are clear. Your goal should be to position related points, chunks of text, and visual elements together so that your reader's understanding of your meaning is unimpeded.

An easy way to evaluate your text's use of proximity is to squint your eyes and see how the page or screen looks. Does your eye move logically from one part to another? If not, you'll want to work on the internal relationships.

Repetition

This principle is important for creating a sense of coherence: A consistent design gives a unified look and helps guide readers through the text.

Repetition can involve elements that are visual, verbal, or both. For example, you'll want to be consistent in the design of typefaces you choose, the placement and use of color, and the positioning of graphic elements, such as a navigational banner on a homepage. One example of repetition in a text-based document is the practice of indenting paragraphs: The seemingly subtle half-inch actually signals the start of a new topic or subtopic and helps your reader keep track of your argument.

Contrast

A page or screen effectively employs contrast when the design attracts the reader's eye and draws him or her in. Contrast helps organize and orient the reader's interactions with a text, guiding the reader around the elements on a page and making the information accessible. Even the simplest, text-based documents employ contrast in the interplay between white space and text. Margins, double-spacing, and unused space around headings or graphics, for instance, frame the text and guide the reader through it. (Take a look at the white space on this page, and try to imagine how the page would look without it, and how difficult it would be to read word after word presented uninterrupted and extending to the borders of the page on all sides.)

Focal points play an important role in establishing contrast. A focal point—a point that the eye travels to first and that the mind uses to organize the other elements in the composition—may be an image, a logo, or a dominant set of words. When you design a page or a screen, you should organize the elements so that the flow of information starts with this point. White space can also create effective contrast.

Formatting and Layout

There are so many formatting and layout elements to consider when designing a document that it's sometimes hard to choose the best elements for a particular layout. There is no one right answer for all situations; what works well in one situation isn't necessarily appropriate in another. The following advice will help you make appropriate decisions, but remember that your assignment or the genre you're working in may have specific requirements.

Color

Color can add visual appeal and impact, so it can play an important role in document design. In brochures, Web pages, newsletters, and similar documents, using color is not only acceptable but expected. In academic papers, however, most instructors still require that texts be printed only in black ink. If you do plan to use color, see the Guidelines for Using Color Effectively on pp. 309–10.

Fonts and Typefaces

With computers, writers have a dazzling—but potentially bewildering—array of fonts to choose from, and they can display them in any size. How can you make the best use of them? For academic assignments, a standard, easy-to-read font such as Times New Roman in an 11- or 12-point type size is best:

This is 11-point Times New Roman.

This is 12-point Times New Roman.

But what if you're composing a brochure, newsletter, or Web site? In keeping with the conventions of these genres, you may want to use a variety of typefaces.

First, you should consider whether to use a *serif* or *sans serif* typeface for particular elements. Serif fonts add small, decorative embellishments to the basic form of the characters.

Guidelines for Using Color Effectively

1. Establish a plan.

| How many colors will you use? | Do you need to consider the costs of printing documents with color? | What role do you want color to play in your overall design? |

2. Use color to emphasize key elements of your text — and do so consistently.

If you're using color to emphasize subheads, for instance, use the same color for all of them.

3. Use color for only the most important elements.

4. Use two — or at most three — colors.

This is definitely a case of more being less: a few colors will direct readers' attention to key features; too many colors will overwhelm or confuse them.

5. Choose colors that will be legible and clear in your final product.

Be aware that colors can look different in different browsers, on different monitors, and on the printed page. If you're submitting a project in print, test a print page.

6. Choose color combinations that offer strong contrast.

For most projects, use dark type on a light background. (Light type on a dark background is generally more difficult to read, except on slides to be shown in a darkened room.) Also, remember: Not all colors are equally legible when printed out.

continued

7. **Be aware that certain colors may be hard for some readers to see comfortably.**

Ask for feedback from representative readers.

8. **If you are writing an academic essay, remember that color should only be used if it enriches the content and readability of your essay.**

Check with your instructor if you are uncertain about the requirements of your assignment.

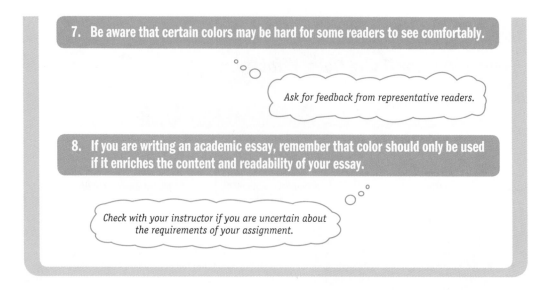

E (serif)   E (sans serif)

Many readers find serif typefaces (such as Times New Roman or Filosofia, which is used for the main text of this book) easier to read for printed texts and sans serif ones (such as Arial, Helvetica, or Verdana) easier to read online and for headings. In some situations, you may want to consider using an unusual font such as **Impact** or Century Gothic to create a particular tone. Remember, though, that script, handwriting, or decorative typefaces call attention to themselves and should be used sparingly.

Even in the types of writing that call for the use of multiple fonts, you'll probably want to limit yourself to two or at most three fonts in a single document. If you shift fonts and sizes too often within a document, you'll distract readers from focusing on your text.

Spacing

Margins and the spacing of elements on a page are important for determining whether your text looks dense or readable. White space—in the margins, between paragraphs and sentences, and around visual or textual elements such as figures and lists—helps draw the reader's eye to the appropriate text or visual elements. For most academic writing, your text should be double-spaced, with one-inch margins and paragraphs indented one-half inch.

Some genres, including résumés, letters, and online texts, should be single-spaced, with no paragraph indents (use an extra line of space between paragraphs instead). When writing in still other genres, including brochures and flyers, you may want to choose different margins, use columns, or include additional white space around visual elements to draw attention to them and balance the visuals with the text.

As with other design decisions, the choices you make for spacing will likely be limited by your instructor, your supervisor, or the discipline in which you're writing, so always check the requirements of your assignment or course. See the examples in Chapter 7 for models of the formatting required by different disciplines.

Pagination

Academic assignments usually require you to follow the formatting and pagination rules of a particular style (MLA, APA, *Chicago*, CSE, and others), depending on the discipline. (For sample papers that show MLA formatting, see pp. 150–53 and 205–15. For a sample APA-style paper, see pp. 381–402.) Cover pages or first pages need clear identifying information—usually including the title of your paper, your name, the date, your instructor's name, and the course title. Since subsequent pages can become disconnected, they should also have identifying information—usually either a shortened version of the title or your last name, along with a page number.

For online texts, the information that would appear on a printed page's header should appear in a navigation bar that unifies the electronic pages and makes it easy for users to locate parts of the text. Additional information that you can attach to each part of an online text includes your name, the date of publication, and links to the text's homepage.

If you haven't received specific information about how to handle the page number and other pagination information for your document, or if you aren't sure, check with your instructor.

✱ bedfordstmartins.com/rewriting
For more help creating effective layouts using your word processor, go to **Re:Writing** *and then click on* **Tutorial Nation**.

Choosing Effective Headings

Headings provide structure to a text and help readers find the information they need. For some academic writing, there are required headings (*Works Cited* or *Abstract*, for example) and guidelines for their typeface and positioning. For texts where you have flexibility in choosing headings, you should consider *wording*, *type size* and *style*, and *positioning*.

Wording

Make headings concise yet informative. They can be single nouns (*Literacy*), a noun phrase (*Literacy in Families*), a gerund phrase (*Testing for Literacy*), or a question or statement (*How Can Literacy Be Measured?*). Make all headings at the same level consistent throughout your text—for example, by using all single nouns or all gerund phrases. Avoid using headings that simply state the name of the section of text (such as *Conclusion*).

Type Size and Style

For academic writing in MLA or APA style, headings need to be set in the same font as the rest of the text. For documents where you have some choice, you can distinguish headings by using color, bold or italics, and type size and style. Using only type, you might distinguish among levels using capitals, bold, and italics, as here:

FIRST-LEVEL HEADING
Second-Level Heading
Third-Level Heading

Positioning

Place headings consistently throughout your text. For MLA style, headings should be aligned left. For APA papers, the first two levels of headings must be centered. For texts where you can choose the placement, centered headings are common for the first level; for secondary-level headings, you may indent, set flush left, or run them in to the text (that is, you can start the section's text on the same line as the heading).

Using Visuals Effectively

Visuals can add to a text's persuasiveness. They're best used when a text truly *needs* them—that is, when they can present information more succinctly and clearly than words alone. ✱ Visuals fall into two broad categories: *tables* and *figures*. Tables summarize data, usually in clearly labeled horizontal rows and vertical columns. Figures include all other visuals: pie charts, line and bar graphs, drawings, diagrams, maps, photographs, and other illustrations. Whether you're using tables or figures, rhetorical common sense can help you make a number of important decisions. (See the guidelines on pp. 313–14.)

✱ See also "Using Visuals to Strengthen Your Argument," pp. 133–37.

Guidelines for Using Visuals Effectively

1. **Use visuals only when they play a key role in communicating your ideas.**

   Never use visuals merely as decoration, particularly in academic writing.

2. **In print texts, refer to the visual before it appears and explain its significance in the body of your text.**

   For example, a student who is writing about the Vietnam War might introduce an important table by noting, "As Table 1 demonstrates, many more Vietnamese than American soldiers lost their lives during this war."

3. **Be sure to number and title all visuals.**

   - Number and label tables and figures (photographs or other visuals) separately.
   - Give a caption to visuals to relate their significance to your text.
   - Label the parts of graphs and charts clearly.

4. **Document all visual sources.**

   This includes data used in graphs.

5. **Edit visuals ethically.**

   Cropping or otherwise altering a visual might mislead your readers. Be clear in your text about how you have altered an image, and be sure that the edited image is an accurate representation of the subject.

continued

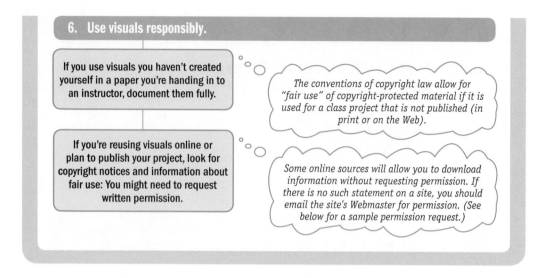

6. Use visuals responsibly.

If you use visuals you haven't created yourself in a paper you're handing in to an instructor, document them fully.

The conventions of copyright law allow for "fair use" of copyright-protected material if it is used for a class project that is not published (in print or on the Web).

If you're reusing visuals online or plan to publish your project, look for copyright notices and information about fair use: You might need to request written permission.

Some online sources will allow you to download information without requesting permission. If there is no such statement on a site, you should email the site's Webmaster for permission. (See below for a sample permission request.)

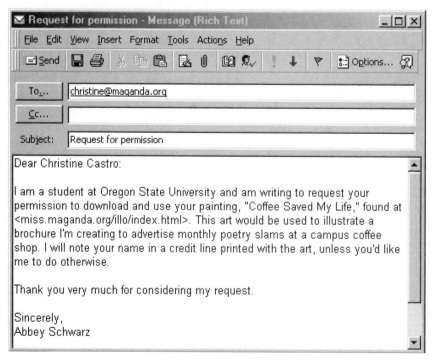

Dear Christine Castro:

I am a student at Oregon State University and am writing to request your permission to download and use your painting, "Coffee Saved My Life," found at <miss.maganda.org/illo/index.html>. This art would be used to illustrate a brochure I'm creating to advertise monthly poetry slams at a campus coffee shop. I will note your name in a credit line printed with the art, unless you'd like me to do otherwise.

Thank you very much for considering my request.

Sincerely,
Abbey Schwarz

Permission Request Email

Remember that different situations call for different visuals. Use visuals that are appropriate to your situation and purpose.

Type of Visual		Purpose
Table		To convey detailed numerical information; to allow readers to make comparisons
Pie Chart		To display how a whole is divided; to show relationships among parts
Bar Graph or Line Graph		To call attention to relationships among data; to show change over time
Diagram or Drawing		To call attention to details; to show processes
Map	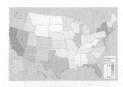	To call attention to locations and spatial relationships
Photograph		To show people, objects, or an event; to convey an emotion or support an argument

* bedfordstmartins.com/rewriting

For more help creating effective visuals, go to **Re:Writing** *and then click on* **Tutorial Nation**.

|||||||||||||||||||||||||||||||||||||||||||||||||||||||||||||||||||||||||||||||||||||||||

FOR EXPLORATION

Review Alletta Brenner's research essay in Chapter 6 on human trafficking in the garment-manufacturing industry (pp. 205–15). As you reread this essay, pay particular attention to its visuals (two photographs). How do these visual elements contribute to her essay's effectiveness? How does Alletta follow the conventions of copyright law in acknowledging the sources of these visuals?

|||||||||||||||||||||||||||||||||||||||||||||||||||||||||||||||||||||||||||||||||||||||||

Making Effective Decisions about Design: Sample Documents

One way to learn how to make effective decisions about document design is to study the decision-making process that others have followed. Collected on pp. 316–20 are sample documents that make effective design moves, annotated with some tips to help you create your own documents.

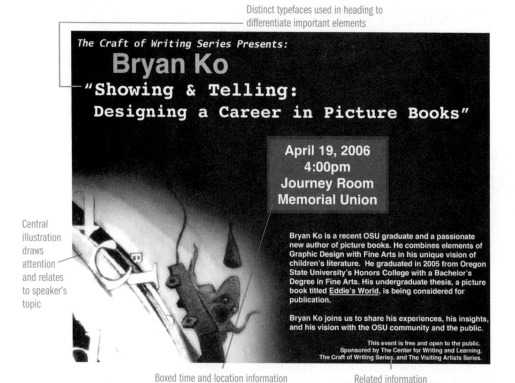

Distinct typefaces used in heading to differentiate important elements

Central illustration draws attention and relates to speaker's topic

Boxed time and location information set off prominently

Related information grouped together

Flyer

Tall, narrow
bifold design

Title in clear,
prominent type

**Questions to ask your local beach
health monitoring official:**

- Which beaches do you monitor and how often?

- What do you test for?

- Where can I see the test results and who can
explain them to me?

- What are the primary sources of pollution that
affect this beach?

Clear, bold
headings

**What to do if your beach is not
monitored regularly:**

- Avoid swimming after a heavy rain.

- Look for storm drains along the beach. Don't
swim near them.

- If the waters of your beach have been designated
as a no-discharge zone for vessel sewage, check
to see if boat pumpout facilities are available and
working.

Bulleted lists
give questions
to ask, steps
to take

- Look for trash and such other signs of pollution
as oil slicks in the water. These kinds of
pollutants may indicate the presence of disease-
causing microorganisms that may also have been
washed into the water.

- If you think your beach water is contaminated,
contact your local health or environmental
protection officials. It is important for them to
know about suspected
beach water
contamination so they
can protect citizens
from exposure.

- Work with your local
authorities to create a
monitoring program.

*In celebration of the 30th anniversary
of the Clean Water Act, EPA presents*

Before You Go
to the Beach...

★ 2002 ★
THE YEAR OF
CLEAN WATER

*Celebration &
Recommitment*

Images layered to draw in reader

Brochure

Logo in distinctive font

Decorative background (used sparingly)

Subsections with distinct type treatments

Links to photos, documents, and further information

Menu

Major heading in large type

Additional spacing between paragraphs

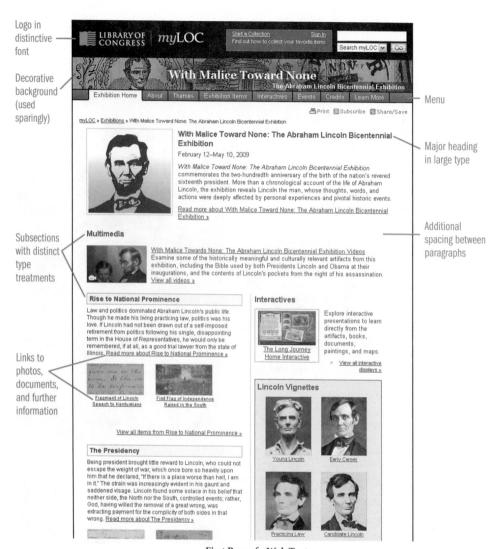

First Page of a Web Text

||||||||||||||||||||||||||||||||||||||||||||||||||||||||||||||||||||||||||||||||||||||||||||||

FOR THOUGHT, DISCUSSION, AND WRITING

1. Look at the introductions to the three articles by Deborah Tannen presented in Chapter 3 on pp. 60–65. Chapter 3's discussion of these introductions touches on issues of document design, noting, for instance, that the article intended for the broadest audience uses the most fully developed visuals. But it doesn't discuss these visuals in depth. Drawing on the guidelines presented in this chapter, analyze the visual design of Tannen's documents and relate the elements of each design to the intended audience.

2. The textbook you're reading right now has, like most books, been designed by a team of editors, designers, and artists. The book's design uses elements such as type fonts and sizes, white space, headings, color, and visuals to increase the text's readability and effectiveness. Drawing on the principles of design discussed in this chapter and also on your own design preferences, write a paragraph in which you evaluate the design of this textbook. Conclude your analysis with one or two suggestions for improving the book's design in future editions.

3. For a community, church, civic, or other group project in which you are currently involved, develop a flyer, brochure, newsletter, or Web page that your group will use as an internal document or share with others. If you aren't currently involved in such a project, develop a document that relates to a project that interests you.

4. "Putin? Never Heard of Her" (p. 320) is from the July 2007 issue of *Wired* magazine. *Wired* is known for its cutting-edge page design, and in this piece the editors developed visuals to represent results from a recent study on Americans' knowledge of current events conducted by an independent research group. Read the text and examine the visuals carefully. In what ways are these visuals effective? What kind of information might be missing? Your instructor may ask you to write several paragraphs analyzing this page.

||||||||||||||||||||||||||||||||||||||||||||||||||||||||||||||||||||||||||||||||||||||||||||||

Putin? Never Heard of Her.

Despite the Internet explosion, Americans remain woefully ill-informed.

More than a decade after the Internet went mainstream, the world's richest information source hasn't necessarily made its users any more informed. A new study from the Pew Research Center for the People & the Press shows that Americans, on average, are less able to correctly answer questions about current events than they were in 1989. Citizens who call the Internet their primary news source know slightly less than fans of TV and radio news. Hmmm ... maybe a little less Perez Hilton and a little more Jim Lehrer. —PATRICK DI JUSTO

Daily Show viewers are more up on current events than Fox News fans.

% of audience that ...

	... could name Vladimir Putin	... could name the Sunni branch of Islam	... could identify Scooter Libby
Major newspaper Web sites	58	52	42
The Daily Show/ The Colbert Report	52	50	44
National Public Radio	51	49	43
News magazines	49	44	41
News from Google, Yahoo, other portals	44	44	33
CNN	41	38	36
Daily newspapers	43	36	35
News blogs	36	35	32
Network evening news	37	31	33
Fox News	38	32	29

Americans now know less about politics than they did in 1989.

% of respondents who ...

	1989	2007
... could name the vice president	74	69
... could name their state's governor	74	66
... could name the president of Russia	47	36
... know whether the US has a trade deficit	81	68
... know which party controls the House	68	76
... know whether the chief justice is conservative	30	37
... could name the Speaker of the House	16	49
... could name the secretary of defense	13	21

Who knows less about the news? Pretty much everyone.

% of people who answered 4 out of 5 questions correctly*

	1989	2007
High school graduate or less	41	30
Some college	59	51
College graduate	80	74

*The five questions: Who is the vice president? Who is your state's governor? Does the US have a trade deficit or surplus? Which party controls the House of Representatives? Is the chief justice of the Supreme Court a liberal, moderate, or conservative?

SOURCE: THE PEW RESEARCH CENTER FOR THE PEOPLE & THE PRESS

Page from *Wired* Magazine, July 2007

CHAPTER 12

Strategies for Revision

Revising can be the most rewarding part of the writing process: It gives you the satisfaction of bringing your ideas to completion in an appropriate form. Revision challenges you to look at your work from a dual perspective: to read your work with your own intentions in mind, and also to consider your readers' perspectives. Although revision occurs throughout the writing process, you'll probably revise most intensively after completing a rough draft that serves as a preliminary statement of your ideas.

This chapter focuses first on revision as a process, explaining how revision differs from editing, or correcting mistakes, and offering strategies for reading your work more objectively so that you can recognize strengths and weaknesses. Next, the chapter describes strategies for revising effectively and efficiently and shows how you can use responses to your draft to help establish priorities for revision. The last section offers ideas for improving your essay's structure and style.

Revising through Re-Vision

You can learn a great deal about revision just by considering the word itself. *Revision* combines the root word *vision* with the prefix *re-*, meaning "again." When you revise, you "see again": You develop a new vision of your essay's logic and organization or of the best way to improve the way it flows.

Revision is very different from editing, which generally occurs at the end of the writing process. Editing is essentially tidying up: When you edit, you're concerned mainly with correctness—with issues of grammar, punctuation, spelling, word choice, and sentence structure.

Unlike editing, revision is a process of discovery where much more than correctness is at stake. Because it generates growth and change, revision sometimes requires you to take risks. Often these risks are minor. If you attempt to fine-tune the details in a paragraph, for instance, you need spend only a little time and can easily revert back to the original version. Sometimes, however, when you revise, you make large-scale decisions with more

Guidelines for Revising Objectively

1. Plan at least a short break between writing and revising.

It's difficult to critique your rough draft when you've just finished composing it; taking a break before revising can help you gain distance and objectivity.

2. Prepare mentally for a revising session.

Review your assignment and your rhetorical analysis.

Reread your draft and ask yourself the following questions:

- What state is your draft in — how rough or near completion?
- To what extent does your draft respond to the assignment and your rhetorical situation?
- How well does your draft meet the goals you established for it?
- What goals should you establish for this revising session, and how can you fulfill them? What should you work on first?

3. Revise from typed or printed copy.

It's generally easier, both for you and for anyone who might be reviewing your draft, to see stylistic and organizational problems in printed drafts.

4. Try reading your work out loud.

If you (or a reader) falter over a phrase or have to read a sentence several times before it makes sense, that may indicate a problem of style or logic.

significant consequences. You might conclude that a different organization is in order, decide to rework your thesis statement, or consider a new approach to your topic altogether. Trying major changes such as these often requires rewriting or discarding whole sections of a draft, but a willingness to experiment can also lead to choices that make revising easier and less frustrating.

See p. 322 for general guidelines for revising objectively.

|||||||||||||||||||||||||||||||||||||||||||||||||||||||||||||||||||||||||||||||||||||||||||||||

FOR EXPLORATION

Think back to earlier writing experiences and freewrite on them for five or ten minutes.

■ When, and for what reasons, have you revised your work, instead of just editing it?

■ How would you characterize these revision experiences? Were they satisfying? Frustrating? Why?

|||||||||||||||||||||||||||||||||||||||||||||||||||||||||||||||||||||||||||||||||||||||||||||||

Asking the Big Questions: Revising for Focus, Content, and Organization

When you revise a draft, begin by asking the big, important questions—questions about how well your essay has responded to your rhetorical situation, and how successfully you've achieved your controlling purpose. If you discover—as writers often do—that your essay hasn't achieved its original purpose or that your purpose evolved into a different one as you wrote, you'll want to make major changes in your draft.

Examining Your Own Writing

From the moment you begin thinking about a writing project until you make your last revision, you must be an analyst and a decision maker. When you examine your work, you look for strengths to build on and weaknesses to remedy. Consequently, you must think about not just what is in your text but also what is *not* there and what *could be* there. You must read the part (the introduction, say, or several paragraphs) while still keeping in mind the whole.

Asking the Questions for Evaluating Focus, Content, and Organization (pp. 324–25) first is a practical approach to revising. Once you're confident that the overall focus, content, and organization of your essay are satisfactory, you'll be better able to recognize less significant but still important stylistic problems.

Questions for Evaluating Focus, Content, and Organization

Focus

What do you hope to accomplish in this essay? How clearly have you defined — and communicated — your working thesis?

How well does your essay respond to your rhetorical situation? If it is an academic essay, does it fulfill the requirements of the assignment?

Have you tried to do too much in this essay? Or are your goals too limited or inconsequential?

How does your essay respond to the needs, interests, and expectations of your readers?

Content

How effectively does your essay fulfill the commitment stated or implied by your working thesis? Do you need to develop it further?

What supporting details and evidence have you provided? Do they relate clearly to your working thesis and to each other?

What additional details, evidence, or counterarguments might strengthen your essay?

Have you included any material that is irrelevant to your working thesis?

How could your introduction and conclusion be more effective?

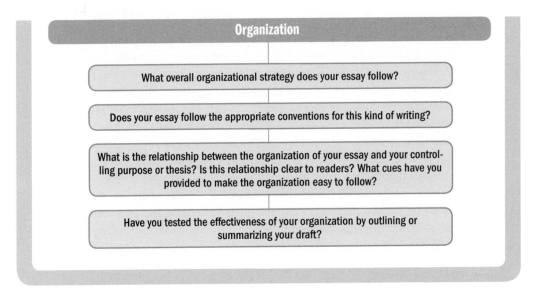

Organization

> What overall organizational strategy does your essay follow?

> Does your essay follow the appropriate conventions for this kind of writing?

> What is the relationship between the organization of your essay and your controlling purpose or thesis? Is this relationship clear to readers? What cues have you provided to make the organization easy to follow?

> Have you tested the effectiveness of your organization by outlining or summarizing your draft?

||||||||||||||||||||||||||||||||||||||||||||||||||||||||||||||||||||||||||||||||

FOR EXPLORATION

Use the Questions for Evaluating Focus, Content, and Organization to evaluate the draft of an essay you are currently working on. Respond as specifically and as concretely as possible, and then take a few moments to reflect on what you have learned about your draft. Use your responses to make a list of goals for revising.

||||||||||||||||||||||||||||||||||||||||||||||||||||||||||||||||||||||||||||||||

One Student Writer's Revision for Focus, Content, and Organization

Here is how one writer, Stevon Roberts, used the Questions for Evaluating Focus, Content, and Organization to establish goals for his revision. For an introductory composition class, Stevon was assigned a four- to five-page essay that proposed a solution to a contemporary problem. Stevon decided to write on something he was truly interested in: Internet privacy. This interest was sparked in part by personal experience, and in part by his analysis of Amitai Etzioni's "Less Privacy Is Good for Us (and You)." ✳

Stevon spent some time discussing the problem with friends and then doing some research online, taking notes as he did so. He reread his notes and then did a freewrite (see p. 326) to determine his rhetorical situation and figure out what he really wanted to get across.

See pp. 101–6. ✳ · · · · · · · · · · ·

I am writing an essay for my composition class in which I'm supposed to propose a solution to a contemporary problem. I've decided to tackle the problem of Internet privacy. Since my readers — my instructor and classmates — almost certainly spend at least some time online, I think they'll be familiar with the general context of my discussion. Since the things we do online vary so widely, though, I've decided to narrow my focus to social media — Facebook, blogs, Twitter, and so on. I do have some practical recommendations to make for ways we can protect our privacy, but I've realized in talking with people and doing some research that making concrete recommendations is not always very helpful: rapid changes in technology mean that they'll rapidly become obsolete. For this reason, I've decided primarily to raise awareness of the problem, emphasizing the need for every person who uses technology to understand the dangers of providing personal information online and be alert to new threats.

Stevon's Early Draft

My name is Stevon Roberts. I'm a videographer, a blogger, a student, and a tech enthusiast (at least, that's what it says on my Twitter profile). My last known location was on the corner of NW Beca Avenue and NW 20th Street, at a place called Coffee Culture, in Corvallis, Oregon.

In the past, I would have guarded this kind of information to prevent marketers, hackers, and identity thieves from building a profile to exploit. Identity thieves have gotten very good at compiling seemingly innocuous pieces of information and using them for purposes like credit card fraud. These threats are still very real, and I still take some measures to protect myself. You probably do, too. Most of us know by now how to recognize phishing scams and other threats to our personal security. But with the advent of social media, we've seen huge changes in the way this information is obtained.

Most of us just give information away for free on Facebook, Twitter, blogs, and other social media services, often compromising security. In the same way that the automobile revolutionized transportation, social media have fundamentally shifted the way we manage our personal information. We learned to mitigate our risks on the road by using safety belts and obeying traffic laws, but most of us probably don't yet have a good understanding of the appropriate precautions for social media. As these services become more integral to our lifestyles, and more revealing of our identities, protecting our identities will become more critical, both online and in real life.

Other security concerns in the digital realm haven't gone away. Spam, for example, has become so pervasive that world spending for anti-spam software was expected to exceed $1.7 billion in 2008, up from $300 million in 2003 ("Anti-Spam Spending Set to Soar," *Global Secure Systems* 24 Feb. 2005). Apart from reducing the annoyance factor, this can also protect from more serious security threats, such as phishing scams, wherein unsuspecting victims will reply to fraudulent emails with personal information—sometimes even giving away bank account numbers!

Clearly, these security issues are still at the forefront of people's minds, and we're taking steps toward better solutions. But let's put the risks in context, and compare our relative response. As of the writing of this essay, Facebook had approximately 300 million users. Many of them are content to settle for the default privacy settings, which aren't all that private. Additionally, many Facebook users will add "applications," including games, quizzes, etc., which have access to many parts of your user profile that you may not want to share. In fact, in a twist of irony, the ACLU has added a quiz that you can take to explain exactly what is exposed when you add these sorts of quizzes (aclunc_privacy_quiz/). The quiz offers some suggestions for changing the privacy settings to protect personal information, but many people simply aren't aware, or don't take the time, to make these adjustments.

But let's not focus on Facebook at the expense of an even larger context. Location services, such as Brightkite, allow you to pinpoint your location on a map. You'd probably be happy to share this information with friends whom you'd like to join you, but you likely wouldn't want to share this information with a stalker, or even an angry ex-boyfriend or -girlfriend. Would you broadcast the location of your home address? Most of us would probably think twice before doing that, but the lines can quickly become blurry. Is it okay to broadcast your location from a friend's house? Your classroom, or your office?

With its instructional tagline, "What are you doing?," Twitter gives its users 140 characters to broadcast activities, locations, Web site URLs, and even pictures (via helper services). An individual post, or "tweet," might cost you a job if, for example, you called in sick for work and then tweeted your location from a restaurant. You might risk being overlooked for an interview if you posted a picture from a drinking party.

Similarly, your political views and feelings may be called into question if you endeavor to start a blog, as I have. My blog is not especially personal, but it occurred to me when I started writing that this might be another potential vector for increased risk. It bothered me so much that I wrote to one of my favorite bloggers (Leo Babauta of Zenhabits. net), asking him whether he was concerned about security. He wrote back (via Twitter), "No, I haven't faced security or privacy issues as a blogger (yet). My readers are 100% really cool, nice (and sexy) people." It's worth pointing out that his blog has over a hundred thousand subscribers.

Still . . . social media, location services, and blogs: These new services all allow you to compromise your own personal identity and security in ways that are unprecedented. And at the same time, participation in all of these environments is almost obligatory. Very few of my friends have not yet succumbed to the peer pressure to be available on Facebook, despite security concerns. And if you're trying to run a business (or promote your blog), avoiding Twitter is tantamount to professional suicide — these venues are key ingredients for successful marketing. In short, your personal name and profile have almost become like a kind of brand that is expected to be proliferated and maintained in cyberspace. And yet censorship levels must be very high to avoid getting passed over for the next opportunity, because heaven forbid that your future employer doesn't agree with you about the last hot political topic (or whatever).

Along with the members of his peer response group, Stevon used the Questions for Evaluating Focus, Content, and Organization to analyze his draft. The following analysis reflects both Stevon's own observations and those of his writing group.

Focus: Some of my readers were confused about my main focus. I think I can correct this by revising my introduction and explaining more clearly that we (my instructor, classmates, and I) are all probably too sophisticated now for the "Nigerian royalty" email scams — we've all been there and learned our lessons — but other dangers exist, and we might not all be aware of them: specifically, the dangers presented in giving personal information away while using social media, which many of us are virtually addicted to.

I made one point that readers found really important — the idea that cutting social media off completely is not really an option for most of us, because it's too important for our social and even professional lives — late in the essay; I think I'll move it up closer to the beginning.

Some of my readers wanted more concrete recommendations for what to do to protect themselves. I have to make it clear from the outset that I think awareness and seeking out solutions that work for you is really the only universal solution anyone can offer — there's too much variety in the kinds of technology people use and it all changes really, really fast. I'm trying to teach them to fish, I guess, instead of giving them fish.

Content: Some of my readers were confused about my opening (where I give away private information about myself — what's my point there, exactly?). I think I just need to make the point more clearly in the second paragraph.

A couple of my readers didn't know what "phishing" was — I have to be careful about assuming too much common knowledge in technical terminology.

I realized on rereading one of my sources that a statistic it offered was a bit out-of-date, so I found a more current source.

I need to provide some more examples of some of the risks that people didn't entirely "get," like how having a blog could cost you a job.

Probably most critical is the fact that my readers didn't like my conclusion: they felt like the discussion just dropped off without really "concluding." I think adding a stronger conclusion, reminding readers of my major points, will make the essay much stronger.

Organization: I did try outlining my draft; it worked out OK, but I realize that I do pingpong a bit, especially in the beginning, between old threats like spam and new threats like Facebook quizzes. I need to work on transitions to make what I'm doing there clearer (because that's where some of the confusion about my focus crept in, I think).

I also have to add some clearer transitions between the different kinds of risks I discuss (the usual stuff with marketers and scam artists, and then other, even scarier stuff, like losing a job or being stalked). In the discussion of the latter risks (like stalkers), I lost some readers when I started out talking about Brightkite (it uses GPS technology but my readers didn't immediately know what I was talking about), so I think I'll reorder the presentation of topics here, and start with Twitter and blogs (which people are more familiar with).

Stevon used this analysis to completely rework his essay. The result follows on pp. 330–34.

Roberts 1

Stevon Roberts
Dr. Mallon
Comp 101
Oct. 10, 2010

Identity, Rebooted

"When you're doing stuff online, you should behave as if you're doing it in public—because increasingly, it is."—Cornell University computer science professor Jon Kleinberg (qtd. in Lohr)

My name is Stevon Roberts. I'm a videographer, a blogger, a student, and a tech enthusiast (at least, that's what it says on my Twitter profile). My last known location was on the corner of NW Beca Avenue and NW 20th Street, at a place called Coffee Culture, in Corvallis, Oregon.

If someone had told me even five years ago that I would one day regularly broadcast this kind of information about myself to people I didn't know, I wouldn't have believed it. If someone I didn't know had asked me back then for information like this, I would have refused to give it, to prevent unscrupulous people from exploiting it. I was well aware of how expert marketers, hackers, and identity thieves had become at compiling such seemingly innocuous pieces of information and using them for unwanted sales pitches, or, even worse, for credit card scams and other kinds of fraud.

These threats are still very real, and I take some measures to protect myself against them. You probably do, too: Most of us are wary of filling out surveys from dubious sources, for example, and most of us know by now how to recognize obvious email scams like the ones purporting to be from "Nigerian royalty." But with the advent of social media, many of us find ourselves in a bind: We want to be connected, so many of us regularly give confidential—and potentially damaging—information away on Facebook, Twitter, blogs, and other social media services.

Stevon added a title to prepare his readers for the content of his essay.

This new epigraph provides thought-provoking expert commentary.

Stevon revised paras. 2 and 3 to clearly reflect his rhetorical situation—writing to media-savvy readers in the age of Facebook—and explain his focus—to make his readers aware of privacy concerns.

Because he wasn't sure his readers would understand "phishing," he replaced the term here with a familiar example.

Stevon moved up this important aspect of his argument: Social media do matter because we all want to be connected.

Roberts 2

In the same way that the automobile revolutionized transportation, social media have fundamentally shifted the way we communicate and share personal information. We learned to mitigate our risks on the road by using safety belts and obeying traffic laws, but most of us probably don't yet have a good understanding of appropriate precautions for social media. As these services become more integral to our lifestyles, protecting our identities from those who might use them for nefarious ends will become even more critical. Given the speed with which social media are developing and changing, it's difficult to give specific recommendations. An important first step, however, is becoming aware of the risks you run in broadcasting personal information.

Stevon clarifies and limits the primary goal of his essay.

These new concerns about privacy and safety in the digital realm have arrived on the heels of older problems that haven't gone away. Spam, for example, has become so pervasive that, according to a 2009 estimate by Ferris Research, annual spending that year for anti-spam software, hardware, and personnel would reach $6.5 billion—$2.1 billion in the United States alone (Jennings). As these figures show, though, in the case of spam, most of us can and do fight back: Anti-spam software eliminates or at least reduces the amount of unwanted email we receive, and it can protect us well from security threats like the "Nigerian royalty" scam mentioned above, wherein unsuspecting victims will reply to fraudulent emails with personal information—sometimes even giving away bank account numbers.

Stevon realized that his original statistics represented a prediction from 2005; because his topic demands currency, he found and cited more recent data.

Most of us are not yet doing anything about the threats posed by the information we publish via social media, however, and many of us are not even fully aware of them. In order to put the problem in context, let's take a closer look at the kinds of social media we're talking about, and the nature and extent of the risks they pose. Participation in social networks like Facebook, Twitter, Flickr, and others has exploded in the last few years: As of the writing of this essay, Facebook alone had approximately 300 million users. Most of those who participate don't think twice about privacy issues, or they assume that the systems' default privacy settings will protect them. Yet recent studies done by researchers at M.I.T., Carnegie Mellon, and the University of Texas have demonstrated that it's possible to determine sexual orientation, match identities to "anonymously" stated preferences, and even

Stevon clarified his transition here—moving from spam (older security concern) to social media.

Stevon added this reference to recent studies to be more specific about what "threats to privacy" might entail.

Roberts 3

piece together social security numbers from profile information on Facebook and other social networks (Lohr).

As if putting basic profile information out there weren't enough, many Facebook users will add applications like games and quizzes that allow outside parties unmediated access to unrelated information from their profiles. In an attempt to raise awareness of the issue, the ACLU has added a quiz(!) to Facebook that explains exactly what is exposed when you add these sorts of quizzes (Conley; see also http://apps.facebook.com/aclunc_privacy_quiz/). The ACLU's quiz offers some suggestions for changing Facebook privacy settings to protect personal information.

The risks you take in revealing personal information via social media go beyond its possible misuse by marketers, hackers, and identity thieves. For example, with its tagline, "What are you doing?" Twitter gives its users 140 characters to broadcast activities, locations, Web site URLs, and even pictures (via helper services). A single post, or "Tweet," however, might cost you a job if you call in sick for work and then tweet your location from a restaurant. You might risk being turned down for an interview if you post a picture from a wild drinking party.

Similarly, your views and opinions, political and otherwise, may become an issue if you start a blog. I have a blog that's not especially personal, but it occurred to me when I started writing that this might be a potential source of risk: What if my boss saw what I wrote, disagreed, and started treating me differently at work? What if my landlord was bothered enough to refuse to renew my lease? I began to worry so much about it that I wrote to one of my favorite bloggers (Leo Babauta of Zenhabits.net), asking him whether he was concerned about security. He wrote back (via Twitter), "No, I haven't faced security or privacy issues as a blogger (yet). My readers are 100% really cool, nice (and sexy) people." It's worth pointing out that his blog has over a hundred thousand subscribers, so maybe I'm worried over nothing. On the other hand, Mr. Babauta lives on the island of Guam, works for himself, and likely doesn't face many of the same identity expectations that I would as a student and young professional.

Stevon added this transition to clarify his move from discussing one kind of risk to another. He also reorganized this section, moving Twitter and blogs to the beginning, as they were likely to be most familiar to his readers.

He provided some examples here to clarify the kinds of risks he might be taking in posting his blog.

Some of his readers were puzzled as to why they should be concerned, if Babauta wasn't — Stevon responds to that question here.

Roberts 4

One last service that's become a recent phenomenon is the use of Global Positioning System (GPS) technology in cell phones. Many cell phones now have GPS receivers built in, and as with some Twitter applications, location services such as Brightkite allow you to pinpoint your location on a map with startling accuracy. Broadcasting your location is optional, but many people do so because the technology's there and they don't see how it could hurt. It could hurt: When you broadcast your location, everyone, not just your friends, will know where you are. How about angry ex-boyfriends or -girlfriends, or potential stalkers? What if someone were casing your home for a break-in and were able to determine via one of these services that you were away?

Clearly, social media allow you to reveal aspects of your identity and (therefore) compromise your security in ways that are unprecedented. At the same time, for many of us participation in these environments is tempting, and at times almost obligatory. Very few of my friends have not yet succumbed to the peer pressure to be available on Facebook, for example. If you're trying to run a business (or promote your blog), avoiding Twitter is tantamount to professional suicide—these venues are key ingredients for successful marketing. In short, your personal name and profile have become a brand that you're expected to proliferate and maintain in cyberspace: Without them, you're nothing. Yet, as I have discussed, the risks that accompany this self-promotion are high.

Because the explosion in social media is relatively new, best practices for mitigating these risks are not clearly identified yet. One friend and professional colleague argues that it's simply impossible to manage your identity online because much of it is revealed by others—your friends will post the embarrassing party pictures for you, school or work will post documents detailing your achievements, and Google will determine what appears in the search results when you type your name in. M.I.T. professor Harold Abelson agrees: "Personal privacy is no longer an individual thing. . . . In today's online world, what your mother told you is true, only more so: people really can judge you by your friends" (qtd. in Lohr).

Some readers of his draft had never heard of Brightkite or thought about GPS technology in cell phones, so Stevon gave this part of his discussion more space.

Stevon added this entire concluding section to clarify his purpose and remind his readers of his key points.

Stevon added a quote from an expert source that bolsters his anonymous friend's claim about the ways in which our identities are revealed online.

Roberts 5

The most positive spin on this perspective is to think of your online identity in terms of a "signal-to-noise" ratio: Assuming you know what you're doing, you are in charge of the "signal" (the information you yourself Tweet or allow to appear on Facebook), and this signal will usually be stronger than the "noise" generated by your friends or others who broadcast information you'd rather not share. The key phrase there is "assuming you know what you're doing," and that's where all of us could use some pointers. If you're going to put your faith in your ability to create a strong, positive signal, you need to follow a few key rules. First, realize that there's a potential problem every time you post something private online. Next, make yourself thoroughly acquainted with the privacy settings of any and all social media you interact with. The default settings for any of these programs are almost certainly inadequate because my security concerns aren't the same as Leo Babauta's, and they're not the same as yours. Finally, keep talking (and blogging and Googling) about the issue, and sharing any best practices you discover. We need to work together to understand and manage these risks if we want to retain control of the "brand" that is us.

Works Cited

The Works Cited page includes all sources in correct MLA format. (*Note:* in an actual MLA-style paper, Works Cited entries start on a new page.)

Babauta, Leo. "Re: Security Concerns?" Message to the author. 11 Nov. 2009. Tweet.

Conley, Chris. "Quiz: What Do Facebook Quizzes Know about You?" *Blog of Rights*. ACLU, 11 June 2009. Web. 13 Apr. 2010.

Jennings, Richi. "Cost of Spam Is Flattening—Our 2009 Predictions." *Ferris.com*. Ferris Research, 28 Jan. 2009. Web. 10 Apr. 2010.

Lohr, Steve. "How Privacy Vanishes Online." *New York Times*. New York Times, 16 Mar. 2010. Web. 11 Apr. 2010.

Snell, Jason. "Think before You Tweet." *Macworld*. Mac Publishing, 18 Mar. 2009. Web. 12 Apr. 2010.

Benefiting from Responses to Work in Progress

You may write alone a good deal of the time, but writing needn't be a lonely process. You can draw on the responses of others to help you re-see your writing and to gain support. When you ask others to respond to your writing, you're asking for feedback so that you can see your writing in fresh and different ways.

Responses can take a number of forms. Sometimes you may find it helpful to ask others simply to describe your writing for you. You might, for example, ask them to summarize in their own words how they understand your main point or what they think you're getting at. Similarly, you might ask them what parts of your draft stood out for them, and what they felt was missing.

On other occasions, you may find more analytical responses helpful. You might ask readers to comment on your essay's organization or how well it responds to their needs and interests. If you're writing an argumentative essay, you might ask readers to look for potential weaknesses in its structure or logic.

To determine what kind of feedback will be most helpful, think commonsensically about your writing. Where are you in your composing process? How do you feel about your draft and the kind of writing you're working on? If you've just completed a rough draft, for instance, you might find descriptive feedback most helpful. After you've worked longer on the essay, you might invite more analytical responses.

As a student, you can turn to many people for feedback. The differences in their situations will influence how they respond; these differences should also influence how you use their responses. No matter whom you approach for feedback, though, learn to distinguish between your writing and yourself. Try not to respond defensively to suggestions for improvement, and don't argue with readers' responses. Instead, use them to gain insight into your writing. Ultimately you are the one who must decide how to interpret and apply other people's comments and criticisms.

NOTE FOR MULTILINGUAL WRITERS

If you were educated in another culture, the process of revising multiple drafts may be new to you. Revising is meant to help you rework your writing to make sure it is as effective and clear as possible. If receiving (and giving) comments on drafts is new to you, be assured that the suggestions and questions from peer and other reviewers should lead to constructive collaboration.

Responses from Friends and Family Members

You can certainly ask the people close to you to respond to your writing, but you should understand their strengths and weaknesses as readers. One important strength is that you trust them. Even if you spend time filling them in, however, friends and family members won't understand the nature of your assignment or your instructor's standards for evaluation; they're also likely to be less objective than other readers. All the same, friends and family members can provide useful responses to your writing if you choose such respondents carefully and draw on their strengths as outsiders. Rather than asking them to respond in detail, you might ask them to give a general impression or a descriptive response to your work. If their understanding of the main idea or controlling purpose of your essay differs substantially from your own, you've gained very useful information.

Responses from Classmates

Because your classmates know your instructor and the assignment as insiders, they can provide particularly effective responses to work in progress. Peers don't need to be experts to provide helpful responses. They simply need to be attentive, honest, supportive readers. Writing groups typically form strong bonds; participants genuinely want group members to do well and to develop as writers. Group members can also read your work more objectively than family members and friends can. To ensure that your writing group provides a helpful balance of support and criticism, follow the Guidelines for Peer Response on pp. 337–38.

|||||||||||||||||||||||||||||||||||||||||||||||||||||||||||||||||||||||||||||||||||||

FOR COLLABORATION

Think about responses to your work that you have received from classmates. Freewrite for five or ten minutes about these experiences, and then draw up a list of statements describing the kinds of responses that have been most helpful.

Meet with a group of your classmates. Begin by having each group member read his or her list. Then, working together, list all the suggestions for peer response. Have one student record all the suggestions and distribute them to everyone in the group for future use.

|||||||||||||||||||||||||||||||||||||||||||||||||||||||||||||||||||||||||||||||||||||

Guidelines for Peer Response

ADVICE FOR WRITERS

1. Prepare for peer response meetings.

Carefully formulate the questions about your work that you most need to have answered.

2. Bring a legible draft to class.

Be sure to bring a working draft, not a jumble of brainstorming ideas, free-writing, and notes.

3. Explain your rhetorical situation.

If you are addressing a specific audience — members of a certain organization, for example, or readers of a particular magazine — be sure to let your classmates know.

4. Maintain your own authority as the writer.

Your fellow students' responses are just that: responses. Treat their comments seriously, but remember that you must always decide what advice to accept and what to reject.

ADVICE FOR READERS

1. Follow the golden rule.

Respond to the writing of others as you would like them to respond to your own work.

continued

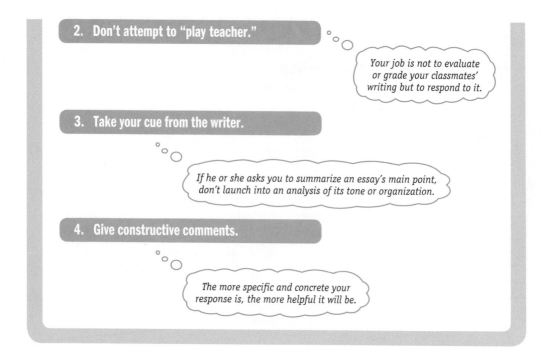

Responses from Writing Center Tutors

Many colleges and universities have writing centers staffed by undergraduate and graduate writing assistants or tutors. Tutors are not professional editors, nor are they faculty aides standing in for instructors who are unavailable or too busy to meet with students. Writing tutors are simply good writers who have been formally trained to respond to peers' work and to make suggestions for improvement. For guidelines on meeting with a tutor, see p. 339.

Responses from Your Instructor and Others

Because your instructor is such an important reader for your written assignments, you want to make good use of any written comments he or she provides. For guidelines on making the most of them, see p. 340.

Friends, family members, classmates, writing tutors, instructors—all can provide helpful responses to your writing. None of these responses, whether criticism or praise, should take the place of your own judgment, however. Your job is to *interpret* and *evaluate* these responses, using them along with your own assessment of your rough draft to establish goals for revising.

Guidelines for Meeting with a Writing Tutor

1. Identify your goals before meeting with a tutor.

Reread your writing, and ask yourself what kind of help you would
benefit most from:

- A discussion of your essay's organization
- An examination of a section of your draft
- Some other activity, such as brainstorming ideas or evaluating possible evidence for your position

2. Begin your conference by sharing your goals with your writing tutor. If at all possible, bring a written description of the assignment to which you are responding.

You might also find it helpful to tell the writing tutor where you are in your process — in the early stages of drafting, for instance, or in the process of final editing.

3. Be realistic about what you can accomplish in the time available.

Recognize, as well, that the writing tutor's job is to respond and advise, not to correct or rewrite your draft.

Keeping Your Readers on Track: Revising for Style

"Proper words in proper places" — that's how the eighteenth-century writer Jonathan Swift defined style. As Swift suggests, writing style reflects all of the choices a writer makes, from global questions of approach and organization to the smallest details about punctuation and grammar. When, in writing, you put the proper words in their proper places, readers will be able to follow your ideas with understanding and interest. In addition, they will probably gain some sense of the person behind the words — that is, of the writer's presence.

Guidelines for Using Your Instructor's Responses

1. Read your instructor's written comments carefully.

They are the clearest, most specific indication of how well you have fulfilled the assignment.

2. Read your instructor's comments more than once.

Read first to understand your instructor's general response to your writing.

Next, read the comments again several times, looking to establish priorities for revision.

3. Distinguish between local and global comments.

Local comments indicate specific questions, problems, or errors.

For example, awkward *is a local comment indicating a problem with a specific sentence.*

Global comments address broader issues, such as organization or the effectiveness of your evidence.

Global comments will help you set large-scale goals for revision.

4. Meet with your instructor if you don't understand his or her comments.

Even if you do understand the comments, you may wish to meet to discuss your plans for revision.

Most writers concern themselves with style *after* writing a rough draft and determining that the essay's focus, content, and organization are effective. At this point, the writer can make changes that enable readers to move through the writing easily and enjoyably.

Achieving Coherence

Most writers are aware that paragraphs and essays need to be *unified* — that is, that they should focus on a single topic. Writing is *coherent* when readers can move easily from word to word, sentence to sentence, and paragraph to paragraph. There are various means of achieving coherence. Some methods, such as *repeating key words and sentence structures* and *using pronouns*, reinforce or emphasize the logical development of ideas. Another method involves *using transitional words* such as *but, although*, and *because* to provide directional cues for readers.

The following introduction to "Home Town," an essay by the popular writer Ian Frazier, uses all of these methods to keep readers on track. The most important means of achieving coherence are italicized.

> *When glaciers* covered much of northern Ohio, the land around Hudson, the town where I grew up, lay under one. *Glaciers* came and went several times, the most recent departing about 14,000 years ago. *When* we studied *glaciers* in an Ohio-history class in grade school, I imagined our *glacier* receding smoothly, like a sheet pulled off a new car. *Actually, glaciers* can move forward *but* they don't back up — *they* melt in place. *Most likely* the *glacier* above Hudson softened, *and* began to trickle underneath; rocks on its surface absorbed sunlight and melted tunnels into *it; it* rotted, *it* dwindled, *it* dripped, *it* ticked; *then it* dropped a pile of the sand and rocks *it* had been carrying around for centuries onto the ground in a heap. Hudson's landscape was hundreds of these little heaps — hills rarely big enough to sled down, a random arrangement made by gravity and smoothed by weather and time.
>
> — Ian Frazier, "Home Town"

When you read your own writing to determine how to strengthen its coherence, use common sense. Your writing is coherent if readers know where they have been and where they are going as they read. Don't assume that your writing will be more coherent if you simply sprinkle key words, pronouns, and transitions throughout your prose. If the logic of your discussion is clear without such devices, don't add them.

Revision for coherence proceeds most effectively if you look first at large-scale issues, such as the relationship among your essay's introduction, body, and conclusion, before considering smaller concerns. For guidelines on revising for coherence, see p. 342.

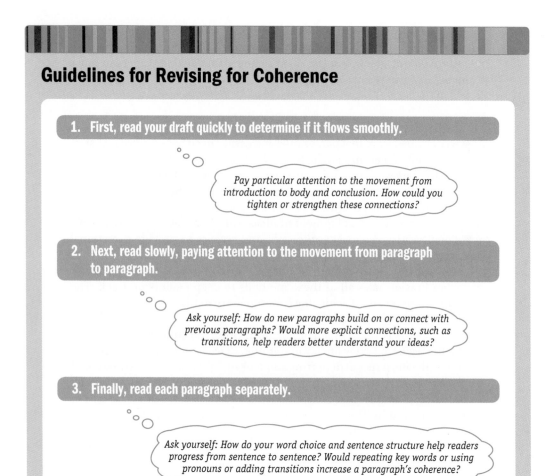

Guidelines for Revising for Coherence

1. First, read your draft quickly to determine if it flows smoothly.

Pay particular attention to the movement from introduction to body and conclusion. How could you tighten or strengthen these connections?

2. Next, read slowly, paying attention to the movement from paragraph to paragraph.

Ask yourself: How do new paragraphs build on or connect with previous paragraphs? Would more explicit connections, such as transitions, help readers better understand your ideas?

3. Finally, read each paragraph separately.

Ask yourself: How do your word choice and sentence structure help readers progress from sentence to sentence? Would repeating key words or using pronouns or adding transitions increase a paragraph's coherence?

Finding an Appropriate Voice

A writer's style reflects his or her individual taste and sensibility. But just as people dress differently for different occasions, so too do effective writers vary their style, depending on their rhetorical situation. As they do so, they are particularly attentive to the *persona*, or voice, they want to convey through their writing.

Sometimes writers present strong and distinctive voices. Here, for instance, is the beginning of an essay by the novelist Ken Kesey on the Pendleton Round-Up, a Northwest rodeo.

My father took me up the Gorge and over the hills to my first one thirty-five years ago. It was on my fourteenth birthday. I had to miss a couple of days' school plus the possibility of suiting up for the varsity game that Friday night. Gives you some idea of the importance Daddy placed on this event.

For this is more than just a world-class rodeo. It is a week-long shindig, a yearly rendezvous dating back beyond the first white trappers, a traditional powwow ground for the Indian nations of the Northwest for nobody knows how many centuries.

— Ken Kesey, "The Blue-Ribbon American Beauty Rose of Rodeo"

Kesey's word choice and sentence structure help create an image of the writer as folksy, relaxed, and yet also forceful—just the right insider to write about a famous rodeo. In other situations, writers may prefer a less personal voice, as is often the case in informative writing for textbooks, academic articles, newspapers, and the like.

If you think rhetorically, always asking questions about your rhetorical situation, you'll naturally consider such major stylistic issues as voice. By considering how much you wish to draw on appeals to reason (*logos*), emotion (*pathos*), and your own credibility as writer (*ethos*), you will more easily determine your own voice and your relationship with readers. ✳

thinking rhetorically

Revising for Effective Prose Style

The stylistic choices that you make as you draft and revise reflect not only your rhetorical awareness but also your awareness of general principles of effective prose style. Perhaps the easiest way to understand these principles is to analyze a passage that illustrates effective prose style in action.

Here is a paragraph from the first chapter of a psycholinguistics textbook. (Psycholinguistics is an interdisciplinary field that studies linguistic behavior and the psychological mechanisms that make verbal communication possible.) As you read it, imagine that you have been assigned to read the textbook for a course in psycholinguistics.

Language stands at the center of human affairs, from the most prosaic to the most profound. It is used for haggling with store clerks, telling off umpires, and gossiping with friends as well as for negotiating contracts, discussing ethics, and explaining religious beliefs. It is the medium through which the manners, morals, and mythology of a society are passed on to the next generation. Indeed, it is a basic ingredient in virtually every social situation. The thread that runs through all these activities is communication, people trying to put their ideas over to others. As the main vehicle of human communication, language is indispensable.

— Herbert H. Clark and Eve V. Clark, *Psychology and Language*

See pp. 40–42 and 51–53. ✳

This paragraph, you would probably agree, embodies effective prose style. It's clearly organized and begins with a topic sentence, which the rest of the paragraph explains. The paragraph is also coherent, with pronouns, key words, and sentence patterns helping readers proceed. But what most distinguishes this paragraph, what makes it so effective, is the authors' use of concrete, precise, economical language and carefully crafted sentences.

Suppose that the paragraph were revised as follows. What would be lost?

Language stands at the center of human affairs, from the most prosaic to the most profound. It is a means of human communication. It is a means of cultural change and regeneration. It is found in every social situation. The element that characterizes all these activities is communication. As the main vehicle of human communication, language is indispensable.

This revision communicates roughly the same ideas as the original paragraph, but it lacks that paragraph's liveliness and interest. Instead of presenting vivid examples—"haggling with store clerks, telling off umpires, and gossiping with friends"—these sentences state only vague generalities. Moreover, they're short and monotonous. Also lost in the revision is any sense of the authors' personalities, as revealed in their writing.

As this example demonstrates, effective prose style doesn't have to be flashy or call attention to itself. The focus in the original passage is on the *ideas* being discussed. The authors don't want readers to stop and think, "My, what a lovely sentence." But they do want their readers to become interested in and engaged with their ideas. So they use strong verbs and vivid, concrete examples whenever possible. They pay careful attention to sentence structure, alternating sequences of sentences with parallel structures with other, more varied sentences. They make sure that the relationships among ideas are clear. As a result of these and other choices, this paragraph succeeds in being both economical and emphatic.

Exploring your stylistic options—developing a style that reflects your understanding of yourself and the world and your feel for language—is one of the pleasures of writing. The Guidelines for Effective Prose Style on p. 345 describe just a few of the ways you can revise your own writing to improve its style.

Guidelines for Effective Prose Style

1. Consider the context.

Decisions about structure and style always depend upon how a passage fits within the work as a whole. To decide whether a sentence is awkward, for instance, you must look at the surrounding paragraph.

2. Vary the length and structure of your sentences.

Short, simple sentences grab readers' attention — but presenting several of them in a row can be boring and repetitive.

Longer, more complex sentences can give weight to important ideas, but they can also test readers' patience.

Avoid overuse of the same sentence structures, such as parenthetical remarks, introductory phrases, or independent clauses connected with semicolons.

3. Use language appropriate to your purpose and situation.

Specific, concrete words can give your writing power and depth. Such language isn't always appropriate, however.

Abstract or general terms can be necessary to convey your meaning, especially when writing about intellectual problems or ideas or emotions.

Abstract terms like *patriotism*, *love*, and *duty* refer to ideas, beliefs, relationships, conditions, and acts that you can't perceive with your senses.

General words designate a group. The word *computer* is general; the word *iMac* identifies a specific machine within that group.

4. Eliminate deadwood.

However, be aware: Knowing whether words are necessary depends on your rhetorical situation. Words that aren't strictly necessary can sometimes enhance emphasis, rhythm, flow, or tone, and strengthen your writing.

|||||||||||||||||||||||||||||||||||||||||||||||||||||||||||||||||||||||||||||||||||||||

FOR THOUGHT, DISCUSSION, AND WRITING

1. To study your own revision process, number and save all your plans, drafts, and revisions for a paper that you're currently writing or have written recently. After you have completed the paper, review these materials, paying particular attention to the revisions you made. Can you describe the revision strategies that you followed and identify ways to improve the effectiveness of this process? Your instructor may ask you to write an essay discussing what you have learned as a result of this analysis.

2. Interview two students in your class about their revision strategies. How do their strategies reflect their preferred composing styles? How are their strategies similar to and different from your own? How do these students feel about revising, and how do their feelings compare with your own? Can you apply any of their strategies to your own writing? What can you learn from these interviews? Your instructor may ask you to write an essay summarizing the results of your interviews.

3. From an essay you are currently working on, choose two or three paragraphs that you suspect could be more coherent or stylistically effective. Using this chapter's discussion as a guide, revise these paragraphs.

4. Read the essay by Jamais Cascio on pp. 261–62 (or choose another essay in this book that interests you), and then answer the following questions.

   ■ How would you describe the general style of this essay? Write three or four sentences describing its style.

   ■ How would you describe the persona, or voice, conveyed by this essay? List at least three characteristics of the writer's voice, and then indicate several passages that exemplify these characteristics.

   ■ Find three passages that demonstrate the principles of effective prose style as discussed in this chapter. Indicate why you believe each passage is stylistically effective.

   ■ What additional comments could you make about the structure and style of this essay? Did anything about the style surprise you? Formulate at least one additional comment about the essay's structure and style.

|||||||||||||||||||||||||||||||||||||||||||||||||||||||||||||||||||||||||||||||||||||||

Writers' References

MLA Documentation Guidelines

The MLA recommends the following format for the manuscript of a research-based essay. It's always a good idea, however, to check with your instructor about formatting before preparing your final draft. For detailed guidelines on formatting a list of works cited, see p. 355. For sample student essays in MLA style, see pp. 47, 101, 150, 205, 222, and 330.

- *First page and title page.* The MLA does not require a title page. Type each of the following items on a separate line on the first page, beginning one inch from the top and flush with the left margin: your name, the instructor's name, the course name and number, and the date. Double-space between each item; then double-space again and center the title. Double-space between the title and the beginning of the text.

- *Margins and spacing.* Leave one-inch margins at the top and bottom and on both sides of each page. Double-space the entire text, including set-off quotations, notes, and the list of works cited. Indent the first line of a paragraph one-half inch.

- *Page numbers.* Include your last name and the page number on each page (including the first), one-half inch below the top and flush with the right margin.

- *Long quotations.* Set off a long quotation (more than four typed lines) in block format by starting it on a new line and indenting each line one inch from the left margin. Do *not* enclose the passage in quotation marks.

- *Headings.* MLA style allows, but does not require, headings. Many students and instructors find them helpful. (See pp. 311–12 for guidelines on using headings.)

- *Visuals.* Place tables, photographs, drawings, charts, graphs, and other figures as near as possible to the relevant text. (See pp. 312–15 for advice on incorporating visuals into your text.) Tables should have a label and number (*Table 1*) and a clear title. The label and title should be aligned on the left, on separate lines. Give the source information below the table. All other visuals should be labeled *Figure* (abbreviated *Fig.*), numbered, and captioned. The label and caption should appear on the same line, followed by the source information (see p. 205 for an example). Remember to refer to each visual in your text, indicating how it contributes to the point(s) you are making.

In-text Citations

MLA style requires documentation in the text of an essay for every quotation, paraphrase, summary, or other material that must be cited. (For more advice about quoting, paraphrasing, and summarizing, see Chapter 6). In-text citations document material from other sources with both signal phrases and parenthetical references. Signal phrases introduce the material, often including the author's name. Parenthetical references direct readers to full bibliographic entries in a list of works cited at the end of the text.

Keep your parenthetical references short, but include enough information in the parentheses to allow readers to locate the full citation in the works-cited list. Place a parenthetical reference as near the relevant material as possible without disrupting the flow of the sentence.

Note in the following examples where punctuation is placed in relation to the parentheses. Except in the case of block quotations, the pattern is as follows: 1) closing quotation mark (if quotes are used); 2) parenthetical reference; and 3) other punctuation. For block quotations, the parenthetical reference falls *after* the final punctuation mark.

1. AUTHOR NAMED IN A SIGNAL PHRASE Ordinarily, you can use the author's name in a signal phrase that introduces the material and cite the page number(s) in parentheses. You may want to use the full name the first time you cite a source, but use just the last name for later references.

Herrera indicates that Kahlo believed in a "vitalistic form of pantheism" (328).

2. AUTHOR NAMED IN A PARENTHETICAL REFERENCE When you don't mention the author in a signal phrase, include the author's last name before the page number(s) in the parentheses. Use no punctuation between the author's name and the page number(s).

In places, Beauvoir "sees Marxists as believing in subjectivity" (Whitmarsh 63).

3. TWO OR THREE AUTHORS Use all the authors' last names in a signal phrase or parenthetical reference.

Gortner, Hebrun, and Nicolson maintain that "opinion leaders" influence other people in an organization because they are respected, not because they hold high positions (175).

4. FOUR OR MORE AUTHORS Use the names of all authors or the first author's name and *et al.* ("and others") in a signal phrase or parenthetical reference.

As Belenky, Clinchy, Goldberger, and Tarule assert, examining the lives of women expands our understanding of human development (7).

5. ORGANIZATION AS AUTHOR Give the organization's full name or a shortened form of it in a signal phrase or parenthetical reference.

Any study of social welfare involves a close analysis of "the impacts, the benefits, and the costs" of its policies (Social Research Corporation iii).

6. UNKNOWN AUTHOR Use the full title of the work or a shortened version in a signal phrase or parenthetical reference.

"Hype," by one analysis, is "an artificially engendered atmosphere of hysteria" ("Today's Marketplace" 51).

7. AUTHOR OF TWO OR MORE WORKS CITED IN THE SAME PROJECT If your list of works cited has more than one work by the same author, give the title of the work you are citing or a shortened version in a signal phrase or parenthetical reference.

Gardner shows readers their own silliness in his description of a "pointless, ridiculous monster, crouched in the shadows, stinking of dead men, murdered children, and martyred cows" (*Grendel* 2).

8. TWO OR MORE AUTHORS WITH THE SAME LAST NAME Include the author's first *and* last names in a signal phrase or first initial and last name in a parenthetical reference.

Children will learn to write if they are allowed to choose their own subjects, James Britton asserts, citing the Schools Council study of the 1960s (37-42).

9. MULTIVOLUME WORK In a parenthetical reference, note the volume number first and then the page number(s), with a colon and one space between them.

Modernist writers prized experimentation and gradually even sought to blur the line between poetry and prose, according to Forster (3: 150).

If you name only one volume of the work in your list of works cited, include only the page number in the parentheses.

10. LITERARY WORK Literary works are often available in many different editions. For a prose work, cite the page number(s) from the edition you used followed by a semicolon, and then give other identifying information that will lead readers to the passage in any edition. Indicate the act and/or scene in a play (*37; sc. 1*). For a novel, indicate the part or chapter (*175; ch. 4*).

Dostoyevsky's character Mitya wonders aloud about the "terrible tragedies realism inflicts on people" (376; bk. 8, ch. 2).

For a poem, instead of page numbers cite the part (if there is one) and line(s), separated by a period. If you are citing only line numbers, use the word *line(s)* in the first reference (*lines 33–34*).

Whitman speculates, "All goes onward and outward, nothing collapses, / And to die is different from what any one supposed, and luckier" (6.129-30).

For a verse play, give only the act, scene, and line numbers, separated by periods.

As *Macbeth* begins, the witches greet Banquo as "Lesser than Macbeth, and greater" (1.3.65).

11. WORK IN AN ANTHOLOGY For an essay, short story, or other piece of prose reprinted in an anthology, use the name of the author of the work, not the editor of the anthology, but use the page number(s) from the anthology.

> Narratives of captivity play a major role in early writing by women in the United States, as Silko demonstrates (219).

12. SACRED TEXT To cite a sacred text such as the Qur'an or the Bible, give the title of the edition you used, followed by location information, such as the book, chapter, and verse, separated by a period. In your text, spell out the names of books. In parenthetical references, use abbreviations for books with names of five or more letters (*Gen.* for *Genesis*).

> He ignored the admonition "Pride goes before destruction, and a haughty spirit before a fall" (*New Oxford Annotated Bible*, Prov. 16.18).

13. INDIRECT SOURCE Use the abbreviation *qtd. in* to indicate that you're quoting from someone else's report of a conversation, interview, letter, or the like.

> Arthur Miller says, "When somebody is destroyed everybody finally contributes to it, but in Willy's case, the end product would be virtually the same" (qtd. in Martin and Meyer 375).

14. TWO OR MORE SOURCES IN ONE CITATION Separate the information with semicolons.

> Some economists recommend that *employment* be redefined to include unpaid domestic labor (Clark 148; Nevins 39).

15. ENTIRE WORK OR ONE-PAGE ARTICLE Include the reference in the text without any page numbers or parentheses.

> Michael Ondaatje's poetic sensibility transfers beautifully to prose in *The English Patient*.

16. WORK WITHOUT PAGE NUMBERS If a work has no page numbers or is only one page long, you may omit the page number. If a work uses paragraph numbers instead, use the abbreviation *par.* (or *pars.*). If a parenthetical reference to a work with paragraph numbers includes the author's name, use a comma after the name.

> Whitman considered their speech "a source of a native grand opera" (Ellison, par. 13).

17. ELECTRONIC OR NONPRINT SOURCE Give enough information in a signal phrase or parenthetical reference for readers to locate the source in the list of works cited. Usually use the author or title under which you list the source. Specify a source's page, section, paragraph, or screen numbers, if numbered, in parentheses.

> Kilgore, the bloodthirsty lieutenant colonel played by Robert Duvall, declares, "I love the smell of napalm in the morning" (*Apocalypse Now*).

> As a *Slate* analysis has noted, "Prominent sports psychologists get praised for their successes and don't get grief for their failures" (Engber).

Explanatory and Bibliographic Notes

MLA style recommends explanatory notes for information or commentary that would not readily fit into your text but is needed for clarification or further explanation. In addition, MLA style permits bibliographic notes for citing several sources for one point and for offering thanks to, information about, or evaluation of a source. Use superscript numbers in the text to refer readers to the notes, which may appear as endnotes (typed under the heading *Notes* on a separate page after the text but before the list of works cited) or as footnotes at the bottom of the page (typed four lines below the last text line, first line indented one-half inch).

SUPERSCRIPT NUMBER IN TEXT

Stewart emphasizes the existence of social contacts in Hawthorne's life so that the audience will accept a different Hawthorne, one more attuned to modern times than the figure in Woodberry.[3]

NOTE

[3]Woodberry does, however, show that Hawthorne *was* often an unsociable individual. He emphasizes the seclusion of Hawthorne's mother, who separated herself from her family after the death of her husband, often even taking meals alone (28). Woodberry seems to imply that Mrs. Hawthorne's isolation rubbed off onto her son.

Directory to MLA style for works-cited entries

List of Works Cited

A list of works cited is an alphabetical list of the sources you have referred to in your essay. (If your instructor asks you to list everything you have read as background, call the list *Works Consulted.*) Here are some guidelines for preparing such a list:

- Start your list on a separate page after the text of your essay and any notes.

- Continue the consecutive numbering of pages.

- Center the heading *Works Cited* an inch from the top of the page; don't underline or italicize it or enclose it in quotation marks. Double-space between the heading and the first entry, and double-space the entire list.

- Start each entry flush with the left margin, and indent subsequent lines one-half inch.

- List your sources alphabetically by author's (or editor's) last name. If the author is unknown, alphabetize the source by the first word of the title, disregarding *A*, *An*, or *The*.

The sample works-cited entries that follow observe MLA's advice to use italics for words that are often italicized in print. Check whether your instructor would prefer underlining.

PRINT SOURCES: BOOKS

The basic format for a works-cited entry for a print book is outlined on pp. 358–59. For an online book, see p. 370.

1. ONE AUTHOR

Winchester, Simon. *The Meaning of Everything: The Story of the Oxford English Dictionary.* New York: Oxford UP, 2003. Print.

2. TWO OR THREE AUTHORS Give the first author listed on the title page, last name first; then list the name(s) of the other author(s) in regular order, with a comma between authors and the word *and* before the last one.

> Martineau, Jane, Desmond Shawe-Taylor, and Jonathon Bate. *Shakespeare in Art*. London: Merrill, 2003. Print.

3. FOUR OR MORE AUTHORS Give the first author listed on the title page, followed by a comma and *et al.* ("and others"), or list all the names, since the use of *et al.* diminishes the importance of the other contributors.

> Lupton, Ellen, Jennifer Tobias, Alicia Imperiale, Grace Jeffers, and Randi Mates. *Skin: Surface, Substance, and Design*. New York: Princeton Architectural, 2002. Print.

4. ORGANIZATION AS AUTHOR Give the name of the group listed on the title page as the author, even if the same group published the book.

> Getty Trust Publications. *Seeing the Getty Center/Seeing the Getty Gardens*. Los Angeles: Getty Trust Publications, 2000. Print.

5. UNKNOWN AUTHOR Begin the entry with the title, and list the work alphabetically by the first word of the title after any initial *A*, *An*, or *The*.

> *New Concise World Atlas*. New York: Oxford UP, 2003. Print.

6. TWO OR MORE BOOKS BY THE SAME AUTHOR(S) Arrange the entries alphabetically by title. Include the name(s) of the author(s) in the first entry, but in subsequent entries, use three hyphens followed by a period.

> Lorde, Audre. *A Burst of Light*. Ithaca: Firebrand, 1988. Print.

> ---. *Sister Outsider*. Trumansburg: Crossing, 1984. Print.

If you cite a work by one author who is also listed as the first coauthor of another work you cite, list the single-author work first, and repeat the author's name in the entry for the coauthored work. Also repeat the author's name if you cite a work in which that author is listed as the first of a different set of coauthors. In other words, use three hyphens only when the work is by *exactly* the same author(s) as the previous entry.

7. EDITOR Treat an editor as an author, but add a comma and *ed.* (or *eds.*).

> Wall, Cheryl A., ed. *Changing Our Own Words: Essays on Criticism, Theory, and Writing by Black Women*. New Brunswick: Rutgers UP, 1989. Print.

8. AUTHOR AND EDITOR If you have cited the body of the text, begin with the author's name. Then list the editor(s), introduced by *Ed.* ("Edited by"), after the title.

> James, Henry. *Portrait of a Lady*. Ed. Leon Edel. Boston: Houghton, 1963.
>   Print.

If you have cited the editor's contribution, begin with the name(s) of the editor(s), followed by a comma and *ed.* (or *eds.*). Then list the author's name, introduced by *By*, after the title.

> Edel, Leon, ed. *Portrait of a Lady*. By Henry James. Boston: Houghton, 1963.
>   Print.

9. WORK IN AN ANTHOLOGY OR CHAPTER IN A BOOK WITH AN EDITOR List the author(s) of the selection or chapter; its title; the title of the book in which the selection or chapter appears; *Ed.* and the name(s) of the editor(s); the publication information; and the inclusive page numbers of the selection or chapter.

> Komunyakaa, Yusef. "Facing It." *The Seagull Reader*. Ed. Joseph Kelly.
>   New York: Norton, 2000. 126-27. Print.

If the selection was originally published in a periodical and you are asked to supply information for this original source, use the following format. *Rpt.* is the abbreviation for *Reprinted*.

> Byatt, A. S. "The Thing in the Forest." *New Yorker* 3 June 2002: 80-89. Rpt.
>   in *The O. Henry Prize Stories 2003*. Ed. Laura Furman. New York: Anchor,
>   2003. 3-22. Print.

For inclusive page numbers up to 99, note all digits in the second number. For numbers above 99, note only the last two digits and any others that change in the second number (115–18, 1378–79, 296–301).

10. TWO OR MORE ITEMS FROM AN ANTHOLOGY Include the anthology itself in your list of works cited. If the title page uses the term *compiler(s)* rather than *editor(s)*, use the abbreviation *comp.* (or *comps.*) instead of *ed.* (or *eds.*).

> Walker, Dale L., ed. *Westward: A Fictional History of the American West*.
>   New York: Forge, 2003. Print.

Also list each selection separately by its author and title, followed by a cross-reference to the anthology. Alphabetize all entries.

> Estleman, Loren D. "Big Tim Magoon and the Wild West." Walker 391-404.
>   Print.

> Salzer, Susan K. "Miss Libbie Tells All." Walker 199-212. Print.

SOURCE MAP: *Citing Print Books Using MLA Style*

Take information from the book's title page and copyright page (on the reverse side of the title page), not from the book's cover or a library catalog.

① *Author.* List the last name first, followed by a comma, the first name, and the middle initial (if given). Omit titles such as *MD*, *PhD*, or *Sir;* include suffixes after the name and a comma (*O'Driscoll, Gerald P., Jr.*). End with a period.

② *Title.* Italicize the title and any subtitle; capitalize all major words. End with a period.

③ *City of publication.* If more than one city is given, use the first one listed. For foreign cities that may be unfamiliar to your readers, add an abbreviation of the country or province (*Cork, Ire.*). Follow it with a colon.

④ *Publisher.* Give a shortened version of the publisher's name (*Harper* for *HarperCollins Publishers; Harcourt* for *Harcourt Brace; Oxford UP* for *Oxford University Press*). Follow it with a comma.

⑤ *Year of publication.* Consult the copyright page. If more than one copyright date is given, use the most recent one. End with a period.

⑥ *Medium of publication.* End with the medium (*Print*) followed by a period.

For a book by one author, use the following format:

Last name, First name. *Title of book.* City: Publisher, Year. Medium.

A citation for the book on p. 359 would look like this:

AUTHOR, LAST NAME FIRST   TITLE AND SUBTITLE OF WORK, ITALICIZED   PUBLISHER'S CITY AND NAME, YEAR OF PUBLICATION

Twitchell, James B. *Living It Up: America's Love Affair with Luxury.* New York:

MEDIUM

Simon, 2002. Print.

DOUBLE-SPACE; INDENT ONE-HALF INCH

① ②

LIVING IT UP

America's Love Affair with 𝓛*uxury*

James B. Twitchell

For Liz

SIMON & SCHUSTER
NEW YORK   LONDON   TORONTO
SYDNEY   SINGAPORE

Simon & Schuster
Rockefeller Center
1230 Avenue of the Americas
New York, NY 10020

Copyright © 2002 by James B. Twitchell
All rights reserved, including the right of reproduction
in whole or in part in any form.

First Simon & Schuster Edition 2003
SIMON & SCHUSTER and colophon are registered trademarks
of Simon & Schuster, Inc.
Published by arrangement with Columbia University Press

For information regarding special discounts for bulk purchases,
please contact Simon & Schuster Special Sales at 1-800-456-6798
or business@simonandschuster.com
Manufactured in the United States of America
10 9 8 7 6 5 4 3 2 1
The Library of Congress Cataloging-in-Publication Data
Twitchell, James B.
  Living it up : our love affair with luxury/James B. Twitchell. —1st Simon
& Schuster ed.
    p.   cm.
  Includes bibliographical references and index.
    1. Affluent consumers—Psychology. 2. Luxuries—Marketing. I. Title.
  HF5415.32.T95   2003   306.3—dc21   2003041507
ISBN 0-7432-4506-7

③ New York   London   Toronto

④ Simon & Schuster

⑤ Copyright © 2002 by James B. Twitchell

11. TRANSLATION Begin the entry with the author's name, and give the translator's name, preceded by *Trans.* ("Translated by"), after the title.

> Hietamies, Laila. *Red Moon over White Sea*. Trans. Borje Vahamaki. Beaverton, OR: Aspasia, 2000. Print.

If you cite a translated selection from an anthology, add *Trans.* and the translator's name before the title of the anthology.

> Horace. *The Art of Poetry*. Trans. Smith Palmer Bovie. *The Critical Tradition: Classic Texts and Contemporary Trends*. Ed. David H. Richter. 2nd ed. Boston: Bedford, 1998. 68-78. Print.

12. BOOK IN A LANGUAGE OTHER THAN ENGLISH If necessary, you may provide a translation of the book's title in brackets. You may also choose to give the English name of a foreign city in brackets.

> Benedetti, Mario. *La borra del café* [*The Coffee Grind*]. Buenos Aires: Sudamericana, 2000. Print.

13. EDITION OTHER THAN THE FIRST Add the information, in abbreviated form, after the title.

> Walker, John A. *Art in the Age of Mass Media*. 3rd ed. London: Pluto, 2001. Print.

14. MULTIVOLUME WORK If you cite only one volume, give the volume number after the title, using the abbreviation *Vol.* You may give the number of volumes in the complete work at the end of the entry, using the abbreviation *vols.*

> Ch'oe, Yong-Ho, Peter Lee, and William Theodore De Barry, eds. *Sources of Korean Tradition*. Vol. 2. New York: Columbia UP, 2000. Print. 2 vols.

If you cite two or more volumes, give the number of volumes in the complete work after the title.

> Ch'oe, Yong-Ho, Peter Lee, and William Theodore De Barry, eds. *Sources of Korean Tradition*. 2 vols. New York: Columbia UP, 2000. Print.

15. PREFACE, FOREWORD, INTRODUCTION, OR AFTERWORD Begin with the author of the item and the item title (not italicized or in quotation marks). Then give the title of the book and the book's author (preceded by the word *By*) or editor (preceded by *Ed.*). If the same person wrote or edited both the book and the cited item, use just the last name after *By* or *Ed.* List the page numbers of the item at the end of the entry.

Atwan, Robert. Foreword. *The Best American Essays 2002*. Ed. Stephen Jay
Gould. Boston: Houghton, 2002. viii-xii. Print.

16. ENTRY IN A REFERENCE WORK List the author of the entry, if known.
If no author is identified, begin with the title. For a well-known reference
work, just note the edition number and year of publication, or designate the
edition by its year of publication. If the entries in the work are in alphabetical
order, you need not give volume or page numbers. (For an electronic version
of a reference work, see p. 371.)

"Hero." *Merriam-Webster's Collegiate Dictionary*. 11th ed. 2003. Print.

Kettering, Alison McNeil. "Art Nouveau." *World Book Encyclopedia*. 2002 ed.
Print.

17. BOOK THAT IS PART OF A SERIES Cite the series name as it appears on
the title page, followed by any series number.

Nichanian, Marc, and Vartan Matiossian, eds. *Yeghishe Charents: Poet of the
Revolution*. Armenian Studies Ser. 5. Costa Mesa: Mazda, 2003. Print.

18. REPUBLICATION To cite a modern edition of an older book, add the
original publication date, followed by a period, after the title.

Scott, Walter. *Kenilworth*. 1821. New York: Dodd, 1956. Print.

19. PUBLISHER'S IMPRINT If a book is published under a publisher's imprint (indicated on the title page), hyphenate the imprint and the publisher's
name.

Gilligan, Carol. *The Birth of Pleasure: A New Map of Love*. New York:
Vintage-Random, 2003. Print.

20. BOOK WITH A TITLE WITHIN THE TITLE Do not italicize the title of a book
within the title of a book you are citing. Enclose in quotation marks the title
of a short work within a book title, and italicize it as you do the rest of the
title.

Mullaney, Julie. *Arundhati Roy's* The God of Small Things: *A Reader's Guide*.
New York: Continuum, 2002. Print.

Rhynes, Martha. *"I, Too, Sing America": The Story of Langston Hughes*.
Greensboro: Morgan, 2002. Print.

21. SACRED TEXT To cite individual published editions of sacred books,
begin with the title. If a specified version is not part of the title, list the

version after the title. If you are not citing a particular edition, do not include sacred texts in the works-cited list.

PRINT SOURCES: PERIODICALS

The basic format for a works-cited entry for a periodical article appears on pp. 364–65.

22. ARTICLE IN A JOURNAL Follow the journal title with the volume number, a period, the issue number (if given), and the year (in parentheses).

> Gigante, Denise. "The Monster in the Rainbow: Keats and the Science of Life." *PMLA* 117.3 (2002): 433-48. Print.

23. ARTICLE IN A JOURNAL WITH MORE THAN ONE SERIES Give the appropriate designation—whether the number of the series (*2nd*, *3rd*, etc.) or the abbreviation *os* (for "old series") or *ns* (for "new series")—between the title and the volume number.

> Fertel, Randy. "Katrina Five Ways." *Kenyon Review* ns 28.3 (2006): 71-84. Print.

24. ARTICLE THAT SKIPS PAGES When an article skips pages, give only the first page number and a plus sign.

> Tyrnauer, Matthew. "Empire by Martha." *Vanity Fair* Sept. 2002: 364+. Print.

25. ARTICLE WITH A TITLE WITHIN THE TITLE Enclose in single quotation marks the title of a short work within an article title. Italicize the title of a book within an article title.

> Frey, Leonard H. "Irony and Point of View in 'That Evening Sun.'" *Faulkner Studies* 2 (1953): 33-40. Print.

26. ARTICLE IN A MONTHLY MAGAZINE Put the month (or months, hyphenated) before the year. Abbreviate months other than *May*, *June*, and *July*. Do not include volume or issue numbers.

> Fonda, Daren. "Saving the Dead." *Life* Apr. 2000: 69-72. Print.

27. ARTICLE IN A WEEKLY MAGAZINE Include the day, month, and year in that order, with no commas between them. Do not include volume or issue numbers.

> Gilgoff, Dan. "Unusual Suspects." *US News and World Report* 26 Nov. 2001: 51. Print.

28. ARTICLE IN A NEWSPAPER After the author and title of the article, give the name of the newspaper as it appears on the front page but without any initial *A*, *An*, or *The*. For locally published newspapers, add the city in brackets after the name if it is not part of the name. Then give the date and the edition (if listed), followed by a colon, a space, the section number or letter (if listed), and the page number(s). If the article does not appear on consecutive pages, give the first page followed by a plus sign.

> Bernstein, Nina. "On Lucille Avenue, the Immigration Debate." *New York Times* 26 June 2006, late ed.: A1+. Print.

29. ARTICLE IN A COLLECTION OF REPRINTED ARTICLES First give the citation for the original publication. Then give the citation for the collection in which the article is reprinted. Insert *Rpt. in* ("Reprinted in") between the two citations. Use *Comp.* to identify the compiler. *Ed.* and *Trans.* are other common abbreviations used in citing a collection.

> Quindlen, Anna. "Playing God on No Sleep." *Newsweek* 2 July 2001: 64. Rpt. in *The Best American Magazine Writing 2002*. Comp. Amer. Soc. of Magazine Eds. New York: Perennial, 2002. 458-62. Print.

30. EDITORIAL OR LETTER TO THE EDITOR Use the label *Editorial* or *Letter*, not italicized or in quotation marks, after the title or, if there is no title, after the author's name, if given.

> Magee, Doug. "Soldier's Home." Editorial. *Nation* 26 Mar. 1988: 400-01. Print.

31. REVIEW List the reviewer's name and the title of the review, if any, followed by *Rev. of* and the title and author, director, or other creator of the work reviewed. Then add the publication information.

> Franklin, Nancy. "Dead On." Rev. of *Deadwood*, by David Milch. *New Yorker* 12 June 2006: 158-59. Print.

32. UNSIGNED ARTICLE Begin with the article title, alphabetizing the entry according to the first word after any initial *A*, *An*, or *The*.

> "Performance of the Week." *Time* 6 Oct. 2003: 18. Print.

ELECTRONIC SOURCES

Electronic sources such as Web sites differ from print sources in the ease with which they can be—and frequently are—changed, updated, or even eliminated. In addition, the various electronic media do not organize their works the same way.

SOURCE MAP: Citing Articles from Print Periodicals Using MLA Style

(1) *Author.* List the last name first, followed by a comma, the first name, and the middle initial (if given). Omit titles such as *MD, PhD,* or *Sir;* include suffixes after the name and a comma (*O'Driscoll, Gerald P., Jr.*). End with a period.

(2) *Article title.* Enclose the title and any subtitle in quotation marks, and capitalize all major words. The closing period goes inside the closing quotation mark.

(3) *Periodical title.* Italicize the periodical title (deleting any initial *A, An,* or *The*), and capitalize all major words. For journals, give the volume number; if each issue starts with page 1, include the issue number as well.

(4) *Date of publication.* For journals, list the year in parentheses, followed by a colon. For monthly magazines, list the month and year. For weekly magazines and newspapers, list the day, month, and year.

(5) *Inclusive page numbers.* For page numbers up to 99, note all digits in the second number. For numbers above 99, note only the last two digits and any others that change in the second number (*115–18, 1378–79, 296–301*). Include section letters for newspapers. End with a period.

(6) *Medium of publication.* End with the medium of publication (*Print*) followed by a period.

For a journal article, use the following format:

> Last name, First name. "Title of article." *Journal* Volume number (year): Page number(s). Print.

For a newspaper article, use the following format:

> Last name, First name. "Title." *Newspaper* Date, Edition (if any): Section number (if any): Page number(s) (including section letter, if any). Print.

For a magazine article, use the following format:

> Last name, First name. "Title of article." *Magazine* Date: Page number(s). Print.

A citation for the magazine article on p. 365 would look like this:

364

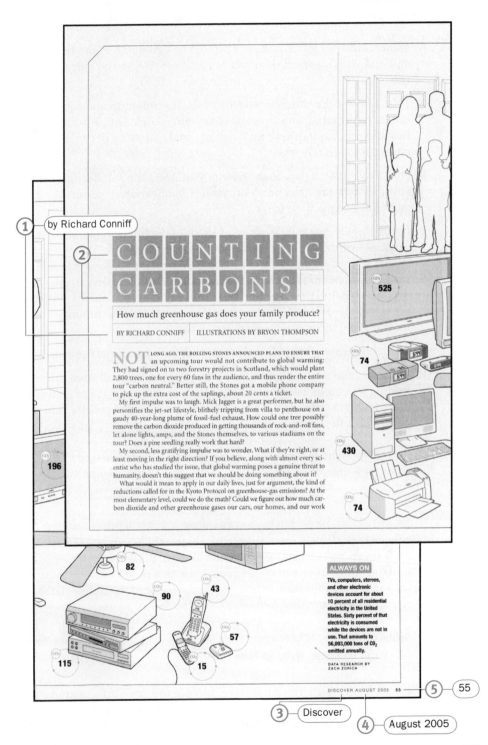

by Richard Conniff

COUNTING CARBONS

How much greenhouse gas does your family produce?

BY RICHARD CONNIFF   ILLUSTRATIONS BY BRYON THOMPSON

NOT LONG AGO, THE ROLLING STONES ANNOUNCED PLANS TO ENSURE THAT an upcoming tour would not contribute to global warming: They had signed on to two forestry projects in Scotland, which would plant 2,800 trees, one for every 60 fans in the audience, and thus render the entire tour "carbon neutral." Better still, the Stones got a mobile phone company to pick up the extra cost of the saplings, about 20 cents a ticket.

My first impulse was to laugh. Mick Jagger is a great performer, but he also personifies the jet-set lifestyle, blithely tripping from villa to penthouse on a gaudy 40-year-long plume of fossil-fuel exhaust. How could one tree possibly remove the carbon dioxide produced in getting thousands of rock-and-roll fans, let alone lights, amps, and the Stones themselves, to various stadiums on the tour? Does a pine seedling really work that hard?

My second, less gratifying impulse was to wonder, What if they're right, or at least moving in the right direction? If you believe, along with almost every scientist who has studied the issue, that global warming poses a genuine threat to humanity, doesn't it suggest that we should be doing something about it?

What would it mean to apply in our daily lives, just for argument, the kind of reductions called for in the Kyoto Protocol on greenhouse-gas emissions? At the most elementary level, could we do the math? Could we figure out how much carbon dioxide and other greenhouse gases our cars, our homes, and our work

CO_2 525

CO_2 74

CO_2 430

CO_2 74

CO_2 196

CO_2 82

CO_2 90

CO_2 43

CO_2 57

CO_2 115

CO_2 15

ALWAYS ON

TVs, computers, stereos, and other electronic devices account for about 10 percent of all residential electricity in the United States. Sixty percent of that electricity is consumed while the devices are not in use. That amounts to 56,093,000 tons of CO_2 emitted annually.

DATA RESEARCH BY ZACH ZORICH

Discover

August 2005

55

The most commonly cited electronic sources are documents from Web sites and databases. The entry for such a source may include up to five basic elements, as in the following list, but must always include the last two:

- *Author*. List the last name first, followed by a comma and the first name, and end with a period. If no author is given, begin the entry with the title.

- *Title*. Enclose the title and subtitle of the document in quotation marks unless you're citing an entire site or an online book, both of which should be italicized. Capitalize all major words, and end with a period inside the closing quotation marks.

- *Print publication information*. Give any information the document provides about a previous or simultaneous publication in print, using the guidelines on pp. 355–63.

- *Electronic publication information*. List all of the following items that you can find, with a period after each one: the title of the site, italicized, with all major words capitalized; the editor(s) of the site, preceded by *Ed.*; the version number of the site, preceded by *Vers.*; the date of electronic publication or of the latest update, with the month, if any, abbreviated except for *May*, *June*, and *July*; the name of any sponsoring institution or organization; and the medium consulted (*Web*).

- *Access information*. Give the most recent date you accessed the source.

- *URLs*. Include a URL only if you think your readers will have difficulty finding your source without one. If you do include a URL, put it after the period following the date of access, enclose it in angle brackets, and put a period after the closing bracket.

Further guidelines for citing electronic sources can be found in the *MLA Handbook for Writers of Research Papers*, Seventh Edition, and online at www.mla.org.

33. ARTICLE FROM AN ONLINE DATABASE OR A SUBSCRIPTION SERVICE The basic format for citing a work from a database appears on pp. 368–69. For a work from an online database, provide all of the following elements that are available: the author's name (if given); the title of the work in quotation marks; any print publication information; the name of the online database, italicized; the medium consulted (*Web*); and the date of access.

Goldman, William. "*The Princess Bride* Shooting Draft." 1987. *Internet Movie Script Database*. Web. 12 June 2008.

For a work from a subscription service, include the same information as for an online database; after the information about the work, give the name of the database, italicized; the medium consulted (*Web*); and the date of access.

Collins, Ross F. "Cattle Barons and Ink Slingers: How Cow Country Journalists Created a Great American Myth." *American Journalism* 24.3 (2007); 7–29. *Communication and Mass Media Complete*. Web. 7 Feb. 2008.

34. WORK FROM A WEB SITE For basic information on citing a work from a Web site, see pp. 372–73. Include all of the following elements that are available: the author; the title of the document in quotation marks; the name of the Web site, italicized; the name of the publisher or sponsor (if none is available, use *N.p.*); the date of publication (if not available, use *n.d.*); the medium consulted (*Web*); and the date of access.

"Hands Off Public Broadcasting." *Media Matters for America*. Media Matters for America, 24 May 2005. Web. 31 May 2005.

Stauder, Ellen Keck. "Darkness Audible: Negative Capability and Mark Doty's 'Nocturne in Black and Gold.'" *Romantic Circles Praxis Series*. Ed. Orrin Wang. 2003. Web. 28 Sept. 2003.

35. ENTIRE WEB SITE Follow the guidelines for a specific work from the Web, beginning with the name of the author, editor, compiler, director, narrator, or translator, followed by the title of the Web site, italicized; the name of the sponsor or publisher (if none, use *N.p.*); the date of publication or last update; the medium of publication (*Web*); and the date of access.

Bernstein, Charles, Kenneth Goldsmith, Martin Spinelli, and Patrick Durgin, eds. *Electronic Poetry Corner*. SUNY Buffalo, 2003. Web. 26 Sept. 2006.

Weather.com. Weather Channel Interactive, 2006. Web. 13 Mar. 2006.

For a personal Web site, include the name of the person who created the site; the title, italicized, or (if there is no title) a description such as *Home page*, not italicized; the publisher or sponsor of the site (if none, use *N.p.*); the date of the last update; the medium of publication (*Web*); and the date of access.

Lunsford, Andrea A. Home page. Stanford U, 27 Mar. 2003. Web. 17 May 2006.

36. ACADEMIC COURSE OR DEPARTMENT WEB SITE For a course site, include the name of the instructor, the title of the course in quotation marks, a description such as *Course home page*, the department name, the institution, the dates of the course, the medium consulted (*Web*), and the access information.

Creekmur, Corey K., and Philip Lutgendorf. "Topics in Asian Cinema; Popular Hindi Cinema." Course home page. Depts. of English, Cinema, and Comparative Literature, U of Iowa, Fall 2004. Web. 13 Mar. 2007.

SOURCE MAP: Citing Articles from Databases Using MLA Style

Library subscriptions—such as InfoTrac, EBSCOhost, ProQuest, and LexisNexis—provide access to huge databases of articles.

① *Author.* List the last name first.

② *Article title.* Enclose the title and any subtitle in quotation marks.

③ *Periodical title.* Italicize it. Exclude any initial *A*, *An*, or *The*.

④ *Print publication information.* List the volume and issue number, if any; the date of publication, including the day (if given), month, and year, in that order; and the inclusive page numbers.

⑤ *Name of databases.* Provide the name of the database, italicized.

⑥ *Medium.* For an online database, use *Web*.

⑦ *Date of access.* Give the day, month, and year, then a period.

For an article from a database, use the following format:

[Citation format for journal, magazine, or newspaper article — see pp. 362–63]. *Name of database*. Medium. Date accessed.

A citation for the article on p. 369 would look like this:

AUTHOR   ARTICLE TITLE   PERIODICAL TITLE
Wallace, Maurice. "Richard Wright's Black Medusa." *Journal of African*

PRINT PUBLICATION INFORMATION   DATABASE
American History 88.1 (2003): 71+ . *Expanded Academic ASAP*.

MEDIUM   ACCESS DATE
Web. 28 July 2005.

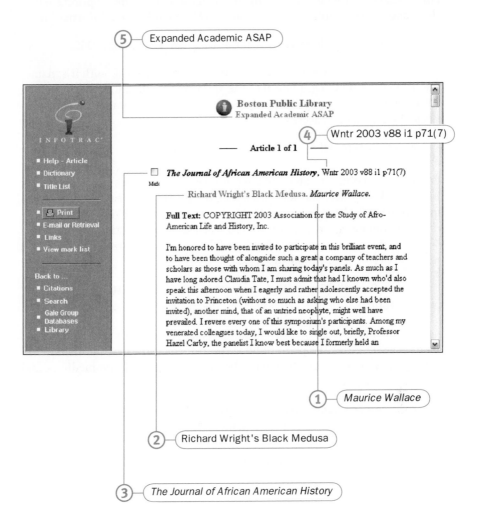

⑤ Expanded Academic ASAP

Boston Public Library
Expanded Academic ASAP

④ Wntr 2003 v88 i1 p71(7)

—— **Article 1 of 1** ——

☐ *The Journal of African American History*, Wntr 2003 v88 i1 p71(7)
Mark

Richard Wright's Black Medusa. *Maurice Wallace.*

Full Text: COPYRIGHT 2003 Association for the Study of Afro-American Life and History, Inc.

I'm honored to have been invited to participate in this brilliant event, and to have been thought of alongside such a great a company of teachers and scholars as those with whom I am sharing today's panels. As much as I have long adored Claudia Tate, I must admit that had I known who'd also speak this afternoon when I eagerly and rather adolescently accepted the invitation to Princeton (without so much as asking who else had been invited), another mind, that of an untried neophyte, might well have prevailed. I revere every one of this symposium's participants. Among my venerated colleagues today, I would like to single out, briefly, Professor Hazel Carby, the panelist I know best because I formerly held an

INFOTRAC

- Help - Article
- Dictionary
- Title List

- 🖶 Print
- E-mail or Retrieval
- Links
- View mark list

Back to ...
- Citations
- Search
- Gale Group Databases
- Library

① Maurice Wallace

② Richard Wright's Black Medusa

③ The Journal of African American History

For a department Web site, give the department name, a description such as *Home page*, the institution, the medium (*Web*), and the access information.

> Dept. of English. Home page. Amherst Coll., n.d. Web. 5 Apr. 2006.

37. WEB LOG (BLOG) For an entire Web log, give the author's name; the title of the Web log, italicized; the sponsor or publisher of the Web log (if there is none, use *N.p.*); the date of the most recent update; the medium (*Web*); and the date of access.

> Atrios. *Eschaton*. N.p., 27 June 2006. Web. 27 June 2006.

For a post or comment on a Web log, follow the guidelines for a short work from a Web site. Give the author's name; the title of the post or comment, in quotation marks (if there is no title, use the description *Web log post* or *Web log comment*, not italicized); the title of the Web log, italicized; the sponsor of the Web log (if there is none, use *N.p.*); the date of the most recent update; the medium (*Web*); and the date of access.

> Parker, Randall. "Growth Rate for Electric Hybrid Vehicle Market Debated." *FuturePundit*. N.p., 20 May 2005. Web. 24 May 2005.

38. ONLINE BOOK Cite an online book as you would a print book (see models 1–21). After the print publication information (city, publisher, and year), if any, give the electronic publication information, the medium, and the date of access.

> Euripides. *The Trojan Women*. Trans. Gilbert Murray. New York: Oxford UP, 1915. Internet Sacred Text Archive. Web. 12 Oct. 2008.

Cite a part of an online book as you would a part of a print book (see models 9 and 15). Give the available print and electronic publication information, the medium, and the date of access.

> Riis, Jacob. "The Genesis of the Gang." *The Battle with the Slum*. New York: Macmillan, 1902. *Bartleby.com: Great Books Online*. 2000. Web. 31 Mar. 2007.

39. ONLINE POEM Include the poet's name and the title of the poem, followed by the print publication information for the poem (if applicable). End with title of the site or database, the medium, and the date of access.

> Dickinson, Emily. "The Grass." *Poems: Emily Dickinson*. Boston: Roberts Brothers, 1891. *Humanities Text Initiative American Verse Project*. Ed. Nancy Kushigian. Web. 6 Jan. 2006.

40. ARTICLE IN AN ONLINE JOURNAL, MAGAZINE, OR NEWSPAPER If the journal, magazine, or newspaper also appears in print, include print publication information, if it is available (see models 22–32). If the print article includes

① by Øyvind Tønnesson

② Mahatma Gandhi, the Missing Laureate

③ http://nobelprize.org/nobel_prizes/peace/articles/gandhi/index.html

④ The Official Web Site of the Nobel Foundation

⑤ 1 December 1999

44. ENTRY IN A WIKI Because wiki content is collectively edited, do not include an author. Treat a wiki as you would a work from a Web site (see model 34). Include the title of the entry; the name of the wiki, italicized; the sponsor or publisher of the wiki (use *N.p.* if there is no sponsor); the date of the latest update; the medium (*Web*); and the date of access. Check with your instructor before using a wiki as a source.

"Fédération Internationale de Football Association." *Wikipedia*. Wikipedia
　　Foundation, 27 June 2006. Web. 27 June 2006.

45. POSTING TO A DISCUSSION GROUP Begin with the author's name and the title of the posting in quotation marks (or the words *online posting*). Follow with the name of the Web site, the sponsor or publisher of the site (use *N.p.* if there is no sponsor), the date of publication, the medium (*Web*), and the date of access.

Daly, Catherine. "Poetry Slams." *Poetics Discussion List*. SUNY Buffalo,
　　29 Aug. 2003. Web. 1 Oct. 2003.

46. POSTING ON A SOCIAL NETWORKING SITE To cite a message on Facebook or another social networking site, include the writer's name, a description of the posting that mentions the recipient, the date of the message, the medium of delivery, and the date of access. (The MLA does not provide guidelines for citing postings on such sites; this model is based on the MLA's guidelines for citing email.)

Ferguson, Sarah. Message to the author. 6 Mar. 2008. Facebook posting.
　　8 Mar. 2008.

47. EMAIL Include the writer's name; the subject line, in quotation marks; *Message to* (not italicized or in quotation marks) followed by the recipient's name; the date of the message; and the medium of delivery (*E-mail*). (MLA style hyphenates *e-mail*.)

Harris, Jay. "Thoughts on Impromptu Stage Productions." Message to the
　　author. 16 July 2006. E-mail.

48. COMPUTER SOFTWARE OR VIDEO GAME Include the title, italicized; version number (if given); and publication information. If you are citing downloaded software, replace the publication information with the medium and the date of access.

The Sims 2. Redwood City: Electronic Arts, 2004. CD-ROM.

Web Cache Illuminator. Vers. 4.02. NorthStar Solutions, n.d. Web. 12 Nov.
　　2003.

49. PERIODICALLY REVISED CD-ROM For a periodically revised CD-ROM, begin with the author, title, and any available print publication information. Then give the place of publication, the name of the company or group producing it, the electronic publication date (month and year, if available), and the medium (*CD-ROM*).

> Ashenfelter, Orley, and Kathryn Graddy. "Auctions and the Price of Art." *Journal of Economic Literature* 41.3 (2003): 763-87. Nashville: Amer. Economic Assn., Sept. 2003. CD-ROM.

50. SINGLE-ISSUE CD-ROM Cite a CD-ROM like a book if it is not regularly updated.

> *Cambridge Advanced Learner's Dictionary*. Cambridge: Cambridge UP, 2003. CD-ROM.

51. MULTIDISC CD-ROM If the CD-ROM includes more than one disc, include either the total number of discs (*3 discs*) or, if you used material from only one, the number of that disc.

> *IRIS: Immigration Research Information Service, LawDesk*. Disc 2. Eagon, MN: West, 2003. CD-ROM.

OTHER SOURCES (INCLUDING ONLINE VERSIONS)

If an online version is not shown here, use the appropriate model for the source and then end with the medium, and the date of access.

52. REPORT OR PAMPHLET Cite a report or pamphlet by following the guidelines for a print or an online book.

> Allen, Katherine, and Lee Rainie. *Parents Online*. Washington: Pew Internet and Amer. Life Project, 2002. Print.

> Environmental Working Group. *Dead in the Water*. Washington: Environmental Working Group. 2006. Web. 24 Apr. 2006.

53. GOVERNMENT PUBLICATION Begin with the author, if identified. Otherwise, start with the name of the government, followed by the agency and any subdivision. Use abbreviations if they can be readily understood. Then give the title. For congressional documents, cite the number, session, and house of Congress (using *S* for Senate and *H* or *HR* for House of Representatives); the type (*Report*, *Resolution*, *Document*) in abbreviated form; and the number of the material. If you cite the *Congressional Record*, give only the date and page number(s). Otherwise, end with the publication information. For print versions of federal documents, the publisher is often the Government Printing Office (GPO). For online versions, follow the models for a work from a Web site (model 34) or an entire Web site (model 35).

Gregg, Judd. *Report to Accompany the Genetic Information Act of 2003*. US
108th Cong., 1st sess. S. Rept. 108-22. Washington: GPO, 2003. Print.

Kinsella, Kevin, and Victoria Velkoff. *An Aging World: 2001*. US Bureau of
the Census. Washington: GPO, 2001. Print.

United States. Environmental Protection Agency. Office of Emergency
and Remedial Response. *This Is Superfund*. Jan. 2000. Environmental
Protection Agency. Web. 16 Aug. 2002.

54. PUBLISHED PROCEEDINGS OF A CONFERENCE Cite proceedings as you
would a book. If the title doesn't include enough information about the conference, add necessary information after the title.

Cleary, John, and Gary Gurtler, eds. *Proceedings of the Boston Area
Colloquium in Ancient Philosophy 2002*. Boston: Brill Academic, 2003.
Print.

55. UNPUBLISHED DISSERTATION OR THESIS Enclose the title in quotation
marks. Add the label *Diss.*, the school, and the year the work was accepted. If
you are citing a thesis, use a label such as *MA thesis* (or whatever is appropriate) instead of *Diss.*

LeCourt, Donna. "The Self in Motion: The Status of the (Student) Subject in
Composition Studies." Diss. Ohio State U, 1993. Print.

56. PUBLISHED DISSERTATION Cite a published dissertation as a book,
adding the identification *Diss.* and the university. If the dissertation was
published by University Microfilms International, end the entry with *Ann
Arbor: UMI*, the year, and the medium.

Yau, Rittchell Ann. *The Portrayal of Immigration in a Selection of Picture
Books Published since 1970*. Diss. U of San Francisco, 2003. Ann Arbor:
UMI, 2003. Print.

57. DISSERTATION ABSTRACT To cite the abstract of a dissertation using
Dissertation Abstracts International (DAI), include the *DAI* volume, year (in parentheses), and page number.

Huang-Tiller, Gillian C. "The Power of the Meta-Genre: Cultural, Sexual,
and Racial Politics of the American Modernist Sonnet." Diss. U of Notre
Dame, 2000. *DAI* 61 (2000): 1401. Print.

58. UNPUBLISHED OR PERSONAL INTERVIEW List the person interviewed,
and then use the label *Telephone interview*, *Personal interview*, or *E-mail interview*. End with the date(s) the interview took place.

Freedman, Sasha. Personal interview. 10 Nov. 2006.

59. PUBLISHED OR BROADCAST INTERVIEW List the person interviewed and then the title of the interview. If the interview has no title, use the label *Interview* and name the interviewer, if relevant. Then identify the source.

> Ebert, Robert. Interview with Matthew Rothschild. *Progressive*. Progressive
> Magazine, Aug. 2003. Web. 5 Oct. 2003.

> Taylor, Max. "Max Taylor on Winning." *Time* 13 Nov. 2000: 66. Print.

To cite a broadcast interview, end with information about the program, the date(s) the interview took place, and the medium.

> Revkin, Andrew. Interview by Terry Gross. *Fresh Air*. Natl. Public Radio.
> WNYC, New York, 14 June 2006. Radio.

60. UNPUBLISHED LETTER Cite a published letter as a work in an anthology (see model 9). If the letter is unpublished, follow this form, including "MS." for manuscript (handwritten) letters, and "TS." (typescript) for typed letters:

> Anzaldúa, Gloria. Letter to the author. 10 Sept. 2002. MS.

61. OTHER UNPUBLISHED WORK Begin with the author's name and the title or, if there is no title, a description of the material. Then note the form of the material (*MS.* for *manuscript* or *TS.* for *typescript*) and any identifying numbers assigned to it. End by giving the name and location of the library or research institution housing the material, if applicable.

> Woolf, Virginia. "The Searchlight." TS. Ser. III, Box 4, Item 184. Papers of
> Virginia Woolf, 1902-1956. Smith Coll., Northampton.

62. LEGAL SOURCE To cite a legal case, give the name of the case, the number of the case (using the abbreviation *No.*), the name of the court, and the date of the decision.

> Eldred v. Ashcroft. No. 01-618. Supreme Ct. of the US. 15 Jan. 2003. Print.

To cite an act, give the name of the act followed by its Public Law (*Pub. L.*) number, the date the act was enacted, and its Statutes at Large (*Stat.*) cataloging number.

> Museum and Library Services Act of 2003. Pub. L. 108-81. 25 Sept. 2003.
> Stat. 117.991. Print.

63. FILM, VIDEO, OR DVD If you cite a particular person's work, start the entry with that person's name. In general, start with the title, italicized; then name the director, the distributor, and the year of release. Other contributors, such as writers or performers, may follow the director. If you cite a video or DVD instead of a theatrical release, include the original film release date (if relevant) and the label *Videocassette* or *DVD*. For material found on a Web site, give the name of the site or database, the medium (*Web*), and the access date.

> Moore, Michael, dir. *Bowling for Columbine*. 2002. *BowlingforColumbine.com*. Web. 30 Sept. 2005.

> *Spirited Away*. Dir. Hiyao Miyazaki. Perf. Daveigh Chase, Suzanne Pleshette, and Jason Marsden. 2001. Walt Disney Video, 2003. DVD.

> *Water*. Dir. Deepa Mehta. Fox Searchlight, 2006. Film.

64. TELEVISION OR RADIO PROGRAM In general, begin with the title of the program, italicized. Then list any important contributors (narrator, writer, director, actors); the network; the local station and city, if any; and the broadcast date and the medium. To cite a particular person's work, begin the entry with that name. To cite a particular episode, begin with the episode title, in quotation marks.

> *Box Office Bombshell: Marilyn Monroe*. Writ. Andy Thomas, Jeff Schefel, and Kevin Burns. Dir. Bill Harris. Narr. Peter Graves. A&E Biography. Arts and Entertainment Network, 23 Oct. 2002. Television.

> "The Fleshy Part of the Thigh." *The Sopranos*. Writ. Diane Frolov and Andrew Schneider. Dir. Alan Taylor. HBO, 2 Apr. 2006. Television.

> Komando, Kim. "E-mail Hacking and the Law." *CBS Radio*. CBS Radio Inc., 28 Oct. 2003. Web. 11 Nov. 2003.

65. SOUND RECORDING Begin with the name of the person or group you wish to emphasize (such as the composer, conductor, or band). Then give the title of the recording or musical composition; the artist(s), if appropriate; the manufacturer; and the year of issue. Give the medium (such as *CD*, *MP3 file*, or *LP*) at the end. If you are citing a particular song or selection, include its title, in quotation marks, before the title of the recording. If you are citing a piece of instrumental music (such as a symphony) that is identified *only* by form, number, and key, do not italicize or enclose it in quotation marks.

> Fountains of Wayne. "Bright Future in Sales." *Welcome Interstate Managers*. S-Curve, 2003. CD.

> Grieg, Edvard. Concerto in A minor, op. 16. Cond. Eugene Ormandy. Philadelphia Orch. LP. RCA, 1989. LP.

> Sonic Youth. "Incinerate." *Rather Ripped*. Geffen, 2006. MP3 file.

66. MUSICAL COMPOSITION When you are *not* citing a specific published version, first give the composer's name, followed by the title. Italicize the title of an opera, a ballet, or a piece of instrumental music that is identified by name.

> Mozart, Wolfgang Amadeus. *Don Giovanni*, K527.

> Mozart, Wolfgang Amadeus. Symphony no. 41 in C major, K551.

Cite a published score as you would a book. If you include the date when the composition was written, do so immediately following the title.

> Schoenberg, Arnold. *Chamber Symphony No. 1 for 15 Solo Instruments,*
> *Op. 9.* 1906. New York: Dover, 2002. Print.

67. LECTURE OR SPEECH List the speaker, the title in quotation marks, the name of the sponsoring institution or group, the place, the date, and the medium. If the speech is untitled, use a label such as *Lecture or Keynote speech*.

> Colbert, Stephen. Speech. White House Correspondents' Association Dinner.
> *YouTube*. YouTube, LLC, 29 Apr. 2006. Web. 20 May 2006.

> Eugenides, Jeffrey. Lecture. Portland Arts and Lectures. Arlene Schnitzer
> Concert Hall, Portland, OR. 30 Sept. 2003. Lecture.

68. LIVE PERFORMANCE List the title, other appropriate details (composer, writer, performer, or director), the place, and the date. To cite a particular person's work, begin the entry with that name.

> *Anything Goes*. By Cole Porter. Perf. Klea Blackhurst. Shubert Theater, New
> Haven. 7 Oct. 2003. Performance.

69. PODCAST Include all of the following that are relevant and available: the speaker, the title of the podcast, the title of the program, the host or performers, the title of the site, the site's sponsor, the date of posting, the medium (such as *MP3 file* or *Web*) and the access date.(This model is based on MLA guidelines for a short work from a Web site.)

> "Seven Arrested in U.S. Terror Raid." *Morning Report*. Host Krishnan Guru-
> Murthy. *4 Radio*. Channel 4 News, 23 June 2006. MP3 file. 27 June
> 2006.

70. WORK OF ART OR PHOTOGRAPH List the artist or photographer; the work's title, italicized; the date of composition (if unknown, use *n.d.*); and the medium of composition (*Oil on Canvas, Bronze*). Then cite the name of the museum or other location and the city. To cite a reproduction in a book, add the publication information. To cite artwork found online, omit the medium of composition, and after the location, add the title of the database or Web site, italicized; the medium consulted (*Web*); and the date of access.

> Chagall, Marc. *The Poet with the Birds*. 1911. Minneapolis Inst. of Arts. *artsmia.org*. Web. 6 Oct. 2003.

> *General William Palmer in Old Age*. 1810. Oil on canvas. National Army Museum, London. *White Mughals: Love and Betrayal in Eighteenth-Century India*. William Dalrymple. New York: Penguin, 2002. 270. Print.

> Kahlo, Frida. *Self-Portrait with Cropped Hair. 1940*. Oil on canvas. Museum of Mod. Art, New York.

71. MAP OR CHART Cite a map or chart as you would a book or a short work within a longer work and include the word *Map* or *Chart* after the title. Add the medium of publication. For an online source, end with the date of access.

> "Australia." Map. *Perry-Castañeda Library Map Collection*. U of Texas, 1999. Web. 4 Nov. 2003.

> *California*. Map. Chicago: Rand, 2002. Print.

72. CARTOON OR COMIC STRIP List the artist's name; the title (if any) of the cartoon or comic strip, in quotation marks; the label *Cartoon* or *Comic strip*; and the usual publication information for a print periodical (see models 22–28) or a work from a Web site (model 34).

> Johnston, Lynn. "For Better or for Worse." Comic strip. *FBorFW.com*. Lynn Johnston Publications, 30 June 2006. Web. 20 July 2006.

> Lewis, Eric. "The Unpublished Freud." Cartoon. *New Yorker* 11 Mar. 2002: 80. Print.

73. ADVERTISEMENT Include the label *Advertisement* after the name of the item or organization being advertised.

> Microsoft. Advertisement. *Harper's* Oct. 2003: 2-3. Print.

> Microsoft. Advertisement. *New York Times*. New York Times, 11 Nov. 2003. Web. 11 Nov. 2010.

APA Documentation Guidelines

The following formatting guidelines are adapted from the APA's recommendations for preparing manuscripts for publication in journals. For detailed guidelines on formatting a list of references, see p. 386. For a sample student essay in APA style, see p. 236.

- *Title page.* Center the title, and include your name, the course name and number, the instructor's name, and the date. In the top right-hand corner, type a short version of the title (fifty characters or fewer, including spaces), skip one space, and type the page number.

- *Margins and spacing.* Leave margins of at least one inch at the top and bottom and on both sides of the page. Do not justify the right margin. Double-space the entire text, including headings, set-off quotations, content notes, and the list of references. Indent the first line of each paragraph one-half inch (or five to seven spaces) from the left margin.

- *Short title and page numbers.* Type the short title and page number in the upper right-hand corner of each page, in the same position as on the title page.

- *Long quotations.* For a long, set-off quotation (one having more than forty words), indent it one-half inch (or five to seven spaces) from the left margin and do not use quotation marks. Place the page reference in parentheses one space after the final punctuation.

- *Abstract.* If your instructor asks for an abstract with your paper—a one-paragraph summary of your major thesis and supporting points—it should go on a separate page immediately after the title page. Center the word *Abstract* about an inch from the top of the page. Double-space the text of the abstract, and begin the first line flush with the left margin. APA recommends that an abstract not exceed 120 words.

- *Headings.* Headings are used within the text of many APA-style papers. In papers with only one or two levels of headings, center the main headings; italicize the subheadings and position them flush with the left margin. Capitalize all major words; however, do not capitalize articles, short prepositions, or coordinating conjunctions unless they are the first word or follow a colon.

■ *Visuals.* Tables should be labeled *Table*, numbered, and captioned. All other visuals (charts, graphs, photographs, and drawings) should be labeled *Figure*, numbered, and captioned with a description and the source information. Remember to refer to each visual in your text, stating how it contributes to the point(s) you are making. Tables and figures should appear near the relevant text; check with your instructor for guidelines on placement of visuals.

In-text Citations

APA style requires parenthetical references in the text to document quotations, paraphrases, summaries, and other material from a source (see Chapter 6). These citations include the year of publication and correspond to full bibliographic entries in the list of references at the end of the text. Note that APA style generally calls for past-tense signal verbs (*Baker showed*) in literature reviews or when describing a past action that occurred at a definite time. Use the present perfect tense (*Baker has shown*) for actions or conditions that are ongoing or didn't happen at a specific time. Use the present tense to discuss results (*the second experiment corroborates*) or widely accepted information (*researchers agree*).

Directory to APA style for in-text citations

1. AUTHOR NAMED IN A SIGNAL PHRASE In most instances, use the author's name in a signal phrase to introduce the cited material, and place the date, in parentheses, immediately after the author's name. For a quotation, the page number, preceded by *p.*, appears in parentheses after the quotation.

> As Fanderclai (2001) observed, older siblings play an important role in the development of language and learning skills.

> Chavez (2003) noted that "six years after slim cigarettes for women were introduced, more than twice as many teenage girls were smoking" (p. 13).

For electronic texts or other works with paragraph numbers but no page numbers, use the paragraph number preceded by the abbreviation *para.*

> Weinberg (2000) has claimed that "the techniques used in group therapy can be verbal, expressive, or psychodramatic" (para. 5).

If paragraph numbers are not given, cite the heading and number of the paragraph in that section, if any: (*Types of Groups section, para. 1*). For a long, set-off quotation (one having more than forty words), place the page reference in parentheses one space after the final punctuation.

2. AUTHOR NAMED IN A PARENTHETICAL REFERENCE When you do not mention the author in a signal phrase in your text, give the author's name and the date, separated by a comma, in parentheses at the end of the cited material.

> One study found that 17% of adopted children in the United States are of a different race than their adoptive parents (Peterson, 2003).

3. TWO AUTHORS Use both names in all citations. Join the names with *and* in a signal phrase, but use an ampersand (&) instead in a parenthetical reference.

> Babcock and Laschever (2003) have suggested that many women do not negotiate their salaries and pay raises as vigorously as their male counterparts do.

> A recent study has suggested that many women do not negotiate their salaries and pay raises as vigorously as their male counterparts do (Babcock & Laschever, 2003).

4. THREE TO FIVE AUTHORS List all the authors' names for the first reference.

Safer, Voccola, Hurd, and Goodwin (2003) reached somewhat different conclusions by designing a study that was less dependent on subjective judgment than were previous studies.

In subsequent references, use just the first author's name plus *et al.* ("and others").

Based on the results, Safer et al. (2003) determined that the apes took significant steps toward self-expression.

5. SIX OR MORE AUTHORS Use only the first author's name and *et al.* ("and others") in every citation, including the first.

As Soleim et al. (2002) demonstrated, advertising holds the potential for manipulating "free-willed" consumers.

6. CORPORATE OR GROUP AUTHOR If the name of the organization or corporation is long, spell it out the first time you use it, followed by an abbreviation in brackets. In later references, use the abbreviation only.

FIRST CITATION   (Centers for Disease Control and Prevention [CDC], 2006)

LATER CITATIONS   (CDC, 2006)

7. UNKNOWN AUTHOR Use the title or its first few words in a signal phrase or in parentheses. Italicize a book or report title; place an article title in quotation marks.

The school profiles for the county substantiate this trend (*Guide to secondary schools*, 2003).

8. TWO OR MORE AUTHORS WITH THE SAME LAST NAME If your list of references includes works by different authors with the same last name, include the authors' initials in each citation.

G. Jones (2001) conducted the groundbreaking study on teenage childbearing.

9. TWO OR MORE WORKS BY AN AUTHOR IN A SINGLE YEAR Assign lowercase letters (*a*, *b*, and so on) alphabetically by title, and include the letters after the year.

Gordon (2004b) examined this trend in more detail.

10. TWO OR MORE SOURCES IN ONE PARENTHETICAL REFERENCE List sources by different authors in alphabetical order by authors' last names, separated by semicolons; list works by the same author in chronological order, separated by commas.

(Cardone, 2004; Lai, 2002)

(Lai, 2000, 2002)

11. SPECIFIC PARTS OF A SOURCE Use abbreviations (*chap.*, *p.*, *para.*, and so on) in a parenthetical reference to name the part of a work you are citing.

Mogolov (2003, chap. 9) has argued that his research yielded the opposite results.

12. EMAIL AND OTHER PERSONAL COMMUNICATION Cite any personal letters, email messages, electronic postings, telephone conversations, or interviews with the person's initial(s) and last name, the identification *personal communication*, and the date. Do not include personal communications in the reference list.

R. Tobin (personal communication, November 4, 2005) supported his claims about music therapy with new evidence.

13. ELECTRONIC DOCUMENT To cite an entire Web site, include its address in parentheses in your text (http://www.gallup.com); you don't need to include it in your list of references. Otherwise, cite a Web or electronic document as you would a print source, using the author's name and date; indicating the chapter or figure, as appropriate; and giving a full citation in your list of references. To cite a quotation, include the page or paragraph numbers.

In her report, Zomkowski stressed the importance of "ensuring equitable access to the Internet" (2003, para. 3).

CONTENT NOTES

APA style allows you to use content notes to expand or supplement your text. Indicate such notes in the text by superscript numerals ([1]). Type the notes themselves on a separate page after the last page of the text, under the heading *Footnotes*, which should be centered at the top of the page. Double-space all entries. Indent the first line of each note one-half inch (or five to seven spaces), but begin subsequent lines at the left margin.

The age of the children involved in the study was an important factor in the selection of items for the questionnaire.[1]

[1]Marjorie Youngston Forman and William Cole of the Child Study Team provided great assistance in identifying appropriate items for the questionnaire.

List of References

The alphabetical list of all the sources cited in your document is called *References*. (If your instructor asks that you list everything you have read as background—not just the sources you cite—call the list *Bibliography*.) Here are guidelines for preparing a list of references:

- Start your list on a separate page after the text of your document but before any appendices or notes. Identify each page with the short title and page number, continuing the numbering of the text.

- Type the heading *References*, neither italicized nor in quotation marks, centered one inch from the top of the page.

- Double-space, and begin your first entry. Unless your instructor suggests otherwise, do not indent the first line of each entry, but indent subsequent lines one-half inch or five to seven spaces. Double-space the entire list.

- List sources alphabetically by authors' (or editors') last names. If the author is unknown, alphabetize the source by the first major word of the title, disregarding *A, An*, or *The*. If the list includes two or more works by the same author, see the examples on pp. 389 and 392. APA style specifies the treatment and placement of four basic elements—author, publication date, title, and other publication information.

- *Author*. List all authors' last names first, and use only initials for first and middle names. Separate the names of multiple authors with commas, and use an ampersand (&) before the last author's name.

- *Publication date*. Enclose the date in parentheses. Use only the year for books and journals; use the year, a comma, and the month or month and day for magazines; use the year, a comma, and the month and day for newspapers. Do not abbreviate.

- *Title*. Italicize titles and subtitles of books and periodicals. Do not enclose titles of articles in quotation marks. For books and articles, capitalize only the first word of the title and subtitle and any proper nouns or proper adjectives. Capitalize all major words in a periodical title.

■ *Publication information*. For a book, list the city and state (or country) of publication, a colon, and the publisher's name, dropping any *Inc.*, *Co.*, or *Publishers*. For a periodical, follow the periodical title with a comma, the volume number (italicized), the issue number (if appropriate) in parentheses and followed by a comma, and the inclusive page numbers of the article. For newspaper articles and for articles or chapters in books, include the abbreviation *p.* ("page") or *pp.* ("pages") before the page numbers.

The sample entries that start on p. 388 use a hanging indent format, in which the first line aligns on the left and the subsequent lines indent one-half inch or five to seven spaces. This is the customary APA format for final copy, including student papers.

Directory to APA style for references

BOOKS

The basic format for a reference-list entry for a book is outlined on pp. 390–91.

1. ONE AUTHOR

Lightman, A. P. (2002). *The diagnosis.* New York, NY: Vintage Books.

2. TWO OR MORE AUTHORS

Walsh, M. E., & Murphy, J. A. (2003). *Children, health, and learning: A guide to the issues.* Westport, CT: Praeger.

3. CORPORATE OR GROUP AUTHOR

Committee on Abrupt Climate Change, National Research Council. (2002). *Abrupt climate change: Inevitable surprises.* Washington, DC: National Academies Press.

Use the word *Author* as the publisher when the organization is both the author and the publisher.

Resources for Rehabilitation. (2003). *A woman's guide to coping with disability.* London, England: Author.

4. UNKNOWN AUTHOR

National Geographic atlas of the Middle East. (2003). Washington, DC: National Geographic Society.

5. EDITOR

Dickens, J. (Ed.). (1995). *Family outing: A guide for parents of gays, lesbians, and bisexuals.* London, England: Peter Owen.

6. SELECTION IN A BOOK WITH AN EDITOR

Burke, W. W., & Nourmair, D. A. (2001). The role of personality assessment in organization development. In J. Waclawski & A. H. Church (Eds.), *Organization development: A data-driven approach to organizational change* (pp. 55-77). San Francisco, CA: Jossey-Bass.

7. TRANSLATION

Al-Farabi, A. N. (1998). *On the perfect state* (R. Walzer, Trans.). Chicago, IL: Kazi.

8. EDITION OTHER THAN THE FIRST

Moore, G. S. (2002). *Living with the earth: Concepts in environmental health science* (2nd ed.). New York, NY: Lewis.

9. MULTIVOLUME WORK

Barnes, J. (Ed.). (1995). *Complete works of Aristotle* (Vols. 1-2). Princeton, NJ: Princeton University Press.

10. ARTICLE IN A REFERENCE WORK   If no author is listed, begin with the title.

Dean, C. (1994). Jaws and teeth. In *The Cambridge encyclopedia of human evolution* (pp. 56-59). Cambridge, England: Cambridge University Press.

11. REPUBLICATION

Piaget, J. (1952). *The language and thought of the child*. London, England: Routledge & Kegan Paul. (Original work published 1932)

12. TWO OR MORE WORKS BY THE SAME AUTHOR(S)   List two or more works by the same author in chronological order (if the works appear in a single year, see model 21). Repeat the author's name in each entry.

Goodall, J. (1999). *Reason for hope: A spiritual journey*. New York, NY: Warner Books.

Goodall, J. (2002). *Performance and evolution in the age of Darwin: Out of the natural order*. New York, NY: Routledge.

PERIODICALS

The basic format for a reference-list entry for an article in a periodical is outlined on pp. 394–95.

13. ARTICLE IN A JOURNAL PAGINATED BY VOLUME

O'Connell, D. C., & Kowal, S. (2003). Psycholinguistics: A half century of monologism. *The American Journal of Psychology, 116,* 191-212.

SOURCE MAP: Citing Books Using APA Style

Take information from the book's title page and copyright page (on the reverse side of the title page), not from the book's cover or a library catalog.

(1) *Author.* List all authors' last names first, and use only initials for first and middle names. Separate the names of multiple authors with commas, and use an ampersand (&) before the last author's name.

(2) *Publication year.* Enclose the year of publication in parentheses.

(3) *Title.* Italicize the title and subtitle. Capitalize only the first word of the title and the subtitle and any proper nouns or proper adjectives.

(4) *City of publication.* List the city and state (or country) of publication followed by a colon.

(5) *Publisher.* Give the publisher's name, dropping any *Inc., Co.,* or *Publishers.*

For a book by one author, use the following format:

> Last name, initial(s). (Year). *Title of book: Subtitle.* City, ST: Publisher.

A citation for the book on p. 391 would look like this:

AUTHOR'S LAST NAME AND INITIAL   YEAR OF PUBLICATION   TITLE AND SUBTITLE, ITALICIZED

Tsutsui, W. (2004). *Godzilla on my mind: Fifty years of the king of monsters.*

PUBLISHER'S CITY AND NAME

New York, NY: Palgrave Macmillan.

DOUBLE-SPACE; INDENT ONE-HALF INCH OR FIVE TO SEVEN SPACES

GODZILLA ON MY MIND
Copyright © William Tsutsui, 2004.

All rights reserved. No part of this book may be used or
reproduced in any manner whatsoever without written permission
except in the case of brief quotations embodied in critical articles
or reviews.

First published 2004 by
PALGRAVE MACMILLAN™
175 Fifth Avenue, New York, N.Y. 10010 and
Houndmills, Basingstoke, Hampshire, England RG21 6XS.
Companies and representatives throughout the world.

PALGR
the Palg
Palgrave
the Uni
is a regi
countrie

ISBN 1-

Library
Tsutsui,
Godzilla
Tsutsui.
    p.
  Inclu
  ISBN
  1. G

PN1995
791.43'6

A catal
Library.

Design

10 9

Printed

GODZILLA®
ON MY MIND

*

*Fifty Years of the
King of Monsters*

WILLIAM TSUTSUI

palgrave
macmillan

14. ARTICLE IN A JOURNAL PAGINATED BY ISSUE

Hall, R. E. (2000). Marriage as vehicle of racism among women of color. *Psychology: A Journal of Human Behavior, 37*(2), 29-40.

15. ARTICLE IN A MAGAZINE

Ricciardi, S. (2003, August 5). Enabling the mobile work force. *PC Magazine, 22,* 46.

16. ARTICLE IN A NEWSPAPER

Faler, B. (2003, August 29). Primary colors: Race and fundraising. *The Washington Post,* p. A5.

17. EDITORIAL OR LETTER TO THE EDITOR

Zelneck, B. (2003, July 18). Serving the public at public universities [Letter to the editor]. *The Chronicle Review,* p. B18.

18. UNSIGNED ARTICLE

Annual meeting announcement. (2003, March). *Cognitive Psychology, 46,* 227.

19. REVIEW

Ringel, S. (2003). [Review of the book *Multiculturalism and the therapeutic process*]. *Clinical Social Work Journal, 31,* 212-213.

20. PUBLISHED INTERVIEW

Smith, H. (2002, October). [Interview with A. Thompson]. *The Sun,* pp. 4-7.

21. TWO OR MORE WORKS BY THE SAME AUTHOR IN THE SAME YEAR List the works alphabetically by title, and place lowercase letters (*a, b,* and so on) after the dates.

Shermer, M. (2002a). On estimating the lifetime of civilizations. *Scientific American, 287*(2), 33.

Shermer, M. (2002b). Readers who question evolution. *Scientific American, 287*(1), 37.

ELECTRONIC SOURCES

The *Publication Manual of the American Psychological Association*, Sixth Edition, includes guidelines for citing various kinds of electronic resources, including Web sites; articles, reports, and abstracts; some types of online communications; and computer software. Updated guidelines are maintained at the APA's Web site (www.apa.org).

The basic entry for most sources accessed via the Internet should include the following elements:

- *Author*. Give the author's name, if available.

- *Publication date*. Include the date of electronic publication or of the latest update, if available. Use *n.d.* ("no date") when the publication date is unavailable.

- *Title*. List the title of the document or subject line of the message, neither italicized nor in quotation marks.

- *Publication information*. For articles from online journals, newspapers, or reference databases, give the publication title and other publishing information as you would for a print periodical.

- *Retrieval information*. For a work from a database, do the following: If the article has a DOI (digital object identifier), include that number after publication information; do not include the name of the database. If there is no DOI, write *Retrieved from* followed by the URL for the journal's home page (not the database URL). For a work found on a Web site, write *Retrieved from* and include the URL.

22. ARTICLE FROM AN ONLINE PERIODICAL   Give the author, date, title, and publication information as you would for a print document. Include both the volume and issue numbers for all journal articles. If the article has a DOI, include it. If there is no DOI, include the URL for the periodical's home page or for the article (if the article is difficult to find from the home page). For newspaper articles accessible from a searchable Web site, give the site's URL only.

> Barringer, F. (2008, February 7). In many communities, it's not easy going green. *The New York Times*. Retrieved from http://www.nytimes.com.

> Cleary, J. M., & Crafti, N. (2007). Basic need satisfaction, emotional eating, and dietary restraint as risk factors for recurrent overeating in a community sample. *E-Journal of Applied Psychology, 2*(3), 27-39. Retrieved from http://ojs.lib.swin.edu.au/index.php/ejap/article/view/90/116

23. ARTICLE OR ABSTRACT FROM A DATABASE   (See pp. 398–99 for the basic format for citing an article from a database.) Give the author, date, title,

SOURCE MAP: Citing Articles from Print Periodicals Using APA Style

① *Author.* List all authors' last names first, and use only initials for first and middle names. Separate the names of multiple authors with commas, and use an ampersand (&) before the last author's name.

② *Publication date.* Enclose the date in parentheses. For journals, use only the year. For magazines and newspapers, use the year, a comma, the month (spelled out), and the day of the month if given.

③ *Article title.* Do not italicize or enclose article titles in quotation marks. Capitalize only the first word of the article title and subtitle and any proper nouns or proper adjectives.

④ *Periodical title.* Italicize the periodical title (and subtitle, if any), and capitalize all major words.

⑤ *Publication information.* Follow the periodical title with a comma, and then give the volume number (italicized) and, without a space in between, the issue number (if given) in parentheses.

⑥ *Page numbers.* Give the inclusive page numbers of the article. For newspapers only, include the abbreviation *p.* ("page") or *pp.* ("pages") before the page numbers. End the citation with a period.

For a basic periodical article, use the following format:

> Last name, First initial. (Year, month day [or year alone for journal]). Title of article. *Title of Periodical, Volume number* (Issue number), Page number(s).

A citation for the magazine article on p. 395 would look like this:

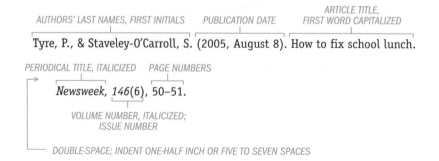

AUTHORS' LAST NAMES, FIRST INITIALS   PUBLICATION DATE   ARTICLE TITLE, FIRST WORD CAPITALIZED

Tyre, P., & Staveley-O'Carroll, S. (2005, August 8). How to fix school lunch.

PERIODICAL TITLE, ITALICIZED   PAGE NUMBERS

Newsweek, 146(6), 50–51.

VOLUME NUMBER, ITALICIZED; ISSUE NUMBER

DOUBLE-SPACE; INDENT ONE-HALF INCH OR FIVE TO SEVEN SPACES

① By Peg Tyre and Sarah Staveley-O'Carroll

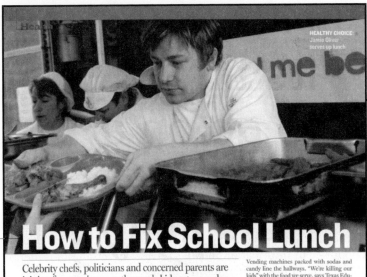

HEALTHY CHOICE
Jamie Oliver
serves up lunch

③ # How to Fix School Lunch

Celebrity chefs, politicians and concerned parents are joining forces to improve the meals kids eat every day.

BY PEG TYRE AND SARAH STAVELEY-O'CARROLL

FOR JORGE COLLAZO, EXECUTIVE chef for the New York City public schools, coming up with the perfect jerk sauce is yet another step toward making the 1.1 million schoolkids he serves healthier. In a little more than a year, he's introduced salad bars and replaced whole milk with skim. Beef patties are now served on whole-wheat buns. Until recently, "every piece of chicken the manufacturers sent us was either breaded or covered in a glaze," says Collazo. Brandishing the might of his $125 million annual food budget, he switched to plain cutlets and asked suppliers to come up with something healthy—and appealing—to put on offering. The ② August 8, 2005 d and doesn't the says with a grimace. Within minutes, the supplier is hard at work on a lower-sodium version.

A cramped public-school test kitchen might seem an unlikely outpost for a food revolution. But Collazo and scores of others across the country—celebrity chefs and

lunch ladies, district superintendents and politicians—say they're determined to improve what kids eat in school. Nearly everyone agrees something must be done. Most school cafeterias are staffed by poorly trained, badly equipped workers who churn out 4.8 billion hot lunches a year. Often the meals, produced for about $1 each, consist of breaded meat patties, french fries and overcooked vegetables. So the kids buy muffins, cookies and ice cream instead—or they feast on fast food from McDonald's, Pizza Hut and Taco Bell, which is available in more than half the schools in the nation.

Vending machines packed with sodas and candy line the hallways. "We're killing our kids" with the food we serve, says Texas Education Commissioner Susan Combs.

As rates of childhood obesity and diabetes skyrocket, public-health officials say schools need to change the way kids eat. It won't be easy. Some kids and their parents don't know better. Home cooking is becoming a forgotten art. And fast-food companies now spend $3 billion a year on television ads aimed at children. Along with reading and writing, schools need to teach kids what to eat to stay healthy, says culinary innovator Alice Waters, who is introducing gardening and fresh produce to 16 schools in California. It's a golden opportunity, she says, "to affect the way children eat for the rest of their lives." Last year star English chef Jamie Oliver took over a school cafeteria in a working-class suburb of London. A documentary about his work shamed the British government into spending $500 million to revamp the nation's school-food program. Oliver says it's the United States' turn now. "If you can put a man on the moon," he says, "you can give kids the food they need to make them lighter, fitter and live longer."

Changing school food takes time. More than a decade ago, when local restaurateur Lynn Walters lobbied school-board members in Santa Fe, N.M., to provide kids with

50 NEWSWEEK AUGUST 8, 2005

TOP TO BOTTOM: JULIAN MAKEY—REX FEATURES, PHOTOGRAPH BY LAUREN FLEISHMAN FOR NEWSWEEK

Newsweek (ISSN 0028-9604), August 8, 2005. Volume CXLVI, No. 6. Newsweek publishes an issue weekly, except when combined issues are published which count as two issues (currently in August and December) and when, from time to time, an additional special issue may be published. A one-year subscription (52 issues) is U.S. $41.08 and Canadian $61.88 a year. In the U.S. send subscription inquiries to Newsweek, P.O. Box 5571, Harlan, IA 51593-1071. In Canada: Newsweek, Inc., P.O. Box 4067, Postal Station A, Toronto, ON M5W2K1. Canada Post International Publications Mail (Canadian Distribution) Sales Agreement No. 40051822. Canadian GST No. 123-321-309. All changes of address: 800-634-6850. All other queries: 800-631-1040. Unless otherwise indicated by source or currency designation, all terms and prices are applicable in the U.S. only and may not apply in Canada. Copyright © 2005 Newsweek, Inc. All rights reserved. 251 West 57th Street, New York, NY 10019-1894. Richard M. Smith, Chairman and Editor-in-Chief. Stephen Fuzesi Jr., Chief Counsel and Secretary. Periodicals postage paid at New York, NY, and at additional mailing offices. POSTMASTERS: send address changes to Newsweek, P.O. Box 9572, Harlan, IA 51593-1072. Printed in U.S.A. We may make a portion of our mailing list available to a select group of companies whose products or services may be of interest of you. If you would prefer that we not disclose your personal information for this purpose, please contact subscriber services by mail, phone or e-mail at mesub@newsweek.com. Your choice will not affect the cost of your service.

④ Newsweek

⑤ Volume CXLVI, No. 6

⑥ 50

395

and publication information as you would for a print document. Include both the volume and issue numbers for journal articles. If the article has a DOI, include it. If there is no DOI, type *Retrieved from* and the URL of the journal's home page (not the URL of the database).

> Crook, S. (2003). Change, uncertainty and the future of sociology. *Journal of Sociology, 39*(1), 7-14. Retrieved from http://jos.sagepub.com

> McCall, R. B. (1988). Science and the press: Like oil and water? *American Psychologist, 43*(2), 87-94. Abstract retrieved from http://www.apa .org/journals/amp/

> Morley, N. J., Ball, L. J., & Ormerod, T. C. (2006). How the detection of insurance fraud succeeds and fails. *Psychology, Crime, & Law, 12*(2), 163-180. doi: 10.1080/10683160512331316325

24. DOCUMENT FROM A WEB SITE (See pp. 400–1 for the basic format for citing a work from a Web site.) Include information as you would for a print document, followed by information about its retrieval. If no author is identified, give the title of the document followed by the date (if available).

> Hacker, J. S. (2006). The privatization of risk and the growing economic insecurity of Americans. *Items and Issues, 5*(4), 16-23. Retrieved from http://publications.ssrc.org/items/items5.4/Hacker.pdf

> What parents should know about treatment of behavioral and emotional disorders in preschool children. (2006). *APA Online*. Retrieved from http://www.apa.org/releases/kidsmed.html

25. CHAPTER OR SECTION OF A WEB DOCUMENT After the chapter or section title, type *In* and give the document title, with identifying information, if any, in parentheses. End with the date of access and the URL.

> Salamon, Andrew. (n.d.). War in Europe. In *Childhood in times of war* (chap. 2). Retrieved April 11, 2005, from http://remember.org/jean

26. EMAIL MESSAGE OR REAL-TIME COMMUNICATION Do not include entries for email messages or real-time communications (such as IMs) in the list of references; instead, cite these sources in your text as forms of personal communication (see in-text model 12 on p. 385).

27. ONLINE POSTING List an online posting in the reference list only if the message is retrievable from a mailing list's archive. Give the author's name and the posting's date and subject line. Include the description [*Electronic mailing list message*] in square brackets. End with the words *Retrieved from* and the URL of the archived message.

Troike, R. C. (2001, June 21). Buttercups and primroses [Electronic mailing list message]. Retrieved from http://listserv.linguistlist.org/archives/ads-l.html

For a newsgroup posting, use the label [*online forum comment*].

Wittenberg, E. (2001, July 11). Gender and the Internet [Online forum comment]. Retrieved from news://comp.edu.composition

28. SOFTWARE OR COMPUTER PROGRAM

PsychMate [Computer software]. (2003). Available from Psychology Software Tools: http://pstnet.com/products/psychmate

OTHER SOURCES (INCLUDING ONLINE VERSIONS)

29. GOVERNMENT PUBLICATION

Office of the Federal Register. (2003). *The United States government manual 2003/2004*. Washington, DC: U.S. Government Printing Office.

For an online government document, add the date of access and the URL.

U.S. Public Health Service. (1999). *The surgeon general's call to action to prevent suicide*. Retrieved November 5, 2003, from http://www.mentalhealth.org/suicideprevention/calltoaction.asp.

30. DISSERTATION ABSTRACT If you retrieve a dissertation from a database, give the database name and the accession number, if one is assigned.

Bandeji, N. (2003). Embedded economies: Foreign direct investment in Central and Eastern Europe. Retrieved from ProQuest Digital Dissertations. (6900033)

31. UNPUBLISHED DISSERTATION If you retrieve a dissertation from a Web site, give the type of dissertation, the institution, and year, and provide a retrieval statement.

Meeks, M. G. (2006). *Between abolition and reform: First-year writing programs, e-literacies, and institutional change* (Doctoral dissertation, University of North Carolina). Retrieved from http://dc.lib.unc.edu/etd

32. TECHNICAL OR RESEARCH REPORT Give the report number, if available, in parentheses after the title.

SOURCE MAP: *Citing Articles from Databases Using APA Style*

Libraries pay for services—such as InfoTrac, EBSCOhost, ProQuest, and Lexis-Nexis—that provide access to large databases of electronic articles.

(1) *Author.* If available, include the author's name as you would for a print source. List all authors' last names first, and use only initials for first and middle names. Separate the names of multiple authors with commas, and use an ampersand (&) before the last author's name.

(2) *Publication date.* Enclose the date in parentheses. For journals, use only the year. For magazines and newspapers, use the year, a comma, the month (spelled out), and the day of the month if given.

(3) *Article title.* Do not italicize or enclose article titles in quotation marks. Capitalize only the first word of the article title and the subtitle and any proper nouns or proper adjectives.

(4) *Periodical title.* Italicize the periodical title (and subtitle, if any), and capitalize all major words.

(5) *Print publication information.* Give the volume number (italicized), the issue number (if given) in parentheses, and the inclusive page numbers. For newspapers, include abbreviation *p.* ("page") or *pp.* ("pages") before the page numbers.

(6) *Retrieval information.* If the article has a DOI (digital object identifier), include that number after the publication information. If there is no DOI, write *Retrieved from* followed by the URL for the home page of the journal (not the database URL).

For a journal article retrieved from a database, use the following format:

> Last name, First initial. (Year). Title of article. *Title of Journal, Volume number* (Issue number), Page number(s). DOI or " Retrieved from" URL.

A citation for the article on p. 399 would look like this:

AUTHORS' LAST NAMES, INITIALS   YEAR OF PUBLICATION   ARTICLE TITLE AND SUBTITLE, FIRST WORD OF EACH CAPITALIZED

Chory-Assad, R. M., & Tamborini, R. (2004). Television sitcom exposure and

PERIODICAL TITLE, ITALICIZED

aggressive communication: A priming perspective. *North American*

VOLUME NUMBER, ITALICIZED, AND ISSUE NUMBER, IF GIVEN   PERIODICAL HOME PAGE

Journal of Psychology, 6(3), 415–422. Retrieved, from http://najp.8m.com

DOUBLE-SPACE; INDENT ONE-HALF INCH OR FIVE TO SEVEN SPACES   PAGE NUMBERS

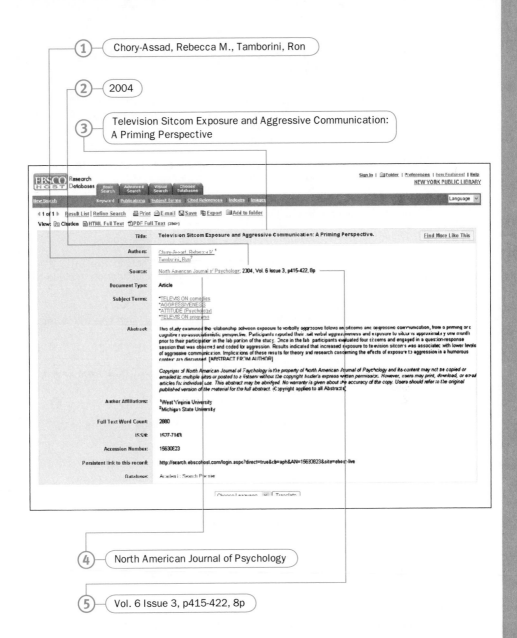

① Chory-Assad, Rebecca M., Tamborini, Ron

② 2004

③ Television Sitcom Exposure and Aggressive Communication: A Priming Perspective

EBSCO Research Databases

Sign In | Folder | Preferences | New Features! | Help
NEW YORK PUBLIC LIBRARY

Basic Search | Advanced Search | Visual Search | Choose Databases

New Search | Keyword | Publications | Subject Terms | Cited References | Indexes | Images

Language

1 of 1 | Result List | Refine Search | Print | E-mail | Save | Export | Add to folder

View: Citation | HTML Full Text | PDF Full Text (394K)

Title:	Television Sitcom Exposure and Aggressive Communication: A Priming Perspective.
Authors:	Chory-Assad, Rebecca M.[1] Tamborini, Ron[2]
Source:	North American Journal of Psychology; 2004, Vol. 6 Issue 3, p415-422, 8p
Document Type:	Article
Subject Terms:	*TELEVISION comedies *AGGRESSIVENESS *ATTITUDE (Psychology) *TELEVISION programs
Abstract:	This study examined the relationship between exposure to verbally aggressive television and aggressive communication, from a priming and cognitive neo-associationistic perspective. Participants reported their own verbal aggressiveness and exposure to sitcoms approximately one month prior to their participation in the lab portion of the study. Once in the lab participants evaluated four sitcoms and engaged in a question-response session that was observed and coded for aggression. Results indicated that increased exposure to television sitcoms was associated with lower levels of aggressive communication. Implications of these results for theory and research concerning the effects of exposure to aggression in a humorous context are discussed [ABSTRACT FROM AUTHOR] Copyright of North American Journal of Psychology is the property of North American Journal of Psychology and its content may not be copied or emailed to multiple sites or posted to a listserv without the copyright holder's express written permission. However, users may print, download, or email articles for individual use. This abstract may be abridged. No warranty is given about the accuracy of the copy. Users should refer to the original published version of the material for the full abstract. (Copyright applies to all Abstracts.)
Author Affiliations:	[1]West Virginia University [2]Michigan State University
Full Text Word Count:	2880
ISSN:	1527-7143
Accession Number:	15630823
Persistent link to this record:	http://search.ebscohost.com/login.aspx?direct=true&db=aph&AN=15630823&site=ehost-live
Database:	Academic Search Premier

Choose Language | Translate

④ North American Journal of Psychology

⑤ Vol. 6 Issue 3, p415-422, 8p

SOURCE MAP: Citing Works from Web Sites Using APA Style

① *Author.* If available, include the author's name as you would for a print source. List authors' last names first, and use initials for first names. The site's sponsor may be the author. If no author is identified, begin the citation with the title of the document.

② *Publication date.* Include the date of publication or latest update. Use *n.d.* ("no date") when no publication date is available.

③ *Title of work.* Capitalize only the first word of the title and subtitle and any proper nouns or proper adjectives.

④ *Title of Web site.* Italicize the title. Capitalize all major words.

⑤ *Retrieval information.* Write *Retrieved from* and include the URL. If the work seems likely to be updated or has no date of publication, include the retrieval date.

For a document found on a Web site with one author, use the following format:

> Last name, First initial. (Publication date). Title of document. *Title of Web Site.* "Retrieved from" URL

A citation for the Web document on p. 401 would look like this:

AUTHOR   PUBL. DATE   TITLE OF WORK

Alexander, M. (2001, August 22). Thirty years later, Stanford Prison

TITLE OF WEB SITE   RETRIEVAL INFO

Experiment lives on. *Stanford Report.* Retrieved from http://news-

service.stanford.edu/news/2001/august22/prison2-822.html

For more on using APA style to cite works from Web sites, see 396–97. (For guidelines and models for using MLA style to cite works from Web sites, see pp. 372–73.)

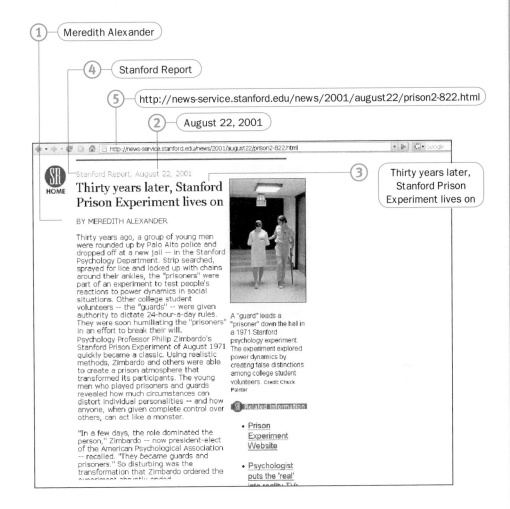

(1) Meredith Alexander

(4) Stanford Report

(5) http://news-service.stanford.edu/news/2001/august22/prison2-822.html

(2) August 22, 2001

http://news-service.stanford.edu/news/2001/august22/prison2-822.html

(3) Thirty years later, Stanford Prison Experiment lives on

Stanford Report, August 22, 2001

SR HOME

Thirty years later, Stanford Prison Experiment lives on

BY MEREDITH ALEXANDER

Thirty years ago, a group of young men were rounded up by Palo Alto police and dropped off at a new jail -- in the Stanford Psychology Department. Strip searched, sprayed for lice and locked up with chains around their ankles, the "prisoners" were part of an experiment to test people's reactions to power dynamics in social situations. Other college student volunteers -- the "guards" -- were given authority to dictate 24-hour-a-day rules. They were soon humiliating the "prisoners" in an effort to break their will. Psychology Professor Philip Zimbardo's Stanford Prison Experiment of August 1971 quickly became a classic. Using realistic methods, Zimbardo and others were able to create a prison atmosphere that transformed its participants. The young men who played prisoners and guards revealed how much circumstances can distort individual personalities -- and how anyone, when given complete control over others, can act like a monster.

"In a few days, the role dominated the person," Zimbardo -- now president-elect of the American Psychological Association -- recalled. "They *became* guards and prisoners." So disturbing was the transformation that Zimbardo ordered the experiment abruptly ended.

A "guard" leads a "prisoner" down the hall in a 1971 Stanford psychology experiment. The experiment explored power dynamics by creating false distinctions among college student volunteers. Credit: Chuck Painter

SR Related Information

- Prison Experiment Website

- Psychologist puts the 'real' into reality TV:

McCool, R., Fikes, R., & McGuinness, D. (2003). *Semantic web tools for enhanced authoring* (Report No. KSL-03-07). Stanford, CA: Knowledge Systems Laboratory.

33. CONFERENCE PROCEEDINGS

Mama, A. (2001). Challenging subjects: Gender and power in African contexts. In *Proceedings of Nordic African Institute Conference: Rethinking power in Africa*. Uppsala, Sweden, 9-18.

34. PAPER PRESENTED AT A MEETING OR SYMPOSIUM, UNPUBLISHED Cite the month of the meeting if it is available.

Jones, J. G. (1999, February). *Mental health intervention in mass casualty disasters*. Paper presented at the Rocky Mountain Region Disaster Mental Health Conference, Laramie, WY.

35. POSTER SESSION

Barnes, Young, L. L. (2003, August). *Cognition, aging, and dementia*. Poster session presented at the 2003 Division 40 APA Convention, Toronto, Ontario, Canada.

36. FILM, VIDEO, OR DVD

Moore, M. (Director). (2003). *Bowling for Columbine* [Motion picture]. United States: MGM.

37. TELEVISION PROGRAM, SINGLE EPISODE

Imperioli, M. (Writer), & Buscemi, S. (Director). (2002). Everybody hurts [Television series episode]. In D. Chase (Executive Producer), *The Sopranos*. New York, NY: HBO.

38. RECORDING

The Avalanches. (2001). Frontier psychiatrist. On *Since I left you* [CD]. Los Angeles: Elektra/Asylum Records.

39. AUDIO PODCAST

O'Brien, K. (Writer). (2008, January 31). Developing countries. *KUSP's life in the fast lane* [Audio file]. Retrieved from http://www.kusp.org/shws/fast.html

Acknowledgments

Amitai Etzoni. Excerpts from "Less Privacy Is Good for Us (And You)." From *The Limits of Privacy*, Copyright © 1999. Reprinted with permission of the author.

Deborah Tannen. "For Argument's Sake: Why Do We Feel Compelled to Fight About Everything?" *The Washington Post*, March 15, 1998. Copyright © 1998 by Deborah Tannen. Reprinted with permission of the author. This article is adapted from *The Argument Culture: Moving for Debate in Dialogue*. New York: Ballantine, 1999. "Agonism in the Academy: Surviving Higher Learning's Argument Culture." Originally published in *The Chronicle of Higher Education*, March 31, 2000. Copyright © 2000 by Deborah Tannen. Reprinted with permission of the author. "Agonism in Academic Discourse." Originally published in the *Journal of Pragmatics*. Copyright © 2002. Reprinted with permission of the Taylor & Francis Group.

Picture Credits

Chapter 1: 2, Reproduced with permission of Yahoo! Inc. © 2010 Yahoo! Inc. Yahoo!, the Yahoo! logo, Flickr and the Flickr logo are registered trademarks of Yahoo! Inc. Photos courtesy Melissa Weintraub. **6,** (top) Edward Hausner/The New York Times/Redux, (bottom) Michael Kamber/The New York Times/Redux. **11,** Reprinted with permission of The Denver Post. **13,** © 2007 Steven Meyer-Rassow. **17, 18,** © 2009 Levi Strauss & Co. **Chapter 2: 22,** Courtesy of Mirlandra Ebert. **26,** Earl Wilson/The New York Times/Redux. **Chapter 3: 71,** National Center for Missing & Exploited Children and The Ad Council. **72,** U.S. Dept of Health & Mental Health Services Administration and The Ad Council. **74,** WWF-US Public Service Campaign. **Chapter 4: 87,** © Amitai Etzoni. **107,** Banque d'Images, ADAGP/Art Resource, NY/ARS. **109,** Courtesy of Christopher Nash. **110,** © Matthew Diffee/Conde Nast Publications/www.cartoonbank.com. **114,** Courtesy of ONDCP. **Chapter 5: 134,** Erik S. Lesser/The New York Times/Redux. **135,** University of Washington Libraries, Special Collections, UW21422. **Chapter 6: 159,** © 2006 Association for Computing Machinery, Inc. Reprinted by permission. Machionini, Gary (2006). "Exploratory Search, from Finding to Understanding" Communications of the ACM 49:4 http://doi.acm.org/10.1145/nnnnnn.nnnnnn. **161,** Courtesy of Wikipedia. **172,** iStockphoto. **173,** (top) © Google, (bottom) image printed with permission from EBSCO Publishing. **175,** Reproduced with permission of the American Psychological Association, publisher of the *Thesaurus of Psychological Index Terms*. Copyright © 2010 by the American Psychological Association, all rights reserved. No further reproduction or distribution is permitted without written permission from the American Psychological Association. **180,** Image courtesy of Wolfram Alpha LLC (www.wolframalpha.com). **205,** National Labor Committee. **206,** National Labor Committee. **Chapter 8: 250,** Sociological

Images, by Lisa Wade & Gwen Sharp. **251,** Source Interlink Companies, Inc. **258,** Sepah News/ AFP/Getty Images/Newscom. **261,** Gluekit. **261–263,** Copyright 2009 The Atlantic Media Co., as first published in The Atlantic Magazine. Distributed by Tribune Media Services. **Chapter 11: 317,** Environmental Protection Agency. **318,** Library of Congress. **Writers' References: 359,** Columbia University Press. Reprinted with permission of the publisher. **365,** Bryon Thompson. **369,** From Gale. *InfoTrac.* © Gale, a part of Cengage Learning, Inc. Reproduced by permission. www.cengage.com/permissions. **373,** Provided by the courtesy of Nobelprize.org, the official Web site of the Nobel Foundation. Copyright © 2010 Nobel Web AB. **391,** William Tsutsui, GODZILLA ON MY MIND, Published 2004, Palgrave, Macmillan, reproduced with the permission of Palgrave Macmillan. **395,** Julian Makey/Rex. **395,** From Newsweek, Aug. 8, 2005, Newsweek, Inc. All rights reserved. Used by permission and protected by the copyright laws of the United States. The printing, copying, redistribution, or retransmission of the material without express written permission is prohibited. **395,** Lauren Fleishman. **399,** Image printed with permission from EBSCO Publishing. **401,** Alexander, Meredith. "Thirty years later, Stanford Prison Experiment lives on." Stanford Report (online), August 22, 2001. http://news.stanford.edu/news/2001/august22/prison2-822.html. Photo credit: Chuck Painter/ Stanford News Service.

Index